Essential
WORLD ATLAS

Essential
WORLD ATLAS

BARNES & NOBLE BOOKS
NEW YORK

This edition published by Barnes & Noble, Inc,
by arrangement with Weldon Owen Inc.

2005 Barnes & Noble Books

M 10 9 8 7 6 5 4 3 2 1

ISBN 0-7607-6763-7

Library of Congress Cataloging-in-Publication Data available
upon request.

Printed and bound in Singapore

Top: At the southern tip of South
America is the mountainous Patagonia
region, an area progressively sculpted by
glacial action. In this image vegetation
appears as red, the glacier white.

Bottom: Surrounded by sand dunes,
Lake Disappointment is an ephemeral
salt lake in one of the most remote
areas of Western Australia.

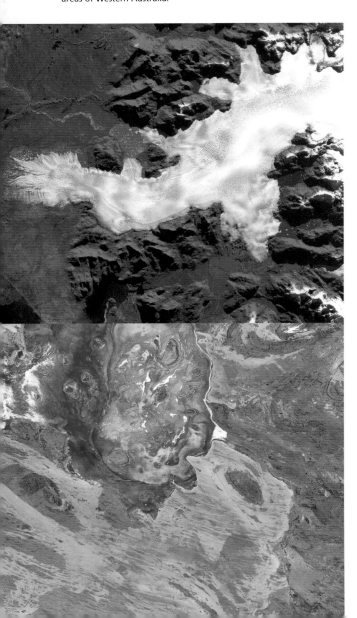

CARTOGRAPHIC CONSULTANTS

Dr William Cartwright
Associate Professor in Multimedia Cartography
School of Mathematical and Geospatial Sciences
RMIT University, Melbourne, Australia
Vice-President, International
Cartographic Association

Professor Michael P. Peterson
Department of Geography/Geology
University of Nebraska at Omaha, U.S.A.
Chair, International Cartographic Association
Commission on Maps and the Internet

REGIONAL MAPPING CONSULTANTS

Imran Ali
Cartographer, Pakistan

M. (John) Balodis
FMSIA Adjunct Professor
Curtin University, Perth, Australia

Professor Jean Carrière
Professeur titulaire
Directeur du Département de géographie
Université du Québec à Montréal, Canada

Dr Prem Chetri
School of Mathematical and Geospatial Sciences
RMIT University, Melbourne, Australia

Professor Benjamin Cohen
Department of Photogrammetry and Cartography
University of Architecture, Civil Engineering and Geodesy,
Sofia, Bulgaria

Igor Drecki
Geographics Unit Manager
School of Geography and Environmental Science
University of Auckland, Auckland, New Zealand

Dr Francisco Escobar
Profesor Titular de Análisis Geográfico Regional
Departamento de Geografía
Universidad de Alcalá de Henares, Spain

Dr David Fairbairn
School of Civil Engineering and Geosciences
University of Newcastle, Newcastle, U.K.

Steve Foldi
Cartographer, Windsor, Australia

Scott Furey
School of Mathematical and Geospatial Sciences
RMIT University, Melbourne, Australia

Professor Dr Georg Gartner
Institut für Kartographie und Geo-Medientechnik
Technische Universitat Wien, Vienna, Austria

Ibrahim Hanna
Hydrogeologist, Syria

Hashim al Hashimi
Geo-Information Analyst
Environmental Research and Wildlife
Development Agency, United Arab Emirates

Dr Stephen Hutchinson
Southampton Oceanography Centre
University of Southampton, Southampton, U.K.

Dr Simon Jones
School of Mathematical and Geospatial Sciences
RMIT University, Melbourne, Australia

Professor Milan Konecny
Department of Geography, Faculty of Science
Masaryk University, Brno, Czech Republic
President, International Cartographic Association

Professor Alexandra Koussoulakou
Department of Cadastre, Photogrammetry
and Cartography
The Aristotle University, Thessaloniki, Greece

Colin Kropman
Geographic Consultant, Sydney, Australia

Hyun Jong (David) Lee
Sung Kyun Kwan University, Seoul, South Korea

Antonio Hernández Navarro
Geodetic Coordinator
National Institute of Statistics,
Geography and Informatics (INEGI)
National Mapping Agency of Mexico,
Aguascaliente, Mexico

Professor Ferjan Ormeling
University of Utrecht, Netherlands
Secretary-General, International
Cartographic Association

Will Pringle
Cartographic Director
Australian Geographic Pty Ltd,
Sydney, Australia

Professor Patrick Quilty
Honorary Research Professor
School of Earth Sciences
University of Tasmania, Hobart, Australia

Cristhiane da Silva Ramos
School of Mathematical and Geospatial Sciences
RMIT University, Melbourne, Australia

Rushan Gul Rozi
School of Mathematical and Geospatial Sciences
RMIT University, Melbourne, Australia

Afshin Alizadeh Shabini
University of Tehran, Tehran, Iran

Hussein Tawansi
Fellow Member, Institute of Quarrying
Sydney, Australia

Professor Dr Theodor Wintges
Munich University of Applied Sciences,
Munich, Germany

Assistant Professor Hiroyuki Yoshida
Faculty of Policy Management
SFC, Keio University, Endo, Japan

Jason Zhang
School of Mathematical and Geospatial Sciences
RMIT University, Melbourne, Australia

HOW TO USE THIS ATLAS

Essential World Atlas contains two world maps—physical and political—and 67 regional spreads, arranged by continent. Each of these features a detailed regional map, supplemented by smaller maps plotting population patterns and an economic profile of the area. Three-dimensional terrain maps, evocative illustrations and photographs, and an informative text enhance the pages. A comprehensive gazetteer of all place names is included.

Grid reference
The location of each place, as listed in the gazetteer, is referenced against the grid frame.

Regional map
Each regional map includes detailed information on the physical landscape of a region, as well as its human geography.

Photographs
Photographs of natural features and human structures are included, with captions.

Locator map
This map indicates the location of the region within its continent.

Illustration
Illustrations highlight significant areas within a major city.

Population Patterns key

Population Patterns map
The population distribution of the area is plotted on this map.

Economic Profile key

Economic Profile map
The regional land use and economic activity are displayed on this map.

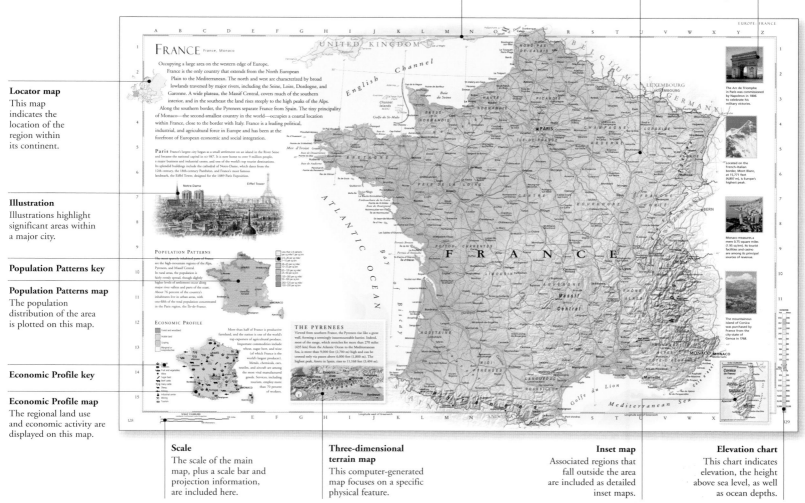

Scale
The scale of the main map, plus a scale bar and projection information, are included here.

Three-dimensional terrain map
This computer-generated map focuses on a specific physical feature.

Inset map
Associated regions that fall outside the area are included as detailed inset maps.

Elevation chart
This chart indicates elevation, the height above sea level, as well as ocean depths.

KEY TO MAPS

PHYSICAL FEATURES

ELEVATION
Feet	Meters
6562	2000
4921	1500
3281	1000
2461	750
1640	500
1312	400
984	300
656	200
328	100
0 / Below sea level	0
656	200
3281	1000
6562	2000
13,123	4000
19,685	6000
26,246	8000
32,808	10,000

PHYSICAL FEATURES

☐ Ice cap
☐ Ice shelf

▲ Mountain peak/volcano *Height, feet (meters)*
+ Pole
△ Geomagnetic Pole
▲ Seamount
▼ Sea trench *Depth, feet (meters)*

WATER FEATURES
◇ Lake
◇ Salt pan/Dry/Intermittent lake
◻ Coastline
〜 Major river
〜 Minor river
✖ River source
▼ Waterfall

GRATICULE FEATURE
125° Graticule number
— Graticule line
--- Tropics/polar circle
— Equator

BORDERS
〜 International border
〜 Defined maritime boundary
〜 Equidistant lines
〜 Disputed border
•••• Demarcation/line of control/ceasefire line
〜 State/territory border (Australia, Canada, U.S.A.)
〜 International Date Line

TRANSPORT
〜 Major road
〜 Main road
〜 Minor road
〜 Railway

NATIONAL/DEPENDENT TERRITORY CAPITAL CITIES
Over 5 million	■ **LONDON**
1–5 million	● **OTTAWA**
100,000–1 million	✴ **HELSINKI**
100,000–1 million	✴ **KINGSTON**
0–100,000	✴ **HONIARA**
0–100,000	✴ **BELMOPAN**

STATE/TERRITORY CAPITAL CITIES
(Australia, Canada, U.S.A.)
Over 5 million	■ **Toronto**
1–5 million	● **Sydney**
100,000–1 million	✴ **Québec**
0–100,000	✴ **Columbia**

OTHER CITIES OR TOWNS
Over 5 million	■ **São Paulo**
1–5 million	● **Calicut**
100,000–1 million	○ Luxor
0–100,000	○ Lillehammer

☐ Research base
🛏 Built-up area

TYPOGRAPHIC KEY

POLITICAL FEATURES
Country	**BELIZE**
Dependent territory with parent state	VIRGIN ISLANDS (to U.S.A.)
Internal administrative region	*UMBRIA*
State/Territory (Australia, Canada, U.S.A.)	V I C T O R I A

PHYSICAL FEATURES
Mountain range	*Allegheny Mountains*
Mountain peak	Mt Davis
Geographic feature	Nullarbor Plain
Peninsula	Cape York Peninsula
Headland/point/cape	Cabo de São Vincent
Island group	Solomon Islands
Island	New Caledonia
Pole	North Pole

WATER FEATURES
Ocean	*PACIFIC OCEAN*
Sea	*Irish Sea*
Bay/gulf	*Gulf of Mexico*
Channel/strait	*Bass Strait*
Undersea ridge	*Carlsberg Ridge*
Seamount/Sea trench	*Golden Dragon Seamount*
Lake/Salt pan/Dry/Intermittent lake	*Lake Titicaca*
Major river	*Nile*
Minor river	*Salween*
River source	*Source of the Amazon*
Waterfall	*Angel Falls*

GRATICULE FEATURES
Tropics/polar circle/equator	Tropic of Capricorn
Date line	International Date Line

CONTENTS

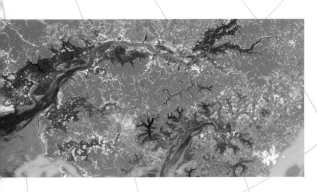
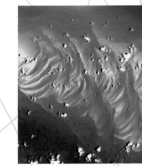
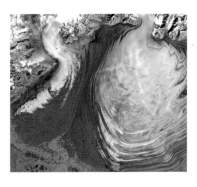
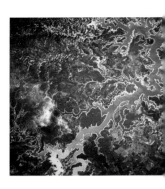

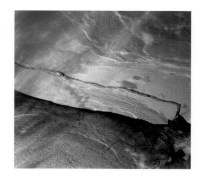

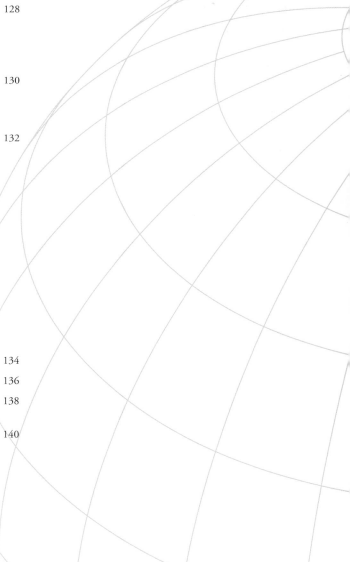

THE PHYSICAL WORLD

Oceans and seas dominate the globe, covering 70.8 percent of its surface. The land between these large bodies of water is traditionally divided into seven major landmasses or continents: Europe, Asia, North America, South America, Africa, Australia, and Antarctica. Europe and Asia form a single landmass, known as Eurasia, but are conventionally identified as separate continents because of their distinct peoples and histories. Though technically a continent in itself, Australia is usually considered part of the large region of Oceania, which includes the other islands of the southwestern Pacific Ocean.

NORTHERN HEMISPHERE

The Northern Hemisphere encompasses more than two-thirds of Earth's land, including all of Europe and North America, and most of Asia and Africa. Its areas of open ocean are further reduced by the presence of a permanent ice cap that surrounds the North Pole, covering most of the Arctic Ocean.

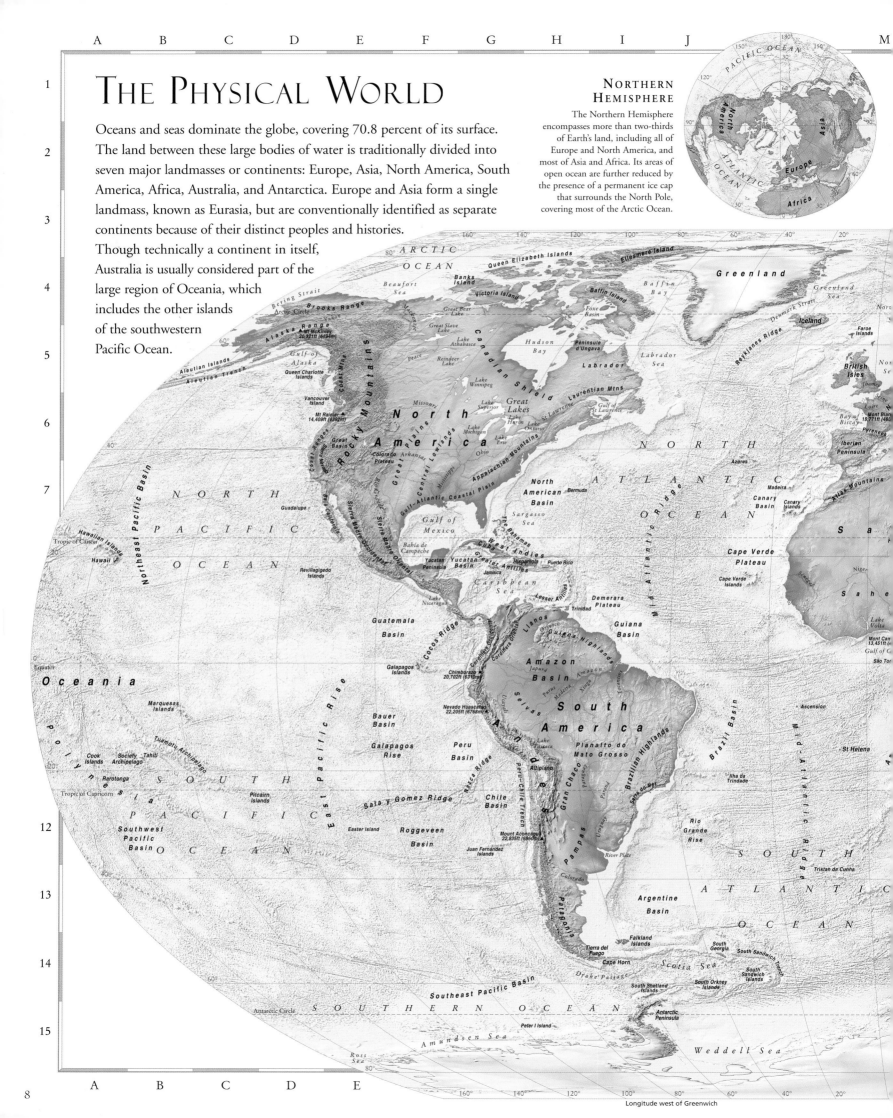

Longitude west of Greenwich

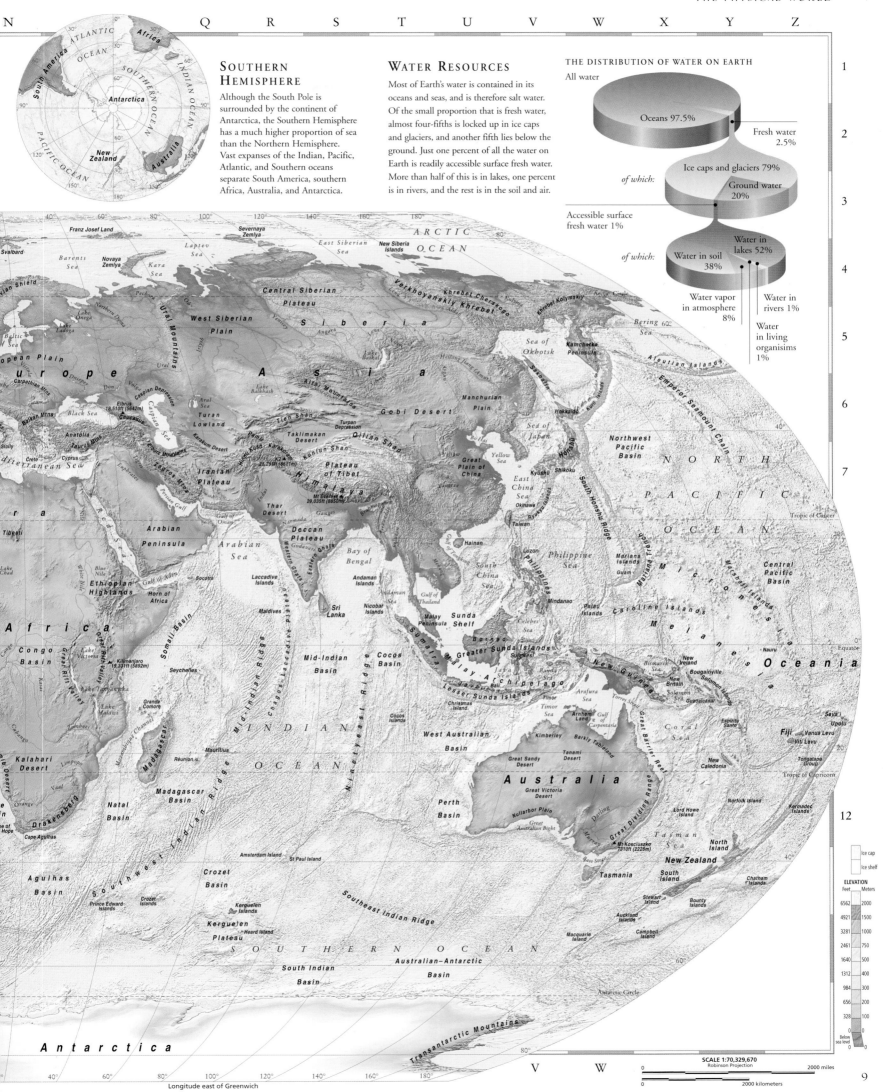

SOUTHERN HEMISPHERE

Although the South Pole is surrounded by the continent of Antarctica, the Southern Hemisphere has a much higher proportion of sea than the Northern Hemisphere. Vast expanses of the Indian, Pacific, Atlantic, and Southern oceans separate South America, southern Africa, Australia, and Antarctica.

WATER RESOURCES

Most of Earth's water is contained in its oceans and seas, and is therefore salt water. Of the small proportion that is fresh water, almost four-fifths is locked up in ice caps and glaciers, and another fifth lies below the ground. Just one percent of all the water on Earth is readily accessible surface fresh water. More than half of this is in lakes, one percent is in rivers, and the rest is in the soil and air.

THE DISTRIBUTION OF WATER ON EARTH

All water

Oceans 97.5%

Fresh water 2.5%

of which:

Ice caps and glaciers 79%

Ground water 20%

Accessible surface fresh water 1%

of which:

Water in lakes 52%

Water in soil 38%

Water vapor in atmosphere 8%

Water in rivers 1%

Water in living organisims 1%

ELEVATION

Feet	Meters
6562	2000
4921	1500
3281	1000
2461	750
1640	500
1312	400
984	300
656	200
328	100
0	0
Below sea level	

Ice cap

Ice shelf

SCALE 1:70,329,670
Robinson Projection

0   2000 miles
0   2000 kilometers

Longitude east of Greenwich

THE POLITICAL WORLD

With the exception of Antarctica, where territorial claims have been suspended, all the land on Earth is divided into 192 independent countries and about 60 dependent territories. The countries range in size from the largest, the vast Russian Federation, to the smallest, the Vatican City, which lies entirely within the city of Rome in Italy. Most dependent territories came about as the result of colonization and belong to a few, mainly European nations. Some areas of land, usually on the fringes of countries, are the focus of territorial disputes.

Dividing the World

About 150,000 miles (250,000 km) of land boundaries separate the world's countries and territories. These borders may follow landforms, waterways, the margins of traditional ethnic territories, lines of latitude or longitude, or arbitrary lines plotted by colonial administrators. Many seaboard nations have also established maritime boundaries. A nation's maritime territorial claim extends 12 nautical miles offshore, but exclusive fishing and economic zones are generally recognized up to 200 nautical miles offshore.

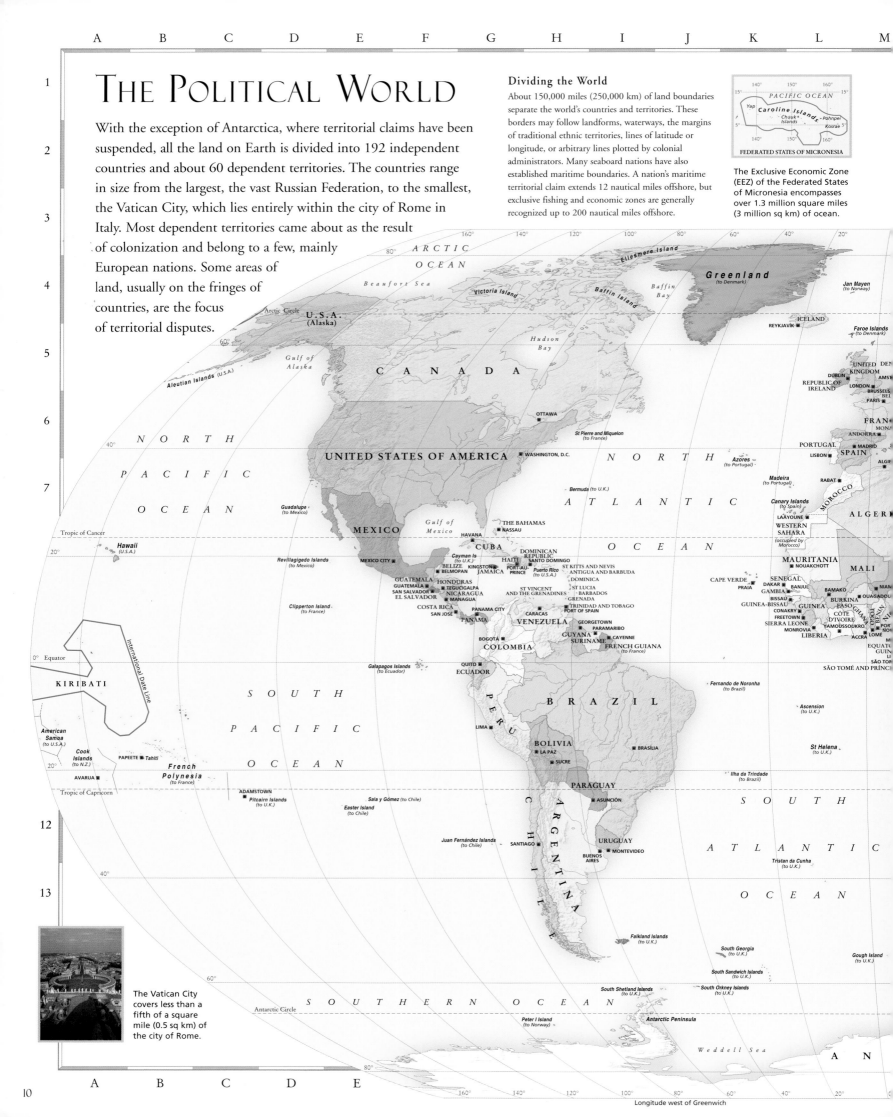

FEDERATED STATES OF MICRONESIA

The Exclusive Economic Zone (EEZ) of the Federated States of Micronesia encompasses over 1.3 million square miles (3 million sq km) of ocean.

The Vatican City covers less than a fifth of a square mile (0.5 sq km) of the city of Rome.

Longitude west of Greenwich

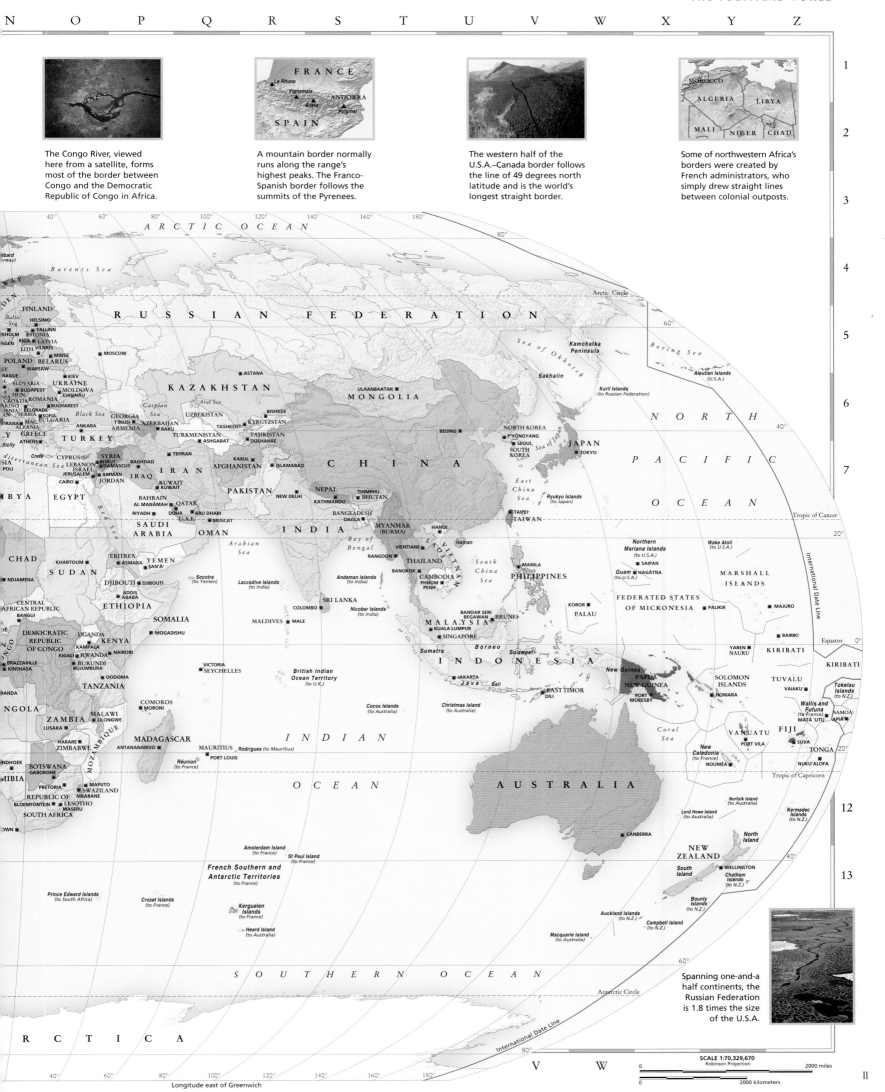

The Congo River, viewed here from a satellite, forms most of the border between Congo and the Democratic Republic of Congo in Africa.

A mountain border normally runs along the range's highest peaks. The Franco-Spanish border follows the summits of the Pyrenees.

The western half of the U.S.A.–Canada border follows the line of 49 degrees north latitude and is the world's longest straight border.

Some of northwestern Africa's borders were created by French administrators, who simply drew straight lines between colonial outposts.

Spanning one-and-a half continents, the Russian Federation is 1.8 times the size of the U.S.A.

SCALE 1:70,329,670
Robinson Projection

2000 miles

2000 kilometers

UNITED STATES OF AMERICA

A federal republic made up of 50 states, the United States of America (U.S.A.) is the world's third-largest country by size and population. Its contiguous 48 states span the center of North America, from the Pacific Ocean to the Atlantic shoreline. The other two states are Alaska, in the far northwest of the continent, and the island state of Hawaii, in the central Pacific Ocean. On the western side of the lower 48, coastal ranges and the central Rocky Mountains enclose a series of high, arid plateaus and peaks. Plains predominate in the center and east, the much-eroded Appalachian Mountains dividing the vast Mississippi River Basin from the Atlantic Coastal Plain. The U.S.A. declared independence from British rule in 1776 and, with help from France, defeated Britain in the Revolutionary War. It has since flourished to become the world's leading economic and political power.

The Rockies attain their highest elevations in Colorado, which has 53 peaks above 14,000 feet (4,270 m).

The Mississippi River nears the end of its 2,339-mile (3,765-km) journey at New Orleans in Louisiana.

POPULATION PATTERNS

The U.S.A. has a large population, but it is distributed over a wide area. Density is higher in the eastern half of the country, especially on the northeastern seaboard, but California is the most populous state. Although the western interior is the least densely inhabited area, it has the fastest-growing state populations. The majority of Americans, 69.1 percent, are non-Hispanic whites; Hispanics make up 12.5 percent of the population, blacks 12.3 percent, Asians 3.6 percent, and Native Americans 0.9 percent.

Less than 2.6 persons per sq mile/1 per sq km
2.6–26 per sq mile/1–10 per sq km
26–65 per sq mile/10–25 per sq km
65–130 per sq mile/25–50 per sq km
130–260 per sq mile/50–100 per sq km
260–520 per sq mile/100–200 per sq km
520–1040 per sq mile/200–400 per sq km
1040–2080 per sq mile/400–800 per sq km

ECONOMIC PROFILE

The U.S.A. is the most productive nation on Earth. It has the world's largest coal reserves and generates 40 percent of its oil. Intensive farming of rich agricultural lands yields half of the world's corn, one-fifth of its meat, and one-tenth of its wheat. The U.S.A. is also the top producer of soybeans and the biggest source of timber. Forestry, mining, and agriculture are far surpassed, however, in terms of contribution to GDP, by manufacturing—led by transport equipment, industrial machinery, electronic components, and computers—and services, which employ 73.5 percent of workers, primarily in the financial and health sectors.

Corn (maize)
Cereals
Fruit
Citrus fruits
Cotton
Tobacco
Soybeans
Groundnuts
Beef cattle
Sheep
Fishing
Shellfish
Industrial center
Mining
Oil production
Tourism
Timber
Winter sports
Potatoes
Wine

Forest and woodland
Arable land
Grazing
Marginal or nonproductive

Longitude west of Greenwich

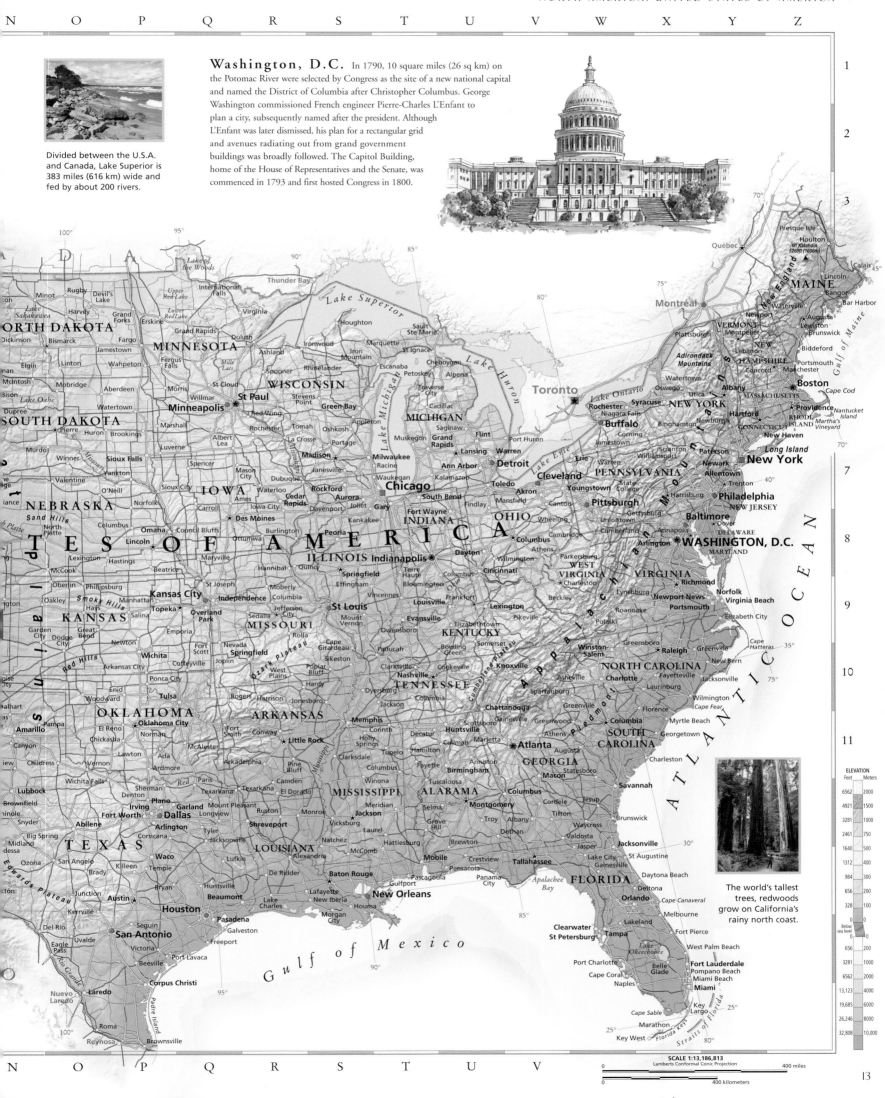

Washington, D.C.

In 1790, 10 square miles (26 sq km) on the Potomac River were selected by Congress as the site of a new national capital and named the District of Columbia after Christopher Columbus. George Washington commissioned French engineer Pierre-Charles L'Enfant to plan a city, subsequently named after the president. Although L'Enfant was later dismissed, his plan for a rectangular grid and avenues radiating out from grand government buildings was broadly followed. The Capitol Building, home of the House of Representatives and the Senate, was commenced in 1793 and first hosted Congress in 1800.

Divided between the U.S.A. and Canada, Lake Superior is 383 miles (616 km) wide and fed by about 200 rivers.

The world's tallest trees, redwoods grow on California's rainy north coast.

ELEVATION

Feet	Meters
6562	2000
4921	1500
3281	1000
2461	750
1640	500
1312	400
984	300
656	200
328	100
0	0
Below sea level	
656	200
3281	1000
6562	2000
13,123	4000
19,685	6000
26,246	8000
32,808	10,000

SCALE 1:13,186,813
Lamberts Conformal Conic Projection

0   400 miles

0   400 kilometers

NORTHEASTERN U.S.A.

Connecticut, Maine, Massachusetts, New Hampshire, New Jersey, New York, Pennsylvania, Rhode Island, Vermont

The site of some of the continent's earliest European settlements and subsequently the entry point to North America for millions of immigrants, the northeastern seaboard is the most densely populated part of the U.S.A. On the southern half of the coastal plain lies a string of cities that have merged to form one massive, almost continuous urban area. Running from Boston south to Washington, D.C., it is sometimes referred to as the megalopolis or BosWash corridor.

In the north, the shoreline is less developed and more rugged, deep bays and promontories lining southern Maine. To the west, the coastal plain is hemmed in by the ancient, forested peaks of the Appalachian Mountains. Studded with lakes and breached by rivers, including the Hudson, Delaware, and Connecticut, the Appalachians reach west to the shores of the Great Lakes, to the Adirondack Mountains, and north into Canada.

Measuring 3,500 miles (5,630 km) in length, the heavily indented Maine coast is fringed by rocky inlets and 1,200 islands.

The strongest winds ever measured were recorded on top of Mount Washington in New Hampshire's White Mountains.

Longitude west of Greenwich

Map grid labels (top): N O P Q R S T U V W X Y Z

Map grid numbers (right): 1 2 3 4 5 6 7 8 9 10 11

Main Map Labels

CANADA

Madawaska, Van Buren, Eagle Lake, Limestone, Caribou, Presque Isle, Ashland, Houlton, Patten, Sherman Mills, Danforth, Vanceboro, Mattawamkeag, Lincoln, Woodland, Calais, Millinocket, Greenville, Milo, Guilford, Old Town, Wesley, Machias, Bangor, Brewer, Skowhegan, Pittsfield, Ellsworth, Cross Island, Lubec, Jackman, Bingham, Solon, Farmington, Winslow, Searsport, Blue Hill, Milbridge, Belfast, Bar Harbor, Rangeley, Stratton, Wilton, Augusta, Camden, Rockland, Wiscasset, Bath, Brunswick, Colebrook, Errol, Groveton, Lancaster, Bethel, South Paris, Lewiston, Bridgton, Lisbon Falls, Portland, Cape Elizabeth, Small Point

Eagle Lake, Chamberlain Lake, Chesuncook Lake, Moosehead Lake, Mt Katahdin 5269ft (1606m), White Cap Mountain 3645ft (1111m), Flagstaff Lake, West Grand Lake, Chiputneticook Lakes, Grand Manan Channel, Grand Manan Island, Great Wass Island, Mount Desert Island, Deer Isle, Swans Island, Isle au Haut, Vinalhaven Island

MAINE

Appalachian Mountains, Longfellow Mountains

NEW HAMPSHIRE, Mt Washington 6293ft (1918m), White Mountains, Conway, Laconia, Lake Winnipesaukee, Sebago Lake, Sanford, Biddeford, Kennebunkport, Rochester, Dover, Newmarket, Concord, Manchester, Derry, Newburyport, Lawrence, Lowell, York Harbor, Portsmouth, Hampton, Gulf of Maine, Casco Bay

MASSACHUSETTS, Cambridge, Concord, Boston, Newton, Weymouth, Brockton, Worcester, Milford, Salem, Gloucester, Cape Ann, Massachusetts Bay, Plymouth, Cape Cod Bay, Cape Cod, Provincetown, Orleans, Barnstable, Monomoy Island, Nantucket Sound, Buzzards Bay, New Bedford, Fall River, Taunton, Providence, RHODE ISLAND, Warwick, Newport, Pawtucket, Woonsocket, Rhode Island Sound, Block Island, Martha's Vineyard, Nantucket, Nantucket Island, Oak Bluffs, Sauk Point, Island Sound

THE HUDSON VALLEY

Numerous waterways cut through the Appalachian Mountains, dividing the system into smaller ranges and separating it from other uplands. In New York State, the southern Hudson River flows between the Taconic Range and the Catskill Mountains. Farther north, the Hudson and slender Lake Champlain separate the Green Mountains of Vermont from the Adirondack Mountains, which are in turn isolated from the Catskills by the Mohawk River Valley. Though often associated with the Appalachians, the Adirondacks are part of the ancient Canadian Shield. Formed 1 billion years ago, they cover about 9,400 square miles (24,300 sq km).

Inset map labels: Adirondack Mountains, Lake Placid, Lake Champlain, Montpelier, Lake Pleasant, Lake George, Ticonderoga, Rome, Little Falls, Great Sacandaga Lake, Hudson Falls, Schenectady, Mohawk, Hudson, Albany, Catskill Mountains, Green Mountains, N

New York City

New York City Originally the territory of Algonquian-speaking Indians, Manhattan Island became the site of a Dutch fur-trading post called New Amsterdam in 1625. Disappointed with its income, the Dutch relinquished the settlement to Britain in 1664 (in return for Suriname). Rechristened New York, the town expanded rapidly following U.S. independence, becoming the world's second-largest city by 1900, with 4.2 million people. In the early 20th century, numerous skyscrapers were built to accommodate Manhattan's thriving businesses. Iconic features of today's Midtown skyline include the Chrysler Building (1930), the Empire State Building (1931)—on completion, the world's tallest building—and the United Nations Headquarters (1952).

Philadelphia's City Hall is capped by a statue of William Penn, who founded Pennsylvania as a refuge for Quakers.

Situated on the U.S.A.–Canada border near Buffalo, Niagara Falls drop approximately 190 feet (58 m).

The deciduous forests of New England are noted for their startling displays of foliage color in fall.

Empire State Building
Chrysler Building
UN Headquarters

POPULATION PATTERNS

Together, the metropolitan areas of New York City, Philadelphia, and Boston accommodate more than 33 million people—almost 12 percent of the American population. Smaller but equally dense agglomerations are taking shape around Buffalo and Pittsburgh. Settlements are more scattered in the Appalachian uplands and in the north—Maine is the least densely populated state east of the Mississippi. Despite its large population, the Northeast experienced the country's lowest level of regional population growth between 1990 and 2000: just 5.5 percent.

Less than 2.6 persons per sq mile/1 per sq km
2.6–26 per sq mile/1–10 per sq km
26–65 per sq mile/10–25 per sq km
65–130 per sq mile/25–50 per sq km
130–260 per sq mile/50–100 per sq km
260–520 per sq mile/100–200 per sq km
520–1040 per sq mile/200–400 per sq km
1040–2080 per sq mile/400–800 per sq km

Map labels: Bangor, Montpelier, Augusta, Concord, Buffalo, Syracuse, Albany, Boston, Erie, Hartford, Providence, Pittsburgh, Harrisburg, New York, Philadelphia

ECONOMIC PROFILE

The Northeast is America's commercial and industrial hub. New York City, seat of the New York Stock Exchange and Wall Street, leads the world in business and finance, and Boston is an important center of banking, insurance, and electronics. The combined port of New York and New Jersey is the nation's largest, and despite a decline in heavy industry Pennsylvania is still one of the nation's leading steel producers. Forests swathe large areas, including 90 percent of Maine, and yield abundant timber. Tourism, generated by attractions as diverse as Niagara Falls and the cultural centers of Manhattan, is also a prime source of revenue.

Legend: Fishing, Dairy cattle, Industrial center, Timber, Fruit, Poultry, Tourism, Mining, Winter sports, Potatoes

Forest and woodland
Arable land

Map labels: Bangor, Montpelier, Augusta, Concord, Buffalo, Syracuse, Albany, Boston, Erie, Hartford, Providence, Pittsburgh, Harrisburg, New York, Philadelphia

ELEVATION

Feet	Meters
6562	2000
4921	1500
3281	1000
2461	750
1640	500
1312	400
984	300
656	200
328	100
Below sea level	0
656	200
3281	1000
6562	2000
13,123	4000
19,685	6000
26,246	8000
32,808	10,000

SCALE 1:3,296,703
Lamberts Conformal Conic Projection
0 ___ 100 miles
0 ___ 100 kilometers

SOUTH ATLANTIC U.S.A.

Delaware, District of Columbia, Kentucky, Maryland, North Carolina, South Carolina, Tennessee, Virginia, West Virginia

The northern perimeter of this region, formed by the Ohio River and the southern border of Pennsylvania—the so-called Mason and Dixon Line—is the traditional divide between North and South: prior to the Civil War it separated slave-owning states from abolitionists. History and terrain have created other regional distinctions. The thickly forested ridges of the Appalachian Mountains form a sparsely populated enclave of mining and timber towns.

To the west lie the pastoral hills of central Tennessee and Kentucky's Bluegrass region, and the heavily cultivated lowlands of the Mississippi and Ohio rivers. In the east, the wooded Appalachian foothills, known as the Piedmont, descend to a broad coastal plain bordered by historic ports and barrier islands.

POPULATION PATTERNS

In the northeast, the population is heavily urbanized and concentrated in the Washington–Baltimore area, home to 7.6 million people. Elsewhere the proportion of rural dwellers is high, rising from 27 percent in Virginia to 51 percent in West Virginia. In Virginia and the Carolinas, people cluster in the Piedmont, but the cities here are relatively small; the largest urban centers outside the northeast are Nashville and Memphis in Tennessee. Population growth between 1990 and 2000 varied markedly, from –5.7 percent in the District of Columbia to 21.4 percent in North Carolina.

ECONOMIC PROFILE

Farming has declined in importance, though this is still the country's main source of tobacco and yields sizable crops of soybeans, corn, and vegetables. Kentucky is also renowned for horse-breeding. Manufacturing industries include whiskey in Kentucky and Tennessee; chemicals in Tennessee, Virginia, and Delaware; and textiles and high-tech goods in North Carolina. Service industries predominate in the northeast, with the government being a major employer. Appalachia has some of America's most productive coal fields. Fishing, mainly of shellfish, remains important around Chesapeake Bay.

Population density legend:
- Less than 2.6 persons per sq mile/1 per sq km
- 2.6–26 per sq mile/1–10 per sq km
- 26–65 per sq mile/10–25 per sq km
- 65–130 per sq mile/25–50 per sq km
- 130–260 per sq mile/50–100 per sq km
- 260–520 per sq mile/100–200 per sq km
- 520–1040 per sq mile/200–400 per sq km
- 1040–2080 per sq mile/400–800 per sq km

Economic legend:
- Corn (maize)
- Cotton
- Shellfish
- Tobacco
- Fishing
- Industrial center
- Timber
- Beef cattle
- Mining
- Fruit
- Poultry
- Soybeans
- Pigs
- Forest and woodland
- Arable land
- Grazing

Longitude west of Greenwich

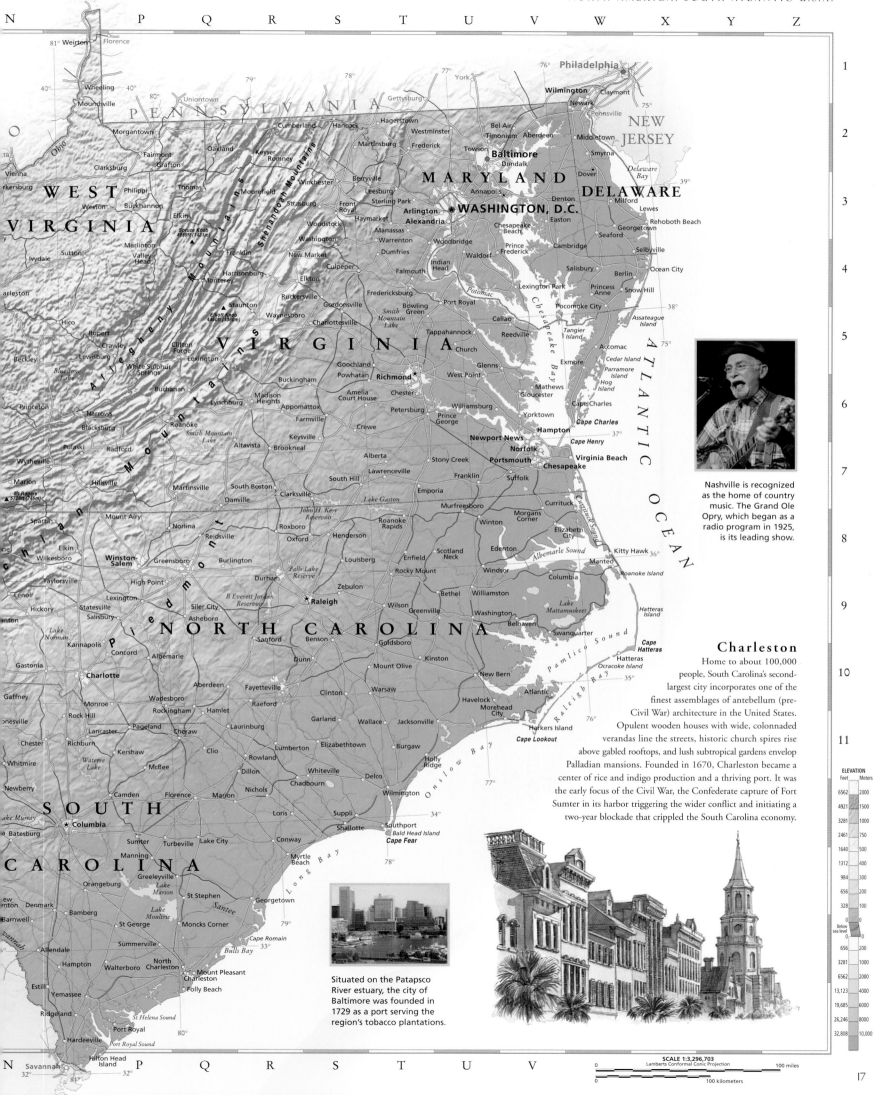

Nashville is recognized as the home of country music. The Grand Ole Opry, which began as a radio program in 1925, is its leading show.

Charleston

Home to about 100,000 people, South Carolina's second-largest city incorporates one of the finest assemblages of antebellum (pre-Civil War) architecture in the United States. Opulent wooden houses with wide, colonnaded verandas line the streets, historic church spires rise above gabled rooftops, and lush subtropical gardens envelop Palladian mansions. Founded in 1670, Charleston became a center of rice and indigo production and a thriving port. It was the early focus of the Civil War, the Confederate capture of Fort Sumter in its harbor triggering the wider conflict and initiating a two-year blockade that crippled the South Carolina economy.

Situated on the Patapsco River estuary, the city of Baltimore was founded in 1729 as a port serving the region's tobacco plantations.

ELEVATION	
Feet	Meters
32,808	10,000
26,246	8000
19,685	6000
13,123	4000
6562	2000
3281	1000
656	200
0	0
Below sea level	
0	0
328	100
656	200
984	300
1312	400
1640	500
2461	750
3281	1000
4921	1500
6562	2000

SCALE 1:3,296,703
Lamberts Conformal Conic Projection

0 — 100 miles
0 — 100 kilometers

SOUTHEASTERN U.S.A.

Alabama, Florida, Georgia, Louisiana, Mississippi

In the southeastern corner of the United States, rolling hills and low plateaus cover much of the interior, rising in northern Alabama and Georgia to the southern edge of the Appalachian Mountains and descending along a broad sweep to the alluvial plain of the Mississippi River, the Gulf and Atlantic coastal plains, and the broad, flat Florida Peninsula. In the 16th century, Spanish explorers became the first Europeans to visit this predominantly swampy coastline, then home to various Indian groups. The Spanish founded the settlement of St Augustine, Florida, in 1565, now the oldest city in the country. In the late 17th century, French traders took control of the Mississippi Basin, establishing a port at New Orleans. Under the Treaty of Paris of 1763, New Orleans and the western Mississippi Valley passed to Spain, while the land to the east of the Mississippi, including Spanish Florida, came under British control. After the Civil War, continuing discrimination against the African-American population made the Southeast the focus of civil-rights protests, which reached a peak in the 1960s with mass demonstrations in Montgomery and Birmingham, Alabama, and the 1963 March on Washington for Jobs and Freedom.

Hurricanes regularly strike the Southeast. In August 1992, Hurricane Andrew caused US$25 billion worth of damage and 23 deaths.

The distinctive architecture of New Orleans reflects the origins of its early inhabitants. Founded by the French in 1718, it was ceded to Spain in 1763.

POPULATION PATTERNS

The Southeast's inhabitants are fairly evenly spread, though coastal wetlands limit settlement in parts of the Gulf Coast (notably the Mississippi Delta) and Florida. Population density and urbanization are lower in the three western states, particularly in Mississippi. In contrast, Georgia and Florida have large urban populations, with settlement focused on cities such as Atlanta (home to half of Georgia's people), Tampa, and Miami. The populations of these two states are growing rapidly, with Florida's projected to reach 20 million by 2010, due in part to its popularity as a retirement destination.

	Less than 2.6 persons per sq mile/1 per sq km
	2.6–26 per sq mile/1–10 per sq km
	26–65 per sq mile/10–25 per sq km
	65–130 per sq mile/25–50 per sq km
	130–260 per sq mile/50–100 per sq km

ECONOMIC PROFILE

Until the early 20th century, the Southeast was dependent on agriculture, especially the cultivation of cotton and tobacco. These crops remain significant, but farmers have diversified into soybeans, corn, peanuts, and, in Florida, citrus fruits. Extensive forests provide abundant timber, and the industrial sector has expanded to include textiles, transportation equipment, electronics, and the aerospace industry. Louisiana is one of the nation's leading producers of oil and gas, Georgia is home to major corporations—Atlanta is the headquarters of Coca-Cola and CNN (Cable News Network)—and Florida has a thriving tourist industry.

Forest and woodland	Corn (maize)
Arable land	Citrus fruits
Grazing	Cotton
Marginal or nonproductive	Tobacco
	Soybeans
	Peanuts
	Fishing
	Shellfish
	Industrial center
	Oil production
	Tourism
	Timber

Longitude west of Greenwich

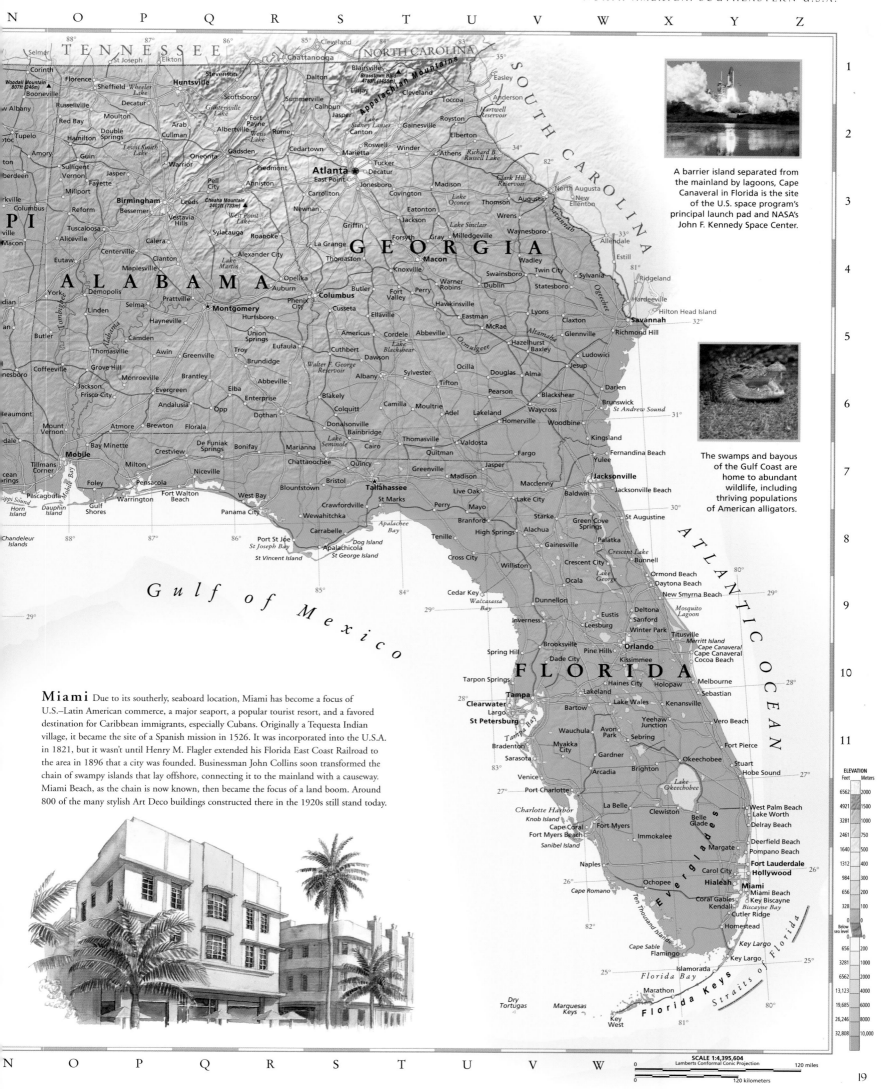

A barrier island separated from the mainland by lagoons, Cape Canaveral in Florida is the site of the U.S. space program's principal launch pad and NASA's John F. Kennedy Space Center.

The swamps and bayous of the Gulf Coast are home to abundant wildlife, including thriving populations of American alligators.

Miami Due to its southerly, seaboard location, Miami has become a focus of U.S.–Latin American commerce, a major seaport, a popular tourist resort, and a favored destination for Caribbean immigrants, especially Cubans. Originally a Tequesta Indian village, it became the site of a Spanish mission in 1526. It was incorporated into the U.S.A. in 1821, but it wasn't until Henry M. Flagler extended his Florida East Coast Railroad to the area in 1896 that a city was founded. Businessman John Collins soon transformed the chain of swampy islands that lay offshore, connecting it to the mainland with a causeway. Miami Beach, as the chain is now known, then became the focus of a land boom. Around 800 of the many stylish Art Deco buildings constructed there in the 1920s still stand today.

ELEVATION	
Feet	Meters
6562	2000
4921	1500
3281	1000
2461	750
1640	500
1312	400
984	300
656	200
328	100
0	0
Below sea level	
656	200
3281	1000
6562	2000
13,123	4000
19,685	6000
26,246	8000
32,808	10,000

SCALE 1:4,395,604
Lamberts Conformal Conic Projection
0   120 miles
0   120 kilometers

GREAT LAKES, U.S.A.

Illinois, Indiana, Michigan, Ohio, Wisconsin

The largest accumulation of fresh water in the world, the Great Lakes, and the lowlands that stretch to the south, were created by a series of ice ages beginning 1 million years ago. During these cold phases, the land was scoured flat by ice sheets that reached south to the Ohio River. At the end of the last ice age, about 13,000 years ago, melting ice flooded wide, shallow basins, forming today's immense bodies of water. Linked to the Atlantic Ocean by the St Lawrence River, the lakes allowed this region to thrive as a transportation center following European settlement. Lakefront cities became distribution points for commodities from the fertile farmland to the south and for timber from the forested, slightly higher terrain around the northern shores. The subsequent discovery of massive deposits of iron ore in Michigan gave rise to industrial centers, which now line the southern shores of Lakes Michigan and Erie.

Sears Tower

Detroit was home to the first U.S. automobile factories, and dominated world production until the 1960s.

Chicago In 1818, when Illinois became a state, Chicago consisted of no more than a cluster of traders' huts on the muddy shore of Lake Michigan. But the opening of the Erie Canal (1825), the construction of the Illinois and Michigan Canal link to the Mississippi River (1842), and the arrival of railroads from the east (1852) resulted in rapid growth. By the late 19th century, this vital transport hub was home to 1 million people. When the downtown area was rebuilt following a fire in 1871, the city became the birthplace of the skyscraper. Between 1885 and 1894, 21 buildings of 12 stories or more were constructed. Today's skyline is dominated by the Sears Tower, which was the world's tallest building from its completion in 1974 until it was surpassed by the Petronas Towers in Kuala Lumpur, Malaysia, in 1996.

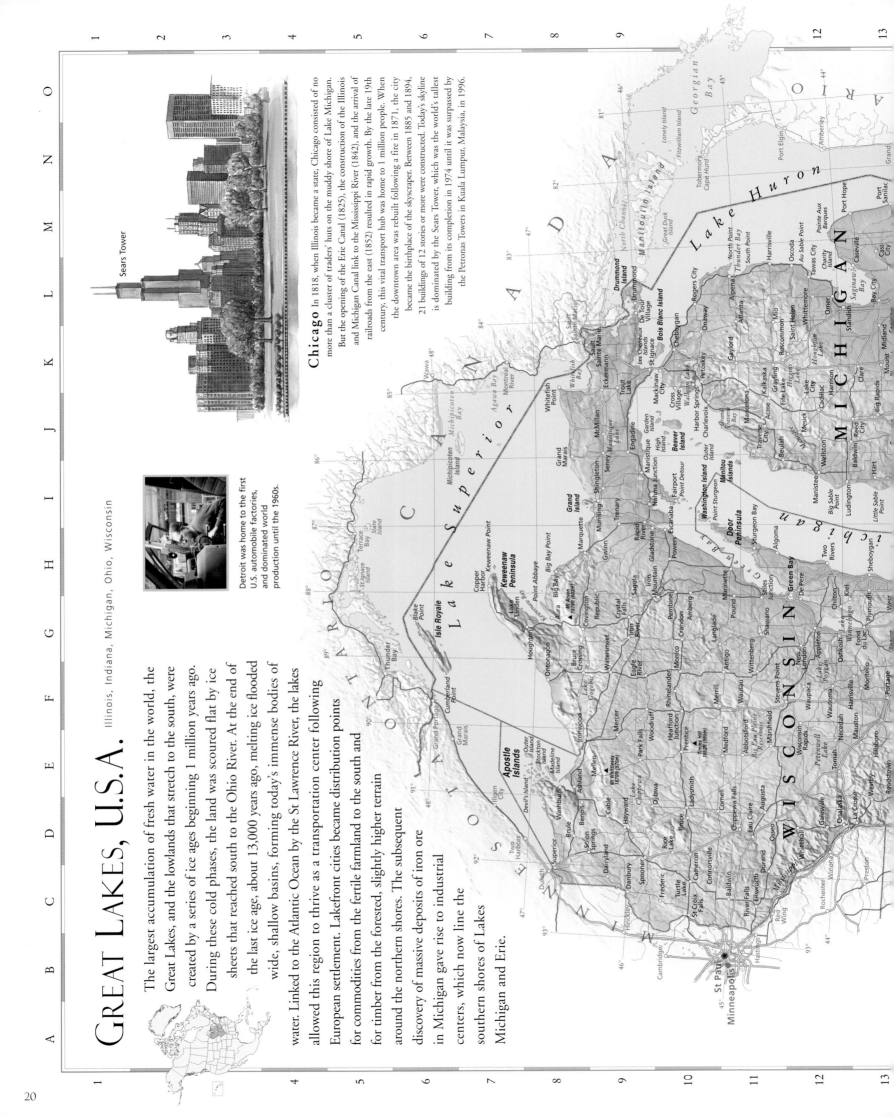

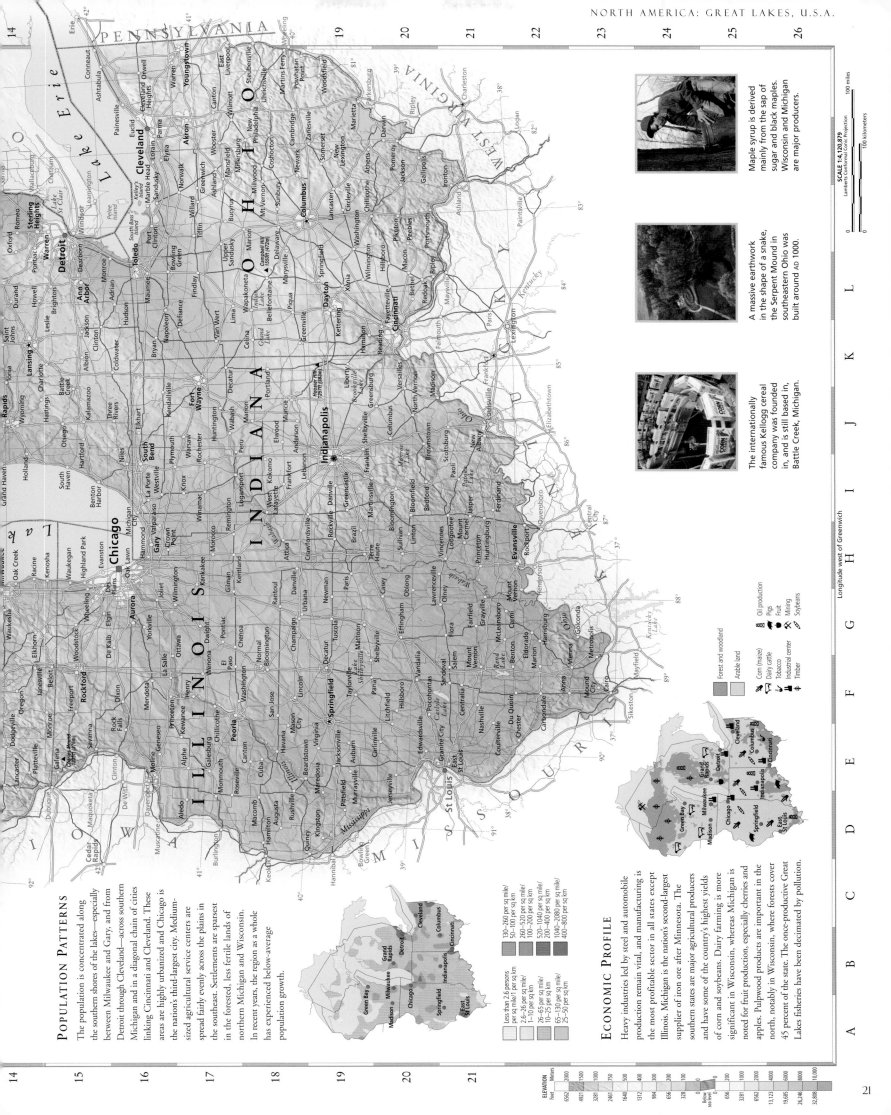

POPULATION PATTERNS

The population is concentrated along the southern shores of the lakes—especially between Milwaukee and Gary, and from Detroit through Cleveland—across southern Michigan and in a diagonal chain of cities linking Cincinnati and Cleveland. These areas are highly urbanized and Chicago is the nation's third-largest city. Medium-sized agricultural service centers are spread fairly evenly across the plains in the southeast. Settlements are sparsest in the forested, less fertile lands of northern Michigan and Wisconsin. In recent years, the region as a whole has experienced below-average population growth.

	less than 2.6 persons per sq mile/1 per sq km
	2.6–26 per sq mile/ 1–10 per sq km
	26–65 per sq mile/ 10–25 per sq km
	65–130 per sq mile/ 25–50 per sq km
	130–260 per sq mile/ 50–100 per sq km
	260–520 per sq mile/ 100–200 per sq km
	520–1040 per sq mile/ 200–400 per sq km
	1040–2080 per sq mile/ 400–800 per sq km

ECONOMIC PROFILE

Heavy industries led by steel and automobile production remain vital, and manufacturing is the most profitable sector in all states except Illinois. Michigan is the nation's second-largest supplier of iron ore after Minnesota. The southern states are major agricultural producers and have some of the country's highest yields of corn and soybeans. Dairy farming is more significant in Wisconsin, whereas Michigan is noted for fruit production, especially cherries and apples. Pulpwood products are important in the north, notably in Wisconsin, where forests cover 45 percent of the state. The once-productive Great Lakes fisheries have been decimated by pollution.

Forest and woodland
Arable land

Corn (maize)
Dairy cattle
Tobacco
Industrial center
Timber

Oil production
Pigs
Fruit
Mining
Soybeans

The internationally famous Kellogg cereal company was founded in, and is still based in, Battle Creek, Michigan.

A massive earthwork in the shape of a snake, the Serpent Mound in southeastern Ohio was built around AD 1000.

Maple syrup is derived mainly from the sap of sugar and black maples. Wisconsin and Michigan are major producers.

SCALE 1:4,120,879
Lamberts Conformal Conic Projection

0   100 miles
0   100 kilometers

Longitude west of Greenwich

ELEVATION
Feet   Meters
6562   2000
4921   1500
3281   1000
2461   750
1640   500
1312   400
984   300
656   200
328   100
0   Below sea level   0
        656   200
        3281   1000
        6562   2000
        13,123 4000
        19,685 6000
        26,246 8000
        32,808 10,000

UPPER MIDWEST, U.S.A.

Iowa, Minnesota, Nebraska,
North Dakota, South Dakota

A seemingly boundless sea of crops is the image
most strongly associated with the Upper Midwest,
and indeed more than half of the land is used for
cultivation and agriculture dominates the economy.
Wheat fields swathe much of the Great Plains
plateau on the western side of the region. Myriad
streams and rivers follow the plateau's gentle
eastward inclination, carving gullies and channels through
hills and badlands, and feeding for the most part into
the Missouri River. Undulating farmland—mainly
fields of corn and soybeans—also covers most of Iowa
and southern Minnesota. In the northeast, the plains
are studded with lakes and marshes formed by the retreat
of glaciers at the end of last ice age. The upper
Mississippi and Missouri were vital transportation routes
for Native Americans and early European explorers and
trappers, but widespread intensive settlement did not take
place until after the arrival of the railroads around 1870.

POPULATION PATTERNS

The western part of this region is one of the most sparsely inhabited parts of the
lower 48, and North and South Dakota are, respectively, the second and fourth
least populous states. The east has larger settlements, especially along major rivers.
The Upper Midwest generally experiences lower than average population growth:
between 1990 and 2000, North Dakota had the country's lowest rate of growth,
a mere 0.5 percent. The overall proportion of rural dwellers is significantly higher
than average, reaching almost half in South Dakota.

	Less than 2.6 persons per sq mile/1 per sq km
	2.6–26 per sq mile/ 1–10 per sq km
	26–65 per sq mile/ 10–25 per sq km
	65–130 per sq mile/ 25–50 per sq km
	130–260 per sq mile/ 50–100 per sq km

ECONOMIC PROFILE

These states are among the nation's largest agricultural producers. The west
forms part of the Great Plains Wheat Belt; the so-called Corn Belt encompasses
eastern Nebraska, Iowa, and southern Minnesota. Grazing of cattle and pigs occurs
throughout the region. Minnesota is the nation's largest producer of iron ore,
Nebraska and North Dakota have modest supplies of petroleum, and South Dakota's
Black Hills are a prime source of gold. Farming is the basis of most manufacturing
and services, though tourism and the insurance industry are also important.

	Forest and woodland
	Arable land
	Grazing
	Cereals
	Corn (maize)
	Beef cattle
	Industrial center
	Mining
	Oil production
	Soybeans
	Pigs

22

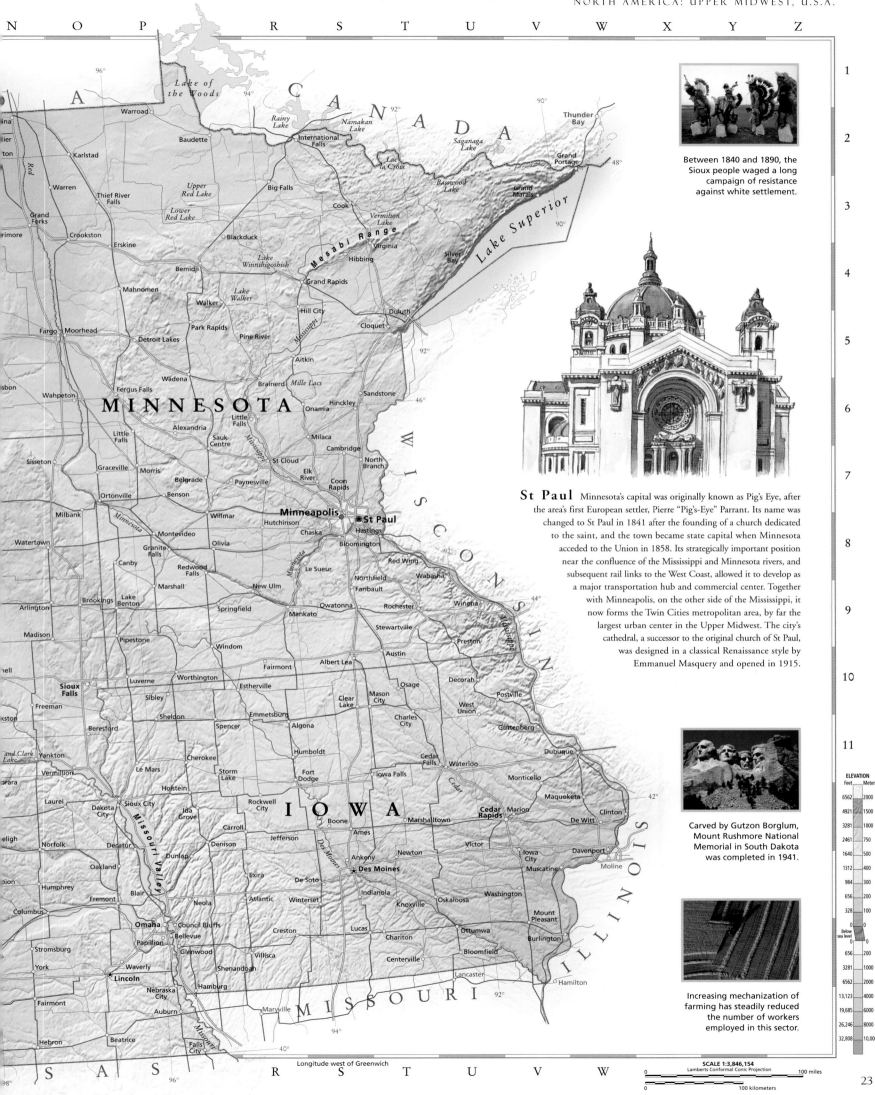

Between 1840 and 1890, the Sioux people waged a long campaign of resistance against white settlement.

St Paul Minnesota's capital was originally known as Pig's Eye, after the area's first European settler, Pierre "Pig's-Eye" Parrant. Its name was changed to St Paul in 1841 after the founding of a church dedicated to the saint, and the town became state capital when Minnesota acceded to the Union in 1858. Its strategically important position near the confluence of the Mississippi and Minnesota rivers, and subsequent rail links to the West Coast, allowed it to develop as a major transportation hub and commercial center. Together with Minneapolis, on the other side of the Mississippi, it now forms the Twin Cities metropolitan area, by far the largest urban center in the Upper Midwest. The city's cathedral, a successor to the original church of St Paul, was designed in a classical Renaissance style by Emmanuel Masquery and opened in 1915.

Carved by Gutzon Borglum, Mount Rushmore National Memorial in South Dakota was completed in 1941.

Increasing mechanization of farming has steadily reduced the number of workers employed in this sector.

ELEVATION

Feet	Meters
6562	2000
4921	1500
3281	1000
2461	750
1640	500
1312	400
984	300
656	200
328	100
0 Below sea level	0
656	200
3281	1000
6562	2000
13,123	4000
19,685	6000
26,246	8000
32,808	10,000

Longitude west of Greenwich

SCALE 1:3,846,154
Lamberts Conformal Conic Projection

0   100 miles

0   100 kilometers

LOWER MIDWEST, U.S.A.

Arkansas, Kansas, Missouri, Oklahoma

From the central Mississippi River, pioneers launched the great wave of westward expansion that began in the 1840s, turning this region into the "Gateway to the West." Most traveled along the Missouri River, over the hills of present-day Kansas and across the treeless plateau of the Great Plains. But the rugged, densely forested terrain of the Ozark Plateau and Ouachita Mountains in the east, the presence of large groups of displaced Native Americans in the so-called Indian Territory of the west, and early reports that the plains were a desert meant that the majority simply passed through. It wasn't until the end of the century that farmers turned the western plains into the major agricultural region that, despite occasional droughts such as those that created the Dust Bowl of the 1930s, it remains today.

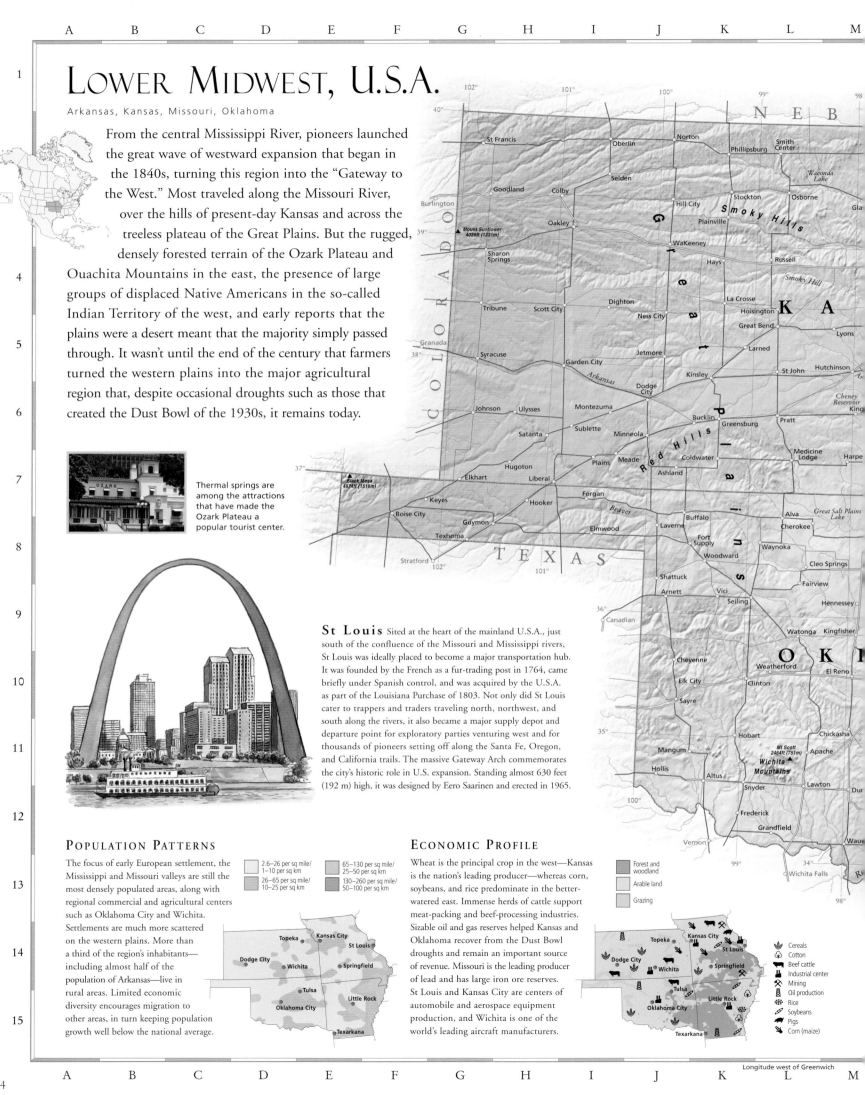

Thermal springs are among the attractions that have made the Ozark Plateau a popular tourist center.

St Louis Sited at the heart of the mainland U.S.A., just south of the confluence of the Missouri and Mississippi rivers, St Louis was ideally placed to become a major transportation hub. It was founded by the French as a fur-trading post in 1764, came briefly under Spanish control, and was acquired by the U.S.A. as part of the Louisiana Purchase of 1803. Not only did St Louis cater to trappers and traders traveling north, northwest, and south along the rivers, it also became a major supply depot and departure point for exploratory parties venturing west and for thousands of pioneers setting off along the Santa Fe, Oregon, and California trails. The massive Gateway Arch commemorates the city's historic role in U.S. expansion. Standing almost 630 feet (192 m) high, it was designed by Eero Saarinen and erected in 1965.

POPULATION PATTERNS

The focus of early European settlement, the Mississippi and Missouri valleys are still the most densely populated areas, along with regional commercial and agricultural centers such as Oklahoma City and Wichita. Settlements are much more scattered on the western plains. More than a third of the region's inhabitants—including almost half of the population of Arkansas—live in rural areas. Limited economic diversity encourages migration to other areas, in turn keeping population growth well below the national average.

- 2.6–26 per sq mile / 1–10 per sq km
- 26–65 per sq mile / 10–25 per sq km
- 65–130 per sq mile / 25–50 per sq km
- 130–260 per sq mile / 50–100 per sq km

ECONOMIC PROFILE

Wheat is the principal crop in the west—Kansas is the nation's leading producer—whereas corn, soybeans, and rice predominate in the better-watered east. Immense herds of cattle support meat-packing and beef-processing industries. Sizable oil and gas reserves helped Kansas and Oklahoma recover from the Dust Bowl droughts and remain an important source of revenue. Missouri is the leading producer of lead and has large iron ore reserves. St Louis and Kansas City are centers of automobile and aerospace equipment production, and Wichita is one of the world's leading aircraft manufacturers.

- Forest and woodland
- Arable land
- Grazing

- Cereals
- Cotton
- Beef cattle
- Industrial center
- Mining
- Oil production
- Rice
- Soybeans
- Pigs
- Corn (maize)

Longitude west of Greenwich

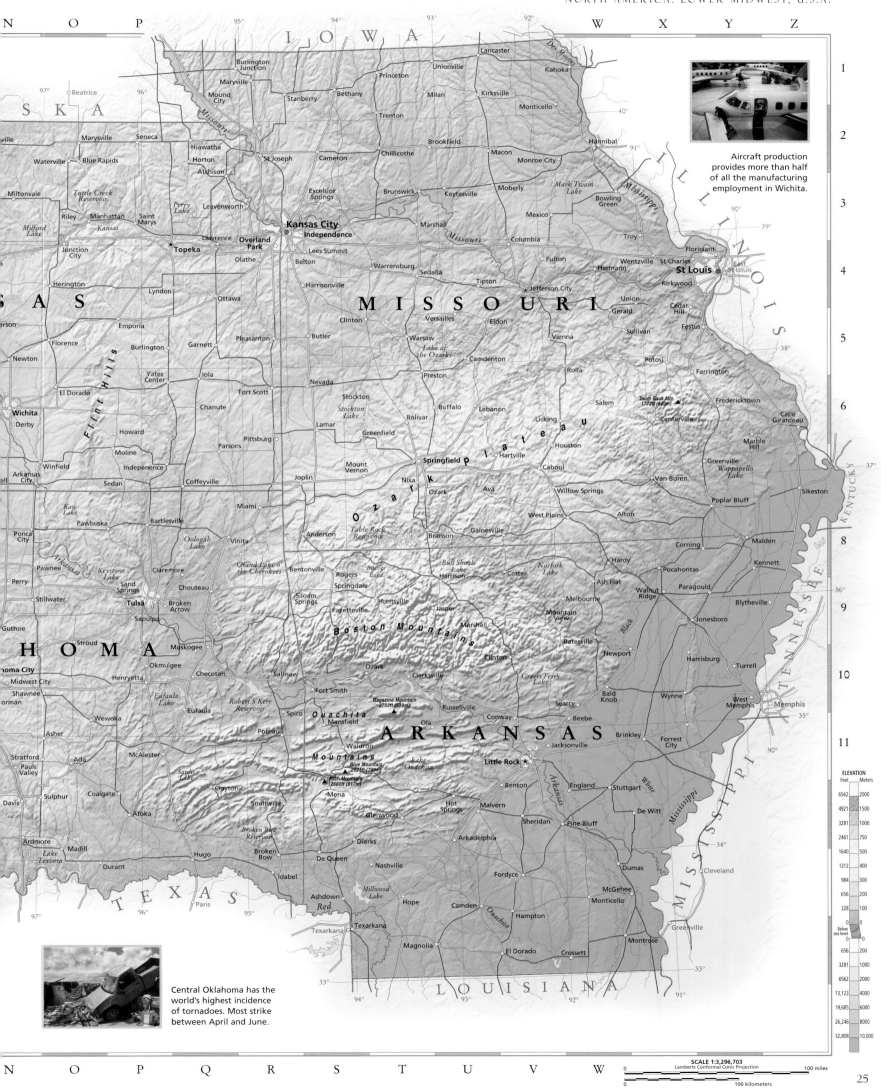

Aircraft production provides more than half of all the manufacturing employment in Wichita.

Central Oklahoma has the world's highest incidence of tornadoes. Most strike between April and June.

SCALE 1:3,296,703
Lambert's Conformal Conic Projection

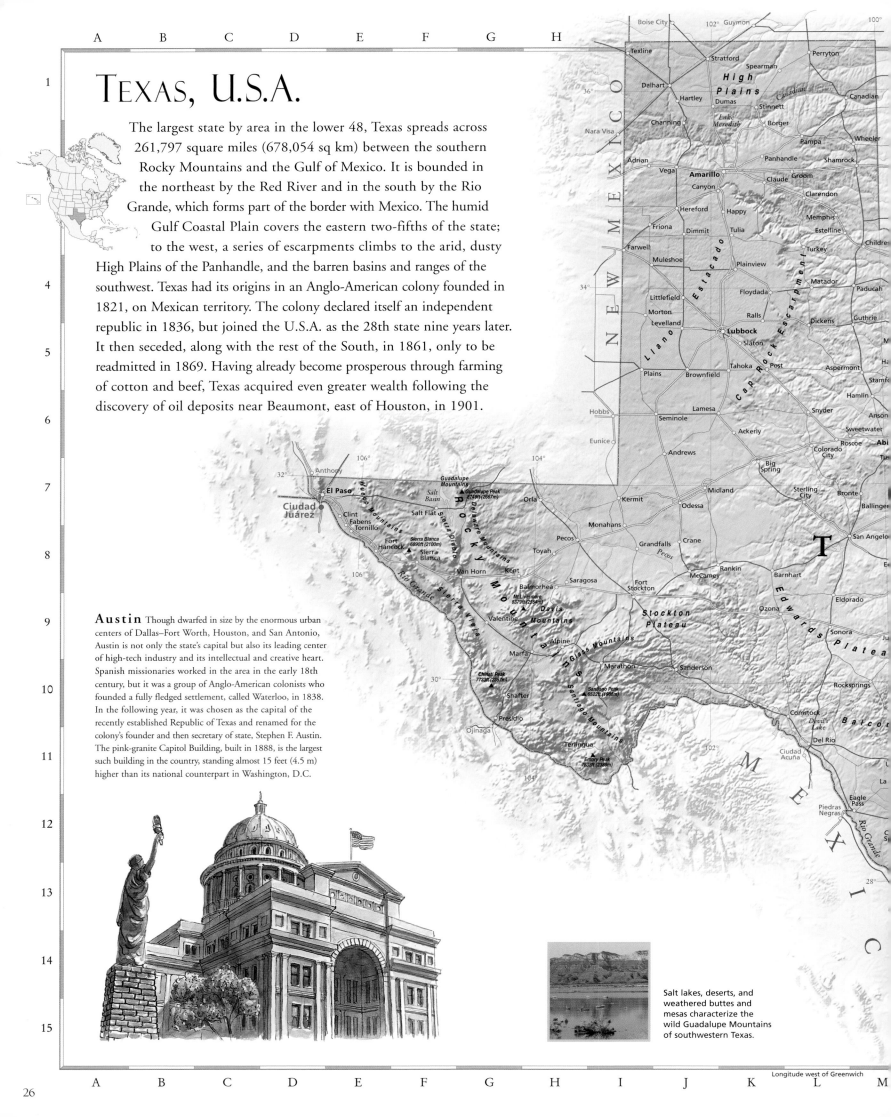

TEXAS, U.S.A.

The largest state by area in the lower 48, Texas spreads across 261,797 square miles (678,054 sq km) between the southern Rocky Mountains and the Gulf of Mexico. It is bounded in the northeast by the Red River and in the south by the Rio Grande, which forms part of the border with Mexico. The humid Gulf Coastal Plain covers the eastern two-fifths of the state; to the west, a series of escarpments climbs to the arid, dusty High Plains of the Panhandle, and the barren basins and ranges of the southwest. Texas had its origins in an Anglo-American colony founded in 1821, on Mexican territory. The colony declared itself an independent republic in 1836, but joined the U.S.A. as the 28th state nine years later. It then seceded, along with the rest of the South, in 1861, only to be readmitted in 1869. Having already become prosperous through farming of cotton and beef, Texas acquired even greater wealth following the discovery of oil deposits near Beaumont, east of Houston, in 1901.

Austin Though dwarfed in size by the enormous urban centers of Dallas–Fort Worth, Houston, and San Antonio, Austin is not only the state's capital but also its leading center of high-tech industry and its intellectual and creative heart. Spanish missionaries worked in the area in the early 18th century, but it was a group of Anglo-American colonists who founded a fully fledged settlement, called Waterloo, in 1838. In the following year, it was chosen as the capital of the recently established Republic of Texas and renamed for the colony's founder and then secretary of state, Stephen F. Austin. The pink-granite Capitol Building, built in 1888, is the largest such building in the country, standing almost 15 feet (4.5 m) higher than its national counterpart in Washington, D.C.

Salt lakes, deserts, and weathered buttes and mesas characterize the wild Guadalupe Mountains of southwestern Texas.

Longitude west of Greenwich

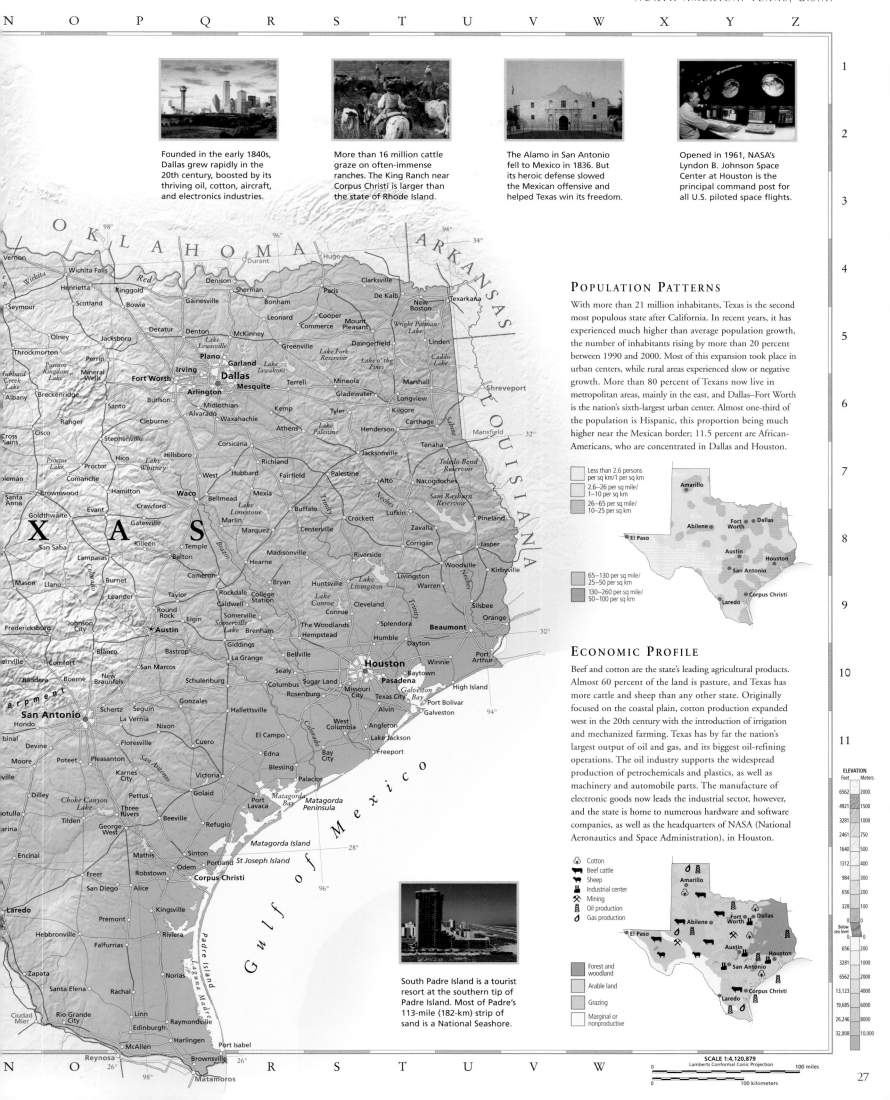

Founded in the early 1840s, Dallas grew rapidly in the 20th century, boosted by its thriving oil, cotton, aircraft, and electronics industries.

More than 16 million cattle graze on often-immense ranches. The King Ranch near Corpus Christi is larger than the state of Rhode Island.

The Alamo in San Antonio fell to Mexico in 1836. But its heroic defense slowed the Mexican offensive and helped Texas win its freedom.

Opened in 1961, NASA's Lyndon B. Johnson Space Center at Houston is the principal command post for all U.S. piloted space flights.

POPULATION PATTERNS

With more than 21 million inhabitants, Texas is the second most populous state after California. In recent years, it has experienced much higher than average population growth, the number of inhabitants rising by more than 20 percent between 1990 and 2000. Most of this expansion took place in urban centers, while rural areas experienced slow or negative growth. More than 80 percent of Texans now live in metropolitan areas, mainly in the east, and Dallas–Fort Worth is the nation's sixth-largest urban center. Almost one-third of the population is Hispanic, this proportion being much higher near the Mexican border; 11.5 percent are African-Americans, who are concentrated in Dallas and Houston.

Less than 2.6 persons per sq km/1 per sq mile

2.6–26 per sq mile/ 1–10 per sq km

26–65 per sq mile/ 10–25 per sq km

65–130 per sq mile/ 25–50 per sq km

130–260 per sq mile/ 50–100 per sq km

ECONOMIC PROFILE

Beef and cotton are the state's leading agricultural products. Almost 60 percent of the land is pasture, and Texas has more cattle and sheep than any other state. Originally focused on the coastal plain, cotton production expanded west in the 20th century with the introduction of irrigation and mechanized farming. Texas has by far the nation's largest output of oil and gas, and its biggest oil-refining operations. The oil industry supports the widespread production of petrochemicals and plastics, as well as machinery and automobile parts. The manufacture of electronic goods now leads the industrial sector, however, and the state is home to numerous hardware and software companies, as well as the headquarters of NASA (National Aeronautics and Space Administration), in Houston.

Cotton
Beef cattle
Sheep
Industrial center
Mining
Oil production
Gas production

Forest and woodland
Arable land
Grazing
Marginal or nonproductive

South Padre Island is a tourist resort at the southern tip of Padre Island. Most of Padre's 113-mile (182-km) strip of sand is a National Seashore.

ELEVATION
Feet / Meters
6562 / 2000
4921 / 1500
3281 / 1000
2461 / 750
1640 / 500
1312 / 400
984 / 300
656 / 200
328 / 100
Below sea level / 0
656 / 200
3281 / 1000
6562 / 2000
13,123 / 4000
19,685 / 6000
26,246 / 8000
32,808 / 10,000

SCALE 1:4,120,879
Lamberts Conformal Conic Projection
0   100 miles
0   100 kilometers

NORTHERN ROCKIES, U.S.A.

Idaho, Montana, Wyoming

The Rocky Mountains form a broad diagonal band across northern Idaho and western Montana and Wyoming. In southern Idaho, the Columbia Plateau and Snake River Plain skirt the mountains. On their eastern flank, the Rockies level out on the Great Plains, an expanse of rolling pastures and wheat fields. Still little developed, the Northern Rockies are the traditional homeland of native peoples such as the Nez Perce, Shoshone, Cheyenne, and Sioux. The first Europeans to visit were Lewis and Clark, during their momentous expedition of 1804–06. Only a trickle of traders and trappers followed, until a gold rush in the early 1860s. Once the boom was over, prospectors turned their hands to mining other minerals, and to forestry and farming—still the foundations of the economy.

Old Faithful is one of 200 or so geysers in Yellowstone National Park, Wyoming. A major tourist destination, Yellowstone also encompasses 10,000 hot springs.

POPULATION PATTERNS

Population density is low—Wyoming is the nation's least populous state, despite being the ninth biggest by area—and there are few large cities, with only Boise's population surpassing 100,000. Towns line the major river valleys, and half of Wyoming's population is concentrated in the southeastern quarter of the state. Wide open spaces separate settlements elsewhere. The population is overwhelmingly white, but includes a much higher than average proportion of Native Americans. In 1990–2000, Idaho was the fifth fastest-growing state and Boise was the nation's seventh fastest-growing metropolitan area.

Less than 2.6 persons per sq mile/1 per sq km
2.6–26 per sq mile/1–10 per sq km
26–65 per sq mile/10–25 per sq km
65–130 per sq mile/25–50 per sq km

ECONOMIC PROFILE

Coal, oil, and gas are major sources of revenue in Montana and especially Wyoming (the nation's top coal producer), whereas mining in Idaho is focused on silver, lead, and molybdenum. Irrigation supports the cultivation of a range of crops, most notably potatoes in Idaho and wheat in the east. Huge numbers of cattle and sheep roam the plateaus and prairies. Forests are extensive, covering one-third of Idaho; timber is a vital resource there and in Montana. Most manufacturing involves the processing of raw materials. Tourism is a leading employer and revenue source.

Forest and woodland
Arable land
Grazing
Marginal or nonproductive

Cereals
Potatoes
Gas production
Beef cattle
Timber
Industrial center
Mining
Oil production
Fruit

THE TETON RANGE

Extending for 40 miles (64 km) across northwestern Wyoming, the Teton Range is one of the youngest and most imposing mountain ranges in the Rockies. Its jagged peaks began to form more than 1 million years ago when the land to the east dropped downward along a 50-mile (80-km) fault line. Today, 13,770-foot (4,197-m) Grand Teton, the highest peak in the range, rises 7,000 feet (2,135 m) above the valley of Jackson Hole.

The Northern Rockies harbor the country's largest bison populations.

The Capitol Building in Boise was completed in 1920, 30 years after Idaho became a state.

ELEVATION
Feet / Meters
6562 / 2000
4921 / 1500
3281 / 1000
2461 / 750
1640 / 500
1312 / 400
984 / 300
656 / 200
328 / 100
0 / 0
Below sea level
0 / 0
656 / 200
3281 / 1000
6562 / 2000
13,123 / 4000
19,685 / 6000
26,246 / 8000
32,808 / 10,000

Longitude west of Greenwich

N O P Q R S T U V W X Y Z

C A N A D A

113°   112°   111°   110°   109°   108°   107°   106°   105°   104°   49°

Cleveland
ft (3184m)   Babb   Sunburst   West Butte   Simpson   Loring   Gr   Opheim   Scobey   Plentywood
Browning   Cut   6980ft (2128m)   Gildford   Chinook   Harlem   Dodson   Saco   Glasgow   Wolf   Poplar   Culbertson
Shelby   Chester   Havre   Malta   Point   Missouri   North   Dakota
Dupuyer   Conrad   Tiber   Big Sandy   Baldy Mountain   Hays   Fort Peck   Nashua   Vida   Sidney
Reservoir   6621ft (2018m)   Missouri   Fort Peck   Circle
Rocky Mountain   Choteau   Fort Benton   Winifred   Reservoir
9393ft (2863m)   Augusta   Great Falls   Roy   Jordan   Glendive   Wibaux
Simms   Armington   M O N T A N A   Great   Plains
Stanford   Lewistown   Roy   Jordan
Wolf Creek   Moore   Grassrange   Winnett   Mosby   Rock   Terry
Big Snow Mtns   Melstone   Ingomar   Springs   Baker
Helena   White Sulphur   8730ft (2661m)   Roundup   Miles City
Drummond   Garrison   Springs   Harlowton   Ryegate   Hysham   Forsyth
Philipsburg   Townsend   Ringling   Lavina   Custer
Crow Peak   Crazy Mtns   Yellowstone   Volborg   Ekalaka
Anaconda   9413ft (2868m)   Clyde Park   Big Timber   Billings   Hardin   Crow Agency   Lame Deer
Mount Evans   Butte   Three   Bozeman   Livingston   Columbus   Laurel   Broadus
10,640ft (3243m)   Forks   Granite Peak   Boyd   Bridger   Lodge   Biddle   Alzada
Wisdom   Ennis   12,800ft (3901m)   Red Lodge   Bighorn   Fort   Grass
Melrose   Twin   Gardiner   Lake   Smith   Wyola   45°
Dillon   Bridges   Virginia   Mammoth Hot   Spotted   Devil's Tower
City   Springs   Powell   Lovell   Sheridan   Horse   5112ft (1558m)   Belle
Lima   Canyon   Trout Peak   Cody   Greybull   Buffalo   Ucross   Fourche
Island   West   12,244ft (3732m)   Basin   Sundance   Spearfish
Spencer   Park   Yellowstone   Old   Yellowstone   Meeteetse   Bighorn   Gillette
Faithful   Lake   Needle Mountain   Basin   Wright
Borah Peak   Dubois   12,129ft (3697m)   Worland   Kaycee
651ft (3859m)   Ashton   Jackson   Grand Teton   Thermopolis   Midwest   Bill
Mackay   Lake   13,770ft (4197m)   Moran   Dubois   Newcastle
Leslie   Moose   Shoshoni   Mule
Moore   Rexburg   Jackson   Gannett Peak   W Y O M I N G   Creek
Terreton   13,785ft (4202m)   Riverton   Casper   North Platte   Edgemont
Idaho Falls   Bondurant   Powder   Lusk   Harrison
Victor   Pinedale   River   Douglas   Orin   Glendo
Blackfoot   Daniel   Lander   Laramie   Glendo   Reservoir
American   Palisades   Moose   Jeffrey   Alcova   Mountains   Guernsey
Falls   Reservoir   Thayne   City   Muddy   Pathfinder
Pocatello   Blackfoot   Smoot   Marbleton   Gap   Reservoir   Medicine   Torrington
American   Reservoir   Great Divide   Seminoe   Bow   Hawk
Falls   Soda   La Barge   Basin   Reservoir   Springs
Minidoka   McCammon   Springs   Farson   Rawlins   Walcott   Chugwater
Downey   Montpelier   Kemmerer   Creston   Laramie
Malad City   Paris   Diamondville   Green   Rock Springs   North Platte
Holbrook   Preston   Saint   Granger   River
Strevell   Charles   Bear   Cokeville   Green
Lake   Evanston   Fort   River   Baggs   Cheyenne
Bridger   Flaming Gorge   C O L O R A D O
Manila   Reservoir

I D A H O

U T A H

S O U T H   D A K O T A

N E B R A S K A

113°   112°   111°   110°   109°   108°   107°   106°   105°   104°

SCALE 1:3,571,429
Lamberts Conformal Conic Projection
0   100 miles
0   100 kilometers

SOUTHWESTERN U.S.A.

Arizona, Colorado, New Mexico, Utah

The immense Colorado Plateau constitutes the core of this arid region. Bounded to the west by basin and range country, to the north and east by the southern Rockies, and to the south by the Sonoran Desert, it is characterized by ancient, eroded landscapes where barren plateaus sit beneath forested, snow-capped peaks, and rivers have carved deep chasms between broad mesas and towering buttes. Scattered cliff-dwellings and pueblos testify to thousands of years of Native American habitation. Historic missions and adobe architecture recall Spanish occupation between the 16th and early 19th centuries, and subsequent Mexican rule over much of the Southwest until 1848. Today, the region's dry, sunny climate, thriving high-tech industries, and astounding scenery make it one of the most-visited and fastest-growing parts of the country.

THE GRAND CANYON

A deep gash in the southwestern corner of the Colorado Plateau, the Grand Canyon was carved over millennia by the Colorado River. Extending 277 miles (446 km) and measuring 15 miles (24 km) across at its widest point, it is up to 6,000 feet (1,800 m) deep. Erosion has exposed rocks at the bottom of the canyon that are about 2 billion years old. Now encompassed by the national park of the same name, the canyon attracts up to 5 million visitors annually.

Salt Lake City In 1846, fleeing persecution in Illinois, 148 Mormons migrated more than 1,000 miles (1,600 km) to present-day Utah. Settling in the Valley of the Great Salt Lake in 1847, they founded a new settlement, initially called Great Salt Lake City. By the late 19th century, it had become, and remains, one of the most important commercial centers in the western U.S.A. Its focal point, and the heart of the Mormon faith, is Temple Square, site of the six-towered Mormon Temple, begun in 1853 and completed 40 years later.

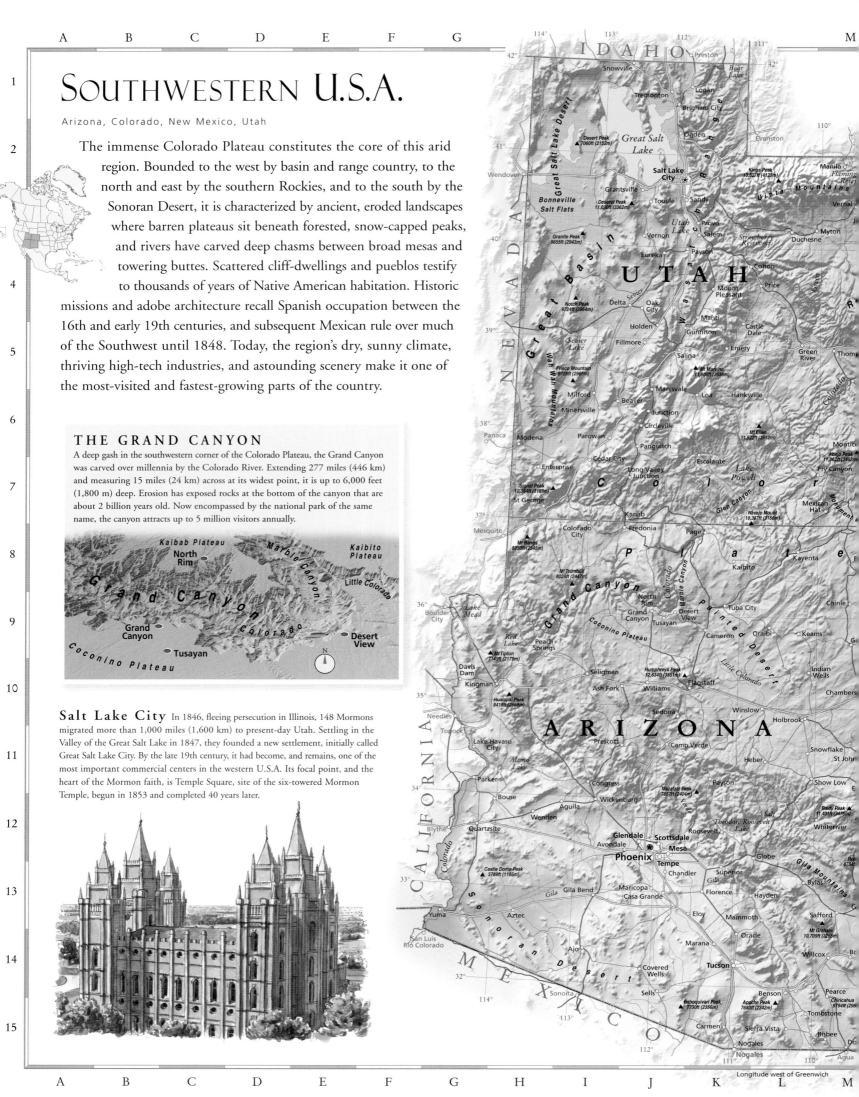

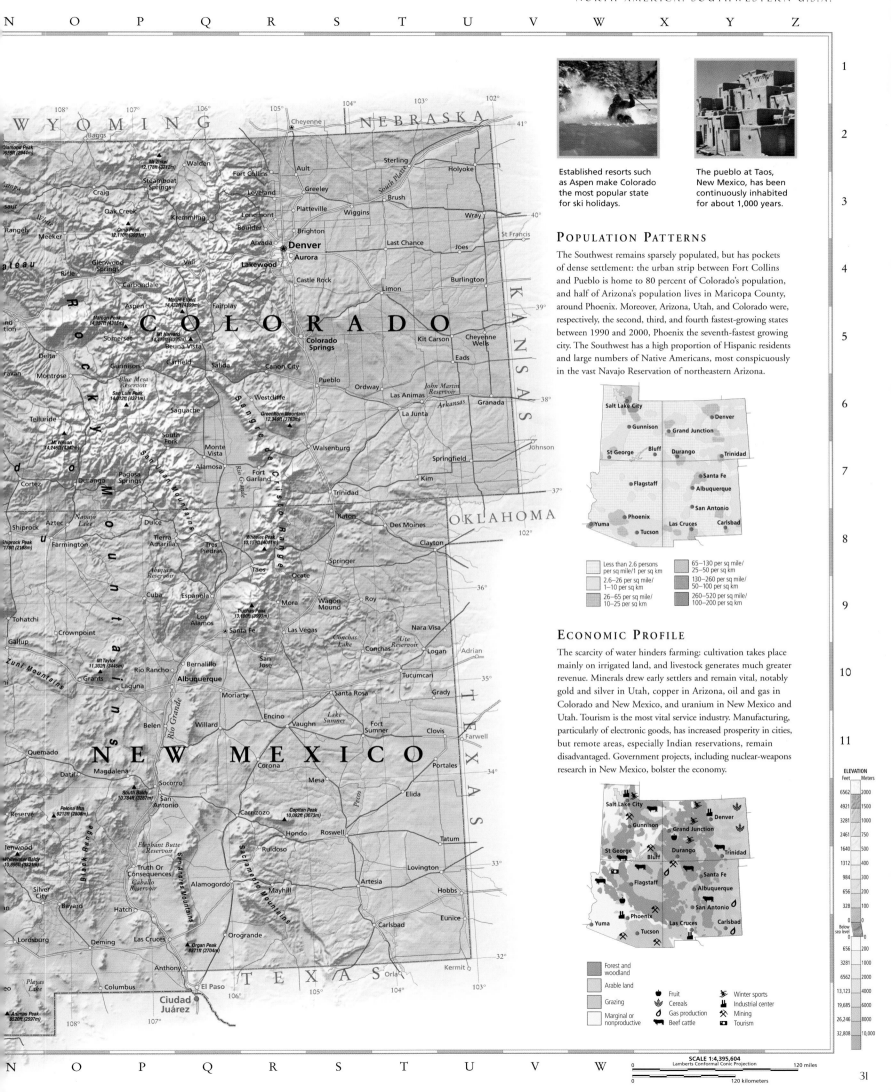

Established resorts such as Aspen make Colorado the most popular state for ski holidays.

The pueblo at Taos, New Mexico, has been continuously inhabited for about 1,000 years.

POPULATION PATTERNS

The Southwest remains sparsely populated, but has pockets of dense settlement: the urban strip between Fort Collins and Pueblo is home to 80 percent of Colorado's population, and half of Arizona's population lives in Maricopa County, around Phoenix. Moreover, Arizona, Utah, and Colorado were, respectively, the second, third, and fourth fastest-growing states between 1990 and 2000, Phoenix the seventh-fastest growing city. The Southwest has a high proportion of Hispanic residents and large numbers of Native Americans, most conspicuously in the vast Navajo Reservation of northeastern Arizona.

Less than 2.6 persons per sq mile/1 per sq km

2.6–26 per sq mile/ 1–10 per sq km

26–65 per sq mile/ 10–25 per sq km

65–130 per sq mile/ 25–50 per sq km

130–260 per sq mile/ 50–100 per sq km

260–520 per sq mile/ 100–200 per sq km

ECONOMIC PROFILE

The scarcity of water hinders farming: cultivation takes place mainly on irrigated land, and livestock generates much greater revenue. Minerals drew early settlers and remain vital, notably gold and silver in Utah, copper in Arizona, oil and gas in Colorado and New Mexico, and uranium in New Mexico and Utah. Tourism is the most vital service industry. Manufacturing, particularly of electronic goods, has increased prosperity in cities, but remote areas, especially Indian reservations, remain disadvantaged. Government projects, including nuclear-weapons research in New Mexico, bolster the economy.

Forest and woodland

Arable land

Grazing

Marginal or nonproductive

Fruit
Cereals
Gas production
Beef cattle

Winter sports
Industrial center
Mining
Tourism

ELEVATION

Feet	Meters
6562	2000
4921	1500
3281	1000
2461	750
1640	500
1312	400
984	300
656	200
328	100
	0
Below sea level	0
656	200
3281	1000
6562	2000
13,123	4000
19,685	6000
26,246	8000
32,808	10,000

SCALE 1:4,395,604
Lamberts Conformal Conic Projection

0 — 120 miles
0 — 120 kilometers

THE FAR WEST, U.S.A.

California, Nevada, Oregon, Washington

Geologically, the U.S. mainland's western fringe is its youngest and most active region. Plate movements here cause regular earthquakes in California and occasional volcanic eruptions in the Pacific Northwest. They have also given rise, over millions of years, to the two long mountain chains that parallel the shoreline. The Coast Ranges climb steeply from the sea, falling to sheltered lowlands, including the Central and Willamette valleys, which are enclosed in turn by the loftier peaks of the Cascade Range and Sierra Nevada. Farther east lies a jumble of arid landforms, including volcanic plateaus in the north, rows of north–south-trending basins and ranges in Nevada, and low-lying deserts in southeastern California. This intimidating terrain deterred early European immigrants, who clustered in coastal settlements and threaded their way along river valleys before being lured into the uplands by the discovery of gold and other minerals in the mid-19th century. In the 20th century, southern California's warm climate, available land, and thriving ports drew millions west, making it one of the nation's most populous regions.

Washington's Mount Rainier is crowned by the largest glacier system in the lower 48 states.

Crater Lake, Oregon, fills a caldera that was once part of an enormous volcano, Mount Mazama.

POPULATION PATTERNS

California has the largest state population, of more than 34 million. More than 90 percent of these people live in urban areas, mainly around Los Angeles and San Diego, and San Francisco and Oakland. One-third of Californians are Hispanic or Latino. In the Pacific Northwest, densely populated areas include the shores of Puget Sound and Oregon's Willamette Valley. In the east, settlements are small and scattered; an exception is Las Vegas, a desert metropolis founded on gambling and tourism. Between 1990 and 2000, Nevada grew faster than any other state, increasing its population by 66 percent.

Less than 2.6 persons per sq mile/1 per sq km
2.6–26 per sq mile/1–10 per sq km
26–65 per sq mile/10–25 per sq km
65–130 per sq mile/25–50 per sq km
130–260 per sq mile/50–100 per sq km
260–520 per sq mile/100–200 per sq km
520–1040 per sq mile/200–400 per sq km

ECONOMIC PROFILE

The region has just a few pockets of arable land, most of which require irrigation, but they include California's productive Central Valley and its Napa Valley vineyards, and the fertile Columbia Basin. The Pacific Northwest has enormous stands of timber and abundant hydroelectric power—Washington generates one-third of U.S. supplies. Nevada benefits from reserves of gold and mercury, and hosts major military test sites—85 percent of the land is government-owned. Seattle and San Francisco's famed Silicon Valley are world leaders in new technologies, and Seattle is also a major aircraft manufacturer. As well as the Hollywood film industry, Los Angeles is home to major TV and music corporations. Tourism is a vital industry throughout the region.

Forest and woodland
Arable land
Grazing
Marginal or nonproductive
Fruit and vegetables
Fruit
Wine
Beef cattle
Fishing
Industrial center
Mining
Tourism
Timber
Cereal
Citrus fruits
Dairy cattle

State and feature labels on map:

UTAH · NEVADA · CALIFORNIA · ARIZONA · MEXICO

PACIFIC OCEAN

Great Basin · Schell Creek Range · Ruby Mountains · Shoshone Mountains · Toiyabe Range · Black Rock Desert · Smoke Creek Desert · Death Valley · Mojave Desert · Sonoran Desert · Colorado Desert · San Bernardino Mountains · Sierra Nevada · Coast Ranges · Diablo Range · Santa Lucia Range · Central Valley · Sacramento Valley · San Joaquin Valley · Channel Islands · California Aqueduct · Colorado

Cities and places (selection): Las Vegas · Los Angeles · San Diego · Tijuana · San Francisco · Oakland · Berkeley · San Jose · Sacramento · Fresno · Bakersfield · Reno · Stockton · Modesto · Riverside · San Bernardino · Santa Ana · Anaheim · Long Beach · Pasadena · Burbank · Oceanside · Escondido · Chula Vista · El Cajon · Mexicali · Calexico · El Centro · Needles · Barstow · Victorville · Mesquite · Overton · Boulder City · Searchlight · Blythe · Parker · Quartzsite · Lake Havasu City

YOSEMITE VALLEY

The granite peaks of the Sierra Nevada were uplifted between 25 and 10 million years ago. Around 1 million years ago, during a major ice age, glaciers covered the highest slopes and snaked downward through valleys, grinding their walls smooth and steep. The results of this glaciation are visible throughout the range, but perhaps nowhere are they as dramatic as in Yosemite Valley. This U-shaped canyon's polished walls rise sheer from the valley floor, forming colossal cliffs surmounted by peaks such as 7,569-foot (2,346-m) El Capitan and 8,842-foot (2,695-m) Half Dome. Between the peaks, mountain streams tumble from hanging valleys, creating some of the world's tallest waterfalls.

Yosemite Valley inset map labels: Moraine Dome · Liberty Cap · Glacier Point · Half Dome · Mirror Lake · Yosemite Village · Sentinel Fall · Bridalveil Fall · El Capitan · Yosemite Falls · Merced

The construction of the Hoover Dam across the Colorado River created Lake Mead in Nevada.

Founded by Spanish settlers in 1781, Los Angeles became part of the U.S.A. in 1846. It is now its second-largest city.

In Death Valley, California, the land drops to 282 feet (86 m) below sea level, North America's lowest point.

SCALE 1:4,945,055
Lambert's Conformal Conic Projection

0 — 120 miles
0 — 120 kilometers

Longitude west of Greenwich

ELEVATION

Feet	Meters
6562	2000
4921	1500
3281	1000
2461	750
1640	500
1312	400
984	300
656	200
328	100
0	0
Below 0	Below 0
656	200
3281	1000
6562	2000
13,123	4000
19,685	6000
26,246	8000
32,808	10,000

ALASKA AND HAWAII, U.S.A.

Alaska and Hawaii are the only two states that are not part of the lower 48, and both became states—the 49th and 50th, respectively—in the same year, 1959. Their territories, however, could hardly be more different. Separated from the rest of the country by western Canada, Alaska is by far the largest state and about 95 times the size of Hawaii—though it has only half as many inhabitants. Its huge, oblong landmass is mountainous, little developed, and mostly inhospitable: winters are severe across most of the state and one-third of the land is barren tundra. Hawaii is a chain of 137 volcanic islands, measuring 1,500 miles (2,400 km) in length and including eight major islands, located in the middle of the Pacific Ocean, about 2,400 miles (3,860 km) west of San Francisco. Cloaked with tracts of tropical forest and fringed by golden beaches, the Hawaiian Islands have fertile soils and are warm and, for the most part, well-watered year-round.

In summer, herds of caribou migrate to Alaska's Arctic tundra to breed.

The Trans-Alaska Oil Pipeline extends from Prudhoe Bay to the port of Valdez.

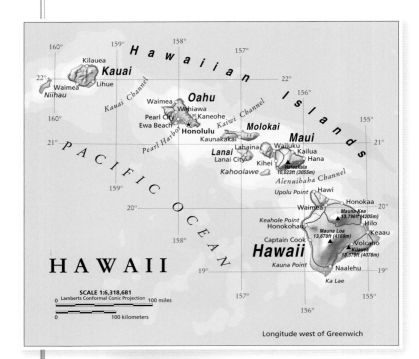

HAWAII

SCALE 1:6,318,681
Lamberts Conformal Conic Projection
0   100 miles
0   100 kilometers

Longitude west of Greenwich

Named Denali by local Native American people, Mount McKinley is the tallest peak in North America, rising to 20,321 feet (6,194 m).

Kilauea, on the island of Hawaii, is the world's largest active volcanic crater. Its regular eruptions generate extensive lava flows.

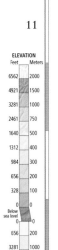

A swamp until the early 20th century, Waikiki Beach, Oahu, is Hawaii's, and one of the world's, best-known beaches.

ELEVATION
Feet	Meters
6562	2000
4921	1500
3281	1000
2461	750
1640	500
1312	400
984	300
656	200
328	100
0	0
Below sea level	0
656	200
3281	1000
6562	2000
13,123	4000
19,685	6000
26,246	8000
32,808	10,000

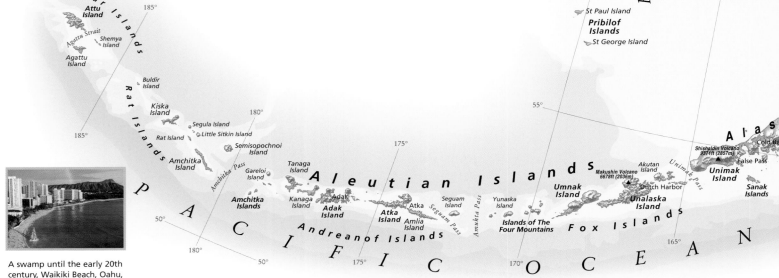

Longitude west of Greenwich

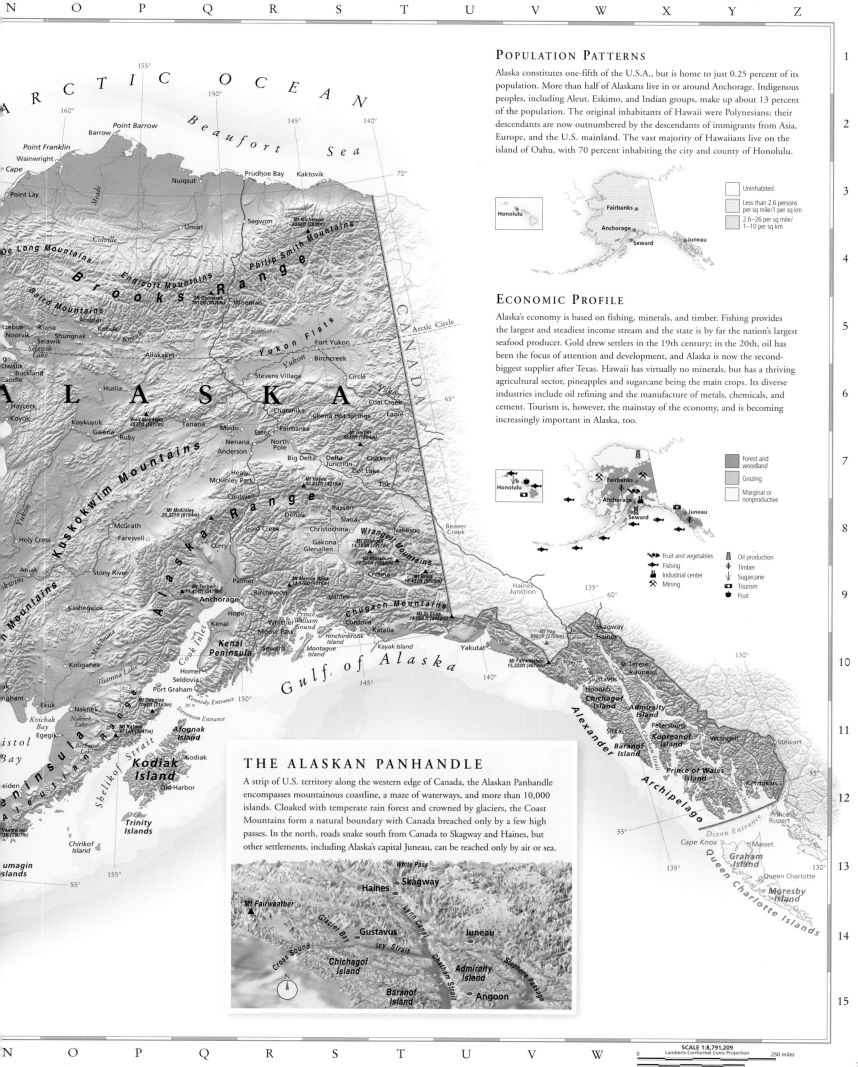

POPULATION PATTERNS

Alaska constitutes one-fifth of the U.S.A., but is home to just 0.25 percent of its population. More than half of Alaskans live in or around Anchorage. Indigenous peoples, including Aleut, Eskimo, and Indian groups, make up about 13 percent of the population. The original inhabitants of Hawaii were Polynesians; their descendants are now outnumbered by the descendants of immigrants from Asia, Europe, and the U.S. mainland. The vast majority of Hawaiians live on the island of Oahu, with 70 percent inhabiting the city and county of Honolulu.

Uninhabited

Less than 2.6 persons per sq mile/1 per sq km

2.6–26 per sq mile/ 1–10 per sq km

ECONOMIC PROFILE

Alaska's economy is based on fishing, minerals, and timber. Fishing provides the largest and steadiest income stream and the state is by far the nation's largest seafood producer. Gold drew settlers in the 19th century; in the 20th, oil has been the focus of attention and development, and Alaska is now the second-biggest supplier after Texas. Hawaii has virtually no minerals, but has a thriving agricultural sector, pineapples and sugarcane being the main crops. Its diverse industries include oil refining and the manufacture of metals, chemicals, and cement. Tourism is, however, the mainstay of the economy, and is becoming increasingly important in Alaska, too.

Forest and woodland

Grazing

Marginal or nonproductive

Fruit and vegetables
Fishing
Industrial center
Mining
Oil production
Timber
Sugarcane
Tourism
Fruit

THE ALASKAN PANHANDLE

A strip of U.S. territory along the western edge of Canada, the Alaskan Panhandle encompasses mountainous coastline, a maze of waterways, and more than 10,000 islands. Cloaked with temperate rain forest and crowned by glaciers, the Coast Mountains form a natural boundary with Canada breached only by a few high passes. In the north, roads snake south from Canada to Skagway and Haines, but other settlements, including Alaska's capital Juneau, can be reached only by air or sea.

SCALE 1:8,791,209
Lamberts Conformal Conic Projection
0 — 250 miles
0 — 250 kilometers

CANADA

Occupying most of the northern third of North America, Canada is the world's second-largest country by area, but also one of its most sparsely inhabited. A band of western ranges, including the Coast and Rocky mountains, and a number of lower, much older mountain chains in the east, enclose the vast Canadian Shield, an ancient, low, bowl-shaped plateau. Originally home to scattered Indian and Inuit peoples, Canada was visited in the 11th century by Viking explorers, who founded a short-lived settlement in Newfoundland. The French laid claim to the St Lawrence River Valley in the 16th century, but by 1763 most of North America was under British control. The self-governing British dominion of Canada was created in 1867. Initially, it included only Ontario, Québec, New Brunswick, and Nova Scotia, but other areas were gradually absorbed into the confederation, which now consists of ten provinces and three territories.

Mostly uninhabited, mountainous Baffin Island is Canada's largest island.

Waterlogged boreal forest, of spruce, fir, and birch, spans the entire country.

Toronto Canada's most populous city, with around 5 million inhabitants, and its leading commercial and financial center, Toronto originated in the 17th century as a trading post founded at the intersection of several Indian trails (Toronto is a Huron word meaning "meeting place"). Despite being chosen as the site for the capital of Ontario in 1793, the settlement remained undeveloped until the arrival of the Grand Trunk and Great Western railways in the 1850s, after which its population rose to more than half a million by 1921. The modern skyline is dominated by the CN Tower, which rises to 1,815 feet (553 m) and is the world's tallest self-supporting structure.

CN Tower

POPULATION PATTERNS

Vast areas of northern Canada are virtually uninhabited: Nunavut and the Yukon and Northwest territories encompass 41 percent of the land, but have just 0.3 percent of the population. Nunavut has no roads. About 80 percent of Canadians live in the temperate south, within 100 miles (160 km) of the U.S. border. The population is highly urbanized, with four-fifths living in towns and cities. It is also ethnically diverse, one-third of Canadians being of mixed descent. Most, however, are of European, especially British or French, origin. Indigenous peoples make up just 3 percent of the population. Both English and French are official languages and bilingualism is encouraged: 17 percent of Canadians can use both languages.

Uninhabited	130–260 per sq mile/50–100 per sq km
Less than 2.6 persons per sq mile/1 per sq km	260–520 per sq mile/100–200 per sq km
2.6–26 per sq mile/1–10 per sq km	520–1040 per sq mile/200–400 per sq km
26–65 per sq mile/10–25 per sq km	1040–2080 per sq mile/400–800 per sq km
65–130 per sq mile/25–50 per sq km	More than 2080 per sq mile/800 per sq km

ECONOMIC PROFILE

Almost half of the country is forested and Canada is the world's leading producer of pulp, paper, and wood. Ample fresh water is harnessed by hydroelectric plants to provide 60 percent of energy needs. Canada is among the world's top sources of zinc, uranium, nickel, bauxite, copper, and gold, and produces far more oil and gas than it uses. Arable land is limited in extent, covering just 7 percent of the country, but productive. Manufacturing is led by transportation equipment, food, machinery, and wood products. Services employ three-quarters of Canadians and generate two-thirds of GDP.

Cereals
Fruit and vegetables
Fruit
Beef cattle
Fishing
Industrial center
Mining
Oil production
Gas production
Timber

Forest and woodland
Arable land
Grazing
Marginal or nonproductive

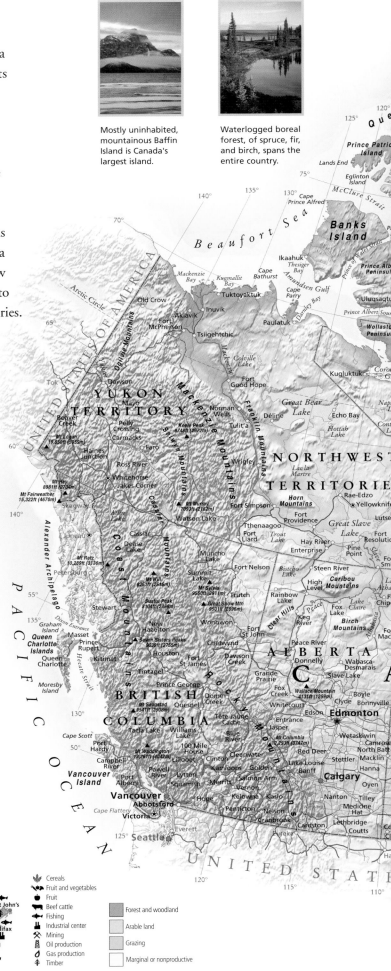

Longitude west of Greenwich

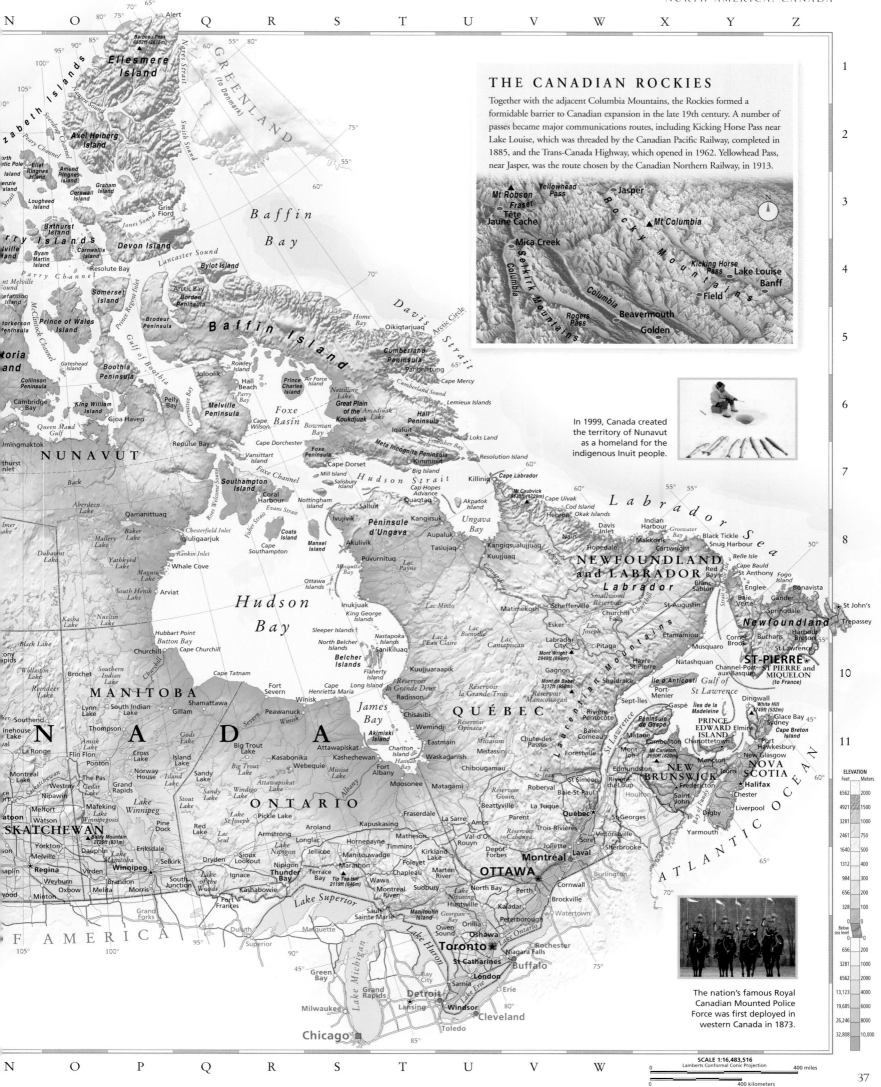

THE CANADIAN ROCKIES

Together with the adjacent Columbia Mountains, the Rockies formed a formidable barrier to Canadian expansion in the late 19th century. A number of passes became major communications routes, including Kicking Horse Pass near Lake Louise, which was threaded by the Canadian Pacific Railway, completed in 1885, and the Trans-Canada Highway, which opened in 1962. Yellowhead Pass, near Jasper, was the route chosen by the Canadian Northern Railway, in 1913.

In 1999, Canada created the territory of Nunavut as a homeland for the indigenous Inuit people.

The nation's famous Royal Canadian Mounted Police Force was first deployed in western Canada in 1873.

ELEVATION	
Feet	Meters
32,808	10,000
26,246	8000
19,685	6000
13,123	4000
6562	2000
3281	1000
656	200
Below sea level	
656	200
328	100
984	300
1312	400
1640	500
2461	750
3281	1000
4921	1500
6562	2000

SCALE 1:16,483,516
Lambert's Conformal Conic Projection

0 — 400 miles

0 — 400 kilometers

WESTERN CANADA

Alberta, British Columbia, Northwest Territories, Nunavut, Saskatchewan, Yukon Territory

The broad belt of mountains that parallels Canada's Pacific shoreline spreads up to 500 miles (800 km) inland. It is bounded in the east by the Coast Mountains, site of the country's highest peaks, and in the west by the Canadian Rockies. On their eastern flank, the Rockies drop to the flatlands of the interior. The Great Plains plateau extends into southern Alberta and Saskatchewan; to the north, immense boreal forests, broken by lakes, gradually yield to swamp and tundra. Settlement of this still relatively undeveloped region was stimulated by gold rushes in British Columbia in 1858 and the Klondike in 1897, as well as the completion of the Canadian Pacific Railway in 1885, which drew hundreds of thousands of immigrants to the fertile plains of Alberta and Saskatchewan.

British Columbia's largest city, Vancouver was founded as a sawmilling town in the 1870s.

Glaciers fashioned Moraine Lake and the dramatic Valley of Ten Peaks near Banff.

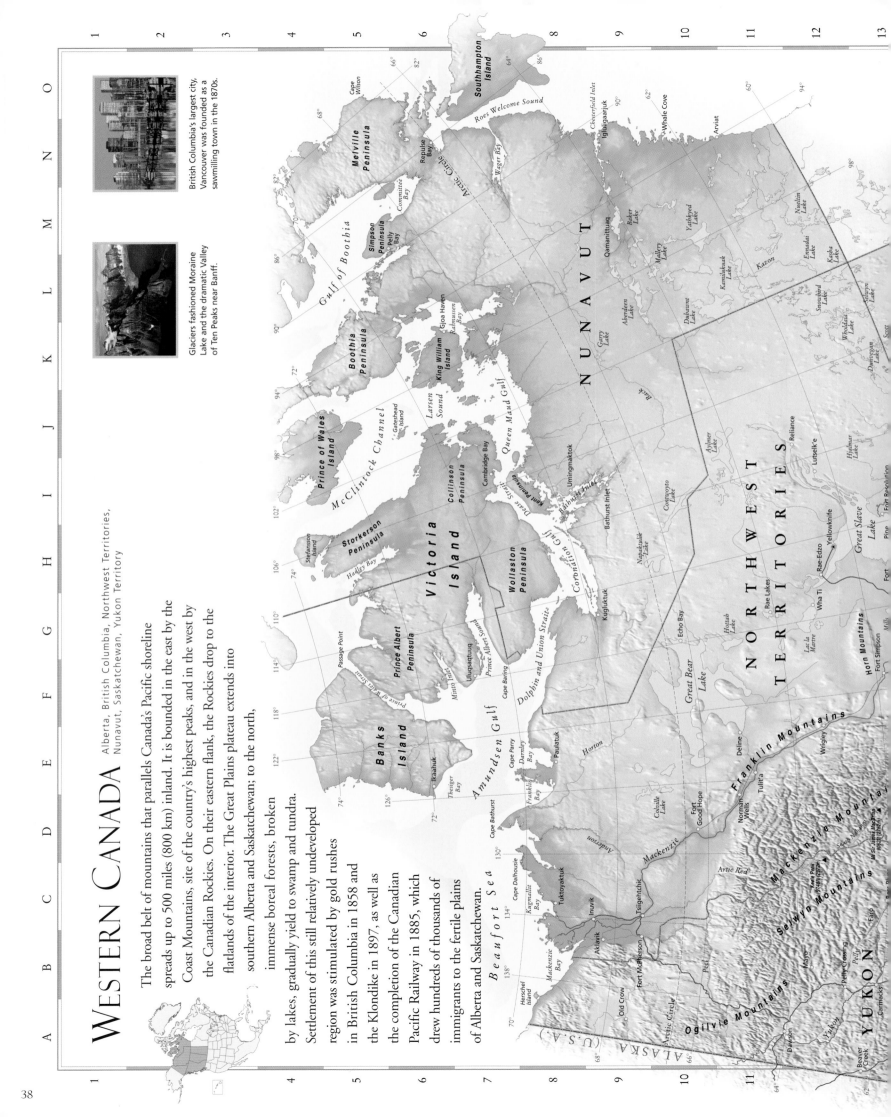

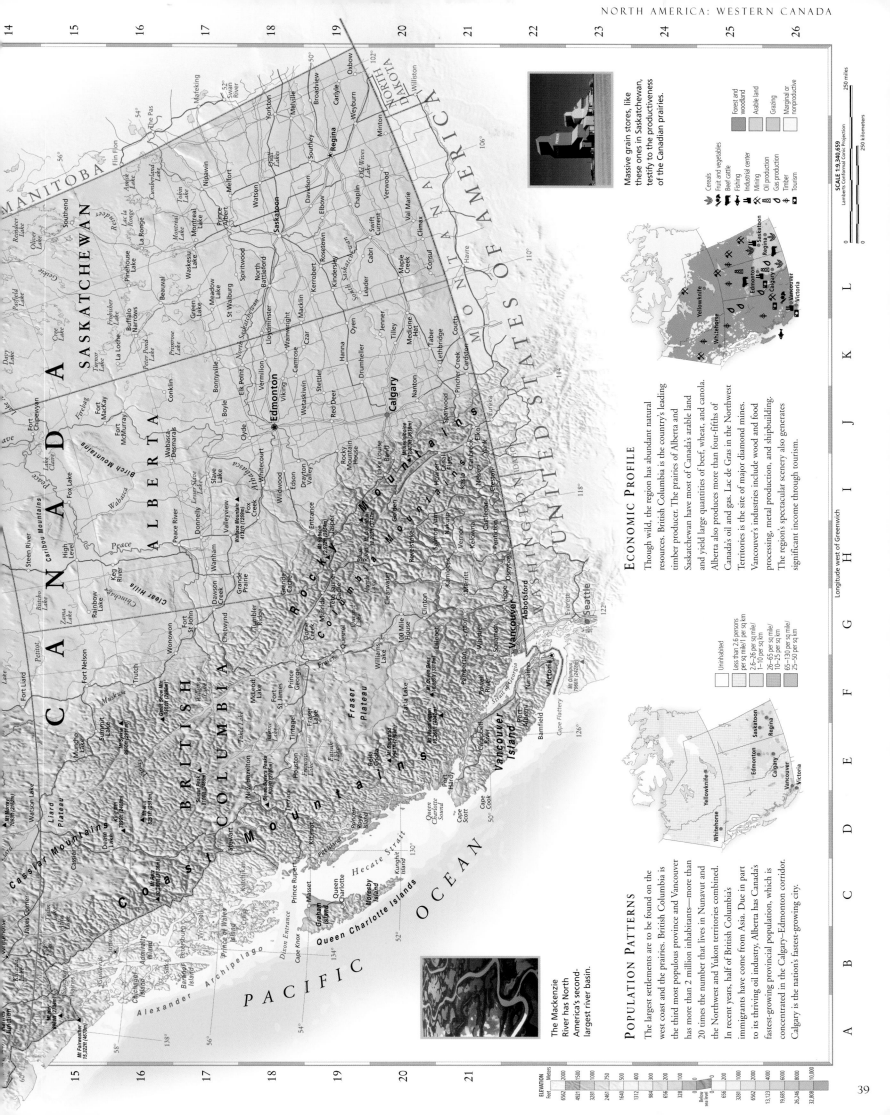

ECONOMIC PROFILE

Though wild, the region has abundant natural resources. British Columbia is the country's leading timber producer. The prairies of Alberta and Saskatchewan have most of Canada's arable land and yield large quantities of beef, wheat, and canola. Alberta also produces more than four-fifths of Canada's oil and gas. Lac de Gras in the Northwest Territories is the site of major diamond mines. Vancouver's industries include wood and food processing, metal production, and shipbuilding. The region's spectacular scenery also generates significant income through tourism.

POPULATION PATTERNS

The largest settlements are to be found on the west coast and the prairies. British Columbia is the third most populous province and Vancouver has more than 2 million inhabitants—more than 20 times the number that lives in Nunavut and the Northwest and Yukon territories combined. In recent years, half of British Columbia's immigrants have come from Asia. Due in part to its thriving oil industry, Alberta has Canada's fastest-growing provincial population, which is concentrated in the Calgary–Edmonton corridor. Calgary is the nation's fastest-growing city.

Massive grain stores, like these ones in Saskatchewan, testify to the productiveness of the Canadian prairies.

The Mackenzie River has North America's second-largest river basin.

SCALE 1:9,340,659
Lamberts Conformal Conic Projection

Longitude west of Greenwich

39

EASTERN CANADA

Manitoba, New Brunswick, Newfoundland and Labrador, Nova Scotia, Nunavut, Ontario, Prince Edward Island, Québec, St Pierre and Miquelon

Underpinned by the ancient Canadian Shield, Eastern Canada consists of a horseshoe-shaped swathe of mostly low-lying land that curls around and inclines gently toward the shores of Hudson Bay. Mountains rise along the eastern fringes of the shield, on Baffin Island, and in Labrador, New Brunswick, and eastern Québec. North America's great belt of lake-studded boreal forest blankets much of Manitoba, Ontario, and Québec, separating the windswept northern tundra from a narrow temperate zone in the south that is home to most of Canada's cities, businesses, and industries, as well as its capital. Before coming under British control in the 18th century, this region was settled by groups of French immigrants. Many remained, and the province of Québec is still culturally distinct from the rest of Canada in that the vast majority of its inhabitants are of French descent and French-speaking. Its demands for greater autonomy constitute Canada's most problematic and potentially disruptive political issue.

In Hudson Bay, polar bears live onshore in summer but hunt seals across the pack ice throughout winter.

Founded in 1642 on an island in the St Lawrence River, Montréal is Canada's second-largest city.

POPULATION PATTERNS

Six out of every ten Canadians live in the provinces of Ontario and Québec, which also encompass 15 of the country's 25 largest cities. Ontario has been the focus of recent immigration to Canada, absorbing half of all incomers in the 1990s. By far the densest settlement occurs along the Great Lakes–St Lawrence lowlands. In Manitoba, the population is concentrated in the productive southern prairies, but mechanization of agricultural processes has kept numbers low. Newfoundland and Labrador's population has dropped sharply in recent years, mainly as a result of migration to other provinces. The north is the site of far-flung indigenous communities and outposts founded on resource exploitation.

Uninhabited

Less than 2.6 persons per sq mile/1 per sq km

2.6–26 per sq mile/ 1–10 per sq km

26–65 per sq mile/ 10–25 per sq km

65–130 per sq mile/ 25–50 per sq km

130–260 per sq mile/ 50–100 per sq km

260–520 per sq mile/ 100–200 per sq km

520–1040 per sq mile/ 200–400 per sq km

1040–2080 per sq mile/ 400–800 per sq km

More than 2080 per sq mile/ 800 per sq km

ECONOMIC PROFILE

Ontario and Québec supply most of Canada's gold, and Sudbury in Ontario produces 20 percent of the world's nickel as well as large amounts of copper, silver, gold, and iron ore. Large gas reserves lie off Cape Sable Island in Nova Scotia, and oil platforms operate off the coast of Newfoundland. Almost all of the energy requirements of Newfoundland and Labrador, Québec, and Manitoba are met by hydroelectric power. Newfoundland's Grand Banks are Canada's richest fisheries, although overfishing has significantly reduced catches since the mid-1970s. Southern Ontario and Québec form the country's industrial and commercial heartland.

Forest and woodland

Arable land

Marginal or nonproductive

Cereals
Fruit
Beef cattle
Fishing
Industrial center
Mining
Timber

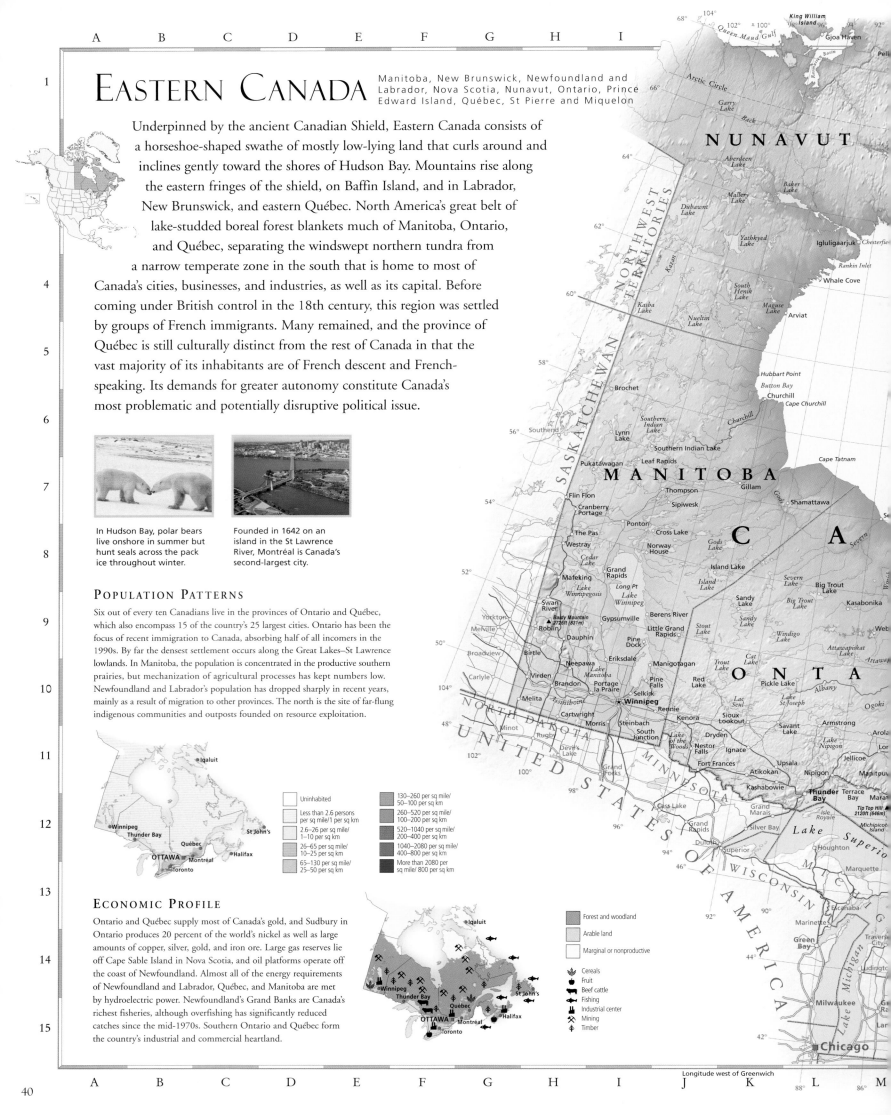

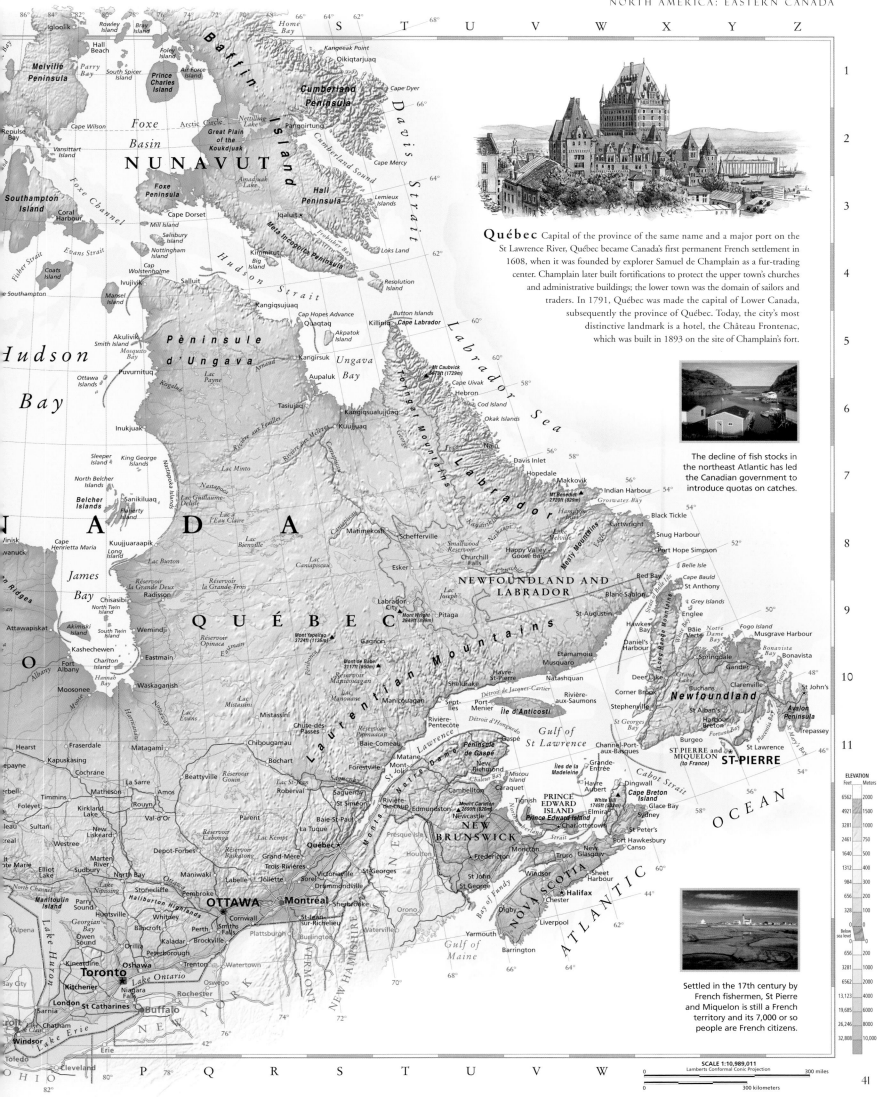

Québec Capital of the province of the same name and a major port on the St Lawrence River, Québec became Canada's first permanent French settlement in 1608, when it was founded by explorer Samuel de Champlain as a fur-trading center. Champlain later built fortifications to protect the upper town's churches and administrative buildings; the lower town was the domain of sailors and traders. In 1791, Québec was made the capital of Lower Canada, subsequently the province of Québec. Today, the city's most distinctive landmark is a hotel, the Château Frontenac, which was built in 1893 on the site of Champlain's fort.

The decline of fish stocks in the northeast Atlantic has led the Canadian government to introduce quotas on catches.

Settled in the 17th century by French fishermen, St Pierre and Miquelon is still a French territory and its 7,000 or so people are French citizens.

SCALE 1:10,989,011
Lamberts Conformal Conic Projection

0 — 300 miles
0 — 300 kilometers

ELEVATION	
Feet	Meters
6562	2000
4921	1500
3281	1000
2461	750
1640	500
1312	400
984	300
656	200
328	100
0 Below sea level	0
656	200
3281	1000
6562	2000
13,123	4000
19,685	6000
26,246	8000
32,808	10,000

SOUTHEASTERN CANADA

New Brunswick, Nova Scotia, Ontario, Prince Edward Island, Québec

Flowing northeast out of Lake Ontario, the St Lawrence River courses for almost 800 miles (1,300 km) to the wide Gulf of St Lawrence and the Atlantic Ocean. The river was the main entry point to the interior for early European adventurers, and in the 17th century the country's first ports were founded on its banks by French explorers. The temperate climate and fertile soils of the river valley and the northern shores of Lakes Ontario and Erie form a stark contrast to the cold, waterlogged plateaus to the north and the wet, precipitous terrain of the Appalachian Mountains to the south. Settlers consequently clustered on these lowlands, and today this is Canada's most populous region, the site of its largest cities, and the home of its national capital, Ottawa.

The commercial center and capital of Nova Scotia, Halifax began as a French fishing port in the 18th century.

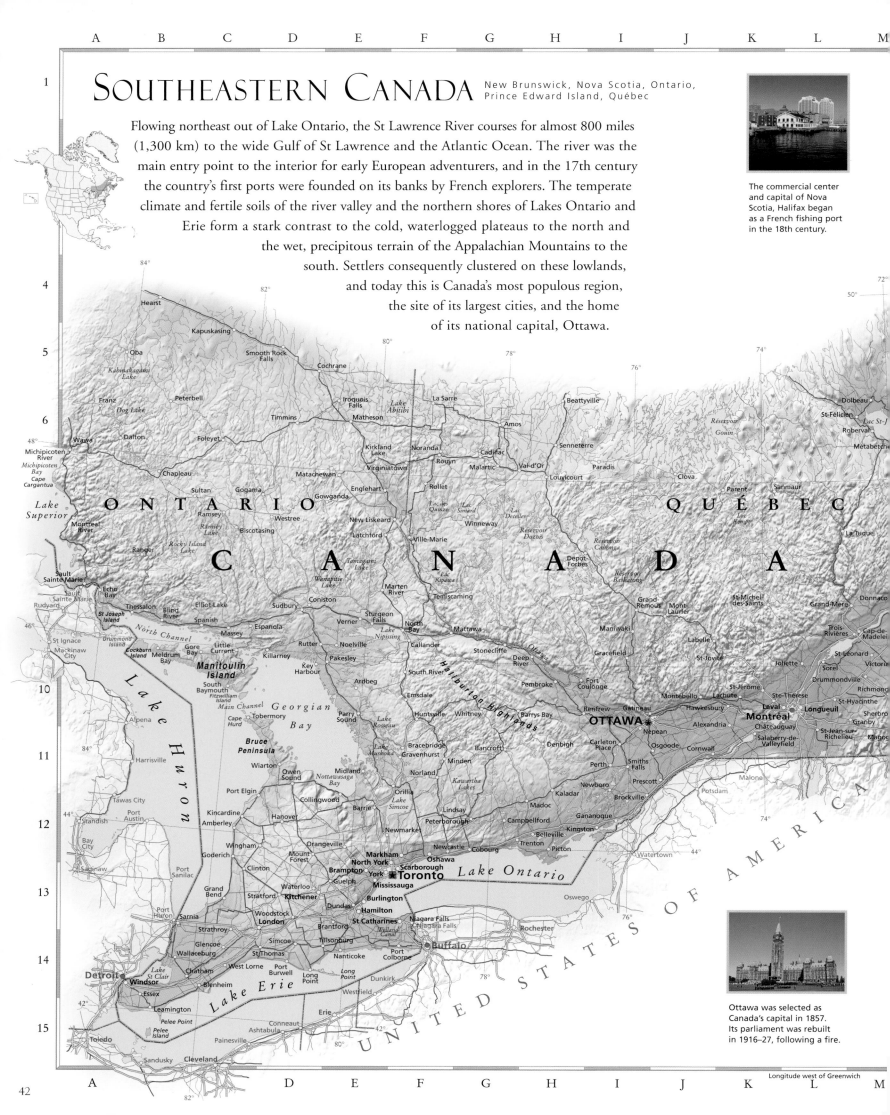

Ottawa was selected as Canada's capital in 1857. Its parliament was rebuilt in 1916–27, following a fire.

Longitude west of Greenwich

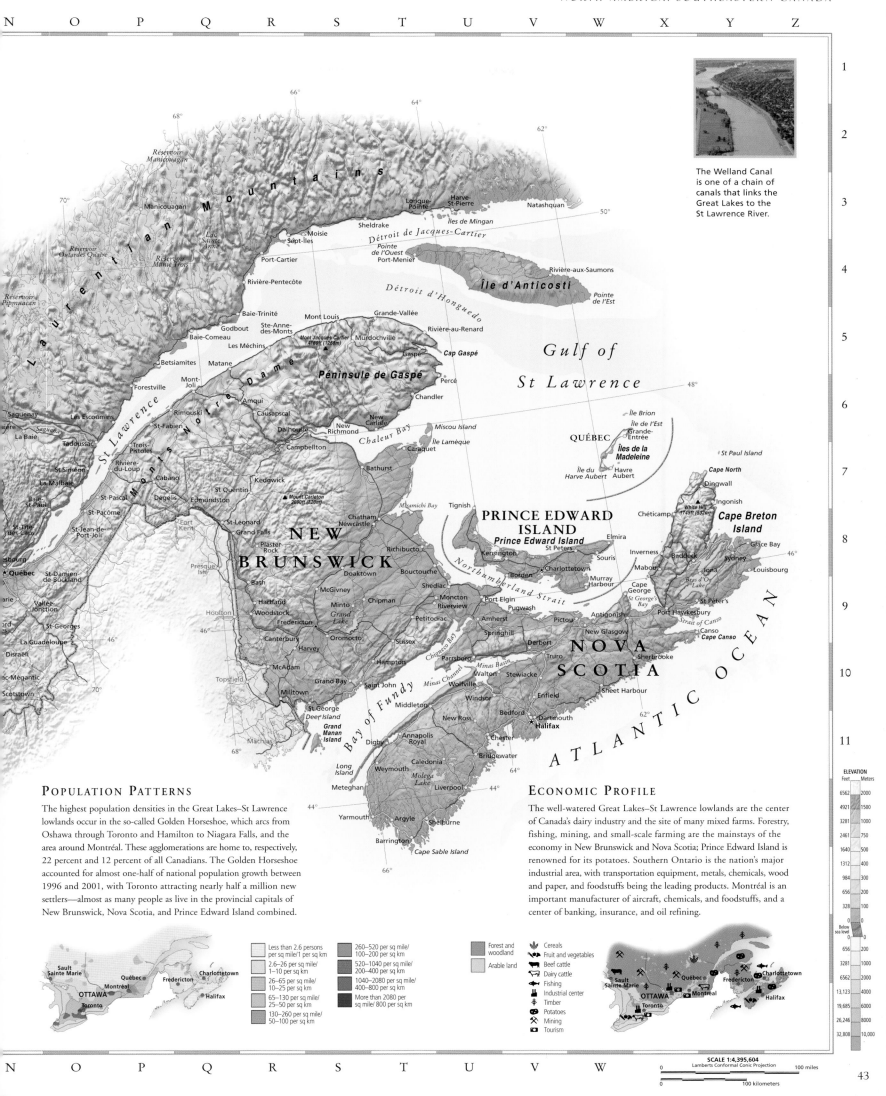

The Welland Canal is one of a chain of canals that links the Great Lakes to the St Lawrence River.

POPULATION PATTERNS

The highest population densities in the Great Lakes–St Lawrence lowlands occur in the so-called Golden Horseshoe, which arcs from Oshawa through Toronto and Hamilton to Niagara Falls, and the area around Montréal. These agglomerations are home to, respectively, 22 percent and 12 percent of all Canadians. The Golden Horseshoe accounted for almost one-half of national population growth between 1996 and 2001, with Toronto attracting nearly half a million new settlers—almost as many people as live in the provincial capitals of New Brunswick, Nova Scotia, and Prince Edward Island combined.

ECONOMIC PROFILE

The well-watered Great Lakes–St Lawrence lowlands are the center of Canada's dairy industry and the site of many mixed farms. Forestry, fishing, mining, and small-scale farming are the mainstays of the economy in New Brunswick and Nova Scotia; Prince Edward Island is renowned for its potatoes. Southern Ontario is the nation's major industrial area, with transportation equipment, metals, chemicals, wood and paper, and foodstuffs being the leading products. Montréal is an important manufacturer of aircraft, chemicals, and foodstuffs, and a center of banking, insurance, and oil refining.

Less than 2.6 persons per sq mile/1 per sq km
2.6–26 per sq mile/ 1–10 per sq km
26–65 per sq mile/ 10–25 per sq km
65–130 per sq mile/ 25–50 per sq km
130–260 per sq mile/ 50–100 per sq km
260–520 per sq mile/ 100–200 per sq km
520–1040 per sq mile/ 200–400 per sq km
1040–2080 per sq mile/ 400–800 per sq km
More than 2080 per sq mile/ 800 per sq km

Forest and woodland
Arable land

Cereals
Fruit and vegetables
Beef cattle
Dairy cattle
Fishing
Industrial center
Timber
Potatoes
Mining
Tourism

ELEVATION
Feet — Meters

SCALE 1:4,395,604
Lamberts Conformal Conic Projection
100 miles
100 kilometers

MEXICO

Mexico's interior is dominated by a vast, V-shaped plateau known as the Mesa Central. Extending from the U.S. border southward beyond Mexico City, it is edged by two major mountain ranges, the Sierra Madre Occidental and the Sierra Madre Oriental. A slender, broken coastal plain runs along the Pacific shore, converging in the far northwest with the long, rugged, and extremely arid arm of Baja California. At the southern end of the wide, humid east-coast lowlands, the Yucatan Peninsula, a flat, low swathe of limestone, juts into the Gulf of Mexico. In the early 16th century, Spain rapidly conquered the prosperous native civilizations of the Aztec and the Maya. Its subsequent colonization of the entire region resulted in the eradication of many Amerindian communities. Mexico shook off Spanish rule in 1821 and became a republic two years later, though it experienced revolutions and civil wars for the next 100 years. In the 20th century, explosive population growth limited the benefits of genuine social and economic progress.

POPULATION PATTERNS

Mexico's population has increased by 500 percent since 1915 and has become highly urbanized in recent decades—75 percent of Mexicans live in towns and cities. By far the most densely populated area is the southern belt linking Guadalajara, Mexico City, Puebla, and Veracruz. Fueled by U.S.-backed industrial expansion, the northern border towns are also growing rapidly. Population density is lowest in the arid north and in Chiapas and eastern Yucatan. About 60 percent of Mexicans are mestizos, 30 percent Amerindian, and 9 percent of European origin.

Less than 2.6 persons per sq mile/1 per sq km
2.6–26 per sq mile/ 1–10 per sq km
26–65 per sq mile/ 10–25 per sq km
65–130 per sq mile/ 25–50 per sq km
130–260 per sq mile/ 50–100 per sq km
260–520 per sq mile/ 100–200 per sq km
520–1040 per sq mile/ 200–400 per sq km

ECONOMIC PROFILE

Mexico has enormous mineral resources, limited arable land, and expanding industries. It is one of the world's largest producers of oil—its main source of income—and the largest supplier of silver; it also has sizable gas and coal reserves. Industries, led by the processing of oil, food, and metals and the manufacture of machinery, chemicals, and textiles, are concentrated in Mexico City. Only about one-fifth of the country is arable; half of this area is given over to corn cultivation. Cattle ranching is the main agricultural activity in the arid north. Tourism is now the nation's second-biggest source of revenue.

Forest and woodland
Arable land
Grazing
Marginal or nonproductive

Corn (maize)
Cotton
Coffee
Sugarcane
Industrial center
Mining
Oil production
Fishing
Beef cattle
Tourism

ELEVATION
Feet / Meters
6562 / 2000
4921 / 1500
3281 / 1000
2461 / 750
1640 / 500
1312 / 400
984 / 300
656 / 200
328 / 100
0 / 0
Below sea level / 0
656 / 200
3281 / 1000
6562 / 2000
13,123 / 4000
19,685 / 6000
26,246 / 8000
32,808 / 10,000

Major offshore oil fields were first discovered near Tampico in 1900, then near Tuxpan and in Tabasco.

Farmers harvest agave cactus to make tequila, a Mexican liquor named for the town of Tequila, west of Guadalajara.

In the 16th century, Guanajuato grew rapidly as a major silver-mining center.

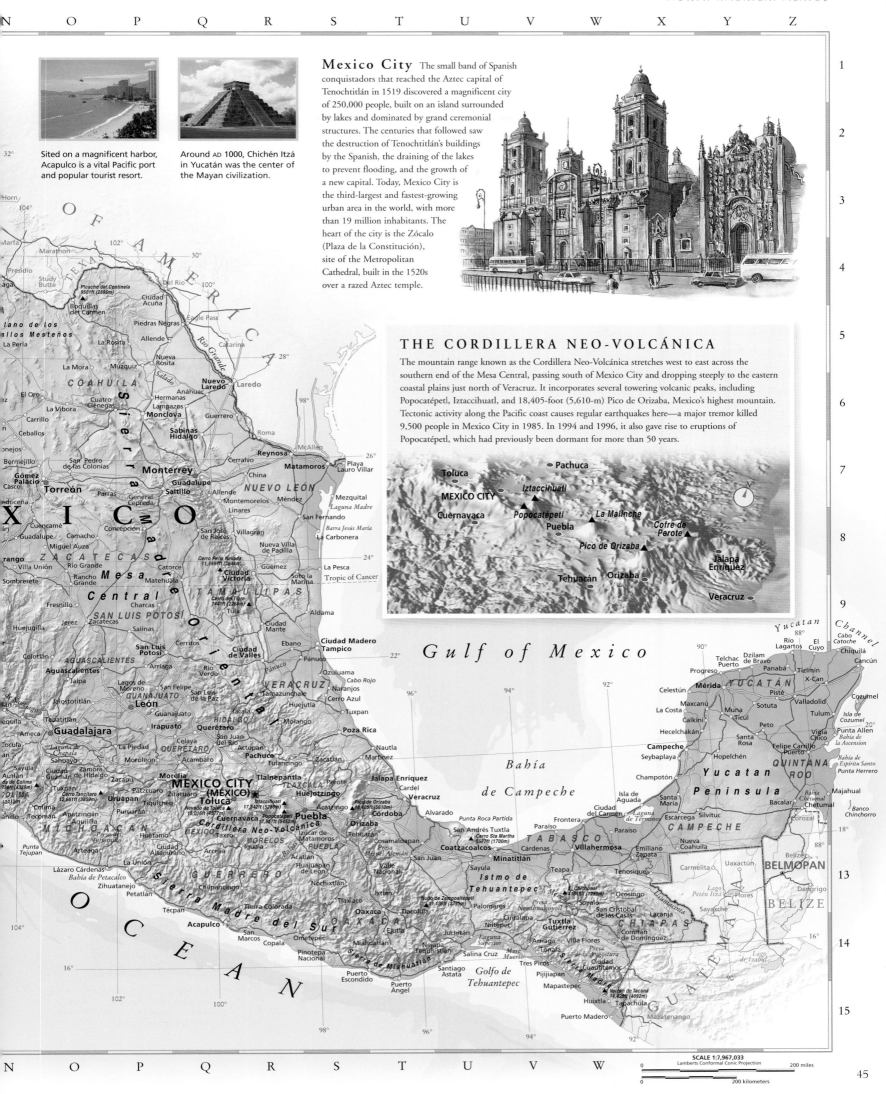

Sited on a magnificent harbor, Acapulco is a vital Pacific port and popular tourist resort.

Around AD 1000, Chichén Itzá in Yucatán was the center of the Mayan civilization.

Mexico City

The small band of Spanish conquistadors that reached the Aztec capital of Tenochtitlán in 1519 discovered a magnificent city of 250,000 people, built on an island surrounded by lakes and dominated by grand ceremonial structures. The centuries that followed saw the destruction of Tenochtitlán's buildings by the Spanish, the draining of the lakes to prevent flooding, and the growth of a new capital. Today, Mexico City is the third-largest and fastest-growing urban area in the world, with more than 19 million inhabitants. The heart of the city is the Zócalo (Plaza de la Constitución), site of the Metropolitan Cathedral, built in the 1520s over a razed Aztec temple.

THE CORDILLERA NEO-VOLCÁNICA

The mountain range known as the Cordillera Neo-Volcánica stretches west to east across the southern end of the Mesa Central, passing south of Mexico City and dropping steeply to the eastern coastal plains just north of Veracruz. It incorporates several towering volcanic peaks, including Popocatépetl, Iztaccihuatl, and 18,405-foot (5,610-m) Pico de Orizaba, Mexico's highest mountain. Tectonic activity along the Pacific coast causes regular earthquakes here—a major tremor killed 9,500 people in Mexico City in 1985. In 1994 and 1996, it also gave rise to eruptions of Popocatépetl, which had previously been dormant for more than 50 years.

SCALE 1:7,967,033
Lamberts Conformal Conic Projection

0   200 miles
0   200 kilometers

CENTRAL AMERICA

Belize, Costa Rica, El Salvador, Guatemala, Honduras, Nicaragua, Panama

From the Mexican border, Central America dog-legs and tapers southeastward, connecting with Colombia in South America at the eastern end of the Isthmus of Panama. Forested mountain ranges parallel the Pacific coast, spreading east across Honduras and northern Nicaragua, and covering four-fifths of the entire landmass. Narrow coastal plains line the Pacific shore; wider, swampy lowlands border the Caribbean Sea. With the exception of the former British colony of Belize, the nations of Central America share a predominantly Hispanic culture stemming from a long period of Spanish domination and shaped to varying degrees by other imported and indigenous cultures. Central America's recent history has been clouded by coups, periods of repressive military rule, and guerilla warfare, especially in the north. The southern nations of Costa Rica and Panama have the highest standards of living and have been more stable, although the U.S.A. invaded Panama in 1989 to remove a corrupt military regime.

POPULATION PATTERNS

Most of the population is mestizo, though the ethnic makeup varies from country to country. Almost one-third of people in Belize are of African origin, and most Costa Ricans are of European descent. Indigenous peoples are in a small minority in most countries except Guatemala, where they form almost half of the population. Settlement has favored the west, especially the cool, fertile uplands, over the humid Caribbean plains, and the north is more populous—one-third of Central Americans live in Guatemala. Urbanization ranges from just over 40 percent in Guatemala to almost 66 percent in El Salvador.

ECONOMIC PROFILE

Development is hampered by political unrest, poor infrastructure, and inequitable distribution of land. Many people grow corn, beans, squashes, and fruit for their own consumption, but much of the best farmland has been turned into large, often foreign-owned, cattle ranches and plantations producing sugar, bananas, and coffee. Mineral resources are, for the most part, scanty or undeveloped. Forests provide timber and chicle (used in chewing gum), but are not harvested sustainably. Industries are limited mainly to food processing and textiles. Services are most significant in Panama, where a free-trade zone is centered on Colón.

Wildlife-rich rain forests are among the attractions that draw over 1 million overseas visitors a year to Costa Rica.

Lake Nicaragua is the world's only freshwater lake that is home to saltwater fish such as sharks and swordfish.

ELEVATION

Feet	Meters
6562	2000
4921	1500
3281	1000
2461	750
1640	500
1312	400
984	300
656	200
328	100
Below sea level	0
656	200
3281	1000
6562	2000
13,123	4000
19,685	6000
26,246	8000
32,808	10,000

Less than 2.6 persons per sq mile/1 per sq km
2.6–26 per sq mile/1–10 per sq km
26–65 per sq mile/10–25 per sq km
65–130 per sq mile/25–50 per sq km
130–260 per sq mile/50–100 per sq km

Fruit
Bananas
Cotton
Coffee
Sugarcane
Shellfish
Beef cattle
Timber
Industrial center

Forest and woodland
Arable land
Grazing
Marginal or nonproductive

SCALE 1:4,395,604
Lamberts Conformal Conic Projection
0   100 miles
0   100 kilometers

Longitude west of Greenwich

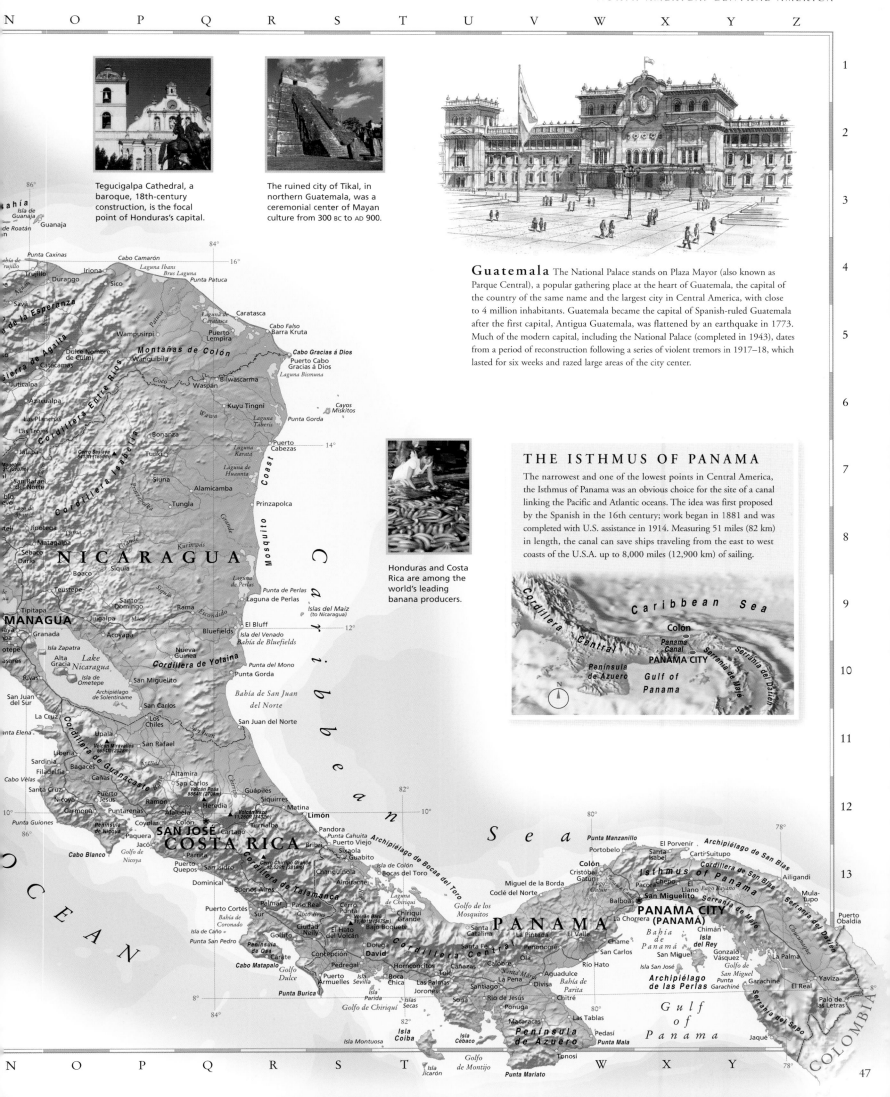

Tegucigalpa Cathedral, a baroque, 18th-century construction, is the focal point of Honduras's capital.

The ruined city of Tikal, in northern Guatemala, was a ceremonial center of Mayan culture from 300 BC to AD 900.

Guatemala The National Palace stands on Plaza Mayor (also known as Parque Central), a popular gathering place at the heart of Guatemala, the capital of the country of the same name and the largest city in Central America, with close to 4 million inhabitants. Guatemala became the capital of Spanish-ruled Guatemala after the first capital, Antigua Guatemala, was flattened by an earthquake in 1773. Much of the modern capital, including the National Palace (completed in 1943), dates from a period of reconstruction following a series of violent tremors in 1917–18, which lasted for six weeks and razed large areas of the city center.

Honduras and Costa Rica are among the world's leading banana producers.

THE ISTHMUS OF PANAMA

The narrowest and one of the lowest points in Central America, the Isthmus of Panama was an obvious choice for the site of a canal linking the Pacific and Atlantic oceans. The idea was first proposed by the Spanish in the 16th century; work began in 1881 and was completed with U.S. assistance in 1914. Measuring 51 miles (82 km) in length, the canal can save ships traveling from the east to west coasts of the U.S.A. up to 8,000 miles (12,900 km) of sailing.

The West Indies

Antigua and Barbuda, The Bahamas, Barbados, Cuba, Dominica, Dominican Republic, Grenada, Haiti, Jamaica, St Kitts and Nevis, St Lucia, St Vincent and the Grenadines, Trinidad and Tobago

Forming the northern boundary of the Caribbean Sea, the islands of the West Indies arc east then south from Florida in the U.S.A. to the north coast of South America. They include two major island groups: the Greater Antilles, consisting of the large islands of Cuba, Hispaniola, Jamaica, and Puerto Rico, and the Lesser Antilles, a string of small, high, chiefly volcanic islands. Following the arrival of Christopher Columbus in 1492 at San Salvador in The Bahamas (his belief that he had reached Asia led to the region being called the "West" Indies), the islands were fought over by various imperial powers, who imported huge numbers of African slaves to work on plantations. Today, this history is reflected in the region's cultural diversity and large number of dependencies, including French Guadeloupe, British Montserrat, and the Netherlands Antilles.

The twin volcanic peaks of the Pitons rise almost sheer from the sea near Soufrière on the island of St Lucia.

Over 100 million tourists visit the West Indies each year. Tourism generates two-fifths of the region's GNP.

ELEVATION

Feet	Meters
6562	2000
4921	1500
3281	1000
2461	750
1640	500
1312	400
984	300
656	200
328	100
0	0
Below sea level	
0	0
656	200
3281	1000
6562	2000
13,123	4000
19,685	6000
26,246	8000
32,808	10,000

UNITED STATES OF AMERICA

THE BAHAMAS

Grand Bahama
Cooper's Town
Marsh Harbour
Freeport
Pelican Point
Great Abaco
Bimini Islands
Alice Town
Cornwall
Mastic Point
New Providence
NASSAU
Eleuthera
Andros Town
Tarpum Ba
Andros Island
Mangrove Cay
Cat Island
Kemp's Bay
Exuma Cays
Geor
Hov
Great Exuma Island
Long Is
Deadman

Straits of Florida
Santaren Channel
Great Bahama Bank
Cay Sal
Anguilla Cay

Tropic of Cancer

HAVANA (LA HABANA)
Guanabacoa
Marianao
Mariel
Matanzas
Archipiélago de Sabana
Artemisa
Güines
Cárdenas
Minas de Matahambre
Los Palacios
Surgidero de Batabanó
Colón
Sagua la Grande
Archipiélago de Camagüey
Guane
Pinar del Río
Lafé
Golfo de Batabanó
Jagüey Grande
Santa Clara
Caibarién
Cayo Romano
Cabo San Antonio
Nueva Gerona
Cienfuegos
Pico San Juan 3793ft (1156m)
Sancti Spíritus
Esmeralda
Cayo Sabinal
Cabo Corrientes
Isla de la Juventud
Santa Fé
Archipiélago de los Canarreros
Trinidad
Ciego de Ávila
Minas
Nuevitas
Cayo del Rosario
Cayo Largo
Camagüey
Puerto Padre

CUBA
Vertientes
Po
Lu

Greater
Archipiélago de los Jardines de la Reina
Las Tunas
Holguín
Santa Cruz del Sur
Bayamo
Cueto
Sagua
Tánam
Golfo de Guacanayabo
Sierra Maestra
Palma Soriano
Guantán
Little Cayman
Cayman Brac
Cabo Cruz
Pilón
Pico Turquino 6578ft (1944m)
Guantán Naval Ba (to U.S.A

GEORGE TOWN
Grand Cayman
CAYMAN ISLANDS (to U.K.)

Cayman Trench
Jamaica Chann

Montego Bay
Falmouth
Ocho Rios
Port Antonio
South Negril Point
Savanna-la-Mar
Mandeville
KINGSTON
Misteriosa Bank
Rosario Bank

BELIZE
BELMOPAN
Dangriga

Swan Islands (to Honduras)

Pedro Bank

JAMAICA

Gulf of Honduras
Islas de la Bahía
Isla de Guanaja
Isla de Utila
Isla de Roatán
Puerto Barrios
La Ceiba
Cabo Camarón
Rosalind Bank
Alice Shoal

HONDURAS
Punta Patuca
Banco Gorda
Serranilla Bank

South Cay
Cabo Gracias á Dios

NICARAGUA
Cayos Miskitos

Mosquito Coast

Isla de Providencia (to Colombia)

C a r i b

Punta de Perlas
Laguna de Perlas
Rama
Isla de San Andrés (to Colombia)
Bluefields
Islas del Maíz (to Nicaragua)
Cayos de Albuquerque (to Colombia)
Acoyapa
Punta del Mono

San Carlos
Bahía de San Juan del Norte
San Juan del Norte
Punta del Mono

COSTA RICA
Cartagena
Limón

SAN JOSÉ

Almirante
Golfo de los Mosquitos
Colón
Gulf of Darién

PANAMA CITY (PANAMÁ)

PANAMA

Isthmus of Panama

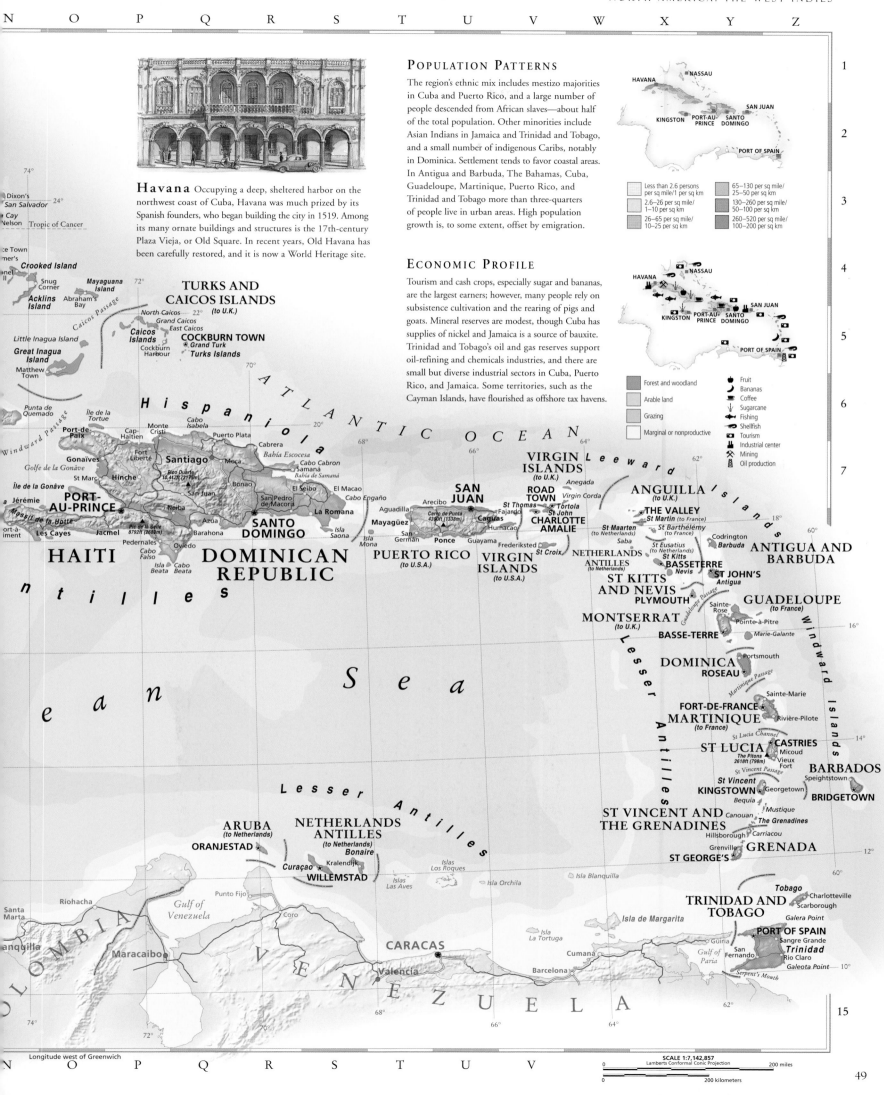

Havana Occupying a deep, sheltered harbor on the northwest coast of Cuba, Havana was much prized by its Spanish founders, who began building the city in 1519. Among its many ornate buildings and structures is the 17th-century Plaza Vieja, or Old Square. In recent years, Old Havana has been carefully restored, and it is now a World Heritage site.

POPULATION PATTERNS

The region's ethnic mix includes mestizo majorities in Cuba and Puerto Rico, and a large number of people descended from African slaves—about half of the total population. Other minorities include Asian Indians in Jamaica and Trinidad and Tobago, and a small number of indigenous Caribs, notably in Dominica. Settlement tends to favor coastal areas. In Antigua and Barbuda, The Bahamas, Cuba, Guadeloupe, Martinique, Puerto Rico, and Trinidad and Tobago more than three-quarters of people live in urban areas. High population growth is, to some extent, offset by emigration.

Less than 2.6 persons per sq mile/1 per sq km
2.6–26 per sq mile/1–10 per sq km
26–65 per sq mile/10–25 per sq km
65–130 per sq mile/25–50 per sq km
130–260 per sq mile/50–100 per sq km
260–520 per sq mile/100–200 per sq km

ECONOMIC PROFILE

Tourism and cash crops, especially sugar and bananas, are the largest earners; however, many people rely on subsistence cultivation and the rearing of pigs and goats. Mineral reserves are modest, though Cuba has supplies of nickel and Jamaica is a source of bauxite. Trinidad and Tobago's oil and gas reserves support oil-refining and chemicals industries, and there are small but diverse industrial sectors in Cuba, Puerto Rico, and Jamaica. Some territories, such as the Cayman Islands, have flourished as offshore tax havens.

Forest and woodland
Arable land
Grazing
Marginal or nonproductive

Fruit
Bananas
Coffee
Sugarcane
Fishing
Shellfish
Tourism
Industrial center
Mining
Oil production

SCALE 1:7,142,857
Lamberts Conformal Conic Projection
200 miles
200 kilometers

Longitude west of Greenwich

NORTHERN SOUTH AMERICA

Colombia, Guyana, Suriname, Venezuela

Nearing their northern limit in southern Colombia, the Andes Mountains divide into three separate chains, forming a rugged hinterland of valleys and ranges. This is paralleled to the east by a broad sweep of low land, including part of the heavily forested Amazon Basin in the south and, in the north, the Llanos, humid savanna grasslands drained by the Orinoco River. Beyond the Orinoco, the flat-topped Guiana Highlands sprawl across southern Venezuela, Guyana, Suriname, and French Guiana, descending in the north to densely forested lowlands and swampy coastal plains. Despite significant natural resources, and for a variety of reasons, the countries in this region have struggled to attain stability and prosperity. Colombia's government has fought a draining struggle against armed guerillas and powerful drug-traffickers; oil-rich Venezuela's progress has been hindered by inefficient economic management and inequitable distribution of wealth; and the less-developed Guyana, Suriname, and French Guiana still lack infrastructure.

THE COLOMBIAN CORDILLERAS

The three northern branches of the Andes—the Cordillera Occidental, Cordillera Central, and Cordillera Oriental—are separated by the fertile valleys of the Cauca and Magdalena rivers. These valleys and adjacent slopes are the site of Colombia's largest cities (including the capital Bogotá) and most productive coffee and sugar plantations. They also contain vital natural resources, including oil, emeralds, and gold. In the north, the Cordillera Oriental splits again, its two arms enclosing the wide ocean inlet of Lake Maracaibo, site of Venezuela's second-largest city, Maracaibo, and the principal source of the country's enormous oil reserves.

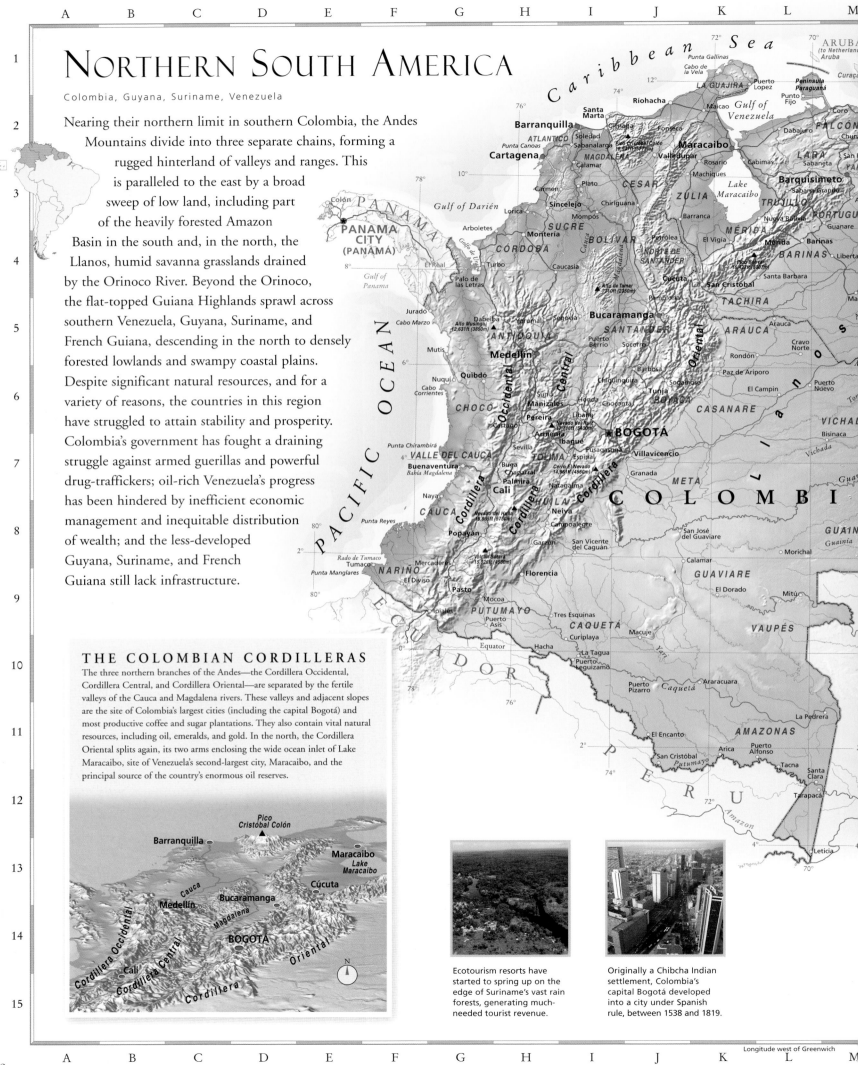

Ecotourism resorts have started to spring up on the edge of Suriname's vast rain forests, generating much-needed tourist revenue.

Originally a Chibcha Indian settlement, Colombia's capital Bogotá developed into a city under Spanish rule, between 1538 and 1819.

Longitude west of Greenwich

50

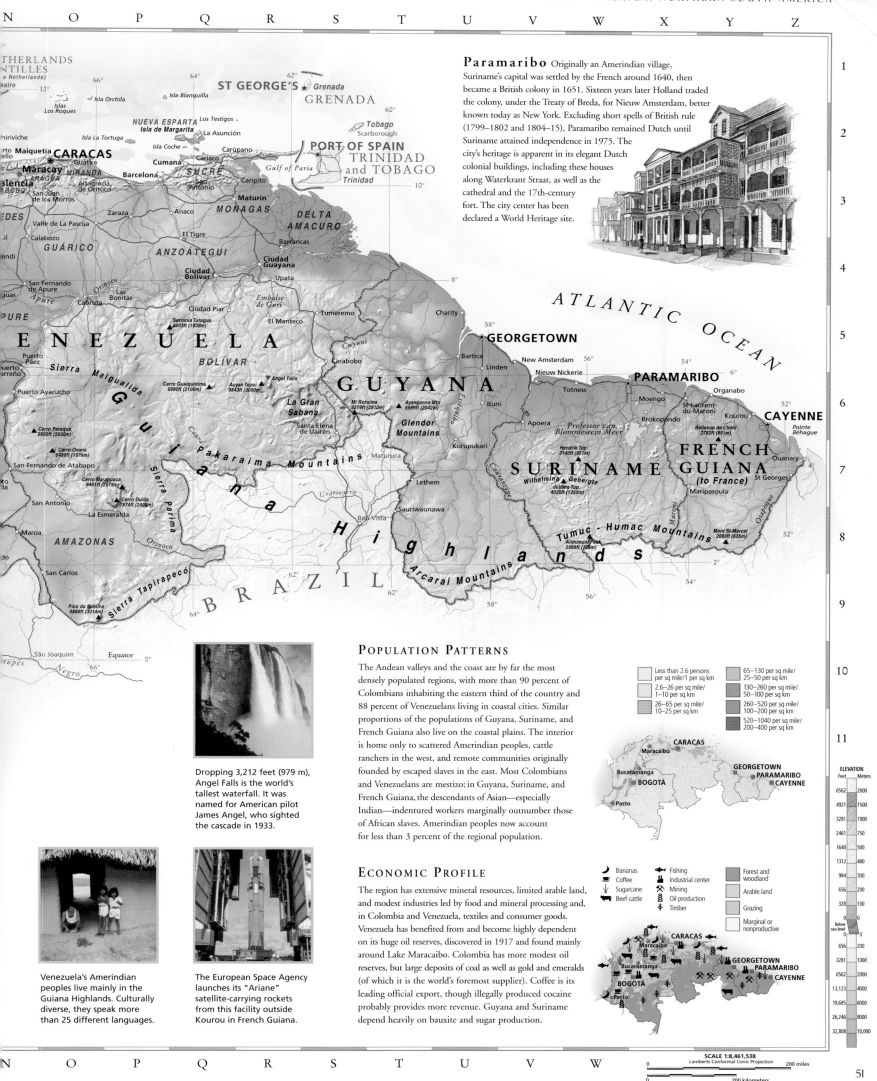

Paramaribo

Originally an Amerindian village, Suriname's capital was settled by the French around 1640, then became a British colony in 1651. Sixteen years later Holland traded the colony, under the Treaty of Breda, for Nieuw Amsterdam, better known today as New York. Excluding short spells of British rule (1799–1802 and 1804–15), Paramaribo remained Dutch until Suriname attained independence in 1975. The city's heritage is apparent in its elegant Dutch colonial buildings, including these houses along Waterkrant Straat, as well as the cathedral and the 17th-century fort. The city center has been declared a World Heritage site.

Dropping 3,212 feet (979 m), Angel Falls is the world's tallest waterfall. It was named for American pilot James Angel, who sighted the cascade in 1933.

Venezuela's Amerindian peoples live mainly in the Guiana Highlands. Culturally diverse, they speak more than 25 different languages.

The European Space Agency launches its "Ariane" satellite-carrying rockets from this facility outside Kourou in French Guiana.

POPULATION PATTERNS

The Andean valleys and the coast are by far the most densely populated regions, with more than 90 percent of Colombians inhabiting the eastern third of the country and 88 percent of Venezuelans living in coastal cities. Similar proportions of the populations of Guyana, Suriname, and French Guiana also live on the coastal plains. The interior is home only to scattered Amerindian peoples, cattle ranchers in the west, and remote communities originally founded by escaped slaves in the east. Most Colombians and Venezuelans are mestizo; in Guyana, Suriname, and French Guiana, the descendants of Asian—especially Indian—indentured workers marginally outnumber those of African slaves. Amerindian peoples now account for less than 3 percent of the regional population.

Population density legend

Less than 2.6 persons per sq mile/1 per sq km	65–130 per sq mile/25–50 per sq km
2.6–26 per sq mile/1–10 per sq km	130–260 per sq mile/50–100 per sq km
26–65 per sq mile/10–25 per sq km	260–520 per sq mile/100–200 per sq km
	520–1040 per sq mile/200–400 per sq km

ECONOMIC PROFILE

The region has extensive mineral resources, limited arable land, and modest industries led by food and mineral processing and, in Colombia and Venezuela, textiles and consumer goods. Venezuela has benefited from and become highly dependent on its huge oil reserves, discovered in 1917 and found mainly around Lake Maracaibo. Colombia has more modest oil reserves, but large deposits of coal as well as gold and emeralds (of which it is the world's foremost supplier). Coffee is its leading official export, though illegally produced cocaine probably provides more revenue. Guyana and Suriname depend heavily on bauxite and sugar production.

Economic legend

- Bananas
- Coffee
- Sugarcane
- Beef cattle
- Fishing
- Industrial center
- Mining
- Oil production
- Timber
- Forest and woodland
- Arable land
- Grazing
- Marginal or nonproductive

ELEVATION

Feet	Meters
6562	2000
4921	1500
3281	1000
2461	750
1640	500
1312	400
984	300
656	200
328	100
0 Below sea level	0
656	200
3281	1000
6562	2000
13,123	4000
19,685	6000
26,246	8000
32,808	10,000

SCALE 1:8,461,538
Lamberts Conformal Conic Projection
0   200 miles
0   200 kilometers

WESTERN SOUTH AMERICA

Bolivia, Ecuador, Peru

Separated from the Pacific Ocean by a slender coastal plain, the towering peaks of the Andes dominate the entire western side of this region, yielding in the east to well-watered, forest-cloaked lowlands, most of which drain into the vast Amazon Basin. Narrower in the north, the Andes broaden in southern Peru and Bolivia, splitting into two parallel chains, the Cordillera Occidental and the Cordillera Oriental. In the south, these ranges enclose an expansive, arid plateau known as the Altiplano. From around 1200 until shortly after the arrival of the Spanish conquistadors, Cuzco in the northern Altiplano was the capital of the Inca empire, which encompassed virtually the entire Andean sector of this region. Spanish rule left most of the region's wealth and resources in the hands of European-dominated elites. Dissatisfaction with this state of affairs has since fueled indigenous uprisings, labor unrest, Maoist guerilla activity in Peru, and repeated changes of government. In turn, this has hampered economic development, especially in Bolivia, South America's poorest nation.

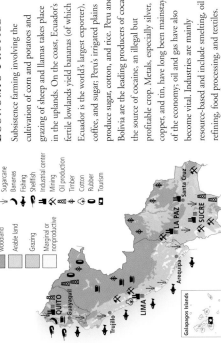

Quito The world's second-highest capital city after La Paz in Bolivia, Ecuador's capital occupies a narrow valley on the slopes of spectacular Pichincha volcano in the Andes. Little trace remains of the Amerindian and Inca settlements that once stood here, but the city's rich array of buildings from the early period of Spanish settlement in the 16th and 17th centuries, including the elegant Monastery of San Francisco, Ecuador's oldest church, make it the best-preserved capital city in South America.

In the 16th century, the silver-mining center of Potosí in Bolivia was the New World's largest city, with 120,000 inhabitants.

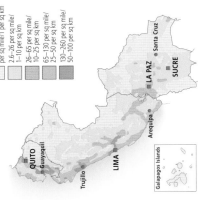

The Galapagos Islands' wildlife includes a host of species unique to the archipelago, including the land iguana.

POPULATION PATTERNS

In Ecuador and Peru, the population is split evenly between coastal and mountain dwellers, with only a minority inhabiting the interior. One-third of Peruvians live in Lima. In Bolivia, the Altiplano is by far the most densely populated region, despite attempts in the late 20th century to encourage people to settle in the east. Relative to other South American nations, all three countries have high proportions of indigenous peoples—25 percent in Ecuador, 45 percent in Peru, and more than 50 percent in Bolivia. They live mainly in the Andean uplands.

Less than 2.6 persons per sq mile/1 per sq km
2.6–26 per sq mile/1–10 per sq km
26–65 per sq mile/10–25 per sq km
65–130 per sq mile/25–50 per sq km
130–260 per sq mile/50–100 per sq km

ECONOMIC PROFILE

Subsistence farming involving the cultivation of corn and potatoes and grazing of sheep and llamas takes place in the uplands. On the coast, Ecuador's fertile lowlands yield bananas (of which Ecuador is the world's largest exporter), coffee, and sugar; Peru's irrigated plains produce sugar, cotton, and rice. Peru and Bolivia are the leading producers of coca, the source of cocaine, an illegal but profitable crop. Metals, especially silver, copper, and tin, have long been mainstays of the economy; oil and gas have also become vital. Industries are mainly resource-based and include smelting, oil refining, food processing, and textiles.

Coffee
Sugarcane
Bananas
Fishing
Shellfish
Mining
Oil production
Timber
Cotton
Rubber
Tourism
Industrial center

Forest and woodland
Arable land
Grazing
Marginal or nonproductive

The mountaintop citadel of Machu Picchu, near Cuzco in southern Peru, was built by the Inca in the mid-15th century.

The Aymara people are native to the Altiplano. Aymara women wear distinctive derby hats and woollen shawls.

SCALE 1:9,340,659
Lambert's Conformal Conic Projection

0   250 miles

0   250 kilometers

Longitude west of Greenwich

La Paz (left) is Bolivia's administrative capital and seat of national government. Sucre is the constitutional capital and home of the supreme court.

THE ALTIPLANO

Consisting of a series of basins located at around 12,000 feet (3,650 m) between the Cordillera Occidental and the Cordillera Oriental, the Altiplano extends for 600 miles (965 km) from southeastern Peru to southwestern Bolivia. Its northernmost basin, situated on the border between Peru and Bolivia, is the site of Lake Titicaca, at an altitude of 12,500 feet (3,810 m) the highest navigable body of water on Earth, and La Paz, the world's highest capital city, which climbs from 10,650 feet (3,250 m) to 13,250 feet (4,050 m). Many of the surrounding mountains, including Nevado de Illimani near La Paz and Bolivia's highest peak Nevado Sajama, rise above 20,000 feet (6,100 m). Just to the northwest of the Altiplano, in the Peruvian Andes, the Amazon River begins its long, transcontinental journey of over 4,000 miles (6,400 km) to the Atlantic Ocean.

Galapagos Islands
(to Ecuador)

SCALE 1:5,494,505

0   60 miles

0   60 kilometers

Longitude west of Greenwich

ELEVATION

Feet	Meters
6562	2000
4921	1500
3281	1000
2461	750
1640	500
1312	400
984	300
656	200
328	100
0	0
Below sea level	Below sea level
656	200
3281	1000
6562	2000
13,123	4000
19,685	6000
26,246	8000
32,808	10,000

EASTERN SOUTH AMERICA
Brazil, Paraguay

Encompassing more than 2.3 million square miles (6 million sq km) between the Andes and the eastern seaboard, the Amazon Basin is the world's largest drainage system. Cloaked with dense tropical rain forest embroidered by more than 1,000 tributaries, it dominates western and northern Brazil, its great river draining into the Atlantic Ocean near the town of Macapá. To the south rises the extensive plateau region of the Brazilian Highlands, which falls steeply to the coast in the east but descends more gently in the west to the swamps of the Pantanal, the low hills of eastern Paraguay, and the plains of Argentina. Here, the main drainage outlets are the Paraná River, which forms Paraguay's eastern boundary, and its major tributary, the Paraguay, which bisects the nation of the same name, dividing its eastern uplands from its semiarid western plains. Relatively small and landlocked, Paraguay has modest natural resources and a predominantly agricultural economy. In contrast, Brazil is South America's biggest and the world's fifth-largest country, with 5,400 miles (8,700 km) of coastline, the continent's largest population, and immense natural resources.

POPULATION PATTERNS

Brazil's population is concentrated on the coast, especially around São Paulo and Rio de Janeiro. About half of Brazilians are of European origin, 6 percent are of African descent, and 38 percent are of mixed African-European or African-Amerindian descent (so-called mulatos or pardos). Just 0.1 percent are Amerindian. These diverse groups are united by the Portuguese language. In Spanish-speaking Paraguay, 95 percent of the population is mestizo. Many Paraguayans also speak the indigenous Guaraní language. Paraguay is sparsely inhabited, and only 5 percent of the population lives west of the Paraguay River.

ECONOMIC PROFILE

Though hyperinflation, inequitable wealth distribution, and social problems have hampered development, Brazil has enormous economic potential. It is the world's second-largest iron-ore producer and third-biggest bauxite producer and it has the world's second-largest forests. Self-sufficient in food, it is the world's third-biggest meat producer and leading supplier of coffee, sugar, and oranges. Almost 90 percent of its energy comes from hydroelectric power. Industries include the manufacture of automobiles, petrochemicals, steel, shoes and textiles, and wood products. Paraguay generates all of its energy from hydroelectricity. It has a large "informal" or cash economy involving the resale of imported goods, often at street stalls.

Population density legend
- Less than 2.6 persons per sq mile/1 per sq km
- 2.6–26 per sq mile/1–10 per sq km
- 26–65 per sq mile/10–25 per sq km
- 65–130 per sq mile/25–50 per sq km
- 130–260 per sq mile/50–100 per sq km
- 260–520 per sq mile/100–200 per sq km

Economic legend
- Coffee
- Cocoa
- Sugarcane
- Soybeans
- Beef cattle
- Fishing
- Industrial center
- Mining
- Timber
- Citrus fruits

Land use legend
- Forest and woodland
- Arable land
- Grazing
- Marginal or nonproductive

THE PANTANAL

In western Brazil, the Planalto do Mato Grosso, an extension of the Brazilian Highlands, borders an immense plain known as the Pantanal. Tumbling down escarpments from the plateau, numerous rivers slow and meander across this plain. During the summer rainy season, the rivers overflow their banks, forming countless lakes and swamps and creating the world's largest freshwater wetland. Covering an area almost as big as Ohio, the Pantanal harbors an extraordinary diversity of wildlife. Though parts of the floodplain are protected by a national park, the ecosystem is threatened by poaching and pollution from mines and farms.

Fortaleza in Brazil derives its name from a 17th-century Dutch (then Portuguese) fort around which the city grew.

Western Paraguay is home to about 10,000 German-speaking Mennonites, whose forebears arrived in the 1920s from Eastern Europe.

Brasília A proposal for a new capital city was first presented to the Brazilian government in 1823 and subsequently incorporated in the constitution of 1891. The site was selected in 1956, partly to entice new settlers to the then-sparsely populated interior. Designed by Brazilian architects Lúcio Costa and Oscar Niemeyer in a monumental modernist style, Brasília became the national capital in 1960 and now has over 2 million inhabitants. Notable structures that helped it gain World Heritage status include its Cathedral and the National Congress—both designed by Niemeyer.

National Congress

Cathedral

Toucans abound in the rain forests of the Amazon Basin, 4 square miles (10 sq km) of which may harbor more than 400 bird species.

Brazil's Iguaçu Falls stand 269 feet (82 m) high and span 1.7 miles (2.7 km)—three times the width of the U.S.A.'s Niagara Falls.

Recife in northeastern Brazil was established in the 16th century by Portugal as a seaport serving the colonial sugar trade.

SCALE 1:15,384,615
Lambert's Conformal Conic Projection
0   400 kilometers
0   400 miles
Longitude west of Greenwich

ELEVATION

Feet	Meters
32,808	10,000
26,246	8000
19,685	6000
13,123	4000
6562	2000
3281	1000
1640	500
984	300
656	200
328	100
0 Below sea level	0
656	200
1640	500
2461	750
3281	1000
4921	1500
6562	2000

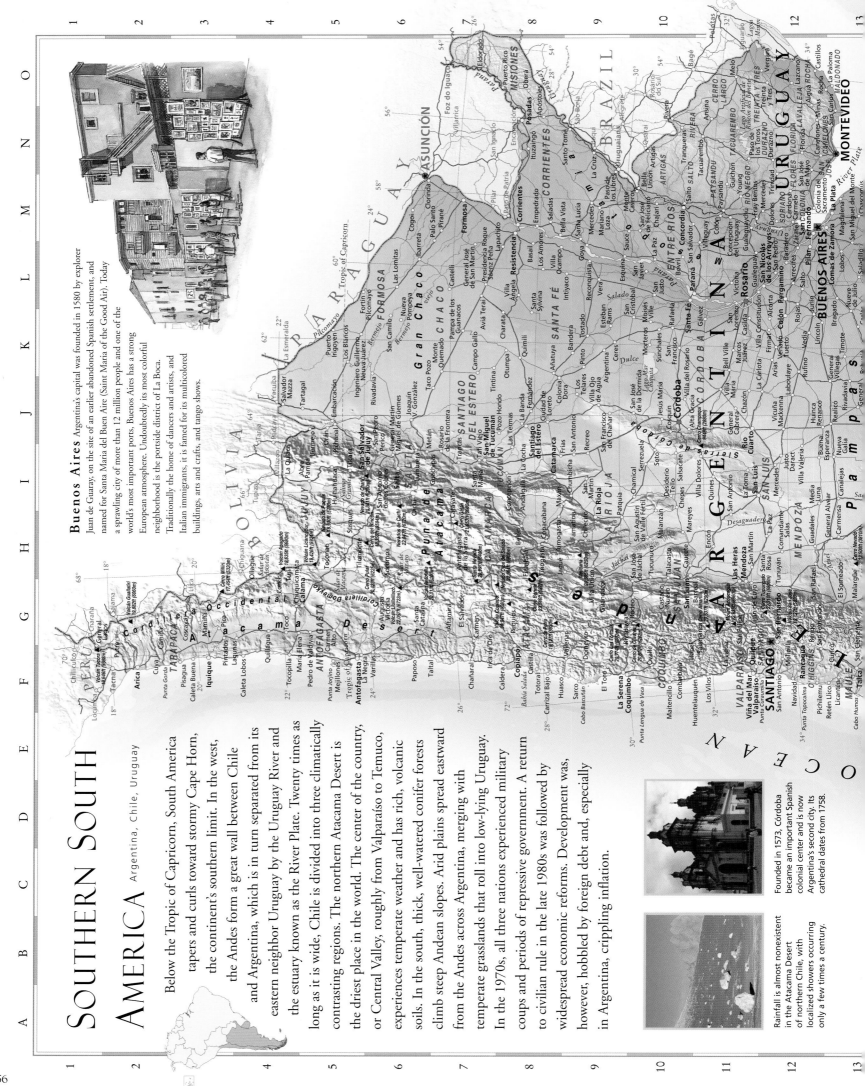

SOUTHERN SOUTH
AMERICA Argentina, Chile, Uruguay

Below the Tropic of Capricorn, South America tapers and curls toward stormy Cape Horn, the continent's southern limit. In the west, the Andes form a great wall between Chile and Argentina, which is in turn separated from its eastern neighbor Uruguay by the Uruguay River and the estuary known as the River Plate. Twenty times as long as it is wide, Chile is divided into three climatically contrasting regions. The northern Atacama Desert is the driest place in the world. The center of the country, or Central Valley, roughly from Valparaíso to Temuco, experiences temperate weather and has rich, volcanic soils. In the south, thick, well-watered conifer forests climb steep Andean slopes. Arid plains spread eastward from the Andes across Argentina, merging with temperate grasslands that roll into low-lying Uruguay. In the 1970s, all three nations experienced military coups and periods of repressive government. A return to civilian rule in the late 1980s was followed by widespread economic reforms. Development was, however, hobbled by foreign debt and, especially in Argentina, crippling inflation.

Buenos Aires Argentina's capital was founded in 1580 by explorer Juan de Guaray, on the site of an earlier abandoned Spanish settlement, and named for Santa Maria del Buen Aire (Saint Maria of the Good Air). Today a sprawling city of more than 12 million people and one of the world's most important ports, Buenos Aires has a strong European atmosphere. Undoubtedly its most colorful neighborhood is the portside district of La Boca. Traditionally the home of dancers and artists, and Italian immigrants, it is famed for its multicolored buildings, arts and crafts, and tango shows.

Founded in 1573, Córdoba became an important Spanish colonial center and is now Argentina's second city. Its cathedral dates from 1758.

Rainfall is almost nonexistent in the Atacama Desert of northern Chile, with localized showers occurring only a few times a century.

POPULATION PATTERNS

Almost 90 percent of the region's inhabitants live in cities, mainly in the central temperate belt, in and around the cities of Santiago in Chile, Buenos Aires and Córdoba in Argentina, and Montevideo in Uruguay. Settlements are sparse on Andean peaks, and in the cold, wet southwest. Chile's population is predominantly mestizo, with a small residual population of mainly Mapuche Indians. Argentina and Uruguay have more varied cultures, influenced by the large numbers of Spanish, Italian, and German immigrants who arrived after 1870. Indigenous groups still inhabit remote parts of Argentina but have almost vanished from Uruguay.

Uninhabited
Less than 2.6 persons per sq mile/1 per sq km
2.6–26 per sq mile/1–10 per sq km
26–65 per sq mile/10–25 per sq km
65–130 per sq mile/25–50 per sq km
130–260 per sq mile/50–100 per sq km
260–520 per sq mile/100–200 per sq km

ECONOMIC PROFILE

All three countries are strong exporters of primary goods. Chile is the world's leading supplier of copper and in the top five fish producers. Its forests provide abundant timber and the Central Valley yields large quantities of wheat, rice, fruit, and vegetables. Beef and wool from livestock grazed on the Pampas are the traditional mainstays of the Argentine and Uruguayan economies. Uruguay has few mineral resources, but Argentina has sizable oil reserves. Chile and Argentina have thriving wine industries, and Argentina is now the world's fifth-largest producer. All three capital cities are important commercial centers.

Leading industries include food processing, chemicals, and textiles.

Forest and woodland
Arable land
Grazing
Marginal or nonproductive

Cereals · Fruit · Wine · Beef cattle · Sheep · Fishing · Industrial center · Mining · Timber · Oil production

SOUTHERN PATAGONIA

On the southern Chile–Argentina border, extensive icefields crown Andean peaks such as Cerro Murallón and Cerro Fitz Roy. Glaciers snake down from these summits, plowing through expansive conifer forests. In the west, they reach the ragged, island-studded coast. In the east, they fall to lakes such as Argentino—site of the huge Moreno Glacier—and Viedma, and fuel mountain streams that drain across the barren Patagonian plateau and feed in turn into major rivers such as the Chico and Gallegos.

The Moreno Glacier forms a 200-foot (60-m) wall of ice across an arm of Lago Argentino in the foothills of the Argentine Andes.

FALKLAND ISLANDS

Argentina has long claimed ownership of the British-ruled Falkland Islands. An Argentine invasion in 1982 led to defeat in a brief war with the U.K.

SCALE 1:9,890,110
Lamberts Conformal Conic Projection

57

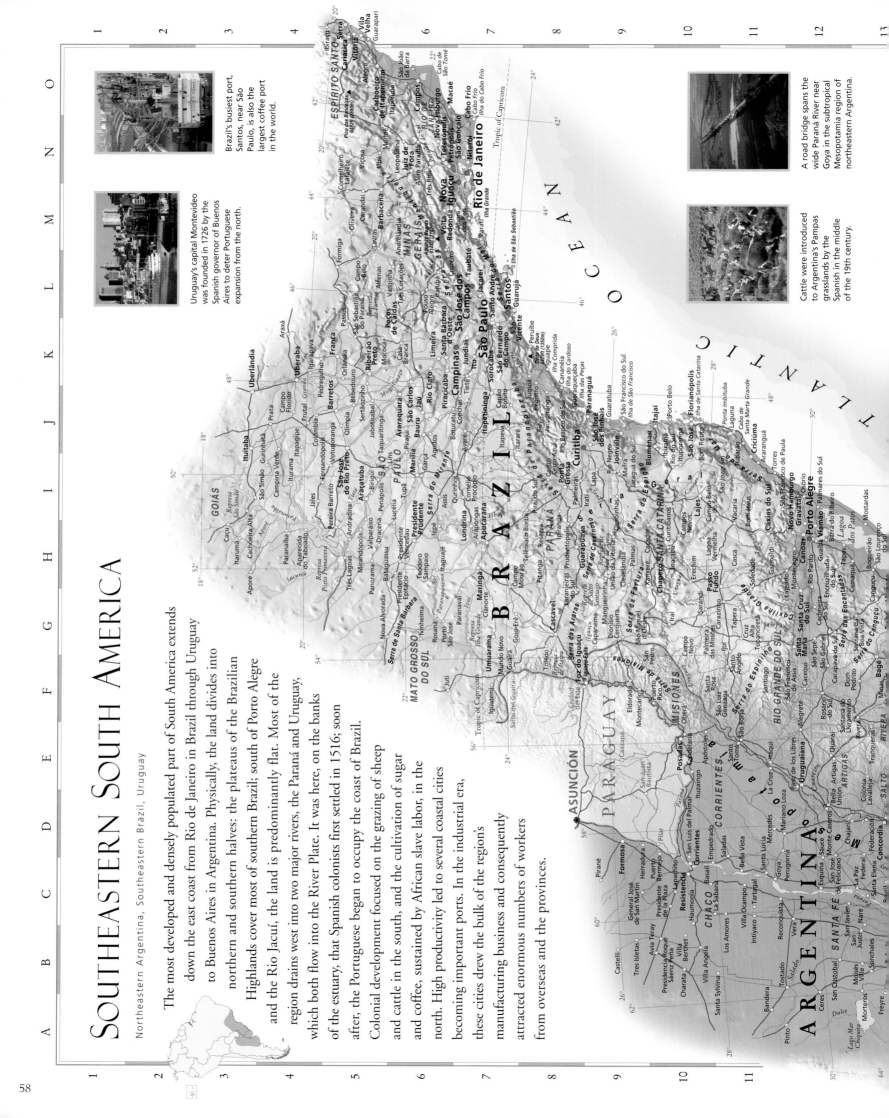

SOUTHEASTERN SOUTH AMERICA

Northeastern Argentina, Southeastern Brazil, Uruguay

The most developed and densely populated part of South America extends down the east coast from Rio de Janeiro in Brazil through Uruguay to Buenos Aires in Argentina. Physically, the land divides into northern and southern halves: the plateaus of the Brazilian Highlands cover most of southern Brazil; south of Porto Alegre and the Rio Jacuí, the land is predominantly flat. Most of the region drains west into two major rivers, the Paraná and Uruguay, which both flow into the River Plate. It was here, on the banks of the estuary, that Spanish colonists first settled in 1516; soon after, the Portuguese began to occupy the coast of Brazil. Colonial development focused on the grazing of sheep and cattle in the south, and the cultivation of sugar and coffee, sustained by African slave labor, in the north. High productivity led to several coastal cities becoming important ports. In the industrial era, these cities drew the bulk of the region's manufacturing business and consequently attracted enormous numbers of workers from overseas and the provinces.

Brazil's busiest port, Santos, near São Paulo, is also the largest coffee port in the world.

Uruguay's capital Montevideo was founded in 1726 by the Spanish governor of Buenos Aires to deter Portuguese expansion from the north.

A road bridge spans the wide Paraná River near Goya in the subtropical Mesopotamia region of northeastern Argentina.

Cattle were introduced to Argentina's Pampas grasslands by the Spanish in the middle of the 19th century.

Population Patterns

The overwhelming majority of the region's inhabitants live in cities. Metropolitan Buenos Aires has more than 12 million people, almost one-third of the national population. Over 1.3 million Uruguayans, 40 percent of the country's inhabitants, live in Montevideo. Elsewhere, Uruguay is sparsely populated: the next largest city, Salto, is less than one-tenth the size of the capital. Southern Brazil includes the country's most populous urban centers, São Paulo and Rio de Janeiro (which accommodate about 17 percent of Brazil's huge population), as well as several other cities, including Curitiba and Porto Alegre. The state of São Paulo alone is home to 37 million people. Its capital's vast citizenry includes the biggest Japanese population outside Japan and South America's largest Jewish community.

Economic Profile

The southern lowlands are used chiefly for raising beef cattle and sheep, though wheat is also cultivated on the Pampas. Fruit, including oranges and bananas, and rice are grown along the Brazilian coast; sugarcane, soybeans, and coffee are planted across the uplands. Livestock exports and food processing underpin the industrial sector in Montevideo and Buenos Aires, though the latter is also a center of automobile production, oil refining, and printing. São Paulo is South America's industrial powerhouse. It generates 40 percent of Brazil's GDP and its factories employ 15 percent of the national population. Its major industries are the manufacture of automobiles, textiles, chemicals, and metals, and oil refining. Services are more significant in Rio de Janeiro, the headquarters of many large businesses.

Uruguay has over 15 million sheep, and wool is one of the country's most valuable exports.

The Serra do Mar

On their eastern flank, the Brazilian Highlands about the coast along a 1,600-mile (2,600-km) escarpment, the southern part of which is known as the Serra do Mar (Sea Range). Averaging 3,000 feet (1,000 m) in height, this range rises almost sheer from the sea at several points. The precipitous slopes provide a mountainous backdrop to Rio de Janeiro and other coastal cities. Associated outcrops have created islands, such as Ilha de São Sebastião and Ilha Grande, and other coastal formations including Rio's famous Sugar Loaf Mountain.

Rio de Janeiro

One of the most distinctive landmarks in South America, the 100-foot (30-m) statue of Christ the Redeemer in Rio de Janiero was built by engineer Heitor da Silva Costa and completed in 1931. From its site atop 2,428-foot (740-m) Mount Corcovado, it overlooks Guanabara Bay and the city of 11 million that spreads inland from the bay's northern and western shores. The name Rio de Janeiro, meaning "January River," was coined by the area's first Portuguese explorers: arriving in January, 1502, they assumed the bay was the mouth of a river. Portuguese settlers returned to occupy the bay in 1565, and a burgeoning sugar trade soon gave rise to a town. In 1763, Rio became the colonial capital, and in 1822, when Brazil achieved independence, it became the national capital, remaining so until 1960, when the country's seat of government was transferred to Brasília.

Sugar Loaf Mountain

Mount Corcovado

SCALE 1:8,241,758
Lambert's Conformal Conic Projection

Longitude east of Greenwich

Population density legend
Less than 2.6 persons per sq mile/1 per sq km
2.6–26 per sq mile/1–10 per sq km
26–65 per sq mile/10–25 per sq km
65–130 per sq mile/25–50 per sq km
130–260 per sq mile/50–100 per sq km
260–520 per sq mile/100–200 per sq km

Economic legend
Coffee
Sugarcane
Soybeans
Beef cattle
Fishing
Mining
Industrial center
Citrus fruits
Cereals
Sheep
Bananas
Tourism

Forest and woodland
Arable land
Grazing

Map labels
Rio de Janeiro
São Paulo
Curitiba
Porto Alegre
MONTEVIDEO
Salto
Santa Fé
Rosario
BUENOS AIRES
Bahía Blanca

URUGUAY
MONTEVIDEO
River Plate
BUENOS AIRES
Mar del Plata
Rosario
CÓRDOBA

ELEVATION
Feet / Meters
32,808 / 10,000
26,246 / 8000
19,685 / 6000
13,123 / 4000
6562 / 2000
3281 / 1000
1640 / 500
984 / 300
656 / 200
328 / 100
Below sea level / 0

THE BRITISH ISLES
Republic of Ireland, United Kingdom

The British Isles consist of two large islands, Great Britain and Ireland, and numerous smaller islands located off the northwest coast of mainland Europe.

Together with the troubled province of Northern Ireland, the once-independent nations of England, Scotland, and Wales make up the United Kingdom (U.K.). The southern part of the island of Ireland became self-governing in 1921. Most of southeastern Britain is low, gently undulating terrain, becoming almost entirely flat in the east-coast Fens region. To the north and west, the land is more rugged, with hills and mountains dominating central northern England, much of Wales, southern and northern Scotland, and parts of Northern Ireland. In southern Ireland, a well-watered central plain is studded with lakes and peat bogs and ringed by coastal uplands. Both the U.K. and Ireland have recently developed closer social and economic ties with other European nations, and a physical link between Britain and the rest of the continent was forged in 1994 with the completion of the Channel Tunnel.

POPULATION PATTERNS

The U.K.'s highly urbanized population—about 90 percent inhabit towns and cities—is heavily concentrated in the southeast and around the industrial centers of Birmingham, Manchester, Leeds, Glasgow, and Belfast. The least densely populated areas are the Scottish Highlands, where sheep far outnumber people, and the uplands of northwest England and Wales. Ireland's population is more evenly distributed, with about 60 percent living in urban areas.

Less than 2.6 persons per sq mile/1 per sq km
2.6–26 per sq mile/1–10 per sq km
26–65 per sq mile/10–25 per sq km
65–130 per sq mile/25–50 per sq km
130–260 per sq mile/50–100 per sq km
260–520 per sq mile/100–200 per sq km

ECONOMIC PROFILE

The decline of the U.K.'s manufacturing industries has been paralleled by the growth in services, which now employ three-quarters of workers. Still-important industries include engineering, chemicals and chemical products, metals, and food and beverages. The nation's most abundant food crops are cereals (especially wheat and barley), potatoes, sugar beet, and oilseed rape. Ireland's farming sector is more dependent on livestock. Its industries experienced a boom in the late 20th century, led by textiles, chemicals, machinery, and computer hardware and software.

Cereals
Potatoes
Sugar beet
Oilseed rape
Beef cattle
Dairy cattle
Sheep

Industrial center
Fishing
Oil production
Gas production
Shellfish
Timber

Forest and woodland
Arable land
Grazing

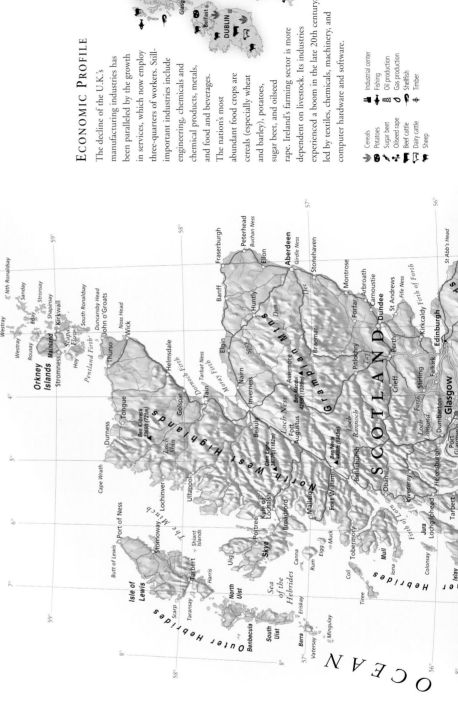

Oxford, England, is a manufacturing center, noted for automobile production. But it is best known as the site of the U.K.'s oldest university, founded in the 12th century.

On the west coast of Ireland, uplands abut the Atlantic Ocean, forming dramatic coastal landforms such as the spectacular Cliffs of Moher, near Hag's Head.

North Sea oil and gas fields have made the U.K. virtually self-sufficient in fossil fuels.

THE HIGHLANDS

The highest part of the British Isles, the Scottish Highlands rise from the Central Lowlands along the Highland Boundary Fault, which extends from Helensburgh in the southwest to Stonehaven in the northeast. They are split in two by another major fault, the Great Glen, which is partially filled by lakes including Loch Ness.

Stonehaven

Edinburgh

Glasgow

Grampian Mtns

Ben Nevis

Fort William

Helensburgh

Inverness

Loch Ness

The Great Glen

SCALE 1:3,296,703
Lamberts Conformal Conic Projection

100 miles

100 kilometers

ELEVATION

feet	meters
6562	2000
4921	1500
3281	1000
2461	750
1640	500
1312	400
984	300
656	200
328	100
0	Below sea level
656	200
3281	1000
6562	2000
13,123	4000
19,685	6000
26,246	8000
32,808	10,000

Longitude west of Greenwich

Map labels

North Sea

North

Great Britain

UNITED KINGDOM

ENGLAND

WALES

NORTHERN IRELAND

ULSTER

REPUBLIC OF IRELAND

Ireland

LEINSTER

MUNSTER

CONNAUGHT

ATLANTIC

Irish Sea

Celtic Sea

English Channel

Strait of Dover

St George's Channel

Bristol Channel

FRANCE

DUBLIN

LONDON

Atlantic coast places: Bloody Foreland, Malin, Donegal Bay, Rossan Point, Sligo, Sligo Bay, Killala Bay, Ballina, Erris Head, Achill Island, Clare Island, Inishturk, Inishbofin, Clifden, Slyne Head, Aran Islands, Inishmore, Inisheer, Galway, Galway Bay, Clifden, Kilkee, Loop Head, Kerry Head, Tralee, Dingle, Dingle Bay, Caherciveen, Cahersiveen, Kenmare, Bantry Bay, Skull, Mizen Head, Cape Clear, Carrantuohill 3415m (1041m), Milltown Malbay, Kilrush, Listowel, Abbeyfeale, Killarney, Macroom, Bandon, Clonakilty, Old Head of Kinsale, Cork, Cobh, Cork Harbour, Youghal, Youghal Bay, Dungarvan, Waterford, Mine Head, Hook Head, New Ross, Enniscorthy, Wexford, Carnsore Point, Rosslare, Gorey, Arklow, Cahore Point, Wicklow, Wicklow Head, Greystones, Bray, Blessington

Inland Ireland: Cavan, Longford, Mullingar, Athlone, Tullamore, Birr, Roscrea, Nenagh, Thurles, Limerick, Tipperary, Cashel, Caher, Clonmel, Mallow, Mitchelstown, Fermoy, Blackwater, Carlow, Kilkenny, Portlaoise, Kildare, Naas, Kells, Navan, Drogheda, Balbriggan, Slane, Trim, Ardee, Dundalk, Dundalk Bay, Carlingford Lough, Newry, Armagh, Portadown, Lurgan, Lough Neagh, Antrim, Ballymena, Larne, Belfast, Belfast Lough, Bangor, Newtownards, Strangford Lough, Downpatrick, Newcastle, Banbridge, Lisburn, Omagh, Enniskillen, Lough Erne, Strabane, Londonderry, Coleraine, Glenties, Donegal, Ballaghaderreen, Castlebar, Westport, Croagh Patrick, Boyle, Roscommon, Tuam, Ballinasloe, Loughrea, Ennis, Shannon, Loughs: Lough Mask, Lough Corrib, Lough Ree, Lough Derg, Lough Allen, Lough Conn

Great Britain places: Mull of Kintyre, Firth of Clyde, Cumnock, Girvan, Ballantrae, Stranraer, Newton Stewart, Whithorn, Wigtown, Mull of Galloway, Castle Douglas, Dumfries, Lockerbie, Thornhill, Castle Douglas, Kirkcudbright, Carlisle, Penrith, Keswick, Workington, Whitehaven, Ramsey, Peel, Douglas, Isle of Man (to U.K.), Barrow-in-Furness, Lancaster, Kendal, Lake District, Cross Fell 2927ft (893m), Pennines, Blackpool, Lytham St Anne's, Southport, Preston, Blackburn, Bolton, Wigan, Liverpool, Birkenhead, St Helens, Warrington, Manchester, Stockport, Oldham, Rochdale, Bury, Wrexham, Chester, Rhyl, Conwy, Bangor, Caernarfon, Holyhead, Anglesey, Carmel Head, Braich y Pwll, Bardsey Island, Pwllheli, Dolgellau, Snowdon 3560ft (1085m), Newtown, Welshpool, Oswestry, Shrewsbury, Telford, Stafford, Stoke-on-Trent, Crewe, Cambrian Mtns, Aberystwyth, Aberaeron, Cardigan Bay, Cardigan, Fishguard, St David's, St David's Head, Haverfordwest, Milford Haven, Pembroke, St Govan's Head, Carmarthen, Carmarthen Bay, Llanelli, Swansea, Neath, Port Talbot, Bridgend, Pontypridd, Merthyr Tydfil, Abergavenny, Builth Wells, Llandrindod Wells, Llandovery, Brecon, Llandeilo, Newport, Cardiff, Monmouth, Weston-super-Mare, Minehead, Ilfracombe, Barnstaple, Bideford, Bude, Hartland Point, Lundy Island, Trevose Head, St Austell, Bodmin, Bodmin Moor, Launceston, Okehampton, Tavistock, Dartmoor, Plymouth, Dodman Point, Truro, Falmouth, Lizard Point, Penzance, St Ives, Land's End, Mount's Bay, Isles of Scilly, Exmoor, Tiverton, Exeter, Exmouth, Torquay, Dartmouth, Start Point, Dorchester, Weymouth, Bill of Portland, Lyme Regis, Lyme Bay, Bridgwater, Taunton, Yeovil

Scotland (inset area) and northern places: Newcastle upon Tyne, Blyth, South Shields, Sunderland, Hartlepool, Redcar, Middlesbrough, Durham, Darlington, Thirsk, Whitby, Scarborough, Bridlington, Spurn Head, Flamborough Head, Mablethorpe, Skegness, Grimsby, Scunthorpe, Louth, Lincoln, Boston, The Wash, King's Lynn, East Dereham, Cromer, Great Yarmouth, Lowestoft, Norwich, Thetford, Bury St Edmunds, Ipswich, Felixstowe, Harwich, Clacton-on-sea, Colchester, Chelmsford, Southend-on-Sea, Margate, Ramsgate, Deal, Dover, Folkestone, Sandgate, Dungeness, Hastings, Bexhill, Eastbourne, Beachy Head, North Foreland, Canterbury, Ashford, Maidstone, Chatham, Rochester, Gravesend, Dartford, Croydon, Brentwood, Ilford, Watford, Hendon, Kingston upon Thames, Slough, Reading, Guildford, Aldershot, Reigate, Crawley, Horsham, Worthing, Brighton, Bognor Regis, Chichester, Portsmouth, Southampton, Cowes, Newport, Isle of Wight, St Catherine's Point, Cowes, Bournemouth, Poole, Swanage, Winchester, Basingstoke, Newbury, Andover, Salisbury, Salisbury Plain, Warminster, Chippenham, Swindon, Cirencester, Gloucester, Cheltenham, Worcester, Hereford, Leominster, Ludlow, Kidderminster, Dudley, Wolverhampton, Birmingham, Coventry, Rugby, Warwick, Stratford-upon-Avon, Redditch, Banbury, Daventry, Milton Keynes, Luton, St Albans, Stevenage, Harlow, Cambridge, Peterborough, The Fens, Huntingdon, Northampton, Leicester, Loughborough, Nottingham, Derby, Mansfield, Grantham, Newark, Rotherham, Sheffield, Barnsley, Chesterfield, Doncaster, Pontefract, Wakefield, Huddersfield, Halifax, Bradford, Leeds, Keighley, Harrogate, York, Oxford, Reading, Windsor, Maidenhead, Chiltern Hills, Cotswolds, North Downs, South Downs, Weald, Severn, Thames, Trent, Ouse, Great Ouse, Avon, Wye, Usk, Mersey, Ribble, Eden, Tyne, Tees, Dee

Channel Islands (to U.K.): Guernsey, St Peter Port, Jersey, St Helier, Sark, Alderney

France: Calais, Cap Gris-Nez, Dunkerque, Boulogne, Le Touquet, Le Tréport, Dieppe, Le Havre, Baie de la Seine, Carentan, Bayeux, Cherbourg

54°, 53°, 52°, 51°, 50°, 55°
10°, 9°, 8°, 7°, 6°, 5°, 4°, 3°, 2°, 1°, 0°, 1°, 2°

61

Southern Great Britain

From the southern flanks of the Pennines, a broad belt of roads, towns, and cities runs southeastward through the low-lying heart of England, the region known as the Midlands, to London, the capital of the U.K. and its largest city. This corridor is by far the most developed part of the country, encompassing the majority of its industrial and commercial centers, the bulk of its freeways, and more than half of its population.

The urban sprawl is, however, broken by sizable tracts of fertile farmland—most notably in the East Midlands—remnants of forests, and scenic ranges of hills, including the Cotswolds and the Chilterns. On the eastern and western fringes lie quieter, culturally and geographically distinctive areas. The Cambrian Mountains dominate the interior of the Celtic nation of Wales, descending to a long, heavily indented coastline. In the east, the formerly swampy Fens isolate the tranquil agricultural plains of East Anglia, and in the far southwest, a picturesque, rocky coastline bounds the narrow, traditionally Celtic enclave of Cornwall and the rolling pastures and moorlands of Devon.

Made of chalk, the famous white cliffs of Dover border the English Channel.

The Royal Liver Building, a Liverpool landmark, was completed in 1911.

Snowdon in northwest Wales has five peaks. The tallest, Yr Wyddfa, is the highest point in England and Wales.

POPULATION PATTERNS

This region has more than two-thirds of the U.K. population, with the highest concentrations occurring in London (home to 7.6 million people), Birmingham, and the cluster of cities between Liverpool and Leeds. Population growth is relatively low and due mainly to natural increase. In the late 20th century, the demise of heavy industry and coal mining in the northwest, Wales, and Scotland accelerated migration to London. However, a concurrent trend saw many people and businesses move out of the capital to peripheral areas such as the East Midlands, East Anglia, and the southwest. One-quarter of people in Wales speak Welsh; the region's other Celtic language, Cornish, has all but died out.

ECONOMIC PROFILE

The economy is dominated by services, particularly finance, retailing, health care, and tourism. While the northwest and Wales have suffered due to the collapse of coal mining and heavy industries, the east and southeast have thrived due to the boom in services and success in attracting light, high-tech industries to areas such as Cambridge and Reading. Southern England has most of the U.K.'s best farmland. The highly mechanized cultivation of wheat, oilseed rape, and sugar beet takes place in the east; dairy and beef cattle are reared in the west; and market gardening (the small-scale cultivation of fruit and vegetables) predominates in the southeast.

Less than 2.6 persons per sq mile/1 per sq km
2.6–26 per sq mile/1–10 per sq km
26–65 per sq mile/10–25 per sq km
65–130 per sq mile/25–50 per sq km
130–260 per sq mile/50–100 per sq km
260–520 per sq mile/100–200 per sq km

Forest and woodland
Arable land
Grazing

Cereals
Sugar beet
Oilseed rape
Beef cattle
Dairy cattle
Sheep
Industrial center
Fishing
Tourism
Mining
Fruit and vegetables

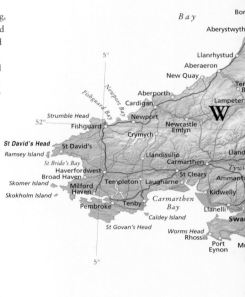

ELEVATION
Feet / Meters

6562 / 2000
4921 / 1500
3281 / 1000
2461 / 750
1640 / 500
1312 / 400
984 / 300
656 / 200
328 / 100
0 / 0 Below sea level
656 / 200
3281 / 1000
6562 / 2000
13,123 / 4000
19,685 / 6000
26,246 / 8000
32,808 / 10,000

London The Romans founded Londinium, as they named it, on the banks of the Thames in the first century AD. After being all but abandoned in the fifth century, the town flourished again under the Saxons and the Normans, whose king, William I (the Conqueror), built a fortress to control local trade. Known as the White Fort and later the Tower of London, it was expanded by several monarchs over the following centuries, becoming a royal residence and, notoriously, a prison and place of execution. The city grew with it, attaining a population of 1 million by 1800 and 6.5 million a century later. Now a popular tourist attraction, the tower still hosts a military garrison and is patrolled by guards, known as "beefeaters," who dress in distinctive Tudor uniforms.

SCALE 1:1,648,352
Lamberts Conformal Conic Projection
0   50 miles
0   50 kilometers

N W X Y Z

From the early 18th century, windmills like this one near Holt, Norfolk, were used to drain marshes in East Anglia.

The precise function of the stone circles at Stonehenge, near Salisbury, begun around 2700 BC, remains uncertain.

ENGLAND

UNITED KINGDOM

Irish Sea

North Sea

Liverpool Bay

East Anglia

The Broads

The Wash

The Fens

Lincolnshire Wolds

Sherwood Forest

Yorkshire Dales

Forest of Bowland

Pennines

Cambrian Mountains

Black Mountains

Brecon Beacons

Cotswold Hills

Chiltern Hills

Marlborough Downs

Salisbury Plain

North Downs

South Downs

The Weald

Mendip Hills

New Forest

Isle of Wight

The Solent

The Needles

English Channel

Strait of Dover

Channel Tunnel

Bristol Channel

Bridgwater Bay

Lyme Bay

Weymouth Bay

Isle of Portland

Bill of Portland

London
Birmingham
Manchester
Leeds
Liverpool
Sheffield
Bristol
Cardiff
Nottingham
Leicester
Coventry
Bradford
Stoke-on-Trent
Derby
Portsmouth
Southampton
Norwich
Ipswich
Peterborough
Cambridge
Oxford
Reading
Swindon
Gloucester
Northampton
Bournemouth
Brighton
Poole
Kingston upon Hull
Blackpool
Preston
Bolton
Oldham
Stockport
Rotherham
Huddersfield
Wolverhampton
Walsall
Dudley
West Bromwich
Sutton Coldfield
Solihull
Telford
Newport
Blackburn
Bury
St Helens
York
Luton
Slough
Croydon
Bromley
Enfield
Barnet
Southend-on-Sea
Richmond upon Thames
Kingston upon Thames

Longitude east of Greenwich

N O P Q R S T U V W X Y Z

63

FRANCE
France, Monaco

Occupying a large area on the western edge of Europe,
France is the only country that extends from the North European
Plain to the Mediterranean. The north and west are characterized by broad
lowlands traversed by major rivers, including the Seine, Loire, Dordogne, and
Garonne. A wide plateau, the Massif Central, covers much of the southern
interior, and in the southeast the land rises steeply to the high peaks of the Alps.
Along the southern border, the Pyrenees separate France from Spain. The tiny principality
of Monaco—the second-smallest country in the world—occupies a coastal location
within France, close to the border with Italy. France is a leading political,
industrial, and agricultural force in Europe and has been at the
forefront of European economic and social integration.

Paris France's largest city began as a small settlement on an island in the River Seine
and became the national capital in AD 987. It is now home to over 9 million people,
a major business and industrial center, and one of the world's top tourist destinations.
Its splendid buildings include the cathedral of Notre-Dame, which dates from the
12th century, the 18th-century Panthéon, and France's most famous
landmark, the Eiffel Tower, designed for the 1889 Paris Exposition.

Notre-Dame

Eiffel Tower

POPULATION PATTERNS

The most sparsely inhabited parts of France
are the high-mountain regions of the Alps,
Pyrenees, and Massif Central.
In rural areas, the population is
fairly evenly spread, though slightly
higher levels of settlement occur along
major river valleys and parts of the coast.
About 76 percent of the country's
inhabitants live in urban areas, with
one-fifth of the total population concentrated
in the Paris region, the Île-de-France.

Less than 2.6 persons per sq mile/1 per sq km

2.6–26 per sq mile/ 1–10 per sq km

26–65 per sq mile/ 10–25 per sq km

65–130 per sq mile/ 25–50 per sq km

130–260 per sq mile/ 50–100 per sq km

260–520 per sq mile/ 100–200 per sq km

Lille · PARIS · Strasbourg · Rennes · Nantes · Dijon · Bordeaux · Clermont-Ferrand · Lyon · Toulouse · MONACO · Marseille · Perpignan · Ajaccio

ECONOMIC PROFILE

Forest and woodland

Arable land

Grazing

Marginal or nonproductive

More than half of France is productive
farmland, and the nation is one of the world's
top exporters of agricultural produce.
Important commodities include
wheat, sugar beet, and wine
(of which France is the
world's largest producer).
Metals, chemicals, cars,
textiles, and aircraft are among
the most vital manufactured
goods. Services, including
tourism, employ more
than 70 percent
of workers.

Cereals
Potatoes
Fruit and vegetables
Wine
Sugar beet
Beef cattle
Dairy cattle
Sheep
Fishing
Industrial center
Mining
Tourism

Lille · PARIS · Rennes · Nantes · Strasbourg · Dijon · Clermont-Ferrand · Lyon · Bordeaux · Toulouse · MONACO · Marseille · Perpignan · Ajaccio

THE PYRENEES

Viewed from southern France, the Pyrenees rise like a great
wall, forming a seemingly insurmountable barrier. Indeed,
most of the range, which stretches for more than 270 miles
(435 km) from the Atlantic Ocean to the Mediterranean
Sea, is more than 9,000 feet (2,700 m) high and can be
crossed only via passes above 6,000 feet (1,800 m). The
highest peak, Aneto in Spain, rises to 11,168 feet (3,404 m).

Barcelona · ANDORRA LA VELLA · Zaragoza · Ebro · Aneto · Vignemale · Pamplona · Perpignan · Pyrenees · Garonne · Biarritz · Toulouse · Bordeaux

SCALE 1:3,296,703
Lamberts Conformal Conic Projection

0 ___ 100 miles
0 ___ 100 kilometers

Longitude west of Greenwich

The Arc de Triomphe in Paris was commissioned by Napoleon in 1806 to celebrate his military victories.

Located on the French–Italian border, Mont Blanc, at 15,771 feet (4,807 m), is the Alps' highest peak.

Monaco measures a mere 0.75 square miles (1.95 sq km). Its tourist facilities and casino are among its principal sources of revenue.

The mountainous island of Corsica was purchased by France from the city-state of Genoa in 1768.

ELEVATION

Feet	Meters
6562	2000
4921	1500
3281	1000
2461	750
1640	500
1312	400
984	300
656	200
328	100
Below sea level	
656	200
3281	1000
6562	2000
13,123	4000
19,685	6000
26,246	8000
32,808	10,000

SCALE 1:4,395,604

Corsica (to France)

THE IBERIAN PENINSULA

Andorra, Portugal, Spain

Located at the southwestern edge of Europe, the wide, almost square-shaped Iberian Peninsula is flanked by the Atlantic Ocean to the west and by the Mediterranean Sea to the east. It is separated from France by the Pyrenees, and from Africa by the Strait of Gibraltar, which is just 8 miles (12.8 km) wide at its narrowest point. Spain occupies more than 80 percent of the landmass, Portugal almost all of the remainder; the tiny principality of Andorra nestles in the eastern Pyrenees. A large plateau, the Meseta, extends across much of the peninsula. It is bisected by the Sistema Central mountain chain and fringed by other ranges. Between the 15th and 17th centuries, Spain and Portugal ruled vast empires. But their 20th-century histories were marred by war and repressive regimes, and their economies are still recovering.

Completed in 1521, the Torre de Belém was built to protect the city of Lisbon.

In Spain's Castilla-La Mancha region, medieval windmills dot flat, semiarid plains.

POPULATION PATTERNS

In Spain, rapid industrial growth in the late 20th century led to significant urbanization, with the result that 78 percent of the population now live in cities—17 percent in Madrid and Barcelona. The temperate coastal areas are generally more densely inhabited than the less fertile Meseta. In Portugal, the south is more sparsely populated than the north, with the exception of Lisbon and the crowded coastal region of the Algarve.

Less than 2.6 persons per sq mile/1 per sq km
2.6–26 per sq mile/1–10 per sq km
26–65 per sq mile/10–25 per sq km
65–130 per sq mile/25–50 per sq km
130–260 per sq mile/50–100 per sq km

ECONOMIC PROFILE

Investment in agriculture is low relative to the European average and small farms are the norm. The region is renowned for its abundant fruit and vegetables; other major crops include cereals, wine grapes, and olives. About one-third of the land is forested, and Portugal is the world's foremost supplier of cork. Textiles and footwear, paper and paper products, chemicals, metals, wine, and tourism are the leading industries; automobile production is also important in Spain. Andorra relies heavily on tourism and its duty-free retail trade.

Cereals
Citrus fruits
Wine
Olives
Beef cattle
Sheep
Industrial center
Mining
Timber
Tourism
Fishing

Forest and woodland
Arable land
Grazing

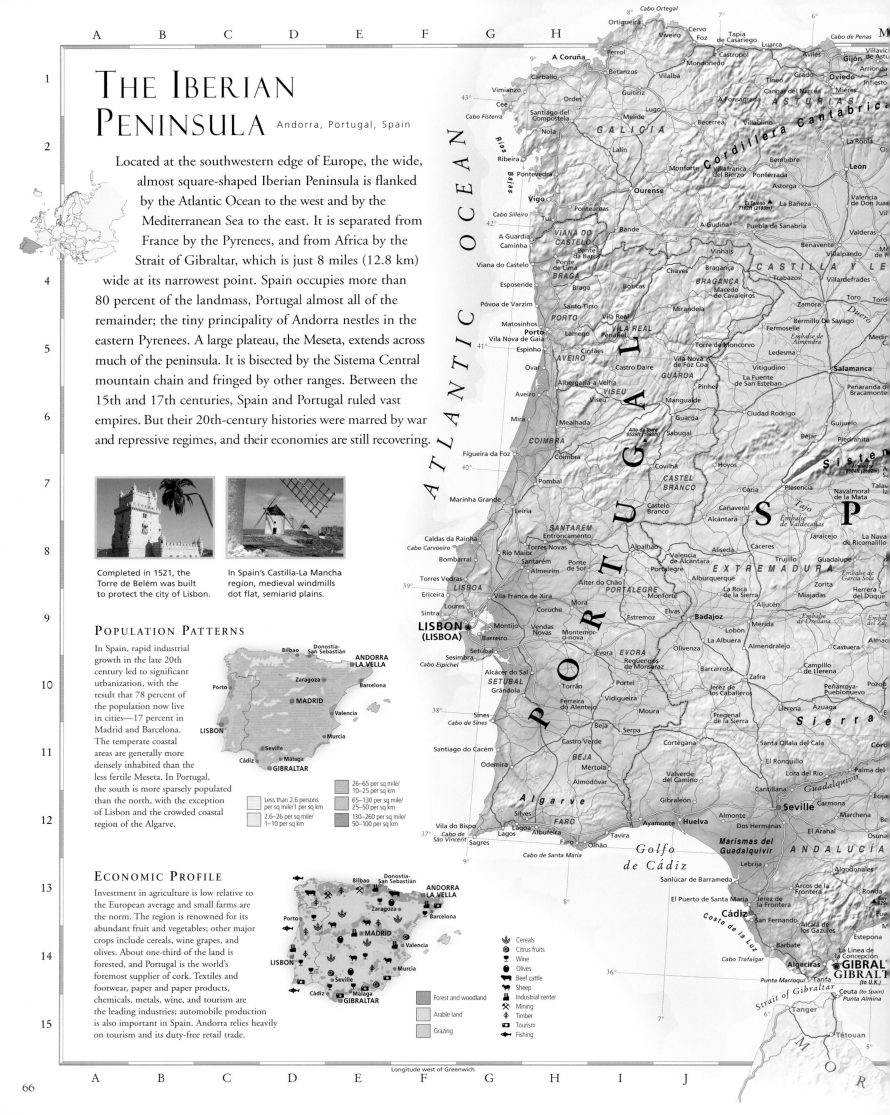

Longitude west of Greenwich

THE SISTEMAS BÉTICOS

In southeastern Spain, a mountain chain, known as the Sistemas Béticos or Baetic Cordillera, extends from Punta Marroquí on the Strait of Gibraltar to Cabo de la Nao on the Costa Blanca. Incorporating numerous small ranges, it rises to its highest point of 11,421 feet (3,481 m) at Mulhacén, northwest of Almería. East of Cabo de la Nao, the chain continues beneath the Mediterranean Sea—the Balearic Islands of Ibiza, Majorca, and Minorca are the summits of its submerged slopes.

ELEVATION	
Feet	Meters
6562	2000
4921	1500
3281	1000
2461	750
1640	500
1312	400
984	300
656	200
328	100
0	0
Below sea level	
0	0
656	200
3281	1000
6562	2000
13,123	4000
19,685	6000
26,246	8000
32,808	10,000

Longitude east of Greenwich

SCALE 1:3,296,703
Lamberts Conformal Conic Projection

0   100 miles

0   100 kilometers

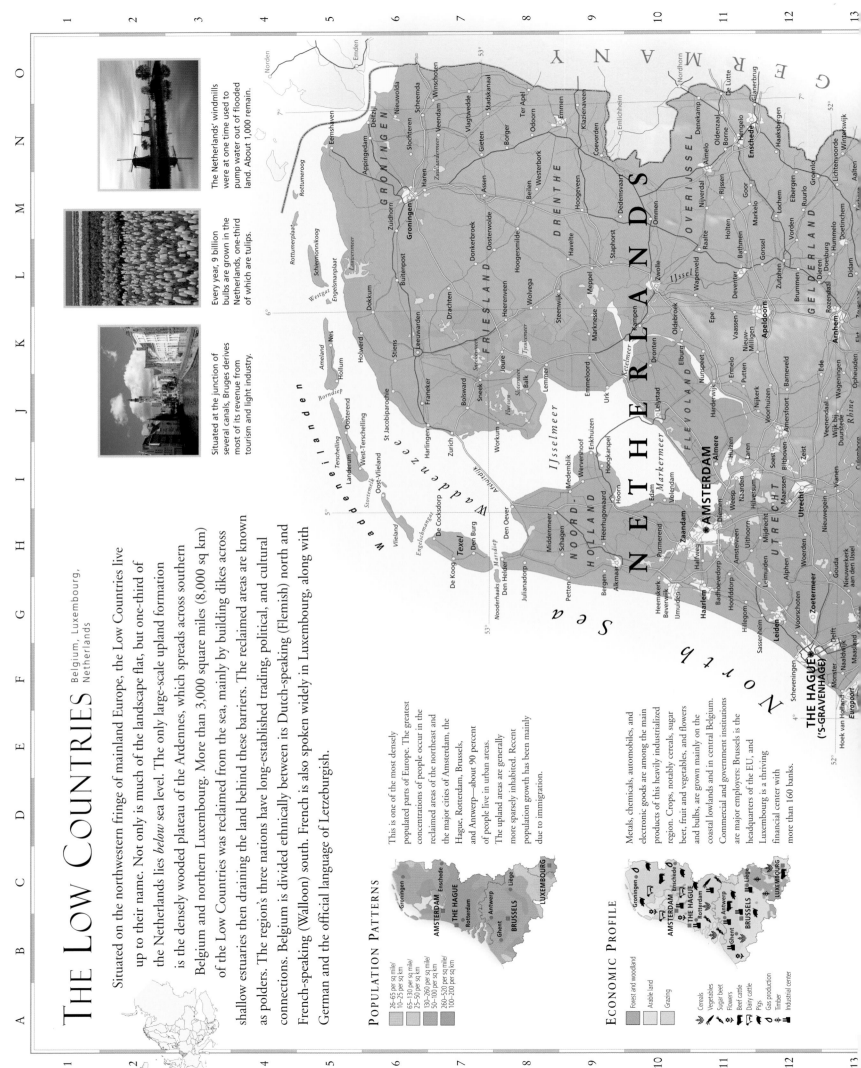

THE LOW COUNTRIES

Belgium, Luxembourg, Netherlands

Situated on the northwestern fringe of mainland Europe, the Low Countries live up to their name. Not only is much of the landscape flat, but one-third of the Netherlands lies *below* sea level. The only large-scale upland formation is the densely wooded plateau of the Ardennes, which spreads across southern Belgium and northern Luxembourg. More than 3,000 square miles (8,000 sq km) of the Low Countries was reclaimed from the sea, mainly by building dikes across shallow estuaries then draining the land behind these barriers. The reclaimed areas are known as polders. The region's three nations have long-established trading, political, and cultural connections. Belgium is divided ethnically between its Dutch-speaking (Flemish) north and French-speaking (Walloon) south. French is also spoken widely in Luxembourg, along with German and the official language of Letzeburgish.

The Netherlands' windmills were at one time used to pump water out of flooded land. About 1,000 remain.

Every year, 9 billion bulbs are grown in the Netherlands, one-third of which are tulips.

Situated at the junction of several canals, Bruges derives most of its revenue from tourism and light industry.

POPULATION PATTERNS

This is one of the most densely populated parts of Europe. The greatest concentrations of people occur in the reclaimed areas of the northeast and the major cities of Amsterdam, the Hague, Rotterdam, Brussels, and Antwerp—about 90 percent of people live in urban areas. The upland areas are generally more sparsely inhabited. Recent population growth has been mainly due to immigration.

26–65 per sq mile/
10–25 per sq km
65–130 per sq mile/
25–50 per sq km
130–260 per sq mile/
50–100 per sq km
260–520 per sq mile/
100–200 per sq km

ECONOMIC PROFILE

Metals, chemicals, automobiles, and electronic goods are among the main products of this heavily industrialized region. Crops, notably cereals, sugar beet, fruit and vegetables, and flowers and bulbs, are grown mainly on the coastal lowlands and in central Belgium. Commercial and government institutions are major employers: Brussels is the headquarters of the EU, and Luxembourg is a thriving financial center with more than 160 banks.

Forest and woodland
Arable land
Grazing

Cereals
Vegetables
Flowers
Beef cattle
Dairy cattle
Pigs
Gas production
Timber
Industrial center

The European Parliament meets at this building in Brussels, as well as others in Luxembourg and in Strasbourg, France.

Luxembourg's Grand Ducal Palace has been the home of the head of state (the Grand Duke) since the 1890s.

Amsterdam

In the 13th century, Amsterdam was a fishing village on the Amstel River. By the late 16th century, following an influx of people and funds from other parts of war-ravaged Europe, it had become the world's foremost financial and commercial center. Now one of the Netherlands' two capitals (the Hague is the seat of national government), Amsterdam spreads across 90 islands linked by more than 1,000 bridges. Elegant churches and gabled houses line the canals, which are plied by tourist boats and traditional wooden barges.

GERMANY

BELGIUM

FRANCE

LUXEMBOURG

NOORD-BRABANT

LIMBURG

ANTWERPEN

OOST-VLAANDEREN

WEST-VLAANDEREN

VLAAMS BRABANT

BRABANT WALLON

HAINAUT

NAMUR

LIÈGE

Ardennes

LUXEMBOURG

ZEELAND

Flanders

Brussels (Brussel/Bruxelles)
Antwerp
Ghent
Bruges
Liège
Maastricht
Eindhoven
Tilburg
Breda
Luxembourg
Diekirch
Grevenmacher
Aachen

SCALE 1:1,208,791
Lambert Conformal Conic Projection
30 miles
30 kilometers

Longitude east of Greenwich

ELEVATION
Feet Meters
32,808 10,000
26,246 8000
19,685 6000
13,123 4000
6562 2000
3281 1000
1640 500
656 200
0 Below sea level

69

SCANDINAVIA
Denmark, Finland, Iceland, Norway, Sweden

Geographically speaking, Scandinavia is the wide peninsula that divides the Norwegian Sea from the Baltic Sea and Gulf of Bothnia. Used in a broader context, however, the name encompasses all of the countries in this region, which share centuries-old historical, cultural, and linguistic ties. Occupied by Norway and Sweden, the Scandinavian Peninsula is dominated by a mountain chain that runs for almost its entire length. In the west, the peaks and plateaus drop steeply to the sea. To the east, they incline more gently toward Sweden's coastal and southern lowlands, and the flat, lake-studded terrain that covers most of Finland. Separated from Sweden by a sliver of sea, Denmark consists of fertile plains and low hills. In stark contrast, far-flung Iceland is a mountainous, mostly barren land that continues to be fashioned by earthquakes, volcanoes, and Europe's largest glaciers.

POPULATION PATTERNS

Less than 2.6 persons per sq mile/1 per sq km
2.6–26 per sq mile/1–10 per sq km
26–65 per sq mile/10–25 per sq km
65–130 per sq mile/25–50 per sq km

About 75 percent of this region's relatively small population lives in urban areas, mainly in the warmer, more fertile south—Denmark has as many inhabitants as either of the much larger countries of Norway and Finland. In the north and Iceland, inhospitable terrain, harsh climates, and a long winter (during which the sun may not rise for a week) have restricted human settlements to more temperate coastal areas and sheltered valleys.

ECONOMIC PROFILE

Scandinavia's natural resources include productive fishing grounds, the rich oil and gas fields of the North Sea (Norway has Europe's largest), and the immense evergreen forests that cover a quarter of Norway, two-thirds of Sweden, and three-quarters of Finland. Industries are service-dominated, but the manufacture of machinery, metals, chemicals, food, and wood products remains vital. Two-thirds of Denmark, but only small areas of the other countries, are cultivated. Generally, Scandinavians enjoy a high standard of living and access to comprehensive welfare systems.

Cereals
Sugar beet
Fishing
Reindeer
Sheep
Beef cattle
Pigs
Industrial center
Mining
Oil production
Gas production
Timber

Forest and woodland
Arable land
Grazing
Marginal or nonproductive

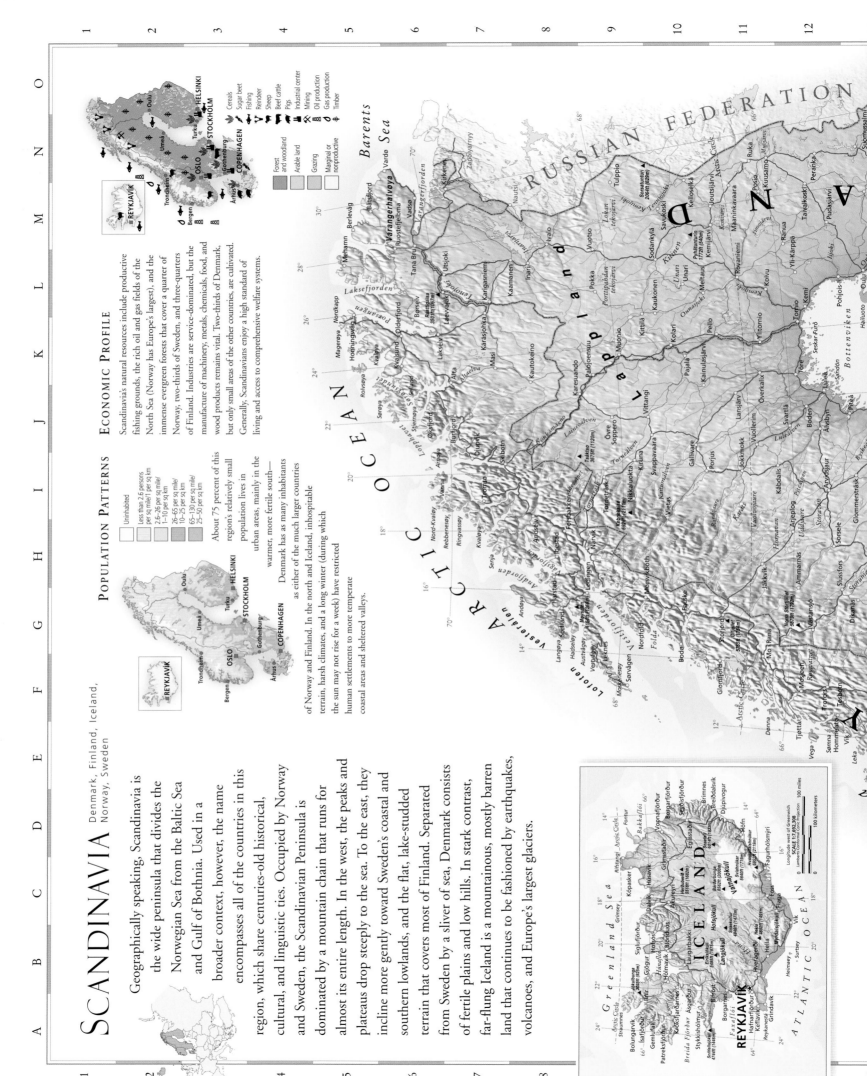

THE FJORDS OF NORWAY

During the last ice age, most of this region was blanketed by thick glaciers. On the western side of the Scandinavian Peninsula, rivers of ice cut deep into existing river valleys, forming U-shaped channels. As the climate warmed and the glaciers retreated, the rising sea filled coastal channels, creating the thousands of steep-sided inlets, or fjords, and the 150,000 islands that now line Norway's coast. The most deeply indented stretch of shoreline lies between Ålesund and Stavanger and includes several major fjords. The largest of these, Sognefjorden (Sogne Fjord), snakes 127 miles (204 km) inland, its walls rising as high as 4,291 feet (1,308 m).

Hardangerfjorden
Leirvik
Bergen
Sognefjorden
Galdhøpiggen
Ålesund
Måløy
Nordfjord

Historic boats and houses line the picturesque harbor in Copenhagen.

The Saami people inhabit northern Sweden, Norway, and Finland.

SCALE 1:4,945,055
Lamberts Conformal Conic Projection

Longitude east of Greenwich

0   120 miles
0   120 kilometers

ELEVATION		
Feet	Meters	
32,808	10,000	
26,246	8000	
19,685	6000	
13,123	4000	
6562	2000	
4921	1500	
3281	1000	
2461	750	
1640	500	
1312	400	
984	300	
656	200	
328	100	
0	0	Sea level
Below sea level	Below sea level	

NORTH Sea

Skagerrak

Kattegat

DENMARK

GERMANY

Norwegian Sea

NORWAY

SWEDEN

FINLAND

Gulf of Bothnia

Baltic Sea

Gulf of Finland

HELSINKI
Espoo
Vantaa
Tampere
Turku

STOCKHOLM
Uppsala

OSLO
Bergen
Stavanger
Trondheim

COPENHAGEN (KØBENHAVN)
Malmö
Odense
Ålborg
Århus

Gotland
Öland
Bornholm (Denmark)
Åland

71

GERMANY

When East Germany and West Germany merged in October 1990, the reunified nation became the most populous country in Europe. More than 80 million people dwell in this broad land, which stretches south from the North and Baltic seas to the northern flank of the Alps. Germany can be divided into three main physical regions. In the northern lowlands, wide rivers, including the Elbe and Weser, meander seaward across expansive, sandy plains.

A complex series of basins, partially wooded plateaus, and mountains extends across the center of the country. In the south, beyond the valley of the Main, stand the nation's highest ranges: the Black Forest, Swabian Alp, and Bavarian Alps. The great Rhine River, a historic artery of trade, defines the nation's southwestern boundaries. Continuing north, it cuts through the central uplands before veering westward across the plains to the Netherlands. Despite the economic and social challenges posed by reunification, Germany has retained its position as Europe's leading industrial power.

Construction of Cologne Cathedral, the largest Gothic church in Northern Europe, began in 1248 but was not completed until 1880.

POPULATION PATTERNS

Until the 19th century, Germany was divided into numerous small states with their own capitals and trading centers. As a result, its population is highly urbanized but fairly evenly distributed. Dense concentrations of inhabitants occur at the confluence of the Rhine and Ruhr rivers—the industrial heartland—and around Leipzig and Dresden in the east. Immigration has been the main contributor to recent population growth—10 million incomers settled in West Germany between 1950 and 1990.

2.6–26 per sq mile/
1–10 per sq km
26–65 per sq mile/
10–25 per sq km
65–130 per sq mile/
25–50 per sq km
130–260 per sq mile/
50–100 per sq km
260–520 per sq mile/
100–200 per sq km

ECONOMIC PROFILE

West Germany staged a remarkable economic recovery after the Second World War, and Germany is now the third-largest industrial power after the U.S.A. and Japan. The mainstays of manufacturing are machinery, automobiles, iron and steel, chemicals, electrical goods, and food and beverages. Two of the most significant agricultural products are wine and beer; cereals, potatoes, and sugar beet are also grown widely. The largest pastures are in the northwest, but dairying takes place throughout the country.

Sheep
Pigs
Industrial center
Mining
Timber

Cereals
Potatoes
Sugar beet
Wine
Beef cattle
Dairy cattle

Forest and woodland
Arable land
Grazing

Berlin

Established in the 13th century as a trading post on the Spree River, Berlin first became the capital of Germany in 1871. Though repeatedly ravaged by conflict, the city retains prominent buildings and landmarks from most periods of its history, including the 19th-century Victory Column.

Linked to the North Sea by the Elbe, Hamburg is one of the world's largest container ports.

A typical Rhine Valley town, Bacharach is crowned by a castle and surrounded by vineyards.

SCALE 1:2,472,527
Lamberts Conformal Conic Projection

0   60 miles
0   60 kilometers

GERMANY

CZECH REPUBLIC

AUSTRIA

SWITZERLAND

FRANCE

LUXEMBOURG

BELGIUM

BRANDENBURG

SACHSEN

THÜRINGEN

HESSEN

NORDRHEIN-WESTFALEN

RHEINLAND-PFALZ

SAARLAND

BADEN-WÜRTTEMBERG

BAYERN

ELEVATION

Feet	Meters
6562	2000
4921	1500
3281	1000
2461	750
1640	500
1312	400
984	300
656	200
328	100
0 (Below sea level)	0
656	200
3281	1000
6562	2000
13,123	4000
19,685	6000
26,246	8000
32,808	10,000

The Alpine Nations
Austria, Liechtenstein, Switzerland

Arcing northeastward from France, the countless peaks and valleys of the Alps sprawl across more than half of Switzerland, the tiny monarchy of Liechtenstein, and two-thirds of Austria. These nations occupy a continental crossroads, their mountain passes permitting the flow of people and goods between north and south, the Danube Valley forming a natural corridor between eastern and western Europe. Despite its strategic importance, Switzerland has remained politically neutral for almost 200 years. This, along with its prosperity and secretive banking practices, has made it a haven for international organizations, businesses, and funds. Austria's more tempestuous past includes periods as the heart of the powerful Holy Roman and Austro-Hungarian empires; its present boundaries were defined after the First World War. Liechtenstein established its independence, and neutrality, in 1866.

Millions of people visit the Alps each year to holiday at winter-sports resorts.

The spectacular Jet d'Eau, a 460-foot (140-m) fountain, is Geneva's best-known landmark.

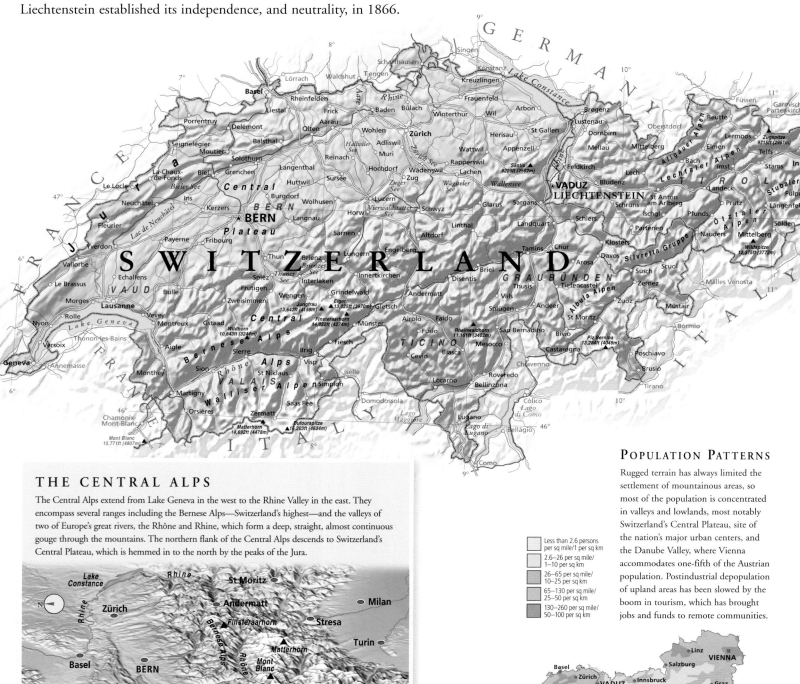

THE CENTRAL ALPS

The Central Alps extend from Lake Geneva in the west to the Rhine Valley in the east. They encompass several ranges including the Bernese Alps—Switzerland's highest—and the valleys of two of Europe's great rivers, the Rhône and Rhine, which form a deep, straight, almost continuous gouge through the mountains. The northern flank of the Central Alps descends to Switzerland's Central Plateau, which is hemmed in to the north by the peaks of the Jura.

POPULATION PATTERNS

Rugged terrain has always limited the settlement of mountainous areas, so most of the population is concentrated in valleys and lowlands, most notably Switzerland's Central Plateau, site of the nation's major urban centers, and the Danube Valley, where Vienna accommodates one-fifth of the Austrian population. Postindustrial depopulation of upland areas has been slowed by the boom in tourism, which has brought jobs and funds to remote communities.

Less than 2.6 persons per sq mile/1 per sq km
2.6–26 per sq mile/ 1–10 per sq km
26–65 per sq mile/ 10–25 per sq km
65–130 per sq mile/ 25–50 per sq km
130–260 per sq mile/ 50–100 per sq km

Longitude east of Greenwi

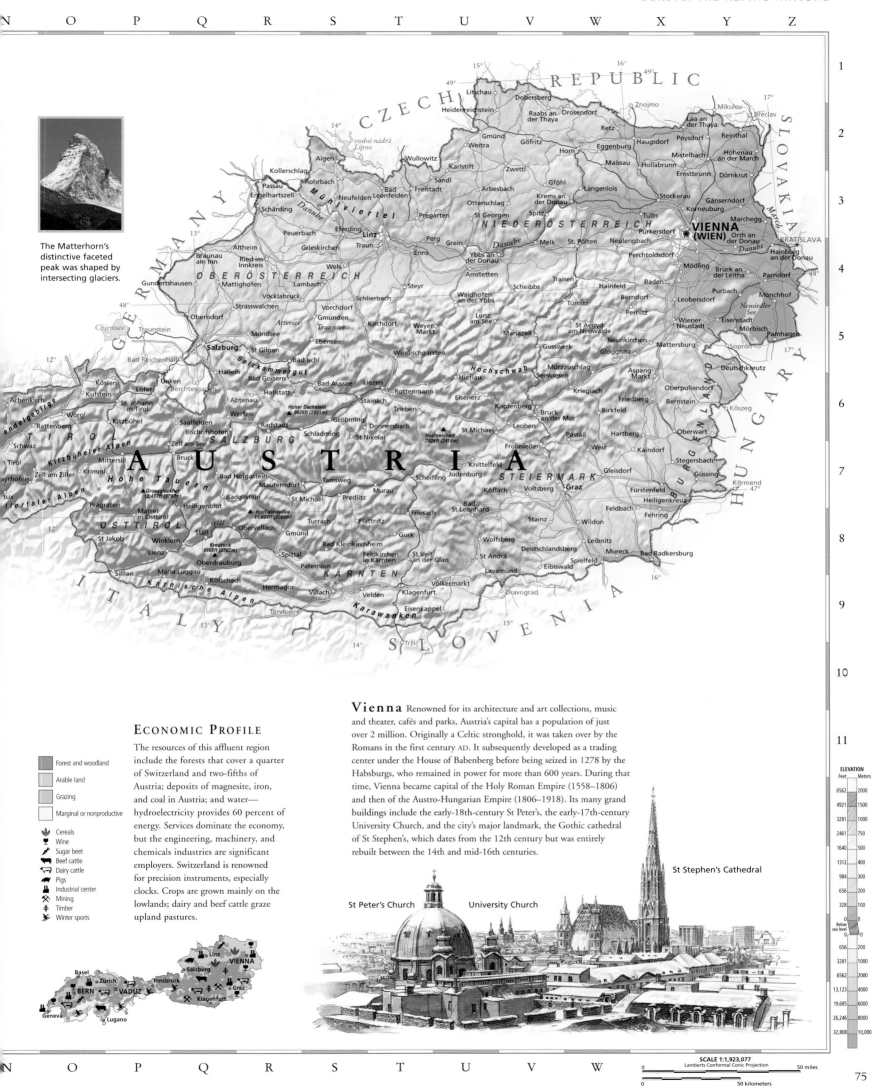

The Matterhorn's distinctive faceted peak was shaped by intersecting glaciers.

ECONOMIC PROFILE

The resources of this affluent region include the forests that cover a quarter of Switzerland and two-fifths of Austria; deposits of magnesite, iron, and coal in Austria; and water—hydroelectricity provides 60 percent of energy. Services dominate the economy, but the engineering, machinery, and chemicals industries are significant employers. Switzerland is renowned for precision instruments, especially clocks. Crops are grown mainly on the lowlands; dairy and beef cattle graze upland pastures.

Forest and woodland
Arable land
Grazing
Marginal or nonproductive

Cereals
Wine
Sugar beet
Beef cattle
Dairy cattle
Pigs
Industrial center
Mining
Timber
Winter sports

Vienna Renowned for its architecture and art collections, music and theater, cafés and parks, Austria's capital has a population of just over 2 million. Originally a Celtic stronghold, it was taken over by the Romans in the first century AD. It subsequently developed as a trading center under the House of Babenberg before being seized in 1278 by the Habsburgs, who remained in power for more than 600 years. During that time, Vienna became capital of the Holy Roman Empire (1558–1806) and then of the Austro-Hungarian Empire (1806–1918). Its many grand buildings include the early-18th-century St Peter's, the early-17th-century University Church, and the city's major landmark, the Gothic cathedral of St Stephen's, which dates from the 12th century but was entirely rebuilt between the 14th and mid-16th centuries.

St Peter's Church   University Church   St Stephen's Cathedral

ELEVATION
Feet	Meters
6562	2000
4921	1500
3281	1000
2461	750
1640	500
1312	400
984	300
656	200
328	100
0 Below sea level	0
656	200
3281	1000
6562	2000
13,123	4000
19,685	6000
26,246	8000
32,808	10,000

SCALE 1:1,923,077
Lamberts Conformal Conic Projection
0   50 miles
0   50 kilometers

ITALY AND MALTA

Italy, Malta, San Marino, Vatican City

Resembling a high-heeled boot, Italy extends from the southern Alps to the middle of the Mediterranean Sea. Apart from the Northern Plain, much of the country is mountainous. Alpine peaks line the northern border, and the Apennines extend down the center of the country like a backbone. Two tiny nations lie within Italy: the Republic of San Marino and the Vatican City, the world's smallest state and the seat of the Roman Catholic Church. Situated 60 miles (100 km) south of Sicily, Malta is an independent republic with a distinctive culture and language.

Colosseum

St Peter's Basilica, Vatican City

Roman Forum

Rome Many of Rome's most famous buildings date from the period when the city was the capital of the vast Roman Empire (27 BC–AD 330). Others, such as St Peter's Basilica, were erected by the Roman Catholic Church, which effectively controlled the city from the 8th century until the unification of Italy in 1870.

POPULATION PATTERNS

During the preindustrial era, Italy's population was concentrated in ports, river valleys, and lowland plains. Following the Industrial Revolution and especially after the Second World War, many Italians from the less affluent south moved to the industrialized north, making this by far the most densely populated part of the country today.

Less than 2.6 persons per sq mile/1 per sq km
2.6–26 per sq mile/ 1–10 per sq km
26–65 per sq mile/ 10–25 per sq km
65–130 per sq mile/ 25–50 per sq km
130–260 per sq mile/ 50–100 per sq km
260–520 per sq mile/ 100–200 per sq km

ECONOMIC PROFILE

Italy is a major producer of vegetables, cereals, citrus fruit, and olives, and is the world's second-largest manufacturer of wine. Most of its crops are grown on the Northern Plain and the coastal plains that flank the Apennines. Manufacturing is concentrated in the north, and automobiles, iron and steel, chemicals, and textiles are the most important products. Tourism is vital to all the countries in this region.

Cereals
Rice
Vegetables
Citrus fruits
Wine
Olives
Beef cattle
Dairy cattle
Sheep
Fishing
Industrial center
Tourism

Forest and woodland
Arable land
Grazing
Marginal or nonproductive

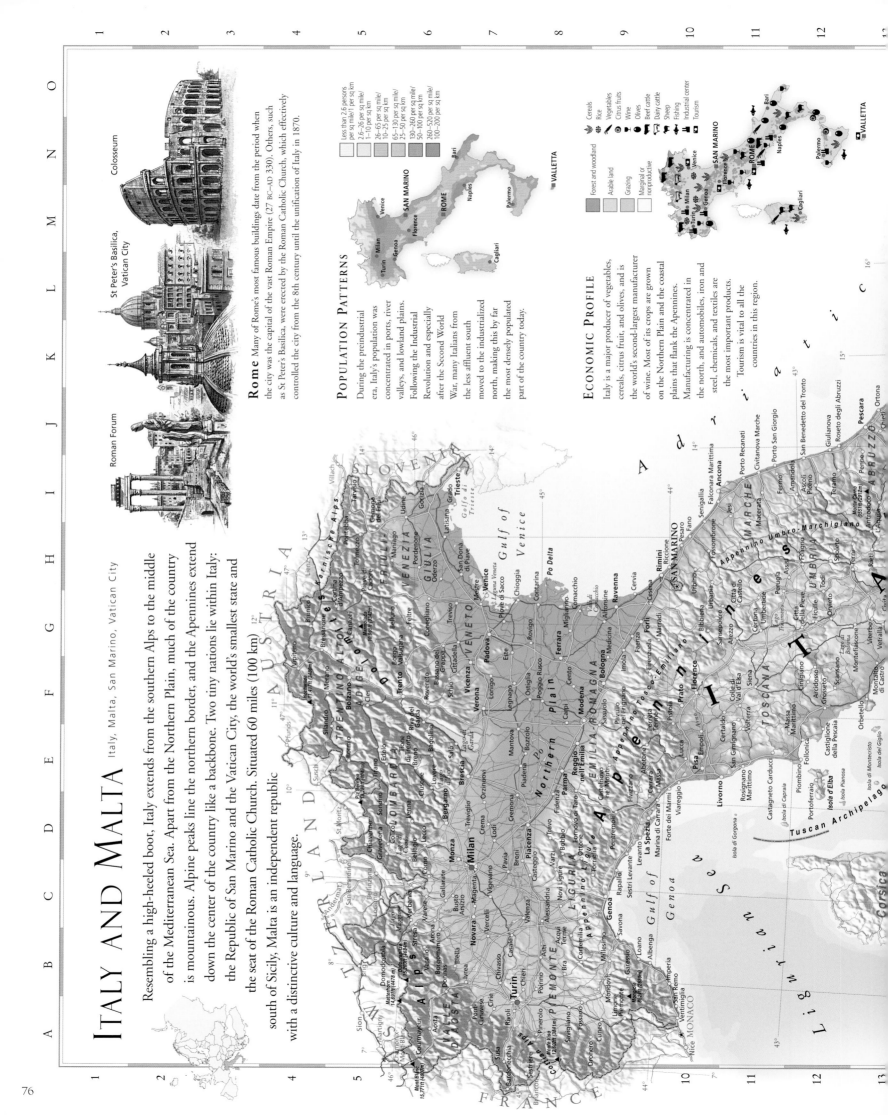

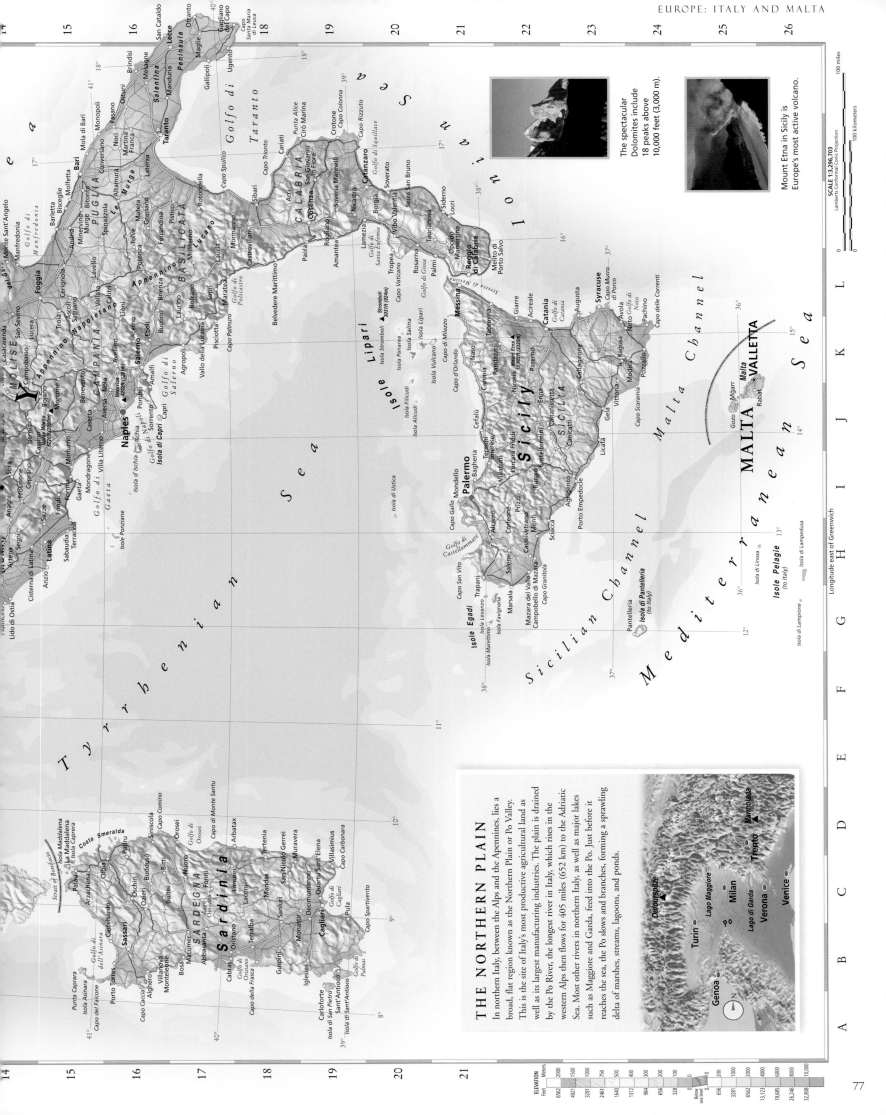

The spectacular Dolomites include 18 peaks above 10,000 feet (3,000 m).

Mount Etna in Sicily is Europe's most active volcano.

SCALE 1:3,296,703
Lamberts Conformal Conic Projection

THE NORTHERN PLAIN

In northern Italy, between the Alps and the Apennines, lies a broad, flat region known as the Northern Plain or Po Valley. This is the site of Italy's most productive agricultural land as well as its largest manufacturing industries. The plain is drained by the Po River, the longest river in Italy, which rises in the western Alps then flows for 405 miles (652 km) to the Adriatic Sea. Most other rivers in northern Italy, as well as major lakes such as Maggiore and Garda, feed into the Po. Just before it reaches the sea, the Po slows and branches, forming a sprawling delta of marshes, streams, lagoons, and ponds.

Longitude east of Greenwich

ELEVATION

Feet	Meters
6562	2000
4921	1500
3281	1000
2461	750
1640	500
1312	400
984	300
656	200
328	100
0	Below sea level
0	0
656	200
3281	1000
6562	2000
13,123	4000
19,685	6000
26,246	8000
32,808	10,000

Northern Central Europe

Czech Republic, Hungary, Poland, Slovakia

The Bohemian Massif and the Carpathian Mountains bisect this region from west to east, separating the flatlands of the North European Plain from those of the Great Hungarian Plain in the south. A ring of mountain ranges around a broad central basin, the Bohemian Massif covers most of the Czech Republic. The heavily forested Carpathians—a continuation of the Alps—occupy northern and central Slovakia, giving way to plains in the south and east. Separated from these two nations by the peaks that line its southern border, Poland otherwise has little high land. Rivers meander across its central lowlands and lake-studded coastal plains, many, notably the Oder and Vistula, flowing all the way to the Baltic Sea. Hungary, too, is mostly flat, the Great Hungarian Plain spreading across more than half of its territory. All of these independent, democratic nations were part of the Eastern bloc until the collapse of communism in 1989. In 1992, Czechoslovakia split into two nations, the Czech Republic and Slovakia.

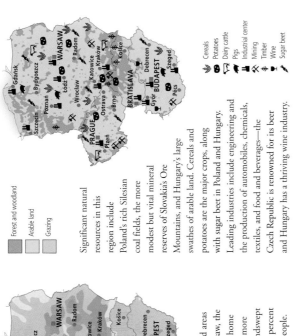

ECONOMIC PROFILE

- Forest and woodland
- Arable land
- Grazing

Significant natural resources in this region include Poland's rich Silesian coal fields, the more modest but vital mineral reserves of Slovakia's Ore Mountains, and Hungary's large swathes of arable land. Cereals and potatoes are the major crops, along with sugar beet in Poland and Hungary. Leading industries include engineering and the production of automobiles, chemicals, textiles, and food and beverages—the Czech Republic is renowned for its beer and Hungary has a thriving wine industry.

- 🌾 Cereals
- 🥔 Potatoes
- Dairy cattle
- Pigs
- ⚒ Mining
- ✕ Industrial center
- ☘ Timber
- Wine
- Sugar beet

POPULATION PATTERNS

- 2.6–26 per sq mile / 1–10 per sq km
- 26–65 per sq mile / 10–25 per sq km
- 65–130 per sq mile / 25–50 per sq km
- 130–260 per sq mile / 50–100 per sq km
- 260–520 per sq mile / 100–200 per sq km

About 65 percent of the region's inhabitants are urban dwellers, with the highest levels in the Czech Republic and the lowest in less-developed Slovakia (which has half the population of its northwestern neighbor). The most densely populated areas are Poland's industrialized south and its capital Warsaw, the northern Czech Republic, and the Budapest region, home to one-quarter of Hungary's people. Settlements are more scattered in the Slovakian mountains and on the windswept and relatively infertile Baltic Sea coast. More than 5 percent of Hungary's population are ethnic Roma (Gypsy) people.

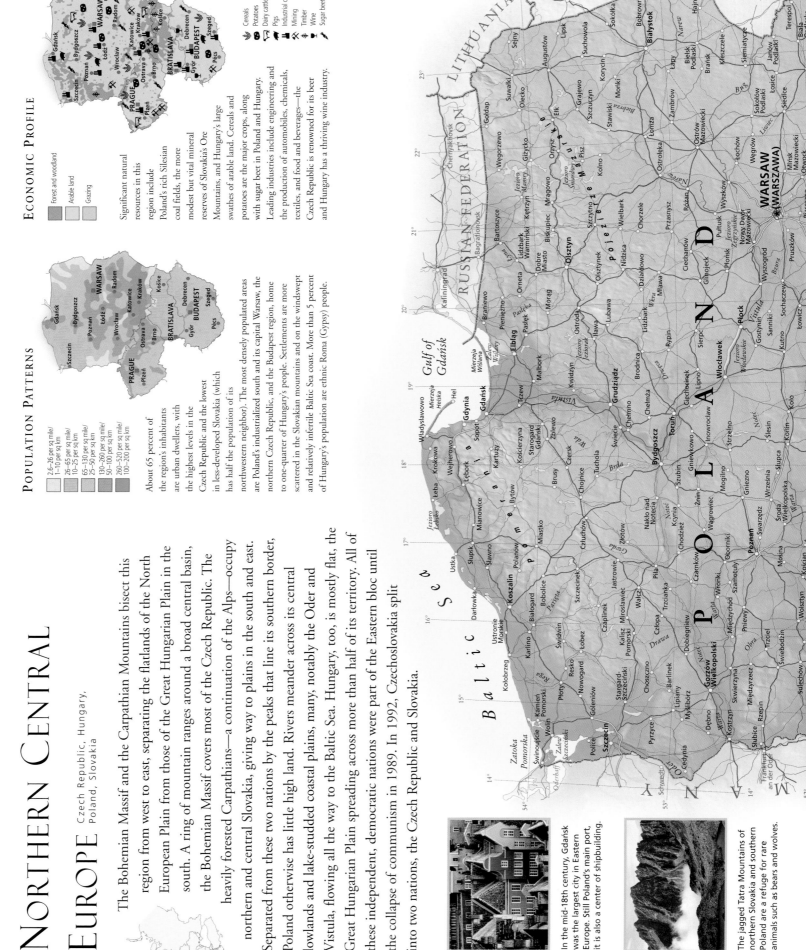

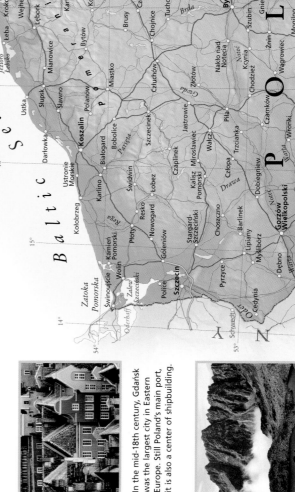

In the mid-18th century, Gdańsk was the largest city in Eastern Europe. Still Poland's main port, it is also a center of shipbuilding.

The jagged Tatra Mountains of northern Slovakia and southern Poland are a refuge for rare animals such as bears and wolves.

Prague Undoubtedly the most famous of the many bridges that cross the Vltava River in the city of Prague, the Charles Bridge dates from 1357. At that time, Prague was the capital of Bohemia and the Holy Roman Empire under Charles IV, and a major trading center. Merchants remained central to the development of the economy until the Industrial Revolution, and were responsible for commissioning many of the magnificent Gothic and Baroque buildings and monuments that today attract a steady influx of visitors. Prague became capital of the nation of Czechoslovakia in 1918 and capital of the newly formed Czech Republic in 1992.

Situated on the east bank of the Danube, Budapest's Parliament was completed in 1902.

SCALE 1:3,021,978
Lambert's Conformal Conic Projection

100 miles
100 kilometers

Longitude east of Greenwich

ELEVATION

Feet	Meters
6562	2000
4921	1500
3281	1000
2461	750
1640	500
984	300
656	200
328	100
Below sea level	0
656	200
3281	1000
6562	2000
13,123	4000
19,685	6000
26,246	8000
32,808	10,000

WESTERN BALKANS

Albania, Bosnia and Herzegovina, Croatia, Serbia and Montenegro, Slovenia

Over the centuries, numerous peoples settled in the Balkans, giving rise to a patchwork of ethnically diverse communities. Until the 20th century, these communities remained relatively isolated from each other, partly as a result of the region's rugged terrain—mountains line the coast and spread across much of the interior, yielding to sizable lowlands only in the north. In the mid-20th century, all of the region's nations adopted communism and all but Albania were united as the Republic of Yugoslavia. The breakup of the republic in 1991 brought ethnic and religious rivalries to a head, resulting in a catastrophic civil war between Croats, Serbs, and Bosnian Muslims (Bosniaks). Peace was restored in 1995, but tensions remain high, especially in the culturally distinct and independently oriented provinces of Montenegro and Kosovo.

THE DINARIC ALPS

Stretching for 350 miles (560 km) along the coast from Slovenia to Albania and rising to 8,274 feet (2,522 m) at Durmitor, the Dinaric Alps form an almost impenetrable barrier between the Adriatic Sea and the Balkan hinterland. A single natural breach, the Neretva River valley, provides Bosnia and Herzegovina with its only coastal access; elsewhere, steep, arid slopes climb directly from the shoreline or narrow coastal plains. In the Dalmatia region of Croatia, the mountains have been partially submerged by the sea, giving rise to a series of long, parallel islands and slender, sheltered channels. The western slopes of the Dinaric Alps consist mainly of porous limestone; in places, the rock is honeycombed with underground channels and pools, and extensive cave systems.

Dubrovnik

Dubrovnik A settlement existed on the site of Dubrovnik at least as far back as the sixth century AD, but the town came to prominence as a trading center only in the 13th century. By the 15th century, Dubrovnik was an independent republic and the most important port in the eastern Adriatic. After falling to Napoleon in 1808, the city became part of Croatia in 1815. During the recent civil war, Dubrovnik was devastated by Serb shelling. However, careful renovation has restored many historic buildings, and tourists are now beginning to return to the city in large numbers.

Mostar is the historical capital of Herzegovina. Its spectacular stone bridge, built in 1566, was destroyed by shelling in 1993.

Site of the pretty Church of St Maria and a dramatic clifftop castle, Lake Bled lies in the foothills of Slovenia's Julian Alps.

Zagreb was originally two medieval cities, Gradec and Kaptol, which merged in the 19th century.

In undeveloped rural Albania, many industrial and agricultural processes are still carried out manually.

The late-19th-century Catholic cathedral is a prominent landmark in Novi Sad, Serbia's second-largest city.

Economic Profile

Economic activity throughout the region was severely disrupted by the civil war, and recovery has been slow. Agriculture is concentrated on the northern plains and the coast; cereals, sugar beet, and vegetables are the leading crops. In the interior, sheep graze hillsides and thick forests provide abundant timber. Sizable mineral resources support the manufacture of metals and machinery in industrial centers. Textile production and food processing are also important, and hydroelectric power stations are widespread.

Forest and woodland
Arable land
Grazing

Cereals
Fruit
Olives
Sugar beet
Dairy cattle
Pigs
Sheep
Industrial center
Timber
Mining

Population Patterns

The interior's mountainous terrain and dense forests have long restricted settlement. In contrast, the north's fertile land and developed industries have resulted in higher population densities, especially around Zagreb and along the Sava, Danube, Tisa, and Morava river valleys. However, only about 50 percent of the region's inhabitants are urban dwellers. The civil war displaced huge numbers of people. About 2.5 million inhabitants of Bosnia and Herzegovina left their homes during the conflict; a decade later, one-third had still not returned.

Less than 2.6 persons per sq mile/1 per sq km
2.6–26 per sq mile/ 1–10 per sq km
26–65 per sq mile/ 10–25 per sq km
65–130 per sq mile/ 25–50 per sq km
130–260 per sq mile/ 50–100 per sq km

ELEVATION

Feet	Meters
6562	2000
4921	1500
3281	1000
2461	750
1640	500
1312	400
984	300
656	200
328	100
0	0
Below sea level	
656	200
3281	1000
6562	2000
13,123	4000
19,685	6000
26,246	8000
32,808	10,000

81

EASTERN
BALKANS

Bulgaria,
Greece, Macedonia

On its eastern side, the Balkan Peninsula is bounded by the Black and Aegean seas, and separated from Asia by the slender straits of the Bosporus and Dardanelles. The Former Yugoslav Republic of Macedonia occupies a high plateau in the interior of the peninsula. In neighboring Bulgaria (also a former communist country), the Balkan Mountains separate the wide plain of the Danube River from the southern lowlands, and the Rhodope Mountains form a natural boundary with Greece. Underpinned by the Pindus Mountains, central Greece stretches south from the Macedonian border, fraying into numerous narrow peninsulas and hundreds of widely scattered islands. Turkey's toehold on Europe is a legacy of that nation's long dominance over the entire Balkan Peninsula, which commenced in the 14th century and ended only in the early 20th century.

POPULATION PATTERNS

This region has a relatively low population density, with the highest concentrations occurring on the Bulgarian lowlands and in European Turkey. In Macedonia and Greece, rugged, arid terrain has restricted development. Since the mid-20th century, industrialization has led to a decline in natural population growth and an increase in urbanization. In Greece, more than 30 percent of the population now lives in Athens and many rural settlements have been abandoned.

Less than 2.6 persons per sq mile/1 per sq km	
2.6–26 per sq mile/ 1–10 per sq km	
26–65 per sq mile/ 10–25 per sq km	
65–130 per sq mile/ 25–50 per sq km	
130–260 per sq mile/ 50–100 per sq km	

ECONOMIC PROFILE

Macedonia and Greece have little fertile farmland, few mineral resources, and undeveloped industrial sectors; consequently, Macedonia is one of Europe's poorest nations. Greece depends heavily on shipping and tourism. Bulgaria has had a difficult transition from a Soviet-style centralized economy to an open market. However, it possesses rich farmland, especially on the Danube floodplain, and sophisticated industries led by metals, chemicals, and textiles.

Forest and woodland
Arable land
Grazing

Cereals
Citrus fruits
Wine
Tobacco
Olives
Sheep
Fishing
Industrial center
Tourism
Flowers

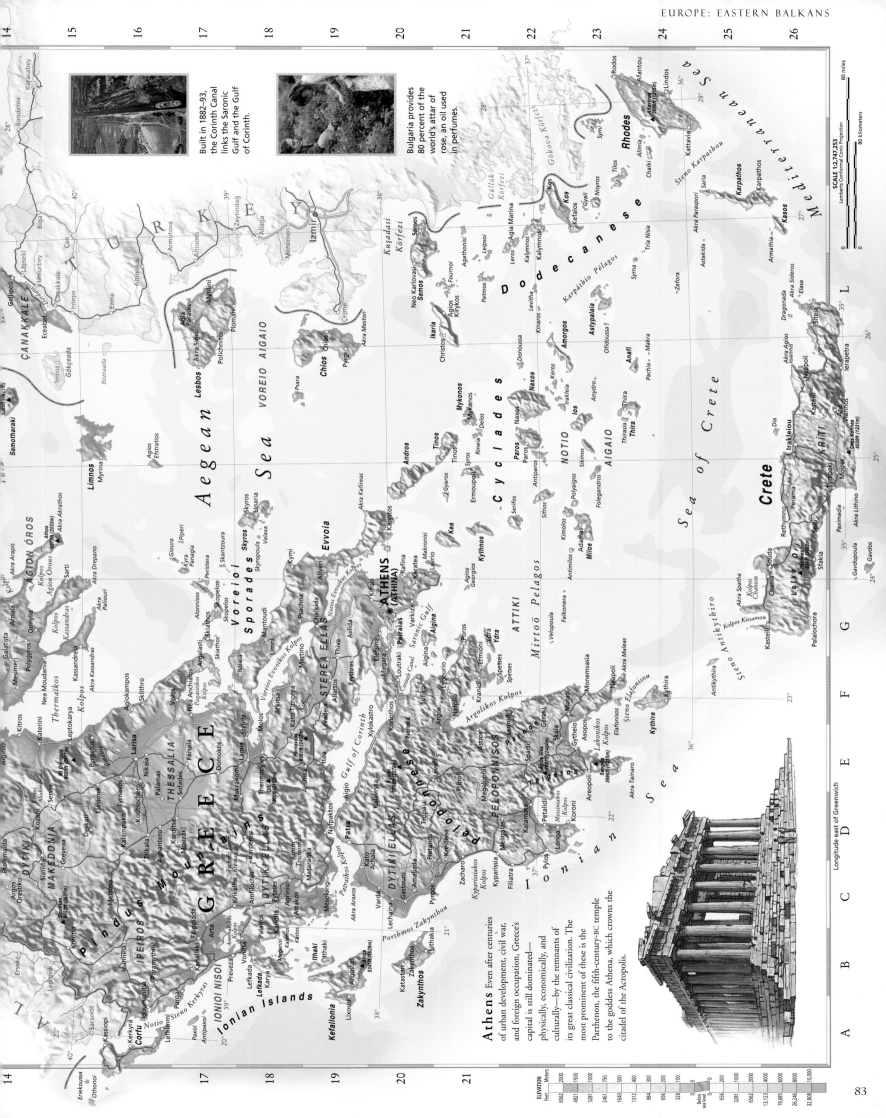

Built in 1882–93, the Corinth Canal links the Saronic Gulf and the Gulf of Corinth.

Bulgaria provides 80 percent of the world's attar of rose, an oil used in perfumes.

Athens Even after centuries of urban development, civil war, and foreign occupation, Greece's capital is still dominated—physically, economically, and culturally—by the remnants of its great classical civilization. The most prominent of these is the Parthenon, the fifth-century-BC temple to the goddess Athena, which crowns the citadel of the Acropolis.

SCALE 1:2,747,253
Lamberts Conformal Conic Projection

80 miles

80 kilometers

ELEVATION

Feet	Meters
6562	2000
4921	1500
3281	1000
2461	750
1640	500
984	300
656	200
328	100
0 Below sea level	0 Below sea level
656	200
3281	1000
6562	2000
13,123	4000
19,685	6000
26,246	8000
32,808	10,000

Longitude east of Greenwich

83

NORTHEASTERN EUROPE
Belarus, Estonia, Latvia, Lithuania

Much of Northeastern Europe's low-lying landscape was fashioned during the last ice age. Across the region, extensive plains, scoured flat by ice, are separated by hills and ridges originally deposited by the wide snouts of glaciers. Innumerable lakes fill hollows, and winding rivers have given rise to some of Europe's largest wetlands. Due to their proximity to the Baltic Sea, the nations of Estonia, Latvia, and Lithuania are often referred to as the Baltic States, even though the three countries are ethnically and linguistically distinct. In common with their southern neighbor Belarus, the Baltic States were, for long periods of their histories, controlled by more powerful nations, including Poland, Russia, Germany, Denmark, and Sweden. In the mid-20th century, all four countries became part of the Soviet Union, but all reasserted their independence soon after the collapse of the Eastern bloc in 1989. The Russian enclave around Kaliningrad is a remnant of the Soviet empire, and a vital Baltic port for the Russian Federation.

POPULATION PATTERNS

Northeastern Europe's population is fairly evenly spread, though it thins out in northern Latvia and on Estonia's chilly Baltic coast—only 14 of Estonia's 1,541 islands are inhabited. About 60 percent of people in Latvia and 70 percent in the other countries are urban dwellers; in both Estonia and Latvia roughly one-third inhabit the capital city. People of Russian origin live throughout the region, but make up 30 percent of the population in Estonia and Latvia, the result of a Soviet policy of encouraging workers from the U.S.S.R. to settle in these states.

2.6–26 per sq mile/ 1–10 per sq km	
26–65 per sq mile/ 10–25 per sq km	
65–130 per sq mile/ 25–50 per sq km	
130–260 per sq mile/ 50–100 per sq km	

ECONOMIC PROFILE

These nations are still dealing with the transition to a market economy, and are still dependent to some extent (especially Belarus) on Russian raw materials and sales. Much of Belarus's arable land was contaminated by fallout from Chernobyl, but it remains a significant supplier of flax as well as potash (widely used for fertilizers), and peat (from its marshlands); its heavy industries produce machinery, tools, tractors, and trucks. Estonia's oil-shale provides much of the Baltic States' energy. The Baltic States are also noted for wood products and textiles, and Lithuania is a major source of amber.

Forest and woodland
Arable land

Cereals
Flax
Potatoes
Vegetables
Dairy cattle
Sugar beet
Pigs
Industrial center
Timber

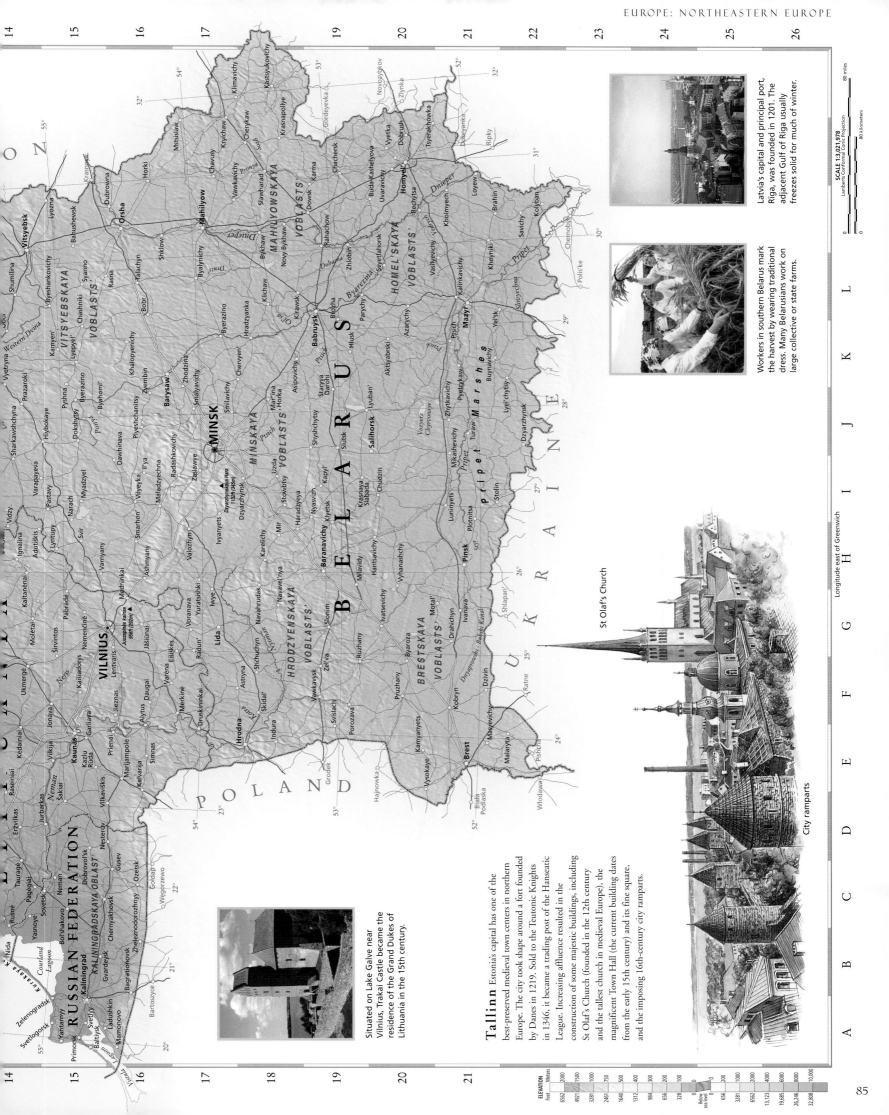

Tallinn Estonia's capital has one of the best-preserved medieval town centers in northern Europe. The city took shape around a fort founded by Danes in 1219. Sold to the Teutonic Knights in 1346, it became a trading post of the Hanseatic League. Increasing affluence resulted in the construction of some majestic buildings, including St Olaf's Church (founded in the 12th century and the tallest church in medieval Europe), the magnificent Town Hall (the current building dates from the early 15th century) and its fine square, and the imposing 16th-century city ramparts.

St Olaf's Church

City ramparts

Situated on Lake Galve near Vilnius, Trakai Castle became the residence of the Grand Dukes of Lithuania in the 15th century.

Latvia's capital and principal port, Riga, was founded in 1201. The adjacent Gulf of Riga usually freezes solid for much of winter.

Workers in southern Belarus mark the harvest by wearing traditional dress. Many Belarusians work on large collective or state farms.

SCALE 1:3,021,978
Lamberts Conformal Conic Projection

85

CENTRAL EASTERN EUROPE

Moldova, Romania, Ukraine

Three major rivers flow through Central Eastern Europe to the north shore of the Black Sea. The Danube courses along Romania's southern border, its vast floodplain contrasting with the mountains of the interior. The Dniester runs from the uplands of western Ukraine along the eastern edge of Moldova; in western Moldova, hundreds of other, mainly short, rivers have carved steep ravines and gorges amid low hills. Flowing first south, then east and west in a great S-shape, the Dnieper River snakes through the immense steppe grasslands that cover most of Ukraine. Formerly part of the Soviet Union, Ukraine is now Europe's largest country. Romania and Moldova share strong linguistic and ethnic links, and most of Moldova was incorporated into Romania from 1918 to 1940. In the mid-20th century, both nations were part of the Eastern bloc; like Ukraine, they are now independent fledgling democracies.

POPULATION PATTERNS

	Less than 2.6 persons per sq mile/1 per sq km
	2.6–26 per sq mile/1–10 per sq km
	26–65 per sq mile/10–25 per sq km
	65–130 per sq mile/25–50 per sq km
	130–260 per sq mile/50–100 per sq km
	260–520 per sq mile/100–200 per sq km

Moldova is the most densely populated of the former Soviet republics, yet the majority of its inhabitants still live in rural areas; one-third of the urban population dwells in the capital. More than half of Romanians and Ukrainians live in towns and cities. Romania has areas of low population density in the mountains and swampy Danube Delta; Ukraine's population is a little more evenly spread, with the highest concentrations in the industrial southeast—home to one-third of the population—and the fertile belt that runs eastward from the Dniester. Ukraine and Moldova have many inhabitants of Russian origin, whereas Romania's largest minorities are ethnic Roma (Gypsy) people and Hungarians.

ECONOMIC PROFILE

Forest and woodland	
Arable land	
Grazing	

⚘	Cereals	⚒	Mining
⚘	Sugar beet	🛢	Oil production
⚘	Flowers	⬢	Gas production
🐄	Dairy cattle	🍷	Wine
🏭	Industrial center	🐟	Fishing

All three countries have productive farmland. Cereals are grown widely in lowland areas, especially on the fertile black-soil plains of Ukraine, formerly known as "the breadbasket of the Soviet Union." Sugar beet (Ukraine is the world's largest producer) and sunflowers are also vital crops, and Romania and Moldova are significant wine producers. Moldova has few mineral resources and remains dependent on agriculture. Romania and Ukraine's reserves of oil, coal, and gas support major industries including the manufacture of metals, machinery, and chemicals. Textiles and footwear are important in Romania. Despite some economic progress, these nations remain among Europe's poorest.

Romania's Transylvanian Alps are heavily forested and contain mineral deposits including coal and iron ore.

Longitude east of Greenwich

In the Soviet era, Ukraine produced one-fifth of the U.S.S.R.'s agricultural goods.

Chişinău's buildings reflect Turkish and Soviet influences.

Kiev The Ukrainian capital's best-known landmark is golden-domed St Sophia Cathedral, which dates from 1037. At that time Kiev was the center of the powerful independent state of Kievan Rus. The city was razed by Mongol invaders in the 13th century and subsequently ruled by Poland, Lithuania, and Russia. It became the capital of newly independent Ukraine in 1991.

TRANSYLVANIA

Viewed from Romania's western border, the Carpathian Mountains and Transylvanian Alps form a vast amphitheater of mountains encompassing the region of Transylvania. Formerly autonomous but also ruled by Hungary for long periods, Transylvania was entirely ceded to Romania only in 1947.

ELEVATION

Feet	Meters
6562	2000
4921	1500
3281	1000
2461	750
1640	500
1312	400
984	300
656	200
328	100
0	0
Below sea level	
656	200
3281	1000
6562	2000
13,123	4000
19,685	6000
26,246	8000
32,808	10,000

SCALE 1:3,846,154
Lamberts Conformal Conic Projection

0   100 miles
0   100 kilometers

THE RUSSIAN FEDERATION

Spanning 11 time zones and most of the Eastern Hemisphere, the Russian Federation is the largest country on Earth. It is divided into European Russia and Asian Russia, or Siberia, by the Ural Mountains, which stretch from the shore of the Kara Sea to Kazakhstan. In European Russia, the site of the nation's largest cities, major rivers divide plains and ranges of low, rolling hills. East of the Urals, an immense, swampy plain stretches to the Yenisey River, where the land climbs to the wide Central Siberian Plateau. High mountains line the Mongolian border and skirt the east coast. An almost unbroken band of boreal forest crosses the entire country, dividing the tundra of the far north from the woodlands and steppe grasslands of the south.

In 1917, after a bloody revolution, Russia became a communist state known as the Soviet Union, or Union of Soviet Socialist Republics (U.S.S.R.). Following the collapse of communism in 1991, ten Soviet republics declared independence. The remainder of the union, about 75 percent of its land area, became the Russian Federation.

St Petersburg's Winter Palace is one of a series of buildings constructed in the mid-18th century by Peter the Great.

Local fishermen harvest more than 50 species of fish from Lake Baikal, the deepest lake in the world.

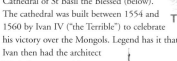

The Chukchi of northeastern Russia live mainly by herding reindeer, fishing, and hunting whales, seals, and walruses.

Moscow The focal point of Russia's capital city, Red Square, dates from the late 15th century and acquired its present name—the Russian word for "red" also means "beautiful"—in the 17th century. It is the site of some of the nation's most important buildings, including the Kremlin, Lenin's Tomb, and the 12-domed Cathedral of St Basil the Blessed (below). The cathedral was built between 1554 and 1560 by Ivan IV ("the Terrible") to celebrate his victory over the Mongols. Legend has it that Ivan then had the architect blinded to prevent him ever building anything to surpass this extraordinary work.

THE KAMCHATKA PENINSULA

Remote, cold, and desolate, the Kamchatka Peninsula extends for 750 miles (1,200 km) southwestward from the eastern edge of Russia, dividing the Sea of Okhotsk from the Bering Sea. Its forbidding landscape is characterized by forest-studded tundra, few towns or roads, hot springs, and more than 120 steep-sided volcanic peaks, including 15,584-foot (4,750-m) Sopka Klyuchevskaya, Siberia's highest mountain. No fewer than 22 of these volcanoes are still active.

Longitude east of Greenwich

POPULATION PATTERNS

European Russia constitutes one-quarter of the country but is home to four-fifths of its inhabitants. Settlement is especially dense around Moscow, along the River Volga, and in the southwest. East of the Urals, Russians cluster around the industrial centers of Omsk and Novosibirsk, the towns strung along the Trans-Siberian railway, and far-flung northern ports and mining centers. Over the past century, Russians have steadily abandoned the countryside for cities; 73 percent now live in urban areas. More than four-fifths are ethnic Russians; the remainder consists of a large number of other ethnic groups, including Ukrainians, Tatars, and Bashkirs.

Uninhabited

Less than 2.6 persons per sq mile/1 per sq km

2.6–26 per sq mile/ 1–10 per sq km

26–65 per sq mile/ 10–25 per sq km

65–130 per sq mile/ 25–50 per sq km

130–260 per sq mile/ 50–100 per sq km

260–520 per sq mile/ 100–200 per sq km

ECONOMIC PROFILE

Much of the Soviet Union's best arable land was located in the now-independent republics of Ukraine and Belarus. Less than one-sixth of the Russian Federation is farmland; wheat, barley, and sugar beet are among the major crops. Russia has the world's largest forests and plentiful supplies of minerals, including coal, oil, gas, gold, copper, and nickel. These support the processing of metals and fossil fuels, and the manufacturing of chemicals and machinery. Communist rule accelerated industrialization, but ultimately stifled development. A shift toward privatization and a more open market is under way.

Forest and woodland

Arable land

Grazing

Marginal or nonproductive

Potatoes

Beef cattle

Industrial center

Mining

Oil production

Gas production

Timber

Reindeer

Fishing

SCALE 1:20,329,670
Lamberts Conformal Conic Projection

ELEVATION

Feet	Meters
6562	2000
4921	1500
3281	1000
2461	750
1640	500
1312	400
984	300
656	200
328	100
	Below sea level
656	200
3281	1000
6562	2000
13,123	4000
19,685	6000
26,246	8000
32,808	10,000

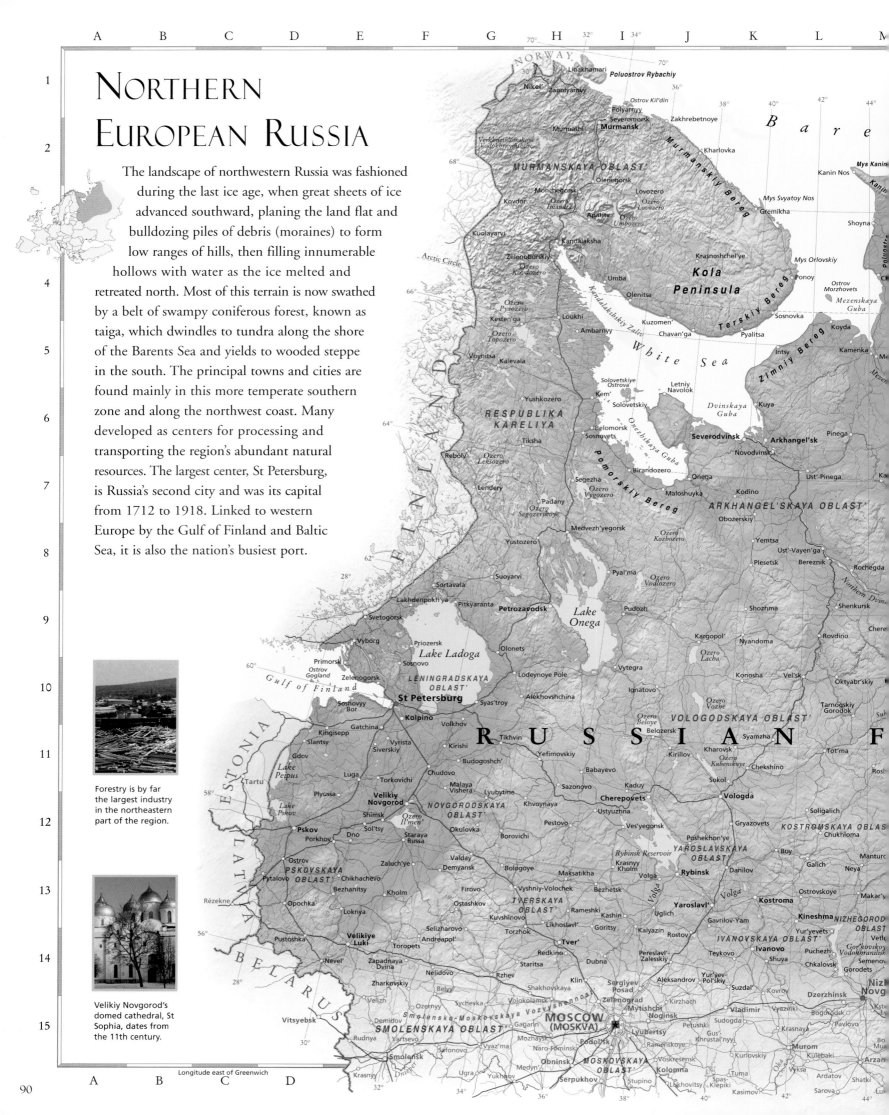

Northern European Russia

The landscape of northwestern Russia was fashioned during the last ice age, when great sheets of ice advanced southward, planing the land flat and bulldozing piles of debris (moraines) to form low ranges of hills, then filling innumerable hollows with water as the ice melted and retreated north. Most of this terrain is now swathed by a belt of swampy coniferous forest, known as taiga, which dwindles to tundra along the shore of the Barents Sea and yields to wooded steppe in the south. The principal towns and cities are found mainly in this more temperate southern zone and along the northwest coast. Many developed as centers for processing and transporting the region's abundant natural resources. The largest center, St Petersburg, is Russia's second city and was its capital from 1712 to 1918. Linked to western Europe by the Gulf of Finland and Baltic Sea, it is also the nation's busiest port.

Forestry is by far the largest industry in the northeastern part of the region.

Velikiy Novgorod's domed cathedral, St Sophia, dates from the 11th century.

Map labels (grid references across top): N O P Q R S T U V W X Y Z

1 2 3 4 5 6 7 8 9 10 11

One of Russia's biggest ports, Murmansk is the largest city in the world north of the Arctic Circle.

These 18th-century churches lie on an island in Lake Onega, Europe's second-largest lake.

POPULATION PATTERNS

The north's inhospitable subarctic climate has confined settlement to sheltered harbors and river valleys, though small groups of Arctic peoples, including the Komi and Nenets, are scattered across the northeast. By far the most populous area is the south, where the highest densities of settlement occur around the industrial centers of Perm' and Kirov in the east, and St Petersburg in the west. St Petersburg alone accommodates almost 4.5 million people.

Uninhabited
Less than 2.6 persons per sq mile/1 per sq km
2.6–26 per sq mile/ 1–10 per sq km
26–65 per sq mile/ 10–25 per sq km
65–130 per sq mile/ 25–50 per sq km
130–260 per sq mile/ 50–100 per sq km

Murmansk · Vorkuta · Pechora · Arkangel'sk · Kotlas · St Petersburg · Kirov · Perm' · Yaroslavl'

ECONOMIC PROFILE

The processing of resources dominates the economy. Local forests provide one-third of Russia's wood products. Oil, gas, and coal reserves are exploited around Pechora, and metal production is also important, notably in Vologda, where it accounts for two-thirds of industrial output. The White and Barents seas yield one-quarter of Russia's fish. Dairying and the cultivation of fodder crops, oats, and rye take place in the southwest. Engineering, chemical production, printing, and food processing are the leading industries in St Petersburg.

Forest and woodland
Arable land
Grazing

Cereals
Industrial center
Mining
Reindeer
Fishing
Dairy cattle
Gas production
Oil production
Timber
Flax
Tourism
Coal

Large quantities of crude oil from western Siberia are piped to Perm' for refining.

ELEVATION

Feet	Meters
32,808	10,000
26,246	8000
19,685	6000
13,123	4000
6562	2000
4921	1500
3281	1000
2461	750
1640	500
1312	400
984	300
656	200
328	100
0 Below sea level	0
656	200
3281	1000
6562	2000
13,123	4000
19,685	6000
26,246	8000
32,808	10,000

SCALE 1:6,043,956
Lamberts Conformal Conic Projection

0 — 150 miles
0 — 150 kilometers

W

Map place names (selection):

Guba Dolgaya, Ostrov Vaygach, Amderma, Yugorskiy Poluostrov, Khrebet Pay-Khoy, Ostrov Dolgiy, Varandey, Khal'mer-Yu, Severnyy, Vorkuta, Ostrov Kolguyev, Bugrino, Tobseda, Chernaya, Nosovaya, NENETSKIY AVTONOMNYY OKRUG, Yeletskiy, Chum, Pomorskiy Proliv, Indiga, Oksino, Nar'yan-Mar, Khorey-Ver, Gora Payyer 4829ft (1472m), Abez', Malozemel'skaya Tundra, Novyy Bor, Pechora, Inta, Bol'shezemel'skaya Tundra, Usinsk, Kos'yu, Synya, Gora Narodnaya 6217ft (1895m), Krestovka, Ust'-Tsil'ma, Myla, Pechora, Timanskiy Kryazh, Vozhgora, Irayel', RESPUBLIKA KOMI, Dutovo, Vuktyl, Polyarnyy Ural, Mezen', Vashka, Sosnogorsk, Gora Tel'pos-Iz 5305ft (1617m), Usogorsk, Vodnyy, Ukhta, Vendinga, Voyvozh, Gora Koyp 3920ft (1195m), Mikun', Yemva, Puzla, Vol'dino, Yarensk, Sindor, Kur'ya, Severnyy Ural, Storozhevsk, Chasovo, Ust'-Kulom, Ust'-Nem, Syktyvkar, Gora Isherim 4357ft (1331m), Koryazhma, Vizinga, Nyrob, Kotlas, KOMI-PERMYATSKIY AVTONOMNYY OKRUG, Ob''yachevo, Gayny, Gora Denezhkin Kamen' 4895ft (1492m), Velikiy Ustyug, Luza, Krasnovishersk, Cherdyn', Gora Konzhakovskiy Kamen' 5148ft (1569m), Solikamsk, Kama, Berezniki, Aleksandrovsk, Kizel, Oparino, Yurla, Gubakha, Nagorsk, Kamskoye Vodokhranilishche, Kirs, Kudymkar, Chermoz, Murashi, Chermoz, Il'inskiy, Dobryanka, Omutninsk, Slobodskoy, Krasnokamsk, Chusovoy, Lys'va, Kirov, Kirovo-Chepetsk, Glazov, Perm, PERMSKAYA OBLAST', Yur'ya, Kotel'nich, KIROVSKAYA OBLAST', Balezino, Ocher, Okhansk, Leninskoye, Suna, Igra, Osa, Kungur, UDMURTSKAYA RESPUBLIKA, Selty, Suksun, Votkinsk, Barda, Uinskoye, Kiknur, Yaransk, Nolinsk, Votkinskoye Vodokhranilishche, Krasnoufimsk, Urzhum, Kil'mez, Izhevsk, Chaykovskiy, Chernushka, Sovetsk, Sernur, Sarapul, Kuyeda, Askino, RESPUBLIKA MARIY EL, Malmyzh, Mozhga, Agryz, Yanaul, Duvan, Yoshkar-Ola, Neftekamsk, UDMURTSKAYA RESPUBLIKA, Vyatskiye Polyany, Sarapul, Koz'modem'yansk, Cheboksary, Novocheboksarsk, Kazan', RESPUBLIKA TATARSTAN, Mamadysh, Nizhnekamsk, Naberezhnyye Chelny, Birsk, Blagoveshchensk, Ufa, Zlatoust, FEDERATION

SOUTHERN EUROPEAN RUSSIA

Europe's second-largest urban center, Moscow is not only the capital of the Russian Federation, but the heart of its most densely populated, developed, and productive region. The city lies on the wide valley of the Moskva River, a tributary of the Oka, which in turn flows east into the Volga, Europe's longest river. A chain of cities lines these waterways, running eastward and veering south with the Volga through Samara to Volgograd. West of the river, the Volga Hills roll down to the banks of the Don, Europe's fifth-longest waterway, which forms the eastern boundary of the Central Russian Uplands, a low plateau. Near Volgograd, the two rivers almost meet and are linked by the Volga–Don Canal. Turning away from each other, the Don and the Volga then drain across arid lowlands into, respectively, the Sea of Azov and the Caspian Sea. In the far south, where the mighty Caucasus range forms Russia's southern frontier and a natural boundary with Asia, a mere 200 miles (320 km) or so divides Europe's lowest point, in the Caspian Depression, from its highest, the towering summit of Elbrus.

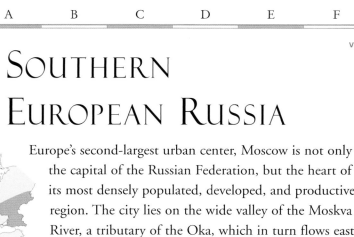

THE CASPIAN DEPRESSION

Covering 77,000 square miles (200,000 sq km), the Caspian Depression is a vast lowland on the northwestern edge of the Caspian Sea. Part of an immense downward fold caused by crumpling of Earth's crust, it descends to 92 feet (28 m) below sea level at the shoreline. In the north, the depression is traversed by the Volga River, which forms Russia's largest delta. Elsewhere, the depression is mainly barren, although beneath its surface lie large deposits of oil and salt.

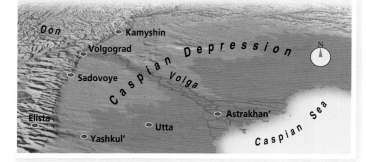

A war between Russian forces and Chechen separatists that began in 1994 has ravaged Chechnya's capital Groznyy.

Governor's Palace

Cathedral of the Annunciation

Suyumbike Tower

Kazan' The westward expansion of the Mongol empire led to the founding of the city of Kazan' in the late 13th century. It became part of the Khanate of the Golden Horde and then an independent khanate. The city's founders, known in the West as Tatars, converted to Islam, creating the northernmost outpost of that religion. In 1552, following an extended siege, Ivan IV (the Terrible) of Russia captured the city, made it a Christian see, and constructed the vast white-walled fortress or kremlin that still stands. It now encompasses a remarkable cluster of historic buildings dating from the 16th to 19th centuries, as well as the remnants of earlier structures from the Tatar period. Kazan' remains a center of Tatar culture and about half of the population of the Republic of Tatarstan is of Tatar origin.

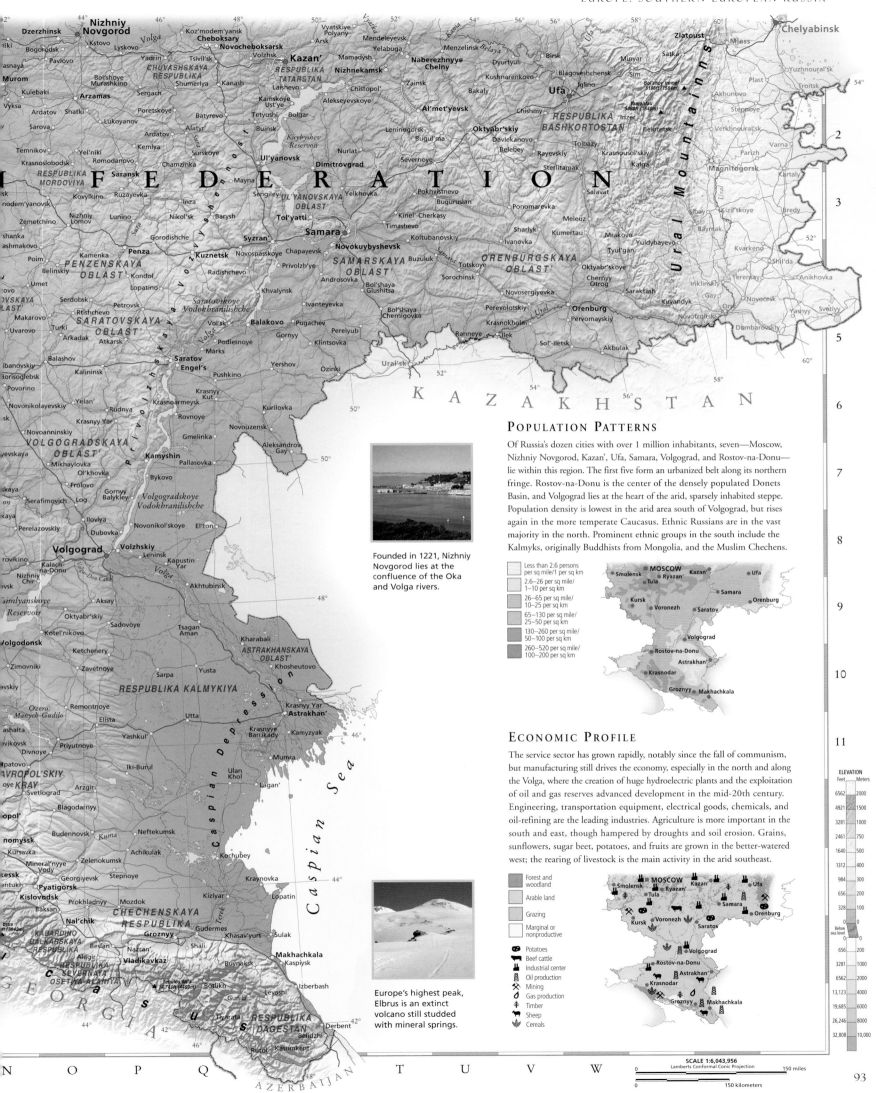

Founded in 1221, Nizhniy Novgorod lies at the confluence of the Oka and Volga rivers.

POPULATION PATTERNS

Of Russia's dozen cities with over 1 million inhabitants, seven—Moscow, Nizhniy Novgorod, Kazan', Ufa, Samara, Volgograd, and Rostov-na-Donu—lie within this region. The first five form an urbanized belt along its northern fringe. Rostov-na-Donu is the center of the densely populated Donets Basin, and Volgograd lies at the heart of the arid, sparsely inhabited steppe. Population density is lowest in the arid area south of Volgograd, but rises again in the more temperate Caucasus. Ethnic Russians are in the vast majority in the north. Prominent ethnic groups in the south include the Kalmyks, originally Buddhists from Mongolia, and the Muslim Chechens.

Less than 2.6 persons per sq mile/1 per sq km
2.6–26 per sq mile/ 1–10 per sq km
26–65 per sq mile/ 10–25 per sq km
65–130 per sq mile/ 25–50 per sq km
130–260 per sq mile/ 50–100 per sq km
260–520 per sq mile/ 100–200 per sq km

ECONOMIC PROFILE

The service sector has grown rapidly, notably since the fall of communism, but manufacturing still drives the economy, especially in the north and along the Volga, where the creation of huge hydroelectric plants and the exploitation of oil and gas reserves advanced development in the mid-20th century. Engineering, transportation equipment, electrical goods, chemicals, and oil-refining are the leading industries. Agriculture is more important in the south and east, though hampered by droughts and soil erosion. Grains, sunflowers, sugar beet, potatoes, and fruits are grown in the better-watered west; the rearing of livestock is the main activity in the arid southeast.

Forest and woodland
Arable land
Grazing
Marginal or nonproductive

Potatoes
Beef cattle
Industrial center
Oil production
Mining
Gas production
Timber
Sheep
Cereals

Europe's highest peak, Elbrus is an extinct volcano still studded with mineral springs.

ELEVATION
Feet / Meters
6562 / 2000
4921 / 1500
3281 / 1000
2461 / 750
1640 / 500
1312 / 400
984 / 300
656 / 200
328 / 100
0 / 0
Below sea level
656 / 200
1640 / 500
6562 / 2000
13,123 / 4000
19,685 / 6000
26,246 / 8000
32,808 / 10,000

SCALE 1:6,043,956
Lamberts Conformal Conic Projection
0 — 150 miles
0 — 150 kilometers

TURKEY, CYPRUS, AND
TRANSCAUCASIA
Armenia, Azerbaijan, Cyprus, Georgia, Turkey

Projecting westward from the Middle East, Turkey forms a land bridge between Europe and Asia. Divided by the Bosporus, it straddles the two continents, its small region of Eastern Thrace lying within Europe and the remainder of the country, Anatolia, forming Asia's westernmost edge. An arid plateau covers much of Anatolia's interior, giving way in the east to a series of ranges that extends into Transcaucasia. Here, the towering Caucasus form another natural boundary between Asia and Europe. Three nations occupy Transcaucasia: Armenia, Azerbaijan, and Georgia. All became Soviet republics in the 20th century before attaining independence in 1991. Turkey was the heart of the Ottoman Empire, which endured from the 12th century to the early 20th century, and from 1573 to 1878 included the mainly Greek island of Cyprus.

THE CAUCASUS

The Caucasus and the associated Lesser Caucasus mountains isolate and define the region known as Transcaucasia. The much higher Caucasus peaks form a great wall that runs from the Black Sea to the shores of the Caspian Sea and reaches Europe's highest point of 18,510 feet (5,642 m) at Elbrus in Russia. The Lesser Caucasus spread to the south across Armenia, merging with the ranges of eastern Turkey. In-between are lowlands and major river valleys, including the Kür–Aras lowlands of Azerbaijan, parts of which lie below sea level.

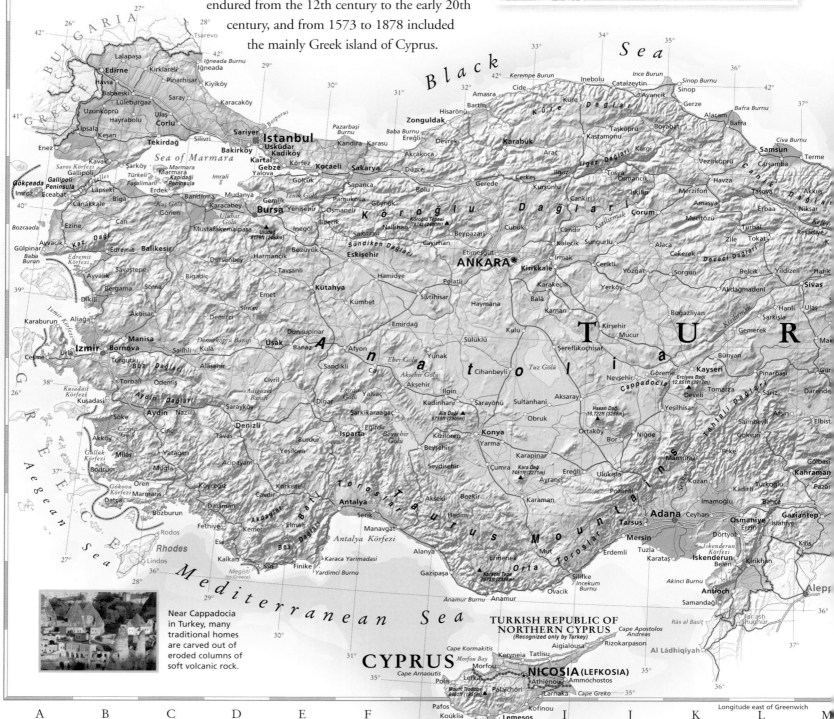

Near Cappadocia in Turkey, many traditional homes are carved out of eroded columns of soft volcanic rock.

POPULATION PATTERNS

In Turkey, the interior is less densely inhabited than the Black Sea and Aegean Sea coasts and European Turkey. Transcaucasia's inhabitants cluster on the Black Sea coast, along river valleys, and on foothills, shunning uplands and the Caspian lowlands. Cyprus is more densely populated in the south. Numerous peoples have fought over and settled in this region and ethnic diversity is high, with over 50 different groups in Transcaucasia alone. Turkey and Azerbaijan's populations are predominantly Muslim, whereas Christians are in the majority elsewhere.

Less than 2.6 persons per sq mile/1 per sq km
2.6–26 per sq mile/1–10 per sq km
26–65 per sq mile/10–25 per sq km
65–130 per sq mile/25–50 per sq km
130–260 per sq mile/50–100 per sq km
260–520 per sq mile/100–200 per sq km
520–1040 per sq mile/200–400 per sq km

ECONOMIC PROFILE

Metallic minerals, including chromium, manganese, mercury, and copper, are fairly widely distributed; the word Cyprus means "copper" in Greek and the island has long been renowned as a source of this metal. Oil reserves located in the Caspian Sea provide Azerbaijan with energy and valuable export revenue; the nation is also a major supplier of caviar. Traditional agriculture predominates in many areas, though industries and services have expanded rapidly in recent years, especially in Turkey. The production of textiles is important, along with metals, machinery, automobiles, food products, and some electronic goods in Transcaucausia.

Citrus fruits
Wine
Cotton
Tobacco
Sugar beet
Fishing
Industrial center
Oil production

Forest and woodland
Arable land
Grazing

Istanbul Turkey's largest urban, commercial, and industrial center occupies a strategic position on the Bosporus. This narrow waterway divides the city into European and Asian sectors, with the former being home to more than three-quarters of the population and most businesses. Founded as a Greek colony called Byzantium in the eighth century BC, the city became the capital of the Roman Empire in AD 330 and was renamed Constantinople. It remained the capital of the Byzantine (eastern Roman) Empire until it fell to the Ottoman Turks in 1453, under whom it became known as Istanbul. Constructed in AD 532–537 by the Emperor Justinian, the church of Hagia Sophia is the city's most remarkable Byzantine building and still its largest monument.

A Turkish invasion of Cyprus in 1974 led to the creation of Turkish and Greek sectors divided by a UN buffer zone.

Azerbaijan's oil is not as much in demand as it once was. Around 1900, Baku provided half the world's supplies.

ELEVATION

Feet	Meters
6562	2000
4921	1500
3281	1000
2461	750
1640	500
1312	400
984	300
656	200
328	100
0	0
Below sea level	
0	0
656	200
3281	1000
6562	2000
13,123	4000
19,685	6000
26,246	8000
32,808	10,000

SCALE 1:4,670,330
Lamberts Conformal Conic Projection
120 miles
120 kilometers

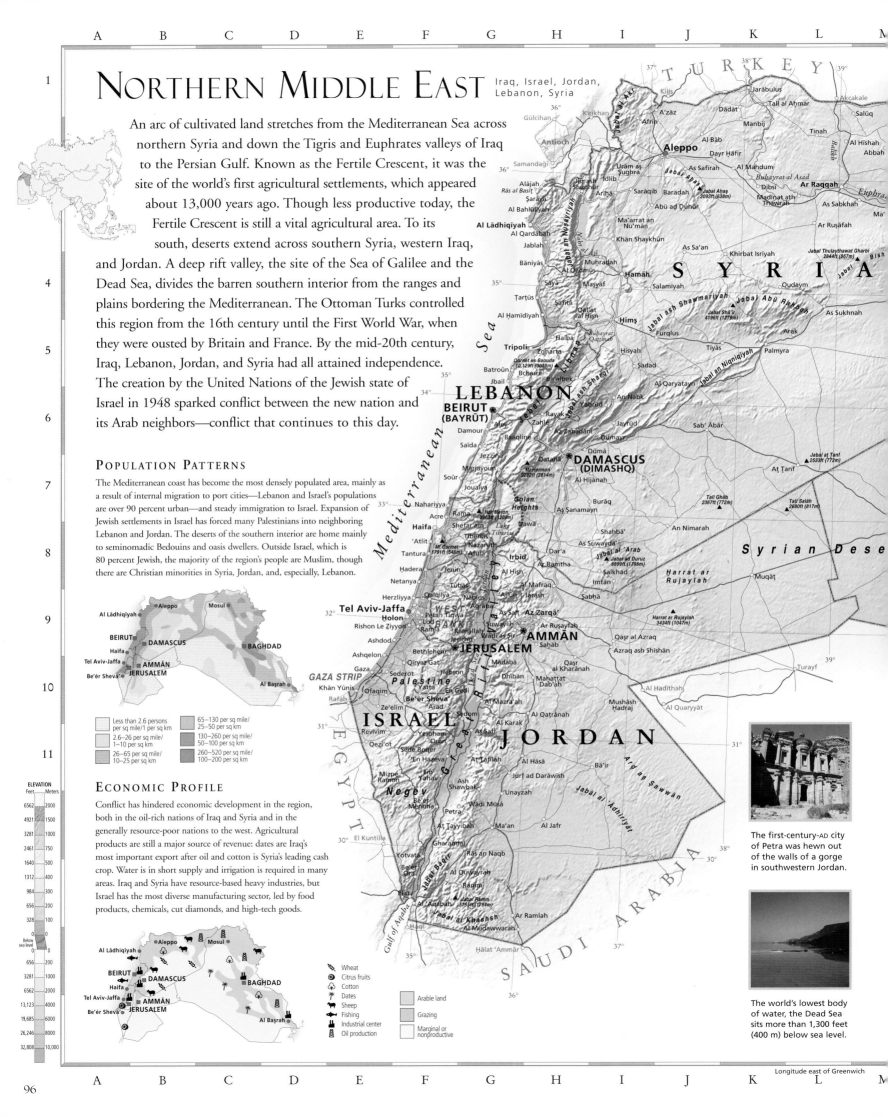

NORTHERN MIDDLE EAST
Iraq, Israel, Jordan, Lebanon, Syria

An arc of cultivated land stretches from the Mediterranean Sea across northern Syria and down the Tigris and Euphrates valleys of Iraq to the Persian Gulf. Known as the Fertile Crescent, it was the site of the world's first agricultural settlements, which appeared about 13,000 years ago. Though less productive today, the Fertile Crescent is still a vital agricultural area. To its south, deserts extend across southern Syria, western Iraq, and Jordan. A deep rift valley, the site of the Sea of Galilee and the Dead Sea, divides the barren southern interior from the ranges and plains bordering the Mediterranean. The Ottoman Turks controlled this region from the 16th century until the First World War, when they were ousted by Britain and France. By the mid-20th century, Iraq, Lebanon, Jordan, and Syria had all attained independence. The creation by the United Nations of the Jewish state of Israel in 1948 sparked conflict between the new nation and its Arab neighbors—conflict that continues to this day.

POPULATION PATTERNS

The Mediterranean coast has become the most densely populated area, mainly as a result of internal migration to port cities—Lebanon and Israel's populations are over 90 percent urban—and steady immigration to Israel. Expansion of Jewish settlements in Israel has forced many Palestinians into neighboring Lebanon and Jordan. The deserts of the southern interior are home mainly to seminomadic Bedouins and oasis dwellers. Outside Israel, which is 80 percent Jewish, the majority of the region's people are Muslim, though there are Christian minorities in Syria, Jordan, and, especially, Lebanon.

Less than 2.6 persons per sq mile/1 per sq km
2.6–26 per sq mile/ 1–10 per sq km
26–65 per sq mile/ 10–25 per sq km
65–130 per sq mile/ 25–50 per sq km
130–260 per sq mile/ 50–100 per sq km
260–520 per sq mile/ 100–200 per sq km

ECONOMIC PROFILE

Conflict has hindered economic development in the region, both in the oil-rich nations of Iraq and Syria and in the generally resource-poor nations to the west. Agricultural products are still a major source of revenue: dates are Iraq's most important export after oil and cotton is Syria's leading cash crop. Water is in short supply and irrigation is required in many areas. Iraq and Syria have resource-based heavy industries, but Israel has the most diverse manufacturing sector, led by food products, chemicals, cut diamonds, and high-tech goods.

Wheat
Citrus fruits
Cotton
Dates
Sheep
Fishing
Industrial center
Oil production

Arable land
Grazing
Marginal or nonproductive

ELEVATION

Feet	Meters
6562	2000
4921	1500
3281	1000
2461	750
1640	500
1312	400
984	300
656	200
328	100
0 Below sea level	0
656	200
3281	1000
6562	2000
13,123	4000
19,685	6000
26,246	8000
32,808	10,000

The first-century-AD city of Petra was hewn out of the walls of a gorge in southwestern Jordan.

The world's lowest body of water, the Dead Sea sits more than 1,300 feet (400 m) below sea level.

Longitude east of Greenwich

N O P 41° P 42° 43° Q 44° R S T U V W X Y Z

1

TURKEY

Cizre

Nusaybin

Al Qāmishlī
Jāghir Bāzār
Ra's al 'Ayn
aş Şafiḥ
Tall Baydar
Tall Tamir
ʿAbd al 'Azīz
(920m)
Kubaybāt
Al Hasakah
Al Hawl
Ghūnā
Ash Shaddādah
Fedghāmī
Abū Ḥardān
As Sayyāl
Abū Kamāl
Anka
Mayādīn
Al 'Ashārah
Ubaylah
Ar Ruţbah
Akāshat

Ḑayr az Zawr
Al Buşayrah

Zakho
Amādīyah
Dahūk
Summēl
Sinjār
Jabal Sinjār
Wardīyah
Al Ba'aj
Al Bādī

Kurdistan

Birkīm
Rānya
Qalā Diza
Koi Sanjaq
Rawāndiz
Salahuddin
Qosh Tepe
Sūrdash
Taqtaq
Altin Köprü

Zēbār
'Aqrah
Kūh-e Hajī Ebrāhīm
11,811ft (3600m)

Arbīl

Chamchamal
Arbat
Halabja
Sadd Darband-i Khān
Penwin

As Sulaymānīyah

Kirkūk
Tāza Khurmātū
Dāqūq
Qādir Karam

Amādīyah
Al Amādīyah

Tall Küjik
Tall 'Uwaynāt
Tall Huqnah
Tall Kayf
Tall 'Afar

Mosul
Ḥammām al 'Alīl

Qayyārah
Makhmūr
Ash Sharqāţ

Al Ḥadr
Guwēr

Little Zab

Great Zab

Tigris

46°

37°
37°
45°
36°
35°

2

3

4

A l   J a z ī r a h
Aş Şuwār
Rāwah
'Ānah
Al Qā'im
Fuhaymī
Euphrates

Jabal Hamrīn

Wadi ath Tharthār

Al Fatḥah
Bayjī
Tikrīt
Ad Dawr
Sāmarrā'
Balad

Tūz Khurmātū
Sulaymān Beg
Kifrī
Kalār
Qara Tepe
Jalawlā
Khānaqīn

Umm al Tūz
Malḥāt

Qaşr-e Shirin

Īlām

I R A Q

5

6

7

8

9

10

Buḥayrat
ath Tharthār
Tharthar
Saniyah
Hīt
Kubaysah
Muḥaywir

Khān al Baghdādī
Abū al Jīr

Ar Ramādī
Al Habbānīyah
Hawr
al Habbānīyah
Al Fallūjah
Al Mahmūdīyah

Kādhimain
**BAGHDAD
(BAGHDĀD)**
Ḥusayn al Ghafūs
Salmān Pāk
Sarābādī
As Suwayrah

Ad Dujayl
Al Khāliş
Ba'qūbah
Diltāwa
Al Muqdādīyah
Mandalī
Balad Rūz

Imām Hamid
Badrah
Mehrān

Tursāq
Shandrūkh

I R A N

33°
34°

Ar Rahhālīyah
Buḥayrat
ar Raẓāzah
Saddat al
Hindīyah
Khan
al Maḥāwīl
Karbalā'
Al Hindīyah
Al Hillah
Bi'r Sābil
Al Hāshimīyah
Khān al Muşallá
Ishaq
Aţ Ţaqţaqānah
Al Kūfah
Khān
Jadwal
An Najaf
Abū Shukhayr

An Nu'mānīyah
'Alī
Hājī Muḥsin
An Nu'mānīyah
Arab
Abdullah
Al Kūt
Ad Daghgharah
'Afak
Al Muwaffaqīyah
Al Ḥayy
Tarād al Kahf
Ad Dīwānīyah
Taḥrīr
Fajir
Qal'at Sukkār
Ar Rifā'ī
Telloh
An Naşr

Jaşşān
Bagsaya
Mūlat
al Mashkhūr
Shaykh Sa'd
'Alī al Gharbī
Shaykh Jūwī
Marhaj Kahlīl
Al Kumayt
Musallam
Somaydeh
Al Halfāyah
Al 'Amārah

Hawr
as Sa'dīyah

Tigris

47°
48°
32°

An Nukhayb

Imām al
Hamzah
Khān ar
Rahbah
Al Ghammās
Ash
Shanāfīyah
Ar Rumaythah
As Samāwah
Al Khidr

Euphrates

An Nāşirīyah
Aradah
Kharfīyah
**Sūq ash
Shuyūkh**
Tall al Laḥm
Jalībah
Al Qusayr

Qal'at Şālih
Al 'Uzayr
Ash Shaţrah
Al Qurnah

Hawr
al Hammār

Al Muzayri'ah
Ad Dayr

31°

Judaidat
al Hamir
Al Ma'ānīyah
Ash Shabakah

As Salmān
Qal'at Abū Ghar
Al Buşayyah

Raudhatain

Al Ma'qil
Shu'aiba
Az Zubayr
Rumaila
Safwān
Umm Qaşr

Al Başrah
Khorramshahr
Abādān
Shaţţ al Arab
Sūsangerd

30°

11

13

14

S a h r ā'   a l   Ḥ i j ā r a
Zahrat al Batn
Nişāb
Ash Shu'bah

Ash Shāmīyah
Wādī al Bāţin
Al Ḥaniyah

K U W A I T

**KUWAIT
(AL KUWAYT)**

Bubiyān
Island

Al Fāw
**Persian
Gulf**

30°

48°

S A U D I   A R A B I A

29°
45°
46°
47°

Jerusalem

Situated in a river valley linking the
Mediterranean coast and the Dead Sea, the
ancient city of Jerusalem is a place of pilgrimage
for the adherents of three major faiths: Judaism,
Christianity, and Islam. The Old City's many shrines
reflect this diversity of beliefs, most notably around the Dome
of the Rock. The oldest remaining Islamic temple and said to be
the scene of Muhammad's ascension to heaven, it backs onto the
Western Wall, the remains of a temple that constitute the most sacred
site of Judaism. Nearby is the Church of the Holy Sepulchre, where
Jesus is said to have been entombed before rising again.

Dome of the Rock

SCALE 1:3,571,429
Lamberts Conformal Conic Projection
0   100 miles
0   100 kilometers

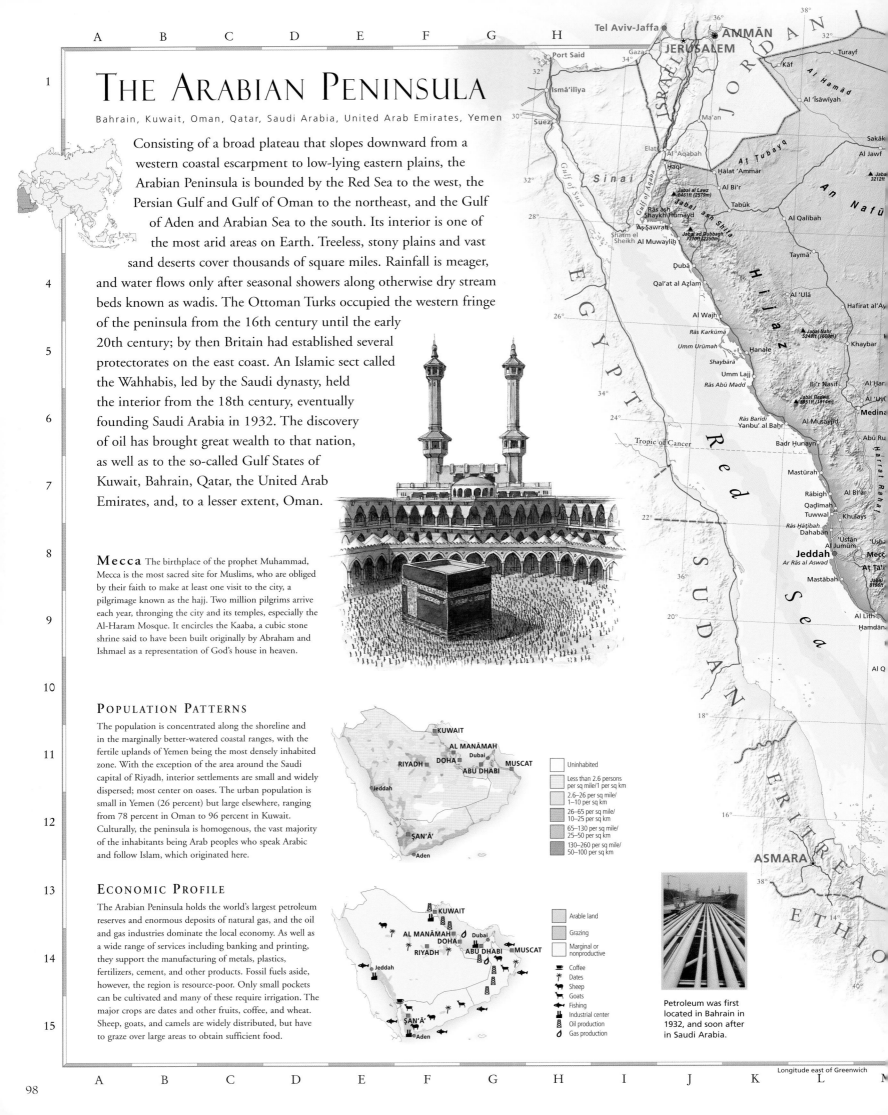

THE ARABIAN PENINSULA

Bahrain, Kuwait, Oman, Qatar, Saudi Arabia, United Arab Emirates, Yemen

Consisting of a broad plateau that slopes downward from a western coastal escarpment to low-lying eastern plains, the Arabian Peninsula is bounded by the Red Sea to the west, the Persian Gulf and Gulf of Oman to the northeast, and the Gulf of Aden and Arabian Sea to the south. Its interior is one of the most arid areas on Earth. Treeless, stony plains and vast sand deserts cover thousands of square miles. Rainfall is meager, and water flows only after seasonal showers along otherwise dry stream beds known as wadis. The Ottoman Turks occupied the western fringe of the peninsula from the 16th century until the early 20th century; by then Britain had established several protectorates on the east coast. An Islamic sect called the Wahhabis, led by the Saudi dynasty, held the interior from the 18th century, eventually founding Saudi Arabia in 1932. The discovery of oil has brought great wealth to that nation, as well as to the so-called Gulf States of Kuwait, Bahrain, Qatar, the United Arab Emirates, and, to a lesser extent, Oman.

Mecca The birthplace of the prophet Muhammad, Mecca is the most sacred site for Muslims, who are obliged by their faith to make at least one visit to the city, a pilgrimage known as the hajj. Two million pilgrims arrive each year, thronging the city and its temples, especially the Al-Haram Mosque. It encircles the Kaaba, a cubic stone shrine said to have been built originally by Abraham and Ishmael as a representation of God's house in heaven.

POPULATION PATTERNS

The population is concentrated along the shoreline and in the marginally better-watered coastal ranges, with the fertile uplands of Yemen being the most densely inhabited zone. With the exception of the area around the Saudi capital of Riyadh, interior settlements are small and widely dispersed; most center on oases. The urban population is small in Yemen (26 percent) but large elsewhere, ranging from 78 percent in Oman to 96 percent in Kuwait. Culturally, the peninsula is homogenous, the vast majority of the inhabitants being Arab peoples who speak Arabic and follow Islam, which originated here.

	Uninhabited
	Less than 2.6 persons per sq mile/1 per sq km
	2.6–26 per sq mile/ 1–10 per sq km
	26–65 per sq mile/ 10–25 per sq km
	65–130 per sq mile/ 25–50 per sq km
	130–260 per sq mile/ 50–100 per sq km

ECONOMIC PROFILE

The Arabian Peninsula holds the world's largest petroleum reserves and enormous deposits of natural gas, and the oil and gas industries dominate the local economy. As well as a wide range of services including banking and printing, they support the manufacturing of metals, plastics, fertilizers, cement, and other products. Fossil fuels aside, however, the region is resource-poor. Only small pockets can be cultivated and many of these require irrigation. The major crops are dates and other fruits, coffee, and wheat. Sheep, goats, and camels are widely distributed, but have to graze over large areas to obtain sufficient food.

	Arable land
	Grazing
	Marginal or nonproductive
	Coffee
	Dates
	Sheep
	Goats
	Fishing
	Industrial center
	Oil production
	Gas production

Petroleum was first located in Bahrain in 1932, and soon after in Saudi Arabia.

Longitude east of Greenwich

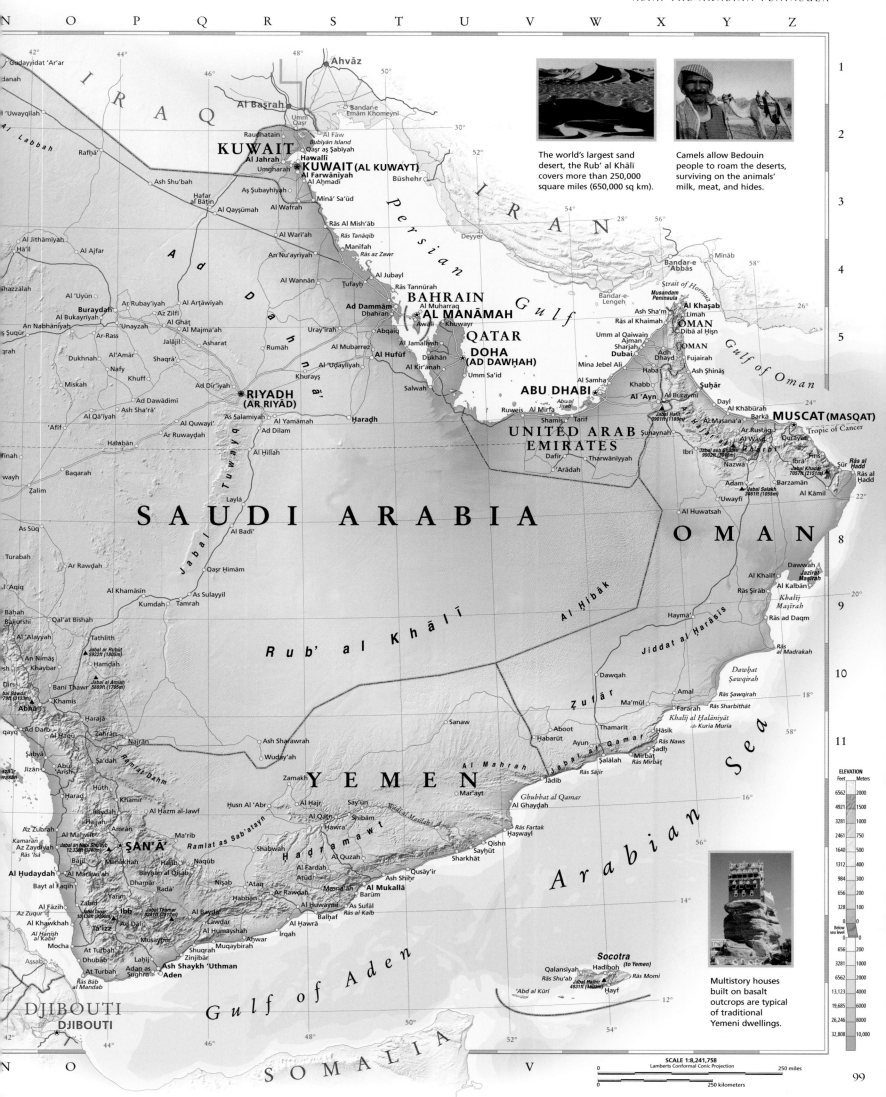

The world's largest sand desert, the Rub' al Khālī covers more than 250,000 square miles (650,000 sq km).

Camels allow Bedouin people to roam the deserts, surviving on the animals' milk, meat, and hides.

Multistory houses built on basalt outcrops are typical of traditional Yemeni dwellings.

ELEVATION

Feet	Meters
6562	2000
4921	1500
3281	1000
2461	750
1640	500
1312	400
984	300
656	200
328	100
0	0
Below sea level	Below sea level
656	200
3281	1000
6562	2000
13,123	4000
19,685	6000
26,246	8000
32,808	10,000

SCALE 1:8,241,758
Lamberts Conformal Conic Projection

0   250 miles

0   250 kilometers

AFGHANISTAN, IRAN, AND PAKISTAN

A high, mainly barren plateau dominates the western half of this region, occupying most of Iran and extending into Afghanistan and Pakistan. It is bounded in the northwest by the forested Elburz Mountains and in the west by the Zagros Mountains. In northeastern Afghanistan, it rises to the lofty summits of the Hindu Kush and the Karakorams, offshoots of the Himalaya; in Pakistan, its crumpled eastern fringe abuts the broad, low valley of the Indus River. More than 97 percent of the inhabitants of this rugged and mostly arid land are Muslims, and their religion has profoundly influenced the region's history. Pakistan was founded in 1947 as a home for India's Muslims; Iran has been ruled by Islamic clerics since a revolution in 1979; and in the late 1990s Afghanistan was run by the Taliban, a fundamentalist Islamic regime that was toppled by a U.S.-led invasion in 2001.

At 28,251 feet (8,611m), K2, in the Karakoram range, is the world's second-highest peak.

Thriving around 2500 BC, Mohenjo Daro, near Sukkur, Pakistan, was one of Indus Valley's first cities.

Iran's Dasht-e Kavir is characterized by vast stony plains and low-lying salt pans (*kavirs*).

Iranian carpets, most of which are still woven by hand, are much in demand overseas.

THE KHYBER PASS

One of just a few passes permitting travel between Central Asia and the Indian Subcontinent, the Khyber Pass has long been of strategic importance to locals and foreign powers, from the Persians, who used it to reach the Indus in the fifth century BC, to the British, who made it the focus of local operations in the late 19th century. Consisting of a narrow opening in the Safed Koh Range, the pass reaches its highest point of 3,543 feet (1,080 m) at Landi Kotal. Its road and rail links facilitate travel between Kabul in Afghanistan and Peshawar in Pakistan.

Longitude east of Greenwich

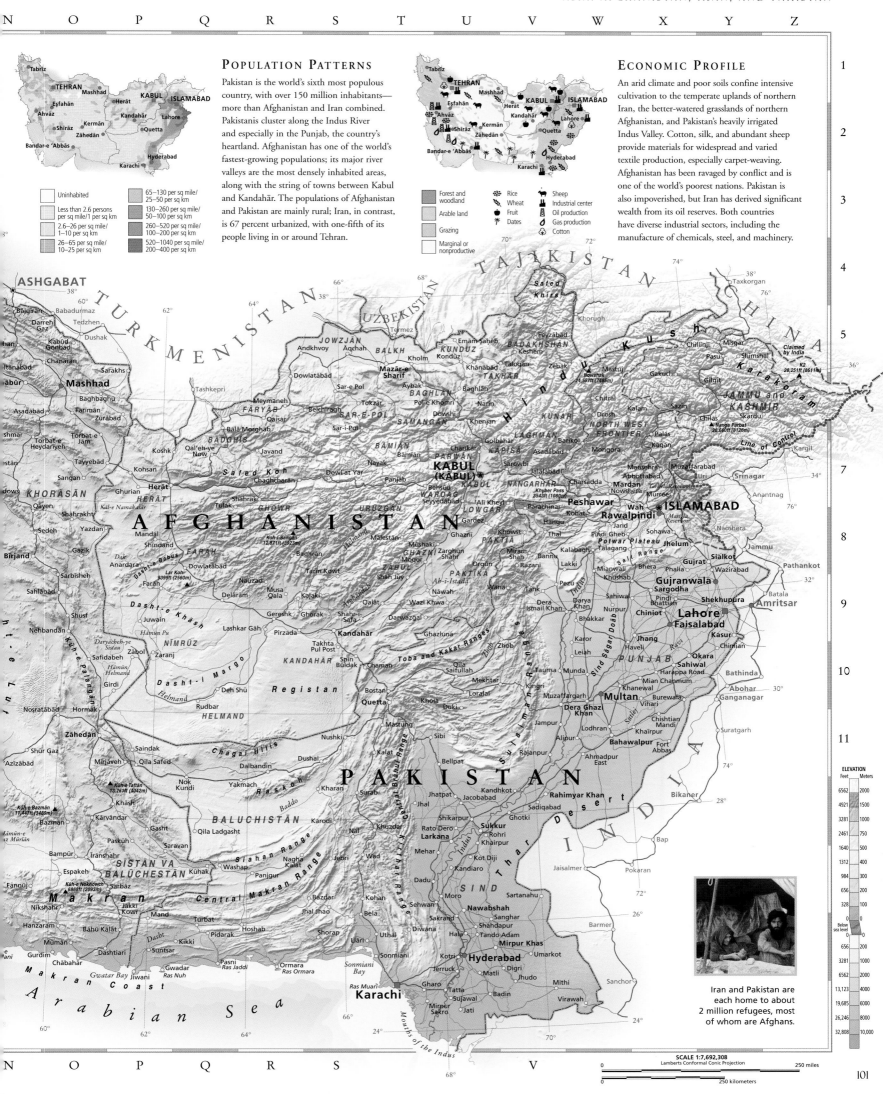

POPULATION PATTERNS

Pakistan is the world's sixth most populous country, with over 150 million inhabitants—more than Afghanistan and Iran combined. Pakistanis cluster along the Indus River and especially in the Punjab, the country's heartland. Afghanistan has one of the world's fastest-growing populations; its major river valleys are the most densely inhabited areas, along with the string of towns between Kabul and Kandahar. The populations of Afghanistan and Pakistan are mainly rural; Iran, in contrast, is 67 percent urbanized, with one-fifth of its people living in or around Tehran.

- Uninhabited
- Less than 2.6 persons per sq mile/1 per sq km
- 2.6–26 per sq mile/1–10 per sq km
- 26–65 per sq mile/10–25 per sq km
- 65–130 per sq mile/25–50 per sq km
- 130–260 per sq mile/50–100 per sq km
- 260–520 per sq mile/100–200 per sq km
- 520–1040 per sq mile/200–400 per sq km

ECONOMIC PROFILE

An arid climate and poor soils confine intensive cultivation to the temperate uplands of northern Iran, the better-watered grasslands of northern Afghanistan, and Pakistan's heavily irrigated Indus Valley. Cotton, silk, and abundant sheep provide materials for widespread and varied textile production, especially carpet-weaving. Afghanistan has been ravaged by conflict and is one of the world's poorest nations. Pakistan is also impoverished, but Iran has derived significant wealth from its oil reserves. Both countries have diverse industrial sectors, including the manufacture of chemicals, steel, and machinery.

- Forest and woodland
- Arable land
- Grazing
- Marginal or nonproductive
- Rice
- Wheat
- Fruit
- Dates
- Sheep
- Industrial center
- Oil production
- Gas production
- Cotton

Iran and Pakistan are each home to about 2 million refugees, most of whom are Afghans.

ELEVATION

Feet	Meters
6562	2000
4921	1500
3281	1000
2461	750
1640	500
1312	400
984	300
656	200
328	100
Below sea level	
656	200
3281	1000
6562	2000
13,123	4000
19,685	6000
26,246	8000
32,808	10,000

SCALE 1:7,692,308
Lamberts Conformal Conic Projection

0 _____ 250 miles
0 _____ 250 kilometers

CENTRAL ASIA
Kazakhstan, Kyrgyzstan, Tajikistan, Turkmenistan, Uzbekistan

The peoples of Central Asia have long been linked by a shared Islamic religious and cultural heritage, traditionally pastoral and seminomadic lifestyles, and related, mainly Turkic languages. During the 19th century, they were brought even closer together when their lands were annexed by the Russian Empire. Subsequent Soviet control transformed an undeveloped region, rapidly industrializing farming, manufacturing, and mining, turning several villages into cities, and creating separate republics for each of the major ethnic groups—the Uzbeks, Kazaks, Tajiks, Turkmens, and Kyrgyz. After the fall of communism in 1991, all five republics became independent states. These nations occupy a wide, mainly arid and low-lying region. The grasslands of the Kazakh Steppe stretch across its northern third, spreading into Russia. South of the Aral Sea, deserts cover the Turan Lowland. In the east, a series of ranges climbs toward the Pamir and Tien Shan ranges, whose soaring peaks divide Central Asia from China.

Cotton is Turkmenistan's principal crop. Production centers on irrigated areas along the Amudar'ya River.

Russia's spacecraft-launching center is near Baykonur in Kazakhstan.

POPULATION PATTERNS

The scarcity of fresh water has restricted dense settlement to upland areas and the banks of major rivers, leaving the deserts and grasslands sparsely inhabited. During the Soviet era, Central Asia's population grew rapidly, due partly to an influx of Russians and Ukrainians and partly to improvements in medical services. Despite this, Central Asian society remains predominantly rural; indeed, with the departure of many Russians after the demise of the Soviet Union, the continuing focus on cotton production, and high birth rates in country areas, rural populations have grown recently, against the prevailing world trend.

Less than 2.6 persons per sq mile/1 per sq km
2.6–26 per sq mile/1–10 per sq km
26–65 per sq mile/10–25 per sq km
65–130 per sq mile/25–50 per sq km
130–260 per sq mile/50–100 per sq km
260–520 per sq mile/100–200 per sq km
520–1040 per sq mile/200–400 per sq km

ECONOMIC PROFILE

Central Asia's mineral reserves include oil and gas deposits near the Caspian Sea and supplies of coal, iron ore, and chromium in Kazakhstan; these support a variety of heavy industries. Three-fifths of the land is desert, and large areas are used for grazing. Crops can be grown only in fertile upland pockets and irrigated areas. Soviet emphasis on the production of coal and oil in Kazakhstan and cotton elsewhere not only created severe environmental problems, but left these nations dependent on just a few commodities. Recent expansion of the gas industry (Turkmenistan has the world's fifth-largest reserves) is part of an attempt to diversify produce and alleviate widespread poverty.

Cereals
Cotton
Beef cattle
Sheep
Fishing
Industrial center
Mining
Oil production
Gas production
Fruit and vegetables

Forest and woodland
Arable land
Grazing
Marginal or nonproductive

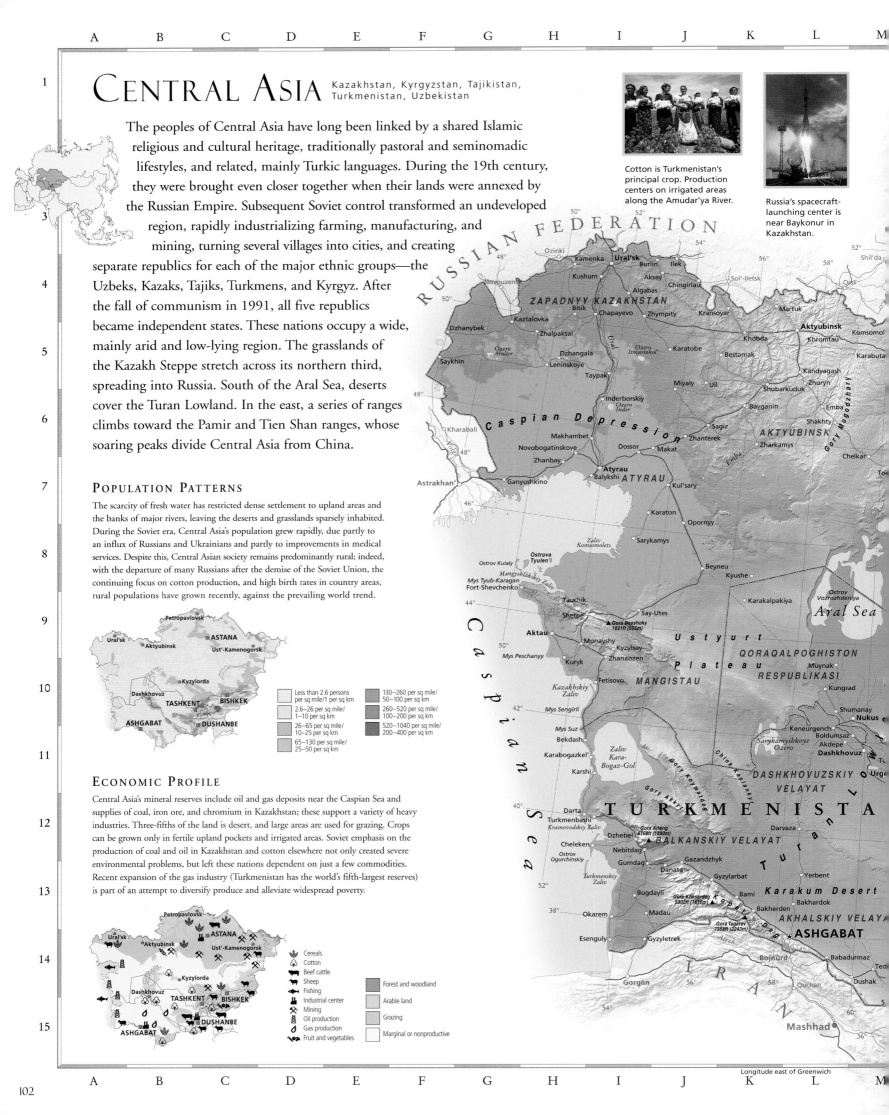

Longitude east of Greenwich

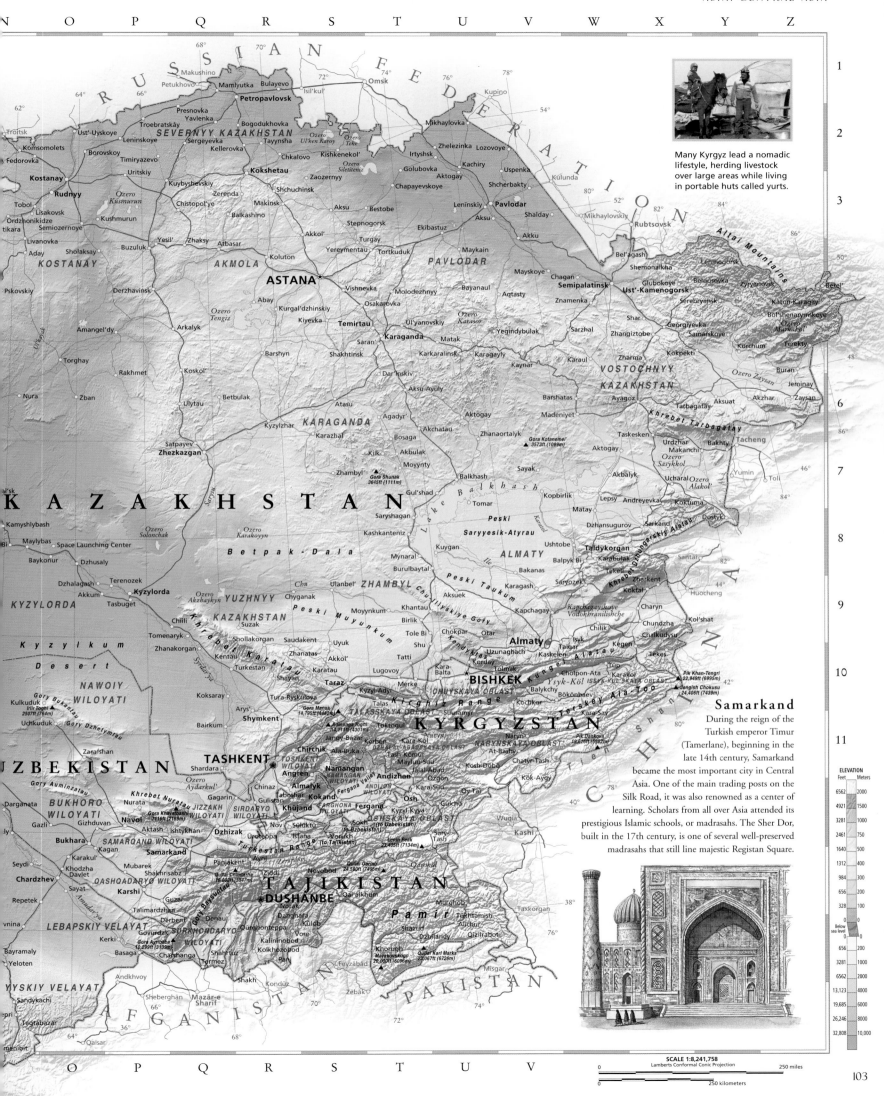

Many Kyrgyz lead a nomadic lifestyle, herding livestock over large areas while living in portable huts called yurts.

Samarkand

During the reign of the Turkish emperor Timur (Tamerlane), beginning in the late 14th century, Samarkand became the most important city in Central Asia. One of the main trading posts on the Silk Road, it was also renowned as a center of learning. Scholars from all over Asia attended its prestigious Islamic schools, or madrasahs. The Sher Dor, built in the 17th century, is one of several well-preserved madrasahs that still line majestic Registan Square.

SCALE 1:8,241,758
Lamberts Conformal Conic Projection

SOUTHERN ASIA

Bangladesh, Bhutan, India, Maldives, Nepal, Sri Lanka

Sometimes referred to as the Subcontinent, this region is dominated by India, the world's seventh-largest and second-most populous country. It also includes the Himalayan kingdoms of Nepal and Bhutan, low-lying Bangladesh, and the island nations of Sri Lanka and the Maldives. From their dizzy heights, the mountains of the Himalaya drop steeply to the wide, low plain of the Ganges River. West of the Gangetic Plain, the Thar Desert spreads into Pakistan; to the south, the triangular Deccan Plateau occupies most of central and southern India. In the early 16th century, much of Southern Asia was united by the Muslim Mughal dynasty, which ruled until it was undermined by the rise of the Hindu Marathas in the 18th century. Britain controlled most of the region from the early 19th century until 1948; before withdrawing, it created the states of West Pakistan and East Pakistan, which later became Pakistan and Bangladesh, and granted independence to Ceylon, now Sri Lanka.

POPULATION PATTERNS

More than one-sixth of the world's population lives in this region. India alone has more than 1 billion inhabitants and, given its growth rate—48,000 babies are born there every day—could surpass China as the world's most populous nation by 2050. High population densities occur on the Gangetic Plain and in the northeast—Bangladesh is one of the world's most densely populated countries—but only one-quarter of people live in cities. Most Indians and Nepalis are Hindu, whereas the majority of Bangladeshis are Muslim; Bhutan and Sri Lanka are predominantly Buddhist. Indigenous languages are many and varied, and English functions as a lingua franca.

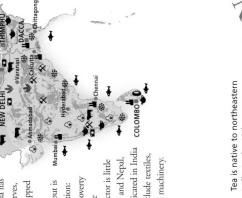

ECONOMIC PROFILE

The region's enormous population places great strain on its resources, which include large tracts of arable land (including 50 percent of India), forests, and minerals—India has the world's fourth-largest coal reserves, and oil and gas fields that have been tapped in many areas. Most people are dependent on agriculture, yet output is insufficient to support the population: half of all Nepalis live below the poverty line and one-quarter of Indians are undernourished. The industrial sector is little developed in Bhutan, Bangladesh, and Nepal, but becoming increasingly sophisticated in India and Sri Lanka, where products include textiles, chemicals, computer software, and machinery.

Tea is native to northeastern India. In the 19th century, the British greatly expanded its commercial cultivation.

In Sri Lanka, Tamil separatists have been waging war on the government since the 1980s.

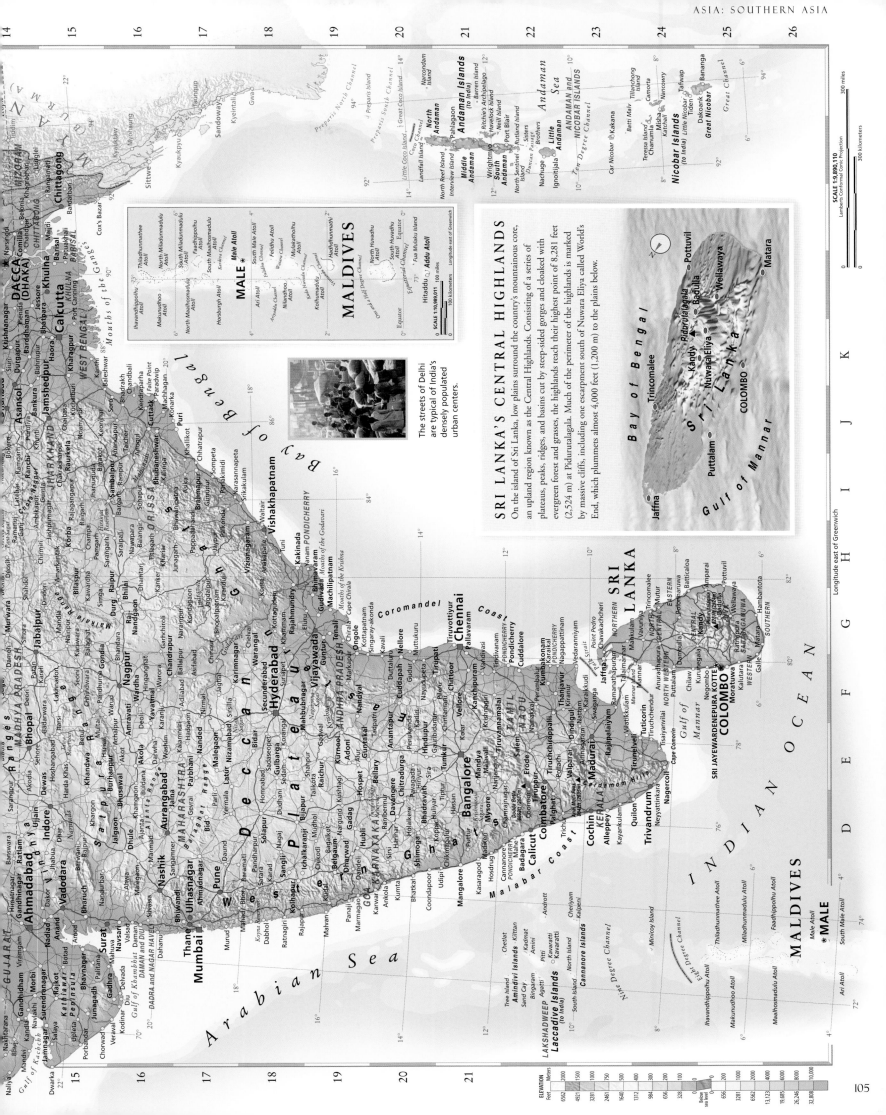

SRI LANKA'S CENTRAL HIGHLANDS

On the island of Sri Lanka, low plains surround the country's mountainous core, an upland region known as the Central Highlands. Consisting of a series of plateaus, peaks, ridges, and basins cut by steep-sided gorges and cloaked with evergreen forest and grasses, the highlands reach their highest point of 8,281 feet (2,524 m) at Pidurutalagala. Much of the perimeter of the highlands is marked by massive cliffs, including one escarpment south of Nuwara Eliya called World's End, which plummets almost 4,000 feet (1,200 m) to the plains below.

The streets of Delhi are typical of India's densely populated urban centers.

THE HIMALAYA AND THE GANGETIC PLAIN

Bangladesh, Bhutan, Nepal, Northern India

The world's tallest mountain range, the Himalaya forms a colossal barrier between the Subcontinent and Central Asia. Rising to the highest point on Earth, 29,035-foot (8,850-m) Mount Everest, it stretches for 1,550 miles (2,500 km) along the northern edge of India. Its southern flank yields abruptly to the densely populated and intensively farmed plain of the Ganges River. From its source in the western Himalaya, the Ganges flows south then east across northern India and into Bangladesh, branching repeatedly as it nears the Bay of Bengal to create one of the world's largest deltas. Cohesive states first took shape on the Gangetic Plain 3,000 years ago, and the valley was the heart of powerful Indian dynasties such as the Gupta (AD 300–550), the Mamluks (1206–1526), and the Mughals (1526–1761). Physical isolation helped preserve the autonomy of the kingdoms of Nepal, Sikkim, and Bhutan, though all were British protectorates during the 19th century, and in 1975 Sikkim acceded to India.

Up to 1,000 climbers a year now attempt an ascent of Mount Everest, which was first conquered in 1953.

Hindus view the Ganges as a holy river and visit places such as Varanasi to bathe in its waters.

The orchards of the fertile Kashmir Valley are one of India's most important sources of fruit and nuts.

POPULATION PATTERNS

This region includes the Subcontinent's least and most crowded areas. Above 16,000 feet (5,000 m), the Himalaya is virtually uninhabited. In contrast, population densities are among the world's highest in Bangladesh, which averages 2,000 people per square mile (770 per sq km); in Calcutta, where up to 100,000 people occupy each square mile of the city (40,000 per sq km); and in irrigated parts of the Gangetic Plain. The majority of people live in rural areas—Bhutan had no towns until the 1960s—and population growth rates are high. The region's peoples are a mix of Indo-European and Tibeto-Burman groups, with the latter, who include the Newar and Sherpa, generally occupying the higher land.

Uninhabited

Less than 2.6 persons per sq mile/1 per sq km

2.6–26 per sq mile/ 1–10 per sq km

26–65 per sq mile/ 10–25 per sq km

65–130 per sq mile/ 25–50 per sq km

130–260 per sq mile/ 50–100 per sq km

260–520 per sq mile/ 100–200 per sq km

520–1040 per sq mile/ 200–400 per sq km

1040–2080 per sq mile/ 400–800 per sq km

More than 2080 per sq mile/800 per sq km

ECONOMIC PROFILE

The region includes many large cities, but is little developed and its people mainly poor. On the Gangetic Plain, irrigation is used to grow wheat, cotton, and sugar. In the wetter Brahmaputra Valley and Bangladesh, tea is cultivated on the hillsides, rice on the plains. Despite its rugged terrain, the Himalaya has extensive arable land—mainly in foothills, basins, and river valleys—which produces wheat, corn, millet, and potatoes. On the upper slopes, sheep, goats, and yaks are herded between seasonal pastures. Minerals, including gold, sapphires, copper, and iron ore, are widespread, though difficult to access. The Himalaya and cities such as Agra, Delhi, and Varanasi are major tourist attractions.

Forest and woodland

Arable land

Grazing

Marginal or nonproductive

Cereals
Rice
Wheat
Fruit
Cotton
Tea
Dairy cattle
Fishing
Industrial center
Tourism

106

Longitude east of Greenwich

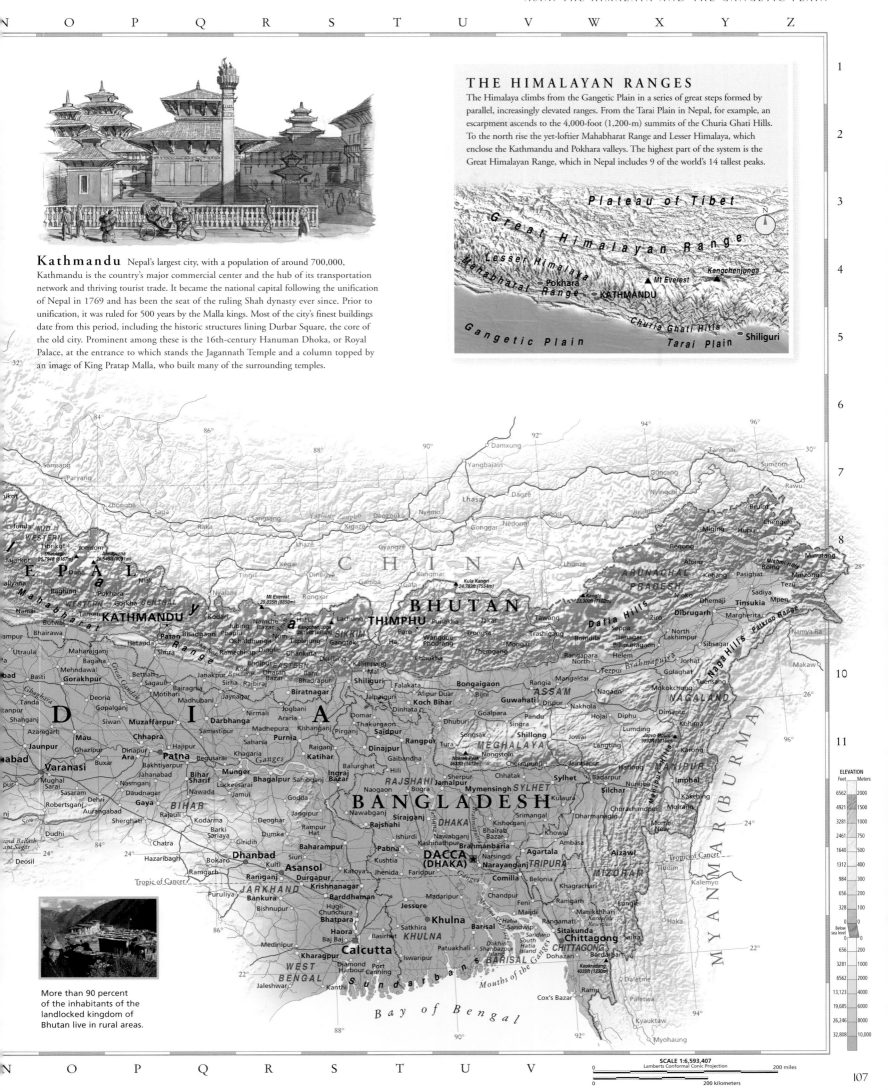

THE HIMALAYAN RANGES

The Himalaya climbs from the Gangetic Plain in a series of great steps formed by parallel, increasingly elevated ranges. From the Tarai Plain in Nepal, for example, an escarpment ascends to the 4,000-foot (1,200-m) summits of the Churia Ghati Hills. To the north rise the yet-loftier Mahabharat Range and Lesser Himalaya, which enclose the Kathmandu and Pokhara valleys. The highest part of the system is the Great Himalayan Range, which in Nepal includes 9 of the world's 14 tallest peaks.

Kathmandu Nepal's largest city, with a population of around 700,000, Kathmandu is the country's major commercial center and the hub of its transportation network and thriving tourist trade. It became the national capital following the unification of Nepal in 1769 and has been the seat of the ruling Shah dynasty ever since. Prior to unification, it was ruled for 500 years by the Malla kings. Most of the city's finest buildings date from this period, including the historic structures lining Durbar Square, the core of the old city. Prominent among these is the 16th-century Hanuman Dhoka, or Royal Palace, at the entrance to which stands the Jagannath Temple and a column topped by an image of King Pratap Malla, who built many of the surrounding temples.

More than 90 percent of the inhabitants of the landlocked kingdom of Bhutan live in rural areas.

ELEVATION

Feet	Meters
6562	2000
4921	1500
3281	1000
2461	750
1640	500
1312	400
984	300
656	200
328	100
0	0
Below sea level	
656	200
3281	1000
6562	2000
13,123	4000
19,685	6000
26,246	8000
32,808	10,000

SCALE 1:6,593,407
Lamberts Conformal Conic Projection
200 miles
200 kilometers

EASTERN ASIA
China, Mongolia, North Korea, South Korea, Taiwan

In both size and population, China dwarfs not only its neighbors, but most other countries. The world's third-largest and most populous country, it occupies 3.7 million square miles (9.6 million sq km) and is home to 1.3 billion people. From the Plateau of Tibet, which covers one-quarter of the country, major rivers, including the Yellow and the Yangtze, run eastward through the central ranges to the intensely cultivated coastal plains. Northward-flowing rivers quickly peter out in the belt of arid land that spans northern China and Mongolia. In the northeast, the forested Changbai Mountains separate China from the Korean Peninsula. Early Chinese civilizations led the world in technology, becoming the first to develop products such as paper, cast iron, silk, and gunpowder. The 20th century saw a power struggle within China between the Nationalist Party and the Communist Party. The latter won out, proclaiming the People's Republic of China in 1949, while the Nationalists repaired to Taiwan. That island's subsequent declaration of independence has yet to be recognized by China.

Cities such as Seoul have absorbed most of the rapid population growth that has occurred in South Korea.

Near Guilin in southeastern China, rice fields form a patchwork between steep, jagged limestone outcrops.

POPULATION PATTERNS

China's population increases by 10 million every year, a situation that helps explain the government's controversial policy of permitting each family to have only one child. Most Chinese live in small villages and two-thirds occupy the eastern lowlands, which constitute less than one-third of the country. The population dwindles in northern and western China—just 2 million or so inhabit the vast Plateau of Tibet—and in Mongolia. The latter is one of the world's least densely populated countries: its 2.5 million people live in an area bigger than Alaska, with an average of just four people occupying each square mile (1.6 per sq km). Tiny Taiwan has almost ten times the population of Mongolia and, like the similarly crowded Korean Peninsula, is highly urbanized.

Uninhabited	130–260 per sq mile/50–100 per sq km
Less than 2.6 persons per sq mile/1 per sq km	260–520 per sq mile/100–200 per sq km
2.6–26 per sq mile/1–10 per sq km	520–1040 per sq mile/200–400 per sq km
26–65 per sq mile/10–25 per sq km	1040–2080 per sq mile/400–800 per sq km
65–130 per sq mile/25–50 per sq km	More than 2080 per sq mile/800 per sq km

ECONOMIC PROFILE

With the world's largest workforce, abundant resources including coal, oil, iron ore, and hydroelectric power, and diverse, developed industries, China has huge economic potential. Until the late 1970s, this was held in check by strict government controls, but recent years have seen a degree of liberalization of production and trade, and consequent rises in productivity. A contrasting reluctance to relax state control has led to recession and food shortages in North Korea. South Korea and Taiwan have taken advantage of U.S. assistance to develop strong, technologically advanced industrial sectors, and both nations are now major producers of electronic goods. Though it has significant mineral reserves, including copper, coal, and oil, Mongolia is still dependent on its pastoral industry.

Forest and woodland	
Arable land	
Grazing	
Marginal or nonproductive	

- Cereals
- Rice
- Beef cattle
- Sheep
- Fishing
- Industrial center
- Oil production
- Timber

Immense dams are being built on the Three Gorges section of the Yangtze River.

About 70 percent of farming in Mongolia involves the rearing of domestic animals.

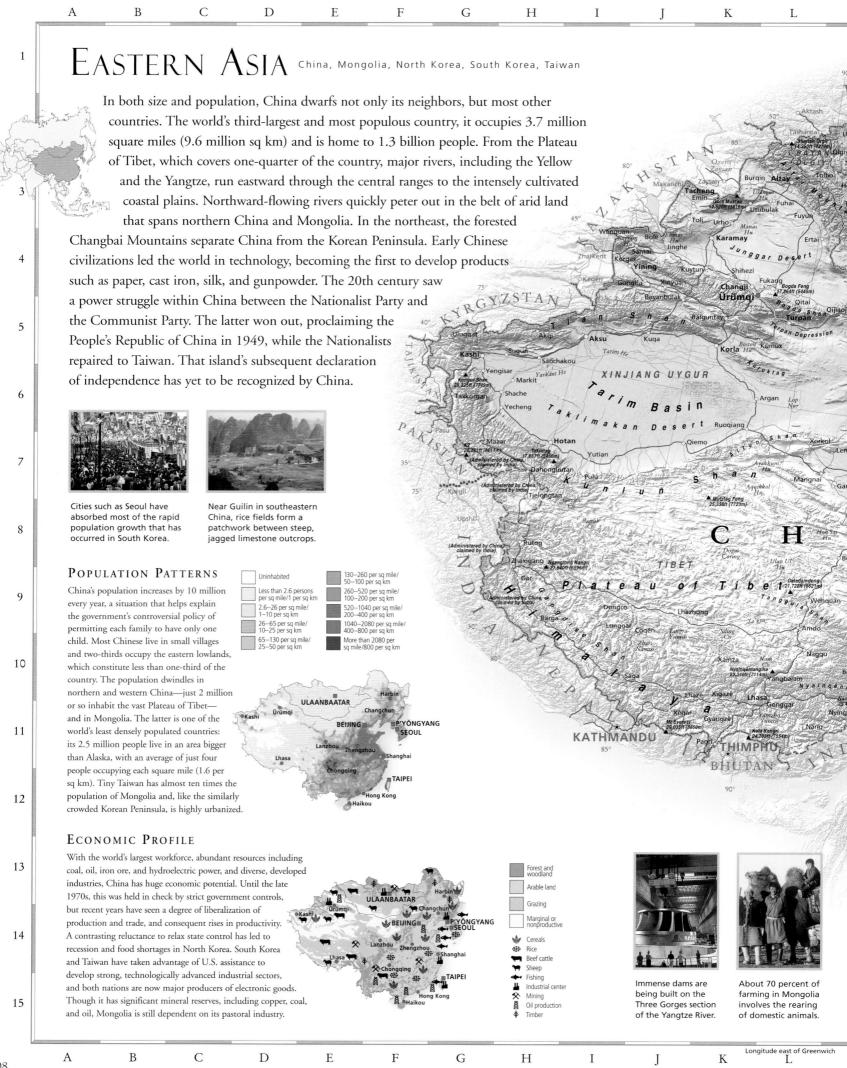

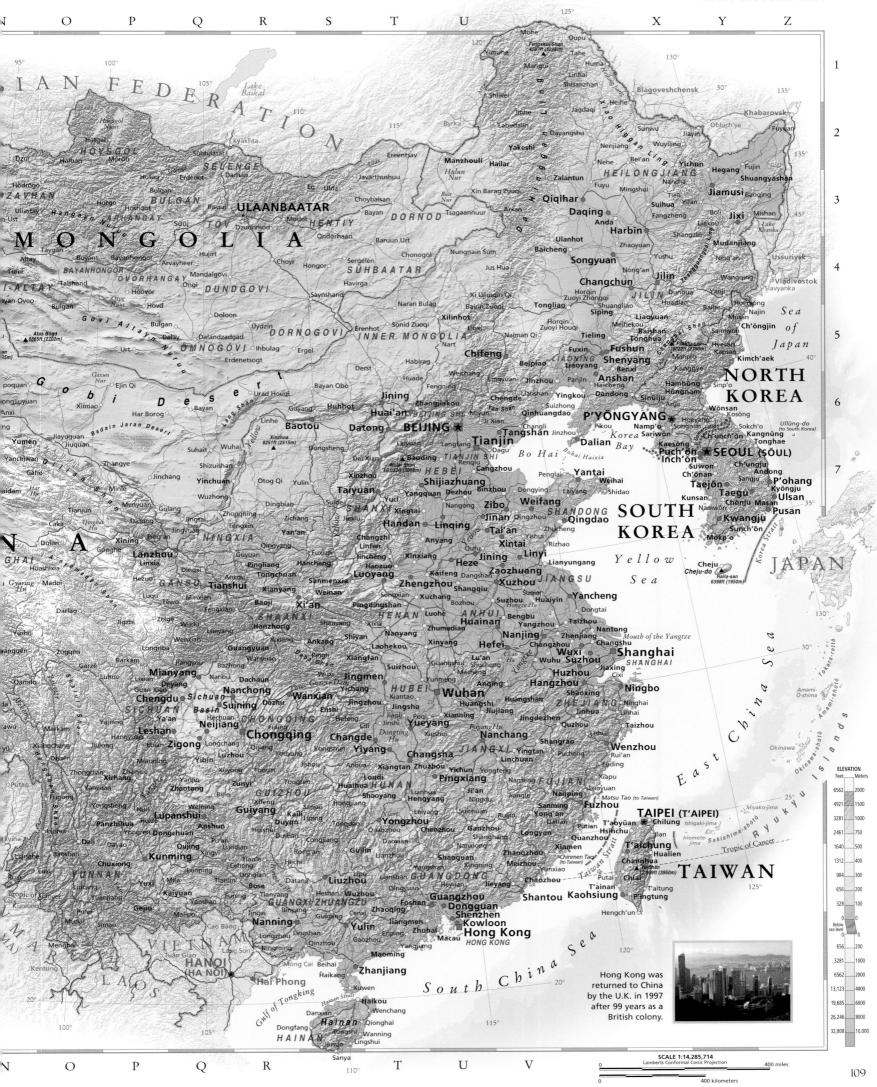

Hong Kong was returned to China by the U.K. in 1997 after 99 years as a British colony.

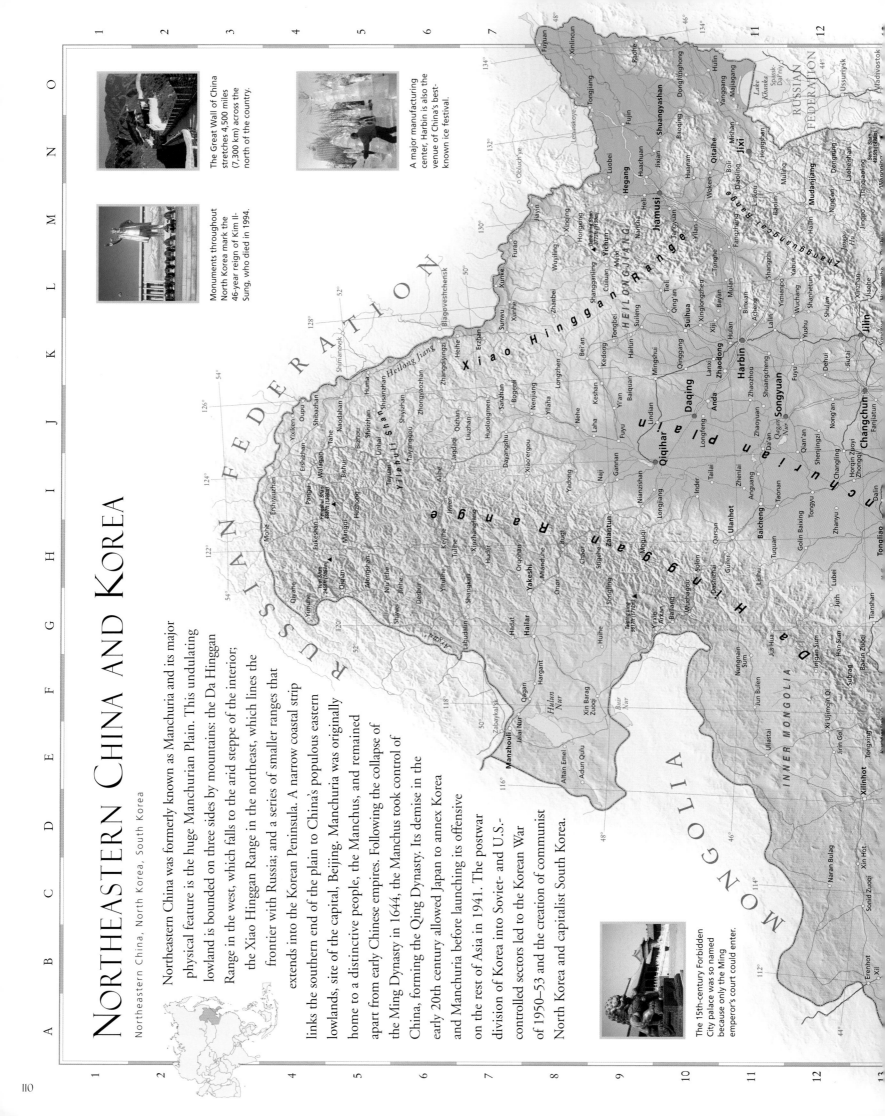

NORTHEASTERN CHINA AND KOREA

Northeastern China, North Korea, South Korea

Northeastern China was formerly known as Manchuria and its major physical feature is the huge Manchurian Plain. This undulating lowland is bounded on three sides by mountains: the Da Hinggan Range in the west, which falls to the arid steppe of the interior; the Xiao Hinggan Range in the northeast, which lines the frontier with Russia; and a series of smaller ranges that extends into the Korean Peninsula. A narrow coastal strip links the southern end of the plain to China's populous eastern lowlands, site of the capital, Beijing. Manchuria was originally home to a distinctive people, the Manchus, and remained apart from early Chinese empires. Following the collapse of the Ming Dynasty in 1644, the Manchus took control of China, forming the Qing Dynasty. Its demise in the early 20th century allowed Japan to annex Korea and Manchuria before launching its offensive on the rest of Asia in 1941. The postwar division of Korea into Soviet- and U.S.-controlled sectors led to the Korean War of 1950–53 and the creation of communist North Korea and capitalist South Korea.

The Great Wall of China stretches 4,500 miles (7,300 km) across the north of the country.

Monuments throughout North Korea mark the 46-year reign of Kim Il-Sung, who died in 1994.

A major manufacturing center, Harbin is also the venue of China's best-known ice festival.

The 15th-century Forbidden City palace was so named because only the Ming emperor's court could enter.

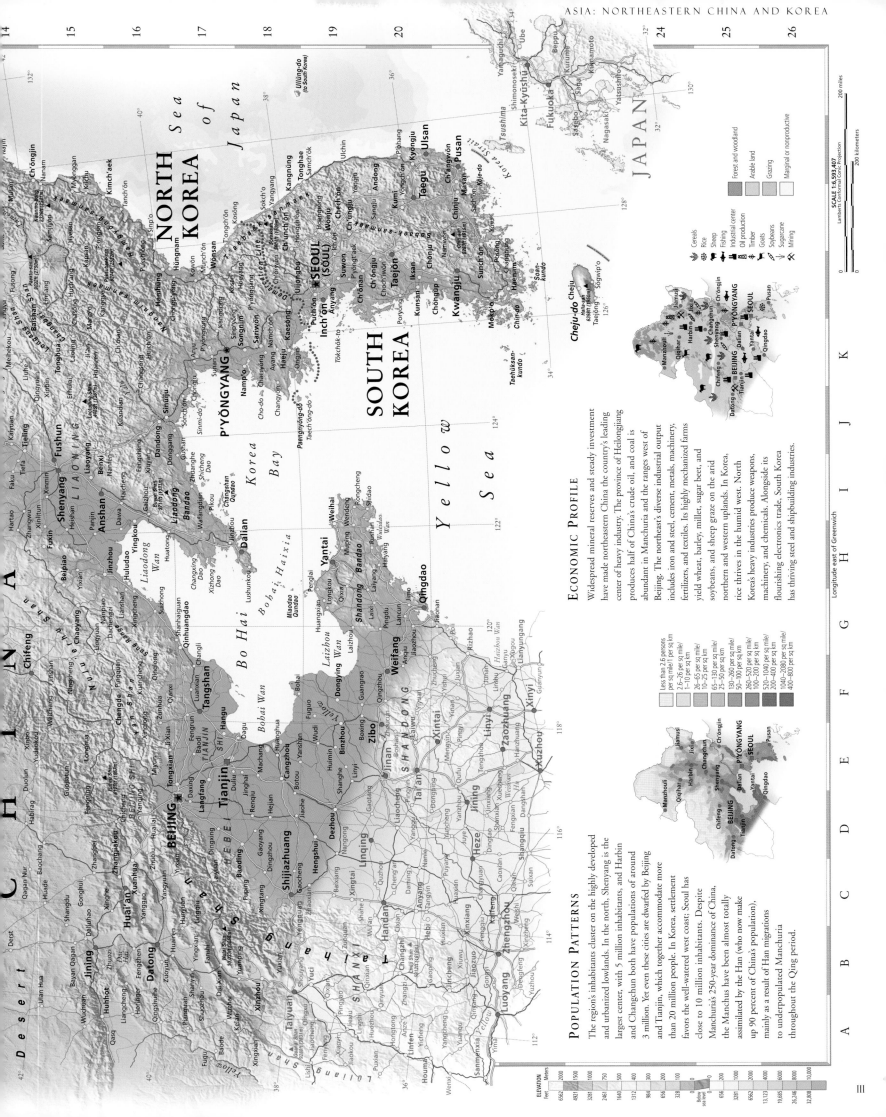

ASIA: NORTHEASTERN CHINA AND KOREA

Economic Profile

Widespread mineral reserves and steady investment have made northeastern China the country's leading center of heavy industry. The province of Heilongjiang produces half of China's crude oil, and coal is abundant in Manchuria and the ranges west of Beijing. The northeast's diverse industrial output includes iron and steel, cement, metals, machinery, fertilizers, and textiles. Its highly mechanized farms yield wheat, barley, millet, sugar beet, and soybeans, and sheep graze on the arid northern and western uplands. In Korea, rice thrives in the humid west. North Korea's heavy industries produce weapons, machinery, and chemicals. Alongside its flourishing electronics trade, South Korea has thriving steel and shipbuilding industries.

Population Patterns

The region's inhabitants cluster on the highly developed and urbanized lowlands. In the north, Shenyang is the largest center, with 5 million inhabitants, and Harbin and Changchun both have populations of around 3 million. Yet even these cities are dwarfed by Beijing and Tianjin, which together accommodate more than 20 million people. In Korea, settlement favors the well-watered west coast; Seoul has close to 10 million inhabitants. Despite Manchuria's 250-year dominance of China, the Manchus have been almost totally assimilated by the Han (who now make up 90 percent of China's population), mainly as a result of Han migrations to underpopulated Manchuria throughout the Qing period.

SCALE 1:6,593,407
Lambert's Conformal Conic Projection

III

SOUTHEASTERN CHINA AND TAIWAN

The valleys of the Yellow and Yangtze rivers were the cradles of Chinese civilization, giving rise to China's first agricultural societies, around 9,000 years ago, and its first urban society, the Shang Dynasty, around 1800 BC. They remained the center of development under the Han, who united most of this region in 221 BC. The Han gradually expanded their territory westward beyond the broad Sichuan Basin to the plateaus of modern-day Gansu and the deep valleys and steep slopes of Yunnan, and southward through the eroded limestone hills of present-day Guangdong to the humid lowlands lining the South China Sea. The Yellow and Yangtze valleys, and the plains that divide them, are still the cultural and economic heart of modern China, and were developed intensively by the communist government during the second half of the 20th century. Taiwan also underwent dramatic economic growth in the 20th century, initially under Japanese rule (1895–1943) and then under the leadership of the Chinese Nationalist Party, which controlled the island until 2000.

An ancient system of waterways dating from the 7th century, China's Grand Canal links Beijing with Hangzhou.

About 6,000 life-size terra-cotta warriors guard the tomb of Emperor Qin Shi Huang (259–210 BC), at Xi'an in Shaanxi province.

POPULATION PATTERNS

The plains between the lower Yellow and Yangtze valleys now encompass 20 or so cities with more than 1 million inhabitants, including Shanghai, the nation's largest city, which has almost 13 million people. Other centers of population include the fertile Sichuan Basin, and the Pearl River Valley in the south. The Han are by far the largest ethnic group, but China's second-largest ethnic group, the Zhuang, cluster in the autonomous region of Guangxi Zhuangzu. Taiwan's mountainous terrain concentrates its large population on the northern and western coastal lowlands. Its indigenous Malayo-Polynesian inhabitants have, for the most part, been assimilated by Chinese immigrants, who began arriving in the 17th century.

Uninhabited

Less than 2.6 persons per sq mile/1 per sq km

2.6–26 per sq mile/1–10 per sq km

26–65 per sq mile/10–25 per sq km

65–130 per sq mile/25–50 per sq km

130–260 per sq mile/50–100 per sq km

260–520 per sq mile/100–200 per sq km

520–1040 per sq mile/200–400 per sq km

1040–2080 per sq mile/400–800 per sq km

More than 2080 per sq mile/800 per sq km

ECONOMIC PROFILE

The rich loess soils of the Yellow River have long provided wheat, millet, and cotton. Intensive farming of the fertile southeast and Sichuan Basin yields up to three crops a year, mainly of rice (of which China is the world's largest producer) and vegetables. Coal is abundant in Shanxi and Sichuan, which also has half of the nation's gas reserves; these resources underpin heavy industries in the interior. However, port cities such as Guangzhou and Shanghai have become the most prosperous centers, thanks to their long-established links with other Asian and Western trading partners and a recent influx of foreign investment. China is now the largest market for the exports—mainly electrical goods, metals, textiles, and plastics—that power Taiwan's thriving economy.

Forest and woodland

Arable land

Grazing

Marginal or nonproductive

Cereals
Rice
Beef cattle
Fishing
Industrial center
Mining
Oil production
Pigs
Gas production
Tea

ELEVATION

Feet	Meters
6562	2000
4921	1500
3281	1000
2461	750
1640	500
1312	400
984	300
656	200
328	100
0	0
Below sea level	
0	0
656	200
3281	1000
6562	2000
13,123	4000
19,685	6000
26,246	8000
32,808	10,000

Though resource-rich, the island of Hainan remains relatively undeveloped. Most of its people live by farming and fishing.

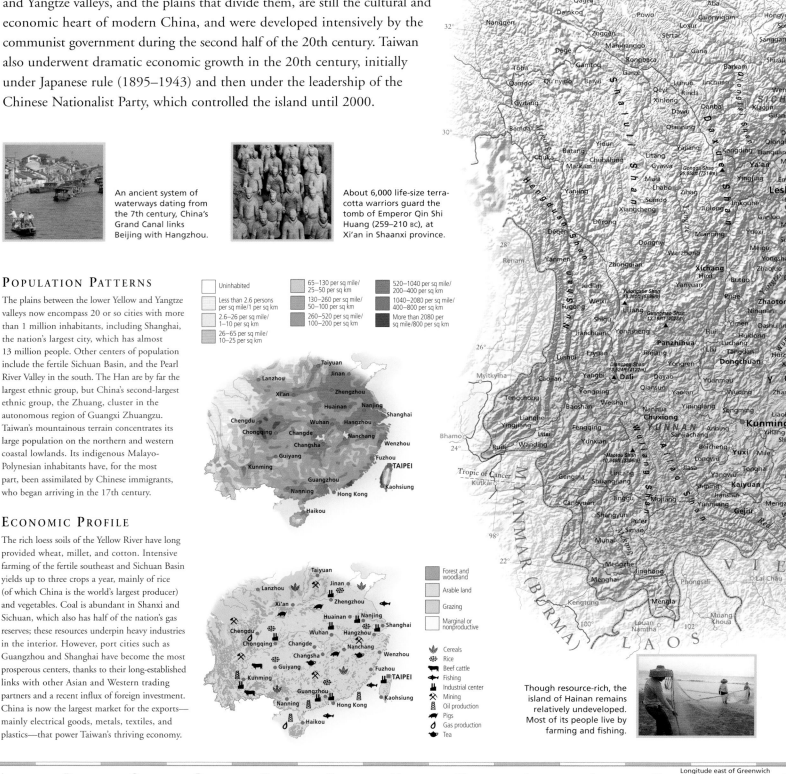

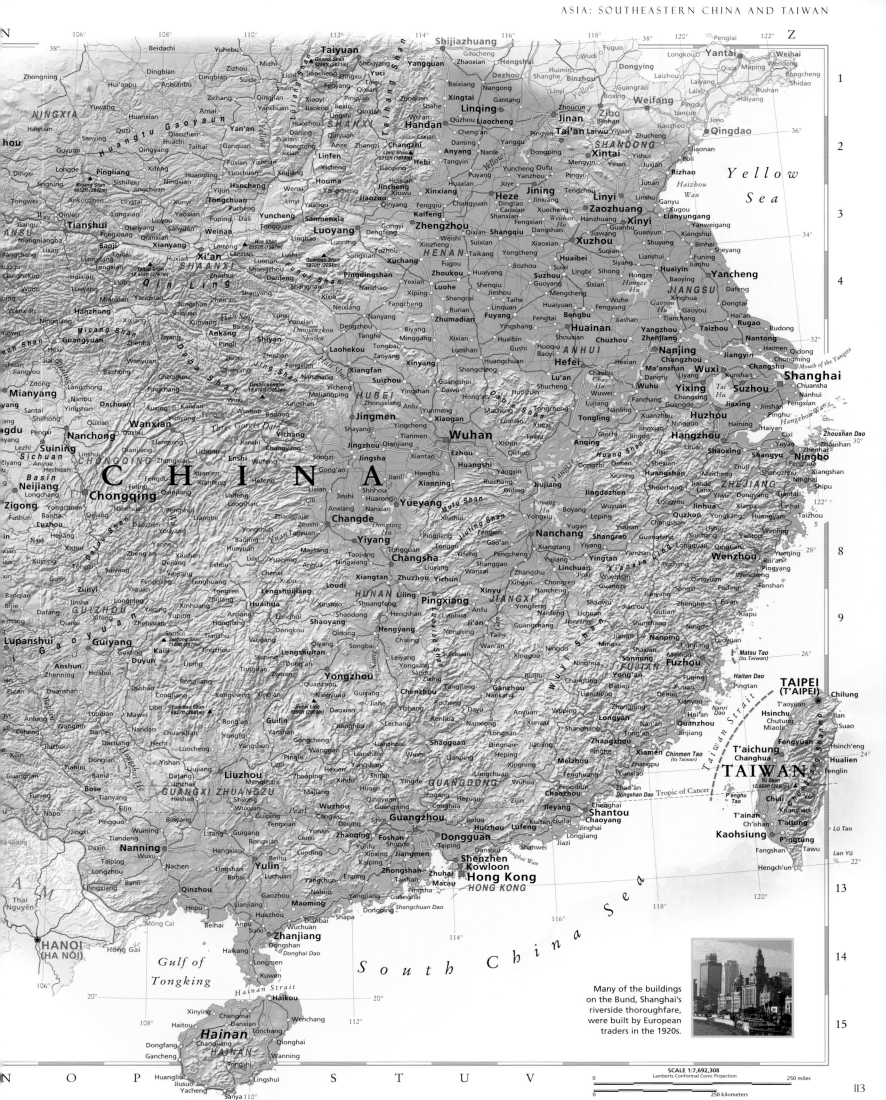

Many of the buildings on the Bund, Shanghai's riverside thoroughfare, were built by European traders in the 1920s.

SCALE 1:7,692,308
Lamberts Conformal Conic Projection

Mainland Southeast Asia

Cambodia, Laos, Myanmar (Burma), Thailand, Vietnam

The Southeast Asian mainland consists of a broad peninsula—sometimes referred to as the Indochina Peninsula—that extends southeastward from the borders of Bangladesh, India, and China, as well as part of its narrow offshoot, the Malay Peninsula. From the Chinese Himalaya, a series of mountain ranges fans out over the north. On the southern lowlands, these rivers, which include the Irrawaddy and the Mekong, have formed wide alluvial plains and deltas. In the 16th century, towns along the coast became bases for European traders. By the late 19th century, Britain controlled Burma (now Myanmar) and France ruled Indochina (present-day Laos, Cambodia, and Vietnam). Post–World War II decolonization led to civil wars in Indochina, including the Vietnam War of 1964–75. Only Thailand resisted colonization throughout its history; its independence and political stability have helped it become the region's leading economic power.

Population Patterns

Ethnically diverse, the inhabitants of Mainland Southeast Asia live mainly in rural villages. They are concentrated along the river valleys and especially the deltas of the Irrawaddy, Chao Phraya, Mekong, and Red rivers; they are sparsest in the heavily forested uplands of Cambodia, Laos, and the Myanmar–Thailand border. Though only about a quarter of the population is urban, the region has several large cities, most notably Bangkok (which is 20 times the size of Thailand's second city, Nonthaburi). Population growth is especially high in Laos and Cambodia; in contrast, Thailand has dramatically slowed its growth through social policies and education.

Eastern Myanmar is the world's second-biggest source of illegal opium.

Economic Profile

Agriculture is still the principal source of employment and many people, especially in the poorer countries of Cambodia, Laos, Vietnam, and Myanmar, depend on subsistence cultivation, mainly of rice, corn, and vegetables. Cash crops including rubber, palm oil, sugar, and tropical fruits make up the bulk of exports, whereas most manufactured goods are imported. Industrial development is most advanced in Thailand, which produces textiles, foodstuffs, and electrical goods, and has a thriving tourist trade. Cambodia, Laos, and Myanmar continue to exploit their extensive forests for timber, whereas Thailand now limits harvesting following overexploitation. The area where Myanmar, Thailand, and Laos meet, known as the "Golden Triangle," is a major source of opium, from which heroin is derived.

Most of the world's high-quality rubies come from mines in northern Myanmar.

Rice is the most widespread crop in Vietnam, covering approximately 80 percent of the country's arable land.

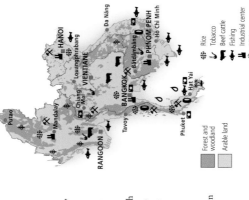

Less than 2.6 persons per sq mile/1 per sq km
2.6–26 per sq mile/1–10 per sq km
26–65 per sq mile/10–25 per sq km
65–130 per sq mile/25–50 per sq km
130–260 per sq mile/50–100 per sq km
260–520 per sq mile/100–200 per sq km
520–1040 per sq mile/200–400 per sq km
1040–2080 per sq mile/400–800 per sq km
More than 2080 per sq mile/800 per sq km

Forest and woodland
Arable land

Rice
Tobacco
Beef cattle
Fishing
Industrial center
Mining
Gas production
Timber
Rubber
Tourism
Palm oil

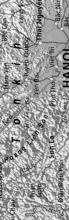

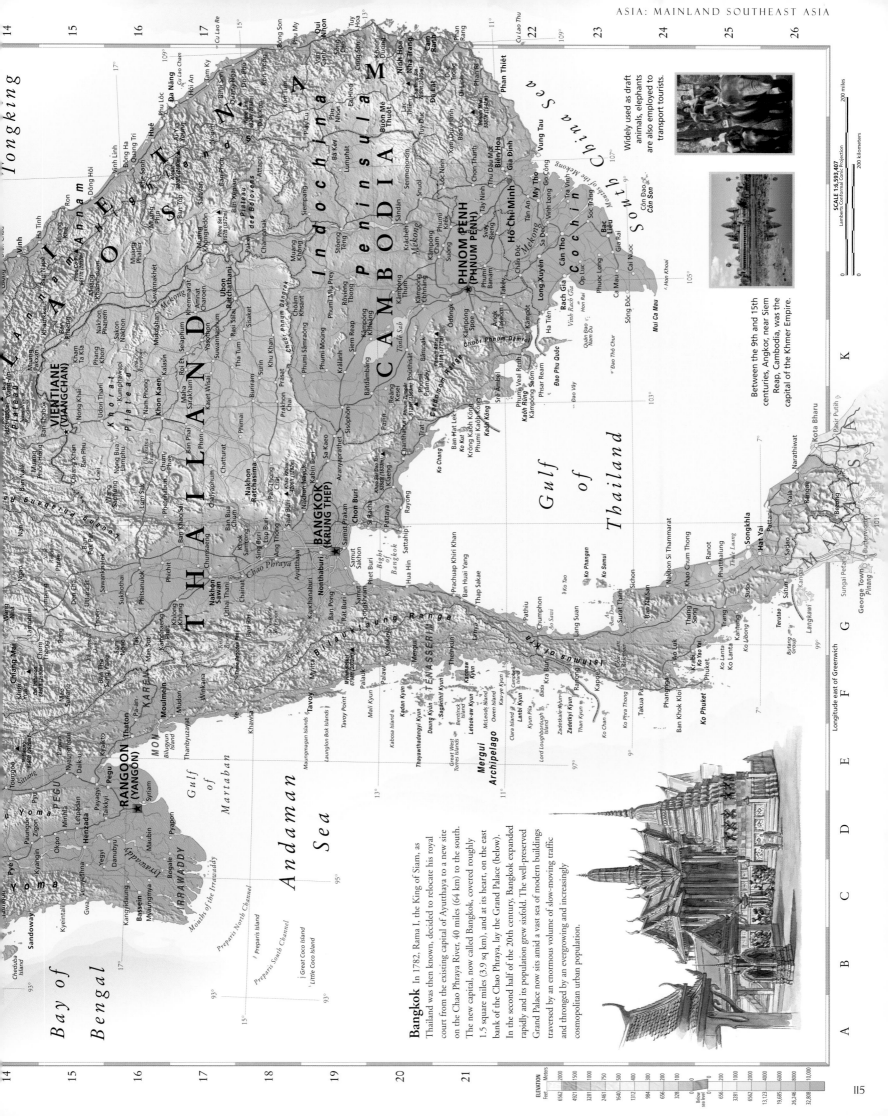

Widely used as draft animals, elephants are also employed to transport tourists.

Between the 9th and 15th centuries, Angkor, near Siem Reap, Cambodia, was the capital of the Khmer Empire.

Bangkok In 1782, Rama I, the King of Siam, as Thailand was then known, decided to relocate his royal court from the existing capital of Ayutthaya to a new site on the Chao Phraya River, 40 miles (64 km) to the south. The new capital, now called Bangkok, covered roughly 1.5 square miles (3.9 sq km), and at its heart, on the east bank of the Chao Phraya, lay the Grand Palace (below). In the second half of the 20th century, Bangkok expanded rapidly and its population grew sixfold. The well-preserved Grand Palace now sits amid a vast sea of modern buildings traversed by an enormous volume of slow-moving traffic and thronged by an evergrowing and increasingly cosmopolitan urban population.

SCALE 16,593,407
Lamberts Conformal Conic Projection

ELEVATION

MARITIME SOUTHEAST ASIA

Brunei, East Timor, Indonesia, Malaysia, Philippines, Singapore

Scattered around the southeastern fringe of the Asian mainland are more than 20,000 islands. Ranging from the massive, rain-forest-cloaked landmass of Borneo—the world's third-largest island—to the tiny atolls of the Banda Sea, they form the largest island group on Earth, the Malay Archipelago. Divided mainly between the large countries of Malaysia (which includes the southern part of the Malay Peninsula), the Philippines, and Indonesia, it is also the site of the small states of Singapore, East Timor, and Brunei. Beginning in the 16th century, intense competition for control of the lucrative spice trade led various European powers to colonize large areas of the region. The Dutch seized most of present-day Indonesia, the British gradually gained control of Malaysia, the Portuguese established a foothold in Timor, and the Spanish occupied the Philippines (from where they were ousted by the U.S.A. in 1898). Since decolonization in the second half of the 20th century, Indonesia and Malaysia, in particular, have become major regional powers.

JAVA'S VOLCANOES

The islands of southern Indonesia formed as a result of subduction of the Indo-Australian Plate beneath the Eurasian Plate. This process continues to fuel the country's 76 volcanoes (more than any other nation), 22 of which are on Java. Sporadic and sometimes destructive volcanic activity takes place at Gunung Semeru in the east, Gunung Merapi near Yogyakarta, and Galunggung in the west. But the largest recorded eruption occurred on August 28, 1883, when Krakatau (Krakatoa) exploded, unleashing a tidal wave that killed 36,000 people.

Native to Borneo and Sumatra, the orangutan has become endangered due to habitat loss.

East Timor attained independence in 2002, following almost 25 years of Indonesian rule.

Controlled by the Dutch from 1619 to 1941, Jakarta became the capital of Indonesia in 1949.

POPULATION PATTERNS

Indonesia has the region's largest and the world's fourth-biggest population, though it is distributed unevenly. Java, Bali, and parts of Sumatra are densely packed, whereas populations are thin in Borneo, the eastern islands, and Irian Jaya. To counter this, the government has sponsored the voluntary resettlement of millions of people. In Malaysia, about four-fifths of the population live on the mainland. Indonesia has the region's lowest level of population growth; in contrast, East Timor has one of the world's highest. East Timor aside, urbanization levels are higher here than in Mainland Southeast Asia, ranging from 50 percent in Indonesia to 100 percent in Singapore.

Less than 2.6 persons per sq mile/1 per sq km
2.6–26 per sq mile/1–10 per sq km
26–65 per sq mile/10–25 per sq km
65–130 per sq mile/25–50 per sq km
130–260 per sq mile/50–100 per sq km
260–520 per sq mile/100–200 per sq km
520–1040 per sq mile/200–400 per sq km
1040–2080 per sq mile/400–800 per sq km
More than 2080 per sq mile/800 per sq km

ECONOMIC PROFILE

Since the mid-20th century, this region has undergone rapid economic growth. Singapore has become a major commercial center; Brunei has used vast oil reserves to fund a modern infrastructure; and Malaysia has become a leading exporter of electronic goods. The other nations are more reliant on farming, but all have raised production levels of subsistence crops, such as rice and corn, and cash crops, including rubber, palm oil, coffee, and cacao. They have also nurtured light industries, such as food processing and textile manufacturing. Other sources of revenue are timber, tourism, and minerals—Malaysia and Indonesia are leading exporters of tin and significant suppliers of oil and gas.

Forest and woodland
Arable land
Grazing

Rice
Coconuts
Rubber
Fishing
Industrial center
Mining
Oil production
Timber
Palm oil

Kuala Lumpur Although it is the nation's capital, with a population of 1.5 million, Kuala Lumpur is young compared to historic Malay cities such as Melaka. Sited at the meeting point of the Keland and Gombak rivers (its name means "muddy confluence"), it was founded by Chinese tin miners in 1857. Rich yields attracted more settlers and funded an intensive phase of construction. Kuala Lumpur became the seat of British administration in 1895, and underwent rapid growth after the Second World War. It was chosen as the capital of Malaya in 1957 and of Malaysia in 1963. In the mid-1990s its international profile was boosted when it became the site of the world's tallest building, the Petronas Towers, designed by Argentine-American architect Cesar Pelli.

ELEVATION
Feet	Meters
6562	2000
4921	1500
3281	1000
2461	750
1640	500
1312	400
984	300
656	200
328	100
Below sea level	0
656	200
3281	1000
6562	2000
13,123	4000
19,685	6000
26,246	8000
32,808	10,000

SCALE 1:12,087,912
Lamberts Conformal Conic Projection
300 miles
300 kilometers

BRUNEI, MALAYSIA, AND SINGAPORE

Malaysia comprises the southern third of the Malay Peninsula and the northern third of the island of Borneo. Divided by the South China Sea, these territories are known, respectively, as West (or Peninsular) Malaysia and East Malaysia (which is made up of the states of Sabah and Sarawak). Nestled on their fringes are two small independent states: Singapore, a tiny island republic on the southern tip of West Malaysia, and Brunei, a sultanate consisting of two enclaves on the north shore of East Malaysia. When the Portuguese arrived in the early 16th century, the Malay Peninsula and northern Borneo were divided into autonomous Islamic sultanates. In the 19th century, most of these states were brought under British control. Following Japanese occupation during the Second World War, the sultanates of the Malay Peninsula gained independence from Britain as Malaya in 1957; in 1963, they invited Singapore, Sabah, Sarawak, and Brunei to unite with them as Malaysia. All but Brunei accepted, though Singapore seceded peacefully in 1965. Today, these three states are among the most prosperous in Southeast Asia.

The jagged summit of Mount Kinabalu, Malaysia's highest peak, looms above a mosque near Kota Kinabalu.

Malaysia's largest port, George Town, occupies a sheltered position on the east side of the island of Pinang.

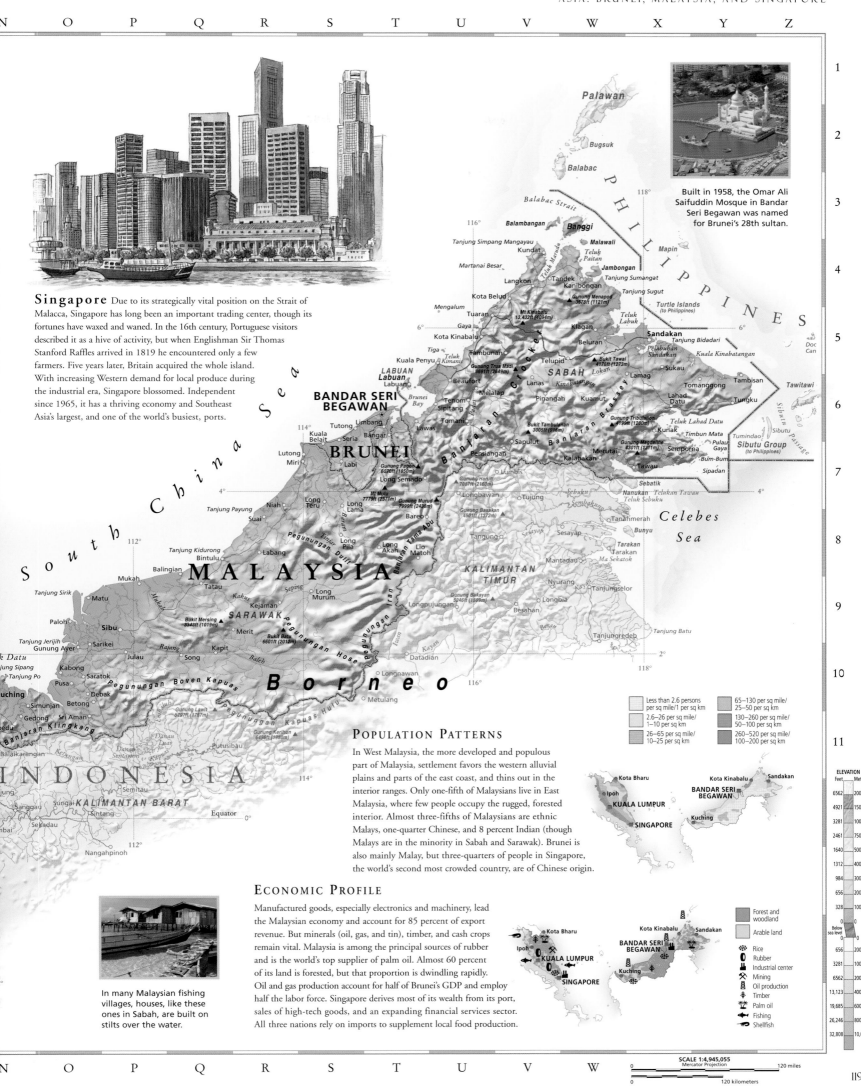

Built in 1958, the Omar Ali Saifuddin Mosque in Bandar Seri Begawan was named for Brunei's 28th sultan.

Singapore Due to its strategically vital position on the Strait of Malacca, Singapore has long been an important trading center, though its fortunes have waxed and waned. In the 16th century, Portuguese visitors described it as a hive of activity, but when Englishman Sir Thomas Stanford Raffles arrived in 1819 he encountered only a few farmers. Five years later, Britain acquired the whole island. With increasing Western demand for local produce during the industrial era, Singapore blossomed. Independent since 1965, it has a thriving economy and Southeast Asia's largest, and one of the world's busiest, ports.

In many Malaysian fishing villages, houses, like these ones in Sabah, are built on stilts over the water.

POPULATION PATTERNS

In West Malaysia, the more developed and populous part of Malaysia, settlement favors the western alluvial plains and parts of the east coast, and thins out in the interior ranges. Only one-fifth of Malaysians live in East Malaysia, where few people occupy the rugged, forested interior. Almost three-fifths of Malaysians are ethnic Malays, one-quarter Chinese, and 8 percent Indian (though Malays are in the minority in Sabah and Sarawak). Brunei is also mainly Malay, but three-quarters of people in Singapore, the world's second most crowded country, are of Chinese origin.

Population density	
Less than 2.6 persons per sq mile/1 per sq km	65–130 per sq mile/ 25–50 per sq km
2.6–26 per sq mile/ 1–10 per sq km	130–260 per sq mile/ 50–100 per sq km
26–65 per sq mile/ 10–25 per sq km	260–520 per sq mile/ 100–200 per sq km

ECONOMIC PROFILE

Manufactured goods, especially electronics and machinery, lead the Malaysian economy and account for 85 percent of export revenue. But minerals (oil, gas, and tin), timber, and cash crops remain vital. Malaysia is among the principal sources of rubber and is the world's top supplier of palm oil. Almost 60 percent of its land is forested, but that proportion is dwindling rapidly. Oil and gas production account for half of Brunei's GDP and employ half the labor force. Singapore derives most of its wealth from its port, sales of high-tech goods, and an expanding financial services sector. All three nations rely on imports to supplement local food production.

Forest and woodland
Arable land

Rice
Rubber
Industrial center
Mining
Oil production
Timber
Palm oil
Fishing
Shellfish

ELEVATION	
Feet	Meters
32,808	10,000
26,246	8000
19,685	6000
13,123	4000
6562	2000
3281	1000
1640	500
656	200
Below sea level	0

SCALE 1:4,945,055
Mercator Projection
0   120 miles
0   120 kilometers

THE PHILIPPINES

A physically fractured country made up of more than 7,000 mainly volcanic islands, the Philippines encompasses 116,000 square miles (300,000 sq km) of land between China and Indonesia. Its two largest islands, Luzon in the north and Mindanao in the south, account for two-thirds of the country's area. Most of the islands are mountainous with narrow coastal plains. The indigenous inhabitants, the Filipinos, are of Malay origin, but modern Philippine society displays conspicuous colonial influences. Following Ferdinand Magellan's visit in 1521, Spain controlled the archipelago (naming it after its king, Philip II) from 1565 until 1898, when it was ceded to the U.S.A. Under Spanish rule, most of the population converted to Catholicism; under the Americans, English became the colony's lingua franca. The Second World War, during which Japan occupied the islands, delayed independence, which was achieved in 1946. In 1986, the repressive, 21-year rule of Ferdinand Marcos was ended by a popular uprising. A fragile democracy has since held, despite attempted coups, economic crises, and violence perpetrated by Muslim separatists, particularly on the islands of Mindanao and Basilan.

These rice terraces near Banaue, Luzon, were first built by the local Ifugao people 2,000 years ago.

Mayon in southeastern Luzon is a highly active volcano that poses a threat to nearby towns.

Manila

Spanish forces arrived in Manila, a trading post dating back to the 12th century, in 1571. Having ousted the local Muslim ruler, they constructed a fortress called Intramuros, whose 20-foot (6-m) walls eventually enclosed a town with 15 churches and 6 monasteries. Much of Intramuros was obliterated during the Second World War. Remnants of the Spanish colony include the church and monastery of San Augustin, built in 1599, and Fort Santiago, which dates from the mid-17th century.

San Augustin Church

Fort Santiago

POPULATION PATTERNS

The archipelago is densely though unevenly populated. The most developed area is central Luzon: Manila alone is home to 10 million people. Other areas, such as central Mindanao, Palawan, and northern Luzon, are sparsely inhabited. The population growth rate is high. Significant migration takes place, to the cities—urbanization has risen from 20 percent in 1900 to 63 percent in 2000—and overseas. More than 70 native languages are spoken; the official languages are Filipino (the Tagalog language of southern Luzon) and English.

ECONOMIC PROFILE

About 20 percent of the land is arable and agriculture is the biggest employer. Rice and corn are the staple crops, sugar and coconuts are the main exports. Fishing is also important. Abundant minerals include some of the world's largest deposits of nickel, copper, and chromite. Electronic goods, mainly assembled in foreign-owned factories using imported parts, account for over half of exports. Other industrial products include textiles, metals, chemicals, and foodstuffs. Substantial income is also derived from tourism.

Population density legend

- Less than 2.6 persons per sq mile/1 per sq km
- 2.6–26 per sq mile/ 1–10 per sq km
- 26–65 per sq mile/ 10–25 per sq km
- 65–130 per sq mile/ 25–50 per sq km
- 130–260 per sq mile/ 50–100 per sq km
- 260–520 per sq mile/ 100–200 per sq km
- 520–1040 per sq mile/ 200–400 per sq km
- 1040–2080 per sq mile/ 400–800 per sq km

Land use legend

- Forest and woodland
- Arable land
- Grazing

- Rice
- Coconuts
- Fishing
- Industrial center
- Mining
- Oil production
- Timber
- Sugarcane

Map labels

Aparri, Dagupan, MANILA, Roxas, Cebu, Zamboanga, Legaspi, Davao

Luzon Strait, Batan Islands, Babuyan Islands, Babuyan Channel, Balintang Channel, Luzon, Philippine Sea

Y'ami, North Island, Mabudis, Siayan, Itbayat, Batan, Ibuhos, Sabtang, Basco, Calayan, Dalupiri, Fuga, Camiguin

Escarpada Point, San Vicente, Palaui, Iligan Point, Cabutunan Point, Valley Head, Baguio Point, Divilacan Bay, Estagno Point, Palanan Point, Palanan, Tarigtig Point, Casiguran, San Ildefonso Peninsula, Casiguran Sound, Baler Bay, Cape Encanto, Dingalan Bay, Baler

Cape Bojeador, Mayraira Point, Bangui, Claveria, Abulug, Aparri, Lal-Lo, Gonzaga, Alcala, Cauayan, Santiago, Cagayan, Tuao, Tuguegarao, Tabuk, Ilagan, Aurora, Infanta, Sierra Madre

Cordillera Central, Mount Pulog, Banaue, Bontoc, Sabangan, Bambang, Bayombong

Bacarra, Laoag, Batac, Badoc, Cabugao, Vigan, Narvacan, Candon, Candon Point, Bauang, San Fernando, Lingayen, Lingayen Gulf, Dagupan, San Carlos, Baguio, Tarlac, Cuyapo, Victoria, Capas, Camiling, Gapan, San Jose, Iba, Botolan, San Antonio, Olongapo, Zambales Mountains, Mount Pinatubo

Anda, Alaminos, Agno, Bani Point, Santa Cruz, Caiman Point, Balanga, Bagac, Mariveles, Bataan Peninsula, Mount Mariveles, Corregidor, Cabra, Lubang, Lubang Islands, Cape Calavite, Golo, Ambil, Lubang, Calapan, Mount Halcon

Rosario, San Fernando, Malolos, Angeles, Mabalacat, Muntinlupa, Cavite, Manila Bay, Quezon City, MANILA, Pasig, Valenzuela, Calamba, Laguna de Bay, San Pablo, Lipa, Batangas, Lucena, Tayabas Bay, Boac, Marinduque, Verde Island Passage

Polillo Islands, Polillo, Polillo Strait, Lamon, Lamon Bay, Jomalig, Patnanongan, Panukulan, Agta Point, Alabat, Lopez, José Panganiban, Jose Panganiban Peninsula, Bondoc Peninsula, Mompog Passage, Calagua Islands, Labo, Daet, San Miguel Bay, Naga, Iriga, Libmanan, Caramoan Peninsula, Mount Isarog, Yog Point, Pandan, Viga, Virac, Catanduanes, San Andres, Batan, San Miguel Islands, Ragay Gulf, Bulig Mountains, Mulahay, Mount Labo, Maqueda Channel, Tabaco

Philippines

Up to 25 typhoons strike the Philippines each year. They are most common in the east around Samar and Leyte.

A distinctively Filipino mode of transport, jeepneys were originally modified U.S.-Army-surplus jeeps.

PHILIPPINES

Philippine Sea

South China Sea

Sulu Sea

Celebes Sea

Bohol Sea

Visayan Sea

Mindanao Sea

Panay Gulf

Leyte Gulf

Davao Gulf

Moro Gulf

Luzon

Mindanao

Samar

Leyte

Cebu

Bohol

Negros

Panay

Masbate

Palawan

Mindoro

Basilan

Zamboanga Peninsula

INDONESIA

MALAYSIA

Kaluku Mountains

Diuata Mountains

Mount Apo 9692ft (2954m)

Mount Kitanglad 9511ft (2899m)

Mount Ragang 9265ft (2825m)

Mount Matutum 7532ft (2296m)

Mount Hilong-hilong 6601ft (2012m)

Mount Dapiak 8901ff (2596m)

Mount Malindang 7956ft (2425m)

Mount Canlaon 8087ft (2465m)

Mount Guiting-guiting 6726ft (2050m)

Mount Capotoan 2769ft (850m)

Victoria Peak 5607ft (1709m)

Cleopatra Needle 5256ft (1593m)

Mount Mantalingajan 6739ft (2054m)

Davao

Cagayan de Oro

Butuan

General Santos

Zamboanga

Cotabato

Iligan

Dipolog

Surigao

Tacloban

Calbayog

Catbalogan

Ormoc

Maasin

Bacolod

Iloilo

Roxas

Cebu

Mandaue

Lapu-Lapu

Tagbilaran

Dumaguete

Puerto Princesa

Cuyo Islands

Cagayan Islands

Calamian Group

Busuanga

Cuyon

Culion

Dumaran

Tubbataha Reefs

Turtle Islands

Sulu Archipelago

Jolo

Tawitawi

Sibutu Group

Sarangani Islands

Miangas (to Philippines)

Kepulauan Talaud

Surigao Strait

Bohol Strait

Cebu Strait

Tanon Strait

Basilan Strait

Balabac Strait

Longitude east of Greenwich

SCALE 1:4,395,604
Lambert's Conformal Conic Projection

0 — 120 miles
0 — 120 kilometers

ELEVATION
Feet / Meters
6562 / 2000
4921 / 1500
3281 / 1000
2461 / 750
1640 / 500
1312 / 400
984 / 300
656 / 200
328 / 100
Below sea level

656 / 200
3281 / 1000
6562 / 2000
13,123 / 4000
19,685 / 6000
26,246 / 8000
32,808 / 10,000

JAPAN

Although it occupies a strategically important position off the northeast coast of Asia, Japan remained isolated from outside influences for long periods of its history. It limited relations with its neighbors from the ninth century and adopted an official policy of isolation in 1639, soon after the arrival of the first Western missionaries and explorers. Only in the mid-19th century did it open up to foreign influences and trade.

Its subsequent attempts to expand its empire led to international conflicts and a devastating defeat in the Second World War. Yet the nation recovered spectacularly to become the world's second-strongest industrial power after the United States and wield an economic and political influence far out of proportion to its small size. Occupying a land area smaller than California, Japan consists of about 4,000 islands, dominated by the large islands of Hokkaidō, Honshū, Shikoku, and Kyūshū. In the interiors of these islands, mountain ranges are separated by river valleys and bounded by narrow coastal plains. Being situated on the Pacific Rim of Fire, the country experiences regular earthquakes and volcanic eruptions, which periodically wreak havoc on the land and its people.

POPULATION PATTERNS

About 80 percent of Japan is mountainous and has low-to-moderate levels of population density; the other 20 percent, however—mainly valleys and coastal plains—supports the bulk of the population and includes some of the world's most densely inhabited areas. Urban dwellers account for 80 percent of the inhabitants and the capital, Tokyo, is the world's largest urban center. The population is ethnically homogenous, with 99 percent being Japanese. About 84% follow both Buddhist and Shinto traditions. In recent years, a declining birth rate and rapidly aging population have heightened concerns about labor shortages and the cost of maintaining social services.

	Less than 2.6 persons per sq mile/1 per sq km
	2.6–26 per sq mile/1–10 per sq km
	26–65 per sq mile/10–25 per sq km
	65–130 per sq mile/25–50 per sq km
	130–260 per sq mile/50–100 per sq km
	260–520 per sq mile/100–200 per sq km
	520–1040 per sq mile/200–400 per sq km
	1040–2080 per sq mile/400–800 per sq km
	More than 2080 per sq mile/ 800 per sq km

ECONOMIC PROFILE

Japan is an economic superpower despite having only a small area of cultivable land and modest mineral resources (small deposits of copper, coal, and iron ore and meager reserves of oil and gas). Its success is due mainly to government support and innovation: large subsidies and intensive farming practices have helped it become virtually self-sufficient in rice and produce large quantities of fruit and vegetables; heavy investment in education, research, and technology have created a sophisticated industrial sector renowned for machinery and electronic goods. Even the nation's impressive fish catches, accounting for 15 percent of world totals, are due in part to the use of technology-loaded, wide-ranging fishing boats. This industrial success has greatly increased export revenue; however, a recession in the late 1990s cast a shadow over the nation's economic future.

- Forest and woodland
- Arable land

- Rice
- Fruit
- Tobacco
- Beef cattle
- Fishing
- Industrial center
- Winter sports

In winter, mountain-dwelling macaque monkeys stay warm by sitting in pools fed by hot springs.

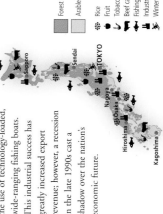

Bullet trains began operating in 1964. They now have a top speed of 160 mph (260 km/h).

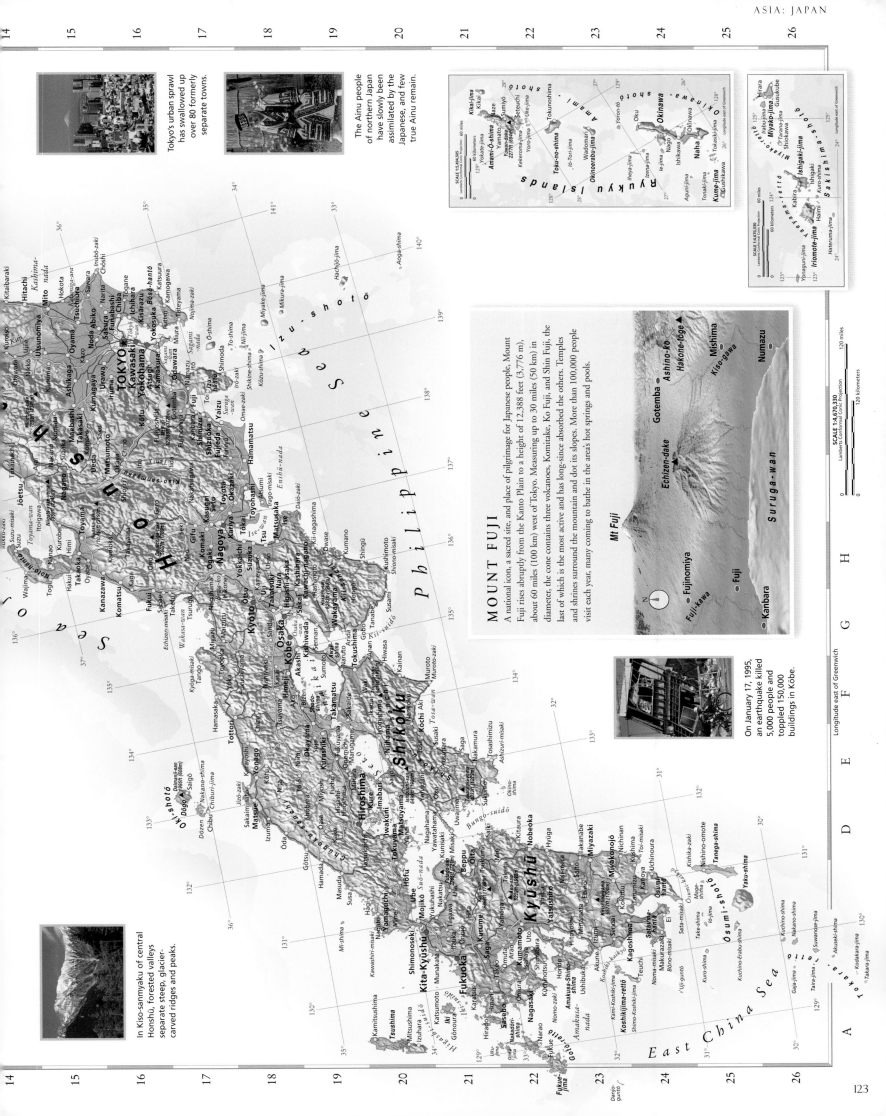

Tokyo's urban sprawl has swallowed up over 80 formerly separate towns.

The Ainu people of northern Japan have slowly been assimilated by the Japanese, and few true Ainu remain.

In Kiso-sanmyaku of central Honshū, forested valleys separate steep, glacier-carved ridges and peaks.

On January 17, 1995, an earthquake killed 5,000 people and toppled 150,000 buildings in Kōbe.

MOUNT FUJI

A national icon, a sacred site, and place of pilgrimage for Japanese people, Mount Fuji rises abruptly from the Kanto Plain to a height of 12,388 feet (3,776 m), about 60 miles (100 km) west of Tokyo. Measuring up to 30 miles (50 km) in diameter, the cone contains three volcanoes, Komitake, Ko Fuji, and Shin Fuji, the last of which is the most active and has long-since absorbed the others. Temples and shrines surround the mountain and dot its slopes. More than 100,000 people visit each year, many coming to bathe in the area's hot springs and pools.

NORTHWESTERN AFRICA

Algeria, Libya, Morocco, Tunisia

Isolated from the rest of the continent by the Sahara Desert, Northwestern Africa is a transitional zone, between sea and remote interior, Europe and Africa, the West and the Middle East. Its distinctive and relatively homogenous culture was flavored by classical European civilizations and its original, nomadic Berber inhabitants, but derives mainly from the Arab peoples who invaded and settled here in the seventh century AD. This Arabic, Islamic heritage not only withstood subsequent occupation by the Ottoman Empire (between the 16th and 19th centuries), European colonial rule, and a torrid phase of decolonization, but also permeated almost every part of a vast, inhospitable region. Bounded by the Atlas Mountains in the northwest, the Sahara Desert occupies more than 80 percent of the land, confining major population centers and communications routes, sedentary farming, and industries to a narrow coastal strip.

POPULATION PATTERNS

The Sahara contains just a few isolated towns, scattered oases, and groups of nomadic pastoralists; the vast majority of the region's inhabitants dwell on the north coast. The population soared in the 20th century (Algeria's population doubled between 1960 and 1990), due to improving health services and persistent high fertility (even today, each woman has an average of four children). Migration to cities began under European rule and accelerated with industrialization, making this the most urbanized part of Africa. Libya is distinctly underpopulated and has to import skilled workers, whereas there is a steady outward flow of migrants from the other countries.

	Uninhabited
	Less than 2.6 persons per sq mile/1 per sq km
	2.6–26 per sq mile/ 1–10 per sq km
	26–65 per sq mile/ 10–25 per sq km
	65–130 per sq mile/ 25–50 per sq km
	130–260 per sq mile/ 50–100 per sq km
	260–520 per sq mile/ 100–200 per sq km

The seminomadic Tuareg people roam the desert lands of Algeria, Libya, Mali, and Niger.

The Atlas Mountains are home to large numbers of Berbers, the region's original inhabitants.

Tangier Befitting a port that has at various times been ruled by the Phoenicians, Romans, Arabs, Spanish, Portuguese, and British, Tangier was for much of the 20th century designated an international zone. Since it became part of Morocco in 1956, many foreign residents have departed, but the city retains a cosmopolitan atmosphere. Encircled by 15th-century ramparts and surmounted by the Great Mosque, its whitewashed buildings climb a craggy limestone outcrop.

Great Mosque

ELEVATION

Feet	Meters
6562	2000
4921	1500
3281	1000
2461	750
1640	500
1312	400
984	300
656	200
328	100
0	0
Below sea level	
656	200
3281	1000
6562	2000
13,123	4000
19,685	6000
26,246	8000
32,808	10,000

Longitude west of Greenwich

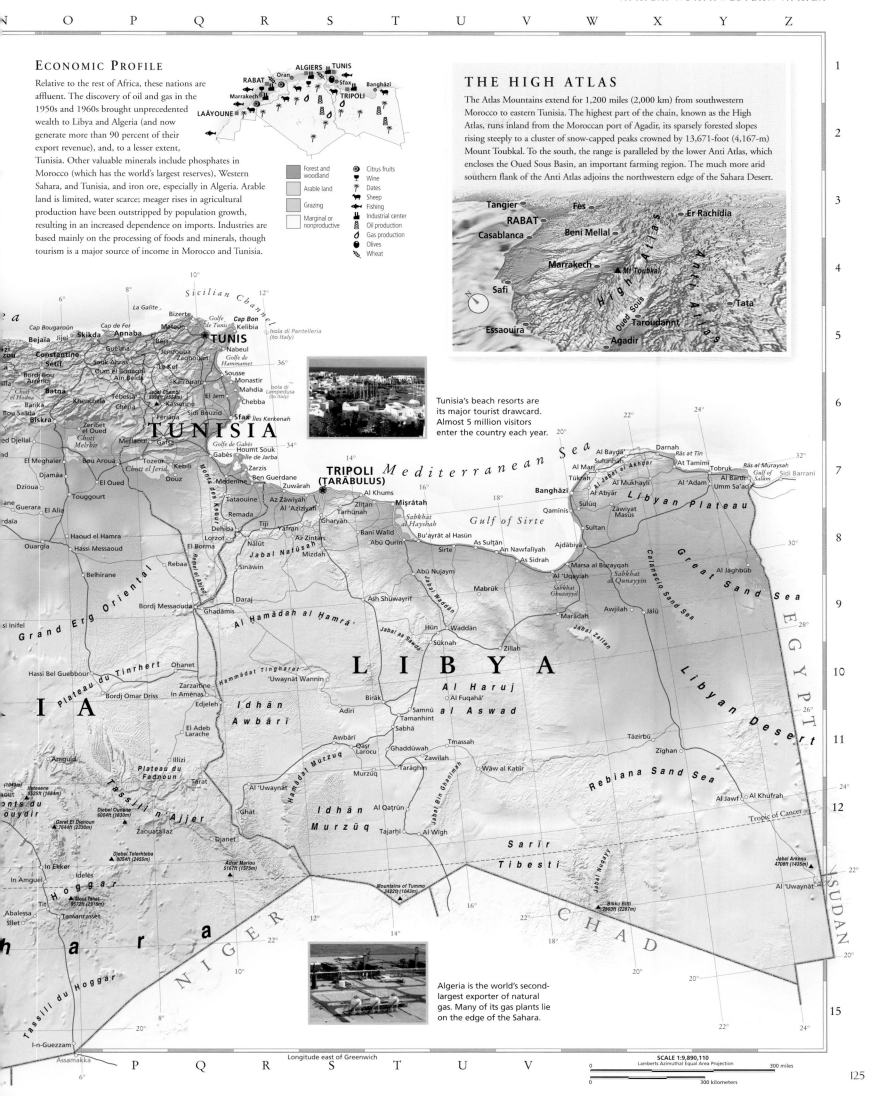

ECONOMIC PROFILE

Relative to the rest of Africa, these nations are affluent. The discovery of oil and gas in the 1950s and 1960s brought unprecedented wealth to Libya and Algeria (and now generate more than 90 percent of their export revenue), and, to a lesser extent, Tunisia. Other valuable minerals include phosphates in Morocco (which has the world's largest reserves), Western Sahara, and Tunisia, and iron ore, especially in Algeria. Arable land is limited, water scarce; meager rises in agricultural production have been outstripped by population growth, resulting in an increased dependence on imports. Industries are based mainly on the processing of foods and minerals, though tourism is a major source of income in Morocco and Tunisia.

Forest and woodland
Arable land
Grazing
Marginal or nonproductive

Citrus fruits
Wine
Dates
Sheep
Fishing
Industrial center
Oil production
Gas production
Olives
Wheat

THE HIGH ATLAS

The Atlas Mountains extend for 1,200 miles (2,000 km) from southwestern Morocco to eastern Tunisia. The highest part of the chain, known as the High Atlas, runs inland from the Moroccan port of Agadir, its sparsely forested slopes rising steeply to a cluster of snow-capped peaks crowned by 13,671-foot (4,167-m) Mount Toubkal. To the south, the range is paralleled by the lower Anti Atlas, which encloses the Oued Sous Basin, an important farming region. The much more arid southern flank of the Anti Atlas adjoins the northwestern edge of the Sahara Desert.

Tunisia's beach resorts are its major tourist drawcard. Almost 5 million visitors enter the country each year.

Algeria is the world's second-largest exporter of natural gas. Many of its gas plants lie on the edge of the Sahara.

Longitude east of Greenwich

SCALE 1:9,890,110
Lamberts Azimuthal Equal Area Projection
0   300 miles
0   300 kilometers

NORTHEASTERN AFRICA

Djibouti, Egypt, Eritrea, Ethiopia, Somalia, Sudan

At the northern end of the Great Rift Valley, the Ethiopian Highlands divides the Horn of Africa in the east from the barren expanses of the Sahara in the west. Rivers that descend from the highlands, and from the East African Plateau to the south, are the lifeblood of this predominantly arid and impoverished land.

The Shebeli and Juba are the only permanent rivers in Somalia and supply most of the nation's water. From Lake Tana, the Blue Nile flows east then west to join the White Nile at Khartoum; continuing north, the Nile forms a riverine oasis that constitutes Egypt's only fertile zone.

Since decolonization took place after the Second World War, the southern part of this region has been crippled by famines and political instability, including a long civil war that saw Eritrea secede from Ethiopia in 1993.

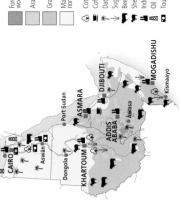

ECONOMIC PROFILE

The regional economy is undeveloped, and most people rely on subsistence farming of cereals, fruit and vegetables, sheep, cattle, goats, and camels—80 percent of Somalians are dependent on livestock. Cash crops include cotton and sugarcane, grown in the Nile Valley, and coffee from the Ethiopian Highlands (from whose Kaffa region the word "coffee" derives). Only Egypt has a developed industrial sector, based on engineering and the manufacture of metals and electronic goods. It also benefits from modest oil reserves, tourism, and revenue from the Suez Canal.

Forest and woodland
Arable land
Grazing
Marginal or nonproductive

Cotton
Coffee
Dates
Sugarcane
Beef cattle
Sheep
Industrial center
Oil production
Tourism

POPULATION PATTERNS

The highest population densities occur in the fertile Ethiopian Highlands and along the major rivers—99 percent of Egyptians live in the Nile Valley, an area that constitutes just 3 percent of the country. The deserts of the eastern Sahara, northern Ethiopia, and Somalia, and the swamps of southern Sudan deter settlement. In semiarid zones, many people, including 70 percent of Somalians, maintain a nomadic lifestyle. The Sahara separates the mainly Arabic peoples of the north from the diverse African groups of the south; however, the Middle East has influenced the entire region and most inhabitants are adherents of Islam.

Uninhabited
Less than 2.6 persons per sq mile/1 per sq km
2.6–26 per sq mile/1 per sq km
26–65 per sq mile/10–25 per sq km
65–130 per sq mile/25–50 per sq km
130–260 per sq mile/50–100 per sq km
260–520 per sq mile/100–200 per sq km
520–1040 per sq mile/200–400 per sq km
1040–2080 per sq mile/400–800 per sq km
More than 2080 per sq mile/800 per sq km

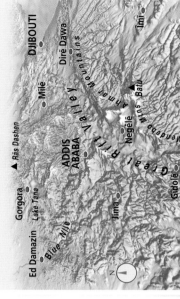

Completed in 1971, the Aswân Dam supplies half of Egypt's electricity.

THE ETHIOPIAN HIGHLANDS

An enormous plateau, the Ethiopian Highlands cover most of Ethiopia and are bisected by the Great Rift Valley. The western highlands encompass the region's highest peak, 14,872-foot (4,533-m) Râs Dashen, Lake Tana, and Ethiopia's capital Addis Ababa, which sits about 8,000 feet (2,500 m) above sea level. The eastern highlands are narrower but almost as high, reaching 14,176 feet (4,321 m) at Batu. South of Addis Ababa, lakes and volcanic peaks stud the floor of the Great Rift Valley; northeast of the capital, the valley widens, the western wall forming a great escarpment that runs north to the Red Sea, the eastern side arcing toward the Gulf of Aden.

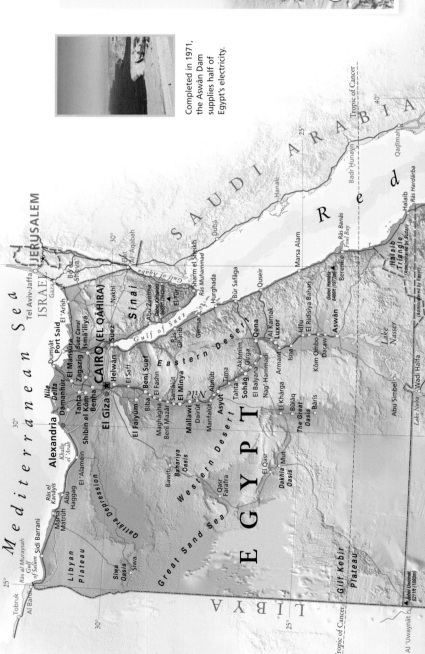

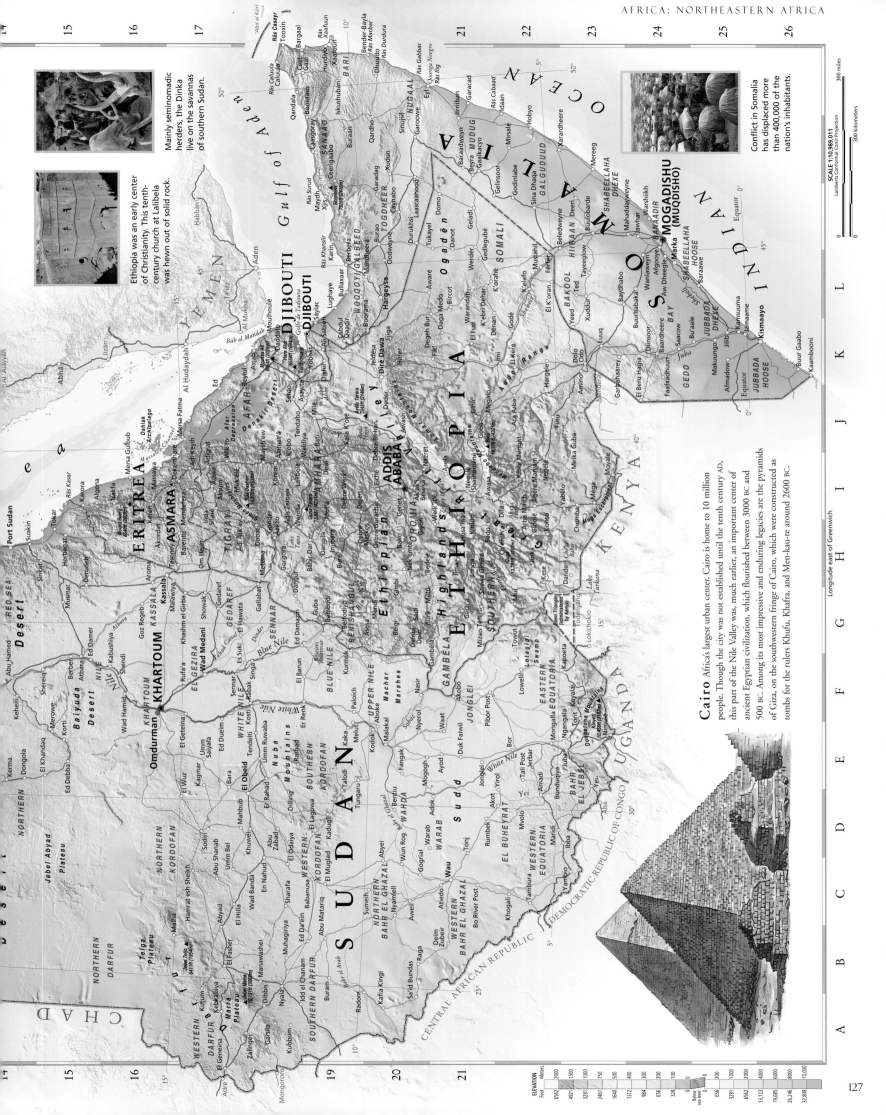

Mainly seminomadic herders, the Dinka live on the savannas of southern Sudan.

Ethiopia was an early center of Christianity. This tenth-century church at Lalibela was hewn out of solid rock.

Conflict in Somalia has displaced more than 400,000 of the nation's inhabitants.

Cairo Africa's largest urban center, Cairo is home to 10 million people. Though the city was not established until the tenth century AD, this part of the Nile Valley was, much earlier, an important center of ancient Egyptian civilization, which flourished between 3000 BC and 500 BC. Among its most impressive and enduring legacies are the pyramids of Giza, on the southwestern fringe of Cairo, which were constructed as tombs for the rulers Khufu, Khafra, and Men-kau-re around 2600 BC.

SCALE 1:10,989,011
Lambert's Conformal Conic Projection

ELEVATION

127

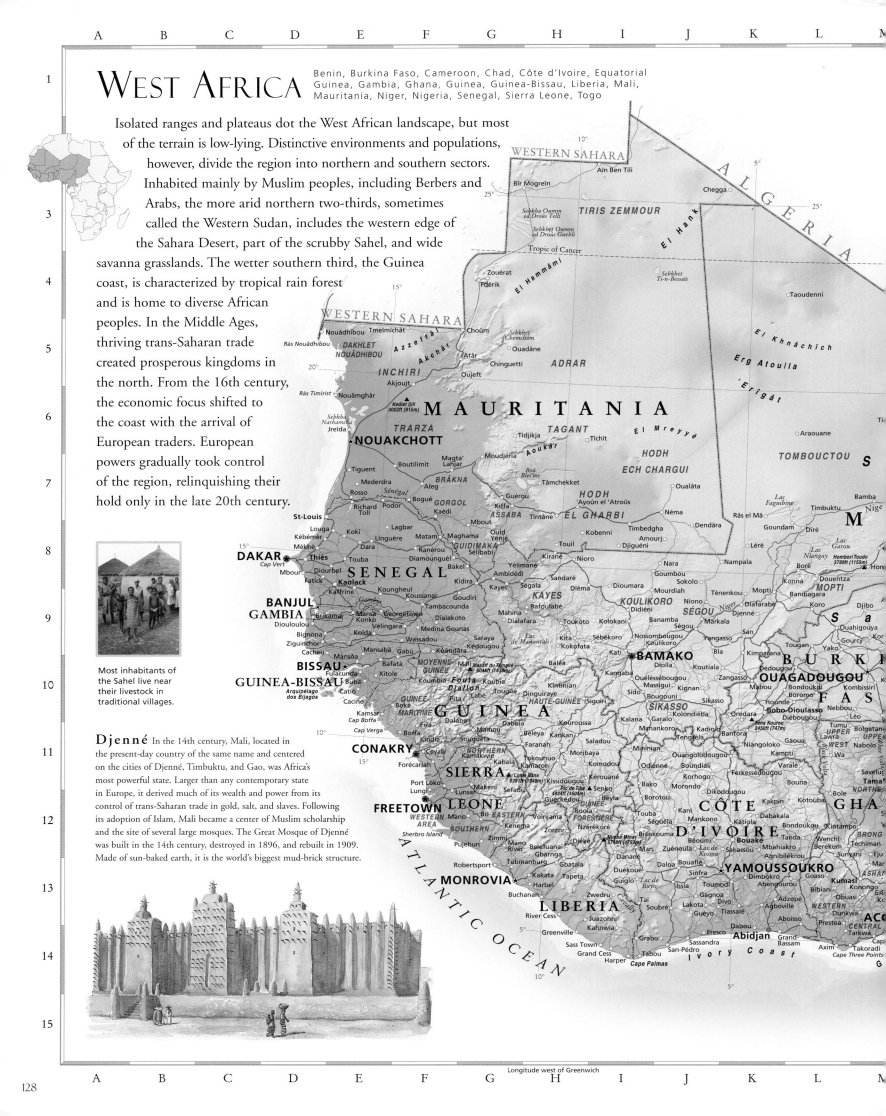

WEST AFRICA

Benin, Burkina Faso, Cameroon, Chad, Côte d'Ivoire, Equatorial Guinea, Gambia, Ghana, Guinea, Guinea-Bissau, Liberia, Mali, Mauritania, Niger, Nigeria, Senegal, Sierra Leone, Togo

Isolated ranges and plateaus dot the West African landscape, but most of the terrain is low-lying. Distinctive environments and populations, however, divide the region into northern and southern sectors. Inhabited mainly by Muslim peoples, including Berbers and Arabs, the more arid northern two-thirds, sometimes called the Western Sudan, includes the western edge of the Sahara Desert, part of the scrubby Sahel, and wide savanna grasslands. The wetter southern third, the Guinea coast, is characterized by tropical rain forest and is home to diverse African peoples. In the Middle Ages, thriving trans-Saharan trade created prosperous kingdoms in the north. From the 16th century, the economic focus shifted to the coast with the arrival of European traders. European powers gradually took control of the region, relinquishing their hold only in the late 20th century.

Most inhabitants of the Sahel live near their livestock in traditional villages.

Djenné In the 14th century, Mali, located in the present-day country of the same name and centered on the cities of Djenné, Timbuktu, and Gao, was Africa's most powerful state. Larger than any contemporary state in Europe, it derived much of its wealth and power from its control of trans-Saharan trade in gold, salt, and slaves. Following its adoption of Islam, Mali became a center of Muslim scholarship and the site of several large mosques. The Great Mosque of Djenné was built in the 14th century, destroyed in 1896, and rebuilt in 1909. Made of sun-baked earth, it is the world's biggest mud-brick structure.

Longitude west of Greenwich

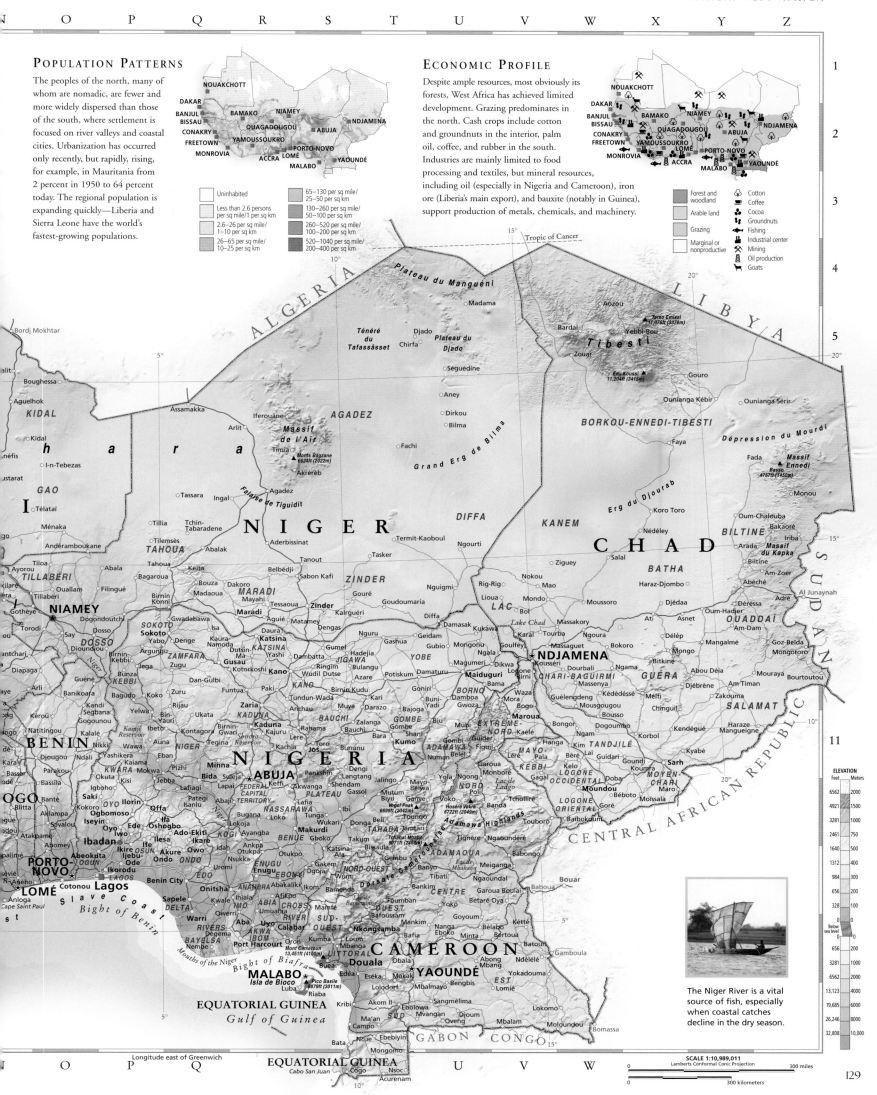

POPULATION PATTERNS

The peoples of the north, many of whom are nomadic, are fewer and more widely dispersed than those of the south, where settlement is focused on river valleys and coastal cities. Urbanization has occurred only recently, but rapidly, rising, for example, in Mauritania from 2 percent in 1950 to 64 percent today. The regional population is expanding quickly—Liberia and Sierra Leone have the world's fastest-growing populations.

Uninhabited
Less than 2.6 persons per sq mile/1 per sq km
2.6–26 per sq mile/1–10 per sq km
26–65 per sq mile/10–25 per sq km
65–130 per sq mile/25–50 per sq km
130–260 per sq mile/50–100 per sq km
260–520 per sq mile/100–200 per sq km
520–1040 per sq mile/200–400 per sq km

ECONOMIC PROFILE

Despite ample resources, most obviously its forests, West Africa has achieved limited development. Grazing predominates in the north. Cash crops include cotton and groundnuts in the interior, palm oil, coffee, and rubber in the south. Industries are mainly limited to food processing and textiles, but mineral resources, including oil (especially in Nigeria and Cameroon), iron ore (Liberia's main export), and bauxite (notably in Guinea), support production of metals, chemicals, and machinery.

Forest and woodland
Arable land
Grazing
Marginal or nonproductive

Cotton
Coffee
Cocoa
Groundnuts
Fishing
Industrial center
Mining
Oil production
Goats

The Niger River is a vital source of fish, especially when coastal catches decline in the dry season.

SCALE 1:10,989,011
Lamberts Conformal Conic Projection
300 miles
300 kilometers

CENTRAL AND EAST AFRICA

Burundi, Central African Republic, Congo, Democratic Republic of Congo, Gabon, Kenya, Rwanda, São Tomé and Príncipe, Tanzania, Uganda

The Congo Basin covers most of Central Africa, extending from the west coast northeastward to the tablelands that cross the Central African Republic, east to the Mitumba and Ruwenzori mountains, and south into Angola and Zambia. A wet climate and dense cover of tropical rain forest make overland travel through the basin notoriously difficult, and the Congo and other rivers are still major communications routes. The dividing line between Central Africa and East Africa is the Great Rift Valley. On its eastern flank, the rain forests yield to savannas roamed by a great diversity of wild animals, as well as herds of cattle and sheep. Violence has plagued these countries in recent decades, including civil wars in Uganda and the Democratic Republic of Congo, and interethnic massacres in Rwanda and Burundi.

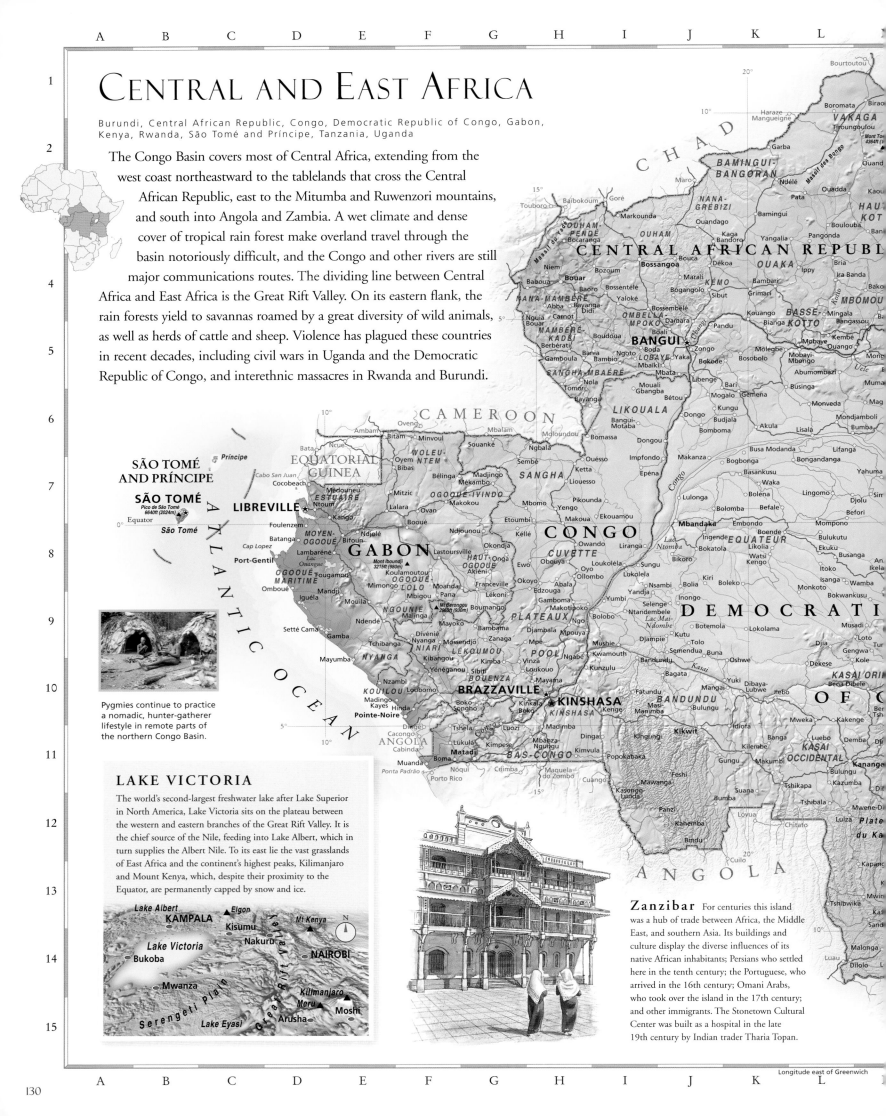

Pygmies continue to practice a nomadic, hunter-gatherer lifestyle in remote parts of the northern Congo Basin.

LAKE VICTORIA

The world's second-largest freshwater lake after Lake Superior in North America, Lake Victoria sits on the plateau between the western and eastern branches of the Great Rift Valley. It is the chief source of the Nile, feeding into Lake Albert, which in turn supplies the Albert Nile. To its east lie the vast grasslands of East Africa and the continent's highest peaks, Kilimanjaro and Mount Kenya, which, despite their proximity to the Equator, are permanently capped by snow and ice.

Zanzibar For centuries this island was a hub of trade between Africa, the Middle East, and southern Asia. Its buildings and culture display the diverse influences of its native African inhabitants; Persians who settled here in the tenth century; the Portuguese, who arrived in the 16th century; Omani Arabs, who took over the island in the 17th century; and other immigrants. The Stonetown Cultural Center was built as a hospital in the late 19th century by Indian trader Tharia Topan.

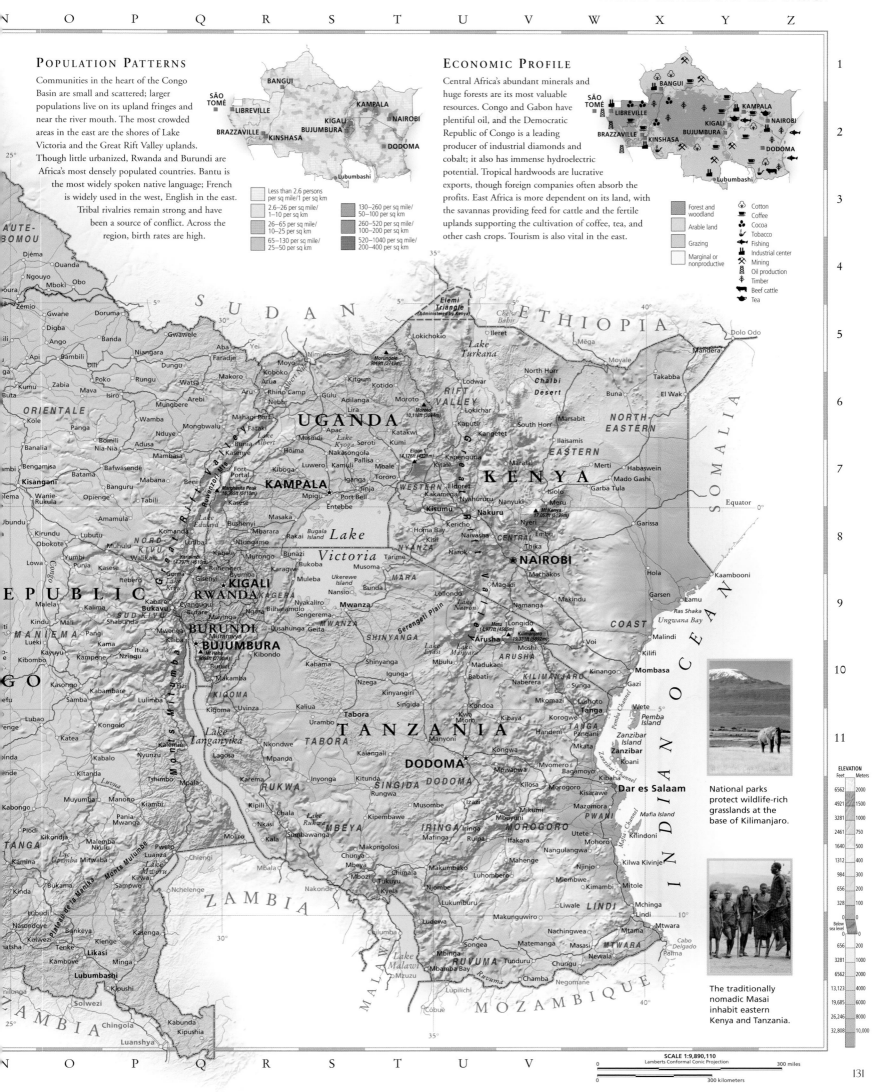

POPULATION PATTERNS

Communities in the heart of the Congo Basin are small and scattered; larger populations live on its upland fringes and near the river mouth. The most crowded areas in the east are the shores of Lake Victoria and the Great Rift Valley uplands. Though little urbanized, Rwanda and Burundi are Africa's most densely populated countries. Bantu is the most widely spoken native language; French is widely used in the west, English in the east. Tribal rivalries remain strong and have been a source of conflict. Across the region, birth rates are high.

Less than 2.6 persons per sq mile/1 per sq km
2.6–26 per sq mile/ 1–10 per sq km
26–65 per sq mile/ 10–25 per sq km
65–130 per sq mile/ 25–50 per sq km
130–260 per sq mile/ 50–100 per sq km
260–520 per sq mile/ 100–200 per sq km
520–1040 per sq mile/ 200–400 per sq km

ECONOMIC PROFILE

Central Africa's abundant minerals and huge forests are its most valuable resources. Congo and Gabon have plentiful oil, and the Democratic Republic of Congo is a leading producer of industrial diamonds and cobalt; it also has immense hydroelectric potential. Tropical hardwoods are lucrative exports, though foreign companies often absorb the profits. East Africa is more dependent on its land, with the savannas providing feed for cattle and the fertile uplands supporting the cultivation of coffee, tea, and other cash crops. Tourism is also vital in the east.

Forest and woodland
Arable land
Grazing
Marginal or nonproductive

Cotton
Coffee
Cocoa
Tobacco
Fishing
Industrial center
Mining
Oil production
Timber
Beef cattle
Tea

National parks protect wildlife-rich grasslands at the base of Kilimanjaro.

The traditionally nomadic Masai inhabit eastern Kenya and Tanzania.

ELEVATION
Feet	Meters
6562	2000
4921	1500
3281	1000
2461	750
1640	500
1312	400
984	300
656	200
328	100
0	0
Below sea level	0
656	200
3281	1000
6562	2000
13,123	4000
19,685	6000
26,246	8000
32,808	10,000

SCALE 1:9,890,110
Lamberts Conformal Conic Projection
300 miles
300 kilometers

SOUTHERN AFRICA

Angola, Botswana, Comoros, Lesotho, Madagascar, Malawi, Mozambique, Namibia, Republic of South Africa, Swaziland, Zambia, Zimbabwe

Consisting of an undulating tableland rimmed by escarpments and narrow coastal plains, the southern African mainland takes in contrasting environments, including the Namib and Kalahari deserts, the tropical forests of northern Mozambique, and the "Highveld" grasslands of South Africa. About 250 miles (400 km) off its east coast lie the culturally and ecologically distinct island of Madagascar and the small Comoros archipelago. As in other parts of Africa, colonialism left the region a legacy of instability and inequality. Portugal's efforts to retain Mozambique and Angola initiated devastating wars from the 1960s to the early 1990s. White-minority rule sparked conflict in postcolonial Zimbabwe, in Namibia, and in South Africa, where racial segregation was enshrined in law in 1948 as the system of apartheid, and formally abolished only in 1994.

POPULATION PATTERNS

The east is more densely populated than the west, with heavy settlement occurring in southern Mozambique, central and southern Zimbabwe, and between Pretoria, Durban, and Port Elizabeth in South Africa. Few people live in the western deserts, and Namibia and Botswana are two of Africa's least densely populated countries. Urbanization remains between 30 and 50 percent in most countries, but reaches 60 percent in South Africa. Most southern Africans belong to Bantu-speaking groups, such as the Zulu, Swazi, and Ndebele (Matabele), but Madagascar's Malagasy peoples originated in Indonesia.

	Uninhabited
	Less than 2.6 persons per sq mile/1 per sq km
	2.6–26 per sq mile/ 1–10 per sq km
	26–65 per sq mile/ 10–25 per sq km
	65–130 per sq mile/ 25–50 per sq km
	130–260 per sq mile/ 50–100 per sq km
	260–520 per sq mile/ 100–200 per sq km

ECONOMIC PROFILE

South Africa has by far the most developed and diversified industrial sector in Africa. Led by iron and steel, transport equipment, and chemicals, it accounts for one-third of the continent's total manufacturing output. The country also has huge mineral reserves, including diamonds, gold (half of world reserves), uranium, and iron ore. Uranium and diamonds are also found in Namibia, gold in Zimbabwe. Angola has sizable oil reserves, Madagascar deposits of graphite. The best arable land lies in the east. Cash crops include tobacco, coffee, tea, and citrus fruits—South Africa is the world's largest producer of grapefruit.

Corn (maize) · Citrus fruits · Coffee · Tea · Wine · Tobacco · Beef cattle · Sheep · Fishing · Industrial center · Mining · Oil production

Forest and woodland · Arable land · Grazing · Marginal or nonproductive

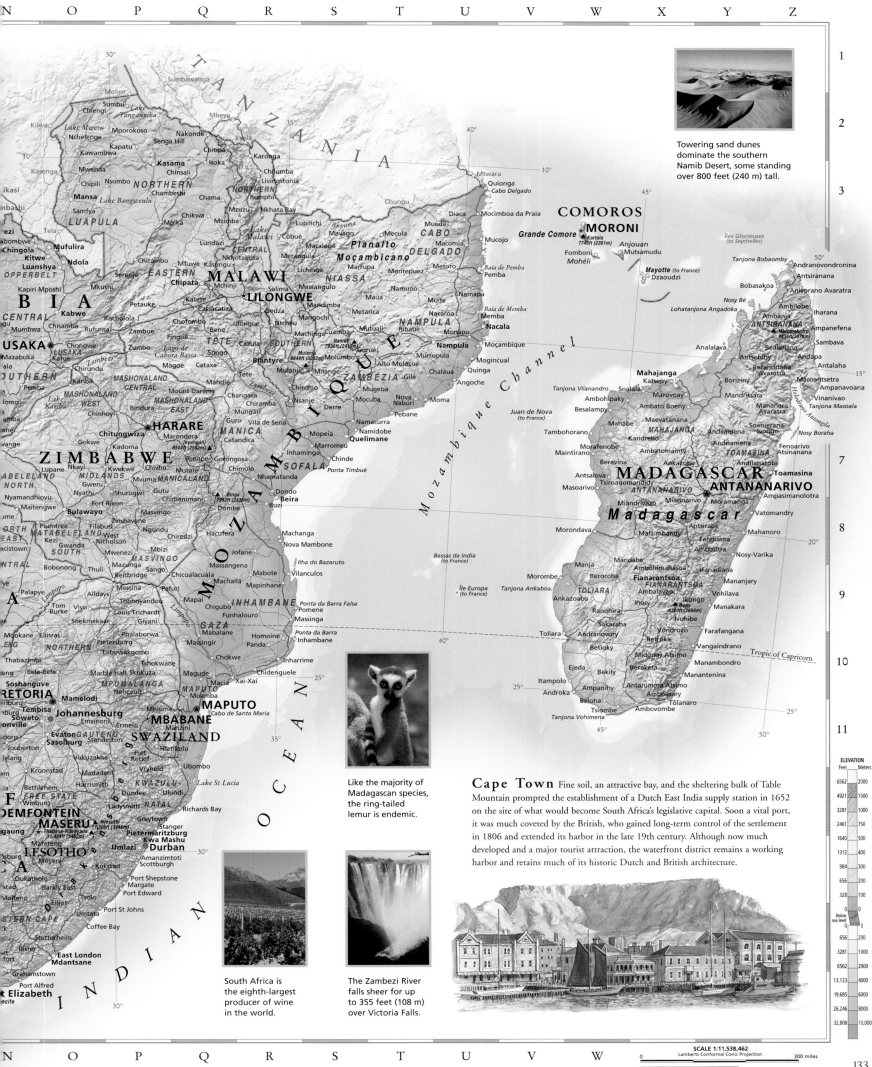

Towering sand dunes dominate the southern Namib Desert, some standing over 800 feet (240 m) tall.

Like the majority of Madagascan species, the ring-tailed lemur is endemic.

South Africa is the eighth-largest producer of wine in the world.

The Zambezi River falls sheer for up to 355 feet (108 m) over Victoria Falls.

Cape Town Fine soil, an attractive bay, and the sheltering bulk of Table Mountain prompted the establishment of a Dutch East India supply station in 1652 on the site of what would become South Africa's legislative capital. Soon a vital port, it was much coveted by the British, who gained long-term control of the settlement in 1806 and extended its harbor in the late 19th century. Although now much developed and a major tourist attraction, the waterfront district remains a working harbor and retains much of its historic Dutch and British architecture.

ELEVATION

Feet	Meters
6562	2000
4921	1500
3281	1000
2461	750
1640	500
1312	400
984	300
656	200
328	100
Below sea level	
656	200
3281	1000
6562	2000
13,123	4000
19,685	6000
26,246	8000
32,808	10,000

SCALE 1:11,538,462
Lamberts Conformal Conic Projection

0 — 300 miles
0 — 300 kilometers

AUSTRALIA

The world's sixth-largest country by area, Australia constitutes an entire continent—the world's smallest, flattest, and (after Antarctica) driest. Its massive landmass consists of an ancient western plateau joined by broad sedimentary lowlands to heavily eroded eastern ranges. Known as the Great Dividing Range, the ranges parallel the Pacific coast, separating the better-watered eastern seaboard from the vast, arid interior or "outback." Despite the continent's poor soils and harsh climate, Aboriginal peoples lived off the land for 60,000 years, developing one of the world's most enduring societies. Europeans began arriving only in the late 18th century after the founding of a British penal colony at Port Jackson, now Sydney, in 1788. This and other British colonies drew increasing numbers of free settlers, especially after the discovery of gold in the southeast in the mid-19th century. In 1901, the colonies agreed to federation, resulting in the creation of the independent nation of Australia.

POPULATION PATTERNS

Recent settlers have shunned the interior, clustering along the temperate east and southwest coasts, where 84 percent of Australians occupy one percent of the land. In the outback, vast areas are devoid of people. Although immigration from Asia has risen in the last 30 years, the majority of Australians are still of European, especially British, origin and English is the official language. Aboriginal and Torres Strait Islander peoples constitute just 2.4 percent of the population. Birth rates are low, and it is estimated that by 2035 immigration will be the country's only source of growth.

Uninhabited

Less than 2.6 persons per sq mile/1 per sq km

2.6–26 per sq mile/ 1–10 per sq km

26–65 per sq mile/ 10–25 per sq km

Cereals
Wine
Sugarcane
Beef cattle
Sheep
Fishing
Industrial center
Mining
Tourism
Timber
Gas production
Oil production

Forest and woodland

Arable land

Grazing

Marginal or nonproductive

ECONOMIC PROFILE

Australia's economy was founded on agriculture, especially the wool industry, and mining. Arable land is limited to the temperate zones and irrigated areas along major rivers. Wheat is the largest crop and Australia is the world's third-largest exporter. The country is self-sufficient in natural gas and has the world's largest reserves of lead, uranium, silver, and zinc. It is also estimated to have 40 percent of world bauxite supplies and at least 20 percent of world coal, iron ore, and diamond reserves. These resources support heavy industries such as the manufacture of steel, machinery, cars, and chemicals, but services, including a thriving retail trade, banking, and tourism, employ 70 percent of the workforce.

Founded in 1939, the Royal Flying Doctor Service provides medical services to people in remote outback communities.

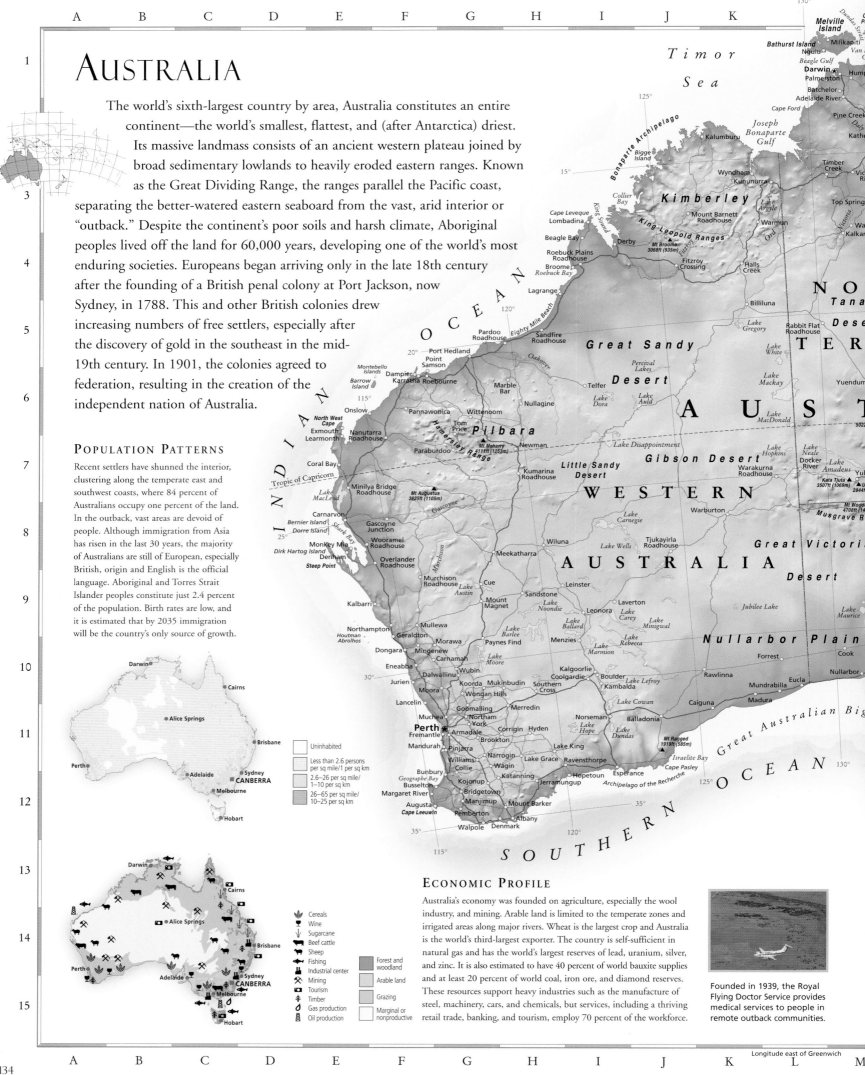

Longitude east of Greenwich

THE GREAT DIVIDING RANGE

More correctly called the Eastern Highlands, the Great Dividing Range stretches from Cape York in northeastern Australia to the island of Tasmania. Rather than a single range, it consists of a chain of eroded plateaus and peaks. The highest part of the range, known as the Australian Alps, lies between Canberra and southern Victoria. Capped by Mount Kosciuszko, the country's tallest peak, the Alps have winter snowfields as large as those of Switzerland, and are the source of the continent's longest waterway, the Murray–Darling.

The rain forests of northern Queensland harbor 3,000 plant species, one-quarter of which grow nowhere else.

Introduced to Australia in 1915 from Hawaii, surfing has become an enormously popular recreational pastime.

Sydney The site of the first major European settlement in Australia, Sydney occupies a large, sheltered, and scenic harbor around which it has grown steadily over the past 200 years. Now home to more than 4 million people, it is Australia's largest urban center, sprawling across almost 4,000 square miles (10,000 sq km)—twice the area of New York City. Two highly distinctive landmarks constructed in the 20th century helped the city establish an international identity and have become national icons: the steel, single-span Sydney Harbour Bridge, completed in 1932, and the adjacent Sydney Opera House, designed by Danish architect Jørn Utzon, which opened in 1973.

The perpetuation of long-established rites and customs is an integral part of life in Aboriginal communities.

ELEVATION	
Feet	Meters
6562	2000
4921	1500
3281	1000
2461	750
1640	500
1312	400
984	300
656	200
328	100
Below sea level	
656	200
3281	1000
6562	2000
13,123	4000
19,685	6000
26,246	8000
32,808	10,000

SCALE 1:12,637,363
Lamberts Conformal Conic Projection

0 — 300 miles
0 — 300 kilometers

135

NEW ZEALAND

Situated 1,000 miles (1,600 km) southeast of Australia, its nearest neighbor, New Zealand consists of two large islands and several smaller ones. Both main islands straddle fault lines between the Indo-Australian and Pacific tectonic plates. Movement along these faults causes sporadic earthquakes and has formed active volcanoes and geysers in the North Island; over millions of years, it has also pushed up the steep-sided peaks of the Southern Alps, which form the backbone of the South Island. This rugged interior and the South Island's generally cold, wet climate concentrated the development of modern infrastructure in the North Island and along the drier, more fertile east coast of the South Island. Annexed by Britain in 1840, New Zealand became a self-governing colony in 1856 and a dominion in 1907, but did not achieve full independence until 1947. The descendants of British colonists now far outnumber the indigenous Maori, but Maori remains an official language and in recent years the government has made some reparations to Maori peoples for loss of traditional lands.

VOLCANO COUNTRY

Volcanic activity has fashioned the landscape of the North Island's central plateau and still has the potential to modify it further. Lake Taupo, the country's largest lake, occupies a crater formed by a massive volcanic explosion thought to have taken place in AD 186. To its south stretches a line of active volcanoes—Tongariro, Ngauruhoe, and Ruapehu—all of which erupted in the 20th century. In 1996, in the country's largest eruption in 400 years, Ruapehu spewed great clouds of steam and ash over the surrounding skifields; fortunately, there were no casualties. Farther west, the huge cone of Mount Taranaki (Mount Egmont) looms over the southwestern corner of the island. Now dormant, it last erupted in the 18th century.

Wellington Though Auckland is by far the largest city in New Zealand, Wellington is the country's national capital and major business center. The city occupies a large sheltered harbor—the flooded crater of an ancient volcano—at the southern end of the North Island. Europeans arrived in 1840 and moved their seat of government here in 1865. The foreshore, much of it reclaimed land, is the site of the commercial district and major government buildings including the parliament, with its distinctive executive office building, widely known as the Beehive. Designed by British architect Sir Basil Spence, it was begun in 1969 and completed in 1980.

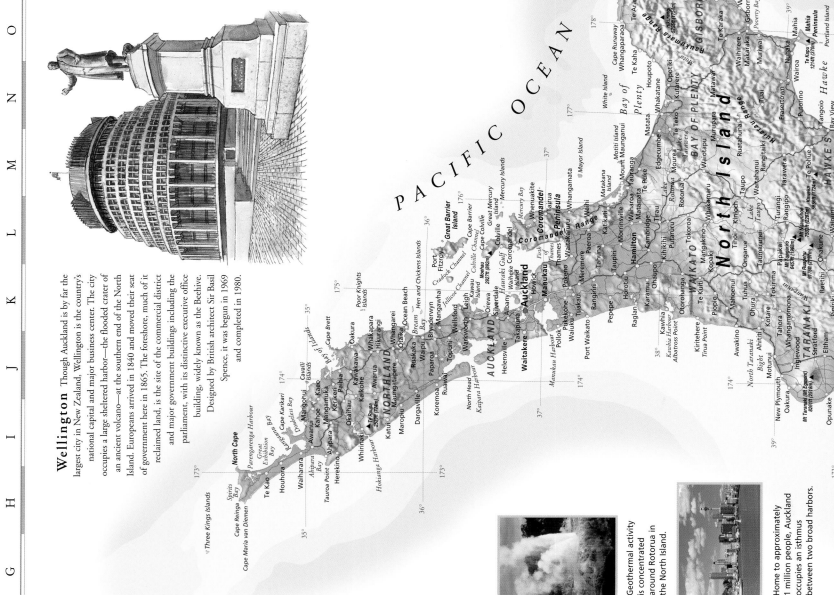

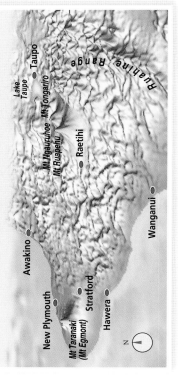

Geothermal activity is concentrated around Rotorua in the North Island.

Home to approximately 1 million people, Auckland occupies an isthmus between two broad harbors.

ELEVATION

Feet / Meters
6562 / 2000
4921 / 1500
3281 / 1000
2461 / 750
1640 / 500
1312 / 400
984 / 300
656 / 200
328 / 100
0 / Below sea level
656 / 200
3281 / 1000
6562 / 2000
13,123 / 4000
19,685 / 6000
26,246 / 8000
32,808 / 10,000

NEW ZEALAND

POPULATION PATTERNS

The North Island constitutes 42 percent of the country but is home to more than three-quarters of the population; indeed, more than 30 percent of New Zealanders live in the Auckland region. About 75 percent of inhabitants live in towns and cities. People of European extraction make up 80 percent of the population, and one in seven New Zealanders is Maori. Ethnic diversity is increasing. The number of residents of Asian origin, for example, climbed 140 percent between 1991 and 2001. Many Pacific Islander people have settled in New Zealand, and Auckland is recognized as the world's largest Polynesian city.

Population density legend:
- Uninhabited
- Less than 2.6 persons per sq mile/1 per sq km
- 2.6–26 per sq mile/1–10 per sq km
- 26–65 per sq mile/10–25 per sq km

ECONOMIC PROFILE

New Zealand has a long association with wool, which was the country's leading agricultural product until the late 1970s. But the sheep population has declined, and dairy products and meat are now the nation's most valuable exports. Forests cover 30 percent of the country and forest products, overwhelmingly from plantations, constitute the third most lucrative export. New Zealand is self-sufficient in all energy sources except oil; two-thirds of its electricity comes from hydroelectric power and over 6 percent from geothermal power. Leading industries include foods and beverages (notably wine), machinery, metals, and textiles. However, services employ 65 percent of workers, with tourism alone generating 10 percent of GDP and supporting one in ten jobs.

Economic legend:
- Forest and woodland
- Arable land
- Grazing
- Marginal or nonproductive
- Fruit
- Wine
- Beef cattle
- Sheep
- Pigs
- Fishing
- Industrial center
- Timber
- Dairy cattle
- Tourism

SCALE 1:3,571,429
Lamberts Conformal Conic Projection
100 miles
100 kilometers

Longitude east of Greenwich

Cathedral Square is the heart of the South Island's largest city, Christchurch.

In the western South Island, Franz Josef Glacier (above) and Fox Glacier descend as far as the coastal lowlands.

The traditional welcome dance, or powhiri, is still performed for visitors to Maori meeting houses.

The southwest coast of the South Island is characterized by deep fjords, including spectacular Milford Sound.

South Island

PACIFIC OCEAN

TASMAN SEA

WELLINGTON

Christchurch

Dunedin

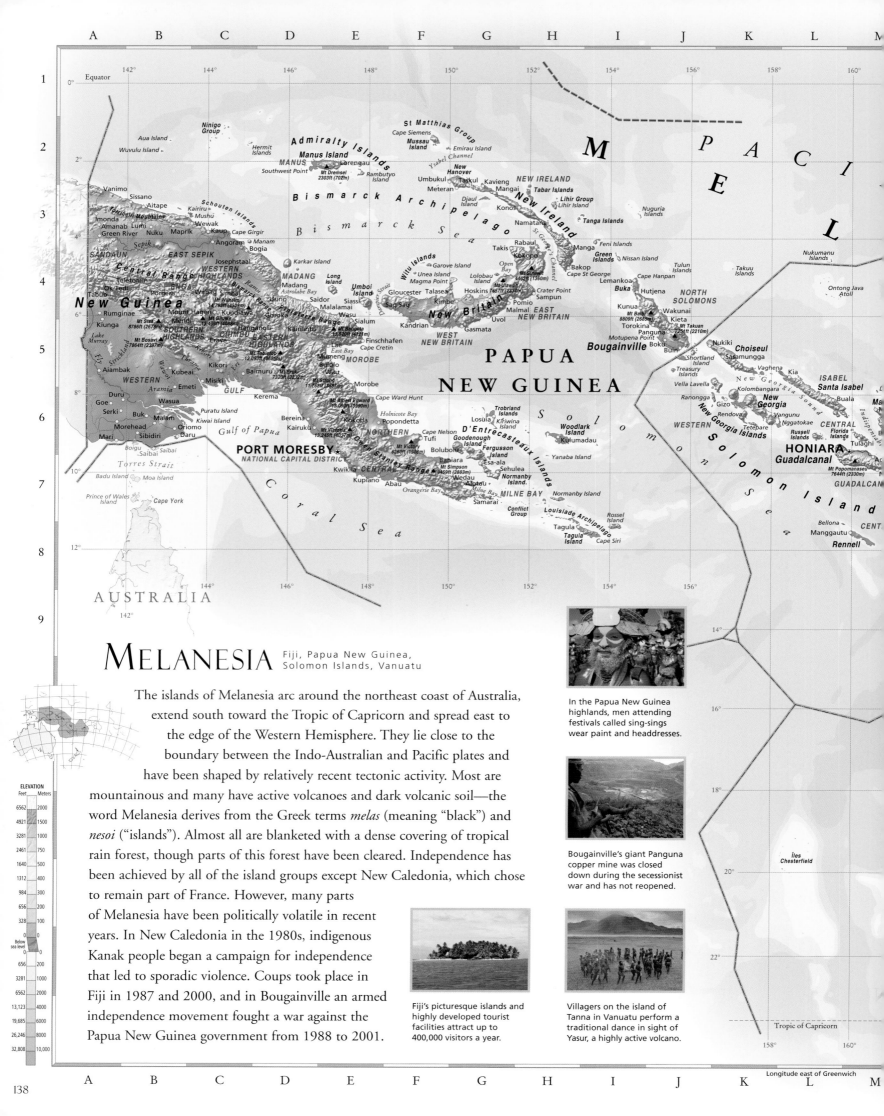

MELANESIA

Fiji, Papua New Guinea,
Solomon Islands, Vanuatu

The islands of Melanesia arc around the northeast coast of Australia, extend south toward the Tropic of Capricorn and spread east to the edge of the Western Hemisphere. They lie close to the boundary between the Indo-Australian and Pacific plates and have been shaped by relatively recent tectonic activity. Most are mountainous and many have active volcanoes and dark volcanic soil—the word Melanesia derives from the Greek terms *melas* (meaning "black") and *nesoi* ("islands"). Almost all are blanketed with a dense covering of tropical rain forest, though parts of this forest have been cleared. Independence has been achieved by all of the island groups except New Caledonia, which chose to remain part of France. However, many parts of Melanesia have been politically volatile in recent years. In New Caledonia in the 1980s, indigenous Kanak people began a campaign for independence that led to sporadic violence. Coups took place in Fiji in 1987 and 2000, and in Bougainville an armed independence movement fought a war against the Papua New Guinea government from 1988 to 2001.

In the Papua New Guinea highlands, men attending festivals called sing-sings wear paint and headdresses.

Bougainville's giant Panguna copper mine was closed down during the secessionist war and has not reopened.

Fiji's picturesque islands and highly developed tourist facilities attract up to 400,000 visitors a year.

Villagers on the island of Tanna in Vanuatu perform a traditional dance in sight of Yasur, a highly active volcano.

ELEVATION

Feet	Meters
6562	2000
4921	1500
3281	1000
2461	750
1640	500
1312	400
984	300
656	200
328	100
Below sea level	0
0	0
656	200
3281	1000
6562	2000
13,123	4000
19,685	6000
26,246	8000
32,808	10,000

POPULATION PATTERNS

Population density and growth rates are high in Melanesia, with steadily increasing numbers of people occupying relatively small islands. In the largest, most populous country, Papua New Guinea, the cooler highlands are the most crowded areas. Four-fifths of the inhabitants of New Caledonia live in the capital, Nouméa, but elsewhere urbanization remains low. An extraordinary variety of languages is spoken in Melanesia: over 700 are in use in Papua New Guinea, and over 100 in much smaller Vanuatu. Pidgin is used as a lingua franca in many areas and English is an official language everywhere except New Caledonia.

Less than 2.6 persons per sq mile/1 per sq km
2.6–26 per sq mile/1–10 per sq km
26–65 per sq mile/10–25 per sq km
65–130 per sq mile/25–50 per sq km

ECONOMIC PROFILE

The majority of people rely on fishing or subsistence farming of sweet potato, yams, taro, or cassava. Cash crops include cocoa, coffee, palm oil, coconuts and copra, tuna, and sugar in Fiji. Exceptionally, Vanuatu has a thriving beef industry. Minerals are abundant and widespread, including deposits of copper and gold in Papua New Guinea (Bougainville has the world's largest copper reserves), 40 percent of the world's nickel in New Caledonia, gold in Fiji, and phosphates in the Solomons. Industries are limited to resource (mainly food) processing, services are dominated by tourism. Vanuatu promotes itself as a tax haven, offering an offshore shipping registry and banking.

Coconuts
Rubber
Fishing
Industrial center
Mining
Tourism
Timber
Coffee
Palm oil

Forest and woodland
Arable land
Grazing

SCALE 1:10,439,560
Mercator Projection

0   200 miles
0   200 kilometers

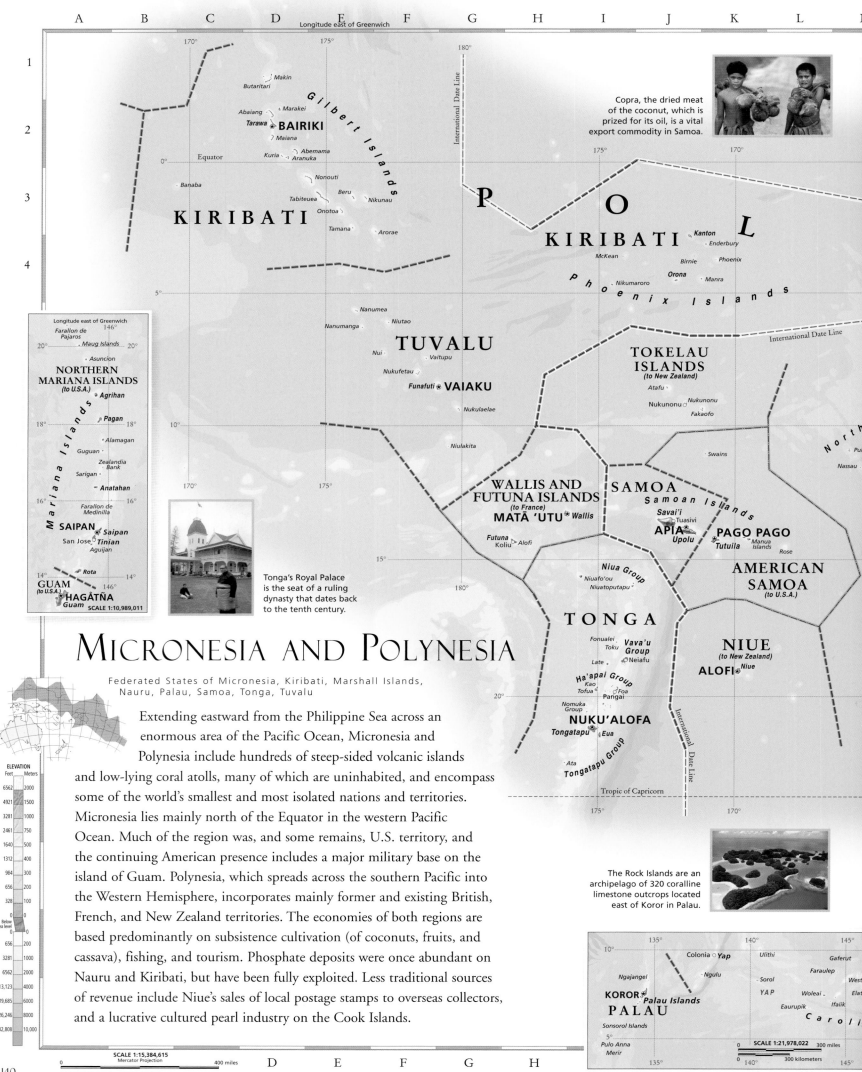

A B C D E F G H I J K L M

1
2
3
4

Makin
Butaritari

Abaiang Marakei
Tarawa ✴ BAIRIKI
Maiana

Equator
Kuria Abemama
Aranuka

Banaba
Nonouti

Beru Nikunau
Tabiteuea
Onotoa Arorae
Tamana

Gilbert Islands

K I R I B A T I

Copra, the dried meat
of the coconut, which is
prized for its oil, is a vital
export commodity in Samoa.

P O L

K I R I B A T I

Kanton
Enderbury
McKean
Birnie Phoenix
Orona
Nikumaroro Manra

Phoenix Islands

International Date Line

Nanumea
Niutao
Nanumanga

Nui Vaitupu
Nukufetau

T U V A L U

Funafuti ✴ VAIAKU

Nukulaelae

Niulakita

TOKELAU ISLANDS
(to New Zealand)
Atafu
Nukunonu Nukunonu
Fakaofo

International Date Line

North

Swains

Puk
Nassau

Longitude east of Greenwich
146°
Farallon de
Pajaros
Maug Islands
Asuncion

**NORTHERN
MARIANA ISLANDS**
(to U.S.A.)

Agrihan
Pagan
Alamagan
Guguan
Zealandia
Bank
Sarigan
Anatahan

Farallon de
Medinilla
SAIPAN Saipan
San Jose Tinian
Aguijan
Rota

GUAM
(to U.S.A.) **HAGÅTÑA**
Guam 146°
SCALE 1:10,989,011

Mariana Islands

**WALLIS AND
FUTUNA ISLANDS**
(to France)
MATÃ 'UTU ✴ Wallis

Futuna
Koliu Alofi

Niulakita

SAMOA
Samoan Islands
Savai'i
Tuasivi
APIA ✴
Upolu

PAGO PAGO
Tutuila Manua
Islands
Rose

**AMERICAN
SAMOA**
(to U.S.A.)

Tonga's Royal Palace
is the seat of a ruling
dynasty that dates back
to the tenth century.

Niua Group
Niuafo'ou
Niuatoputapu

T O N G A

Fonualei
Toku **Vava'u
Group**
Late Neiafu

Ha'apai Group
Kao
Tofua Foa
Pangai
Nomuka
Group

NUKU'ALOFA
Tongatapu Eua

Ata
Tongatapu Group

NIUE
(to New Zealand)
ALOFI ✴ Niue

International Date Line

Tropic of Capricorn

MICRONESIA AND POLYNESIA

Federated States of Micronesia, Kiribati, Marshall Islands,
Nauru, Palau, Samoa, Tonga, Tuvalu

Extending eastward from the Philippine Sea across an
enormous area of the Pacific Ocean, Micronesia and
Polynesia include hundreds of steep-sided volcanic islands
and low-lying coral atolls, many of which are uninhabited, and encompass
some of the world's smallest and most isolated nations and territories.
Micronesia lies mainly north of the Equator in the western Pacific
Ocean. Much of the region was, and some remains, U.S. territory, and
the continuing American presence includes a major military base on the
island of Guam. Polynesia, which spreads across the southern Pacific into
the Western Hemisphere, incorporates mainly former and existing British,
French, and New Zealand territories. The economies of both regions are
based predominantly on subsistence cultivation (of coconuts, fruits, and
cassava), fishing, and tourism. Phosphate deposits were once abundant on
Nauru and Kiribati, but have been fully exploited. Less traditional sources
of revenue include Niue's sales of local postage stamps to overseas collectors,
and a lucrative cultured pearl industry on the Cook Islands.

ELEVATION
Feet Meters

6562 2000
4921 1500
3281 1000
2461 750
1640 500
1312 400
984 300
656 200
328 100
0 0
Below
sea level
0 0
656 200
3281 1000
6562 2000
13,123 4000
19,685 6000
26,246 8000
32,808 10,000

The Rock Islands are an
archipelago of 320 coralline
limestone outcrops located
east of Koror in Palau.

135° 140° 145°

Colonia **Yap** Ulithi
Ngajangel Ngulu Gaferut
Sorol Faraulep
West
YAP Woleai Elate
Eaurupik Ifalik
KOROR ✴
Palau Islands
PALAU
Sonsorol Islands
Caroli
Pulo Anna
Merir SCALE 1:21,978,022
300 miles
300 kilometers
135° 140° 145°

SCALE 1:15,384,615
Mercator Projection
400 miles
400 kilometers
D E F G H

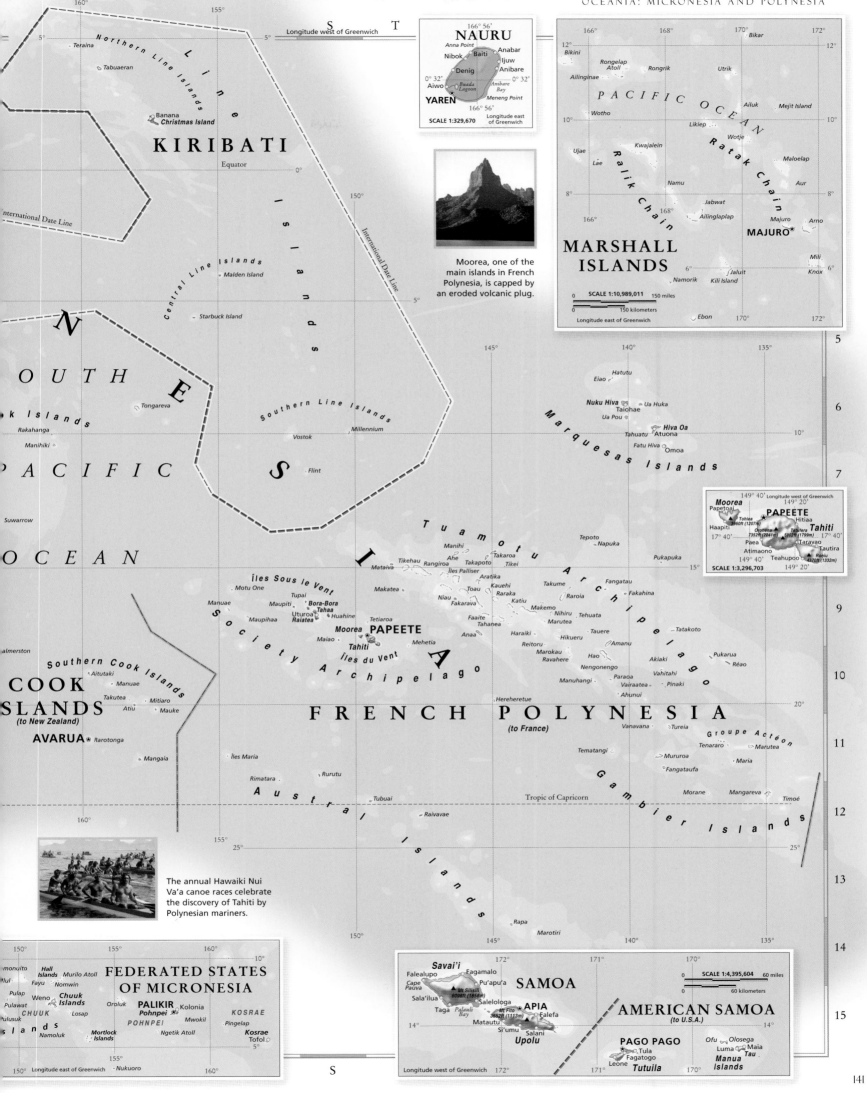

Moorea, one of the main islands in French Polynesia, is capped by an eroded volcanic plug.

The annual Hawaiki Nui Va'a canoe races celebrate the discovery of Tahiti by Polynesian mariners.

THE ARCTIC

Covering 5.5 million square miles (14.1 million sq km), the Arctic Ocean is the world's smallest ocean. It is ringed by the continental fringes of North America, Europe, and Asia, as well as associated islands, including the largest island on Earth, Greenland. The ocean reaches depths of over 18,000 feet (5,500 m) and is divided into major basins by extensive undersea ranges, the largest of which, the Lomonosov Ridge, surpasses 10,000 feet (3,000 m) in height. Pack ice covers most of the sea surface year-round, expanding to reach most surrounding landmasses in winter. This shoreline has been inhabited by indigenous groups such as the North American Inuit, Asian Yakut, and European Saami for thousands of years. They have learned to cope with the Arctic's extreme climate, including months of darkness in winter, and exploit its restricted range of biological resources. Europeans first explored the Arctic Ocean in the 16th century, searching for a shortcut between Europe and Asia. More recently, outsiders have been lured here by the discovery of potentially vast undersea mineral reserves.

The polar ice pack is 10 feet (3 m) thick on average, but ridges form that may be up to three times that depth.

Directly beneath the North Pole, the ocean is 13,410 feet (4,087 m) deep.

NATURAL RESOURCES

The Arctic Ocean's pack ice blocks sunlight, inhibiting photosynthetic processes and limiting marine life, but rich fisheries exist in areas of open ocean such as the Barents, Greenland, and Bering seas. Seals and whales were long a valuable resource for native peoples and, from the late 17th century, the basis of lucrative commercial trades operated by Europeans. Whaling is now banned, but sealing still takes place in Newfoundland and the White Sea. Sparse grazing lands fringe the ocean, providing food for wild caribou in North America and about 3 million domesticated reindeer in Scandinavia and Russia. Huge reserves of oil, coal, and gas have been tapped in northern Siberia and Alaska; even larger supplies are thought to lie offshore, but so far remain inaccessible.

- 🐑 Sheep
- 🐟 Fishing
- 🦐 Shellfish
- ⛏ Mining
- Oil
- Gas
- Reindeer
- Coal

GREENLAND AND ICELAND

At the boundary between the Arctic and Atlantic oceans, the narrow Denmark Strait divides Greenland from the much smaller island of Iceland. About two-thirds of Greenland lies within the Arctic Circle, and the northern tip of the island lies just 500 miles (800 km) from the North Pole. More than 80 percent of the landmass is blanketed by the world's second-largest ice sheet. Cupped within a basin encircled by coastal peaks, it has an average thickness of about 5,000 feet (1,500 m). Iceland sits astride the Reykjanes Ridge, part of the Mid-Atlantic Ridge. Divergence of tectonic plates along this boundary steadily tears the island apart, giving rise to great faults as well as volcanoes and geysers.

In winter, the Arctic fox grows a white coat to blend in with the snow.

About 3,000 people live on Svalbard, working mainly in coal extraction.

Yakut hunters in the Siberian Arctic employ modern means to catch traditional prey, including seals and walruses.

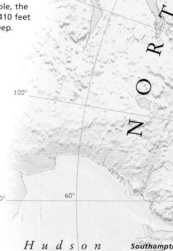

ELEVATION

Feet	Meters
Ice cap	
Ice shelf	
6562	2000
4921	1500
3281	1000
2461	750
1640	500
1312	400
984	300
656	200
328	100
0	0
Below sea level	0

SCALE 1:21,978,022
Lamberts Azimuthal Equal Area Projection

600 miles

600 kilometers

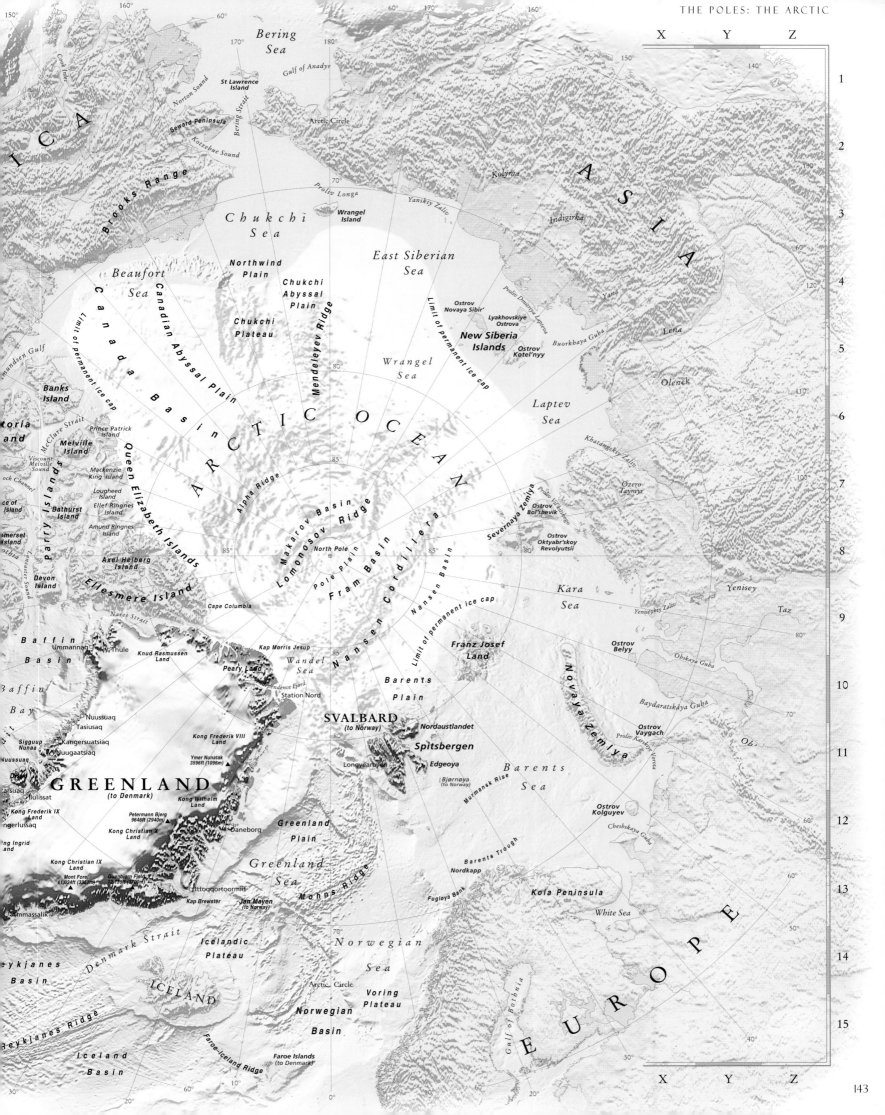

ARCTIC OCEAN
ASIA
EUROPE
GREENLAND
(to Denmark)
ICELAND
SVALBARD
(to Norway)
Bering Sea
Chukchi Sea
East Siberian Sea
Beaufort Sea
Laptev Sea
Kara Sea
Barents Sea
Greenland Sea
Norwegian Sea
Wrangel Sea
Wandel Sea
Baffin Bay
White Sea
Canada Basin
Canadian Abyssal Plain
Northwind Plain
Chukchi Abyssal Plain
Chukchi Plateau
Mendeleyev Ridge
Alpha Ridge
Makarov Basin
Lomonosov Ridge
Pole Plain
Fram Basin
Nansen Cordillera
Nansen Basin
Barents Plain
Greenland Plain
Mohns Ridge
Icelandic Plateau
Voring Plateau
Norwegian Basin
Iceland Basin
Reykjanes Ridge
Reykjanes Basin
Faroe-Iceland Ridge
Baffin Basin
Barents Trough
Murmansk Rise
Fugløya Bank
North Pole
Limit of permanent ice cap
Arctic Circle
Wrangel Island
New Siberia Islands
Ostrov Novaya Sibir'
Lyakhovskiye Ostrova
Ostrov Kotel'nyy
Severnaya Zemlya
Ostrov Bol'shevik
Ostrov Oktyabr'skoy Revolyutsii
Franz Josef Land
Novaya Zemlya
Ostrov Vaygach
Ostrov Kolguyev
Ostrov Belyy
Nordaustlandet
Spitsbergen
Edgeoya
Longyearbyen
Bjørnøya (to Norway)
Jan Mayen (to Norway)
Faroe Islands (to Denmark)
Queen Elizabeth Islands
Ellesmere Island
Axel Heiberg Island
Devon Island
Banks Island
Melville Island
Prince Patrick Island
Bathurst Island
Parry Islands
Cape Columbia
Kap Morris Jesup
Peary Land
Station Nord
Knud Rasmussen Land
Thule
Ummannaq
Kong Frederik VIII Land
Ymer Nunatak 3596ft (1096m)
Kong Wilhelm Land
Petermann Bjerg 9646ft (2940m)
Kong Christian X Land
Kong Christian IX Land
Mont Forel 11,024ft (3360m)
Gunnbjørn Fjeld 12,139ft (3700m)
Daneborg
Ittoqqortoormiit
Kap Brewster
Ammassalik
Nuussuaq
Tasiusaq
Kangersuatsiaq
Nuugaatsiaq
Sigguup Nunaa
Ilulissat
Kong Frederik IX Land
St Lawrence Island
Seward Peninsula
Brooks Range
Gulf of Anadyr
Bering Strait
Norton Sound
Kotzebue Sound
Cook Inlet
Proliv Longa
Yanskiy Zaliv
Proliv Dmitriya Lapteva
Buorkhaya Guba
Khatangskiy Zaliv
Proliv Vil'kitskogo
Ozero Taymyr
Yeniseyskiy Zaliv
Obskaya Guba
Baydaratskaya Guba
Proliv Karskiye Vorota
Cheshskaya Guba
Kola Peninsula
Nordkapp
Gulf of Bothnia
Denmark Strait
Nares Strait
McClure Strait
Viscount Melville Sound
Lancaster Sound
Kolyma
Indigirka
Yana
Lena
Olenek
Yenisey
Taz
Ob
X Y Z
1 2 3 4 5 6 7 8 9 10 11 12 13 14 15

Antarctica

An almost circular landmass centered on the South Pole, Antarctica is the world's fifth-largest as well as its coldest, windiest, driest, and, on average, highest continent. A vast ice sheet covers 98 percent of the land. Among the few topographical features not totally obscured by the ice are the Transantarctic Mountains, which divide the continent into East and West Antarctica. In the east, the ice sheet hides a high plateau; to the west, it conceals a mountainous archipelago. Much of the surrounding ocean freezes in winter, effectively doubling the size of Antarctica, and for much of that season the sun does not rise. These severe conditions drastically restrict animal and plant distribution, and have prohibited permanent human occupation. Nevertheless, Antarctica is home to a fluctuating population of scientists and support staff based at a total of 42 research stations. Their numbers swell annually from around 1,000 in winter to approximately 4,000 in summer.

Icebergs abound in coastal waters, often providing a place for penguins to roost.

THE ANTARCTIC PENINSULA

The roughly circular outline of Antarctica is interrupted by the narrow Antarctic Peninsula, which extends 800 miles (1,300 km) toward the southern tip of South America. The peninsula is mountainous—rising to 13,747 feet (4,190 m) at Mount Jackson—capped by ice sheets and glaciers, and fringed by numerous islands, slender channels, and ice shelves. Nevertheless, it experiences the continent's mildest conditions and includes most of its few patches of ice-free land. From the end of the peninsula, an undersea ridge known as the Scotia Arc runs east then west, forming a great loop that eventually connects with Cape Horn in South America.

Completed in 1975, the U.S. Amundsen–Scott Base at the South Pole is covered by a huge aluminum dome.

THE ANTARCTIC TREATY

Seven countries—Argentina, Australia, Chile, France, New Zealand, Norway, and the United Kingdom—have at one time or other asserted sovereignty over parts of Antarctica. However, by becoming signatories to the Antarctic Treaty of 1959, they and 38 other nations have since agreed to suspend territorial claims and preserve the continent for nonmilitary scientific research. The Antarctic Treaty arose out of a worldwide scientific project called the International Geophysical Year, which began in 1957 and saw 12 nations establish numerous research stations across Antarctica.

NATURAL RESOURCES

Early sealers and whalers almost wiped out the continent's originally abundant marine mammals, but populations of seals and whales have recovered in recent years, especially since the International Whaling Commission declared most of the Southern Ocean a whale sanctuary in 1994. Although 23 countries have agreed to manage Antarctic fisheries for sustainability, illegal fishing is steadily depleting stocks of Antarctic cod, finfish, and toothfish. Geologists concur that Antarctica may harbor great mineral wealth, including copper, gold, platinum, and oil. No economically exploitable reserves have been found, however, and, in any case, mining is banned under the Antarctic Treaty. Tourism is proving a more viable economic activity, with visitor numbers rising steadily.

Fishing
Gas
Tourism
Coal
Precious metals and minerals
Metallic minerals
Whales

Marginal or nonproductive

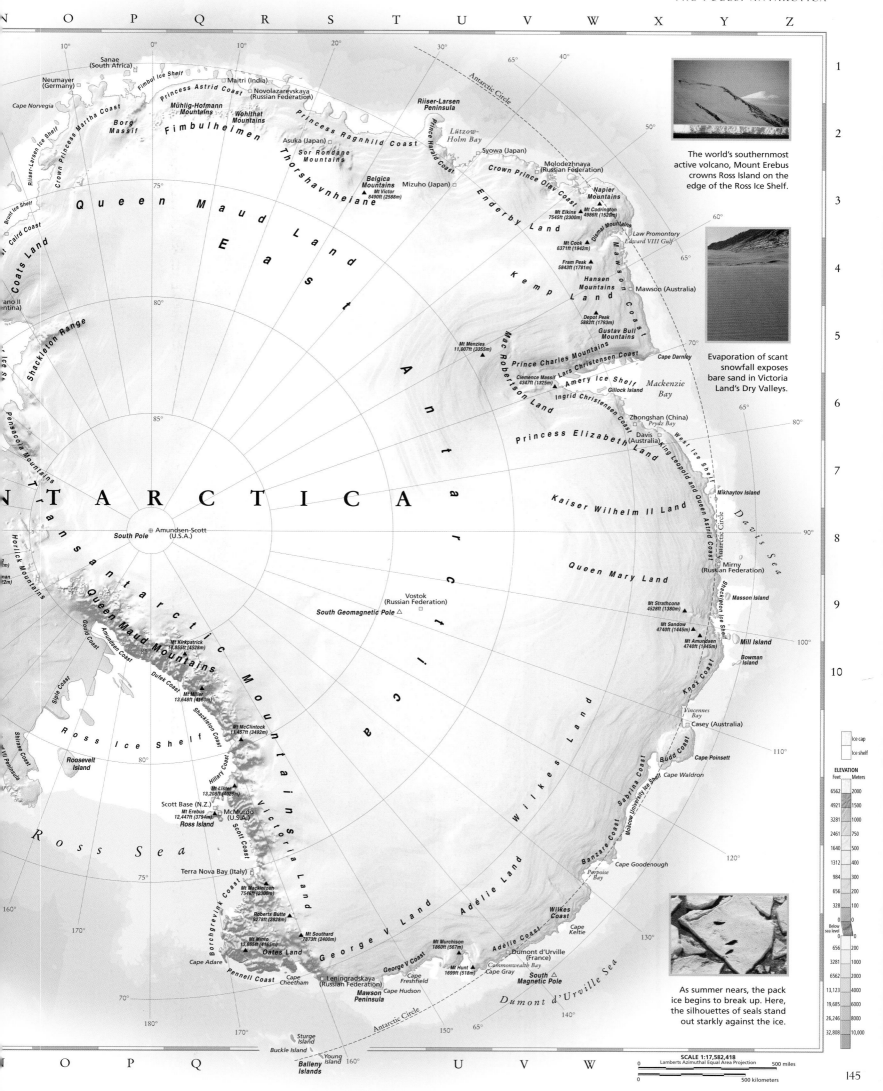

The world's southernmost active volcano, Mount Erebus crowns Ross Island on the edge of the Ross Ice Shelf.

Evaporation of scant snowfall exposes bare sand in Victoria Land's Dry Valleys.

As summer nears, the pack ice begins to break up. Here, the silhouettes of seals stand out starkly against the ice.

Ice cap
Ice shelf

ELEVATION

Feet	Meters
6562	2000
4921	1500
3281	1000
2461	750
1640	500
1312	400
984	300
656	200
328	100
0	0
Below sea level	Below sea level
656	200
3281	1000
6562	2000
13,123	4000
19,685	6000
26,246	8000
32,808	10,000

SCALE 1:17,582,418
Lamberts Azimuthal Equal Area Projection

0   500 miles

0   500 kilometers

145

100 Mile House – Alah

Abbreviations

United States of America

AL	Alabama
AK	Alaska
AZ	Arizona
AR	Arkansas
CA	California
CO	Colorado
CT	Connecticut
DE	Delaware
DC	District of Columbia
FL	Florida
GA	Georgia
HI	Hawaii
ID	Idaho
IL	Illinois
IN	Indiana
IA	Iowa
KS	Kansas
KY	Kentucky
LA	Louisiana
ME	Maine
MD	Maryland
MA	Massachusetts
MI	Michigan
MN	Minnesota
MS	Mississippi
MO	Missouri
MT	Montana
NE	Nebraska
NV	Nevada
NH	New Hampshire
NJ	New Jersey
NM	New Mexico
NY	New York
NC	North Carolina
ND	North Dakota
OH	Ohio
OK	Oklahoma
OR	Oregon
PA	Pennsylvania
RI	Rhode Island
SC	South Carolina
SD	South Dakota
TN	Tennessee
TX	Texas
UT	Utah
VT	Vermont
VA	Virginia
WA	Washington
WV	West Virginia
WI	Wisconsin
WY	Wyoming

Canada

AB	Alberta
BC	British Columbia
MB	Manitoba
NB	New Brunswick
NL	Newfoundland and Labrador
NT	Northwest Territories
NS	Nova Scotia
NU	Nunavut
ON	Ontario
PE	Prince Edward Island
QC	Québec
SK	Saskatchewan
YT	Yukon Territory

Australia

ACT	Australian Capital Territory
NSW	New South Wales
NT	Northern Territory
QLD	Queensland
SA	South Australia
TAS	Tasmania
VIC	Victoria
WA	Western Australia

1

39 G 20 **100 Mile House**, BC, Canada

A

66 H 1 **A Coruña**, Spain
66 J 1 **A Fonsagrada**, Spain
66 G 3 **A Guardia**, Spain
66 J 3 **A Gudiña**, Spain
73 B 17 **Aachen**, Germany
73 H 22 **Aalen**, Germany
69 J 16 **Aalst**, Netherlands
69 E 18 **Aalst**, Luxembourg
68 M 13 **Aalten**, Netherlands
69 D 17 **Aalter**, Belgium
74 F 6 **Aarau**, Switzerland
74 F 6 **Aare**, Switzerland
69 H 18 **Aarschot**, Belgium
69 F 17 **Aartselaar**, Belgium
101 T 9 **Ab-i-Istada**, Afghanistan
112 L 4 **Aba**, China
129 R 14 **Aba**, Nigeria
131 Q 5 **Aba**, Democratic Republic of Congo
100 G 9 **Ābādān**, Iran
100 J 9 **Ābādeh**, Iran
124 J 8 **Abadla**, Algeria
140 D 2 **Abaiang**, Kiribati
129 R 12 **Abaji**, Nigeria
30 M 6 **Abajo Peak**, UT, U.S.A.
129 R 13 **Abakaliki**, Nigeria
89 N 13 **Abakan**, Russian Federation
129 P 8 **Abala**, Niger
130 H 8 **Abala**, Congo
129 Q 8 **Abalak**, Niger
125 N 14 **Abalessa**, Algeria
53 F 17 **Abancay**, Peru
100 J 9 **Abarqū**, Iran
122 L 3 **Abashiri**, Japan
122 L 4 **Abashiri-ko**, Japan
138 F 7 **Abau**, Papua New Guinea
103 R 4 **Abay**, Kazakhstan
127 I 22 **Ābaya Hāyk'**, Ethiopia
89 N 13 **Abaza**, Russian Federation
130 H 4 **Abba**, Central African Republic
96 M 2 **Abbah**, Syria
77 B 17 **Abbasanta**, Italy
16 M 12 **Abbeville**, SC, U.S.A.
18 J 8 **Abbeville**, LA, U.S.A.
19 R 6 **Abbeville**, AL, U.S.A.
19 U 5 **Abbeville**, GA, U.S.A.
65 P 2 **Abbeville**, France
61 B 20 **Abbeyfeale**, Republic of Ireland
144 J 8 **Abbot Ice Shelf**, Antarctica
63 P 14 **Abbotsbury**, U.K.
20 E 11 **Abbotsford**, WI, U.S.A.
39 G 22 **Abbotsford**, BC, Canada
101 X 7 **Abbottabad**, Pakistan
99 V 15 **'Abd al Kūrī**, Yemen
129 Y 9 **Abéché**, Chad
69 A 19 **Abele**, Belgium
140 D 2 **Abemama**, Kiribati
128 L 13 **Abengourou**, Côte d'Ivoire
71 B 26 **Åbenrå**, Denmark
129 P 13 **Abeokuta**, Nigeria
62 M 8 **Aberaeron**, U.K.
63 O 10 **Aberdare**, U.K.
62 L 6 **Aberdaron**, U.K.
17 V 2 **Aberdeen**, MD, U.S.A.
17 Q 10 **Aberdeen**, NC, U.S.A.
19 N 3 **Aberdeen**, MS, U.S.A.
22 M 7 **Aberdeen**, SD, U.S.A.
32 F 7 **Aberdeen**, WA, U.S.A.
60 J 10 **Aberdeen**, U.K.
132 M 14 **Aberdeen**, Republic of South Africa
40 K 2 **Aberdeen Lake**, NU, Canada
62 M 7 **Aberdyfi**, U.K.
63 P 9 **Abergavenny**, U.K.
62 L 8 **Aberporth**, U.K.
62 L 6 **Abersoch**, U.K.
63 O 10 **Abertillery**, U.K.
62 M 7 **Aberystwyth**, U.K.
76 E 9 **Abetone**, Italy
91 T 3 **Abez'**, Russian Federation
99 N 11 **Abhā**, Saudi Arabia
100 H 5 **Abhar**, Iran
129 R 13 **Abia**, Nigeria
128 K 14 **Abidjan**, Côte d'Ivoire
123 K 15 **Abiko**, Japan
26 M 6 **Abilene**, TX, U.S.A.
16 M 7 **Abingdon**, VA, U.S.A.
63 T 10 **Abingdon**, U.K.
14 I 13 **Abington**, PA, U.S.A.
31 P 8 **Abiquia Reservoir**, NM, U.S.A.
126 E 10 **Abnûb**, Egypt
106 G 7 **Abohar**, India
128 L 13 **Aboisso**, Côte d'Ivoire
127 E 20 **Aboke**, Sudan
129 O 13 **Abomey**, Benin
129 U 14 **Abong Mbang**, Cameroon
99 V 11 **Aboot**, Oman
121 C 19 **Aborlan**, Philippines
129 Y 10 **Abou Déia**, Chad
99 T 5 **Abqaiq**, Saudi Arabia
120 F 7 **Abra**, Philippines
56 I 5 **Abra Pampa**, Argentina
49 O 4 **Abraham's Bay**, The Bahamas
126 D 13 **'Abri**, Sudan
86 H 10 **Abrud**, Romania
84 D 8 **Abruka**, Estonia
76 I 13 **Abruzzo**, Italy
12 K 6 **Absaroka Range**, MT/WY, U.S.A.
75 R 6 **Abtenau**, Austria
96 I 3 **Abū aḍ Ḍuhūr**, Syria
97 R 7 **Abū al Jīr**, Iraq
99 W 6 **Abu al Jirab**, United Arab Emirates
99 O 11 **Abū 'Arīsh**, Saudi Arabia
99 W 6 **Abu Dhabi**, United Arab Emirates
126 D 8 **Abu Haggag**, Egypt
127 F 14 **Abu Hamed**, Sudan
97 O 5 **Abū Ḥardān**, Syria
97 O 5 **Abū Kamāl**, Syria
127 B 19 **Abu Matariq**, Sudan
100 K 13 **Abu Musa**, Iran
125 T 8 **Abū Nujaym**, Libya
125 T 8 **Abū Qurīn**, Libya
98 M 6 **Abū Rubayq**, Saudi Arabia
127 C 17 **Abu Shanab**, Sudan
126 E 12 **Abu Simbel**, Egypt
97 T 9 **Abū Şukhayr**, Iraq
127 D 18 **Abu Zabad**, Sudan
126 F 9 **Abu Zenîma**, Egypt
129 R 12 **Abuja**, Nigeria
120 G 5 **Abulog**, Philippines
130 L 5 **Abumombazi**, Democratic Republic of Congo
54 D 13 **Abunā**, Brazil
122 J 6 **Abuta**, Japan
127 C 17 **Abyad**, Sudan
127 C 20 **Abyei**, Sudan
54 K 11 **Açailândia**, Brazil
46 I 7 **Acajutla**, El Salvador
67 P 6 **Acalá de Henares**, Spain
45 Q 11 **Acambaro**, Mexico
44 M 10 **Acaponeta**, Mexico
45 Q 14 **Acapulco**, Mexico
54 K 10 **Acará**, Brazil
54 N 11 **Acaraú**, Brazil
54 F 9 **Acari Mountains**, Brazil
50 M 3 **Acarigua**, Venezuela
86 H 8 **Acâş**, Romania
45 S 13 **Acatlan**, Mexico
45 S 12 **Acatzingo**, Mexico
17 W 5 **Accomac**, VA, U.S.A.
128 M 13 **Accra**, Ghana
116 B 8 **Aceh**, Indonesia
77 K 16 **Acerno**, Italy
51 N 4 **Achaguas**, Venezuela
105 E 16 **Achalpur**, India
95 U 6 **Achaseli**, Georgia
110 K 11 **Acheng**, China
75 N 6 **Achenkirch**, Austria
93 P 13 **Achikulak**, Russian Federation
61 A 16 **Achill Island**, Republic of Ireland
89 N 12 **Achinsk**, Russian Federation
92 J 11 **Achuyevo**, Russian Federation
94 D 12 **Acipayam**, Turkey
77 K 22 **Acireale**, Italy
26 K 6 **Ackerly**, TX, U.S.A.
49 N 4 **Acklins Island**, The Bahamas
63 Z 6 **Acle**, U.K.
20 J 11 **Acme**, MI, U.S.A.
47 P 9 **Acoyapa**, Nicaragua
76 C 8 **Acqui Terme**, Italy
54 B 13 **Acre**, Brazil
96 F 7 **Acre**, Israel
77 M 18 **Acri**, Italy
45 R 11 **Actopan**, Mexico
54 O 12 **Açu**, Brazil
129 T 15 **Acurenam**, Equatorial Guinea
99 N 7 **Ad Dafīnah**, Saudi Arabia
97 U 9 **Ad Daghgharah**, Iraq
99 P 4 **Ad Dahnā'**, Saudi Arabia
124 B 12 **Ad Dakhla**, Western Sahara
99 P 14 **Aḍ Ḍāli'**, Yemen
99 T 5 **Ad Dammām**, Saudi Arabia
99 N 11 **Ad Darb**, Saudi Arabia
99 P 6 **Ad Dawādimī**, Saudi Arabia
97 S 5 **Ad Dawr**, Iraq
97 Y 11 **Ad Dayr**, Iraq
99 R 6 **Ad Dilam**, Saudi Arabia
99 Q 6 **Ad Dir'īyah**, Saudi Arabia
97 U 9 **Ad Dīwānīyah**, Iraq
97 T 6 **Ad Dujayl**, Iraq
25 O 11 **Ada**, OK, U.S.A.
80 K 8 **Ada**, Serbia and Montenegro
34 F 14 **Adak**, AK, U.S.A.
34 F 14 **Adak Island**, AK, U.S.A.
99 Y 7 **Adam**, Oman
129 U 13 **Adamaoua**, Cameroon
83 H 23 **Adamas**, Greece
129 U 11 **Adamawa**, Nigeria
129 U 12 **Adamawa Highlands**, Cameroon
14 H 7 **Adams**, NY, U.S.A.
10 C 12 **Adamstown**, Pitcairn Island
99 P 14 **Adan as Sughra**, Yemen
94 K 13 **Adana**, Turkey
122 K 13 **Adatara-san**, Japan
135 S 7 **Adavale**, QLD, Australia
33 M 19 **Adaven**, NV, U.S.A.
103 N 4 **Aday**, Kazakhstan
127 I 20 **Addis Ababa**, Ethiopia
105 L 20 **Addu Atoll**, Maldives
19 U 6 **Adel**, GA, U.S.A.
135 P 12 **Adelaide**, SA, Australia
144 H 5 **Adelaide Island**, Antarctica
134 M 2 **Adelaide River**, NT, Australia
145 U 14 **Adélie Coast**, Antarctica
145 U 14 **Adélie Land**, Antarctica
103 S 11 **Adelunga Toghi**, Uzbekistan
67 S 7 **Ademuz**, Spain
99 P 14 **Aden**, Yemen
129 R 8 **Aderbissinat**, Niger
99 X 5 **Adh Dhayd**, United Arab Emirates
117 U 13 **Adi**, Indonesia
127 I 18 **Ādī Ārk'ay**, Ethiopia
127 I 17 **Adi Keyih**, Eritrea
127 I 17 **Ādīgrat**, Ethiopia
94 D 11 **Adigüzel Baraji**, Turkey
105 F 17 **Adilabad**, India
131 T 6 **Adilanga**, Uganda
95 S 10 **Adilcevaz**, Turkey
33 H 15 **Adin**, CA, U.S.A.
69 A 18 **Adinkerke**, Belgium
125 S 11 **Adīrī**, Libya
14 J 8 **Adirondack Mountains**, NY, U.S.A.
127 H 18 **Ādīs Zemen**, Ethiopia
95 N 12 **Adiyaman**, Turkey
86 L 10 **Adjud**, Romania
92 L 14 **Adler**, Russian Federation
74 G 7 **Adliswil**, Switzerland
32 G 6 **Admiralty Inlet**, WA, U.S.A.
35 X 11 **Admiralty Island**, AK, U.S.A.
138 D 2 **Admiralty Islands**, Papua New Guinea
129 Q 12 **Ado-Ekiti**, Nigeria
127 D 21 **Adok**, Sudan
117 P 15 **Adonara**, Indonesia
105 E 19 **Adoni**, India
67 P 13 **Adra**, Spain
124 K 11 **Adrar**, Algeria
128 H 5 **Adrar**, Mauritania
125 R 13 **Adrar Mariou**, Algeria
124 B 14 **Adrar Souttouf**, Western Sahara
129 Z 9 **Adré**, Chad
21 L 16 **Adrian**, MI, U.S.A.
26 I 2 **Adrian**, TX, U.S.A.
76 I 9 **Adriatic Sea**, Europe
110 E 8 **Adun Qulu**, China
131 P 7 **Adusa**, Democratic Republic of Congo
85 H 14 **Adutiškis**, Lithuania
127 I 17 **Ādwa**, Ethiopia
128 K 13 **Adzopé**, Côte d'Ivoire
91 S 4 **Adz'va**, Russian Federation
91 S 4 **Adz'vavom**, Russian Federation
83 I 17 **Aegean Sea**, Greece
84 G 6 **Aegviidu**, Estonia
97 V 9 **'Afak**, Iraq
83 O 24 **Afantou**, Greece
127 J 18 **Afar**, Ethiopia
127 J 17 **Afar Depression**, Ethiopia
101 R 8 **Afghanistan**, Asia
127 M 24 **Afgooye**, Somalia
99 O 6 **'Afif**, Saudi Arabia
129 R 13 **Afikpo**, Nigeria
124 M 7 **Aflou**, Algeria
127 K 25 **Afmadow**, Somalia
35 Q 11 **Afognak Island**, AK, U.S.A.
54 M 13 **Afrânio**, Brazil
96 J 2 **'Afrīn**, Syria
94 L 11 **Afşin**, Turkey
68 I 8 **Afsluitdijk**, Netherlands
54 I 9 **Afuá**, Brazil
96 G 8 **'Afula**, Israel
94 F 10 **Afyon**, Turkey
129 R 7 **Agadez**, Niger
129 S 6 **Agadez**, Niger
124 F 9 **Agadir**, Morocco
103 T 6 **Agadyr'**, Kazakhstan
107 V 13 **Agartala**, India
83 M 21 **Agathonisi**, Greece
117 X 13 **Agats**, Indonesia
105 B 22 **Agatti**, India
34 B 12 **Agattu Island**, AK, U.S.A.
34 B 12 **Agattu Strait**, AK, U.S.A.
128 K 13 **Agboville**, Côte d'Ivoire
120 G 6 **Agbulu**, Philippines
95 W 9 **Ağcabädi**, Azerbaijan
95 W 9 **Ağdam**, Azerbaijan
95 W 8 **Ağdaş**, Azerbaijan
65 R 14 **Agde**, France
65 N 13 **Agen**, France
127 I 22 **Āgere Maryam**, Ethiopia
95 W 10 **Aghband**, Azerbaijan
83 M 22 **Agia Marina**, Greece
83 K 17 **Agia Paraskevi**, Greece
89 R 14 **Aginskoye**, Russian Federation
83 F 16 **Agiokampos**, Greece
83 H 14 **Ágion Óros**, Greece
83 I 16 **Agios Efstratios**, Greece
83 H 21 **Agios Georgios**, Greece
83 E 22 **Ágios Ilías**, Greece
83 L 21 **Agios Kirykos**, Greece
83 D 16 **Agnantero**, Greece
32 E 13 **Agness**, OR, U.S.A.
128 K 13 **Agnibilékrou**, Côte d'Ivoire
120 E 9 **Agno**, Philippines
106 J 10 **Agra**, India
67 R 4 **Ágreda**, Spain
95 S 9 **Ağri**, Turkey
77 I 23 **Agrigento**, Italy
140 B 6 **Agrihan**, Northern Mariana Islands
83 C 18 **Agrinio**, Greece
77 K 17 **Agropoli**, Italy
91 R 14 **Agryz**, Russian Federation
95 X 8 **Ağsu**, Azerbaijan
120 H 11 **Agta Point**, Philippines
44 J 3 **Agua Prieta**, Mexico
57 I 16 **Aguada Cecilio**, Argentina
49 T 8 **Aguadilla**, Puerto Rico
47 V 14 **Aguadulce**, Panama
47 N 4 **Agúan**, Honduras
45 O 10 **Aguascalientes**, Mexico
45 O 10 **Aguascalientes**, Mexico
58 J 6 **Agudos**, Brazil
129 N 6 **Aguelhok**, Mali
129 R 9 **Aguié**, Niger
140 B 8 **Aguijan**, Northern Mariana Islands
30 I 12 **Aguila**, AZ, U.S.A.
67 N 2 **Aguilar de Campóo**, Spain
46 I 7 **Aguilares**, El Salvador
67 R 12 **Águilas**, Spain
45 O 12 **Aguililla**, Mexico
58 M 6 **Agulhas Negras**, Brazil
123 N 24 **Aguni-jima**, Japan
121 M 20 **Agusan**, Philippines
121 G 16 **Agutaya**, Philippines
100 G 3 **Ahar**, Iran
137 G 18 **Ahaura**, New Zealand
73 C 14 **Ahaus**, Germany
136 I 5 **Ahipara**, New Zealand
136 I 5 **Ahipara Bay**, New Zealand
136 J 12 **Ahititi**, New Zealand
35 O 13 **Ahklun Mountains**, AK, U.S.A.
95 R 11 **Ahlat**, Turkey
73 E 15 **Ahlen**, Germany
105 C 14 **Ahmadabad**, India
105 C 17 **Ahmadnagar**, India
101 W 11 **Ahmadpur East**, Pakistan
127 J 21 **Ahmar Mountains**, Ethiopia
44 J 7 **Ahome**, Mexico
100 G 9 **Āhū**, Iran
46 I 7 **Ahuachapán**, El Salvador
100 G 9 **Ahvāz**, Iran
105 C 16 **Ahwa**, India
99 R 14 **Aḥwar**, Yemen
115 N 17 **Ai Yin Young**, Vietnam
138 A 5 **Aiambak**, Papua New Guinea
73 J 23 **Aichach**, Germany
75 S 2 **Aigen**, Austria
94 I 15 **Aigialousa**, Cyprus
83 G 21 **Aigina**, Greece
83 G 20 **Aigina**, Greece
83 E 14 **Aiginio**, Greece
83 D 19 **Aigio**, Greece
74 C 10 **Aigle**, Switzerland
59 F 15 **Aiguá**, Uruguay
122 I 13 **Aikawa**, Japan
112 K 11 **Ailao Shan**, China
135 N 6 **Aileron**, NT, Australia
47 Z 13 **Ailigandi**, Panama
141 W 1 **Ailinginae**, Marshall Islands
141 Y 3 **Ailinglaplap**, Marshall Islands
141 Y 2 **Ailuk**, Marshall Islands
56 H 8 **Aimogasta**, Argentina
125 P 6 **Aïn Beïda**, Algeria
128 I 2 **Aïn Ben Tili**, Mauritania
124 J 7 **Aïn Beni Mathar**, Morocco
124 M 5 **Aïn Defla**, Algeria
124 M 6 **Aïn Deheb**, Algeria
125 N 6 **Aïn el Hadjel**, Algeria
124 K 8 **Aïn Sefra**, Algeria
124 K 6 **Aïn Temouchent**, Algeria
84 F 9 **Ainaži**, Latvia
83 B 19 **Ainos**, Greece
67 U 3 **Ainsa**, Spain
22 K 12 **Ainsworth**, NE, U.S.A.
53 K 20 **Aiquile**, Bolivia
116 G 9 **Air**, Indonesia
41 Q 1 **Air Force Island**, NU, Canada
116 D 10 **Airbangis**, Indonesia
64 M 14 **Aire-sur-l'Adour**, France
74 G 9 **Airolo**, Switzerland
117 R 14 **Airpanas**, Indonesia
57 F 20 **Aisén**, Chile
67 T 9 **Aitana**, Spain
138 B 3 **Aitape**, Papua New Guinea
23 R 5 **Aitkin**, MN, U.S.A.
141 P 10 **Aitutaki**, Cook Islands
86 I 10 **Aiud**, Romania
84 H 11 **Aiviekste**, Latvia
141 U 1 **Aiwo**, Nauru
65 U 14 **Aix-en-Provence**, France
65 V 10 **Aix-les-Bains**, France
107 W 13 **Aizawl**, India
84 G 11 **Aizkraukle**, Latvia
84 C 11 **Aizpute**, Latvia
122 K 13 **Aizu-Wakamatsu**, Japan
65 X 15 **Ajaccio**, France
106 L 12 **Ajaigarh**, India
105 D 16 **Ajanta**, India
105 D 16 **Ajanta Range**, India
125 W 8 **Ajdābiyā**, Libya
80 A 7 **Ajdovščina**, Slovenia
96 G 9 **'Ajlūn**, Jordan
99 X 5 **Ajman**, United Arab Emirates
104 D 12 **Ajmer**, India
106 H 5 **Ajnala**, India
30 I 14 **Ajo**, AZ, U.S.A.
122 K 5 **Akabira**, Japan
124 L 11 **Akabli**, Algeria
127 I 20 **Āk'ak'ī**, Ethiopia
137 H 21 **Akaroa**, New Zealand
137 I 21 **Akaroa Harbour**, New Zealand
97 N 6 **Akāshat**, Iraq
123 G 18 **Akashi**, Japan
103 W 7 **Akbalyk**, Kazakhstan
93 W 5 **Akbulak**, Russian Federation
103 T 7 **Akbulak**, Kazakhstan
95 N 11 **Akşşadağ**, Turkey
95 O 13 **Akşşakale**, Turkey
94 G 7 **Akşşakoca**, Turkey
128 F 5 **Akchâr**, Mauritania
103 T 6 **Akchatau**, Kazakhstan
94 D 13 **Akdağlar**, Turkey
94 K 10 **Akdağmadeni**, Turkey
102 L 11 **Akdepe**, Turkmenistan
117 S 10 **Akelamo**, Indonesia
130 M 6 **Aketi**, Democratic Republic of Congo
95 S 7 **Akhalk'alak'i**, Georgia
102 L 13 **Akhalskiy Velayat**, Turkmenistan
95 S 7 **Akhalts'ikhe**, Georgia
94 C 10 **Akhisar**, Turkey
126 E 10 **Akhmîm**, Egypt
106 H 4 **Akhnoor**, India
93 Q 9 **Akhtubinsk**, Russian Federation
123 F 20 **Aki**, Japan
130 G 8 **Akiéni**, Gabon
41 O 9 **Akimiski Island**, QC, Canada
94 K 14 **Akinci Burnu**, Turkey
122 J 10 **Akita**, Japan
128 F 5 **Akjoujt**, Mauritania
124 G 9 **Akka**, Morocco
122 M 5 **Akkeshi**, Japan
122 M 5 **Akkeshi-wan**, Japan
103 S 10 **Akkol'**, Kazakhstan
103 S 3 **Akkol'**, Kazakhstan
94 B 12 **Akköy**, Turkey
103 V 3 **Akku**, Kazakhstan
103 O 9 **Akkum**, Kazakhstan
94 M 8 **Akkuş**, Turkey
129 O 12 **Aklampa**, Benin
38 B 9 **Aklavik**, NT, Canada
103 R 4 **Akmola**, Kazakhstan
84 H 12 **Aknīste**, Latvia
123 F 18 **Akō**, Japan
127 F 21 **Akobo**, Sudan
105 E 14 **Akodia**, India
105 E 16 **Akola**, India
129 T 15 **Akom II**, Cameroon
127 H 16 **Akordat**, Eritrea
105 E 16 **Akot**, India
127 D 22 **Akot**, Sudan
41 S 5 **Akpatok Island**, NU, Canada
108 H 5 **Akqi**, China
83 K 26 **Akra Agios Ioannis**, Greece
83 H 15 **Akra Akrathos**, Greece
83 H 14 **Akra Arapis**, Greece
83 C 19 **Akra Araxos**, Greece
83 H 15 **Akra Drepano**, Greece
83 I 19 **Akra Kafireas**, Greece
83 G 15 **Akra Kassandras**, Greece
83 I 26 **Akra Lithino**, Greece
83 F 23 **Akra Maleas**, Greece
83 K 19 **Akra Meston**, Greece
83 G 15 **Akra Paliouri**, Greece
83 M 25 **Akra Paraspori**, Greece
83 L 26 **Akra Sideros**, Greece
83 K 17 **Akra Sigri**, Greece
83 G 25 **Akra Spatha**, Greece
83 E 24 **Akra Tainaro**, Greece
129 S 7 **Akrérèb**, Niger
21 N 17 **Akron**, OH, U.S.A.
106 L 3 **Aksai Chin**, India
82 N 7 **Aksakovo**, Bulgaria
94 I 11 **Aksaray**, Turkey
93 O 9 **Aksay**, Russian Federation
102 J 4 **Aksay**, Kazakhstan
94 G 11 **Akşehir**, Turkey
94 F 11 **Aksehir Gölü**, Turkey
94 G 13 **Akseki**, Turkey
103 S 3 **Aksu**, Kazakhstan
103 U 3 **Aksu**, Kazakhstan
108 I 5 **Aksu**, China
103 T 6 **Aksu-Ayuly**, Kazakhstan
103 Y 6 **Aksuat**, Kazakhstan
103 U 9 **Aksuek**, Kazakhstan
127 I 17 **Āksum**, Ethiopia
103 P 12 **Aktash**, Uzbekistan
102 H 9 **Aktau**, Kazakhstan
103 U 3 **Aktogay**, Kazakhstan
103 U 6 **Aktogay**, Kazakhstan
103 W 7 **Aktogay**, Kazakhstan
85 K 20 **Aktsyabrski**, Belarus
102 L 6 **Aktyubinsk**, Kazakhstan
102 L 5 **Aktyubinsk**, Kazakhstan
130 K 6 **Akula**, Democratic Republic of Congo
41 P 5 **Akulivik**, QC, Canada
123 B 23 **Akune**, Japan
129 Q 13 **Akure**, Nigeria
70 C 10 **Akureyri**, Iceland
123 B 26 **Akuseki-shima**, Japan
34 K 13 **Akutan Island**, AK, U.S.A.
129 R 14 **Akwa Ibom**, Nigeria
129 R 12 **Akwanga**, Nigeria
103 Y 6 **Akzhar**, Kazakhstan
95 O 12 **Akziyaret**, Turkey
125 W 7 **Al Abyār**, Libya
125 Y 7 **Al 'Adam**, Libya
99 S 3 **Al Aḥmadī**, Kuwait
99 O 4 **Al Ajfar**, Saudi Arabia
99 N 9 **Al 'Alayyah**, Saudi Arabia
97 S 1 **Al Amādīyah**, Iraq
97 Y 9 **Al 'Amārah**, Iraq
96 F 13 **Al 'Aqabah**, Jordan
99 N 9 **Al 'Aqīq**, Saudi Arabia
124 B 12 **Al Argoub**, Western Sahara
99 Q 4 **Al Arţāwīyah**, Saudi Arabia
97 O 4 **Al 'Ashārah**, Syria
99 X 6 **Al 'Ayn**, United Arab Emirates
97 U 8 **Al 'Azīzīyah**, Iraq
125 S 8 **Al 'Azīzīyah**, Libya
97 P 2 **Al Ba'āj**, Iraq
96 J 2 **Al Bāb**, Syria
97 P 3 **Al Bādī**, Iraq
99 Q 8 **Al Badī'**, Saudi Arabia
99 N 9 **Al Bāḩah**, Saudi Arabia
96 H 3 **Al Bahlūlīyah**, Syria
125 Y 7 **Al Bardī**, Libya
97 Z 11 **Al Başrah**, Iraq
99 Q 13 **Al Bayḑā'**, Yemen
125 W 7 **Al Bayḑā'**, Libya
98 M 7 **Al Bi'ār**, Saudi Arabia
98 K 3 **Al Bi'r**, Saudi Arabia
99 N 11 **Al Birk**, Saudi Arabia
99 O 5 **Al Bukayrīyah**, Saudi Arabia
99 X 6 **Al Buraymī**, Oman
97 N 4 **Al Buşayrah**, Syria
97 W 12 **Al Buşayyah**, Iraq
97 S 7 **Al Fallūjah**, Iraq
99 S 13 **Al Fardah**, Yemen
99 S 3 **Al Farwānīyah**, Kuwait
97 S 4 **Al Fatḩah**, Iraq
97 Z 12 **Al Fāw**, Iraq
99 O 13 **Al Fāzih**, Yemen
125 U 10 **Al Fuqahā'**, Libya
97 U 10 **Al Ghammās**, Iraq
99 P 5 **Al Ghāţ**, Saudi Arabia
99 V 12 **Al Ghayḑah**, Yemen
97 S 7 **Al Ḩabbānīyah**, Iraq
97 Q 6 **Al Ḩadīthah**, Iraq
97 R 3 **Al Ḩaḑr**, Iraq
124 E 10 **Al Haggounia**, Western Sahara
99 X 6 **Al Hajar'al Gharbī**, Oman
99 R 12 **Al Ḩajr**, Yemen
97 Y 9 **Al Ḩalfāyah**, Iraq
98 L 1 **Al Hamād**, Saudi Arabia
125 Q 9 **Al Ḩamādah al Ḩamrā'**, Libya
96 H 4 **Al Ḩamīdīyah**, Syria
98 M 6 **Al Ḩanākīyah**, Saudi Arabia
99 O 14 **Al Ḩanīsh al Kabīr**, Yemen
97 W 14 **Al Haniyah**, Iraq
99 O 11 **Al Haqū**, Saudi Arabia
125 U 10 **Al Haruj al Aswad**, Libya
96 G 11 **Al Hāsā**, Jordan
97 O 2 **Al Ḩasakah**, Syria
97 U 9 **Al Hāshimīyah**, Iraq
97 O 2 **Al Hawl**, Syria
99 R 14 **Al Ḩawrā**, Yemen
97 W 9 **Al Ḩayy**, Iraq
99 P 12 **Al Ḩazm al-Jawf**, Yemen
99 V 9 **Al Ḩibāk**, Saudi Arabia
96 H 7 **Al Hījānah**, Syria
97 T 8 **Al Ḩillah**, Iraq
99 R 7 **Al Ḩillah**, Saudi Arabia
97 T 8 **Al Hindīyah**, Iraq
96 L 2 **Al Hīshah**, Syria
96 G 8 **Al Ḩişn**, Jordan
124 J 6 **Al Hoceima**, Morocco
99 O 13 **Al Ḩudaydah**, Yemen
99 T 5 **Al Hufūf**, Saudi Arabia
99 Q 14 **Al Ḩumayshah**, Yemen
99 X 8 **Al Huwatsah**, Oman
99 S 13 **Al Ḩuwaymi**, Yemen
98 L 1 **Al 'Īsāwīyah**, Saudi Arabia
125 W 7 **Al Jabal al Akhḑar**, Libya
96 H 12 **Al Jafr**, Jordan
125 Y 8 **Al Jaghbūb**, Libya
99 R 2 **Al Jahrah**, Kuwait
99 U 5 **Al Jamalīyah**, Qatar
98 M 2 **Al Jawf**, Saudi Arabia
125 Y 12 **Al Jawf**, Libya
97 N 2 **Al Jazīrah**, Syria
99 N 4 **Al Jithāmīyah**, Saudi Arabia
99 T 4 **Al Jubayl**, Saudi Arabia
98 M 8 **Al Jumūm**, Saudi Arabia
99 Z 9 **Al Kalbān**, Oman
96 G 11 **Al Karak**, Jordan
126 F 11 **Al Karnak**, Egypt
99 Y 6 **Al Khābūrah**, Oman
99 Z 9 **Al Khalīf**, Oman
97 U 6 **Al Khāliş**, Iraq
99 P 9 **Al Khamāsīn**, Saudi Arabia
99 Y 5 **Al Khaşab**, Oman
99 O 14 **Al Khawkhah**, Yemen
97 V 10 **Al Khiḑr**, Iraq
125 Y 12 **Al Khufrah**, Libya
125 T 7 **Al Khums**, Libya
97 T 9 **Al Kifl**, Iraq
99 U 5 **Al Kir'ānah**, Qatar
97 T 9 **Al Kūfah**, Iraq
97 X 9 **Al Kumayt**, Iraq
97 W 8 **Al Kūt**, Iraq
99 N 2 **Al Labbah**, Saudi Arabia
96 H 3 **Al Lādhiqīyah**, Syria
98 M 9 **Al Līth**, Saudi Arabia
97 R 11 **Al Ma'ānīyah**, Iraq
96 H 8 **Al Mafraq**, Jordan
124 F 10 **Al Mahbas**, Western Sahara
96 K 2 **Al Mahdum**, Syria
97 T 7 **Al Maḩmūdīyah**, Iraq
99 U 11 **Al Mahrah**, Yemen
99 O 12 **Al Maḩwīt**, Yemen
99 Q 5 **Al Majma'ah**, Saudi Arabia
97 Q 1 **Al Mālikīyah**, Syria
99 T 5 **Al Manāmah**, Bahrain
97 Z 11 **Al Ma'qil**, Iraq
99 O 13 **Al Marāwi'ah**, Yemen
125 W 7 **Al Marj**, Libya
99 Y 6 **Al Masana'a**, Oman
97 N 4 **Al Mayādīn**, Syria
96 G 10 **Al Mazra'ah**, Jordan
99 V 6 **Al Mirfa**, United Arab Emirates
99 T 5 **Al Mubarrez**, Saudi Arabia
96 G 14 **Al Mudawwarah**, Jordan
99 T 5 **Al Muharraq**, Bahrain
99 T 13 **Al Mukallā**, Yemen
125 X 7 **Al Mukhaylī**, Libya
97 U 6 **Al Muqdādīyah**, Iraq
98 L 6 **Al Musayjīd**, Saudi Arabia
97 W 9 **Al Muwaffaqīyah**, Iraq
99 N 7 **Al Muwayh**, Saudi Arabia
98 J 3 **Al Muwayliḩ**, Saudi Arabia
97 Y 11 **Al Muzayri'ah**, Iraq
96 H 4 **Al Qadmūs**, Syria
97 P 5 **Al Qā'im**, Iraq
99 O 6 **Al Qā'īyah**, Saudi Arabia
98 L 3 **Al Qalībah**, Saudi Arabia
97 O 1 **Al Qāmishlī**, Syria
96 H 3 **Al Qardābah**, Syria
96 I 5 **Al Qaryatayn**, Syria
99 S 12 **Al Qaţn**, Yemen
96 H 10 **Al Qaţrānah**, Jordan
125 T 12 **Al Qaţrūn**, Libya
99 Q 3 **Al Qayşūmah**, Saudi Arabia
98 M 10 **Al Qunfidhah**, Saudi Arabia
97 Y 11 **Al Qurnah**, Iraq
97 W 11 **Al Qusayr**, Iraq
99 Q 6 **Al Quwayi'**, Saudi Arabia
96 F 13 **Al Quwayrah**, Jordan
99 S 13 **Al Quzah**, Yemen
99 W 6 **Al Samha**, United Arab Emirates
99 S 5 **Al 'Uḑaylīyah**, Saudi Arabia
98 L 4 **Al 'Ulā**, Saudi Arabia
125 V 9 **Al 'Uqaylah**, Libya
125 R 12 **Al 'Uwaynāt**, Libya
125 Z 13 **Al 'Uwaynāt**, Libya
99 O 2 **Al 'Uwayqīlah**, Saudi Arabia
98 M 6 **Al 'Uyūn**, Saudi Arabia
99 O 4 **Al 'Uyūn**, Saudi Arabia
97 Y 10 **Al 'Uzayr**, Iraq
99 S 3 **Al Wafrah**, Kuwait
98 J 4 **Al Wajh**, Saudi Arabia
99 S 4 **Al Wannān**, Saudi Arabia
99 R 3 **Al Warī'ah**, Saudi Arabia
99 Y 6 **Al Wāsiţ**, Oman
125 T 12 **Al Wīgh**, Libya
99 R 6 **Al Yamāmah**, Saudi Arabia
103 S 11 **Ala-Buka**, Kyrgyzstan
94 G 11 **Ala Dağl**, Turkey
19 O 4 **Alabama**, U.S.A.
19 O 5 **Alabama**, AL, U.S.A.
120 H 12 **Alabat**, Philippines
94 J 9 **Alaca**, Turkey
94 K 7 **Alaşşam**, Turkey
19 V 8 **Alachua**, FL, U.S.A.
93 O 14 **Alagir**, Russian Federation
54 O 13 **Alagoas**, Brazil
55 N 14 **Alagoinhas**, Brazil
67 S 4 **Alagón**, Spain
121 L 22 **Alah**, Philippines

Country · Internal administrative region: State/Province/Territory/Dependent territory · Capital city · Mountain range/Undersea ridge · Mountain peak/Volcano/Seamount · Geographic feature · Headland/Point/Cape/Peninsula · Desert · Island/Island group · Antarctic base · Ocean · Sea · Bay/Gulf/Channel/Strait · Lake · Salt pan/Dry/Intermittent lake

Alājah – Ar Ruwayḍah

H 3 **Alājah**, Syria
P 12 **Alajuela**, Costa Rica
B 7 **Alamagan**, Northern Mariana Islands
P 5 **Al'Amār**, Saudi Arabia
I 18 **Ālamat'ā**, Ethiopia
Q 7 **Alamicamba**, Nicaragua
E 9 **Alaminos**, Philippines
M 20 **Alamo**, NV, U.S.A.
H 11 **Alamo Lake**, AZ, U.S.A.
Q 13 **Alamogordo**, NM, U.S.A.
Q 7 **Alamosa**, CO, U.S.A.
I 19 **Åland**, Finland
I 19 **Ålands Hav**, Finland
G 13 **Alanya**, Turkey
C 11 **Alaşehir**, Turkey
P 6 **Alaska**, U.S.A.
P 9 **Alaska Range**, AK, U.S.A.
L 13 **Alaskan Peninsula**, AK, U.S.A.
Z 8 **Ālāt**, Azerbaijan
Q 2 **Alatyr'**, Russian Federation
B 10 **Alausí**, Ecuador
T 8 **Alaverdi**, Armenia
K 16 **Alavus**, Finland
V 7 **Alazeya**, Russian Federation
R 9 **Albacete**, Spain
K 17 **Albania**, Europe
K 9 **Albany**, NY, U.S.A.
H 7 **Albany**, KY, U.S.A.
S 6 **Albany**, GA, U.S.A.
N 6 **Albany**, TX, U.S.A.
G 10 **Albany**, OR, U.S.A.
L 10 **Albany**, ON, Canada
H 12 **Albany**, WA, Australia
K 8 **Albany**, New Zealand
G 13 **Albasserdam**, Netherlands
R 1 **Albatross Bay**, QLD, Australia
K 10 **Albatross Point**, New Zealand
K 13 **Albay Gulf**, Philippines
P 10 **Albemarle**, NC, U.S.A.
V 8 **Albemarle Sound**, NC, U.S.A.
B 9 **Albenga**, Italy
G 20 **Alberdi**, Paraguay
O 8 **Alberga**, SA, Australia
H 5 **Albergaria-a-Velha**, Portugal
O 2 **Albert**, France
S 10 **Albert Lea**, MN, U.S.A.
R 6 **Albert Nile**, Uganda
T 7 **Alberta**, VA, U.S.A.
I 16 **Alberta**, Canada
J 23 **Albertirsa**, Hungary
R 2 **Albertville**, AL, U.S.A.
V 10 **Albertville**, France
Q 13 **Albi**, France
A 10 **Albion**, PA, U.S.A.
K 15 **Albion**, MI, U.S.A.
N 13 **Albion**, NE, U.S.A.
O 14 **Alboran Sea**, Africa/Spain
C 23 **Ålborg**, Denmark
H 12 **Albufeira**, Portugal
I 9 **Albula Alpen**, Switzerland
Q 10 **Albuquerque**, NM, U.S.A.
J 8 **Alburquerque**, Spain
T 12 **Albury**, NSW, Australia
H 10 **Alcácer do Sal**, Portugal
H 6 **Alcala**, Philippines
L 13 **Alcalá de los Gazules**, Spain
O 12 **Alcalá la Real**, Spain
H 22 **Alcamo**, Italy
T 5 **Alcañiz**, Spain
J 8 **Alcántara**, Spain
Q 10 **Alcaraz**, Spain
N 12 **Alcaudete**, Spain
P 8 **Alcázar de San Juan**, Spain
S 8 **Alcester**, U.K.
Y 6 **Alchevs'k**, Ukraine
T 6 **Alcorisa**, Spain
P 15 **Alcorta**, Argentina
U 7 **Alcossebre**, Spain
W 12 **Alcova**, WY, U.S.A.
T 9 **Alcoy**, Spain
Y 7 **Alcúdia**, Spain
S 9 **Aldama**, Mexico
U 11 **Aldan**, Russian Federation
T 12 **Aldan**, Russian Federation
Z 8 **Aldeburgh**, U.K.
I 7 **Alder Creek**, NY, U.S.A.
J 25 **Alderney**, U.K.
U 11 **Aldershot**, U.K.
D 17 **Aledo**, IL, U.S.A.
F 7 **Aleg**, Mauritania
O 5 **Alegre**, Brazil
E 12 **Alegrete**, Brazil
H 10 **Alekhovshchina**, Russian Federation
J 14 **Aleksandrov**, Russian Federation
R 7 **Aleksandrov Gay**, Russian Federation
I 7 **Aleksandrovo**, Bulgaria
T 11 **Aleksandrovsk**, Russian Federation
X 13 **Aleksandrovsk-Sakhalinskiy**, Russian Federation
L 6 **Alekseyevka**, Russian Federation
N 7 **Alekseyevskaya**, Russian Federation
S 12 **Alekseyevskoye**, Russian Federation
K 2 **Aleksin**, Russian Federation
N 12 **Aleksinac**, Serbia and Montenegro
N 6 **Além Paraiba**, Brazil
N 5 **Alençon**, France
H 10 **Alenquer**, Brazil
D 8 **Alenuihaha Channel**, HI, U.S.A.
J 2 **Aleppo**, Syria
Z 15 **Aléria**, France
P 1 **Alert**, NU, Canada
G 15 **Alerta**, Peru
S 13 **Alès**, France
G 8 **Aleşd**, Romania
C 8 **Alessandria**, Italy
B 16 **Ålesund**, Norway
E 13 **Aleutian Islands**, AK, U.S.A.
N 12 **Aleutian Range**, AK, U.S.A.
W 11 **Alexander Archipelago**, AK, U.S.A.
I 12 **Alexander Bay**, Republic of South Africa
Q 4 **Alexander City**, AL, U.S.A.
I 6 **Alexander Island**, Antarctica
D 23 **Alexandra**, New Zealand
U 3 **Alexandria**, VA, U.S.A.
I 6 **Alexandria**, LA, U.S.A.
P 6 **Alexandria**, MN, U.S.A.
J 10 **Alexandria**, ON, Canada
J 13 **Alexandria**, Romania
D 7 **Alexandria**, Egypt
H 6 **Alexandria Bay**, NY, U.S.A.
K 13 **Alexandroupoli**, Greece
G 6 **'Aley**, Lebanon
J 13 **Aleysk**, Russian Federation
M 6 **Alfatar**, Bulgaria
L 5 **Alfenas**, Brazil
G 9 **Alfonsine**, Italy
63 W 4 **Alford**, U.K.
63 S 5 **Alfreton**, U.K.
102 I 4 **Algabas**, Kazakhstan
66 G 12 **Algarve**, Portugal
66 L 14 **Algeciras**, Spain
127 I 15 **Algena**, Eritrea
124 K 11 **Algeria**, Africa
77 A 16 **Alghero**, Italy
124 M 5 **Algiers**, Algeria
67 T 9 **Alginet**, Spain
66 L 13 **Algodonales**, Spain
20 H 11 **Algoma**, WI, U.S.A.
23 R 11 **Algona**, IA, U.S.A.
97 V 8 **'Alī**, Iraq
97 X 8 **'Alī al Gharbī**, Iraq
95 Y 9 **Əli Bayramli**, Azerbaijan
101 V 7 **'Alī Kheyl**, Afghanistan
127 K 19 **Ali Sabieh**, Djibouti
94 B 10 **Aliağa**, Turkey
83 F 19 **Aliartos**, Greece
80 L 10 **Alibunar**, Serbia and Montenegro
67 T 10 **Alicante**, Spain
27 P 13 **Alice**, TX, U.S.A.
48 J 10 **Alice Shoal**, Jamaica
135 O 6 **Alice Springs**, NT, Australia
48 J 2 **Alice Town**, The Bahamas
19 O 4 **Aliceville**, AL, U.S.A.
103 U 14 **Alichur**, Tajikistan
106 J 9 **Aligarh**, India
110 I 6 **Alihe**, China
83 N 24 **Alimia**, Greece
51 W 8 **Alimimuni Peak**, Suriname
121 H 22 **Alimpaya Point**, Philippines
101 W 11 **Alipur**, Pakistan
107 T 10 **Alipur Duar**, India
66 J 8 **Aliseda**, Spain
83 H 19 **Aliveri**, Greece
66 K 9 **Aljucén**, Spain
33 M 19 **Alkali Flat**, NV, U.S.A.
68 H 9 **Alkmaar**, Netherlands
107 N 11 **Allahabad**, India
35 Q 5 **Allakaket**, AK, U.S.A.
89 V 10 **Allakh-Yun'**, Russian Federation
133 O 9 **Alldays**, Republic of South Africa
14 E 10 **Allegeny Plateau**, NY, U.S.A.
14 C 14 **Allegheny Mountains**, PA/WV, U.S.A.
121 K 14 **Allen**, Philippines
17 O 14 **Allendale**, SC, U.S.A.
45 P 5 **Allende**, Mexico
45 Q 7 **Allende**, Mexico
14 H 13 **Allentown**, PA, U.S.A.
105 D 23 **Alleppey**, India
74 K 7 **Allgäuer Alpen**, Austria/Germany
22 H 12 **Alliance**, NE, U.S.A.
105 E 23 **Allinagaram**, India
19 V 6 **Alma**, GA, U.S.A.
20 K 13 **Alma**, MI, U.S.A.
22 L 15 **Alma**, NE, U.S.A.
42 M 6 **Alma**, QC, Canada
67 U 4 **Almacelles**, Spain
66 M 9 **Almadén**, Spain
67 O 9 **Almagro**, Spain
103 S 12 **Almalyk**, Uzbekistan
67 S 9 **Almansa**, Spain
66 M 7 **Almanzor**, Spain
55 K 14 **Almas**, Brazil
103 V 8 **Almaty**, Kazakhstan
103 V 10 **Almaty**, Kazakhstan
67 Q 4 **Almazán**, Spain
54 I 10 **Almeirim**, Brazil
66 H 8 **Almeirim**, Portugal
68 N 11 **Almelo**, Netherlands
67 Q 4 **Almenar de Soria**, Spain
66 K 9 **Almendralejo**, Spain
68 I 11 **Almere**, Netherlands
67 Q 13 **Almeria**, Spain
93 T 2 **Al'met'yevsk**, Russian Federation
71 F 24 **Älmhult**, Sweden
47 S 13 **Almirante**, Panama
66 H 11 **Almodôvar**, Portugal
66 J 12 **Almonte**, Spain
106 L 7 **Almora**, India
129 N 7 **Almoustarat**, Mali
67 O 13 **Almuñécar**, Spain
61 J 14 **Alnwick**, U.K.
140 J 10 **Alofi**, Niue
140 H 8 **Alofi**, Wallis and Futuna Islands
84 G 9 **Aloja**, Latvia
107 X 8 **Along**, India
110 G 5 **Alongshan**, China
83 G 17 **Alonnisos**, Greece
117 Q 15 **Alor**, Indonesia
118 A 5 **Alor Setar**, Malaysia
137 G 7 **Alotau**, Papua New Guinea
66 I 8 **Alpalhao**, Portugal
20 L 11 **Alpena**, MI, U.S.A.
135 T 7 **Alpha**, QLD, Australia
143 R 7 **Alpha Ridge**, Arctic Ocean
21 E 17 **Alphe**, IL, U.S.A.
68 G 12 **Alphen**, Netherlands
26 H 9 **Alpine**, TX, U.S.A.
30 M 12 **Alpine**, AZ, U.S.A.
74 A 6 **Alps**, Europe
135 P 5 **Alpurrurulam**, NT, Australia
65 W 5 **Alsace**, France
67 Q 2 **Alsasua**, Spain
73 G 17 **Alsfeld**, Germany
84 C 11 **Alsunga**, Latvia
70 K 7 **Alta**, Norway
47 O 10 **Alta Gracia**, Nicaragua
62 J 10 **Alta Gracia**, Argentina
70 K 7 **Altaelva**, Norway
47 O 2 **Altagracia de Orituco**, Venezuela
108 L 2 **Altai Mountains**, Asia
19 V 5 **Altamaha**, GA, U.S.A.
47 P 11 **Altamira**, Costa Rica
54 I 10 **Altamira**, Brazil
56 G 7 **Altamira**, Chile
77 M 16 **Altamura**, Italy
110 E 8 **Altan Emel**, China
27 Q 7 **Altavista**, VA, U.S.A.
108 L 3 **Altay**, China
109 N 4 **Altay**, Mongolia
74 G 8 **Altdorf**, Switzerland
67 U 10 **Altea**, Spain
73 N 17 **Altenberg**, Germany
73 L 17 **Altenburg**, Germany
66 I 8 **Alter do Chão**, Portugal
70 I 8 **Altevatnet**, Norway
75 Q 4 **Altheim**, Austria
97 T 3 **Altin Köprü**, Iraq
53 H 20 **Altiplano**, Bolivia
27 T 7 **Alto**, TX, U.S.A.
55 H 16 **Alto Araguaia**, Brazil
132 J 3 **Alto Chicapa**, Angola
46 F 4 **Alto Cuchumatanes**, Guatemala
66 I 6 **Alto da Torre**, Portugal
50 I 4 **Alto de Tamar**, Colombia
55 H 16 **Alto Garças**, Brazil
133 T 6 **Alto Molócuè**, Mozambique
50 G 5 **Alto Musinga**, Colombia
54 K 13 **Alto Parnaíba**, Brazil
53 G 15 **Alto Purús**, Peru
57 G 19 **Alto Rio Senguerr**, Argentina
25 W 8 **Alton**, MO, U.S.A.
63 U 12 **Alton**, U.K.
14 D 13 **Altoona**, PA, U.S.A.
73 L 24 **Altötting**, Germany
63 Q 4 **Altrincham**, U.K.
108 K 7 **Altun Shan**, China
33 I 15 **Alturas**, CA, U.S.A.
24 K 11 **Altus**, OK, U.S.A.
87 S 2 **Altynivka**, Ukraine
84 I 10 **Alūksne**, Latvia
87 U 13 **Alupka**, Ukraine
105 E 19 **Alur**, India
87 U 12 **Alushta**, Ukraine
24 L 8 **Alva**, OK, U.S.A.
27 Q 6 **Alvarado**, TX, U.S.A.
45 T 12 **Alvarado**, Mexico
54 D 11 **Alvarães**, Brazil
71 D 17 **Alvdal**, Norway
71 E 18 **Älvdalen**, Sweden
71 F 18 **Älvdalen**, Sweden
71 A 18 **Alvik**, Norway
27 T 11 **Alvin**, TX, U.S.A.
71 H 19 **Älvkarleby**, Sweden
70 J 12 **Älvsbyn**, Sweden
106 I 9 **Alwar**, India
85 F 16 **Alytus**, Lithuania
29 Z 8 **Alzada**, MT, U.S.A.
73 E 20 **Alzey**, Germany
129 Y 9 **Am-Dam**, Chad
129 Y 10 **Am Timan**, Chad
129 Z 8 **Am-Zoer**, Chad
127 D 22 **Amadi**, Sudan
97 S 1 **Amādīyah**, Iraq
41 Q 3 **Amadjuak Lake**, NU, Canada
117 S 12 **Amahai**, Indonesia
123 A 23 **Amakusa-nada**, Japan
123 B 23 **Amakusa-Shimo-shima**, Japan
71 E 21 **Åmål**, Sweden
99 X 10 **Amal**, Oman
77 K 16 **Amalfi**, Italy
83 C 20 **Amaliada**, Greece
117 X 13 **Amamapare**, Indonesia
55 H 19 **Amambai**, Brazil
123 N 21 **Amami-Ō-shima**, Japan
123 N 23 **Amami shotō**, Japan
131 P 8 **Amamula**, Democratic Republic of Congo
138 A 3 **Amanab**, Papua New Guinea
76 I 12 **Amandola**, Italy
103 P 5 **Amangel'dy**, Kazakhstan
77 M 19 **Amantea**, Italy
133 P 13 **Amanzimtoti**, Republic of South Africa
54 I 8 **Amapá**, Brazil
54 I 9 **Amapá**, Brazil
114 D 11 **Amarapura**, Myanmar
33 L 21 **Amargosa Valley**, NV, U.S.A.
26 J 2 **Amarillo**, TX, U.S.A.
105 H 15 **Amarkantak**, India
94 H 7 **Amasra**, Turkey
94 K 8 **Amasya**, Turkey
54 C 11 **Amataurá**, Brazil
69 I 20 **Amay**, Belgium
54 F 11 **Amazon**, Brazil/Peru
54 C 11 **Amazon Basin**, Brazil
50 L 11 **Amazonas**, Colombia
51 O 8 **Amazonas**, Venezuela
52 C 11 **Amazonas**, Peru
54 D 11 **Amazonas**, Brazil
106 I 7 **Ambala**, India
133 X 9 **Ambalavao**, Madgascar
133 Z 5 **Ambanja**, Madgascar
89 W 7 **Ambarchik**, Russian Federation
90 H 5 **Ambarnyy**, Russian Federation
107 V 12 **Ambāsa**, India
52 B 9 **Ambato**, Ecuador
133 X 6 **Ambato Boeny**, Madgascar
133 X 7 **Ambatomainty**, Madgascar
117 R 12 **Ambelau**, Indonesia
20 G 10 **Amberg**, WI, U.S.A.
73 K 21 **Amberg**, Germany
46 L 1 **Ambergris Cay**, Belize
65 U 9 **Ambérieu-en-Bugey**, France
42 C 12 **Amberley**, ON, Canada
137 H 19 **Amberley**, New Zealand
128 G 8 **Ambidédi**, Mali
105 H 14 **Ambikapur**, India
120 F 12 **Ambil**, Philippines
133 Z 5 **Ambilobe**, Madgascar
35 O 5 **Ambler**, AK, U.S.A.
53 D 15 **Ambo**, Peru
133 X 10 **Amboasary**, Madgascar
133 X 9 **Ambohimahasoa**, Madgascar
133 W 6 **Ambohipaky**, Madgascar
117 S 12 **Ambon**, Indonesia
117 S 12 **Ambon**, Indonesia
133 X 8 **Ambositra**, Madgascar
133 X 11 **Ambovombe**, Madgascar
33 M 24 **Amboy**, CA, U.S.A.
132 F 2 **Ambriz**, Angola
139 R 10 **Ambrym**, Vanuatu
34 D 13 **Amchitka Island**, AK, U.S.A.
34 E 14 **Amchitka Islands**, AK, U.S.A.
34 D 14 **Amchitka Pass**, AK, U.S.A.
91 S 1 **Amderma**, Russian Federation
108 L 9 **Amdo**, China
45 N 11 **Ameca**, Mexico
68 K 5 **Ameland**, Netherlands
17 S 6 **Amelia Court House**, VA, U.S.A.
29 O 12 **American Falls**, ID, U.S.A.
29 O 12 **American Falls Reservoir**, ID, U.S.A.
140 L 9 **American Samoa**, U.S.A.
19 S 5 **Americus**, GA, U.S.A.
68 J 12 **Amersfoort**, Netherlands
63 V 10 **Amersham**, U.K.
145 W 6 **Amery Ice Shelf**, Antarctica
23 S 12 **Ames**, IA, U.S.A.
63 S 12 **Amesbury**, U.K.
83 C 18 **Amfilochia**, Greece
83 E 19 **Amfissa**, Greece
89 T 11 **Amga**, Russian Federation
89 U 11 **Amga**, Russian Federation
89 W 15 **Amgu**, Russian Federation
89 Z 6 **Amguema**, Russian Federation
125 O 11 **Amguid**, Algeria
89 V 13 **Amgun**, Russian Federation
127 I 19 **Āmhara**, Ethiopia
14 M 9 **Amherst**, MA, U.S.A.
43 U 9 **Amherst**, NS, Canada
65 Q 2 **Amiens**, France
105 A 22 **Amindivi Islands**, India
105 B 22 **Amini**, India
127 K 23 **Amino**, Ethiopia
132 J 10 **Aminuis**, Namibia
39 N 16 **Amisk Lake**, SK, Canada
18 L 7 **Amite**, LA, U.S.A.
34 G 14 **Amlia Island**, AK, U.S.A.
62 L 4 **Amlwch**, U.K.
96 H 9 **Ammān**, Jordan
62 M 9 **Ammanford**, U.K.
70 H 12 **Ammarnäs**, Sweden
143 N 13 **Ammassalik**, Greenland
73 J 25 **Ammersee**, Germany
94 I 15 **Ammóchostos**, Cyprus
115 L 17 **Amnat Charoen**, Thailand
105 C 15 **Amod**, India
100 J 5 **Amol**, Iran
67 Q 1 **Amorebieta**, Spain
83 K 23 **Amorgos**, Greece
19 N 2 **Amory**, MS, U.S.A.
42 G 6 **Amos**, QC, Canada
71 B 20 **Åmot**, Norway
128 J 8 **Amourj**, Mauritania
46 L 8 **Ampala**, Honduras
133 Z 6 **Ampanavoana**, Madgascar
133 Z 5 **Ampanefena**, Madgascar
133 W 10 **Ampanihy**, Madgascar
105 H 25 **Amparai**, Sri Lanka
133 Z 8 **Ampasimanolotra**, Madgascar
117 O 11 **Ampoa**, Indonesia
67 U 6 **Amposta**, Spain
63 V 9 **Ampthill**, U.K.
43 R 6 **Amqui**, QC, Canada
99 P 12 **Amrān**, Yemen
105 E 16 **Amravati**, India
106 H 5 **Amritsar**, India
72 E 7 **Amrum**, Germany
68 H 11 **Amstelveen**, Netherlands
68 H 11 **Amsterdam**, Netherlands
75 U 4 **Amstetten**, Austria
103 O 13 **Amudar'ya**, Turkmenistan
34 H 15 **Amukta Pass**, AK, U.S.A.
37 O 3 **Amund Ringnes Island**, NU, Canada
143 P 8 **Amund Ringnes Island**, Canada
145 P 9 **Amundsen Coast**, Antarctica
38 D 7 **Amundsen Gulf**, NT, Canada
143 N 6 **Amundsen Gulf**, Arctic Ocean
145 Q 8 **Amundsen-Scott**, Antarctica
144 I 9 **Amundsen Sea**, Antarctica
116 L 12 **Amuntai**, Indonesia
89 U 14 **Amur**, Russian Federation
117 Q 10 **Amurang**, Indonesia
67 P 2 **Amurrio**, Spain
89 V 13 **Amursk**, Russian Federation
83 B 17 **Amvrakikos Kolpos**, Greece
87 Y 7 **Amvrosiyivka**, Ukraine
99 O 5 **An Nabhānīyah**, Saudi Arabia
96 I 6 **An Nabk**, Syria
98 L 2 **An Nafūd**, Saudi Arabia
97 T 9 **An Najaf**, Iraq
97 W 11 **An Nāṣirīyah**, Iraq
97 W 10 **An Naṣr**, Iraq
125 V 8 **An Nawfalīyah**, Libya
96 J 8 **An Nimarah**, Syria
99 N 10 **An Nimāṣ**, Saudi Arabia
99 S 4 **An Nu'ayrīyah**, Saudi Arabia
97 Q 9 **An Nukhayb**, Iraq
97 U 8 **An Nu'mānīyah**, Iraq
97 V 8 **An Nu'mānīyah**, Iraq
141 V 1 **Anabar**, Nauru
51 Q 3 **Anaco**, Venezuela
29 O 6 **Anaconda**, MT, U.S.A.
89 Z 7 **Anadyr'**, Russian Federation
83 K 24 **Anafi**, Greece
55 M 12 **Anagé**, Brazil
77 I 14 **Anagni**, Italy
97 P 5 **'Ānah**, Iraq
33 K 25 **Anaheim**, CA, U.S.A.
45 Q 6 **Anáhuac**, Mexico
105 D 23 **Anai Mudi Peak**, India
105 H 18 **Anakapalle**, India
133 Y 5 **Analalava**, Madgascar
54 E 11 **Anamã**, Brazil
129 R 13 **Anambra**, Nigeria
94 H 14 **Anamur**, Turkey
94 H 14 **Anamur Burnu**, Turkey
123 G 20 **Anan**, Japan
105 C 15 **Anand**, India
105 J 16 **Anandapur**, India
105 E 20 **Anantapur**, India
106 H 4 **Anantnag**, India
92 J 12 **Anapa**, Russian Federation
55 J 16 **Anápolis**, Brazil
100 K 10 **Anār**, Iran
100 K 8 **Anārak**, Iran
101 P 8 **Anardara**, Afghanistan
140 A 7 **Anatahan**, Northern Mariana Islands
94 D 10 **Anatolia**, Turkey
82 I 12 **Anatoliki Makedonia Kai Thraki**, Greece
139 S 13 **Anatom**, Vanuatu
56 K 8 **Añatuya**, Argentina
113 P 1 **Anbianbu**, China
53 C 14 **Ancash**, Peru
64 L 7 **Ancenis**, France
129 R 11 **Anchau**, Nigeria
35 R 9 **Anchorage**, AK, U.S.A.
53 C 16 **Ancón**, Peru
76 I 11 **Ancona**, Italy
57 E 17 **Ancud**, Chile
110 J 10 **Anda**, China
120 E 8 **Anda**, Philippines
53 E 17 **Andahuaylas**, Peru
56 I 8 **Andalgalá**, Argentina
66 L 12 **Andalucia**, Spain
19 Q 6 **Andalusia**, AL, U.S.A.
105 O 23 **Andaman and Nicobar Islands**, India
105 O 21 **Andaman Islands**, India
115 D 18 **Andaman Sea**, Asia
135 P 9 **Andamooka**, SA, Australia
133 Z 5 **Andapa**, Madgascar
74 I 9 **Andeer**, Switzerland
69 I 21 **Andenne**, Belgium
129 O 8 **Andéramboukane**, Mali
69 F 21 **Anderlues**, Belgium
74 G 9 **Andermatt**, Switzerland
64 L 12 **Andernos-les-Bains**, France
16 L 11 **Anderson**, SC, U.S.A.
21 J 18 **Anderson**, IN, U.S.A.
25 S 8 **Anderson**, MO, U.S.A.
35 R 7 **Anderson**, AK, U.S.A.
38 C 9 **Anderson**, NT, Canada
56 G 13 **Andes**, South America
70 G 8 **Andfjorden**, Norway
105 F 19 **Andhra Pradesh**, India
103 T 12 **Andijon Wiloyati**, Uzbekistan
133 Y 7 **Andilamena**, Madgascar
133 Y 7 **Andilanatoby**, Madgascar
100 G 8 **Andimeshk**, Iran
103 T 12 **Andizhan**, Uzbekistan
101 R 5 **Andkhvoy**, Afghanistan
52 D 10 **Andoas**, Peru
111 M 20 **Andong**, South Korea
67 W 2 **Andorra**, Europe
67 W 2 **Andorra La Vella**, Andorra
63 S 11 **Andover**, U.K.
70 G 8 **Andøya**, Norway
58 H 5 **Andradina**, Brazil
133 Z 4 **Andranovondronina**, Madgascar
133 W 10 **Andranovory**, Madgascar
67 X 8 **Andratx**, Spain
34 E 14 **Andreanof Islands**, AK, U.S.A.
90 F 14 **Andreapol'**, Russian Federation
58 M 6 **Andrelândia**, Brazil
26 J 6 **Andrews**, TX, U.S.A.
103 X 7 **Andreyevka**, Kazakhstan
77 M 15 **Andria**, Italy
133 Y 7 **Andriamena**, Madgascar
87 X 8 **Andriyivka**, Ukraine
133 W 10 **Androka**, Madgascar
83 I 20 **Andros**, Greece
48 K 3 **Andros Island**, The Bahamas
48 K 2 **Andros Town**, The Bahamas
93 S 4 **Androsovka**, Russian Federation
105 C 22 **Andrott**, India
70 I 8 **Andselv**, Norway
67 N 11 **Andújar**, Spain
132 H 4 **Andulo**, Angola
129 N 7 **Anéfis**, Mali
49 W 7 **Anegada**, Virgin Islands, U.K.
129 N 13 **Anèho**, Togo
121 C 18 **Anepahan**, Philippines
67 U 2 **Aneto**, Spain
129 U 6 **Aney**, Niger
113 U 9 **Anfu**, China
115 H 18 **Ang Thong**, Thailand
89 O 11 **Angara**, Russian Federation
89 P 13 **Angarsk**, Russian Federation
71 G 16 **Ånge**, Sweden
51 R 6 **Angel Falls**, Venezuela
120 F 10 **Angeles**, Philippines
71 E 24 **Ängelholm**, Sweden
72 N 12 **Angermünde**, Germany
64 M 7 **Angers**, France
71 J 15 **Ångesön**, Sweden
115 L 21 **Ângk Tasaôm**, Cambodia
62 L 4 **Anglesey**, U.K.
27 S 11 **Angleton**, TX, U.S.A.
131 O 5 **Ango**, Democratic Republic of Congo
133 U 6 **Angoche**, Mozambique
100 M 13 **Angohrān**, Iran
57 F 15 **Angol**, Chile
132 H 3 **Angola**, Africa
138 C 3 **Angoram**, Papua New Guinea
65 N 10 **Angoulême**, France
58 M 7 **Angra dos Reis**, Brazil
103 S 11 **Angren**, Uzbekistan
131 N 5 **Angu**, Democratic Republic of Congo
110 I 11 **Anguang**, China
67 T 3 **Angüés**, Spain
49 X 7 **Anguilla**, U.K.
48 J 3 **Anguilla Cay**, The Bahamas
71 D 24 **Anholt**, Denmark
113 S 8 **Anhua**, China
113 W 5 **Anhui**, China
55 H 16 **Anhumas**, Brazil
122 J 10 **Ani**, Japan
35 N 9 **Aniak**, AK, U.S.A.
141 V 1 **Anibare**, Nauru
141 V 1 **Anibare Bay**, Nauru
31 N 15 **Animas Peak**, NM, U.S.A.
121 M 15 **Anitaguipan Point**, Philippines
133 Z 4 **Anivorano Avaratra**, Madgascar
139 S 12 **Aniwa**, Vanuatu
113 R 9 **Anjiang**, China
133 W 4 **Anjouan**, Comoros
111 K 17 **Anju**, North Korea
97 O 5 **Anka**, Iraq
113 Q 5 **Ankang**, China
94 H 9 **Ankara**, Turkey
133 V 9 **Ankazoabo**, Madgascar
133 Y 7 **Ankazobe**, Madgascar
23 S 13 **Ankeny**, IA, U.S.A.
72 M 9 **Anklam**, Germany
105 C 20 **Ankola**, India
109 R 9 **Ankou**, China
113 P 3 **Ankouzhen**, China
129 R 13 **Ankpa**, Nigeria
129 N 13 **Anloga**, Ghana
113 N 10 **Anlong**, China
113 T 6 **Anlu**, China
21 L 15 **Ann Arbor**, MI, U.S.A.
21 F 22 **Anna**, IL, U.S.A.
92 M 5 **Anna**, Russian Federation
141 U 1 **Anna Point**, Nauru
125 P 5 **Annaba**, Algeria
115 M 15 **Annam**, Vietnam
115 K 14 **Annam Highlands**, Laos
17 V 3 **Annapolis**, MD, U.S.A.
43 T 11 **Annapolis Royal**, NS, Canada
107 P 8 **Annapurna**, Nepal
65 V 9 **Annecy**, France
112 L 11 **Anning**, China
19 R 3 **Anniston**, AL, U.S.A.
65 T 11 **Annonay**, France
83 J 26 **Ano Viannos**, Greece
113 R 14 **Anpu**, China
113 W 6 **Anqing**, China
111 F 20 **Anqiu**, China
69 J 20 **Ans**, Belgium
113 Q 1 **Ansai**, China
73 I 21 **Ansbach**, Germany
111 H 16 **Anshan**, China
113 O 10 **Anshun**, China
58 F 13 **Ansina**, Uruguay
22 L 14 **Ansley**, NE, U.S.A.
26 M 6 **Anson**, TX, U.S.A.
129 N 8 **Ansongo**, Mali
117 Y 11 **Ansudu**, Indonesia
53 F 18 **Antabamba**, Peru
133 Z 6 **Antalaha**, Madgascar
94 F 13 **Antalya**, Turkey
94 F 13 **Antalya Körfezi**, Turkey
133 Y 7 **Antananarivo**, Madgascar
133 X 7 **Antananarivo**, Madgascar
133 W 10 **Antanimora Atsimo**, Madgascar
144 H 4 **Antarctic Peninsula**, Antarctica
145 Q 7 **Antarctica**, 0
67 N 13 **Antequera**, Spain
31 Q 14 **Anthony**, NM, U.S.A.
124 F 9 **Anti Atlas**, Morocco
65 X 14 **Antibes**, France
20 F 11 **Antigo**, WI, U.S.A.
43 W 9 **Antigonish**, NS, Canada
46 H 6 **Antigua**, Guatemala
49 Y 9 **Antigua**, Antigua and Barbuda
49 Z 8 **Antigua and Barbuda**, North America
83 F 25 **Antikythira**, Greece
83 H 23 **Antimilos**, Greece
94 L 14 **Antioch**, Turkey
50 H 5 **Antioquia**, Colombia
83 I 22 **Antiparos**, Greece
83 A 17 **Antipaxoi**, Greece
88 M 8 **Antipayuta**, Russian Federation
56 F 5 **Antofagasta**, Chile
56 F 5 **Antofagasta**, Chile
56 H 7 **Antofagasta de la Sierra**, Argentina
57 I 21 **Antonio de Biedma**, Argentina
61 F 15 **Antrim**, U.K.
76 H 13 **Antrodoco**, Italy
133 W 7 **Antsalova**, Madgascar
133 X 8 **Antsirabe**, Madgascar
133 Z 4 **Antsiranana**, Madgascar
133 Z 5 **Antsiranana**, Madgascar
84 H 9 **Antsla**, Estonia
133 Y 5 **Antsohihy**, Madgascar
111 M 14 **Antu**, China
57 F 14 **Antuco**, Chile
69 G 17 **Antwerp**, Belgium
69 G 17 **Antwerpen**, Belgium
105 I 16 **Anugul**, India
104 C 11 **Anupgarh**, India
105 G 24 **Anuradhapura**, Sri Lanka
139 S 8 **Anuta**, Solomon Islands
144 H 4 **Anvers Island**, Antarctica
109 N 6 **Anxi**, China
113 S 7 **Anxiang**, China
135 O 11 **Anxious Bay**, SA, Australia
111 L 19 **Anyang**, South Korea
113 U 2 **Anyang**, China
83 K 23 **Anydro**, Greece
109 O 8 **A'nyêmaqên Shan**, China
85 G 14 **Anykščiai**, Lithuania
113 V 10 **Anyuan**, China
113 N 7 **Anyue**, China
113 S 2 **Anze**, China
69 D 19 **Anzegem**, Belgium
130 M 8 **Anzi**, Democratic Republic of Congo
77 H 15 **Anzio**, Italy
51 Q 4 **Anzoátegui**, Venezuela
115 G 23 **Ao Ban Don**, Thailand
115 F 24 **Ao Luk**, Thailand
115 G 22 **Ao Sawi**, Thailand
139 Q 10 **Aoba**, Vanuatu
123 L 20 **Aoga-shima**, Japan
138 M 7 **Aola**, Solomon Islands
122 J 9 **Aomori**, Japan
106 K 9 **Aonla**, India
76 A 6 **Aosta**, Italy
124 C 11 **Aoufist**, Western Sahara
128 G 7 **Aoukâr**, Mauritania
124 L 11 **Aoulef**, Algeria
129 W 5 **Aozou**, Chad
131 S 6 **Apac**, Uganda
24 M 11 **Apache**, OK, U.S.A.
30 L 15 **Apache Peak**, AZ, U.S.A.
19 T 8 **Apalachee Bay**, FL, U.S.A.
19 S 8 **Apalachicola**, FL, U.S.A.
58 H 4 **Aparecida do Taboado**, Brazil
120 H 5 **Aparri**, Philippines
80 I 8 **Apatin**, Serbia and Montenegro
90 H 3 **Apatity**, Russian Federation
45 O 12 **Apatzingán**, Mexico
84 I 9 **Ape**, Latvia
68 L 12 **Apeldoorn**, Netherlands
76 D 9 **Apennines**, Italy
106 M 7 **Api**, Nepal
131 N 5 **Api**, Democratic Republic of Congo
140 J 8 **Apia**, Samoa
53 F 19 **Aplao**, Peru
54 N 12 **Apodi**, Brazil
51 V 6 **Apoera**, Suriname
135 R 14 **Apollo Bay**, VIC, Australia
53 I 18 **Apolo**, Bolivia
58 H 3 **Aporé**, Brazil
58 H 4 **Aporé**, Brazil
120 H 5 **Aparri**, Philippines
20 E 7 **Apostle Islands**, WI, U.S.A.
142 M 14 **Apostolens Tommefinger**, Greenland
58 E 10 **Apóstoles**, Argentina
87 T 8 **Apostolove**, Ukraine
13 U 11 **Appalachian Mountains**, GA, U.S.A.
76 I 13 **Appennino Abruzzese**, Italy
76 B 9 **Appennino Ligure**, Italy
77 L 16 **Appennino Lucano**, Italy
77 K 15 **Appennino Napoletano**, Italy
76 E 9 **Appennino Tosco-Emiliano**, Italy
76 H 11 **Appennino Umbro-Marchigiano**, Italy
74 I 7 **Appenzell**, Switzerland
68 N 6 **Appingedam**, Netherlands
20 G 12 **Appleton**, WI, U.S.A.
17 S 6 **Appomattox**, VA, U.S.A.
92 L 13 **Apsheronsk**, Russian Federation
65 U 13 **Apt**, France
58 H 7 **Apucarana**, Brazil
51 N 5 **Apure**, Venezuela
51 N 4 **Apure**, Venezuela
53 F 18 **Apurimac**, Peru
53 E 16 **Apurímac**, Peru
101 S 5 **Āqchah**, Afghanistan
100 K 8 **Āqdā**, Iran
108 K 7 **Aqqikkol Hu**, China
96 G 9 **'Aqraba**, Israel
97 S 1 **'Aqrah**, Iraq
103 V 4 **Aqtasty**, Kazakhstan
55 G 18 **Aquidauana**, Brazil
64 L 12 **Aquitaine**, France
97 S 8 **Ar Raḥḥālīyah**, Iraq
97 S 7 **Ar Ramādī**, Iraq
96 G 13 **Ar Ramlah**, Jordan
96 H 8 **Ar Ramtha**, Jordan
96 L 3 **Ar Raqqah**, Syria
98 L 8 **Ar Rās al Aswad**, Saudi Arabia
99 O 5 **Ar-Rass**, Saudi Arabia
99 O 8 **Ar Rawḍah**, Saudi Arabia
99 R 13 **Ar Rawḍah**, Yemen
97 W 10 **Ar Rifā'ī**, Iraq
97 V 10 **Ar Riḥāb**, Iraq
99 P 5 **Ar Rubay'iyah**, Saudi Arabia
97 V 10 **Ar Rumaythah**, Iraq
96 L 3 **Ar Ruṣāfah**, Syria
96 H 9 **Ar Ruṣayfah**, Jordan
99 Z 6 **Ar Rustāq**, Oman
97 N 8 **Ar Ruṭbah**, Iraq
99 P 6 **Ar Ruwayḍah**, Saudi Arabia

ountry ■ Internal administrative region: State/Province/Territory/Dependent territory ▲ Capital city ▲ Mountain range/ Undersea ridge ▲ Mountain peak/ Volcano/Seamount ◇ Geographic feature ▶ Headland/Point/ Cape/Peninsula ▲ Desert Island/Island group Antarctic base Ocean Sea Bay/Gulf/Channel/Strait Lake Salt pan/Dry/ Intermittent lake River

Ara – Bafia

107 P 11 **Ara**, India
127 J 22 **Āra Ārba**, Ethiopia
19 Q 2 **Arab**, AL, U.S.A.
97 V 8 **Arab Abdullah**, Iraq
99 V 13 **Arabian Sea**, 0
94 I 7 **Araş**, Turkey
55 O 14 **Aracaju**, Brazil
54 O 11 **Aracati**, Brazil
58 I 5 **Araçatuba**, Brazil
86 F 10 **Arad**, Romania
96 F 10 **'Arad**, Israel
129 Y 8 **Arada**, Chad
97 Y 11 **Aradah**, Iraq
99 V 7 **'Arādah**, United Arab Emirates
117 V 14 **Arafura Sea**, Asia/Oceania
95 T 8 **Aragats Lerr**, Armenia
67 S 5 **Aragón**, Spain
51 O 3 **Aragua**, Venezuela
55 J 14 **Araguaçu**, Brazil
54 J 13 **Araguaia**, Brazil
54 J 12 **Araguaína**, Brazil
55 J 17 **Araguari**, Brazil
123 I 14 **Arai**, Japan
96 L 5 **Arak**, Syria
100 H 7 **Arāk**, Iran
125 N 12 **Arak**, Algeria
114 B 13 **Arakan**, Myanmar
114 B 12 **Arakan Yoma**, Myanmar
102 L 9 **Aral Sea**, Kazakhstan/Uzbekistan
103 N 7 **Aral'sk**, Kazakhstan
135 S 6 **Aramac**, QLD, Australia
138 B 6 **Aramia**, Papua New Guinea
63 N 6 **Aran Fawddwy**, U.K.
61 A 18 **Aran Islands**, Republic of Ireland
67 O 4 **Aranda de Duero**, Spain
80 L 11 **Aranđelovac**, Serbia and Montenegro
67 O 7 **Aranjuez**, Spain
132 J 10 **Aranos**, Namibia
140 D 2 **Aranuka**, Kiribati
115 J 19 **Aranyaprathet**, Thailand
123 B 22 **Arao**, Japan
128 L 6 **Araouane**, Mali
22 K 15 **Arapahoe**, NE, U.S.A.
137 J 16 **Arapawa Island**, New Zealand
54 O 13 **Arapiraca**, Brazil
95 N 10 **Arapkir**, Turkey
58 H 7 **Arapongas**, Brazil
99 N 1 **'Ar'ar**, Saudi Arabia
50 K 10 **Araracuara**, Colombia
58 I 11 **Araranguá**, Brazil
58 J 6 **Araraquara**, Brazil
54 H 12 **Araras**, Brazil
135 R 13 **Ararat**, VIC, Australia
107 R 11 **Araria**, India
95 R 9 **Aras**, Turkey
95 S 9 **Aras**, Azerbaijan/Turkey
95 R 10 **Aras Güneyi Dağlari**, Turkey
95 N 12 **Aratürk Baraji**, Turkey
50 K 5 **Arauca**, Colombia
50 L 5 **Arauca**, Colombia
50 M 5 **Arauca**, Venezuela
57 F 15 **Araucania**, Chile
57 E 14 **Arauco**, Chile
104 C 13 **Aravalli Range**, India
55 K 17 **Araxá**, Brazil
95 W 10 **Araz**, Azerbaijan
127 H 22 **Ārba Minch**, Ethiopia
97 V 4 **Arbat**, Iraq
77 D 18 **Arbatax**, Italy
75 U 3 **Arbesbach**, Austria
97 T 2 **Arbīl**, Iraq
71 G 20 **Arboga**, Sweden
50 G 4 **Arboletes**, Colombia
74 I 6 **Arbon**, Switzerland
60 I 12 **Arbroath**, U.K.
64 L 12 **Arcachon**, France
14 D 9 **Arcade**, NY, U.S.A.
18 I 4 **Arcadia**, LA, U.S.A.
19 W 11 **Arcadia**, FL, U.S.A.
51 T 8 **Arcarai Mountains**, Guyana
33 E 15 **Arcata**, CA, U.S.A.
45 Q 13 **Arcelia**, Mexico
134 I 12 **Archipelago of the Recherche**, WA, Australia
47 S 12 **Archipiélago de Bocas del Toro**, Panama
48 J 4 **Archipiélago de Camagüey**, Cuba
57 E 23 **Archipiélago de la Reina Adelaida**, Chile
47 X 15 **Archipiélago de las Perlas**, Panama
48 G 4 **Archipiélago de los Canarreros**, Cuba
48 J 5 **Archipiélago de los Jardines de la Reina**, Cuba
57 E 20 **Archipiélago de los Chonos**, Chile
48 H 3 **Archipiélago de Sabana**, Cuba
47 Y 12 **Archipiélago de San Blas**, Panama
47 P 10 **Archipiélago de Solentiname**, Nicaragua
76 F 12 **Arcidosso**, Italy
29 N 11 **Arco**, ID, U.S.A.
66 L 13 **Arcos de la Frontera**, Spain
37 Q 4 **Arctic Bay**, NU, Canada
143 Q 8 **Arctic Ocean**, 0
144 G 3 **Arctowski**, Antarctica
95 U 8 **Arcvašen**, Armenia
96 I 11 **Arḑ aş Şawwān**, Jordan
82 J 11 **Arda**, Bulgaria
100 H 3 **Ardabīl**, Iran
100 H 3 **Ardabīl**, Iran
95 S 8 **Ardahan**, Turkey
100 K 8 **Ardakān**, Iran
93 Q 2 **Ardatov**, Russian Federation
42 E 10 **Ardbeg**, ON, Canada
61 E 17 **Ardee**, Republic of Ireland
69 H 23 **Ardennes**, Belgium
100 J 7 **Ardestān**, Iran
25 N 12 **Ardmore**, OK, U.S.A.
86 H 7 **Ardusat**, Romania
71 F 15 **Åre**, Sweden
131 Q 6 **Arebi**, Democratic Republic of Congo
49 U 7 **Arecibo**, Puerto Rico
121 F 19 **Arena**, Philippines
47 P 11 **Arenal**, Costa Rica
55 G 15 **Arenápolis**, Brazil
66 M 7 **Arenas de San Pedro**, Spain
71 B 21 **Arendal**, Norway
69 H 16 **Arendonk**, Belgium
83 E 23 **Areopoli**, Greece
53 G 19 **Arequipa**, Peru
53 F 20 **Arequipa**, Peru
76 G 11 **Arezzo**, Italy
83 F 17 **Argalasti**, Greece
108 L 6 **Argan**, China
67 O 7 **Arganda**, Spain
65 N 4 **Argentan**, France
56 J 11 **Argentina**, South America
56 J 9 **Argentina**, Argentina
101 S 9 **Arghandab**, Afghanistan
83 E 21 **Argolikos Kolpos**, Greece
83 E 21 **Argos**, Greece
83 C 14 **Argos Orestiko**, Greece
83 B 19 **Argostoli**, Greece
110 G 6 **Argun'**, China
129 P 10 **Argungu**, Nigeria
43 T 12 **Argyle**, NS, Canada
109 P 3 **Arhangay**, Mongolia
71 C 24 **Århus**, Denmark
105 L 18 **Ari Atoll**, Maldives
117 Q 8 **Ariaga**, Indonesia
132 J 12 **Ariamsvlei**, Namibia
59 B 15 **Arias**, Argentina
128 M 9 **Aribinda**, Burkina Faso
50 K 11 **Arica**, Colombia
52 D 9 **Arica**, Peru
56 F 2 **Arica**, Chile
123 G 19 **Arida**, Japan
96 I 3 **Arīḩā**, Syria
80 K 13 **Arilje**, Serbia and Montenegro
55 G 14 **Arinos**, Brazil
54 F 12 **Aripuanã**, Brazil
54 E 13 **Ariquemes**, Brazil
51 N 4 **Arismendi**, Venezuela
105 K 18 **Ariyaddu Channel**, Maldives
67 Q 5 **Ariza**, Spain
30 H 11 **Arizona**, U.S.A.
71 E 20 **Årjäng**, Sweden
70 H 12 **Arjeplog**, Sweden
93 O 5 **Arkadak**, Russian Federation
25 U 12 **Arkadelphia**, AR, U.S.A.
103 Q 5 **Arkalyk**, Kazakhstan
25 T 11 **Arkansas**, U.S.A.
25 O 8 **Arkansas**, U.S.A., U.S.A.
25 N 7 **Arkansas City**, KS, U.S.A.
90 K 6 **Arkhangel'sk**, Russian Federation
90 L 7 **Arkhangel'skaya Oblast'**, Russian Federation
89 P 6 **Arkhipelag Nordenshel'da**, Russian Federation
83 F 18 **Arkitsa**, Greece
61 F 19 **Arklow**, Republic of Ireland
65 T 14 **Arles**, France
129 N 10 **Arli**, Burkina Faso
17 U 3 **Arlington**, DC, U.S.A.
23 O 9 **Arlington**, SD, U.S.A.
27 Q 6 **Arlington**, TX, U.S.A.
129 Q 6 **Arlit**, Niger
69 K 25 **Arlon**, Belgium
134 G 11 **Armadale**, WA, Australia
61 E 16 **Armagh**, U.K.
126 F 11 **Armant**, Egypt
83 M 26 **Armathia**, Greece
92 M 12 **Armavir**, Russian Federation
50 H 7 **Armenia**, Colombia
95 T 8 **Armenia**, Asia
135 V 10 **Armidale**, NSW, Australia
29 Q 4 **Armington**, MT, U.S.A.
40 L 10 **Armstrong**, ON, Canada
83 G 14 **Arnaia**, Greece
41 R 5 **Arnaud**, QC, Canada
69 D 15 **Arnemuiden**, Netherlands
24 J 9 **Arnett**, OK, U.S.A.
68 K 13 **Arnhem**, Netherlands
82 D 13 **Arnissa**, Greece
76 E 10 **Arno**, Italy
141 Z 3 **Arno**, Marshall Islands
70 I 6 **Arnøya**, Norway
73 I 17 **Arnstadt**, Germany
132 K 11 **Aroab**, Namibia
40 M 11 **Aroland**, ON, Canada
127 H 16 **Aroma**, Sudan
76 C 6 **Arona**, Italy
140 F 3 **Arorae**, Kiribati
121 J 14 **Aroroy**, Philippines
74 I 8 **Arosa**, Switzerland
128 D 10 **Arquipélago dos Bijagós**, Guinea-Bissau
60 G 13 **Arran**, U.K.
65 Q 2 **Arras**, France
65 N 15 **Arreau**, France
59 C 15 **Arrecifes**, Argentina
45 P 10 **Arriaga**, Mexico
45 V 14 **Arriaga**, Mexico
66 M 1 **Arriondas**, Spain
59 G 14 **Arroio Grande**, Brazil
33 H 23 **Arroyo Grande**, CA, U.S.A.
71 C 23 **Års**, Denmark
93 S 1 **Arsk**, Russian Federation
67 Z 8 **Artà**, Spain
83 C 17 **Arta**, Greece
95 U 9 **Artashat**, Armenia
45 O 13 **Arteaga**, Mexico
48 G 4 **Artemisa**, Cuba
87 X 6 **Artemivs'k**, Ukraine
77 H 14 **Artena**, Italy
73 J 16 **Artern**, Germany
67 V 4 **Artesa de Segre**, Spain
31 S 13 **Artesia**, NM, U.S.A.
22 I 13 **Arthur**, NE, U.S.A.
137 G 19 **Arthur's Pass**, New Zealand
38 C 10 **Artic Red**, NT, Canada
58 E 12 **Artigas**, Uruguay
58 E 12 **Artigas**, Uruguay
95 T 8 **Art'ik**, Armenia
87 O 10 **Artsyz**, Ukraine
95 Q 7 **Artvin**, Turkey
131 R 6 **Aru**, Democratic Republic of Congo
131 R 6 **Arua**, Uganda
55 I 15 **Aruanã**, Brazil
49 R 12 **Aruba**, The Netherlands, The Netherlands
54 E 11 **Arumã**, Brazil
107 R 9 **Arun**, Nepal
107 X 8 **Arunachal Pradesh**, India
63 V 13 **Arundel**, U.K.
131 V 10 **Arusha**, Tanzania
131 V 10 **Arusha**, Tanzania
31 R 4 **Arvada**, CO, U.S.A.
109 P 4 **Arvayheer**, Mongolia
38 N 11 **Arviat**, NU, Canada
40 L 4 **Arviat**, NU, Canada
70 I 12 **Arvidsjaur**, Sweden
71 E 20 **Arvika**, Sweden
117 R 14 **Arwala**, Indonesia
110 G 10 **Arxan**, China
103 R 11 **Arys'**, Kazakhstan
77 C 15 **Arzachena**, Italy
93 O 1 **Arzamas**, Russian Federation
124 L 6 **Arzew**, Algeria
93 O 12 **Arzgir**, Russian Federation
96 J 3 **As Sa'an**, Syria
96 M 3 **As Sabkhah**, Syria
96 G 11 **Aş Şafi**, Jordan
97 N 1 **Aş Şafiḩ**, Syria
96 J 2 **As Safīrah**, Syria
99 R 6 **As Salamiyah**, Saudi Arabia
97 U 12 **As Salmān**, Iraq
96 G 9 **As Salţ**, Jordan
97 V 10 **As Samāwah**, Iraq
96 H 7 **Aş Şanamayn**, Syria
98 J 3 **Aş Şawrah**, Saudi Arabia
97 O 5 **As Sayyāl**, Syria
125 V 8 **As Sidrah**, Libya
99 R 3 **Aş Şubayhīyah**, Kuwait
99 S 13 **As Sufāl**, Yemen
96 L 4 **As Sukhnah**, Syria
97 U 3 **As Sulaymānīyah**, Iraq
99 Q 9 **As Sulayyil**, Saudi Arabia
125 U 8 **As Sulţān**, Libya
99 O 8 **As Sūq**, Saudi Arabia
97 O 3 **Aş Şuwār**, Syria
96 H 8 **As Suwaydā'**, Syria
97 T 8 **As Suwayrah**, Iraq
100 G 6 **Asadābād**, Iran
101 O 6 **Asadābād**, Iran
101 V 7 **Asadābād**, Afghanistan
95 V 8 **Asaği**, Azerbaijan
122 K 4 **Asahi-dake**, Japan
122 K 4 **Asahikawa**, Japan
100 H 4 **Asālem**, Iran
107 R 13 **Asansol**, India
127 J 19 **Āsayita**, Ethiopia
14 J 13 **Asbury Park**, NJ, U.S.A.
10 L 10 **Ascension**, U.K.
44 L 3 **Ascensión**, Mexico
73 F 19 **Aschaffenburg**, Germany
76 I 12 **Ascoli Piceno**, Italy
77 L 15 **Ascoli Satriano**, Italy
127 I 21 **Āsela**, Ethiopia
71 H 14 **Åsele**, Sweden
82 I 10 **Asenovgrad**, Bulgaria
70 B 10 **Ásgarður**, Iceland
25 W 9 **Ash Flat**, AR, U.S.A.
30 J 10 **Ash Fork**, AZ, U.S.A.
97 S 11 **Ash Shabakah**, Iraq
97 O 2 **Ash Shaddādah**, Syria
99 X 5 **Ash Sha'm**, United Arab Emirates
97 V 12 **Ash Shāmīyah**, Iraq
97 U 10 **Ash Shanāfīyah**, Iraq
99 P 6 **Ash Sha'rā'**, Saudi Arabia
99 R 11 **Ash Sharawrah**, Saudi Arabia
97 S 3 **Ash Sharqāţ**, Iraq
97 W 10 **Ash Shaţrah**, Iraq
96 G 11 **Ash Shawbak**, Jordan
99 P 14 **Ash Shaykh 'Uthman**, Yemen
99 T 13 **Ash Shiḩr**, Yemen
99 X 5 **Ash Şhināş**, Oman
99 P 3 **Ash Shu'bah**, Saudi Arabia
99 N 11 **Ash Shuqayq**, Saudi Arabia
125 T 9 **Ash Shuwayrif**, Libya
128 M 13 **Ashanti**, Ghana
99 Q 5 **Asharat**, Saudi Arabia
63 S 5 **Ashbourne**, U.K.
137 G 21 **Ashburton**, New Zealand
63 S 6 **Ashby de la Zouch**, U.K.
96 E 9 **Ashdod**, Israel
25 S 13 **Ashdown**, AR, U.S.A.
17 Q 9 **Asheboro**, NC, U.S.A.
25 O 11 **Asher**, OK, U.S.A.
16 M 9 **Asheville**, NC, U.S.A.
63 Y 12 **Ashford**, U.K.
102 L 14 **Ashgabat**, Turkmenistan
122 K 5 **Ashibetsu**, Japan
123 J 15 **Ashikaga**, Japan
122 K 10 **Ashiro**, Japan
123 E 22 **Ashizuri-misaki**, Japan
15 R 1 **Ashland**, ME, U.S.A.
16 L 4 **Ashland**, KY, U.S.A.
20 E 8 **Ashland**, WI, U.S.A.
21 N 17 **Ashland**, OH, U.S.A.
24 J 7 **Ashland**, KS, U.S.A.
33 G 14 **Ashland**, OR, U.S.A.
22 L 6 **Ashley**, ND, U.S.A.
85 H 16 **Ashmyany**, Belarus
122 L 5 **Ashoro**, Japan
96 E 10 **Ashqelon**, Israel
21 O 15 **Ashtabula**, OH, U.S.A.
95 T 8 **Ashtarak**, Armenia
29 Q 10 **Ashton**, ID, U.S.A.
121 J 15 **Asid Gulf**, Philippines
105 F 17 **Asifabad**, India
105 I 17 **Asika**, India
124 I 6 **Asilah**, Morocco
88 M 12 **Asino**, Russian Federation
85 K 18 **Asipovichy**, Belarus
95 P 9 **Aşkale**, Turkey
63 T 3 **Askern**, U.K.
71 D 20 **Askim**, Norway
91 T 14 **Askino**, Russian Federation
71 A 18 **Askøy**, Norway
100 G 2 **Aşlāndūz**, Iran
127 I 17 **Asmara**, Eritrea
71 F 24 **Åsnen**, Sweden
129 X 9 **Asnet**, Chad
123 C 22 **Aso-san**, Japan
83 F 23 **Asopos**, Greece
127 G 20 **Āsosa**, Ethiopia
75 X 5 **Aspang-Markt**, Austria
31 P 5 **Aspen**, CO, U.S.A.
26 M 5 **Aspermont**, TX, U.S.A.
127 K 18 **Assab**, Eritrea
128 G 7 **Assaba**, Mauritania
107 V 10 **Assam**, India
129 Q 6 **Assamakka**, Niger
17 X 5 **Assateague Island**, VA, U.S.A.
69 F 18 **Asse**, Belgium
68 M 7 **Assen**, Netherlands
69 I 21 **Assesse**, Belgium
40 H 10 **Assiniboine**, MB, Canada
58 I 6 **Assis**, Brazil
55 B 14 **Assis Brasil**, Brazil
76 H 12 **Assisi**, Italy
71 D 18 **Åsta**, Norway
83 M 25 **Astakida**, Greece
83 C 18 **Astakos**, Greece
103 R 4 **Astana**, Kazakhstan
100 H 3 **Āstārā**, Iran
69 K 16 **Asten**, Netherlands
76 B 8 **Asti**, Italy
53 H 17 **Astillero**, Peru
63 T 4 **Aston**, U.K.
66 L 3 **Astorga**, Spain
32 F 8 **Astoria**, OR, U.S.A.
93 R 11 **Astrakhan'**, Russian Federation
87 V 9 **Astrakhanka**, Ukraine
93 R 10 **Astrakhanskaya Oblast'**, Russian Federation
138 D 4 **Astrolabe Bay**, Papua New Guinea
83 E 21 **Astros**, Greece
85 F 18 **Astryna**, Belarus
66 L 1 **Asturias**, Spain
83 L 23 **Astypalaia**, Greece
145 S 2 **Asuka**, Antarctica
53 I 16 **Asunción**, Bolivia
55 G 20 **Asunción**, Paraguay
140 A 5 **Asuncion**, Northern Mariana Islands
46 I 6 **Asunción Mita**, Guatemala
84 J 13 **Asvyeya**, Belarus
126 F 12 **Aswân**, Egypt
126 E 10 **Asyût**, Egypt
103 U 11 **At-Bashy**, Kyrgyzstan
96 G 11 **Aţ Ţafīlah**, Jordan
98 M 8 **Aţ Ţā'if**, Saudi Arabia
125 X 7 **At Tamīmī**, Libya
96 L 7 **Aţ Ţanf**, Syria
97 T 9 **Aţ Ţaqţaqānah**, Iraq
96 G 12 **Aţ Ţayyibah**, Jordan
97 N 3 **At Tibnī**, Syria
98 K 2 **Aţ Ţubayq**, Saudi Arabia
99 O 14 **At Turbah**, Yemen
99 P 14 **At Turbah**, Yemen
140 H 11 **Ata**, Tonga
56 F 8 **Atacama**, Chile
56 F 2 **Atacama Desert**, Chile
140 J 6 **Atafu**, Tokelau Islands
129 N 12 **Atakpamé**, Togo
53 E 15 **Atalaya**, Peru
99 R 13 **'Ataq**, Yemen
128 G 5 **Atâr**, Mauritania
109 O 5 **Atas Bogd**, Mongolia
103 S 6 **Atasu**, Kazakhstan
117 Q 15 **Atauro**, Indonesia
127 F 15 **Atbara**, Sudan
127 G 16 **Atbara**, Sudan
103 Q 4 **Atbasar**, Kazakhstan
18 J 9 **Atchafalaya Bay**, LA, U.S.A.
25 Q 3 **Atchison**, KS, U.S.A.
128 M 12 **Atebubu**, Ghana
69 E 20 **Ath**, Belgium
39 I 18 **Athabasca**, AB, Canada
16 I 10 **Athens**, TN, U.S.A.
19 U 2 **Athens**, GA, U.S.A.
21 N 19 **Athens**, OH, U.S.A.
27 R 6 **Athens**, TX, U.S.A.
83 G 20 **Athens**, Greece
94 H 15 **Athiénou**, Cyprus
61 D 18 **Athlone**, Republic of Ireland
14 M 9 **Athol**, MA, U.S.A.
83 H 15 **Athos**, Greece
129 X 9 **Ati**, Chad
53 E 19 **Atico**, Peru
127 C 21 **Atiedo**, Sudan
67 P 5 **Atienza**, Spain
40 K 11 **Atikokan**, ON, Canada
46 I 7 **Atiquizaya**, El Salvador
46 G 6 **Atitlán**, Guatemala
141 P 10 **Atiu**, Cook Islands
34 G 14 **Atka**, AK, U.S.A.
89 X 10 **Atka**, Russian Federation
34 G 14 **Atka Island**, AK, U.S.A.
93 P 5 **Atkarsk**, Russian Federation
117 T 11 **Atkri**, Indonesia
19 S 3 **Atlanta**, GA, U.S.A.
20 K 11 **Atlanta**, MI, U.S.A.
28 L 10 **Atlanta**, ID, U.S.A.
17 V 10 **Atlantic**, NC, U.S.A.
23 R 13 **Atlantic**, IA, U.S.A.
14 J 15 **Atlantic City**, NJ, U.S.A.
8 K 9 **Atlantic Ocean**, 0
50 H 2 **Atlantico**, Colombia
124 H 9 **Atlas Mountains**, Morocco
124 L 7 **Atlas Saharien**, Algeria
39 B 15 **Atlin Lake**, BC, Canada
96 F 8 **'Atlit**, Israel
19 P 6 **Atmore**, AL, U.S.A.
53 J 22 **Atocha**, Bolivia
25 P 12 **Atoka**, OK, U.S.A.
115 N 17 **Atouat**, Laos
100 M 4 **Atrak**, Iran
123 K 16 **Atsugi**, Japan
122 J 12 **Atsumi**, Japan
123 I 18 **Atsumi**, Japan
122 J 5 **Atsuta**, Japan
115 N 18 **Attapu**, Laos
83 O 24 **Attavyros**, Greece
40 M 10 **Attawapiskat**, ON, Canada
41 O 9 **Attawapiskat**, ON, Canada
40 L 9 **Attawapiskat Lake**, ON, Canada
75 R 5 **Attersee**, Austria
69 K 25 **Attert**, Belgium
14 D 8 **Attica**, NY, U.S.A.
21 H 18 **Attica**, IN, U.S.A.
83 G 22 **Attiki**, Greece
63 Y 7 **Attleborough**, U.K.
34 B 11 **Attu Island**, AK, U.S.A.
99 S 13 **Atūd**, Yemen
57 H 14 **Atuel**, Argentina
102 I 7 **Atyrau**, Kazakhstan
102 I 7 **Atyrau**, Kazakhstan
20 L 12 **Au Sable Point**, MI, U.S.A.
138 B 2 **Aua Island**, Papua New Guinea
69 K 26 **Aubange**, Belgium
65 S 12 **Aubenas**, France
65 Q 7 **Aubigny-sur-Nère**, France
65 Q 12 **Aubin**, France
14 G 8 **Auburn**, NY, U.S.A.
15 N 10 **Auburn**, MA, U.S.A.
19 R 4 **Auburn**, AL, U.S.A.
21 E 19 **Auburn**, IL, U.S.A.
23 Q 15 **Auburn**, NE, U.S.A.
32 G 7 **Auburn**, WA, U.S.A.
33 H 18 **Auburn**, CA, U.S.A.
65 Q 9 **Aubusson**, France
84 D 12 **Auce**, Latvia
65 N 14 **Auch**, France
136 K 8 **Auckland**, New Zealand
136 J 8 **Auckland**, New Zealand
64 H 5 **Audierne**, France
127 J 22 **Audo Range**, Ethiopia
73 L 18 **Aue**, Germany
73 L 18 **Auerbach**, Germany
135 T 7 **Augathella**, QLD, Australia
73 I 24 **Augsburg**, Germany
84 H 13 **Augšzemes Augstiene**, Latvia
15 P 6 **Augusta**, ME, U.S.A.
19 V 3 **Augusta**, GA, U.S.A.
20 D 11 **Augusta**, WI, U.S.A.
21 D 18 **Augusta**, IL, U.S.A.
29 P 4 **Augusta**, MT, U.S.A.
77 L 23 **Augusta**, Italy
134 F 12 **Augusta**, WA, Australia
56 G 6 **Augusta Victoria**, Chile
78 N 9 **Augustów**, Poland
138 M 6 **Auki**, Solomon Islands
31 R 2 **Ault**, CO, U.S.A.
129 P 11 **Auna**, Nigeria
41 S 6 **Aupaluk**, QC, Canada
117 R 12 **Auponhia**, Indonesia
116 F 9 **Aur**, Malaysia
141 Z 3 **Aur**, Marshall Islands
20 G 8 **Aura**, MI, U.S.A.
106 L 10 **Auraiya**, India
107 P 12 **Aurangabad**, India
64 J 6 **Auray**, France
72 D 10 **Aurich**, Germany
65 Q 11 **Aurillac**, France
71 B 18 **Aurlandsvangen**, Norway
21 G 16 **Aurora**, IL, U.S.A.
31 R 4 **Aurora**, CO, U.S.A.
120 H 8 **Aurora**, Philippines
54 K 10 **Aurora do Pará**, Brazil
135 R 2 **Aurukun**, QLD, Australia
132 I 11 **Aus**, Namibia
23 T 10 **Austin**, MN, U.S.A.
27 P 9 **Austin**, TX, U.S.A.
33 L 17 **Austin**, NV, U.S.A.
135 N 6 **Australia**, Oceania
135 U 12 **Australian Capital Territory**, Australia
75 P 7 **Austria**, Europe
70 G 9 **Austvågøy**, Norway
54 F 11 **Autazes**, Brazil
45 N 11 **Autlán**, Mexico
65 S 8 **Autun**, France
65 Q 10 **Auvergne**, France
65 R 6 **Auxerre**, France
51 R 6 **Auyan Tepuí**, Venezuela
25 U 7 **Ava**, MO, U.S.A.
65 S 7 **Avallon**, France
14 I 15 **Avalon**, NJ, U.S.A.
41 Z 10 **Avalon Peninsula**, NL, Canada
58 J 7 **Avaré**, Brazil
141 N 11 **Avarua**, Cook Islands
63 R 11 **Avebury**, U.K.
54 H 11 **Aveiro**, Brazil
66 H 5 **Aveiro**, Portugal
66 H 6 **Aveiro**, Portugal
77 K 16 **Avellino**, Italy
77 J 16 **Aversa**, Italy
28 K 4 **Avery**, ID, U.S.A.
65 S 2 **Avesnes-sur-Helpe**, France
71 G 19 **Avesta**, Sweden
56 L 7 **Aviá Terai**, Argentina
58 C 10 **Avia Teray**, Argentina
60 H 10 **Aviemore**, U.K.
65 T 13 **Avignon**, France
67 N 6 **Ávila**, Spain
66 L 1 **Avilés**, Spain
84 I 6 **Avinurme**, Estonia
83 G 19 **Avlida**, Greece
77 K 23 **Avola**, Italy
14 E 8 **Avon**, NY, U.S.A.
63 R 9 **Avon**, U.K.
19 W 11 **Avon Park**, FL, U.S.A.
30 I 12 **Avondale**, AZ, U.S.A.
64 L 4 **Avranches**, France
86 I 11 **Avrig**, Romania
127 L 24 **Aw Dheegle**, Somalia
122 J 12 **Awa-shima**, Japan
123 G 19 **Awaji-shima**, Japan
136 K 11 **Awakino**, New Zealand
99 T 5 **Awālī**, Bahrain
136 I 5 **Awanui**, New Zealand
127 L 21 **Āwarē**, Ethiopia
136 J 6 **Awarua**, New Zealand
137 B 21 **Awarua Point**, New Zealand
127 I 21 **Āwasa**, Ethiopia
127 J 20 **Āwash**, Ethiopia
127 J 19 **Āwash**, Ethiopia
137 I 17 **Awatere**, New Zealand
125 S 11 **Awbārī**, Libya
127 C 20 **Aweil**, Sudan
19 P 5 **Awin**, AL, U.S.A.
125 X 9 **Awjilah**, Libya
124 C 13 **Awserd**, Western Sahara
37 O 2 **Axel Heiberg Island**, NU, Canada
128 L 14 **Axim**, Ghana
82 E 13 **Axios**, Greece
63 O 13 **Axminster**, U.K.
53 E 17 **Ayacucho**, Peru
53 E 18 **Ayacucho**, Peru
59 D 18 **Ayacucho**, Argentina
103 X 6 **Ayagoz**, Kazakhstan
108 L 7 **Ayakkum Hu**, China
66 I 12 **Ayamonte**, Spain
89 V 12 **Ayan**, Russian Federation
94 J 7 **Ayancik**, Turkey
111 K 18 **Ayang**, North Korea
51 T 6 **Ayanganna Mountain**, Guyana
129 R 12 **Ayangba**, Nigeria
53 G 18 **Ayaviri**, Peru
101 T 6 **Āybak**, Afghanistan
87 Y 5 **Aydar**, Ukraine
94 C 11 **Aydin**, Turkey
94 B 11 **Aydin Dağlari**, Turkey
127 J 19 **Āyelu Terara**, Ethiopia
118 E 10 **Ayer Hitam**, Malaysia
67 S 3 **Ayerbe**, Spain
89 R 10 **Aykhal**, Russian Federation
63 U 9 **Aylesbury**, U.K.
137 H 20 **Aylesbury**, New Zealand
67 P 5 **Ayllón**, Spain
38 J 10 **Aylmer Lake**, NT, Canada
63 Z 6 **Aylsham**, U.K.
103 R 13 **Ayní**, Tajikistan
127 E 21 **Ayod**, Sudan
67 S 9 **Ayora**, Spain
129 N 8 **Ayorou**, Niger
128 H 7 **'Ayoûn el 'Atroûs**, Mauritania
61 G 14 **Ayr**, U.K.
135 U 5 **Ayr**, QLD, Australia
94 I 12 **Ayranci**, Turkey
103 N 8 **Ayteke Bi**, Kazakhstan
82 M 9 **Aytos**, Bulgaria
99 W 11 **Ayun**, Oman
115 H 18 **Ayutthaya**, Thailand
94 A 9 **Ayvacik**, Turkey
94 B 9 **Ayvalik**, Turkey
96 H 6 **Az Zabadānī**, Syria
96 H 9 **Az Zarqā'**, Jordan
125 S 7 **Az Zāwīyah**, Libya
99 O 13 **Az Zaydīyah**, Yemen
99 P 5 **Az Zilfī**, Saudi Arabia
125 R 8 **Az Zintān**, Libya
97 Z 12 **Az Zubayr**, Iraq
99 O 12 **Az Zuhrah**, Yemen
99 O 14 **Az Zuqur**, Yemen
47 N 6 **Azacualpa**, Honduras
32 F 13 **Azalea**, OR, U.S.A.
107 O 11 **Azamgarh**, India
100 F 4 **Āzarbāyjān-e Gharbī**, Iran
100 G 3 **Āzarbāyjān-e Sharqī**, Iran
129 S 10 **Azare**, Nigeria
85 L 20 **Azarychy**, Belarus
96 J 1 **A'zāz**, Syria
124 G 7 **Azemmour**, Morocco
95 V 10 **Azerbaijan**, Asia
127 H 18 **Āzezo**, Ethiopia
124 H 8 **Azilal**, Morocco
101 N 11 **'Azīzābād**, Iran
10 K 6 **Azores**, Portugal
92 L 10 **Azov**, Russian Federation
96 I 9 **Azraq ash Shīshān**, Jordan
124 I 7 **Azrou**, Morocco
30 H 13 **Aztec**, AZ, U.S.A.
31 O 8 **Aztec**, NM, U.S.A.
49 Q 8 **Azua**, Dominican Republic
66 L 10 **Azuaga**, Spain
52 B 10 **Azuay**, Ecuador
59 C 17 **Azul**, Argentina
128 E 5 **Azzeffâl**, Mauritania

B

17 R 9 **B. Everett Jordan Reservoir**, NC, U.S.A.
115 N 19 **Bâ Kêv**, Cambodia
117 P 15 **Baa**, Indonesia
96 H 5 **Ba'albek**, Lebanon
96 G 6 **Baaqline**, Lebanon
127 L 24 **Baardheere**, Somalia
127 K 17 **Bāb al Mandab**, Africa/Asia
94 G 7 **Baba Burnu**, Turkey
94 A 9 **Baba Burun**, Turkey
87 N 12 **Babadag**, Romania
95 X 7 **Babadağ Dağl**, Azerbaijan
102 L 14 **Babadurmaz**, Turkmenistan
94 B 7 **Babaeski**, Turkey
127 C 19 **Babanusa**, Sudan
117 T 14 **Babar**, Indonesia
131 U 10 **Babati**, Tanzania
90 I 11 **Babayevo**, Russian Federation
29 O 2 **Babb**, MT, U.S.A.
63 N 14 **Babbacombe Bay**, U.K.
118 F 9 **Babi Besar**, Malaysia
39 E 18 **Babine Lake**, BC, Canada
117 U 12 **Babo**, Indonesia
100 J 5 **Bābol**, Iran
129 V 13 **Babongo**, Cameroon
30 K 15 **Baboquivari Peak**, AZ, U.S.A.
130 G 4 **Baboua**, Central African Republic
85 L 19 **Babruysk**, Belarus
120 H 4 **Babuyan**, Philippines
121 D 18 **Babuyan**, Philippines
120 G 5 **Babuyan Channel**, Philippines
120 H 4 **Babuyan Islands**, Philippines
114 M 11 **Băc Can**, Vietnam
114 M 12 **Băc Giang**, Vietnam
114 L 10 **Bac Lac**, Vietnam
115 M 23 **Bac Liêu**, Vietnam
114 M 12 **Băc Ninh**, Vietnam
114 L 11 **Băc Quang**, Vietnam
127 N 21 **Bacaadweyn**, Somalia
54 L 11 **Bacabal**, Brazil
54 I 11 **Bacajá**, Brazil
45 Z 12 **Bacalar**, Mexico
117 R 11 **Bacan**, Indonesia
120 F 6 **Bacarra**, Philippines
86 L 9 **Bacău**, Romania
65 V 5 **Baccarat**, France
74 K 7 **Bach**, Austria
73 D 19 **Bacharach**, Germany
40 K 1 **Back**, NU, Canada
80 J 9 **Baćka Palanka**, Serbia and Montene
80 J 8 **Bačka Topola**, Serbia and Monteneg
73 G 22 **Backnang**, Germany
121 J 17 **Bacolod**, Philippines
44 J 6 **Bácum**, Mexico
75 S 6 **Bad Aussee**, Austria
73 D 22 **Bad Bergzabern**, Germany
72 H 9 **Bad Bramstedt**, Germany
72 N 12 **Bad Freienwalde**, Germany
75 R 6 **Bad Goisern**, Austria
75 Q 7 **Bad Hofgastein**, Austria
73 E 14 **Bad Iburg**, Germany
75 R 5 **Bad Ischl**, Austria
75 S 8 **Bad Kleinkirchheim**, Austria
73 D 20 **Bad Kreuznach**, Germany
73 I 17 **Bad Langensalza**, Germany
75 T 3 **Bad Leonfelden**, Austria
73 H 21 **Bad Mergentheim**, Germany
73 H 19 **Bad Neustadt an der Saale**, Germany
72 H 10 **Bad Oldesloe**, Germany
75 X 8 **Bad Radkersburg**, Austria
73 L 25 **Bad Reichenhall**, Germany
73 H 17 **Bad Salzungen**, Germany
72 H 9 **Bad Segeberg**, Germany
75 U 7 **Bad St Leonhard**, Austria
73 J 25 **Bad Tölz**, Germany
73 G 25 **Bad Waldsee**, Germany
115 F 22 **Bada**, Myanmar
105 D 22 **Badagara**, India
113 N 11 **Badahe**, China
109 O 7 **Badain Jaran Desert**, China
66 J 9 **Badajoz**, Spain
101 V 5 **Badakhshān**, Afghanistan
99 N 1 **Badanah**, Saudi Arabia
104 F 9 **Badarinath Peaks**, India
107 W 11 **Badarpur**, India
43 X 8 **Baddeck**, NS, Canada
101 R 12 **Baddo**, Pakistan
75 X 4 **Baden**, Austria
73 E 22 **Baden Baden**, Germany
73 E 23 **Baden-wurttemberg**, Germany
75 Q 7 **Badgastein**, Austria
101 Q 7 **Bādghīs**, Afghanistan
68 H 11 **Badhoevedorp**, Netherlands
67 Z 7 **Badia d'Alcúdia**, Spain
67 X 8 **Badia de Palma**, Spain
101 U 15 **Badin**, Pakistan
22 G 6 **Badlands**, ND, U.S.A.
120 F 6 **Badoc**, Philippines
113 R 6 **Badong**, China
129 N 12 **Badou**, Togo
98 L 6 **Badr Ḩunayn**, Saudi Arabia
97 W 7 **Badrah**, Iraq
106 L 6 **Badrinath Peaks**, India
135 R 1 **Badu Island**, QLD, Australia
105 G 25 **Badulla**, Sri Lanka
67 N 12 **Baena**, Spain
67 O 11 **Baeza**, Spain
128 E 10 **Bafatá**, Guinea-Bissau
143 O 9 **Baffin Basin**, Arctic Ocean
143 N 10 **Baffin Bay**, Arctic Ocean
41 Q 1 **Baffin Island**, NU, Canada
129 T 14 **Bafia**, Cameroon

Country · Internal administrative region: State/Province/Territory/Dependent territory · Capital city · Mountain range/Undersea ridge · Mountain peak/Volcano/Seamount · Geographic feature · Headland/Point/Cape/Peninsula · Desert · Island/Island group · Antarctic base · Ocean · Sea · Bay/Gulf/Channel/Strait · Lake · Salt pan/Dry/Intermittent lake

Bafoulabé – Bayḩan al Qişab

H 9 Bafoulabé, Mali
T 14 Bafoussam, Cameroon
L 9 Bāfq, Iran
K 7 Bafra, Turkey
L 7 Bafra Burnu, Turkey
P 7 Bafwasende, Democratic Republic of Congo
G 8 Bagabag, Philippines
F 11 Bagac, Philippines
F 11 Bagac Bay, Philippines
O 11 Bagaces, Costa Rica
O 10 Bagaha, India
D 19 Bagalkot, India
W 11 Bagamoyo, Tanzania
N 21 Baganga, Philippines
K 7 Bagani, Namibia
J 22 Baganian Peninsula, Philippines
D 9 Bagansiapiapi, Indonesia
P 9 Bagaroua, Niger
J 10 Bagata, Democratic Republic of Congo
F 13 Bagé, Brazil
L 7 Bageshwar, India
V 15 Baggs, WY, U.S.A.
M 12 Baggy Point, U.K.
O 6 Baghbaghū, Iran
T 7 Baghdad, Iraq
I 21 Bagheria, Italy
L 10 Bāghīn, Iran
T 6 Baghlān, Afghanistan
U 6 Baghlān, Afghanistan
R 8 Baghrān, Afghanistan
O 9 Baglung, Nepal
I 17 Bago, Philippines
E 6 Bagolino, Italy
B 16 Bagrationovsk, Russian Federation
J 10 Bagre, Brazil
W 8 Bagsaya, Iraq
U 11 Bagshot, U.K.
B 12 Bagua, Peru
P 10 Bagudo, Nigeria
F 8 Baguio, Philippines
H 9 Baguio Point, Philippines
K 1 Bahamas, The, North America
R 13 Baharampur, India
D 9 Bahariya Oasis, Egypt
W 7 Bahatyr, Ukraine
D 9 Bahau, Malaysia
W 11 Bahawalpur, Pakistan
L 13 Bahşe, Turkey
M 14 Bahia, Brazil
K 16 Bahía Anegada, Argentina
G 6 Bahía Asunción, Mexico
B 19 Bahía Blanca, Argentina
B 19 Bahía Blanca, Argentina
I 19 Bahía Bustamante, Argentina
I 19 Bahía Camarones, Argentina
Z 12 Bahía Chetumal, Mexico
J 4 Bahía de Amatique, Guatemala
B 7 Bahía de Ancón de Sardinas, Ecuador
G 6 Bahía de Ballenas, Mexico
M 11 Bahía de Banderas, Mexico
R 10 Bahía de Bluefields, Nicaragua
V 11 Bahía de Campeche, Mexico
A 9 Bahía de Caráquez, Ecuador
L 1 Bahía de Chetumal, Belize
G 26 Bahía de Cook, Chile
Q 14 Bahía de Coronado, Costa Rica
Z 11 Bahía de Espíritu Santo, Mexico
K 8 Bahía de Jiquilisco, El Salvador
Z 14 Bahía de la Ascensión, Mexico
I 8 Bahía de La Paz, Mexico
G 4 Bahía de los Ángeles, Mexico
A 9 Bahía de Manta, Ecuador
X 14 Bahía de Panamá, Panama
W 15 Bahía de Parita, Panama
P 13 Bahía de Petacalco, Mexico
R 7 Bahía de Samaná, Dominican Republic
R 10 Bahía de San Juan del Norte, Nicaragua
H 24 Bahía de San Sebastián, Argentina
A 9 Bahía de Santa Elena, Ecuador
K 7 Bahía de Santa María, Mexico
A 12 Bahía de Sechura, Peru
N 4 Bahía de Trujillo, Honduras
R 7 Bahía Escocesa, Dominican Republic
H 23 Bahía Grande, Argentina
I 4 Bahía Kino, Mexico
I 21 Bahía Laura, Argentina
H 8 Bahía Magdalena, Mexico
G 7 Bahía Magdalena, Colombia
I 26 Bahía Nassau, Chile
G 18 Bahía Negra, Paraguay
F 25 Bahía Otway, Chile
F 8 Bahía Salada, Chile
E 23 Bahía Salvación, Chile
E 16 Bahía Samborombón, Argentina
E 18 Bahía San Nicolás, Peru
G 5 Bahía Sebastián Vizcaíno, Mexico
I 19 Bahía Solano, Argentina
F 5 Bahía Tortugas, Mexico
B 20 Bahía Unión, Argentina
H 19 Bahir Dar, Ethiopia
A 19 Bahr el Arab, Sudan
D 20 Bahr el Ghazal, Sudan
E 23 Bahr el Jebel, Sudan
M 9 Bahraich, India
U 4 Bahrain, Asia
P 14 Bāhū Kālāt, Iran
M 15 Bahushewsk, Belarus
L 13 Bai Thuong, Vietnam
N 12 Baia, Romania
J 10 Baia de Marajó, Brazil
U 5 Baia de Memba, Mozambique
U 4 Baia de Pemba, Mozambique
L 10 Baia de São Marcos, Brazil
F 6 Baía dos Tigres, Angola
F 4 Baia Farta, Angola
I 8 Baia Mare, Romania
J 10 Baião, Brazil
L 8 Baiazeh, Iran
W 12 Baïbokoum, Chad
H 11 Baicheng, China
K 12 Băicoi, Romania
Q 5 Baie-Comeau, QC, Canada
H 6 Baie de Audierne, France
K 7 Baie de Bourgneuf, France
H 5 Baie de Douarnenez, France
M 3 Baie de Seine, France
J 4 Baie de St-Brieuc, France
N 7 Baie-St-Paul, QC, Canada
R 5 Baie-Trinité, QC, Canada
X 9 Baie Verte, NL, Canada
M 14 Baihe, China
R 5 Baihe, China
G 10 Bailang, China
86 K 10 Băile Tuşnad, Romania
67 O 11 Bailén, Spain
54 J 9 Bailique, Brazil
69 J 22 Baillonville, Belgium
132 H 4 Bailundo, Angola
112 K 4 Baima, China
138 C 5 Baimuru, Papua New Guinea
19 S 6 Bainbridge, GA, U.S.A.
117 O 15 Baing, Indonesia
110 K 9 Baiquan, China
96 I 11 Bā'ir, Jordan
108 I 8 Bairab Co, China
107 Q 10 Bairagnia, India
35 O 5 Baird Mountains, AK, U.S.A.
140 D 2 Bairiki, Kiribati
110 F 13 Bairin Qiao, China
110 F 13 Bairin Zuoqi, China
103 Q 11 Bairkum, Kazakhstan
135 T 13 Bairnsdale, VIC, Australia
113 O 7 Baisha, China
111 K 14 Baishan, China
111 L 14 Baishan, China
106 M 8 Baitadi, Nepal
112 I 4 Baitang, China
141 U 1 Baiti, Nauru
113 U 1 Baixiang, China
132 J 6 Baixo-Longa, Angola
112 J 5 Baiyü, China
127 F 15 Baiyuda Desert, Sudan
107 S 14 Baj Baj, India
79 I 25 Baja, Hungary
44 F 2 Baja California, Mexico
44 F 4 Baja California Norte, Mexico
44 G 7 Baja California Sur, Mexico
106 M 8 Bajang, Nepal
116 G 9 Bajau, Indonesia
101 N 7 Bajestān, Iran
101 O 5 Bājgīrān, Iran
99 O 13 Bājil, Yemen
47 S 14 Bajo Boquete, Panama
57 G 21 Bajo Caracoles, Argentina
129 T 11 Bajoga, Nigeria
93 U 1 Bakaly, Russian Federation
103 W 8 Bakanas, Kazakhstan
129 Z 8 Bakaoré, Chad
128 G 8 Bakel, Senegal
29 Z 6 Baker, MT, U.S.A.
32 K 11 Baker, OR, U.S.A.
33 L 23 Baker, CA, U.S.A.
40 K 3 Baker Lake, NU, Canada
33 J 23 Bakersfield, CA, U.S.A.
63 S 4 Bakewell, U.K.
102 L 13 Bakhardok, Turkmenistan
87 T 12 Bakhcysaray, Ukraine
102 K 13 Bakherden, Turkmenistan
87 S 2 Bakhmach, Ukraine
89 N 10 Bakhta, Russian Federation
107 Q 11 Bakhtiyarpur, India
103 Y 7 Bakhty, Kazakhstan
94 D 7 Bakırköy, Turkey
82 O 13 Bakiröy, Turkey
70 D 10 Bakkaflói, Iceland
106 H 5 Bakloh, India
127 H 20 Bako, Ethiopia
128 I 11 Bako, Côte d'Ivoire
79 G 24 Bakony, Hungary
127 L 23 Bakool, Somalia
138 H 4 Bakop, Papua New Guinea
130 M 4 Bakouma, Central African Republic
93 O 13 Baksan, Russian Federation
95 Z 8 Baku, Azerbaijan
95 S 7 Bakuriani, Georgia
144 K 10 Bakutis Coast, Antarctica
63 N 5 Bala, U.K.
94 H 10 Bala, Turkey
101 Q 6 Bālā Morghāb, Afghanistan
121 B 21 Balabac, Philippines
121 A 21 Balabac, Philippines
121 A 21 Balabac Strait, Philippines
87 U 7 Balabyne, Ukraine
97 T 6 Balad, Iraq
97 U 6 Balad Rūz, Iraq
105 G 15 Balaghat, India
105 D 17 Balaghat Range, India
67 V 4 Balaguer, Spain
95 V 6 Balakān, Azerbaijan
87 T 13 Balaklava, Ukraine
87 W 5 Balakliya, Ukraine
93 R 5 Balakovo, Russian Federation
119 V 3 Balambangan, Malaysia
120 F 11 Balanga, Philippines
105 H 16 Balangir, India
93 O 5 Balashov, Russian Federation
79 J 21 Balassagyarmat, Hungary
79 G 24 Balaton, Hungary
120 G 7 Balbalan, Philippines
54 F 10 Balbina, Brazil
47 W 13 Balboa, Panama
61 F 17 Balbriggan, Republic of Ireland
59 D 18 Balcarce, Argentina
82 N 7 Balchik, Bulgaria
137 E 25 Balclutha, New Zealand
26 N 10 Balcones Escarpment, TX, U.S.A.
17 T 12 Bald Head Island, NC, U.S.A.
25 W 10 Bald Knob, AR, U.S.A.
19 W 7 Baldwin, FL, U.S.A.
20 C 11 Baldwin, WI, U.S.A.
20 J 13 Baldwin, MI, U.S.A.
14 G 8 Baldwinsville, NY, U.S.A.
29 S 3 Baldy Mountain, MT, U.S.A.
40 H 9 Baldy Mountain, MB, Canada
30 M 12 Baldy Peak, AZ, U.S.A.
128 H 10 Baléa, Mali
67 V 9 Balearic Islands, Spain
119 R 10 Baleh, Malaysia
120 H 9 Baler, Philippines
120 H 9 Baler Bay, Philippines
105 K 16 Baleshwar, India
91 Q 13 Balezino, Russian Federation
108 K 5 Balguntay, China
99 S 14 Balḩaf, Yemen
104 C 13 Bali, India
116 L 14 Bali, Indonesia
116 L 15 Bali, Indonesia
116 K 14 Bali Sea, Indonesia
116 D 9 Balige, Indonesia
94 C 9 Balıkesir, Turkey
96 L 2 Balīkh, Syria
116 M 11 Balikpapan, Indonesia
121 E 25 Balimbing, Philippines
121 L 20 Balingasag, Philippines
73 F 24 Balingen, Germany
119 P 8 Balingian, Malaysia
121 L 19 Balingoan, Philippines
120 G 3 Balintang Channel, Philippines
130 M 5 Balitondo, Central African Republic
99 N 9 Baljurshi, Saudi Arabia
68 J 8 Balk, Netherlands
82 F 8 Balkan Mountains, Bulgaria
102 J 12 Balkanskiy Velayat, Turkmenistan
103 Q 3 Balkashino, Kazakhstan
101 T 5 Balkh, Afghanistan
103 U 7 Balkhash, Kazakhstan
60 G 11 Ballachulish, U.K.
134 J 11 Balladonia, WA, Australia
61 C 17 Ballaghaderreen, Republic of Ireland
105 F 17 Ballalpur, India
61 G 14 Ballantrae, U.K.
135 R 13 Ballarat, VIC, Australia
145 S 15 Balleny Islands, Antarctica
61 B 16 Ballina, Republic of Ireland
135 W 9 Ballina, NSW, Australia
61 C 18 Ballinasloe, Republic of Ireland
26 M 7 Ballinger, TX, U.S.A.
61 F 15 Ballymena, U.K.
61 C 16 Ballysadare, Republic of Ireland
57 G 20 Balmaceda, Chile
26 H 8 Balmorhea, TX, U.S.A.
132 G 4 Balombo, Angola
104 B 13 Balotra, India
103 W 8 Balpyk Bi, Kazakhstan
107 N 9 Balrampur, India
135 R 11 Balranald, NSW, Australia
86 I 13 Balş, Romania
47 P 12 Balsa, Costa Rica
45 R 13 Balsas, Mexico
52 C 13 Balsas, Peru
54 K 12 Balsas, Brazil
74 E 7 Balsthal, Switzerland
87 O 7 Balta, Ukraine
80 O 13 Balta Berilovac, Serbia and Montenegro
86 M 8 Bălţi, Moldova
71 G 26 Baltic Sea, Europe
17 U 2 Baltimore, MD, U.S.A.
85 A 15 Baltiysk, Russian Federation
101 R 12 Baluchistān, Pakistan
121 J 15 Balud, Philippines
107 S 11 Balurghat, India
121 M 25 Balut, Philippines
84 I 10 Balvi, Latvia
103 V 10 Balykchy, Kyrgyzstan
102 I 7 Balykshi, Kazakhstan
101 N 11 Bam, Iran
113 P 11 Bama, China
129 U 10 Bama, Nigeria
135 R 1 Bamaga, QLD, Australia
128 J 10 Bamako, Mali
128 M 7 Bamba, Mali
130 G 9 Bambama, Congo
132 K 6 Bambangando, Angola
130 K 4 Bambari, Central African Republic
17 O 14 Bamberg, SC, U.S.A.
73 I 20 Bamberg, Germany
131 O 5 Bambili, Democratic Republic of Congo
130 I 5 Bambio, Central African Republic
127 G 19 Bambudi, Ethiopia
55 K 17 Bambuí, Brazil
112 I 6 Bamda, China
129 S 13 Bamenda, Cameroon
39 F 22 Bamfield, BC, Canada
102 K 13 Bami, Turkmenistan
101 T 7 Bāmīān, Afghanistan
101 T 7 Bāmīān, Afghanistan
110 J 13 Bamiancheng, China
130 K 3 Bamingui, Central African Republic
130 K 2 Bamingui-Bangoran, Central African Republic
115 K 20 Bāmnak, Cambodia
63 N 12 Bampton, U.K.
101 O 13 Bampūr, Iran
114 K 13 Ban Ban, Laos
114 I 12 Ban Boun Tai, Laos
115 I 17 Ban Bua Chum, Thailand
115 J 21 Ban Hat Lek, Thailand
114 H 13 Ban Houayxay, Laos
115 G 21 Ban Huai Yang, Thailand
115 H 17 Ban Khao Sai, Thailand
115 E 24 Ban Khok Kloi, Thailand
115 G 24 Ban Na San, Thailand
115 I 14 Ban Nalè, Laos
115 L 15 Ban Napè, Laos
115 H 15 Ban Pak Pat, Thailand
115 K 15 Ban Phaeng, Laos
115 J 17 Ban Phai, Thailand
115 M 17 Ban Phon, Laos
115 J 15 Ban Phu, Thailand
115 G 19 Ban Pong, Thailand
115 G 18 Ban Rai, Thailand
115 F 15 Ban Tha Song Yang, Thailand
115 J 15 Ban Thabôk, Laos
115 M 17 Ban Tôp, Laos
115 K 14 Ban Vang-An, Laos
115 M 18 Ban Xepian, Laos
127 M 24 Banaadir, Somalia
140 C 3 Banaba, Kiribati
131 N 7 Banalia, Democratic Republic of Congo
128 I 9 Banamba, Mali
141 P 2 Banana, Kiribati
105 O 25 Bananga, India
82 M 13 Banarli, Turkey
104 D 13 Banas, India
120 G 8 Banaue, Philippines
94 E 10 Banaz, Turkey
108 M 10 Banbar, China
61 F 16 Banbridge, U.K.
63 S 8 Banbury, U.K.
45 Z 12 Banco Chinchorro, Mexico
48 G 10 Banco Gorda, Jamaica
121 D 21 Bancoran, Philippines
42 G 11 Bancroft, ON, Canada
106 L 11 Banda, India
129 U 12 Banda, Cameroon
131 P 5 Banda, Democratic Republic of Congo
116 B 8 Banda Aceh, Indonesia
117 S 13 Banda Sea, Indonesia
117 T 13 Bandaneira, Indonesia
100 L 12 Bandar-e 'Abbās, Iran
100 H 4 Bandar-e Anzalī, Iran
100 G 9 Bandar-e Emām Khomeynī, Iran
100 K 13 Bandar-e Lengeh, Iran
100 J 13 Bandar-e Moghūyeh, Iran
116 G 13 Bandar Lampung, Indonesia
119 S 6 Bandar Seri Begawan, Brunei
66 I 3 Bande, Spain
27 N 10 Bandera, TX, U.S.A.
56 K 9 Bandera, Argentina
128 L 9 Bandiagara, Mali
106 H 3 Bandipur, India
94 C 8 Bandırma, Turkey
32 E 12 Bandon, OR, U.S.A.
130 J 10 Bandundu, Democratic Republic of Congo
130 I 10 Bandundu, Democratic Republic of Congo
116 H 14 Bandung, Indonesia
86 M 13 Băneasa, Romania
48 M 6 Banes, Cuba
39 I 20 Banff, AB, Canada
60 I 9 Banff, U.K.
128 K 11 Banfora, Burkina Faso
121 L 23 Banga, Philippines
130 K 11 Banga, Democratic Republic of Congo
121 N 21 Bangai Point, Philippines
105 D 21 Bangalore, India
119 T 6 Bangar, Malaysia
130 M 5 Bangassou, Central African Republic
117 P 11 Banggai, Indonesia
119 W 3 Banggi, Malaysia
125 W 7 Banghāzī, Libya
116 G 11 Bangka, Indonesia
117 Q 10 Bangka, Indonesia
116 K 14 Bangkalan, Indonesia
116 D 10 Bangkinang, Indonesia
116 F 11 Bangko, Indonesia
115 I 19 Bangkok, Thailand
107 U 12 Bangladesh, Asia
15 R 5 Bangor, ME, U.S.A.
62 M 4 Bangor, U.K.
120 F 7 Bangued, Philippines
120 F 5 Bangui, Philippines
130 J 5 Bangui, Central African Republic
130 I 6 Bangui-Motaba, Congo
131 P 7 Banguru, Democratic Republic of Congo
130 M 3 Bani, Central African Republic
120 E 10 Bani Point, Philippines
99 O 10 Bani Thawr, Saudi Arabia
125 S 8 Banī Walīd, Libya
130 H 5 Bania, Central African Republic
138 G 7 Baniara, Papua New Guinea
129 O 10 Banikoara, Benin
96 H 4 Bāniyās, Syria
80 G 10 Banja Luka, Bosnia and Herzegovina
119 V 7 Banjaran Brassey, Malaysia
119 U 7 Banjaran Crocker, Malaysia
119 N 11 Banjaran Klingkang, Malaysia
119 T 9 Banjaran Tama Abu, Malaysia
116 L 12 Banjarmasin, Indonesia
128 D 9 Banjul, Gambia
129 N 9 Bankilaré, Niger
129 T 13 Bankim, Cameroon
28 K 9 Banks, ID, U.S.A.
38 E 15 Banks Island, NT, Canada
139 R 9 Banks Islands, Vanuatu
32 J 6 Banks Lake, WA, U.S.A.
137 I 20 Banks Peninsula, New Zealand
107 R 13 Bankura, India
113 P 13 Banli, China
101 V 8 Bannu, Pakistan
113 N 9 Banqiao, China
79 J 20 Banská Bystrica, Slovakia
82 G 11 Bansko, Bulgaria
105 C 14 Banswara, India
117 O 13 Bantaeng, Indonesia
121 K 16 Bantayan, Philippines
121 J 16 Bantayan, Philippines
129 O 12 Bantè, Benin
61 A 21 Bantry Bay, Republic of Ireland
129 U 13 Banyo, Cameroon
116 K 14 Banyuwangi, Indonesia
145 W 13 Banzare Coast, Antarctica
115 N 21 Bao Lôc, Vietnam
115 C 15 Baochang, China
111 A 17 Baode, China
111 E 17 Baodi, China
111 D 18 Baoding, China
113 P 3 Baoji, China
113 R 8 Baojing, China
110 M 11 Baolin, China
111 O 10 Baoqing, China
130 H 4 Baoro, Central African Republic
112 J 10 Baoshan, China
109 S 6 Baotou, China
113 V 5 Baoyi, China
113 X 4 Baoying, China
104 C 12 Bap, India
99 O 7 Baqarah, Saudi Arabia
97 U 6 Ba'qūbah, Iraq
81 I 17 Bar, Serbia and Montenegro
86 M 6 Bar, Ukraine
15 S 6 Bar Harbor, ME, U.S.A.
65 T 4 Bar-le-Duc, France
117 R 12 Bara, Indonesia
127 E 17 Bara, Sudan
129 T 11 Bara, Nigeria
106 M 10 Bara Banki, India
127 L 25 Baraawe, Somalia
96 J 3 Baradah, Syria
59 C 15 Baradero, Argentina
49 Q 8 Barahona, Dominican Republic
105 I 15 Barakot, India
119 S 7 Baram, Malaysia
105 C 18 Baramati, India
106 H 3 Baramula, India
85 H 19 Baranavichy, Belarus
35 W 11 Baranof Island, AK, U.S.A.
69 J 22 Baraque de Fraiture, Belgium
117 P 15 Barate, Indonesia
55 L 18 Barbacena, Brazil
58 M 5 Barbacena, Brazil
49 Z 11 Barbados, North America
73 D 26 Barbastro, Spain
66 K 14 Barbate, Spain
41 P 1 Barbeau Peak, NU, Canada
64 M 10 Barbezieux-St-Hilaire, France
50 J 6 Barbosa, Colombia
49 Y 8 Barbuda, Antigua and Barbuda
135 S 6 Barcaldine, QLD, Australia
66 J 10 Barcarrota, Spain
51 P 3 Barcelona, Venezuela
67 X 5 Barcelona, Spain
54 E 10 Barcelos, Brazil
79 G 26 Barcs, Hungary
91 T 13 Barda, Russian Federation
129 W 5 Bardai, Chad
107 W 14 Bardarban, Bangladesh
70 C 11 Bárðarbunga, Iceland
56 G 13 Bardas Blancas, Argentina
107 S 13 Barddhaman, India
79 L 19 Bardejov, Slovakia
76 A 7 Bardonecchia, Italy
62 K 6 Bardsey Island, U.K.
62 K 6 Bardsey Sound, U.K.
61 G 19 Bardsley Island, U.K.
16 H 5 Bardstown, KY, U.S.A.
106 L 9 Bareilly, India
143 T 10 Barents Plain, Arctic Ocean
70 N 5 Barents Sea, Europe
143 U 13 Barents Trough, Arctic Ocean
127 H 17 Barentu, Eritrea
119 T 8 Bareo, Malaysia
108 H 9 Barga, China
127 O 19 Bargaal, Somalia
105 I 16 Bargarh, India
63 Z 11 Barham, U.K.
77 N 15 Bari, Italy
127 O 19 Bari, Somalia
130 K 6 Bari, Democratic Republic of Congo
125 O 6 Barika, Algeria
101 W 7 Barikoi, Afghanistan
50 L 4 Barinas, Venezuela
50 L 4 Barinas, Venezuela
126 E 11 Bārīs, Egypt
107 U 14 Barisal, Bangladesh
107 V 14 Barisal, Bangladesh
116 L 11 Barito, Indonesia
99 Y 6 Barkā, Oman
112 L 5 Barkam, China
84 H 11 Barkava, Latvia
107 Q 12 Barki Sariaya, India
16 D 7 Barkley Lake, KY, U.S.A.
133 O 13 Barkly East, Republic of South Africa
135 P 5 Barkly Homestead Roadhouse, NT, Australia
135 O 3 Barkly Tableland, NT, Australia
108 M 5 Barkol, China
86 M 10 Bârlad, Romania
77 M 15 Barletta, Italy
78 E 11 Barlinek, Poland
104 B 13 Barmer, India
62 M 6 Barmouth, U.K.
62 M 6 Barmouth Bay, U.K.
88 M 13 Barnaul, Russian Federation
63 V 10 Barnet, U.K.
68 J 12 Barneveld, Netherlands
26 K 8 Barnhart, TX, U.S.A.
63 S 3 Barnsley, U.K.
15 P 11 Barnstable, MA, U.S.A.
62 M 12 Barnstaple, U.K.
17 N 14 Barnwell, SC, U.S.A.
50 L 3 Barquisimeto, Venezuela
55 L 14 Barra, Brazil
60 D 11 Barra, U.K.
54 G 12 Barra de São Manuel, Brazil
55 G 15 Barra do Bugres, Brazil
54 L 12 Barra do Corda, Brazil
55 I 16 Barra do Garças, Brazil
58 H 12 Barra do Ribeiro, Brazil
45 S 8 Barra Jesús María, Mexico
47 S 5 Barra Kruta, Honduras
54 L 13 Barragem de Sobradinho, Brazil
55 J 17 Barragem de São Simão, Brazil
50 J 3 Barranca, Venezuela
53 C 15 Barranca, Peru
51 R 4 Barrancas, Venezuela
50 I 2 Barranquilla, Colombia
14 M 9 Barre, MA, U.S.A.
56 G 11 Barreal, Argentina
55 L 14 Barreiras, Brazil
54 E 12 Barreirinha do Baeta, Brazil
66 G 9 Barreiro, Portugal
105 O 21 Barren Island, India
58 K 5 Barretos, Brazil
42 E 12 Barrie, ON, Canada
43 T 12 Barrington, NS, Canada
135 S 9 Barringun, NSW, Australia
35 O 2 Barrow, AK, U.S.A.
61 E 19 Barrow, Republic of Ireland
135 N 5 Barrow Creek, NT, Australia
63 O 1 Barrow-in-Furness, U.K.
134 E 6 Barrow Island, WA, Australia
63 O 11 Barry, U.K.
42 H 10 Barrys Bay, ON, Canada
103 W 6 Barshatas, Kazakhstan
103 R 5 Barshyn, Kazakhstan
33 L 23 Barstow, CA, U.S.A.
84 C 12 Bārta, Latvia
72 L 8 Barth, Germany
51 U 5 Bartica, Guyana
94 H 7 Bartın, Turkey
135 T 3 Bartle Frere, QLD, Australia
25 P 8 Bartlesville, OK, U.S.A.
16 A 10 Bartlett, TN, U.S.A.
22 M 13 Bartlett, NE, U.S.A.
14 M 5 Barton, VT, U.S.A.
63 U 3 Barton-upon-Humber, U.K.
78 K 8 Bartoszyce, Poland
19 W 11 Bartow, FL, U.S.A.
99 S 13 Barūm, Yemen
116 M 10 Barung, Indonesia
116 K 15 Barung, Indonesia
116 C 9 Barus, Indonesia
109 T 4 Baruun Urt, Mongolia
105 C 15 Barwani, India
79 F 14 Barycz, Poland
85 K 16 Barysaw, Belarus
93 Q 3 Barysh, Russian Federation
99 Z 7 Barzamān, Oman
130 H 11 Bas-Congo, Democratic Republic of Congo
103 P 14 Basaga, Turkmenistan
56 L 8 Basail, Argentina
13 J 19 Basalt, NV, U.S.A.
130 K 7 Basankusu, Democratic Republic of Congo
120 H 2 Basco, Philippines
73 D 26 Basel, Germany
74 D 6 Basel, Switzerland
93 O 4 Bashmakovo, Russian Federation
100 H 10 Bāsht, Iran
87 S 8 Bashtanka, Ukraine
121 H 23 Basilan, Philippines
121 H 23 Basilan Strait, Philippines
63 X 10 Basildon, U.K.
77 M 17 Basilicata, Italy
29 U 9 Basin, WY, U.S.A.
63 T 11 Basingstoke, U.K.
107 T 14 Basirhat, India
80 C 10 Baška, Croatia
95 T 11 Başkale, Turkey
130 M 7 Basoko, Democratic Republic of Congo
33 K 14 Basque, OR, U.S.A.
135 S 14 Bass Strait, TAS, Australia
76 G 6 Bassano del Grappa, Italy
129 N 11 Bassar, Togo
133 U 8 Bassas da India, France
130 L 4 Basse-Kotto, Central African Republic
64 L 4 Basse-Normandie, France
49 Y 9 Basse-Terre, Guadeloupe
115 C 16 Bassein, Myanmar
67 V 3 Bassella, Spain
49 X 8 Basseterre, St Kitts and Nevis
22 L 12 Bassett, NE, U.S.A.
129 O 12 Bassila, Benin
129 Z 7 Basso, Chad
23 U 3 Basswood Lake, MN, U.S.A.
100 K 12 Bastak, Iran
100 G 3 Bastānābād, Iran
107 N 10 Basti, India
65 Z 14 Bastia, France
69 K 23 Bastogne, Belgium
18 J 4 Bastrop, LA, U.S.A.
27 Q 10 Bastrop, TX, U.S.A.
129 S 15 Bata, Equatorial Guinea
120 F 11 Bataan Peninsula, Philippines
120 F 6 Batac, Philippines
89 T 9 Batagay, Russian Federation
58 H 5 Bataguassu, Brazil
82 H 11 Batak, Bulgaria
116 L 13 Batakan, Indonesia
106 H 5 Batala, India
116 F 10 Batam, Indonesia
131 O 7 Batama, Democratic Republic of Congo
97 T 10 Batamay, Russian Federation
120 H 2 Batan, Philippines
120 K 13 Batan, Philippines
120 H 3 Batan Islands, Philippines
112 J 7 Batang, China
130 D 8 Batanga, Gabon
120 G 12 Batangas, Philippines
121 E 16 Batas, Philippines
14 D 8 Batavia, NY, U.S.A.
92 L 10 Bataysk, Russian Federation
121 H 16 Batbatan, Philippines
134 M 1 Batchelor, NT, Australia
115 J 20 Bătdâmbâng, Cambodia
135 U 12 Batemans Bay, NSW, Australia
17 N 12 Batesburg, SC, U.S.A.
18 M 2 Batesville, MS, U.S.A.
25 W 9 Batesville, AR, U.S.A.
27 N 12 Batesville, TX, U.S.A.
14 F 9 Bath, NY, U.S.A.
15 P 6 Bath, ME, U.S.A.
43 R 9 Bath, NB, Canada
63 Q 11 Bath, U.K.
129 X 8 Batha, Chad
106 H 7 Bathinda, India
68 L 11 Bathmen, Netherlands
43 S 7 Bathurst, NB, Canada
135 U 11 Bathurst, NSW, Australia
143 O 7 Bathurst Island, Canada
38 H 9 Bathurst Inlet, NU, Canada
38 I 8 Bathurst Inlet, NU, Canada
37 O 3 Bathurst Island, NU, Canada
134 L 1 Bathurst Island, NT, Australia
127 J 19 Bati, Ethiopia
94 E 13 Bati Toroslar, Turkey
95 Q 12 Batman, Turkey
125 O 6 Batna, Algeria
80 L 12 Batočina, Serbia and Montenegro
18 K 7 Baton Rouge, LA, U.S.A.
106 H 4 Batote, India
129 V 14 Batouri, Cameroon
96 G 5 Batroûn, Lebanon
70 M 5 Båtsfjord, Norway
105 N 24 Batti Malv, India
105 G 24 Batticaloa, Sri Lanka
63 X 12 Battle, U.K.
21 J 15 Battle Creek, MI, U.S.A.
33 L 16 Battle Mountain, NV, U.S.A.
127 J 21 Batu, Ethiopia
118 B 7 Batu Gajah, Malaysia
118 D 10 Batu Pahat, Malaysia
117 O 11 Batudaka, Indonesia
121 M 24 Batulaki, Philippines
95 Q 7 Bat'umi, Georgia
116 F 13 Baturaja, Indonesia
87 R 2 Baturyn, Ukraine
93 Q 2 Batyrevo, Russian Federation
119 N 10 Bau, Malaysia
120 F 8 Bauang, Philippines
117 P 13 Baubau, Indonesia
129 S 11 Bauchi, Nigeria
129 S 11 Bauchi, Nigeria
23 Q 2 Baudette, MN, U.S.A.
117 R 15 Baukau, East Timor
138 M 6 Baunani, Solomon Islands
58 J 6 Bauru, Brazil
55 H 17 Baús, Brazil
84 F 12 Bauska, Latvia
73 O 16 Bautzen, Germany
73 L 25 Bavarian Alps, Germany
44 K 4 Bavispe, Mexico
116 I 12 Bawal, Indonesia
116 K 13 Bawean, Indonesia
126 D 9 Bawiti, Egypt
63 T 3 Bawtry, U.K.
19 V 5 Baxley, GA, U.S.A.
127 L 24 Bay, Somalia
20 L 13 Bay City, MI, U.S.A.
27 S 11 Bay City, TX, U.S.A.
19 P 7 Bay Minette, AL, U.S.A.
107 S 15 Bay of Bengal, Asia
64 I 7 Bay of Biscay, France
43 S 11 Bay of Fundy, NS, Canada
136 J 5 Bay of Islands, New Zealand
136 N 10 Bay of Plenty, New Zealand
136 N 11 Bay of Plenty, New Zealand
18 M 5 Bay Springs, MS, U.S.A.
136 N 13 Bay View, New Zealand
48 L 6 Bayamo, Cuba
109 T 3 Bayan, Mongolia
110 L 11 Bayan, China
112 J 3 Bayan Har Shan, China
109 S 6 Bayan Obo, China
108 L 2 Bayan-Ölgiy, Mongolia
109 N 4 Bayan-Ovoo, Mongolia
111 B 15 Bayan Qagan, China
103 U 4 Bayanaul, Kazakhstan
108 J 5 Bayanbulak, China
130 H 6 Bayanga, Central African Republic
130 H 4 Bayanga-Didi, Central African Republic
109 O 4 Bayanhongor, Mongolia
109 P 4 Bayanhongor, Mongolia
31 O 13 Bayard, NM, U.S.A.
121 I 19 Bayawan, Philippines
100 L 10 Bayāz, Iran
121 L 17 Baybay, Philippines
95 P 9 Bayburt, Turkey
88 L 7 Baydaratskaya Guba, Russian Federation
143 X 10 Baydaratskaya Guba, Arctic Ocean
127 L 23 Baydhabo, Somalia
129 Q 14 Bayelsa, Nigeria
73 L 22 Bayerischer Wald, Germany
73 J 22 Bayern, Germany
64 M 3 Bayeux, France
102 K 6 Bayganin, Kazakhstan
99 Q 13 Bayḩan al Qişab, Yemen

Country ▪ Internal administrative region: State/Province/Territory/Dependent territory ▪ Capital city ▪ Mountain range/Undersea ridge ▪ Mountain peak/Volcano/Seamount ◇ Geographic feature ▶ Headland/Point/Cape/Peninsula ▲ Desert ▪ Island/Island group ▪ Antarctic base ▪ Ocean ▪ Sea ▪ Bay/Gulf/Channel/Strait ▪ Lake ▪ Salt pan/Dry/Intermittent lake ▪ River

Bayjī – Blenheim

97 S 4 Bayjī, Iraq
89 O 11 Baykit, Russian Federation
103 N 8 Baykonur, Kazakhstan
121 H 17 Bayo Point, Philippines
64 K 14 Bayonne, France
52 A 12 Bayóvar, Peru
103 N 14 Bayramaly, Turkmenistan
73 J 20 Bayreuth, Germany
99 O 13 Bayt al Faqih, Yemen
27 T 10 Baytown, TX, U.S.A.
117 P 12 Bayu, Indonesia
121 M 20 Bayugan, Philippines
116 F 12 Bayunglincir, Indonesia
67 P 12 Baza, Spain
87 O 2 Bazar, Ukraine
95 X 7 Bazardüzü Dağı, Azerbaijan
64 M 12 Bazas, France
101 S 13 Bazdar, Pakistan
113 O 5 Bazhong, China
86 F 12 Baziaș, Romania
101 O 12 Bazmān, Iran
96 H 5 Bcharre, Lebanon
22 G 5 Beach, ND, U.S.A.
63 X 13 Beachy Head, U.K.
63 U 10 Beaconsfield, U.K.
134 I 4 Beagle Bay, WA, Australia
134 M 1 Beagle Gulf, NT, Australia
133 Z 5 Bealanana, Madgascar
63 P 13 Beaminster, U.K.
16 K 8 Bean Station, TN, U.S.A.
29 Q 13 Bear Lake, ID, U.S.A.
30 K 1 Bear Lake, UT, U.S.A.
144 K 10 Bear Peninsula, Antarctica
21 E 19 Beardstown, IL, U.S.A.
67 P 10 Beas de Segura, Spain
23 O 15 Beatrice, NE, U.S.A.
33 L 21 Beatty, NV, U.S.A.
42 H 6 Beattyville, QC, Canada
57 L 24 Beauchene Island, Falkland Islands
119 U 6 Beaufort, Malaysia
143 P 4 Beaufort Sea, Canada/U.S.A.
132 L 14 Beaufort West, Republic of South Africa
60 G 10 Beauly, U.K.
19 N 6 Beaumont, MS, U.S.A.
27 U 9 Beaumont, TX, U.S.A.
69 F 22 Beaumont, Belgium
65 O 13 Beaumont-de-Lomagne, France
65 T 8 Beaune, France
69 H 23 Beauraing, Belgium
65 P 3 Beauvais, France
39 L 16 Beauval, SK, Canada
24 I 7 Beaver, OK, U.S.A.
30 J 6 Beaver, UT, U.S.A.
38 A 13 Beaver Creek, YT, Canada
20 G 13 Beaver Dam, WI, U.S.A.
14 A 12 Beaver Falls, PA, U.S.A.
20 J 10 Beaver Island, MI, U.S.A.
25 T 8 Beaver Lake, AR, U.S.A.
29 N 7 Beaverhead Mountains, MT, U.S.A.
104 D 12 Beawar, India
58 J 5 Bebedouro, Brazil
129 W 12 Béboto, Chad
73 G 17 Bebra, Germany
63 Z 7 Beccles, U.K.
80 K 8 Bečej, Serbia and Montenegro
66 J 2 Becerreá, Spain
124 J 8 Béchar, Algeria
35 O 11 Becharof Lake, AK, U.S.A.
17 N 5 Beckley, WV, U.S.A.
86 I 8 Beclean, Romania
127 J 19 Beda Hāyk', Ethiopia
63 S 1 Bedale, U.K.
127 H 21 Bedelē, Ethiopia
14 D 14 Bedford, PA, U.S.A.
16 H 4 Bedford, KY, U.S.A.
21 I 20 Bedford, IN, U.S.A.
43 V 11 Bedford, NS, Canada
63 V 8 Bedford, U.K.
93 O 3 Bednodem'yanovsk, Russian Federation
135 Q 7 Bedourie, QLD, Australia
25 W 11 Beebe, AR, U.S.A.
69 J 15 Beek, Netherlands
96 F 12 Be'ér Menuha, Israel
96 F 13 Be'ér Ora, Israel
96 F 10 Be'ér Sheva', Israel
69 C 17 Beernem, Belgium
73 N 14 Beeskow, Germany
144 J 6 Beethoven Peninsula, Antarctica
27 P 12 Beeville, TX, U.S.A.
130 K 7 Befale, Democratic Republic of Congo
133 Z 6 Befandriana Avaratra, Madgascar
130 L 7 Befori, Democratic Republic of Congo
135 U 13 Bega, NSW, Australia
107 Q 11 Begusarai, India
100 H 9 Behbahān, Iran
100 K 5 Behshahr, Iran
101 T 7 Behsūd, Afghanistan
110 K 8 Bei'an, China
112 L 11 Beicheng, China
113 N 5 Beichuan, China
113 P 1 Beidachi, China
127 G 20 Beigi, Ethiopia
113 Q 14 Beihai, China
111 D 17 Beijing, China
111 D 16 Beijing Shi, China
68 M 8 Beilen, Netherlands
113 R 13 Beiliu, China
73 J 22 Beilngries, Germany
108 M 8 Beiluheyan, China
111 H 15 Beipiao, China
70 B 10 Bňir, Iceland
133 R 8 Beira, Mozambique
96 G 6 Beirut, Lebanon
133 P 9 Beitbridge, Zimbabwe
86 G 9 Beiuș, Romania
66 H 11 Beja, Portugal
66 I 11 Beja, Portugal
125 Q 5 Béja, Tunisia
125 N 5 Bejaïa, Algeria
66 L 6 Béjar, Spain
66 M 12 Beji, Spain
102 H 11 Bekdash, Turkmenistan
79 L 24 Békés, Hungary
79 L 24 Békéscsaba, Hungary
133 W 10 Bekily, Madgascar
17 V 2 Bel Air, MD, U.S.A.
101 S 14 Bela, Pakistan
107 N 11 Bela, India
133 O 10 Bela-Bela, Republic of South Africa
80 M 10 Bela Crkva, Serbia and Montenegro
81 O 14 Bela Palanka, Serbia and Montenegro
129 U 14 Bélabo, Cameroon
103 W 4 Bel'agash, Kazakhstan
85 G 19 Belarus, Europe
116 C 9 Belawan, Indonesia
93 U 1 Belaya, Russian Federation
92 M 11 Belaya Glina, Russian Federation
129 R 8 Belbédji, Niger
79 J 15 Bełchatów, Poland
37 S 10 Belcher Islands, NU, Canada
101 S 6 Belchiragh, Afghanistan
67 S 5 Belchite, Spain
94 L 9 Belcik, Turkey
33 H 17 Belden, CA, U.S.A.
21 J 14 Belding, MI, U.S.A.
93 V 2 Belebey, Russian Federation
127 M 23 Beledweyne, Somalia
128 H 12 Belefuanai, Liberia
129 U 11 Belel, Nigeria
54 J 10 Belém, Brazil
31 P 11 Belen, NM, U.S.A.
56 H 8 Belén, Argentina
94 L 14 Belen, Turkey
92 J 3 Belev, Russian Federation
128 H 11 Bèlèya, Guinea
15 Q 5 Belfast, ME, U.S.A.
61 F 15 Belfast, U.K.
61 F 15 Belfast Lough, U.K.
22 G 5 Belfield, ND, U.S.A.
127 G 19 Bēlfodiyo, Ethiopia
65 V 6 Belfort, France
105 C 19 Belgaum, India
145 T 3 Belgica Mountains, Antarctica
69 E 20 Belgium, Europe
92 J 6 Belgorod, Russian Federation
92 J 6 Belgorodskaya Oblast', Russian Federation
23 Q 7 Belgrade, MN, U.S.A.
80 L 10 Belgrade, Serbia and Montenegro
145 N 5 Belgrano II, Antarctica
137 I 16 Belgrove, New Zealand
17 V 9 Belhaven, NC, U.S.A.
125 O 9 Belhirane, Algeria
129 T 12 Beli, Nigeria
80 I 8 Beli Manastir, Croatia
93 R 15 Belidzhi, Russian Federation
116 F 13 Belimbing, Indonesia
130 F 7 Bélinga, Gabon
93 O 4 Belinskiy, Russian Federation
116 G 11 Belinyu, Indonesia
116 H 12 Belitung, Indonesia
46 J 3 Belize, North America
46 K 2 Belize, Belize
46 J 2 Belize, Belize
132 F 1 Belize, Angola
56 K 11 Bell Ville, Argentina
39 E 20 Bella Coola, BC, Canada
58 D 12 Bella Unión, Uruguay
58 G 24 Bella Vista, Argentina
58 C 11 Bella Vista, Argentina
65 O 9 Bellac, France
76 C 6 Bellagio, Italy
105 E 20 Bellary, India
22 G 8 Belle Fourche, SD, U.S.A.
19 Y 12 Belle Glade, FL, U.S.A.
64 I 7 Belle-Île, France
41 X 8 Belle Isle, NL, Canada
21 L 18 Bellefontaine, OH, U.S.A.
65 U 9 Bellegarde-sur-Valserine, France
25 N 2 Belleville, KS, U.S.A.
42 H 12 Belleville, ON, Canada
23 P 14 Bellevue, IA, U.S.A.
28 M 11 Bellevue, ID, U.S.A.
32 H 7 Bellevue, WA, U.S.A.
51 Y 6 Bellevue de l'Inini, French Guiana
65 U 10 Belley, France
32 G 5 Bellingham, WA, U.S.A.
144 H 8 Bellingshausen Sea, Antarctica
74 H 10 Bellinzona, Switzerland
27 Q 7 Bellmead, TX, U.S.A.
138 L 8 Bellona, Solomon Islands
101 U 11 Bellpat, Pakistan
76 G 6 Belluno, Italy
27 R 10 Bellville, TX, U.S.A.
14 E 10 Belmont, NY, U.S.A.
46 K 2 Belmopan, Belize
55 L 18 Belo Horizonte, Brazil
89 U 14 Belogorsk, Russian Federation
82 F 7 Belogradchik, Bulgaria
133 W 11 Beloha, Madgascar
21 F 15 Beloit, WI, U.S.A.
90 I 6 Belomorsk, Russian Federation
107 V 13 Belonia, India
67 P 3 Belorado, Spain
92 L 12 Belorechensk, Russian Federation
93 X 2 Beloretsk, Russian Federation
82 F 7 Belotintsi, Bulgaria
103 Y 4 Belousovka, Kazakhstan
90 J 11 Belozersk, Russian Federation
54 H 10 Belterra, Brazil
16 M 11 Belton, SC, U.S.A.
25 R 4 Belton, MO, U.S.A.
27 P 8 Belton, TX, U.S.A.
63 Z 6 Belton, U.K.
119 W 5 Beluran, Malaysia
77 L 18 Belvedere Marittimo, Italy
92 I 1 Belyy, Russian Federation
88 M 11 Belyy Yar, Russian Federation
79 O 16 Bełżec, Poland
73 L 14 Belzig, Germany
132 G 1 Bembe, Angola
66 K 2 Bembibre, Spain
63 T 13 Bembridge, U.K.
23 Q 4 Bemidji, MN, U.S.A.
68 K 13 Bemmel, Netherlands
117 T 12 Bemu, Indonesia
125 R 7 Ben Guerdane, Tunisia
60 G 8 Ben Klibreck, U.K.
60 H 11 Ben Macdui, U.K.
60 G 11 Ben Nevis, U.K.
124 H 7 Ben Slimane, Morocco
130 M 10 Bena Dibele, Democratic Republic of Congo
130 M 10 Bena-Tshadi, Democratic Republic of Congo
67 U 3 Benabarre, Spain
116 L 11 Benagin, Indonesia
135 S 13 Benalla, VIC, Australia
66 L 4 Benavente, Spain
62 C 10 Benbecula, U.K.
32 H 11 Bend, OR, U.S.A.
127 O 20 Bender-Bayla, Somalia
135 S 13 Bendigo, VIC, Australia
133 Q 5 Bene, Mozambique
68 J 13 Beneden-Leeuwen, Netherlands
77 K 15 Benevento, Italy
131 N 7 Bengamisa, Democratic Republic of Congo
129 U 15 Bengbis, Cameroon
113 W 4 Bengbu, China
116 E 12 Bengkulu, Indonesia
116 D 12 Bengkulu, Indonesia
132 F 2 Bengo, Angola
132 G 4 Benguela, Angola
132 G 5 Benguela, Angola
126 E 8 Benha, Egypt
53 J 18 Beni, Bolivia
53 J 17 Beni, Bolivia
131 Q 7 Beni, Democratic Republic of Congo
124 K 9 Beni-Abbès, Algeria
126 E 9 Beni Mazâr, Egypt
124 H 8 Beni Mellal, Morocco
124 K 8 Beni-Ounif, Algeria
124 K 6 Beni-Saf, Algeria
126 E 9 Beni Suef, Egypt
67 U 7 Benicasim, Spain
67 T 10 Benidorm, Spain
129 N 11 Benin, Africa
129 Q 13 Benin City, Nigeria
127 G 19 Benishangul, Ethiopia
59 C 18 Benito Juárez, Argentina
44 I 3 Benjamin Hill, Mexico
117 V 13 Benjina, Indonesia
122 I 6 Benkei-misaki, Japan
137 C 25 Benmore, New Zealand
14 L 9 Bennington, VT, U.S.A.
20 D 8 Benoit, WI, U.S.A.
17 S 9 Benson, NC, U.S.A.
23 P 7 Benson, MN, U.S.A.
30 L 14 Benson, AZ, U.S.A.
117 O 14 Benteng, Indonesia
132 F 5 Bentiaba, Angola
115 F 21 Bentinck Island, Myanmar
135 Q 3 Bentinck Island, QLD, Australia
127 D 20 Bentiu, Sudan
21 F 22 Benton, IL, U.S.A.
25 V 12 Benton, AR, U.S.A.
21 I 15 Benton Harbor, MI, U.S.A.
25 S 8 Bentonville, AR, U.S.A.
116 H 10 Benua, Indonesia
129 R 12 Benue, Nigeria
118 E 10 Benut, Malaysia
111 I 15 Benxi, China
117 R 9 Beo, Indonesia
106 M 13 Beohari, India
128 J 12 Béoumi, Côte d'Ivoire
113 O 10 Bepian, China
123 C 21 Beppu, Japan
49 Y 12 Bequia, St Vincent and the Grenadines
133 X 10 Beraketa, Madgascar
81 K 15 Berane, Serbia and Montenegro
133 W 7 Beravina, Madgascar
127 F 15 Berber, Sudan
127 L 19 Berbera, Somalia
130 H 5 Berbérati, Central African Republic
73 M 25 Berchtesgaden, Germany
65 P 1 Berck, France
89 T 10 Berdigestyakh, Russian Federation
87 X 9 Berdyans'k, Ukraine
87 W 9 Berdyans'ka Kosa, Ukraine
87 W 9 Berdyans'ka Zatoka, Ukraine
87 N 4 Berdychiv, Ukraine
129 W 11 Béré, Chad
117 S 9 Berebere, Indonesia
86 H 6 Berehove, Ukraine
138 D 6 Bereina, Papua New Guinea
128 L 12 Berekum, Ghana
103 Z 4 Berel', Kazakhstan
126 G 12 Berenice, Egypt
40 I 9 Berens River, MB, Canada
23 O 11 Beresford, SD, U.S.A.
79 M 23 Berettyóújfalu, Hungary
86 J 5 Berezhany, Ukraine
87 Q 9 Berezivka, Ukraine
87 Q 2 Berezna, Ukraine
86 L 2 Berezne, Ukraine
90 L 8 Bereznik, Russian Federation
91 S 11 Berezniki, Russian Federation
88 K 9 Berezovo, Russian Federation
91 V 13 Berezovyy, Russian Federation
67 W 3 Berga, Spain
94 B 9 Bergama, Turkey
76 D 6 Bergamo, Italy
68 H 9 Bergen, Netherlands
71 A 18 Bergen, Norway
72 M 8 Bergen, Germany
69 F 15 Bergen op Zoom, Netherlands
65 N 11 Bergerac, France
73 C 17 Bergisch Gladbach, Germany
89 Z 9 Bering Sea, Russian Federation/U.S.A.
89 Z 5 Bering Strait, Russian Federation/U.S.A.
69 K 16 Beringe, Netherlands
69 I 18 Beringen, Belgium
89 Z 7 Beringovskiy, Russian Federation
67 P 13 Berja, Spain
124 J 6 Berkane, Morocco
33 G 19 Berkeley, CA, U.S.A.
144 M 5 Berkner Island, Antarctica
82 F 8 Berkovitsa, Bulgaria
70 M 5 Berlevåg, Norway
14 C 14 Berlin, PA, U.S.A.
17 W 4 Berlin, MD, U.S.A.
72 M 13 Berlin, Germany
72 M 13 Berlin, Germany
45 N 7 Bermejillo, Mexico
56 J 5 Bermejo, Argentina/Bolivia
56 K 6 Bermejo, Argentina/Bolivia
56 K 6 Bermejo viejo, Argentina
66 L 5 Bermillo De Sayago, Spain
10 H 7 Bermuda, U.K.
74 D 8 Bern, Switzerland
74 E 8 Bern, Switzerland
31 Q 10 Bernalillo, NM, U.S.A.
57 J 14 Bernasconi, Argentina
72 M 12 Bernau, Germany
65 O 4 Bernay, France
73 J 15 Bernburg, Germany
75 X 4 Berndorf, Austria
74 C 10 Bernese Alps, Switzerland
18 I 4 Bernice, LA, U.S.A.
134 E 8 Bernier Island, WA, Australia
75 X 6 Bernstein, Austria
133 W 9 Beroroha, Madgascar
82 F 11 Berovo, Macedonia (F.Y.R.O.M.)
124 H 7 Berrechid, Morocco
135 Q 11 Berri, SA, Australia
125 N 7 Berriane, Algeria
17 S 3 Berryville, VA, U.S.A.
132 J 11 Berseba, Namibia
72 E 13 Bersenbrück, Germany
87 O 7 Bershad', Ukraine
54 L 12 Bertolínia, Brazil
129 V 14 Bertoua, Cameroon
140 E 3 Beru, Kiribati
54 E 11 Beruri, Brazil
14 G 12 Berwick, PA, U.S.A.
60 J 13 Berwick-upon-Tweed, U.K.
87 T 9 Beryslav, Ukraine
133 W 6 Besalampy, Madgascar
65 V 7 Besançon, France
100 K 11 Beshneh, Iran
95 Q 12 Beşiri, Turkey
93 P 14 Beslan, Russian Federation
82 G 11 Beslet, Bulgaria
94 M 12 Besni, Turkey
19 P 3 Bessemer, AL, U.S.A.
69 J 15 Best, Netherlands
102 K 5 Bestamak, Kazakhstan
103 T 3 Bestobe, Kazakhstan
53 K 21 Betanzos, Bolivia
66 I 1 Betanzos, Spain
129 V 13 Bétaré Oya, Cameroon
103 Q 6 Betbulak, Kazakhstan
132 I 11 Bethanie, Namibia
25 S 1 Bethany, MO, U.S.A.
15 O 6 Bethel, ME, U.S.A.
17 U 9 Bethel, NC, U.S.A.
21 L 20 Bethel, OH, U.S.A.
34 M 9 Bethel, AK, U.S.A.
96 F 9 Bethlehem, Israel
133 O 12 Bethlehem, Republic of South Africa
133 W 10 Betioky, Madgascar
115 I 26 Betong, Thailand
119 O 10 Betong, Malaysia
135 Q 7 Betoota, QLD, Australia
130 J 6 Bétou, Congo
103 Q 8 Betpak-Dala, Kazakhstan
133 X 10 Betroka, Madgascar
43 P 5 Betsiamites, QC, Canada
107 P 10 Bettiah, India
105 E 15 Betul, India
63 N 5 Betws-y-coed, U.K.
73 E 17 Betzdorf, Germany
21 I 11 Beulah, MI, U.S.A.
31 Q 5 Beuna Vista, CO, U.S.A.
65 N 3 Beuzeville, France
63 V 2 Beverley, U.K.
73 G 15 Beverungen, Germany
68 G 10 Beverwijk, Netherlands
63 X 13 Bexhill, U.K.
95 N 10 Bey Dağl, Turkey
94 D 13 Bey Dağları, Turkey
128 I 12 Beyla, Guinea
95 X 9 Beyläqan, Azerbaijan
127 K 18 Beylul, Eritrea
102 J 8 Beyneu, Kazakhstan
94 G 9 Beypazarı, Turkey
127 N 21 Beyra, Somalia
94 G 12 Beyşehir, Turkey
94 F 12 Beyşehir Gölü, Turkey
95 S 12 Beytüşşebap, Turkey
90 E 13 Bezhanitsy, Russian Federation
90 I 13 Bezhetsk, Russian Federation
65 R 14 Béziers, France
106 I 4 Bhadarwah, India
107 Q 9 Bhadgaon, Nepal
105 J 16 Bhadrakh, India
107 S 10 Bhadrapur, Nepal
105 D 20 Bhadravati, India
107 R 12 Bhagalpur, India
107 U 12 Bhairab Bazar, Bangladesh
107 O 9 Bhairawa, Nepal
101 W 9 Bhakkar, Pakistan
114 E 9 Bhamo, Myanmar
105 F 16 Bhandara, India
106 I 10 Bharatpur, India
105 C 15 Bharuch, India
105 C 20 Bhatkal, India
107 S 14 Bhatpara, India
105 B 15 Bhavnagar, India
105 H 17 Bhawanipatna, India
101 X 8 Bhera, Pakistan
105 G 16 Bhilai, India
104 D 13 Bhilwara, India
105 G 19 Bhimavaram, India
106 K 10 Bhind, India
104 B 13 Bhinmal, India
105 C 17 Bhiwandi, India
106 I 8 Bhiwani, India
107 R 10 Bhojpur, Nepal
105 E 14 Bhopal, India
105 G 18 Bhopalpatnam, India
105 C 18 Bhor, India
105 J 16 Bhubaneshwar, India
105 A 14 Bhuj, India
115 G 15 Bhumiphol Dam, Thailand
105 D 16 Bhusawal, India
107 U 9 Bhutan, Asia
117 W 11 Biak, Indonesia
117 W 11 Biak, Indonesia
78 N 13 Biała Podlaska, Poland
78 F 9 Białogard, Poland
78 N 11 Białystok, Poland
130 K 5 Bianga, Central African Republic
128 I 12 Biankouma, Côte d'Ivoire
105 E 14 Biaora, India
100 L 6 Biārjmand, Iran
117 Q 10 Biaro, Indonesia
64 K 14 Biarritz, France
74 H 10 Biasca, Switzerland
126 E 9 Biba, Egypt
130 F 7 Bibas, Gabon
76 G 10 Bibbiena, Italy
73 G 24 Biberach, Germany
128 L 13 Bibiani, Ghana
86 K 9 Bicaz, Romania
63 T 9 Bicester, U.K.
135 T 15 Bicheno, TAS, Australia
95 P 5 Bichvint'a, Georgia
105 D 17 Bid, India
129 Q 12 Bida, Nigeria
64 L 14 Bidache, France
105 E 18 Bidar, India
15 P 7 Biddeford, ME, U.S.A.
29 Y 8 Biddle, MT, U.S.A.
62 M 12 Bideford, U.K.
62 L 12 Bideford Bay, U.K.
118 B 7 Bidor, Malaysia
132 I 5 Bié, Angola
33 H 15 Bieber, CA, U.S.A.
78 M 10 Biebrza, Poland
79 L 18 Biecz, Poland
74 D 7 Biel, Switzerland
73 F 14 Bielefeld, Germany
74 C 7 Bieler See, Switzerland
76 B 7 Biella, Italy
78 N 11 Bielsk Podlaski, Poland
79 I 18 Bielsko-Biała, Poland
115 N 22 Biên Hoa, Vietnam
69 I 24 Bièvre, Belgium
130 E 8 Bifoun, Gabon
70 B 11 Bifröst, Iceland
20 H 8 Big Bay, MI, U.S.A.
137 B 22 Big Bay, New Zealand
20 H 8 Big Bay Point, MI, U.S.A.
29 P 5 Big Belt Mountains, MT, U.S.A.
28 L 8 Big Creek, ID, U.S.A.
35 S 7 Big Delta, AK, U.S.A.
20 E 11 Big Eau Pleine Reservoir, WI, U.S.A.
23 R 3 Big Falls, MN, U.S.A.
41 R 4 Big Island, NU, Canada
33 J 15 Big Mountain, NV, U.S.A.
33 J 20 Big Pine, CA, U.S.A.
20 J 13 Big Rapids, MI, U.S.A.
20 I 12 Big Sable Point, MI, U.S.A.
29 R 3 Big Sandy, MT, U.S.A.
29 S 5 Big Snow Mountain, MT, U.S.A.
137 B 26 Big South Cape Island, New Zealand
26 K 7 Big Spring, TX, U.S.A.
16 L 7 Big Stone Gap, VA, U.S.A.
33 G 21 Big Sur, CA, U.S.A.
29 S 7 Big Timber, MT, U.S.A.
40 L 9 Big Trout Lake, ON, Canada
40 L 8 Big Trout Lake, ON, Canada
94 B 8 Biga, Turkey
94 C 9 Bigadiş, Turkey
62 M 15 Bigbury Bay, U.K.
29 N 3 Bigfork, MT, U.S.A.
134 J 2 Bigge Island, WA, Australia
63 V 8 Biggleswade, U.K.
29 U 8 Bighorn, MT, U.S.A.
29 U 8 Bighorn Basin, WY, U.S.A.
29 U 8 Bighorn Lake, MT, U.S.A.
29 U 8 Bighorn Mountains, WY, U.S.A.
115 H 20 Bight of Bangkok, Thailand
129 O 14 Bight of Benin, Nigeria
129 Q 14 Bight of Biafra, Nigeria
128 D 9 Bignona, Senegal
80 D 10 Bihać, Bosnia and Herzegovina
107 Q 12 Bihar, India
107 Q 11 Bihar Sharif, India
86 H 9 Bihor Massif, Romania
107 X 10 Bihpuriagaon, India
105 D 19 Bijapur, India
100 G 5 Bījār, Iran
80 J 10 Bijeljina, Bosnia and Herzegovina
81 K 14 Bijelo Polje, Serbia and Montenegro
113 N 9 Bijie, China
107 U 10 Bijni, India
106 K 8 Bijnor, India
104 C 11 Bikaner, India
141 Z 1 Bikar, Marshall Islands
89 V 14 Bikin, Russian Federation
141 W 1 Bikini, Marshall Islands
125 W 13 Bikku Bitti, Libya
130 J 8 Bikoro, Democratic Republic of Congo
87 P 4 Bila Tserkva, Ukraine
106 I 6 Bilaspur, India
95 Y 9 Biläsuvar, Azerbaijan
115 F 19 Bilauktaung Range, Myanmar
67 P 1 Bilbao, Spain
79 G 20 Bílé Karpaty, Slovakia
81 H 15 Bileča, Bosnia and Herzegovina
94 E 8 Bilecik, Turkey
95 Z 8 Bilgjach, Azerbaijan
79 N 16 Biłgoraj, Poland
131 R 9 Bilharamulo, Tanzania
87 P 10 Bilhorod-Dnistrovs'kyy, Ukraine
131 N 5 Bili, Democratic Republic of Congo
89 X 7 Bilibino, Russian Federation
121 L 16 Biliran, Philippines
81 L 20 Bilisht, Albania
29 Y 11 Bill, WY, U.S.A.
63 Q 14 Bill of Portland, U.K.
63 X 10 Billericay, U.K.
134 K 5 Billiluna, WA, Australia
63 V 5 Billinghay, U.K.
29 T 7 Billings, MT, U.S.A.
63 V 12 Billingshurst, U.K.
22 I 9 Billsburg, SD, U.S.A.
129 U 6 Bilma, Niger
135 V 7 Biloela, QLD, Australia
87 U 12 Bilohirs'k, Ukraine
87 V 6 Bilokurakyne, Ukraine
87 Z 4 Bilolut's'k, Ukraine
87 T 2 Bilopillya, Ukraine
87 Z 5 Bilovods'k, Ukraine
19 N 7 Biloxi, MS, U.S.A.
135 Q 7 Bilpa Morea Claypan, QLD, Australia
68 I 12 Bilthoven, Netherlands
129 Y 8 Biltine, Chad
129 Y 8 Biltine, Chad
115 E 16 Bilugyun Island, Myanmar
47 Q 6 Bilwascarma, Nicaragua
69 J 19 Bilzen, Belgium
129 N 12 Bimbila, Ghana
48 J 1 Bimini Islands, The Bahamas
129 Q 11 Bin-Yauri, Nigeria
69 F 21 Binche, Belgium
130 J 12 Bindu, Democratic Republic of Congo
133 P 6 Bindura, Zimbabwe
133 Q 7 Binga, Mozambique
105 B 22 Bingaram, India
73 D 19 Bingen, Germany
15 P 4 Bingham, ME, U.S.A.
14 H 10 Binghamton, NY, U.S.A.
95 P 11 Bingöl, Turkey
115 O 17 Binh Son, Vietnam
113 Y 3 Binhai, China
116 C 9 Binjai, Indonesia
117 Q 13 Binongko, Indonesia
116 G 10 Bintan, Indonesia
116 F 13 Bintuhan, Indonesia
119 Q 8 Bintulu, Malaysia
110 L 11 Binxian, China
113 Q 12 Binyang, China
111 E 19 Binzhou, China
57 F 14 Bio Bio, Chile
57 F 15 Biobio, Chile
80 D 12 Biograd na Moru, Croatia
124 C 12 Bir Anzarane, Western Sahara
124 A 14 Bir-Gandouz, Western Sahara
128 G 3 Bir Mogrein, Mauritania
98 L 6 Bi'r Nasif, Saudi Arabia
97 S 9 Bi'r Sābil, Iraq
125 T 10 Birāk, Libya
90 I 7 Birandozero, Russian Federation
130 M 1 Birao, Central African Republic
107 S 10 Biratnagar, Nepal
39 I 16 Birch Mountains, AB, Canada
35 S 5 Birchcreek, AK, U.S.A.
35 R 9 Birchwood, AK, U.S.A.
127 L 21 Bircot, Ethiopia
79 N 18 Bircza, Poland
135 Q 7 Birdsville, QLD, Australia
95 N 13 Birecik, Turkey
106 M 8 Birendranagar, Nepal
116 B 8 Bireun, Indonesia
121 L 14 Biri, Philippines
58 I 5 Birigüi, Brazil
101 N 8 Birjand, Iran
63 P 4 Birkenhead, U.K.
75 W 6 Birkfeld, Austria
97 U 1 Birkim, Iraq
103 T 9 Birlik, Kazakhstan
19 P 3 Birmingham, AL, U.S.A.
63 R 7 Birmingham, U.K.
140 J 4 Birnie, Kiribati
129 Q 11 Birnin-Gwari, Nigeria
129 P 10 Birnin-Kebbi, Nigeria
129 Q 9 Birnin Konni, Niger
129 S 10 Birnin Kudu, Nigeria
89 V 14 Birobidzhan, Russian Federation
121 C 19 Birong, Philippines
61 D 18 Birr, Republic of Ireland
93 V 1 Birsk, Russian Federation
40 H 9 Birtle, MB, Canada
84 F 12 Biržai, Lithuania
84 H 12 Birži, Latvia
30 M 15 Bisbee, AZ, U.S.A.
19 Y 13 Biscayne Bay, FL, U.S.A.
77 M 15 Bisceglie, Italy
75 Q 6 Bischofshofen, Austria
144 H 4 Biscoe Islands, Antarctica
42 C 8 Biscotasing, ON, Canada
82 L 6 Bisertsi, Bulgaria
81 E 14 Biševo, Croatia
103 U 10 Bishkek, Kyrgyzstan
107 R 13 Bishnupur, India
133 N 14 Bisho, Republic of South Africa
33 J 20 Bishop, CA, U.S.A.
63 O 12 Bishop's Lydeard, U.K.
63 W 9 Bishop's Stortford, U.K.
81 I 18 Bishti i Pallës, Albania
110 I 5 Bishui, China
50 M 7 Bisinaca, Colombia
125 O 6 Biskra, Algeria
78 L 9 Biskupiec, Poland
121 N 20 Bislig, Philippines
22 J 5 Bismarck, ND, U.S.A.
138 D 3 Bismarck Archipelago, Papua New Guinea
138 C 4 Bismarck Range, Papua New Guinea
138 D 3 Bismarck Sea, Papua New Guinea
95 Q 12 Bismil, Turkey
22 H 7 Bison, SD, U.S.A.
128 E 10 Bissau, Guinea-Bissau
129 T 13 Bissaula, Nigeria
39 G 14 Bistcho Lake, AB, Canada
86 J 8 Bistrița, Romania
106 M 9 Biswan, India
130 E 6 Bitam, Gabon
73 B 19 Bitburg, Germany
102 H 4 Bitik, Kazakhstan
129 X 10 Bitkine, Chad
95 R 11 Bitlis, Turkey
82 C 13 Bitola, Macedonia (F.Y.R.O.M.)
77 M 15 Bitonto, Italy
132 J 14 Bitterfontein, Republic of South Africa
28 L 4 Bitterroot Range, MT, U.S.A.
77 C 16 Bitti, Italy
117 Q 10 Bitung, Indonesia
129 U 11 Biu, Nigeria
74 I 9 Bivio, Switzerland
86 M 8 Bivolari, Romania
123 G 17 Biwa-ko, Japan
113 T 5 Biyang, China
88 M 13 Biysk, Russian Federation
123 F 19 Bizen, Japan
125 Q 5 Bizerte, Tunisia
110 J 5 Bizhou, China
80 F 8 Bjelovar, Croatia
71 I 15 Björna, Sweden
143 U 11 Bjørnøya, Norway
71 I 15 Bjurholm, Sweden
128 J 9 Bla, Mali
25 W 10 Black, AR, U.S.A.
114 J 11 Black, Vietnam
144 J 5 Black Coast, Antarctica
73 D 25 Black Forest, Germany
22 G 9 Black Hills, SD, U.S.A.
38 L 13 Black Lake, SK, Canada
24 E 7 Black Mesa, OK, U.S.A.
16 K 7 Black Mountain, KY, U.S.A.
63 N 9 Black Mountain, U.K.
63 O 9 Black Mountains, U.K.
31 O 13 Black Range, NM, U.S.A.
33 J 16 Black Rock Desert, NV, U.S.A.
137 B 26 Black Rock Point, New Zealand
94 G 6 Black Sea, Asia/Europe
41 X 8 Black Tickle, NL, Canada
128 L 11 Black Volta, Burkina Faso
135 S 7 Blackall, QLD, Australia
62 Q 2 Blackburn, U.K.
23 Q 3 Blackduck, MN, U.S.A.
29 P 11 Blackfoot, ID, U.S.A.
29 Q 12 Blackfoot Reservoir, ID, U.S.A.
63 P 2 Blackpool, U.K.
17 P 6 Blacksburg, VA, U.S.A.
19 V 6 Blackshear, GA, U.S.A.
61 C 20 Blackwater, Republic of Ireland
63 Y 10 Blackwater, U.K.
135 U 6 Blackwater, QLD, Australia
69 I 16 Bladel, Netherlands
63 N 5 Blaenau Ffestiniog, U.K.
93 O 12 Blagodarnyy, Russian Federation
82 G 13 Blagoevgrad, Bulgaria
82 F 10 Blagoevgrad, Bulgaria
89 U 14 Blagoveshchensk, Russian Federation
93 W 1 Blagoveshchensk, Russian Federation
14 E 13 Blain, PA, U.S.A.
32 H 5 Blaine, WA, U.S.A.
23 P 13 Blair, NE, U.S.A.
14 C 13 Blairsville, PA, U.S.A.
19 S 1 Blairsville, GA, U.S.A.
20 G 6 Blake Point, MI, U.S.A.
19 S 6 Blakely, GA, U.S.A.
63 S 7 Blakeney, U.K.
63 Y 6 Blakeney Point, U.K.
37 Y 9 Blanc-Sablon, NL, Canada
27 O 10 Blanco, TX, U.S.A.
53 L 17 Blanco, Bolivia
63 Q 13 Blandford Forum, U.K.
67 Y 4 Blanes, Spain
116 B 8 Blangkejeren, Indonesia
69 C 16 Blankenberge, Belgium
73 C 18 Blankenheim, Germany
133 R 5 Blantyre, Malawi
64 M 11 Blaye, France
80 B 6 Bled, Slovenia
69 C 20 Bléharies, Belgium
42 C 14 Blenheim, ON, Canada

Country · Internal administrative region: State/Province/Territory/Dependent territory · Capital city · Mountain range/Undersea ridge · Mountain peak/Volcano/Seamount · Geographic feature · Headland/Point/Cape/Peninsula · Desert · Island/Island group · Antarctic base · Ocean · Sea · Bay/Gulf/Channel/Strait · Lake · Salt pan/Dry/Intermittent lake · Ri

Blenheim – Buitepos

J 17 **Blenheim**, New Zealand
R 11 **Blessing**, TX, U.S.A.
E 18 **Blessington**, Republic of Ireland
U 9 **Bletchley**, U.K.
M 5 **Blida**, Algeria
A 22 **Bligh Sound**, New Zealand
B 9 **Blind River**, ON, Canada
L 12 **Bliss**, ID, U.S.A.
J 15 **Blitar**, Indonesia
N 12 **Blitta**, Togo
N 12 **Block Island**, RI, U.S.A.
N 11 **Block Island Sound**, RI, U.S.A.
N 12 **Bloemfontein**, Republic of South Africa
M 12 **Bloemhof**, Republic of South Africa
O 7 **Blois**, France
B 10 **Blönduós**, Iceland
C 14 **Bloody Foreland**, Republic of Ireland
I 20 **Bloomfield**, IN, U.S.A.
U 14 **Bloomfield**, IA, U.S.A.
F 18 **Bloomington**, IL, U.S.A.
I 20 **Bloomington**, IN, U.S.A.
T 8 **Bloomington**, MN, U.S.A.
R 7 **Blountstown**, FL, U.S.A.
J 7 **Bludenz**, Austria
R 5 **Blue Hill**, ME, U.S.A.
P 6 **Blue Mesa Reservoir**, CO, U.S.A.
J 7 **Blue Mountain**, NY, U.S.A.
S 11 **Blue Mountain**, AR, U.S.A.
J 11 **Blue Mountains**, OR, U.S.A.
O 2 **Blue Mud Bay**, NT, Australia
G 19 **Blue Nile**, Ethiopia/Sudan
F 19 **Blue Nile**, Sudan
O 2 **Blue Rapids**, KS, U.S.A.
H 19 **Blue River**, BC, Canada
Q 9 **Bluefields**, Nicaragua
O 6 **Bluestone Lake**, WV, U.S.A.
M 7 **Bluff**, UT, U.S.A.
C 26 **Bluff**, New Zealand
J 9 **Blumenau**, Brazil
K 9 **Blunt**, SD, U.S.A.
T 4 **Blyth**, U.K.
N 25 **Blythe**, CA, U.S.A.
Z 9 **Blytheville**, AR, U.S.A.
U 3 **Blyton**, U.K.
G 12 **Bo**, Sierra Leone
F 18 **Bo Hai**, China
C 21 **Bo River Post**, Sudan
E 8 **Boa Vista**, Brazil
H 13 **Boac**, Philippines
O 9 **Boaco**, Nicaragua
J 5 **Boali**, Central African Republic
R 12 **Boano**, Indonesia
D 17 **Boayan**, Philippines
R 13 **Bobai**, China
Z 4 **Bobasakoa**, Madgascar
D 8 **Bobbio**, Italy
I 24 **Bobingen**, Germany
L 10 **Bobo-Dioulasso**, Burkina Faso
F 9 **Bobolice**, Poland
O 9 **Bobonong**, Botswana
E 15 **Bóbr**, Poland
L 16 **Bobr**, Belarus
M 6 **Bobrov**, Russian Federation
Q 3 **Bobrovytsya**, Ukraine
O 10 **Bobrowniki**, Poland
R 7 **Bobrynets'**, Ukraine
M 4 **Bobso**, China
X 9 **Boby**, Madgascar
L 1 **Boca Bacalar Chico**, Belize
T 14 **Boca Chica**, Panama
C 13 **Boca do Acre**, Brazil
H 3 **Bocaranga**, Central African Republic
T 13 **Bocas del Toro**, Panama
R 11 **Bochart**, QC, Canada
C 14 **Bocholt**, Germany
C 16 **Bochum**, Germany
G 4 **Bocoio**, Angola
F 11 **Bocșa**, Romania
H 23 **Böda**, Sweden
I 5 **Boda**, Central African Republic
R 12 **Bodaybo**, Russian Federation
J 12 **Boden**, Sweden
P 8 **Bodenham**, U.K.
G 26 **Bodensee**, Germany
L 14 **Bodmin**, U.K.
L 14 **Bodmin Moor**, U.K.
G 10 **Bodø**, Norway
B 12 **Bodrum**, Turkey
K 8 **Boende**, Democratic Republic of Congo
O 10 **Boerne**, TX, U.S.A.
F 11 **Boffa**, Guinea
D 17 **Bogale**, Myanmar
M 7 **Bogalusa**, LA, U.S.A.
J 4 **Bogangolo**, Central African Republic
K 10 **Boğazliyan**, Turkey
K 7 **Bogbonga**, Democratic Republic of Congo
L 4 **Bogda Feng**, China
L 4 **Bogda Shan**, China
E 12 **Bogdanci**, Macedonia (F.Y.R.O.M.)
J 7 **Bogenli**, China
C 3 **Bogia**, Papua New Guinea
U 13 **Bognor Regis**, U.K.
K 16 **Bogo**, Philippines
V 10 **Bogo**, Cameroon
R 2 **Bogodukhovka**, Kazakhstan
H 14 **Bogor**, Indonesia
O 1 **Bogorodsk**, Russian Federation
I 7 **Bogotá**, Colombia
N 12 **Bogotol**, Russian Federation
T 12 **Bogra**, Bangladesh
O 12 **Boguchany**, Russian Federation
M 7 **Boguchar**, Russian Federation
F 7 **Bogué**, Mauritania
F 18 **Bohai**, China
G 18 **Bohai Haixia**, China
E 18 **Bohai Wan**, China
B 18 **Bohemia**, Czech Republic
A 18 **Bohemian Forest**, Czech Republic/Germany
D 19 **Bohemian Massif**, Czech Republic
E 13 **Bohmte**, Germany
V 4 **Bohodukhiv**, Ukraine
K 18 **Bohol**, Philippines
K 19 **Bohol Sea**, Philippines
J 18 **Bohol Strait**, Philippines
L 10 **Bois Blanc Island**, MI, U.S.A.
K 10 **Boise**, ID, U.S.A.
F 7 **Boise City**, OK, U.S.A.
H 11 **Boizenburg**, Germany
J 15 **Bojano**, Italy
M 5 **Bojnürd**, Iran
Q 13 **Bokaro**, India
J 8 **Bokatola**, Democratic Republic of Congo
F 10 **Boké**, Guinea
71 A 20 **Boknafjorden**, Norway
130 G 10 **Boko**, Congo
130 G 10 **Boko-Songho**, Congo
130 J 5 **Bokode**, Democratic Republic of Congo
103 V 10 **Bökönbaev**, Kyrgyzstan
129 W 10 **Bokoro**, Chad
93 N 8 **Bokovskaya**, Russian Federation
132 K 11 **Bokspits**, Botswana
138 J 5 **Boku**, Papua New Guinea
130 M 9 **Bokwankusu**, Democratic Republic of Congo
129 V 9 **Bol**, Chad
131 N 9 **Bolaiti**, Democratic Republic of Congo
65 N 3 **Bolbec**, France
86 L 11 **Boldu**, Romania
102 M 11 **Boldumsaz**, Turkmenistan
108 J 4 **Bole**, China
128 L 12 **Bole**, Ghana
130 K 8 **Boleko**, Democratic Republic of Congo
130 K 7 **Bolena**, Democratic Republic of Congo
79 E 15 **Bolesławiec**, Poland
93 R 2 **Bolgar**, Russian Federation
128 M 11 **Bolgatanga**, Ghana
87 N 11 **Bolhrad**, Ukraine
110 N 11 **Boli**, China
130 J 8 **Bolia**, Democratic Republic of Congo
117 N 3 **Bolinao**, Philippines
16 B 10 **Bolivar**, TN, U.S.A.
25 T 6 **Bolivar**, MO, U.S.A.
50 I 4 **Bolívar**, Colombia
51 Q 5 **Bolívar**, Venezuela
52 B 9 **Bolívar**, Ecuador
53 J 19 **Bolivia**, South America
80 N 12 **Boljevac**, Serbia and Montenegro
92 J 3 **Bolkhov**, Russian Federation
65 T 13 **Bollene**, France
71 G 18 **Bollnäs**, Sweden
135 T 8 **Bollon**, QLD, Australia
71 H 16 **Bollstabruk**, Sweden
71 E 24 **Bolmen**, Sweden
130 I 9 **Bolobo**, Democratic Republic of Congo
76 F 9 **Bologna**, Italy
52 F 13 **Bolognesi**, Peru
53 E 15 **Bolognesi**, Peru
90 G 13 **Bologoye**, Russian Federation
130 J 7 **Bolomba**, Democratic Republic of Congo
121 I 22 **Bolong**, Philippines
85 C 15 **Bol'shakovo**, Russian Federation
93 T 5 **Bol'shaya Chernigovka**, Russian Federation
93 T 4 **Bol'shaya Glushitsa**, Russian Federation
103 Z 5 **Bol'shenarymskoye**, Kazakhstan
91 P 4 **Bol'shezemel'skaya Tundra**, Russian Federation
93 X 1 **Bol'shoy Iremel'**, Russian Federation
89 O 9 **Bol'shoy Porog**, Russian Federation
93 P 1 **Bol'shoye Murashkino**, Russian Federation
63 T 4 **Bolsover**, U.K.
68 J 7 **Bolsward**, Netherlands
67 T 3 **Boltaña**, Spain
63 Q 3 **Bolton**, U.K.
94 G 8 **Bolu**, Turkey
138 G 6 **Bolubolu**, Papua New Guinea
70 A 9 **Bolungarvík**, Iceland
113 U 12 **Boluo**, China
76 F 5 **Bolzano**, Italy
58 I 11 **Bom Jesus**, Brazil
55 L 15 **Bom Jesus da Lapa**, Brazil
58 I 10 **Bom Retiro**, Brazil
130 F 11 **Boma**, Democratic Republic of Congo
130 H 6 **Bomassa**, Congo
135 U 13 **Bombala**, NSW, Australia
66 G 8 **Bombarral**, Portugal
130 J 6 **Bomboma**, Democratic Republic of Congo
107 W 9 **Bomdila**, India
131 O 7 **Bomili**, Democratic Republic of Congo
71 A 19 **Bømlo**, Norway
100 F 4 **Bonāb**, Iran
49 S 13 **Bonaire**, Netherlands Antilles
47 P 6 **Bonanza**, Nicaragua
49 Q 7 **Bonao**, Dominican Republic
134 I 3 **Bonaparte Archipelago**, WA, Australia
41 Z 10 **Bonavista**, NL, Canada
41 Y 10 **Bonavista Bay**, NL, Canada
130 M 5 **Bondo**, Democratic Republic of Congo
120 H 12 **Bondoc Peninsula**, Philippines
128 L 12 **Bondoukou**, Côte d'Ivoire
128 L 10 **Bondoukui**, Burkina Faso
29 R 11 **Bondurant**, WY, U.S.A.
117 O 14 **Bonerate**, Indonesia
115 O 18 **Bông Son**, Vietnam
127 H 21 **Bonga**, Ethiopia
121 H 14 **Bongabong**, Philippines
107 U 10 **Bongaigaon**, India
130 L 7 **Bongandanga**, Democratic Republic of Congo
121 E 25 **Bongao**, Philippines
121 K 22 **Bongo**, Philippines
129 V 11 **Bongor**, Chad
27 R 4 **Bonham**, TX, U.S.A.
65 Y 15 **Bonifacio**, France
19 Q 7 **Bonifay**, FL, U.S.A.
55 G 18 **Bonito**, Brazil
73 C 17 **Bonn**, Germany
65 P 9 **Bonnat**, France
28 K 2 **Bonners Ferry**, ID, U.S.A.
65 V 9 **Bonneville**, France
30 I 3 **Bonneville Salt Flats**, UT, U.S.A.
39 K 17 **Bonnyville**, AB, Canada
123 B 24 **Bōno-misaki**, Japan
115 O 21 **Bonom Mhai**, Vietnam
135 V 9 **Bonshaw**, NSW, Australia
116 M 11 **Bontang**, Indonesia
120 G 7 **Bontoc**, Philippines
117 N 13 **Bontosunggu**, Indonesia
79 I 25 **Bonyhád**, Hungary
128 I 12 **Boola**, Guinea
17 N 8 **Boone**, NC, U.S.A.
23 S 12 **Boone**, IA, U.S.A.
19 N 1 **Booneville**, MS, U.S.A.
127 K 20 **Boorama**, Somalia
69 G 18 **Boortmeerbeek**, Belgium
127 O 19 **Boosaaso**, Somalia
38 K 5 **Boothia Peninsula**, NU, Canada
63 O 3 **Bootle**, U.K.
130 F 8 **Booué**, Gabon
73 D 19 **Boppard**, Germany
58 H 13 **Boqueirão**, Brazil
45 O 5 **Boquillas del Carmen**, Mexico
79 A 18 **Bor**, Czech Republic
80 N 12 **Bor**, Serbia and Montenegro
94 J 12 **Bor**, Turkey
127 E 22 **Bor**, Sudan
108 M 4 **Bor- Üdzüür**, Mongolia
29 N 10 **Borah Peak**, ID, U.S.A.
71 E 22 **Borås**, Sweden
100 H 10 **Borāzjān**, Iran
54 F 11 **Borba**, Brazil
145 Q 14 **Borchgrevink Coast**, Antarctica
95 Q 7 **Borşşka**, Turkey
64 M 11 **Bordeaux**, France
43 V 9 **Borden**, PE, Canada
37 N 3 **Borden Island**, NT, Canada
37 Q 4 **Borden Peninsula**, NU, Canada
135 Q 12 **Bordertown**, SA, Australia
125 O 6 **Bordj Bou Arréridj**, Algeria
125 Q 9 **Bordj Messaouda**, Algeria
124 L 14 **Bordj Mokhtar**, Algeria
125 P 10 **Bordj Omar Driss**, Algeria
128 L 8 **Boré**, Mali
145 P 2 **Borg Massif**, Antarctica
70 D 10 **Borgarfjörður**, Iceland
70 A 11 **Borgarnes**, Iceland
26 K 2 **Borger**, TX, U.S.A.
68 N 8 **Borger**, Netherlands
71 H 24 **Borgholm**, Sweden
77 M 20 **Borgia**, Italy
76 F 6 **Borgo Valsugana**, Italy
76 B 6 **Borgomanero**, Italy
93 N 6 **Borisoglebsk**, Russian Federation
133 Y 6 **Boriziny**, Madgascar
52 C 11 **Borja**, Peru
67 R 4 **Borja**, Spain
84 J 13 **Borkavichy**, Belarus
73 C 15 **Borken**, Germany
129 X 6 **Borkou-Ennedi-Tibesti**, Chad
72 C 10 **Borkum**, Germany
71 G 19 **Borlänge**, Sweden
76 E 5 **Bormio**, Italy
73 L 16 **Borna**, Germany
68 J 5 **Borndiep**, Netherlands
68 N 11 **Borne**, Netherlands
116 J 10 **Borneo**, Indonesia
71 F 26 **Bornholm**, Denmark
129 U 10 **Borno**, Nigeria
94 B 10 **Bornova**, Turkey
87 O 10 **Borodino**, Ukraine
87 O 3 **Borodyanka**, Ukraine
130 L 1 **Boromata**, Central African Republic
128 L 10 **Boromo**, Burkina Faso
121 M 16 **Borongan**, Philippines
128 I 12 **Borotou**, Côte d'Ivoire
63 S 1 **Boroughbridge**, U.K.
87 X 5 **Borova**, Ukraine
90 G 12 **Borovichi**, Russian Federation
103 O 2 **Borovskoy**, Kazakhstan
135 O 3 **Borroloola**, NT, Australia
86 J 8 **Borşa**, Romania
70 K 6 **Børselv**, Norway
62 M 7 **Borth**, U.K.
100 G 7 **Borūjerd**, Iran
87 Q 3 **Boryspil'**, Ukraine
87 R 2 **Borzna**, Ukraine
89 S 14 **Borzya**, Russian Federation
77 B 17 **Bosa**, Italy
103 T 6 **Bosaga**, Kazakhstan
80 F 9 **Bosanska Dubica**, Bosnia and Herzegovina
80 F 9 **Bosanska Gradiška**, Bosnia and Herzegovina
80 E 11 **Bosanski Petrovac**, Bosnia and Herzegovina
62 K 13 **Boscastle**, U.K.
113 O 12 **Bose**, China
113 W 2 **Boshan**, China
80 H 10 **Bosna**, Bosnia and Herzegovina
80 G 11 **Bosnia and Herzegovina**, Europe
123 L 16 **Bōsō-hantō**, Japan
130 K 5 **Bosobolo**, Democratic Republic of Congo
94 D 7 **Bosporus**, Turkey
130 I 4 **Bossangoa**, Central African Republic
130 I 4 **Bossembélé**, Central African Republic
130 I 4 **Bossentélé**, Central African Republic
18 H 4 **Bossier City**, LA, U.S.A.
101 T 10 **Bostan**, Pakistan
108 K 5 **Bosten Hu**, China
15 O 9 **Boston**, MA, U.S.A.
63 W 5 **Boston**, U.K.
25 S 9 **Boston Mountains**, AR, U.S.A.
14 C 13 **Boswell**, PA, U.S.A.
105 B 15 **Botad**, India
135 V 12 **Botany Bay**, NSW, Australia
130 J 9 **Botemola**, Democratic Republic of Congo
82 I 9 **Botev**, Bulgaria
82 G 8 **Botevgrad**, Bulgaria
66 I 4 **Boticas**, Portugal
93 Q 15 **Botlikh**, Russian Federation
120 E 10 **Botolan**, Philippines
86 L 8 **Botoşani**, Romania
111 E 18 **Botou**, China
71 I 14 **Botsmark**, Sweden
132 K 9 **Botswana**, Africa
70 K 13 **Bottenviken**, Sweden
73 C 15 **Bottrop**, Germany
58 J 6 **Botucatu**, Brazil
82 B 12 **Botun**, Macedonia (F.Y.R.O.M.)
125 P 7 **Bou Aroua**, Algeria
128 H 7 **Boû Bleï'îne**, Mauritania
124 F 9 **Bou Izakarn**, Morocco
125 N 6 **Bou Saâda**, Algeria
128 J 13 **Bouaflé**, Côte d'Ivoire
128 K 12 **Bouaké**, Côte d'Ivoire
130 H 4 **Bouar**, Central African Republic
124 K 8 **Bouârfa**, Morocco
130 J 4 **Bouca**, Central African Republic
43 U 8 **Bouctouche**, NB, Canada
130 I 5 **Boudoua**, Central African Republic
130 G 10 **Bouenza**, Congo
138 I 5 **Bougainville**, Papua New Guinea
129 O 6 **Boughessa**, Mali
128 I 10 **Bougouni**, Mali
124 L 7 **Bougtob**, Algeria
69 I 24 **Bouillon**, Belgium
125 N 5 **Bouira**, Algeria
124 C 11 **Boujdour**, Western Sahara
124 D 11 **Boukra**, Western Sahara
31 R 3 **Boulder**, CO, U.S.A.
134 I 10 **Boulder**, WA, Australia
33 N 22 **Boulder City**, NV, U.S.A.
124 I 7 **Boulemane**, Morocco
135 Q 6 **Boulia**, QLD, Australia
65 O 1 **Boulogne-sur-Mer**, France
130 L 3 **Boulouba**, Central African Republic
124 H 8 **Boumalne Dadès**, Morocco
130 G 9 **Boumango**, Gabon
128 L 11 **Bouna**, Côte d'Ivoire
33 J 19 **Boundary Peak**, NV, U.S.A.
128 J 11 **Boundiali**, Côte d'Ivoire
139 P 14 **Bourail**, New Caledonia
65 U 9 **Bourg-en-Bresse**, France
65 W 10 **Bourg-St-Maurice**, France
65 P 10 **Bourganeuf**, France
65 Q 7 **Bourges**, France
65 R 7 **Bourgogne**, France
65 T 10 **Bourgoin-Jallieu**, France
135 S 9 **Bourke**, NSW, Australia
63 V 6 **Bourne**, U.K.
63 R 13 **Bournemouth**, U.K.
69 L 24 **Bourscheid**, Luxembourg
129 Z 10 **Bourtoutou**, Chad
30 H 12 **Bouse**, AZ, U.S.A.
129 W 11 **Bousso**, Chad
69 H 19 **Boutersem**, Belgium
128 F 7 **Boutilimit**, Mauritania
129 Q 9 **Bouza**, Niger
63 N 14 **Bovey Tracey**, U.K.
28 K 5 **Bovill**, ID, U.S.A.
58 C 13 **Bovril**, Argentina
22 I 2 **Bowbells**, ND, U.S.A.
135 U 5 **Bowen**, QLD, Australia
27 P 5 **Bowie**, TX, U.S.A.
30 M 14 **Bowie**, AZ, U.S.A.
16 F 7 **Bowling Green**, KY, U.S.A.
17 T 5 **Bowling Green**, VA, U.S.A.
21 L 17 **Bowling Green**, OH, U.S.A.
25 W 3 **Bowling Green**, MO, U.S.A.
22 G 6 **Bowman**, ND, U.S.A.
37 S 6 **Bowman Bay**, NU, Canada
144 H 4 **Bowman Coast**, Antarctica
145 Y 10 **Bowman Island**, Antarctica
135 U 12 **Bowral**, NSW, Australia
111 F 19 **Boxing**, China
69 K 15 **Boxmeer**, Netherlands
69 I 15 **Boxtel**, Netherlands
94 J 7 **Boyabat**, Turkey
50 J 6 **Boyaca**, Colombia
113 W 7 **Boyang**, China
18 I 6 **Boyce**, LA, U.S.A.
29 T 7 **Boyd**, MT, U.S.A.
39 J 17 **Boyle**, AB, Canada
61 C 16 **Boyle**, Republic of Ireland
53 L 22 **Boyuibe**, Bolivia
94 B 11 **Boz Dağlari**, Turkey
94 C 13 **Bozburun**, Turkey
94 A 9 **Bozcaada**, Turkey
29 Q 7 **Bozeman**, MT, U.S.A.
113 V 4 **Bozhou**, China
94 G 13 **Bozkir**, Turkey
130 I 4 **Bozoum**, Central African Republic
95 N 12 **Bozova**, Turkey
94 E 9 **Bozüyük**, Turkey
76 E 8 **Bozzolo**, Italy
76 B 8 **Bra**, Italy
144 H 4 **Brabant Island**, Antarctica
69 F 19 **Brabant Wallon**, Belgium
80 E 13 **Brač**, Croatia
42 F 11 **Bracebridge**, ON, Canada
63 T 9 **Brackley**, U.K.
63 U 11 **Bracknell**, U.K.
86 G 10 **Brad**, Romania
19 V 11 **Bradenton**, FL, U.S.A.
63 S 2 **Bradford**, U.K.
63 Q 11 **Bradford-on-Avon**, U.K.
27 N 8 **Brady**, TX, U.S.A.
60 J 4 **Brae**, U.K.
60 I 11 **Braemar**, U.K.
66 H 4 **Braga**, Portugal
66 H 4 **Braga**, Portugal
59 C 16 **Bragado**, Argentina
54 K 10 **Bragança**, Brazil
66 J 4 **Bragança**, Portugal
66 K 4 **Bragança**, Portugal
85 M 21 **Brahin**, Belarus
107 V 13 **Brahmanbaria**, Bangladesh
105 I 17 **Brahmapur**, India
107 W 10 **Brahmaputra**, India
62 K 6 **Braich y Pwll**, U.K.
86 M 11 **Brăila**, Romania
69 F 20 **Braine-l'Alleud**, Belgium
23 R 6 **Brainerd**, MN, U.S.A.
63 X 9 **Braintree**, U.K.
72 E 11 **Brake**, Germany
128 F 7 **Brâkna**, Mauritania
42 E 13 **Brampton**, ON, Canada
63 Z 7 **Brampton**, U.K.
72 E 13 **Bramsche**, Germany
54 E 9 **Branco**, Brazil
132 G 9 **Brandberg**, Namibia
71 D 19 **Brandbu**, Norway
72 L 13 **Brandenburg**, Germany
73 M 14 **Brandenburg**, Germany
40 H 10 **Brandon**, MB, Canada
63 X 7 **Brandon**, U.K.
132 K 13 **Brandvlei**, Republic of South Africa
19 U 8 **Branford**, FL, U.S.A.
78 J 8 **Braniewo**, Poland
144 H 3 **Bransfield Strait**, Antarctica
78 N 11 **Brańsk**, Poland
25 T 8 **Branson**, MO, U.S.A.
42 E 13 **Brantford**, ON, Canada
19 Q 6 **Brantley**, AL, U.S.A.
43 Y 9 **Bras d'Or Lake**, NS, Canada
54 A 11 **Brasil**, Brazil
55 C 14 **Brasiléia**, Brazil
55 J 16 **Brasília**, Brazil
85 I 14 **Braslaw**, Belarus
86 K 11 **Braşov**, Romania
69 G 17 **Brasschaat**, Belgium
19 T 1 **Brasstown Bald**, GA, U.S.A.
79 G 21 **Bratislava**, Slovakia
89 P 12 **Bratsk**, Russian Federation
89 P 12 **Bratskoye Vodokhranilishche**, Russian Federation
14 M 9 **Brattleboro**, VT, U.S.A.
87 O 11 **Braţul Chilia**, Romania
87 N 12 **Braţul Sfântu Gheorghe**, Romania
87 O 12 **Braţul Sulina**, Romania
75 Q 4 **Braunau am Inn**, Austria
73 I 15 **Braunlage**, Germany
72 I 13 **Braunschweig**, Germany
62 M 12 **Braunton**, U.K.
33 M 26 **Brawley**, CA, U.S.A.
41 P 1 **Bray Island**, NU, Canada
21 H 19 **Brazil**, IN, U.S.A.
54 H 13 **Brazil**, South America
55 K 16 **Brazilian Highlands**, Brazil
27 Q 7 **Brazos**, TX, U.S.A.
130 H 10 **Brazzaville**, Congo
80 I 10 **Brčko**, Bosnia and Herzegovina
78 H 10 **Brda**, Poland
137 A 24 **Breaksea Island**, New Zealand
136 K 6 **Bream Bay**, New Zealand
69 G 16 **Brecht**, Belgium
27 N 6 **Breckenridge**, TX, U.S.A.
79 F 20 **Břeclav**, Czech Republic
63 O 9 **Brecon**, U.K.
63 N 9 **Brecon Beacons**, U.K.
69 H 15 **Breda**, Netherlands
132 K 15 **Bredasdorp**, Republic of South Africa
72 F 7 **Bredstedt**, Germany
69 J 17 **Bree**, Belgium
82 E 11 **Bregalnica**, Macedonia (F.Y.R.O.M.)
73 G 26 **Bregenz**, Germany
74 J 6 **Bregenz**, Austria
82 E 6 **Bregovo**, Bulgaria
70 A 10 **Breida Fjörður**, Iceland
70 D 11 **Breiðdalsvík**, Iceland
22 J 6 **Breien**, ND, U.S.A.
54 M 11 **Brejo**, Brazil
72 F 11 **Bremen**, Germany
72 F 11 **Bremen**, Germany
72 F 10 **Bremerhaven**, Germany
32 G 7 **Bremerton**, WA, U.S.A.
72 G 10 **Bremervörde**, Germany
27 R 9 **Brenham**, TX, U.S.A.
74 M 8 **Brenner**, Austria
76 E 6 **Breno**, Italy
63 W 10 **Brentwood**, U.K.
76 E 7 **Brescia**, Italy
69 D 16 **Breskens**, Netherlands
76 G 4 **Bressanone**, Italy
60 K 5 **Bressay**, U.K.
64 M 8 **Bressuire**, France
64 H 5 **Brest**, France
85 E 21 **Brest**, Belarus
85 G 20 **Brestskaya Voblasts'**, Belarus
64 I 5 **Bretagne**, France
65 Q 3 **Breteuil**, France
18 M 8 **Breton Sound**, LA, U.S.A.
73 F 22 **Bretten**, Germany
16 L 10 **Brevard**, NC, U.S.A.
54 J 10 **Breves**, Brazil
34 L 6 **Brevig Mission**, AK, U.S.A.
135 T 9 **Brewarrina**, NSW, Australia
15 R 5 **Brewer**, ME, U.S.A.
32 J 6 **Brewster**, WA, U.S.A.
19 P 6 **Brewton**, AL, U.S.A.
82 F 9 **Breznik**, Bulgaria
86 I 11 **Brezoi**, Romania
130 L 4 **Bria**, Central African Republic
65 W 11 **Briançon**, France
47 S 13 **Bribri**, Costa Rica
86 M 7 **Briceni**, Moldova
63 N 10 **Bridgend**, U.K.
14 L 12 **Bridgeport**, CT, U.S.A.
22 G 13 **Bridgeport**, NE, U.S.A.
33 I 19 **Bridgeport**, CA, U.S.A.
29 T 8 **Bridger**, MT, U.S.A.
14 I 15 **Bridgeton**, NJ, U.S.A.
49 Z 12 **Bridgetown**, Barbados
134 G 12 **Bridgetown**, WA, Australia
43 U 11 **Bridgewater**, NS, Canada
63 P 7 **Bridgnorth**, U.K.
15 O 6 **Bridgton**, ME, U.S.A.
63 P 12 **Bridgwater**, U.K.
63 O 11 **Bridgwater Bay**, U.K.
63 V 1 **Bridlington**, U.K.
63 V 1 **Bridlington Bay**, U.K.
63 P 13 **Bridport**, U.K.
74 H 8 **Briel**, Switzerland
65 T 5 **Brienne-le-Château**, France
74 F 8 **Brienz**, Switzerland
77 L 16 **Brienza**, Italy
74 E 8 **Brienzer See**, Switzerland
74 E 10 **Brig**, Switzerland
63 V 3 **Brigg**, U.K.
30 J 1 **Brigham City**, UT, U.S.A.
135 S 13 **Bright**, VIC, Australia
19 X 11 **Brighton**, FL, U.S.A.
21 L 15 **Brighton**, MI, U.S.A.
31 R 3 **Brighton**, CO, U.S.A.
63 W 13 **Brighton**, U.K.
137 E 25 **Brighton**, New Zealand
128 D 9 **Brikama**, Gambia
70 D 10 **Brimnes**, Iceland
77 O 16 **Brindisi**, Italy
25 X 11 **Brinkley**, AR, U.S.A.
65 R 11 **Brioude**, France
135 W 9 **Brisbane**, QLD, Australia
16 M 8 **Bristol**, TN, U.S.A.
19 S 7 **Bristol**, FL, U.S.A.
63 P 11 **Bristol**, U.K.
35 N 11 **Bristol Bay**, AK, U.S.A.
62 M 11 **Bristol Channel**, U.K.
33 M 24 **Bristol Lake**, CA, U.S.A.
39 E 17 **British Columbia**, Canada
65 P 11 **Brive-la-Gaillarde**, France
67 P 2 **Briviesca**, Spain
63 N 14 **Brixham**, U.K.
79 F 19 **Brno**, Czech Republic
62 J 9 **Broad Haven**, U.K.
60 F 10 **Broadford**, U.K.
63 Z 11 **Broadstairs**, U.K.
29 X 7 **Broadus**, MT, U.S.A.
39 O 19 **Broadview**, SK, Canada
63 R 9 **Broadway**, U.K.
40 I 6 **Brochet**, MB, Canada
15 O 10 **Brockton**, MA, U.S.A.
42 I 12 **Brockville**, ON, Canada
14 D 11 **Brockway**, PA, U.S.A.
82 C 11 **Brod**, Macedonia (F.Y.R.O.M.)
37 P 5 **Brodeur Peninsula**, NU, Canada
78 J 10 **Brodnica**, Poland
86 J 4 **Brody**, Ukraine
32 K 11 **Brogan**, OR, U.S.A.
25 Q 9 **Broken Arrow**, OK, U.S.A.
25 R 13 **Broken Bow**, OK, U.S.A.
25 R 12 **Broken Bow Reservoir**, OK, U.S.A.
135 R 10 **Broken Hill**, NSW, Australia
51 X 6 **Brokopondo**, Suriname
63 W 11 **Bromley**, U.K.
63 R 7 **Bromsgrove**, U.K.
71 C 23 **Brønderslev**, Denmark
128 M 12 **Brong-Ahafo**, Ghana
76 C 7 **Broni**, Italy
26 M 7 **Bronte**, TX, U.S.A.
135 T 15 **Bronte Park**, TAS, Australia
121 C 20 **Brooke's Point**, Philippines
25 T 2 **Brookfield**, MO, U.S.A.
18 L 6 **Brookhaven**, MS, U.S.A.
23 P 9 **Brookings**, SD, U.S.A.
33 E 14 **Brookings**, OR, U.S.A.
17 R 7 **Brookneal**, VA, U.S.A.
35 O 4 **Brooks Range**, AK, U.S.A.
19 V 10 **Brooksville**, FL, U.S.A.
134 G 11 **Brookton**, WA, Australia
21 K 19 **Brookville Lake**, IN, U.S.A.
134 I 4 **Broome**, WA, Australia
86 K 8 **Broşteni**, Romania
105 N 22 **Brothers**, India
65 O 5 **Brou**, France
87 Q 3 **Brovary**, Ukraine
26 K 5 **Brownfield**, TX, U.S.A.
29 O 2 **Browning**, MT, U.S.A.
21 I 20 **Brownstown**, IN, U.S.A.
16 A 9 **Brownsville**, TN, U.S.A.
27 Q 15 **Brownsville**, TX, U.S.A.
27 N 7 **Brownwood**, TX, U.S.A.
85 L 19 **Brozha**, Belarus
18 M 2 **Bruce**, MS, U.S.A.
20 D 10 **Bruce**, WI, U.S.A.
20 G 8 **Bruce Crossing**, MI, U.S.A.
42 C 11 **Bruce Peninsula**, ON, Canada
73 F 22 **Bruchsal**, Germany
75 Q 7 **Bruck**, Austria
75 Y 4 **Bruck an der Leitha**, Austria
75 V 6 **Bruck an der Mur**, Austria
116 A 8 **Brueuh**, Indonesia
69 C 17 **Bruges**, Belgium
107 Z 7 **Bruint**, India
20 D 8 **Brule**, WI, U.S.A.
69 G 24 **Brûly**, Belgium
55 M 15 **Brumado**, Brazil
68 L 12 **Brummen**, Netherlands
19 R 5 **Brundidge**, AL, U.S.A.
119 T 7 **Brunei**, Asia
119 T 6 **Brunei Bay**, Malaysia
76 G 4 **Brunico**, Italy
72 F 9 **Brunsbüttel**, Germany
15 P 7 **Brunswick**, ME, U.S.A.
19 W 6 **Brunswick**, GA, U.S.A.
25 T 3 **Brunswick**, MO, U.S.A.
145 N 3 **Brunt Ice Shelf**, Antarctica
79 G 17 **Bruntál**, Czech Republic
135 T 15 **Bruny Island**, TAS, Australia
80 M 13 **Brus**, Serbia and Montenegro
47 P 4 **Brus Laguna**, Honduras
31 T 3 **Brush**, CO, U.S.A.
74 K 10 **Brusio**, Switzerland
69 E 19 **Brussels**, Belgium
78 H 9 **Brusy**, Poland
87 O 4 **Brusyliv**, Ukraine
21 K 16 **Bryan**, OH, U.S.A.
27 R 9 **Bryan**, TX, U.S.A.
144 J 8 **Bryan Coast**, Antarctica
87 Y 6 **Bryanka**, Ukraine
92 I 3 **Bryansk**, Russian Federation
92 H 4 **Bryanskaya Oblast'**, Russian Federation
63 N 9 **Brynamman**, U.K.
136 J 7 **Brynderwyn**, New Zealand
16 K 10 **Bryson City**, NC, U.S.A.
80 O 11 **Brza**, Serbia and Montenegro
79 G 15 **Brzeg**, Poland
127 K 25 **Bu'aale**, Somalia
141 U 1 **Buada Lagoon**, Nauru
138 L 6 **Buala**, Solomon Islands
125 T 8 **Bu'ayrāt al Hasūn**, Libya
128 E 10 **Buba**, Guinea-Bissau
99 S 2 **Bubīyān Island**, Kuwait
139 Y 11 **Buca**, Fiji
50 J 5 **Bucaramanga**, Colombia
121 N 19 **Bucas Grande**, Philippines
77 K 16 **Buccino**, Italy
60 J 10 **Buchan Ness**, U.K.
17 Q 6 **Buchanan**, VA, U.S.A.
128 H 13 **Buchanan**, Liberia
41 X 10 **Buchans**, NL, Canada
86 J 13 **Bucharest**, Romania
63 N 14 **Buckfastleigh**, U.K.
17 P 3 **Buckhannon**, WV, U.S.A.
17 S 6 **Buckingham**, VA, U.S.A.
35 N 6 **Buckland**, AK, U.S.A.
145 S 15 **Buckle Island**, Antarctica
24 K 6 **Bucklin**, KS, U.S.A.
79 G 19 **Bučovice**, Czech Republic
21 M 17 **Bucyrus**, OH, U.S.A.
85 M 20 **Buda-Kashelyova**, Belarus
79 I 23 **Budapest**, Hungary
106 K 9 **Budaun**, India
145 X 11 **Budd Coast**, Antarctica
77 C 16 **Buddusò**, Italy
18 K 6 **Bude**, MS, U.S.A.
62 L 13 **Bude**, U.K.
62 K 13 **Bude Bay**, U.K.
69 J 17 **Budel**, Netherlands
93 O 12 **Budennovsk**, Russian Federation
86 L 13 **Budeşti**, Romania
130 K 6 **Budjala**, Democratic Republic of Congo
90 G 11 **Budogoshch'**, Russian Federation
81 I 16 **Budva**, Serbia and Montenegro
129 S 14 **Buea**, Cameroon
57 H 19 **Buen Pasto**, Argentina
56 I 12 **Buena Esperanza**, Argentina
33 I 23 **Buena Vista Lake Bed**, CA, U.S.A.
44 L 4 **Buenaventura**, Mexico
50 G 7 **Buenaventura**, Colombia
44 J 8 **Buenavista**, Mexico
120 H 13 **Buenavista**, Philippines
47 R 13 **Buenos Aires**, Costa Rica
59 D 16 **Buenos Aires**, Argentina
59 C 17 **Buenos Aires**, Argentina
44 M 6 **Búfalo**, Mexico
14 D 8 **Buffalo**, NY, U.S.A.
16 D 9 **Buffalo**, TN, U.S.A.
22 G 7 **Buffalo**, SD, U.S.A.
24 J 8 **Buffalo**, OK, U.S.A.
25 U 6 **Buffalo**, MO, U.S.A.
27 R 8 **Buffalo**, TX, U.S.A.
29 W 9 **Buffalo**, WY, U.S.A.
39 K 16 **Buffalo Narrows**, SK, Canada
86 K 12 **Buftea**, Romania
78 N 12 **Bug**, Poland
50 H 7 **Buga**, Colombia
131 S 8 **Bugala Island**, Uganda
129 R 12 **Bugana**, Nigeria
121 H 16 **Bugasong**, Philippines
102 I 13 **Bugdayli**, Turkmenistan
91 O 2 **Bugrino**, Russian Federation
121 B 20 **Bugsuk**, Philippines
110 H 8 **Bugt**, China
121 J 14 **Bugui Point**, Philippines
93 U 2 **Bugul'ma**, Russian Federation
93 U 3 **Buguruslan**, Russian Federation
96 K 2 **Buḩayrat al Asad**, Syria
97 S 8 **Buḩayrat ar Razāzah**, Iraq
97 S 6 **Buḩayrat ath Tharthār**, Iraq
96 I 5 **Buḩayrat Qaţţīnah**, Syria
28 L 12 **Buhl**, ID, U.S.A.
86 L 9 **Buhuşi**, Romania
63 O 8 **Builth Wells**, U.K.
138 J 5 **Buin**, Papua New Guinea
93 R 2 **Buinsk**, Russian Federation
109 U 3 **Buir Nur**, China
68 L 6 **Buitenpost**, Netherlands
132 K 9 **Buitepos**, Namibia

Country ■ Internal administrative region: State/Province/Territory/Dependent territory · Capital city · Mountain range/Undersea ridge · Mountain peak/Volcano/Seamount · Geographic feature · Headland/Point/Cape/Peninsula · Desert · Island/Island group · Antarctic base · Ocean · Sea · Bay/Gulf/Channel/Strait · Lake · Salt pan/Dry/Intermittent lake · River

□ Country ■ Internal administrative region: State/Province/Territory/Dependent territory ⚓ Capital city ▲ Mountain range/Undersea ridge ▲ Mountain peak/Volcano/Seamount ◇ Geographic feature ▶ Headland/Point/Cape/Peninsula ✦ Desert ⚏ Island/Island group ⊞ Antarctic base ⦵ Ocean ≈ Sea ≈ Bay/Gulf/Channel/Strait ↳ Lake ⮡ Salt pan/Dry/Intermittent lake

T 15 **Cape Hudson**, Antarctica ►
C 10 **Cape Hurd**, ON, Canada ►
Q 13 **Cape Jaffa**, SA, Australia ►
I 4 **Cape Karikari**, New Zealand ►
W 14 **Cape Keltie**, Antarctica ►
N 13 **Cape Kidnappers**, New Zealand ►
B 18 **Cape Knox**, BC, Canada ►
H 15 **Cape Kormakitis**, Cyprus ►
T 5 **Cape Labrador**, NL, Canada ►
G 12 **Cape Leeuwin**, WA, Australia ►
I 3 **Cape Leveque**, WA, Australia ►
V 11 **Cape Lookout**, NC, U.S.A. ►
K 5 **Cape Mackintosh**, Antarctica ►
H 4 **Cape Maria van Diemen**, New Zealand ►
I 15 **Cape May**, NJ, U.S.A. ►
I 15 **Cape May**, NJ, U.S.A.
A 21 **Cape Melville**, Philippines ►
S 2 **Cape Melville**, QLD, Australia ►
E 16 **Cape Mendocino**, CA, U.S.A. ►
T 2 **Cape Mercy**, NU, Canada ►
K 24 **Cape Meredith**, Falkland Islands ►
K 9 **Cape Mohican**, AK, U.S.A. ►
F 6 **Cape Nelson**, Papua New Guinea ►
M 11 **Cape Newenham**, AK, U.S.A. ►
M 7 **Cape Nome**, AK, U.S.A. ►
Y 7 **Cape North**, NS, Canada ►
O 2 **Cape Norvegia**, Antarctica ►
J 15 **Cape of Good Hope**, Republic of South Africa ►
R 14 **Cape Otway**, VIC, Australia ►
L 17 **Cape Palliser**, New Zealand ►
I 14 **Cape Palmas**, Côte d'Ivoire ►
E 7 **Cape Parry**, NT, Canada ►
J 11 **Cape Pasley**, WA, Australia ►
Y 11 **Cape Poinsett**, Antarctica ►
L 4 **Cape Prince Alfred**, NT, Canada ►
A 25 **Cape Providence**, New Zealand ►
N 15 **Cape Recife**, Republic of South Africa ►
H 4 **Cape Reinga**, New Zealand ►
R 14 **Cape Romain**, SC, U.S.A. ►
W 13 **Cape Romano**, FL, U.S.A. ►
O 10 **Cape Runaway**, New Zealand ►
X 14 **Cape Sable**, FL, U.S.A. ►
T 13 **Cape Sable Island**, NS, Canada ►
N 13 **Cape Saint Paul**, Ghana ►
N 23 **Cape San Agustin**, Philippines ►
D 21 **Cape Scott**, BC, Canada ►
M 15 **Cape Seal**, Republic of South Africa ►
O 1 **Cape Shield**, NT, Australia ►
F 2 **Cape Siemens**, Papua New Guinea ►
I 8 **Cape Siri**, Papua New Guinea ►
N 4 **Cape Southampton**, NU, Canada ►
P 12 **Cape Spencer**, SA, Australia ►
H 4 **Cape St George**, Papua New Guinea ►
J 15 **Cape Stephens**, New Zealand ►
L 7 **Cape Tatnam**, MB, Canada ►
J 16 **Cape Terawhiti**, New Zealand ►
L 14 **Cape Three Points**, Ghana ►
J 15 **Cape Town**, Republic of South Africa ▟
M 15 **Cape Turnagain**, New Zealand ►
U 6 **Cape Uivak**, NL, Canada ►
K 8 **Cape Verde**, Atlantic Ocean □
X 12 **Cape Waldron**, Antarctica ►
E 6 **Cape Ward Hunt**, Papua New Guinea ►
O 1 **Cape Wessel**, NT, Australia ►
O 2 **Cape Wilson**, NU, Canada ►
G 8 **Cape Wrath**, U.K. ►
R 1 **Cape York**, QLD, Australia ►
R 1 **Cape York Peninsula**, QLD, Australia ►
M 16 **Capelinha**, Brazil
U 6 **Capella**, QLD, Australia
G 13 **Capelle aan den IJssel**, Netherlands
L 25 **Capellen**, Luxembourg
I 2 **Capenda-Camulemba**, Angola
I 13 **Capestrano**, Italy
R 12 **Capitan Peak**, NM, U.S.A. ▲
G 17 **Capnoyan**, Philippines 🏝
A 16 **Capo Caccia**, Italy ►
C 19 **Capo Carbonara**, Italy ►
N 19 **Capo Colonna**, Italy ►
D 16 **Capo Comino**, Italy ►
B 15 **Capo del Falcone**, Italy ►
B 18 **Capo della Frasca**, Italy ►
K 24 **Capo delle Correnti**, Italy ►
K 21 **Capo di Milazzo**, Italy ►
D 17 **Capo di Monte Santu**, Italy ►
K 21 **Capo d'Orlando**, Italy ►
I 21 **Capo Gallo**, Italy ►
L 23 **Capo Murro di Porco**, Italy ►
L 17 **Capo Palinuro**, Italy ►
N 20 **Capo Rizzuto**, Italy ►
H 21 **Capo San Vito**, Italy ►
O 18 **Capo Santa Maria di Leuca**, Italy ►
J 24 **Capo Scaramia**, Italy ►
B 20 **Capo Spartivento**, Italy ►
N 17 **Capo Spulico**, Italy ►
N 18 **Capo Trionto**, Italy ►
L 20 **Capo Vaticano**, Italy ►
G 3 **Capolo**, Angola
J 11 **Cappadocia**, Turkey ◇
J 16 **Capri**, Italy
L 7 **Caprivi**, Namibia ▣
K 7 **Caprivi Strip**, Namibia ◇
D 9 **Captain Cook**, HI, U.S.A.
I 9 **Caquetá**, Colombia ▣
J 10 **Caquetá**, Colombia 〰
N 23 **Car Nicobar**, India 🏝
H 15 **Carabao**, Philippines 🏝
N 3 **Carabobo**, Venezuela ▣
S 5 **Carabobo**, Venezuela
I 13 **Caracal**, Romania
E 8 **Caracaraí**, Brazil
O 2 **Caracas**, Venezuela ▟
L 13 **Caracol**, Brazil
I 20 **Caracollo**, Bolivia
N 22 **Caraga**, Philippines
F 15 **Carahue**, Chile
J 12 **Caramoan Peninsula**, Philippines ►
M 5 **Carandaí**, Brazil
G 11 **Caransebeș**, Romania
T 7 **Caraquet**, NB, Canada
A 9 **Caráquez**, Ecuador
Q 5 **Caratasca**, Honduras
R 14 **Carate**, Costa Rica
C 11 **Carauari**, Brazil
R 11 **Caravaca de la Cruz**, Spain
N 17 **Caravelas**, Brazil
G 11 **Carazinho**, Brazil
H 1 **Carballo**, Spain
H 11 **Carbondale**, PA, U.S.A.
F 22 **Carbondale**, IL, U.S.A.
P 4 **Carbondale**, CO, U.S.A.
67 R 13 **Carboneras**, Spain
67 R 7 **Carboneras de Guadazaón**, Spain
59 B 15 **Carcaraña**, Argentina 〰
65 Q 14 **Carcassonne**, France
52 B 8 **Carchi**, Ecuador ▣
105 E 22 **Cardamom Hills**, India ⛰
45 T 12 **Cardel**, Mexico
67 N 10 **Cárdena**, Spain
45 V 13 **Cárdenas**, Mexico
48 H 4 **Cárdenas**, Cuba
63 O 11 **Cardiff**, U.K.
62 K 8 **Cardigan**, U.K.
62 L 7 **Cardigan Bay**, U.K. ≈
115 J 21 **Cardomom Range**, Cambodia ⛰
59 E 15 **Cardona**, Uruguay
137 D 23 **Cardrona**, New Zealand
39 K 21 **Cardston**, AB, Canada
135 T 4 **Cardwell**, QLD, Australia
86 G 7 **Carei**, Romania
64 L 3 **Carentan**, France
28 M 11 **Carey**, ID, U.S.A.
64 I 5 **Carhaix-Plouguer**, France
58 O 5 **Cariacica**, Brazil
51 Q 2 **Cariaco**, Venezuela
52 B 11 **Cariamanga**, Ecuador
77 N 18 **Cariati**, Italy
48 I 13 **Caribbean Sea**, North America 🌊
15 R 1 **Caribou**, ME, U.S.A.
39 H 15 **Caribou Mountains**, AB, Canada ⛰
121 L 16 **Carigara**, Philippines
67 S 5 **Cariñena**, Spain
55 L 15 **Carinhanha**, Brazil
51 R 3 **Caripito**, Venezuela
42 I 11 **Carleton Place**, ON, Canada
133 N 11 **Carletonville**, Republic of South Africa
33 M 16 **Carlin**, NV, U.S.A.
21 E 20 **Carlinville**, IL, U.S.A.
14 F 13 **Carlisle**, PA, U.S.A.
61 I 15 **Carlisle**, U.K.
77 B 19 **Carloforte**, Italy
59 B 16 **Carlos Casares**, Argentina
61 E 19 **Carlow**, Republic of Ireland
31 T 14 **Carlsbad**, NM, U.S.A.
39 O 19 **Carlyle**, SK, Canada
21 F 21 **Carlyle Lake**, IL, U.S.A. ∽
38 B 13 **Carmacks**, YT, Canada
62 L 9 **Carmarthen**, U.K.
62 L 10 **Carmarthen Bay**, U.K. ≈
65 P 13 **Carmaux**, France
62 L 3 **Carmel Head**, U.K. ►
46 I 2 **Carmelita**, Guatemala
59 D 15 **Carmelo**, Uruguay
30 K 15 **Carmen**, AZ, U.S.A.
50 I 3 **Carmen**, Colombia
56 G 7 **Carmen**, Chile
56 G 5 **Carmen Alto**, Chile
59 B 20 **Carmen de Patagones**, Argentina
56 H 13 **Carmensa**, Argentina
21 G 22 **Carmi**, IL, U.S.A.
47 O 12 **Carmona**, Costa Rica
66 L 12 **Carmona**, Spain
60 G 10 **Carn Eighe**, U.K. ▲
134 G 10 **Carnamah**, WA, Australia
132 L 13 **Carnarvon**, Republic of South Africa
134 E 8 **Carnarvon**, WA, Australia
144 K 11 **Carney Island**, Antarctica 🏝
63 P 1 **Carnforth**, U.K.
130 H 4 **Carnot**, Central African Republic
60 I 12 **Carnoustie**, U.K.
61 F 20 **Carnsore Point**, Republic of Ireland ►
19 Y 13 **Carol City**, FL, U.S.A.
54 K 12 **Carolina**, Brazil
140 L 15 **Caroline Islands**, Federated States of Micronesia 🏝
77 J 21 **Caronia**, Italy
79 J 18 **Carpathian Mountains**, Europe ⛰
65 T 13 **Carpentras**, France
76 F 8 **Carpi**, Italy
33 I 24 **Carpinteria**, CA, U.S.A.
19 S 8 **Carrabelle**, FL, U.S.A.
76 D 9 **Carrara**, Italy
67 P 7 **Carrascosa del Campo**, Spain
61 A 20 **Carrauntuohil**, Republic of Ireland ▲
49 Y 12 **Carriacou**, Grenada 🏝
45 N 6 **Carrillo**, Mexico
22 L 4 **Carrington**, ND, U.S.A.
56 F 8 **Carrizal Bajo**, Chile
26 M 12 **Carrizo Springs**, TX, U.S.A.
31 R 12 **Carrizozo**, NM, U.S.A.
23 R 12 **Carroll**, IA, U.S.A.
19 S 3 **Carrollton**, GA, U.S.A.
94 L 8 **Carșamba**, Turkey
76 I 13 **Carsoli**, Italy
33 I 18 **Carson City**, NV, U.S.A.
50 H 2 **Cartagena**, Colombia
67 S 12 **Cartagena**, Spain
47 Q 12 **Cartago**, Costa Rica
50 H 6 **Cartago**, Colombia
16 G 8 **Carthage**, TN, U.S.A.
18 M 4 **Carthage**, MS, U.S.A.
27 T 6 **Carthage**, TX, U.S.A.
47 X 13 **Carti Suitupo**, Panama
40 H 10 **Cartwright**, MB, Canada
41 W 8 **Cartwright**, NL, Canada
54 O 13 **Caruarú**, Brazil
51 Q 2 **Carúpano**, Venezuela
121 D 17 **Caruray**, Philippines
54 K 10 **Carutapera**, Brazil
33 K 18 **Carvers**, NV, U.S.A.
58 K 6 **Casa Branca**, Brazil
30 J 13 **Casa Grande**, AZ, U.S.A.
124 H 7 **Casablanca**, Morocco
77 K 14 **Casacalenda**, Italy
76 B 7 **Casale**, Italy
50 K 6 **Casanare**, Colombia ▣
47 N 10 **Casares**, Nicaragua
44 L 3 **Casas Grandes**, Mexico
67 R 9 **Casas Ibáñez**, Spain
58 H 11 **Casca**, Brazil
28 K 9 **Cascade**, ID, U.S.A.
137 C 21 **Cascade Point**, New Zealand ►
32 G 13 **Cascade Range**, Canada/U.S.A. ⛰
28 K 9 **Cascade Reservoir**, ID, U.S.A. ∽
54 N 11 **Cascavel**, Brazil
58 G 8 **Cascavel**, Brazil
15 P 7 **Casco Bay**, ME, U.S.A. ≈
77 J 15 **Caserta**, Italy
20 L 13 **Caseville**, MI, U.S.A.
21 G 20 **Casey**, IL, U.S.A.
145 Y 11 **Casey**, Antarctica ⁙
120 I 9 **Casiguran**, Philippines
120 H 9 **Casiguran Sound**, Philippines ≈
59 B 15 **Casilda**, Argentina
135 W 9 **Casino**, NSW, Australia
53 B 15 **Casma**, Peru
67 T 5 **Caspe**, Spain
29 W 12 **Casper**, WY, U.S.A.
102 G 6 **Caspian Depression**, Kazakhstan/Russian Federation ◇
93 S 14 **Caspian Sea**, Asia/Europe 🌊
20 M 13 **Cass City**, MI, U.S.A.
133 Q 5 **Cassacatiza**, Mozambique
132 J 4 **Cassamba**, Angola
39 D 15 **Cassiar**, BC, Canada
39 C 14 **Cassiar Mountains**, YT, Canada ⛰
55 I 17 **Cassilândia**, Brazil
132 H 5 **Cassinga**, Angola
77 I 15 **Cassino**, Italy
132 H 4 **Cassongue**, Angola
108 M 2 **Cast Uul**, Mongolia ▲
76 D 11 **Castagneto Carducci**, Italy
54 F 12 **Castanha**, Brazil
54 K 10 **Castanhal**, Brazil
56 G 10 **Castaño**, Argentina
74 I 10 **Castasegna**, Switzerland
76 C 8 **Casteggio**, Italy
66 J 7 **Castel Branco**, Portugal ▣
77 J 14 **Castél di Sangro**, Italy
65 V 13 **Castellane**, France
56 L 7 **Castelli**, Argentina
59 D 17 **Castelli**, Argentina
67 U 7 **Castelló de la Plana**, Spain
65 P 14 **Castelnaudary**, France
76 E 9 **Castelnovo ne' Monti**, Italy
66 I 7 **Castelo Branco**, Portugal
77 B 16 **Castelsardo**, Italy
77 I 22 **Casteltermini**, Italy
77 H 22 **Castelvetrano**, Italy
135 Q 13 **Casterton**, VIC, Australia
76 E 12 **Castiglione della Pescaia**, Italy
56 F 8 **Castilla**, Chile
67 Q 8 **Castilla-La Mancha**, Spain ▣
66 K 4 **Castilla Y Leõn**, Spain ▣
59 G 15 **Castillos**, Uruguay
63 P 12 **Castle Cary**, U.K.
30 L 5 **Castle Dale**, UT, U.S.A.
30 H 13 **Castle Dome Peak**, AZ, U.S.A. ▲
63 S 6 **Castle Donnington**, U.K.
61 H 15 **Castle Douglas**, U.K.
28 M 10 **Castle Peak**, ID, U.S.A. ▲
31 R 4 **Castle Rock**, CO, U.S.A.
61 B 17 **Castlebar**, Republic of Ireland
63 T 2 **Castleford**, U.K.
39 I 21 **Castlegar**, BC, Canada
65 Q 14 **Castres**, France
49 Z 11 **Castries**, St Lucia ▟
57 F 18 **Castro**, Chile
58 I 8 **Castro**, Brazil
66 I 5 **Castro Daire**, Portugal
66 H 11 **Castro Verde**, Portugal
66 J 1 **Castropol**, Spain
77 M 18 **Castrovillari**, Italy
66 L 9 **Castuera**, Spain
137 A 23 **Caswell Sound**, New Zealand ≈
95 Q 9 **Cat**, Turkey
48 L 3 **Cat Island**, The Bahamas 🏝
40 K 10 **Cat Lake**, ON, Canada ∽
47 N 5 **Catacamas**, Honduras
18 J 6 **Catahoula Lake**, LA, U.S.A. ∽
95 S 12 **Çatak**, Turkey
55 J 17 **Catalão**, Brazil
82 O 12 **Çatalca**, Turkey
67 W 4 **Cataluña**, Spain ▣
94 J 6 **Catalzeytin**, Turkey
56 I 8 **Catamarca**, Argentina
56 H 7 **Catamarca**, Argentina ▣
57 G 16 **Catán Lil**, Argentina
133 Q 7 **Catandica**, Mozambique
120 L 12 **Catanduanes**, Philippines 🏝
77 K 22 **Catania**, Italy
77 M 20 **Catanzaro**, Italy
27 N 12 **Catarina**, TX, U.S.A.
121 L 14 **Catarman**, Philippines
133 Q 6 **Cataxa**, Mozambique
121 L 15 **Catbalogan**, Philippines
121 N 21 **Cateel**, Philippines
128 E 10 **Catió**, Guinea-Bissau
137 D 25 **Catlins**, New Zealand ⛰
45 Q 8 **Catorce**, Mexico
57 H 15 **Catriel**, Argentina
56 J 13 **Catriló**, Argentina
14 K 10 **Catskill**, NY, U.S.A.
14 I 10 **Catskill Mountains**, NY, U.S.A. ⛰
120 H 8 **Cauayan**, Philippines
121 I 18 **Cauayan**, Philippines
50 G 8 **Cauca**, Colombia ▣
50 I 4 **Cauca**, Colombia 〰
50 H 4 **Caucasia**, Colombia
92 L 13 **Caucasus**, Russian Federation ⛰
95 Q 5 **Caucasus**, Georgia ⛰
56 H 10 **Caucete**, Argentina
121 N 19 **Cauit Point**, Philippines ►
132 I 2 **Caungula**, Angola
56 F 13 **Cauquenes**, Chile
51 Q 6 **Caura**, Venezuela 〰
43 R 6 **Causapscal**, QC, Canada
23 N 2 **Cavalier**, ND, U.S.A.
136 J 5 **Cavalli Islands**, New Zealand 🏝
128 I 13 **Cavally**, Liberia 〰
61 D 16 **Cavan**, Republic of Ireland
94 E 13 **Cavdir**, Turkey
137 F 21 **Cave**, New Zealand
16 K 5 **Cave Run Lake**, KY, U.S.A. ∽
121 G 19 **Cavili**, Philippines 🏝
120 G 11 **Cavite**, Philippines
54 L 11 **Caxias**, Brazil
58 H 11 **Caxias do Sul**, Brazil
132 G 2 **Caxito**, Angola
94 F 11 **Cay**, Turkey
48 I 3 **Cay Sal**, The Bahamas 🏝
52 C 8 **Cayambe**, Ecuador ▲
95 P 8 **Cayeli**, Turkey
51 Z 6 **Cayenne**, French Guiana ▟
94 G 9 **Cayirhan**, Turkey
48 I 7 **Cayman Brac**, Cayman Islands 🏝
48 I 7 **Cayman Islands**, U.K. ▣
48 H 8 **Cayman Trench**, Cayman Islands ≈
127 M 20 **Caynabo**, Somalia
48 G 5 **Cayo del Rosario**, Cuba 🏝
48 H 5 **Cayo Largo**, Cuba 🏝
48 K 4 **Cayo Romano**, Cuba 🏝
48 K 5 **Cayo Sabinal**, Cuba 🏝
47 S 6 **Cayos Miskitos**, Nicaragua 🏝
86 L 12 **Căzănești**, Romania
65 O 14 **Cazères**, France
132 L 4 **Cazombo**, Angola
133 R 5 **Cazula**, Mozambique
54 N 12 **Ceará**, Brazil ▣
45 N 6 **Ceballos**, Mexico
67 P 4 **Cebollera**, Spain ▲
121 K 18 **Cebu**, Philippines
121 K 17 **Cebu**, Philippines 🏝
79 I 24 **Cece**, Hungary
23 T 11 **Cedar**, IA, U.S.A. 〰
30 I 7 **Cedar City**, UT, U.S.A.
23 T 11 **Cedar Falls**, IA, U.S.A.
25 X 4 **Cedar Hill**, MO, U.S.A.
17 W 5 **Cedar Island**, VA, U.S.A. 🏝
19 U 9 **Cedar Key**, FL, U.S.A.
40 H 8 **Cedar Lake**, MB, Canada ∽
23 U 12 **Cedar Rapids**, IA, U.S.A.
19 S 2 **Cedartown**, GA, U.S.A.
46 L 8 **Cedeño**, Honduras
135 N 10 **Ceduna**, SA, Australia
78 D 11 **Cedynia**, Poland
66 G 1 **Cée**, Spain
127 O 19 **Ceel Gaal**, Somalia
127 N 19 **Ceerigaabo**, Somalia
77 J 21 **Cefalù**, Italy
79 J 23 **Cegléd**, Hungary
113 O 11 **Ceheng**, China
94 K 9 **Cekerek**, Turkey
45 Q 11 **Celaya**, Mexico
117 P 8 **Celebes Sea**, Asia 🌊
45 X 10 **Celestún**, Mexico
16 H 8 **Celina**, TN, U.S.A.
21 K 18 **Celina**, OH, U.S.A.
80 D 7 **Celje**, Slovenia
72 H 13 **Celle**, Germany
69 D 20 **Celles**, Belgium
95 T 11 **Çelo Daglari**, Turkey ▲
61 D 21 **Celtic Sea**, Republic of Ireland 🌊
16 G 9 **Center Hill Lake**, TN, U.S.A. ∽
19 P 4 **Centerville**, AL, U.S.A.
23 T 14 **Centerville**, IA, U.S.A.
25 X 6 **Centerville**, MO, U.S.A.
27 R 8 **Centerville**, TX, U.S.A.
76 F 8 **Cento**, Italy
105 G 24 **Central**, Sri Lanka ▣
107 P 9 **Central**, Nepal ▣
128 M 14 **Central**, Ghana ▣
131 V 8 **Central**, Kenya ▣
133 N 5 **Central**, Zambia ▣
133 N 9 **Central**, Botswana ▣
133 Q 4 **Central**, Malawi ▣
138 E 7 **Central**, Papua New Guinea ▣
138 L 6 **Central**, Solomon Islands ▣
138 M 8 **Central**, Solomon Islands ▣
130 H 4 **Central African Republic**, Africa □
74 E 9 **Central Alps**, Switzerland ◇
101 T 12 **Central Brāhui Range**, Pakistan ⛰
16 F 6 **Central City**, KY, U.S.A.
84 H 11 **Central Highlands of Vidzemes**, Latvia ⛰
141 Q 5 **Central Line Islands**, Kiribati 🏝
101 Q 13 **Central Makran Range**, Pakistan ⛰
74 D 7 **Central Plateau**, Switzerland ◇
138 A 4 **Central Range**, Papua New Guinea ⛰
89 Q 9 **Central Siberian Plateau**, Russian Federation ◇
33 H 16 **Central Valley**, CA, U.S.A. ◇
57 F 14 **Central Valley**, Chile ◇
21 F 21 **Centralia**, IL, U.S.A.
32 G 8 **Centralia**, WA, U.S.A.
65 P 7 **Centre**, France ▣
129 U 13 **Centre**, Cameroon ▣
137 B 25 **Centre Island**, New Zealand 🏝
113 R 12 **Cenxi**, China
80 I 8 **Čepin**, Croatia
77 I 14 **Ceprano**, Italy
56 K 9 **Ceres**, Argentina
77 L 15 **Cerignola**, Italy
94 I 9 **Cerikli**, Turkey
94 H 8 **Cerkeș**, Turkey
82 N 12 **Cerkezköy**, Turkey
80 B 8 **Cerknica**, Slovenia
95 O 12 **Cermik**, Turkey
87 N 12 **Cerna**, Romania
86 M 13 **Cernavodă**, Romania
45 Q 7 **Cerralvo**, Mexico
81 K 19 **Cërrik**, Albania
45 Q 10 **Cerritos**, Mexico
56 G 11 **Cerro Amarillo**, Argentina ▲
57 F 21 **Cerro Arenales**, Chile ▲
53 A 19 **Cerro Azol**, Ecuador ▲
45 S 10 **Cerro Azul**, Mexico
58 J 8 **Cerro Azul**, Brazil
53 J 23 **Cerro Bonete**, Bolivia ▲
56 G 8 **Cerro Bonete**, Argentina ▲
59 F 15 **Cerro Catedral**, Uruguay ▲
57 F 23 **Cerro Cervantes**, Argentina ▲
56 J 11 **Cerro Champaqui**, Argentina ▲
47 R 13 **Cerro Chirripó Grande**, Costa Rica ▲
57 H 20 **Cerro Cojudo Blanco**, Argentina ▲
44 F 2 **Cerro de La Encantada**, Mexico ▲
56 G 10 **Cerro de Olivares**, Chile ▲
53 D 15 **Cerro de Pasco**, Peru
56 G 8 **Cerro de Petro**, Chile ▲
49 U 8 **Cerro de Punta**, Puerto Rico ▲
56 H 6 **Cerro del Rincón**, Argentina ▲
45 R 9 **Cerro del Tigre**, Mexico ▲
51 P 7 **Cerro Duida**, Venezuela ▲
50 I 7 **Cerro El Nevado**, Colombia ▲
44 H 6 **Cerro Encantado**, Mexico ▲
57 F 22 **Cerro Fitz Roy**, Argentina ▲
56 H 7 **Cerro Galán**, Argentina ▲
51 Q 6 **Cerro Guaiquinima**, Venezuela ▲
57 F 20 **Cerro Hudson**, Chile ▲
44 L 8 **Cerro Huehueto**, Mexico ▲
58 F 13 **Cerro Largo**, Uruguay ▣
46 K 6 **Cerro Las Minas**, Honduras ▲
56 F 9 **Cerro Las Tórtolas**, Chile ▲
57 F 22 **Cerro Lautaron**, Chile ▲
51 O 7 **Cerro Marahuaca**, Venezuela ▲
57 F 21 **Cerro Mellizo Sur**, Chile ▲
53 I 22 **Cerro Milliri**, Bolivia/Chile ▲
57 F 22 **Cerro Murallón**, Chile ▲
56 H 13 **Cerro Nevado**, Argentina ▲
51 O 7 **Cerro Ovana**, Venezuela ▲
57 F 23 **Cerro Paine**, Chile ▲
51 O 6 **Cerro Paraque**, Venezuela ▲
57 H 14 **Cerro Payún**, Argentina ▲
45 R 8 **Cerro Peña Nevada**, Mexico ▲
56 H 6 **Cerro Pular**, Chile ▲
47 S 13 **Cerro Punta**, Panama
57 F 21 **Cerro San Lorenzo**, Argentina ▲
55 G 20 **Cerro San Rafael**, Paraguay ▲
57 F 20 **Cerro San Valentín**, Chile ▲
47 O 7 **Cerro Saslaya**, Nicaragua ▲
44 J 5 **Cerro Seberi**, Mexico ▲
45 U 12 **Cerro Sta Martha**, Mexico ▲
45 O 12 **Cerro Tancitaro**, Mexico ▲
59 B 19 **Cerro Tres Picos**, Argentina ▲
56 G 12 **Cerro Tupungato**, Argentina ▲
44 H 3 **Cerro Viejo**, Mexico ▲
53 C 15 **Cerro Yerupaja**, Peru ▲
76 F 11 **Certaldo**, Italy
67 V 4 **Cervera**, Spain
76 H 9 **Cervia**, Italy
66 J 1 **Cervo**, Spain
50 J 3 **Cesar**, Colombia ▣
76 G 9 **Cesena**, Italy
84 G 10 **Cēsis**, Latvia
79 D 16 **Česká Lípa**, Czech Republic
79 F 17 **Česká Třebová**, Czech Republic
79 C 19 **České Budějovice**, Czech Republic
79 C 20 **Český Krumlov**, Czech Republic
80 F 8 **Česma**, Croatia 〰
94 A 11 **Ceșme**, Turkey
135 V 11 **Cessnock**, NSW, Australia
84 H 11 **Cesvaine**, Latvia
66 L 14 **Ceuta**, Spain
74 G 10 **Cevio**, Switzerland
94 K 13 **Ceyhan**, Turkey
95 P 13 **Ceylanpinar**, Turkey
101 O 14 **Chābahār**, Iran
52 C 12 **Chachapoyas**, Peru
85 N 19 **Chachersk**, Belarus
56 K 7 **Chaco**, Argentina ▣
129 W 8 **Chad**, Africa □
17 R 12 **Chadbourn**, NC, U.S.A.
57 I 14 **Chadileo**, Argentina 〰
22 H 11 **Chadron**, NE, U.S.A.
111 K 18 **Chaeryŏng**, North Korea
101 P 11 **Chagai Hills**, Pakistan ⛰
103 W 4 **Chagan**, Kazakhstan
101 R 7 **Chaghcharān**, Afghanistan
100 I 8 **Chahār Mahall Va Bakhtīārī**, Iran ▣
105 J 15 **Chaibasa**, India
115 H 18 **Chainat**, Thailand
57 F 18 **Chaitén**, Chile
115 I 17 **Chaiyaphum**, Thailand
58 D 13 **Chajarí**, Argentina
105 J 15 **Chakradharpur**, India
106 J 6 **Chakrata**, India
53 E 19 **Chala**, Peru
131 R 12 **Chala**, Tanzania
65 N 11 **Chalais**, France
46 J 6 **Chalatenango**, El Salvador
133 T 6 **Chaláua**, Mozambique
131 V 6 **Chalbi Desert**, Kenya ◇
63 T 14 **Chale**, U.K.
43 S 7 **Chaleur Bay**, NB, Canada ≈
113 T 9 **Chaling**, China
83 N 24 **Chalki**, Greece 🏝
83 G 19 **Chalkida**, Greece
103 X 9 **Chalkudysu**, Kazakhstan
64 K 8 **Challans**, France
53 J 21 **Challapata**, Bolivia
28 M 9 **Challis**, ID, U.S.A.
65 T 8 **Chalon-sur-Saône**, France
65 S 4 **Châlons-en-Champagne**, France
100 I 5 **Chālūs**, Iran
73 L 21 **Cham**, Germany
133 Q 3 **Chama**, Zambia
101 S 10 **Chaman**, Pakistan
106 I 5 **Chamba**, India
131 V 15 **Chamba**, Tanzania
22 L 10 **Chamberlain**, SD, U.S.A.
15 Q 2 **Chamberlain Lake**, ME, U.S.A. ∽
30 M 10 **Chambers**, AZ, U.S.A.
14 E 14 **Chambersburg**, PA, U.S.A.
65 V 10 **Chambéry**, France
133 P 3 **Chambeshi**, Zambia
97 U 3 **Chamchamāl**, Iraq
47 W 14 **Chame**, Panama
46 J 5 **Chamelec**, Honduras 〰
56 I 10 **Chamical**, Argentina
106 L 7 **Chamoli**, India
65 W 9 **Chamonix-Mont-Blanc**, France
105 H 15 **Champa**, India
65 T 4 **Champagne-Ardenne**, France ▣
21 G 18 **Champaign**, IL, U.S.A.
115 L 18 **Champasak**, Laos
14 K 5 **Champlain**, NY, U.S.A.
45 X 12 **Champotón**, Mexico
105 D 22 **Chamrajnagar**, India
93 P 2 **Chamzinka**, Russian Federation
56 F 7 **Chañaral**, Chile
101 O 5 **Chanārān**, Iran
56 F 13 **Chanco**, Chile
106 K 8 **Chandausi**, India
105 J 16 **Chandbali**, India
19 N 8 **Chandeleur Islands**, MS, U.S.A. 🏝
19 N 8 **Chandeleur Sound**, MS, U.S.A. ≈
104 E 13 **Chanderi**, India
106 J 6 **Chandigarh**, India
30 J 13 **Chandler**, AZ, U.S.A.
43 T 6 **Chandler**, QC, Canada
107 U 13 **Chandpur**, Bangladesh
105 F 17 **Chandrapur**, India
133 Q 6 **Changara**, Mozambique
111 K 15 **Changbai Shan**, China ⛰
110 J 13 **Changchun**, China
113 S 8 **Changde**, China
113 Z 11 **Changhua**, Taiwan
111 L 22 **Changhŭng**, South Korea
118 C 14 **Changi**, Singapore
108 K 4 **Changji**, China
113 Q 15 **Changjiang**, China
111 F 17 **Changli**, China
110 I 12 **Changling**, China
113 T 8 **Changsha**, China
113 X 8 **Changshan**, China
111 I 17 **Changshan Qundao**, China 🏝
113 Y 5 **Changshu**, China
111 J 16 **Changsong**, North Korea
113 W 10 **Changting**, China
111 J 14 **Changtu**, China
47 S 13 **Changuinola**, Panama
111 N 21 **Ch'angwŏn**, South Korea
113 Y 6 **Changxing**, China
111 H 17 **Changxing Dao**, China 🏝
113 S 6 **Changyang**, China
111 J 18 **Changyŏn**, North Korea
113 U 3 **Changyuan**, China
113 T 2 **Changzhi**, China
113 Y 5 **Changzhou**, China
83 H 26 **Chania**, Greece
33 I 24 **Channel Islands**, CA, U.S.A. 🏝
61 J 26 **Channel Islands**, U.K. 🏝
41 X 11 **Channel-Port-aux-Basques**, NL, Canada
63 Z 12 **Channel Tunnel**, France/United Kingdom ◇
26 J 2 **Channing**, TX, U.S.A.
89 Z 6 **Chantal'skiy**, Russian Federation ▲
115 I 20 **Chanthaburi**, Thailand
64 L 8 **Chantonnay**, France
105 N 24 **Chanumla**, India
25 Q 6 **Chanute**, KS, U.S.A.
53 B 14 **Chao**, Peru
113 W 5 **Chao Hu**, China ∽
115 G 17 **Chao Phraya**, Thailand 〰
113 W 5 **Chaohu**, China
110 H 8 **Chaor**, China
124 I 6 **Chaouèn**, Morocco
111 G 15 **Chaoyang**, China
113 W 12 **Chaoyang**, China
113 W 12 **Chaozhou**, China
50 H 7 **Chaparral**, Colombia
102 I 4 **Chapayevo**, Kazakhstan
93 S 4 **Chapayevsk**, Russian Federation
103 T 3 **Chapayevskoye**, Kazakhstan
58 G 10 **Chapecó**, Brazil
63 R 4 **Chapel-en-le-Frith**, U.K.
42 B 7 **Chapleau**, ON, Canada
39 M 19 **Chaplin**, SK, Canada
92 M 4 **Chaplygin**, Russian Federation
87 T 10 **Chaplynka**, Ukraine
16 M 5 **Chapmanville**, WV, U.S.A.
53 L 22 **Charagua**, Bolivia
53 H 20 **Charana**, Bolivia
56 K 8 **Charata**, Argentina
45 P 9 **Charcas**, Mexico
144 I 6 **Charcot Island**, Antarctica 🏝
63 P 13 **Chard**, U.K.
103 O 13 **Chardzhev**, Turkmenistan
129 W 10 **Chari-Baguirmi**, Chad ▣
101 U 7 **Chārīkār**, Afghanistan
23 T 14 **Chariton**, IA, U.S.A.
51 U 5 **Charity**, Guyana
20 L 12 **Charity Island**, MI, U.S.A. 🏝
106 I 8 **Charkhi Dadri**, India
69 G 21 **Charleroi**, Belgium
23 T 11 **Charles City**, IA, U.S.A.
21 E 15 **Charles Mound**, IL, U.S.A. ▲
43 N 8 **Charlesbourg**, QC, Canada
17 Q 15 **Charleston**, SC, U.S.A.
17 N 4 **Charleston**, WV, U.S.A.
137 F 17 **Charleston**, New Zealand
33 M 21 **Charleston Peak**, NV, U.S.A. ▲
135 T 8 **Charleville**, QLD, Australia
65 S 3 **Charleville-Mézières**, France
20 J 10 **Charlevoix**, MI, U.S.A.
17 O 10 **Charlotte**, NC, U.S.A.
21 K 14 **Charlotte**, MI, U.S.A.
49 V 8 **Charlotte Amalie**, Virgin Islands, U.S.A. ▟
19 W 12 **Charlotte Harbor**, FL, U.S.A. ≈
17 S 5 **Charlottesville**, VA, U.S.A.
43 V 8 **Charlottetown**, PE, Canada
49 Z 13 **Charlotteville**, Trinidad and Tobago
135 R 12 **Charlton**, VIC, Australia
37 T 11 **Charlton Island**, NU, Canada 🏝
65 V 5 **Charmes**, France
63 P 13 **Charmouth**, U.K.
101 W 7 **Charsadda**, Pakistan
103 P 14 **Charshanga**, Turkmenistan
135 T 5 **Charters Towers**, QLD, Australia
65 P 5 **Chartres**, France
103 X 9 **Charyn**, Kazakhstan
59 D 16 **Chascomús**, Argentina
85 K 15 **Chashniki**, Belarus
23 S 8 **Chaska**, MN, U.S.A.
111 K 15 **Chasŏng**, North Korea
91 P 9 **Chasovo**, Russian Federation
35 S 6 **Chatanika**, AK, U.S.A.
65 S 7 **Château-Chinon**, France
65 N 6 **Château-du-Loir**, France
65 R 4 **Château-Thierry**, France
64 L 6 **Châteaubriant**, France
65 O 6 **Châteaudun**, France
42 L 11 **Châteauguay**, QC, Canada
64 H 5 **Châteaulin**, France
65 P 8 **Châteauroux**, France
65 N 8 **Châtellerault**, France
42 B 14 **Chatham**, ON, Canada
43 T 8 **Chatham**, NB, Canada
63 X 11 **Chatham**, U.K.
35 X 11 **Chatham Strait**, AK, U.S.A. ≈
65 O 8 **Châtillon-sur-Indre**, France
65 T 6 **Châtillon-sur-Seine**, France
107 P 12 **Chatra**, India
16 H 10 **Chattanooga**, TN, U.S.A.
19 S 7 **Chattaoochee**, FL, U.S.A.
63 W 7 **Chatteris**, U.K.
115 I 17 **Chatturat**, Thailand
103 V 11 **Chatyr-Tash**, Kyrgyzstan
115 L 22 **Châu Đôc**, Vietnam
114 C 12 **Chauk**, Myanmar
106 L 9 **Chauka**, India 〰
65 T 5 **Chaumont**, France
105 G 23 **Chavakachcheri**, Sri Lanka
90 J 5 **Chavan'ga**, Russian Federation
54 J 9 **Chaves**, Brazil
66 J 4 **Chaves**, Portugal
132 L 4 **Chavuma**, Zambia
85 N 17 **Chavusy**, Belarus
91 S 14 **Chaykovskiy**, Russian Federation
56 J 11 **Chazón**, Argentina
19 Q 3 **Cheaha Mountain**, AL, U.S.A. ▲
79 A 17 **Cheb**, Czech Republic
125 R 6 **Chebba**, Tunisia
93 R 1 **Cheboksary**, Russian Federation
20 K 10 **Cheboygan**, MI, U.S.A.
93 P 13 **Chechenskaya Respublika**, Russian Federation ▣
111 M 19 **Chech'ŏn**, South Korea
79 K 16 **Chęciny**, Poland
25 Q 10 **Checotah**, OK, U.S.A.
63 P 11 **Cheddar**, U.K.
115 B 14 **Cheduba Island**, Myanmar 🏝
34 L 9 **Chefornak**, AK, U.S.A.
128 K 3 **Chegga**, Mauritania
32 G 8 **Chehalis**, WA, U.S.A.
111 L 23 **Cheju**, South Korea
111 L 23 **Cheju-do**, South Korea 🏝
90 K 11 **Chekshino**, Russian Federation
102 I 12 **Cheleken**, Turkmenistan
57 I 15 **Chelforó**, Argentina
102 M 7 **Chelkar**, Kazakhstan
79 O 15 **Chełm**, Poland
78 I 10 **Chełmno**, Poland
63 X 10 **Chelmsford**, U.K.
78 I 11 **Chełmża**, Poland
63 Q 9 **Cheltenham**, U.K.

□ Country ▣ Internal administrative region: State/Province/Territory/Dependent territory ▟ Capital city ⛰ Mountain range/Undersea ridge ▲ Mountain peak/Volcano/Seamount ◇ Geographic feature ► Headland/Point/Cape/Peninsula ◢ Desert 🏝 Island/Island group ⁙ Antarctic base 🌀 Ocean 🌊 Sea ≈ Bay/Gulf/Channel/Strait ∽ Lake ◰ Salt pan/Dry/Intermittent lake 〰 River

Cheltenham – Comacchio

137 L 14 **Cheltenham**, New Zealand
67 S 8 **Chelva**, Spain
105 G 18 **Chelvai**, India
88 I 11 **Chelyabinsk**, Russian Federation
89 Q 6 **Chelyuskin**, Russian Federation
124 G 8 **Chemaïa**, Morocco
103 N 15 **Chemenibit**, Turkmenistan
73 L 17 **Chemnitz**, Germany
32 H 12 **Chemult**, OR, U.S.A.
35 S 6 **Chena Hot Springs**, AK, U.S.A.
124 I 11 **Chenachane**, Algeria
127 H 22 **Ch'ench'a**, Ethiopia
24 M 6 **Cheney Reservoir**, KS, U.S.A.
113 U 2 **Cheng'an**, China
111 E 16 **Chengde**, China
113 N 6 **Chengdu**, China
107 Z 8 **Chengele**, India
113 W 12 **Chenghai**, China
113 Q 5 **Chengkou**, China
113 R 15 **Chengmai**, China
105 G 21 **Chennai**, India
21 G 18 **Chenoa**, IL, U.S.A.
113 R 8 **Chenxi**, China
113 T 10 **Chenzhou**, China
82 I 11 **Chepelare**, Bulgaria
52 B 13 **Chepén**, Peru
56 I 10 **Chepes**, Argentina
47 X 13 **Chepo**, Panama
63 P 10 **Chepstow**, U.K.
17 Q 11 **Cheraw**, SC, U.S.A.
64 L 3 **Cherbourg**, France
91 S 10 **Cherdyn'**, Russian Federation
88 M 12 **Cherepanovo**, Russian Federation
90 I 12 **Cherepovets**, Russian Federation
90 M 9 **Cherevkovo**, Russian Federation
125 P 6 **Chéria**, Algeria
105 C 23 **Cheriyam**, India
87 R 5 **Cherkasy**, Ukraine
93 N 13 **Cherkessk**, Russian Federation
88 K 12 **Cherlak**, Russian Federation
91 S 12 **Chermoz**, Russian Federation
91 Q 2 **Chernaya**, Russian Federation
82 F 9 **Cherni Vrŭkh**, Bulgaria
87 Q 2 **Chernihiv**, Ukraine
87 W 8 **Cherninivka**, Ukraine
86 K 7 **Chernivtsi**, Ukraine
87 P 2 **Chernobyl**, Ukraine
89 N 10 **Chernoostrovskoye**, Russian Federation
91 T 14 **Chernushka**, Russian Federation
87 N 3 **Chernyakhiv**, Ukraine
85 C 16 **Chernyakhovsk**, Russian Federation
89 S 13 **Chernyshevsk**, Russian Federation
89 R 10 **Chernyshevskiy**, Russian Federation
93 W 4 **Chernyy Otrog**, Russian Federation
23 Q 11 **Cherokee**, IA, U.S.A.
24 L 8 **Cherokee**, OK, U.S.A.
16 K 8 **Cherokee Lake**, TN, U.S.A.
107 V 11 **Cherrapunji**, India
14 I 14 **Cherry Hill**, NJ, U.S.A.
89 W 7 **Cherskiy**, Russian Federation
86 J 3 **Chervonohrad**, Ukraine
87 Y 5 **Chervonooskil's'ke Vodoskhovyshche**, Ukraine
87 P 9 **Chervonoznam"yanka**, Ukraine
85 K 18 **Chervyen'**, Belarus
85 N 18 **Cherykaw**, Belarus
21 L 14 **Chesaning**, MI, U.S.A.
17 V 7 **Chesapeake**, VA, U.S.A.
17 V 4 **Chesapeake Bay**, MD, U.S.A.
17 V 3 **Chesapeake Beach**, MD, U.S.A.
91 N 4 **Cheshskaya Guba**, Russian Federation
17 O 11 **Chester**, SC, U.S.A.
17 T 6 **Chester**, VA, U.S.A.
21 E 22 **Chester**, IL, U.S.A.
29 Q 2 **Chester**, MT, U.S.A.
33 H 16 **Chester**, CA, U.S.A.
43 U 11 **Chester**, NS, Canada
63 P 4 **Chester**, U.K.
63 S 4 **Chesterfield**, U.K.
40 M 3 **Chesterfield Inlet**, NU, Canada
15 Q 3 **Chesuncook Lake**, ME, U.S.A.
43 X 8 **Chéticamp**, NS, Canada
105 B 22 **Chetlat**, India
45 Z 12 **Chetumal**, Mexico
137 J 15 **Chetwode Islands**, New Zealand
39 G 17 **Chetwynd**, BC, Canada
34 L 9 **Chevak**, AK, U.S.A.
137 I 19 **Cheviot**, New Zealand
127 H 23 **Che'w Bahir**, Ethiopia
32 K 6 **Chewelah**, WA, U.S.A.
24 J 10 **Cheyenne**, OK, U.S.A.
29 Z 14 **Cheyenne**, WY, U.S.A.
29 Y 11 **Cheyenne**, WY/UT, U.S.A.
31 U 5 **Cheyenne Wells**, CO, U.S.A.
107 P 11 **Chhapra**, India
107 V 11 **Chhatak**, Bangladesh
106 L 12 **Chhatarpur**, India
105 I 17 **Chhatrapur**, India
105 F 15 **Chhindwara**, India
107 T 10 **Chhukha**, Bhutan
113 Z 12 **Chiai**, Taiwan
115 I 15 **Chiang Khan**, Thailand
115 G 14 **Chiang Mai**, Thailand
114 H 13 **Chiang Rai**, Thailand
45 X 14 **Chiapas**, Mexico
95 S 6 **Chiat'ura**, Georgia
76 D 5 **Chiavenno**, Italy
123 L 16 **Chiba**, Japan
132 G 6 **Chibemba**, Angola
132 G 6 **Chibia**, Angola
41 R 11 **Chibougamau**, QC, Canada
123 D 17 **Chibu**, Japan
123 D 17 **Chiburi-jima**, Japan
21 H 16 **Chicago**, IL, U.S.A.
35 W 11 **Chichagof Island**, AK, U.S.A.
124 G 8 **Chichaoua**, Morocco
46 G 5 **Chiché**, Guatemala
111 D 16 **Chicheng**, China
63 U 13 **Chichester**, U.K.
51 N 2 **Chichiriviche**, Venezuela
16 I 10 **Chickamauga Lake**, TN, U.S.A.
24 L 11 **Chickasha**, OK, U.S.A.
35 T 7 **Chicken**, AK, U.S.A.
52 B 13 **Chiclayo**, Peru
33 G 17 **Chico**, CA, U.S.A.
57 H 19 **Chico**, Argentina
132 H 5 **Chicomba**, Angola
133 Q 9 **Chicualacuala**, Mozambique
133 R 10 **Chidenguele**, Mozambique
73 L 25 **Chiemsee**, Germany
133 O 2 **Chiengi**, Zambia
115 F 23 **Chieo Lan Reservoir**, Thailand
76 B 8 **Chieri**, Italy
76 J 13 **Chieti**, Italy
111 F 14 **Chifeng**, China
43 T 10 **Chigneco Bay**, NB, Canada
53 I 22 **Chiguana**, Bolivia
133 Q 9 **Chigubo**, Mozambique
44 M 5 **Chihuahua**, Mexico
44 M 5 **Chihuahua**, Mexico
103 Q 9 **Chiili**, Kazakhstan
90 E 13 **Chikhachevo**, Russian Federation
105 C 21 **Chikmagalur**, India
105 C 19 **Chikodi**, India
133 Q 3 **Chikwa**, Zambia
122 J 7 **Chikyū-misaki**, Japan
132 G 4 **Chila**, Angola
101 Y 6 **Chilas**, Pakistan
106 H 2 **Chilas**, India
105 F 24 **Chilaw**, Sri Lanka
135 V 7 **Childers**, QLD, Australia
26 M 3 **Childress**, TX, U.S.A.
57 F 15 **Chile**, South America
57 G 20 **Chile Chico**, Chile
56 H 9 **Chilecito**, Argentina
63 Y 11 **Chilham**, U.K.
103 W 9 **Chilik**, Kazakhstan
133 N 4 **Chililabombwe**, Zambia
135 S 3 **Chillagoe**, QLD, Australia
57 F 14 **Chillán**, Chile
59 C 18 **Chillar**, Argentina
21 F 17 **Chillicothe**, IL, U.S.A.
21 M 19 **Chillicothe**, OH, U.S.A.
25 T 2 **Chillicothe**, MO, U.S.A.
53 H 20 **Chilliculco**, Peru
101 Y 5 **Chillinji**, Pakistan
32 G 13 **Chiloquin**, OR, U.S.A.
45 R 13 **Chilpancingo**, Mexico
63 T 10 **Chiltern Hills**, U.K.
20 G 12 **Chilton**, WI, U.S.A.
133 R 3 **Chilumba**, Malawi
113 Z 10 **Chilung**, Taiwan
131 T 13 **Chimala**, Tanzania
46 G 6 **Chimaltenango**, Guatemala
47 X 14 **Chimán**, Panama
133 Q 8 **Chimanimani**, Zimbabwe
69 F 23 **Chimay**, Belgium
52 B 9 **Chimborazo**, Ecuador
52 B 9 **Chimborazo**, Ecuador
53 B 14 **Chimbote**, Peru
138 C 5 **Chimbu**, Papua New Guinea
101 Y 10 **Chimian**, Pakistan
133 Q 7 **Chimoio**, Mozambique
114 B 11 **Chin**, Myanmar
111 L 22 **Chin-do**, South Korea
45 R 7 **China**, Mexico
111 E 14 **China**, Asia
46 H 4 **Chinajá**, Guatemala
46 M 8 **Chinandega**, Nicaragua
26 G 10 **Chinati Peak**, TX, U.S.A.
103 R 12 **Chinaz**, Uzbekistan
53 D 17 **Chincha Alta**, Peru
39 G 16 **Chinchaga**, AB, Canada
135 V 8 **Chinchilla**, QLD, Australia
133 S 7 **Chinde**, Mozambique
112 H 4 **Chindu**, China
114 C 8 **Chindwin**, Myanmar
102 J 4 **Chingirlau**, Kazakhstan
133 N 4 **Chingola**, Zambia
132 H 4 **Chinguar**, Angola
128 G 5 **Chinguetti**, Mauritania
129 X 11 **Chinguil**, Chad
133 P 6 **Chinhoyi**, Zimbabwe
101 X 9 **Chiniot**, Pakistan
111 M 21 **Chinju**, South Korea
102 J 11 **Chink Kaplankyr**, Uzbekistan
30 M 9 **Chinle**, AZ, U.S.A.
113 X 11 **Chinmen Tao**, Taiwan
105 F 17 **Chinnur**, India
123 I 16 **Chino**, Japan
65 N 7 **Chinon**, France
29 S 2 **Chinook**, MT, U.S.A.
133 Q 3 **Chinsali**, Zambia
105 E 21 **Chintamani**, India
76 G 7 **Chioggia**, Italy
83 K 19 **Chios**, Greece
83 K 19 **Chios**, Greece
133 Q 4 **Chipata**, Zambia
133 O 3 **Chipili**, Zambia
43 S 9 **Chipman**, NB, Canada
132 J 4 **Chipoia**, Angola
63 R 11 **Chippenham**, U.K.
20 D 11 **Chippewa Falls**, WI, U.S.A.
63 S 8 **Chipping Campden**, U.K.
63 S 9 **Chipping Norton**, U.K.
63 W 9 **Chipping Ongar**, U.K.
63 Q 10 **Chipping Sodbury**, U.K.
15 R 3 **Chiputneticook Lakes**, ME, U.S.A.
53 D 15 **Chiquian**, Peru
45 Z 10 **Chiquilá**, Mexico
46 I 5 **Chiquimula**, Guatemala
50 I 6 **Chiquinquira**, Colombia
93 N 8 **Chir**, Russian Federation
105 G 19 **Chirala**, India
133 R 6 **Chiramba**, Mozambique
106 I 8 **Chirawa**, India
103 R 11 **Chirchik**, Uzbekistan
133 P 8 **Chiredzi**, Zimbabwe
129 T 5 **Chirfa**, Niger
111 M 21 **Chiri-san**, South Korea
30 M 15 **Chiricahua Peak**, AZ, U.S.A.
50 J 3 **Chiriguana**, Colombia
35 O 13 **Chirikof Island**, AK, U.S.A.
47 T 14 **Chiriquí Grande**, Panama
105 H 15 **Chirmiri**, India
133 R 6 **Chiromo**, Mozambique
82 J 10 **Chirpan**, Bulgaria
47 Q 11 **Chirripo**, Costa Rica
133 O 6 **Chirundu**, Zambia
100 J 13 **Chirūyeh**, Iran
133 O 5 **Chisamba**, Zambia
41 P 9 **Chisasibi**, QC, Canada
46 H 4 **Chisec**, Guatemala
113 Z 12 **Ch'ishan**, Taiwan
93 V 2 **Chishmy**, Russian Federation
101 X 11 **Chishtian Mandi**, Pakistan
87 O 9 **Chişinău**, Moldova
86 F 9 **Chişineu-Criş**, Romania
93 S 1 **Chistopol'**, Russian Federation
103 Q 3 **Chistopol'ye**, Kazakhstan
89 R 14 **Chita**, Russian Federation
132 G 7 **Chitado**, Angola
133 P 4 **Chitambo**, Zambia
132 K 1 **Chitato**, Angola
35 S 9 **Chitina**, AK, U.S.A.
133 Q 2 **Chitipa**, Malawi
122 K 6 **Chitose**, Japan
105 D 20 **Chitradurga**, India
101 W 6 **Chitral**, Pakistan
47 V 15 **Chitré**, Panama
107 W 14 **Chittagong**, Bangladesh
107 W 14 **Chittagong**, Bangladesh
104 D 13 **Chittaurgarh**, India
105 F 21 **Chittoor**, India
133 O 7 **Chitungwiza**, Zimbabwe
132 K 5 **Chiume**, Angola
76 B 7 **Chivasso**, Italy
133 P 7 **Chivhu**, Zimbabwe
46 G 4 **Chixoy**, Guatemala
90 M 4 **Chizha**, Russian Federation
123 F 18 **Chizu**, Japan
103 R 2 **Chkalovo**, Kazakhstan
90 L 14 **Chkalovsk**, Russian Federation
79 L 16 **Chmielnik**, Poland
111 J 18 **Cho-do**, North Korea
115 L 18 **Chŏâm Khsant**, Cambodia
132 M 7 **Chobe**, Botswana
111 L 20 **Choch'iwŏn**, South Korea
50 G 6 **Chocó**, Colombia
121 K 18 **Chocolate Hills**, Philippines
50 J 6 **Chocontá**, Colombia
78 G 11 **Chodzież**, Poland
57 I 15 **Choele Choel**, Argentina
133 Q 5 **Chofombo**, Mozambique
138 K 5 **Choiseul**, Solomon Islands
57 L 24 **Choiseul Sound**, Falkland Islands
44 K 6 **Choix**, Mexico
78 H 10 **Chojnice**, Poland
122 K 11 **Chōkai-san**, Japan
27 O 12 **Choke Canyon Lake**, TX, U.S.A.
103 U 9 **Chokpar**, Kazakhstan
89 V 7 **Chokurdakh**, Russian Federation
133 Q 10 **Chókwe**, Mozambique
64 M 7 **Cholet**, France
57 G 18 **Cholila**, Argentina
103 V 10 **Cholpon-Ata**, Kyrgyzstan
46 M 8 **Choluteca**, Honduras
115 G 15 **Chom Thong**, Thailand
133 N 6 **Choma**, Zambia
79 B 16 **Chomutov**, Czech Republic
115 H 19 **Chon Buri**, Thailand
115 N 21 **Chon Thanh**, Vietnam
111 L 19 **Ch'ŏnan**, South Korea
52 A 9 **Chone**, Ecuador
111 N 14 **Ch'ŏngjin**, North Korea
111 L 20 **Ch'ŏngju**, South Korea
111 J 17 **Chŏngju**, North Korea
113 Z 5 **Chongming**, China
132 F 5 **Chongoroi**, Angola
111 K 17 **Chŏngp'yŏng**, North Korea
113 O 7 **Chongqing**, China
113 P 7 **Chongqing**, China
113 V 8 **Chongren**, China
111 L 21 **Chŏngŭp**, South Korea
133 O 5 **Chongwe**, Zambia
111 L 21 **Chŏnju**, South Korea
109 T 4 **Chonogol**, Mongolia
86 G 6 **Chop**, Ukraine
63 P 3 **Chorley**, U.K.
86 K 6 **Chortkiv**, Ukraine
105 A 15 **Chorwad**, India
111 L 18 **Ch'ŏrwŏn**, South Korea
78 L 10 **Chorzele**, Poland
57 G 14 **Chos Malal**, Argentina
111 K 16 **Ch'osan**, North Korea
123 L 16 **Chōshi**, Japan
78 E 11 **Choszczno**, Poland
52 B 13 **Chota**, Peru
105 I 14 **Chota Nagpur**, India
29 P 4 **Choteau**, MT, U.S.A.
124 L 6 **Chott ech Chergui**, Algeria
125 N 6 **Chott el Hodna**, Algeria
125 P 7 **Chott el Jerid**, Tunisia
125 O 7 **Chott Melrhir**, Algeria
128 G 5 **Choûm**, Mauritania
25 Q 9 **Chouteau**, OK, U.S.A.
109 S 3 **Choybalsan**, Mongolia
109 R 4 **Choyr**, Mongolia
63 S 13 **Christchurch**, U.K.
137 H 20 **Christchurch**, New Zealand
116 G 15 **Christmas Island**, Australia
141 P 2 **Christmas Island**, Kiribati
35 S 8 **Christochina**, AK, U.S.A.
83 K 21 **Christos**, Greece
79 E 17 **Chrudim**, Czech Republic
82 I 13 **Chrysoupoli**, Greece
79 J 17 **Chrzanów**, Poland
103 R 9 **Chu**, Kazakhstan
103 T 9 **Chu-Iliyskiye Gory**, Kazakhstan
115 O 20 **Chu Yang Sin**, Vietnam
113 Z 6 **Chuansha**, China
113 P 11 **Chuanshan**, China
112 J 7 **Chubalung**, China
57 H 18 **Chubut**, Argentina
57 H 18 **Chubut**, Argentina
89 Z 5 **Chuckchi Sea**, Russian Federation/U.S.A.
47 Z 14 **Chucunaque**, Panama
87 N 4 **Chudniv**, Ukraine
90 F 11 **Chudovo**, Russian Federation
85 I 20 **Chudzin**, Belarus
35 S 9 **Chugach Mountains**, AK, U.S.A.
123 D 19 **Chūgoku-sanchi**, Japan
29 Z 13 **Chugwater**, WY, U.S.A.
87 W 4 **Chuhuyiv**, Ukraine
112 I 7 **Chuka**, China
143 S 4 **Chukchi Abyssal Plain**, Arctic Ocean
143 R 5 **Chukchi Plateau**, Arctic Ocean
34 J 3 **Chukchi Sea**, Russian Federation/U.S.A.
90 L 12 **Chukhloma**, Russian Federation
89 Z 6 **Chukotskiy Poluostrov**, Russian Federation
33 K 26 **Chula Vista**, CA, U.S.A.
89 T 12 **Chul'man**, Russian Federation
62 M 13 **Chulmleigh**, U.K.
88 L 12 **Chulym**, Russian Federation
91 T 3 **Chum**, Russian Federation
115 I 16 **Chum Phae**, Thailand
106 K 4 **Chumatang**, India
127 I 23 **Chumba**, Ethiopia
56 I 9 **Chumbicha**, Argentina
112 I 4 **Chumda**, China
89 V 12 **Chumikan**, Russian Federation
115 G 22 **Chumphon**, Thailand
115 H 17 **Chumsaeng**, Thailand
111 M 18 **Ch'unch'ŏn**, South Korea
103 X 9 **Chundzha**, Kazakhstan
132 M 5 **Chunga**, Zambia
111 M 19 **Ch'ungju**, South Korea
131 W 14 **Chungu**, Tanzania
113 Z 12 **Chungyang Shanmo**, Taiwan
131 S 13 **Chunya**, Tanzania
115 K 21 **Chuŏr Phnum Dâmrei**, Cambodia
115 K 18 **Chuŏr Phnum Dângrek**, Thailand
56 G 4 **Chuquicamata**, Chile
53 K 22 **Chuquisaca**, Bolivia
74 I 8 **Chur**, Switzerland
107 X 12 **Churachandpur**, India
89 U 10 **Churapcha**, Russian Federation
17 U 5 **Church**, VA, U.S.A.
63 P 7 **Church Stretton**, U.K.
37 P 10 **Churchill**, Canada
40 K 6 **Churchill**, MB, Canada
41 U 8 **Churchill Falls**, NL, Canada
106 H 8 **Churu**, India
50 M 2 **Churuguara**, Venezuela
122 L 6 **Chūrui**, Japan
106 K 4 **Chushul**, India
91 T 12 **Chusovoy**, Russian Federation
41 S 11 **Chute-des-Passes**, QC, Canada
87 U 4 **Chutove**, Ukraine
113 Z 11 **Chutung**, Taiwan
141 O 15 **Chuuk**, Federated States of Micronesia
141 O 15 **Chuuk Islands**, Federated States of Micronesia
93 Q 1 **Chuvashskaya Respublika**, Russian Federation
112 K 10 **Chuxiong**, China
103 U 10 **Chuyskaya Oblast'**, Kyrgyzstan
113 W 5 **Chuzhou**, China
103 R 9 **Chyganak**, Kazakhstan
87 S 5 **Chyhyryn**, Ukraine
87 N 10 **Ciadîr-Lunga**, Moldova
116 H 14 **Ciamis**, Indonesia
116 H 14 **Cianjur**, Indonesia
58 G 7 **Cianorte**, Brazil
80 M 12 **Ćićevac**, Serbia and Montenegro
139 Y 11 **Cicia**, Fiji
94 H 7 **Cide**, Turkey
78 K 11 **Ciechanów**, Poland
78 I 11 **Ciechocinek**, Poland
48 J 5 **Ciego de Ávila**, Cuba
50 I 2 **Ciénaga**, Colombia
48 I 5 **Cienfuegos**, Cuba
79 O 16 **Cieszanów**, Poland
79 I 18 **Cieszyn**, Poland
67 R 10 **Cieza**, Spain
94 H 11 **Cihanbeyli**, Turkey
45 N 12 **Cihuatlán**, Mexico
139 Y 10 **Cikobia**, Fiji
116 I 14 **Cilacap**, Indonesia
95 S 8 **Cildir Gölö**, Turkey
113 S 7 **Cili**, China
67 O 2 **Cilleruelo de Bezana**, Spain
95 Z 8 **Ciloy Adasi**, Azerbaijan
87 N 10 **Cimişlia**, Moldova
95 P 12 **Cinar**, Turkey
80 F 12 **Cincar**, Bosnia and Herzegovina
21 K 20 **Cincinnati**, OH, U.S.A.
94 C 12 **Cine**, Turkey
69 I 22 **Ciney**, Belgium
66 H 5 **Cinfães**, Portugal
76 F 12 **Cinigiano**, Italy
45 V 14 **Cintalapa**, Mexico
67 R 3 **Cintruénigo**, Spain
55 N 14 **Cipó**, Brazil
29 X 4 **Circle**, MT, U.S.A.
35 S 6 **Circle**, AK, U.S.A.
21 M 19 **Circleville**, OH, U.S.A.
30 J 6 **Circleville**, UT, U.S.A.
116 H 14 **Cirebon**, Indonesia
63 R 10 **Cirencester**, U.K.
76 A 7 **Cirie**, Italy
77 N 19 **Cirò Marina**, Italy
27 N 6 **Cisco**, TX, U.S.A.
79 N 19 **Cisna**, Poland
77 H 14 **Cisterna di Latina**, Italy
66 M 2 **Cistierna**, Spain
33 G 18 **Citrus Heights**, CA, U.S.A.
132 K 14 **Citrusdal**, Republic of South Africa
76 G 12 **Città della Pieve**, Italy
76 G 11 **Città di Castello**, Italy
76 F 6 **Cittadella**, Italy
86 H 8 **Ciucea**, Romania
45 P 4 **Ciudad Acuña**, Mexico
45 P 13 **Ciudad Altamirano**, Mexico
51 Q 4 **Ciudad Bolívar**, Venezuela
44 M 6 **Ciudad Camargo**, Mexico
44 I 7 **Ciudad Constitución**, Mexico
45 W 14 **Ciudad Cuauhtémoc**, Mexico
56 J 8 **Ciudad de Loreto**, Argentina
45 R 10 **Ciudad de Valles**, Mexico
45 W 12 **Ciudad del Carmen**, Mexico
44 M 5 **Ciudad Delicias**, Mexico
51 R 4 **Ciudad Guayana**, Venezuela
45 O 11 **Ciudad Guzmán**, Mexico
44 L 3 **Ciudad Juárez**, Mexico
45 S 10 **Ciudad Madero**, Mexico
45 R 9 **Ciudad Mante**, Mexico
47 S 14 **Ciudad Neily**, Costa Rica
44 J 6 **Ciudad Obregón**, Mexico
51 Q 5 **Ciudad Piar**, Venezuela
67 N 9 **Ciudad Real**, Spain
66 K 6 **Ciudad Rodrigo**, Spain
45 Q 8 **Ciudad Victoria**, Mexico
67 Z 7 **Ciutadella de Menorca**, Spain
94 L 7 **Civa Burnu**, Turkey
76 G 13 **Civita Castellana**, Italy
76 I 11 **Civitanova Marche**, Italy
76 G 13 **Civitavecchia**, Italy
65 N 9 **Civray**, France
94 E 11 **Civril**, Turkey
113 Z 6 **Cixi**, China
113 U 2 **Cixian**, China
95 R 12 **Cizre**, Turkey
63 Z 9 **Clacton-on-Sea**, U.K.
65 R 7 **Clamecy**, France
19 Q 4 **Clanton**, AL, U.S.A.
132 J 14 **Clanwilliam**, Republic of South Africa
115 F 22 **Clara Island**, Myanmar
20 K 13 **Clare**, MI, U.S.A.
61 A 17 **Clare Island**, Republic of Ireland
14 M 7 **Claremont**, NH, U.S.A.
25 Q 8 **Claremore**, OK, U.S.A.
137 J 18 **Clarence**, New Zealand
137 I 18 **Clarence**, New Zealand
144 H 2 **Clarence Island**, Antarctica
35 Y 12 **Clarence Strait**, AK, U.S.A.
49 N 4 **Clarence Town**, The Bahamas
26 L 3 **Clarendon**, TX, U.S.A.
41 Y 10 **Clarenville**, NL, Canada
14 C 11 **Clarion**, PA, U.S.A.
28 K 3 **Clark Fork**, ID, U.S.A.
16 M 13 **Clark Hill Reservoir**, SC, U.S.A.
19 V 3 **Clark Hill Reservoir**, GA, U.S.A.
135 T 15 **Clarke Island**, TAS, Australia
17 P 3 **Clarksburg**, WV, U.S.A.
18 L 2 **Clarksdale**, MS, U.S.A.
32 K 8 **Clarkston**, WA, U.S.A.
16 E 8 **Clarksville**, TN, U.S.A.
17 S 7 **Clarksville**, VA, U.S.A.
25 T 10 **Clarksville**, AR, U.S.A.
27 S 4 **Clarksville**, TX, U.S.A.
137 E 25 **Clarksville**, New Zealand
26 K 2 **Claude**, TX, U.S.A.
120 G 5 **Claveria**, Philippines
19 V 5 **Claxton**, GA, U.S.A.
63 Y 8 **Claydon**, U.K.
17 W 1 **Claymont**, DE, U.S.A.
18 J 5 **Clayton**, LA, U.S.A.
25 Q 12 **Clayton**, OK, U.S.A.
28 M 9 **Clayton**, ID, U.S.A.
31 T 8 **Clayton**, NM, U.S.A.
39 G 16 **Clear Hills**, AB, Canada
23 S 10 **Clear Lake**, IA, U.S.A.
33 F 18 **Clear Lake**, CA, U.S.A.
33 H 14 **Clear Lake Reservoir**, CA, U.S.A.
14 D 12 **Clearfield**, PA, U.S.A.
19 V 10 **Clearwater**, FL, U.S.A.
28 L 6 **Clearwater**, ID, U.S.A.
39 H 20 **Clearwater**, BC, Canada
28 L 6 **Clearwater Mountains**, ID, U.S.A.
27 P 6 **Cleburne**, TX, U.S.A.
63 W 3 **Cleethorpes**, U.K.
145 V 6 **Clemence Massif**, Antarctica
118 A 14 **Clementi**, Singapore
24 L 8 **Cleo Springs**, OK, U.S.A.
121 D 18 **Cleopatra Needle**, Philippines
65 Q 3 **Clermont**, France
135 U 6 **Clermont**, QLD, Australia
65 R 10 **Clermont-Ferrand**, France
69 L 23 **Clervaux**, Luxembourg
76 F 5 **Cles**, Italy
63 P 11 **Clevedon**, U.K.
16 I 10 **Cleveland**, TN, U.S.A.
18 L 3 **Cleveland**, MS, U.S.A.
19 T 1 **Cleveland**, GA, U.S.A.
21 N 16 **Cleveland**, OH, U.S.A.
27 S 9 **Cleveland**, TX, U.S.A.
21 O 16 **Cleveland Heights**, OH, U.S.A.
58 H 9 **Clevelândia**, Brazil
61 B 17 **Clew Bay**, Republic of Ireland
19 X 12 **Clewiston**, FL, U.S.A.
61 A 17 **Clifden**, Republic of Ireland
137 J 17 **Clifford Bay**, New Zealand
17 Q 5 **Clifton Forge**, VA, U.S.A.
39 M 20 **Climax**, SK, Canada
16 L 7 **Clinchport**, VA, U.S.A.
16 J 9 **Clingmans Dome**, NC, U.S.A.
26 E 7 **Clint**, TX, U.S.A.
14 M 11 **Clinton**, CT, U.S.A.
16 M 11 **Clinton**, SC, U.S.A.
17 S 10 **Clinton**, NC, U.S.A.
18 K 6 **Clinton**, LA, U.S.A.
18 L 5 **Clinton**, MS, U.S.A.
21 K 15 **Clinton**, MI, U.S.A.
23 W 12 **Clinton**, IA, U.S.A.
24 K 10 **Clinton**, OK, U.S.A.
25 S 5 **Clinton**, MO, U.S.A.
25 V 10 **Clinton**, AR, U.S.A.
39 G 20 **Clinton**, BC, Canada
42 C 13 **Clinton**, ON, Canada
17 Q 11 **Clio**, SC, U.S.A.
64 L 7 **Clisson**, France
63 Q 2 **Clitheroe**, U.K.
61 B 21 **Clonakilty**, Republic of Ireland
135 Q 5 **Cloncurry**, QLD, Australia
61 D 20 **Clonmel**, Republic of Ireland
72 D 12 **Cloppenburg**, Germany
23 T 5 **Cloquet**, MN, U.S.A.
56 M 6 **Clorinda**, Argentina
137 J 16 **Cloudy Bay**, New Zealand
42 J 7 **Clova**, QC, Canada
62 L 12 **Clovelly**, U.K.
33 F 18 **Cloverdale**, CA, U.S.A.
31 U 11 **Clovis**, NM, U.S.A.
86 H 9 **Cluj-Napoca**, Romania
63 P 7 **Clun**, U.K.
65 S 9 **Cluny**, France
65 W 9 **Cluses**, France
76 D 6 **Clusone**, Italy
137 D 24 **Clutha**, New Zealand
39 J 18 **Clyde**, AB, Canada
60 H 13 **Clyde**, U.K.
29 R 7 **Clyde Park**, MT, U.S.A.
137 D 25 **Clydevale**, New Zealand
114 K 12 **Co Nôi**, Vietnam
33 L 25 **Coachella**, CA, U.S.A.
45 O 6 **Coahuila**, Mexico
35 S 6 **Coal Creek**, AK, U.S.A.
33 K 19 **Coaldale**, NV, U.S.A.
25 P 12 **Coalgate**, OK, U.S.A.
54 E 11 **Coari**, Brazil
54 D 12 **Coari**, Brazil
131 X 9 **Coast**, Kenya
39 C 16 **Coast Mountains**, BC, Canada
33 E 15 **Coast Ranges**, U.S.A., U.S.A.
46 F 5 **Coatepeque**, Guatemala
41 O 4 **Coats Island**, NU, Canada
145 N 4 **Coats Land**, Antarctica
45 U 13 **Coatzacoalcos**, Mexico
46 H 5 **Cobán**, Guatemala
135 S 10 **Cobar**, NSW, Australia
53 I 16 **Cobija**, Bolivia
14 J 9 **Cobleskill**, NY, U.S.A.
42 G 12 **Cobourg**, ON, Canada
134 M 1 **Cobourg Peninsula**, NT, Australia
133 R 4 **Cóbuè**, Mozambique
73 I 19 **Coburg**, Germany
53 G 20 **Cocachacra**, Peru
55 I 15 **Cocalinho**, Brazil
53 J 20 **Cochabamba**, Bolivia
53 J 19 **Cochabamba**, Bolivia
57 F 17 **Cochamó**, Chile
73 C 19 **Cochem**, Germany
105 D 23 **Cochin**, India
115 M 23 **Cochin**, Vietnam
42 D 5 **Cochrane**, ON, Canada
57 F 21 **Cochrane**, Chile
135 Q 10 **Cockburn**, SA, Australia
49 P 5 **Cockburn Harbour**, Turks and Caicos Islands
42 B 9 **Cockburn Island**, ON, Canada
49 Q 5 **Cockburn Town**, Turks and Caicos Islands
63 P 2 **Cockerham**, U.K.
47 V 13 **Coclé del Norte**, Panama
47 P 6 **Coco**, Nicaragua/Honduras
105 N 20 **Coco Channel**, India
19 X 10 **Cocoa Beach**, FL, U.S.A.
130 D 7 **Cocobeach**, Gabon
30 I 9 **Coconino Plateau**, AZ, U.S.A.
55 L 15 **Cocos**, Brazil
11 T 11 **Cocos Islands**, Australia
45 N 11 **Cocula**, Mexico
41 U 6 **Cod Island**, NL, Canada
54 E 11 **Codajás**, Brazil
137 B 26 **Codfish Island**, New Zealand
54 L 11 **Codó**, Brazil
49 Y 8 **Codrington**, Antigua and Barbuda
29 T 9 **Cody**, WY, U.S.A.
135 S 2 **Coen**, QLD, Australia
73 D 14 **Coesfeld**, Germany
28 K 3 **Coeur**, ID, U.S.A.
28 K 4 **Coeur d'Alene Lake**, ID, U.S.A.
68 N 9 **Coevorden**, Netherlands
133 O 14 **Coffee Bay**, Republic of South Africa
19 N 6 **Coffeeville**, AL, U.S.A.
25 Q 7 **Coffeyville**, KS, U.S.A.
135 O 11 **Coffin Bay**, SA, Australia
135 O 12 **Coffin Bay**, SA, Australia
135 O 11 **Coffin Bay Peninsula**, SA, Australia
135 W 10 **Coffs Harbour**, NSW, Australia
46 K 5 **Cofradiá**, Honduras
87 N 13 **Cogealac**, Romania
63 X 9 **Coggeshall**, U.K.
64 M 10 **Cognac**, France
129 T 15 **Cogo**, Equatorial Guinea
56 M 6 **Cogoi**, Argentina
57 F 20 **Coihaique**, Chile
105 E 22 **Coimbatore**, India
66 H 6 **Coimbra**, Portugal
66 H 7 **Coimbra**, Portugal
51 N 3 **Cojedes**, Venezuela
46 J 7 **Cojutepeque**, El Salvador
29 Q 13 **Cokeville**, WY, U.S.A.
135 R 13 **Colac**, VIC, Australia
137 B 25 **Colac**, New Zealand
55 M 17 **Colatina**, Brazil
24 H 3 **Colby**, KS, U.S.A.
63 Y 9 **Colchester**, U.K.
34 L 13 **Cold Bay**, AK, U.S.A.
33 K 17 **Cold Spring**, NV, U.S.A.
21 K 16 **Coldwater**, MI, U.S.A.
24 K 7 **Coldwater**, KS, U.S.A.
15 N 5 **Colebrook**, NH, U.S.A.
27 N 7 **Coleman**, TX, U.S.A.
61 E 14 **Coleraine**, U.K.
18 I 6 **Colfax**, LA, U.S.A.
32 L 8 **Colfax**, WA, U.S.A.
33 H 18 **Colfax**, CA, U.S.A.
76 D 6 **Colico**, Italy
69 E 15 **Colijnsplaat**, Netherlands
45 N 12 **Colima**, Mexico
45 N 12 **Colima**, Mexico
54 L 12 **Colinas**, Brazil
60 E 11 **Coll**, U.K.
67 O 6 **Collado Villalba**, Spain
76 F 11 **Colle di Val d'Elsa**, Italy
27 R 9 **College Station**, TX, U.S.A.
134 G 11 **Collie**, WA, Australia
134 I 3 **Collier Bay**, WA, Australia
16 A 10 **Collierville**, TN, U.S.A.
42 E 12 **Collingwood**, ON, Canada
137 I 15 **Collingwood**, New Zealand
18 M 6 **Collins**, MS, U.S.A.
38 I 6 **Collinson Peninsula**, NU, Canada
135 U 5 **Collinsville**, QLD, Australia
57 F 15 **Collipulli**, Chile
65 W 5 **Colmar**, France
63 R 2 **Colne**, U.K.
73 C 17 **Cologne**, Germany
50 I 8 **Colombia**, Colombia
58 J 4 **Colômbia**, Brazil
105 F 25 **Colombo**, Sri Lanka
47 Q 12 **Colón**, Costa Rica
47 W 13 **Colón**, Panama
48 I 4 **Colón**, Cuba
59 B 15 **Colón**, Argentina
59 D 14 **Colón**, Argentina
49 N 4 **Colonel Hill**, The Bahamas
44 F 3 **Colonet**, Mexico
59 D 15 **Colonia**, Uruguay
140 K 14 **Colonia**, Federated States of Microne
59 D 15 **Colonia del Sacramento**, Uruguay
56 J 8 **Colonia Dora**, Argentina
57 H 20 **Colonia Las Heras**, Argentina
58 E 13 **Colonia Lavalleja**, Uruguay
60 F 13 **Colonsay**, U.K.
30 M 6 **Colorado**, UT/AZ, U.S.A.
31 P 5 **Colorado**, U.S.A.
44 F 2 **Colorado**, Mexico
57 H 14 **Colorado**, Argentina
26 L 6 **Colorado City**, TX, U.S.A.
30 I 8 **Colorado City**, AZ, U.S.A.
33 L 25 **Colorado Desert**, CA, U.S.A.
30 L 7 **Colorado Plateau**, UT, U.S.A.
31 S 5 **Colorado Springs**, CO, U.S.A.
45 O 10 **Colotlán**, Mexico
19 S 6 **Colquitt**, GA, U.S.A.
63 Z 6 **Coltishall**, U.K.
30 L 4 **Colton**, UT, U.S.A.
16 E 9 **Columbia**, TN, U.S.A.
17 V 9 **Columbia**, NC, U.S.A.
17 O 12 **Columbia**, SC, U.S.A.
18 I 5 **Columbia**, LA, U.S.A.
18 M 6 **Columbia**, MS, U.S.A.
25 V 4 **Columbia**, MO, U.S.A.
32 I 9 **Columbia**, U.S.A., U.S.A.
32 K 8 **Columbia Basin**, WA, U.S.A.
29 N 3 **Columbia Falls**, MT, U.S.A.
39 G 19 **Columbia Mountains**, BC, Canada
28 J 11 **Columbia Plateau**, ID, U.S.A.
16 M 10 **Columbus**, NC, U.S.A.
19 S 4 **Columbus**, GA, U.S.A.
19 N 3 **Columbus**, MS, U.S.A.
20 F 13 **Columbus**, WI, U.S.A.
21 M 18 **Columbus**, OH, U.S.A.
21 J 20 **Columbus**, IN, U.S.A.
23 N 13 **Columbus**, NE, U.S.A.
27 R 10 **Columbus**, TX, U.S.A.
29 S 7 **Columbus**, MT, U.S.A.
31 O 15 **Columbus**, NM, U.S.A.
32 K 6 **Colville**, WA, U.S.A.
35 O 4 **Colville**, AK, U.S.A.
136 L 8 **Colville**, New Zealand
136 K 7 **Colville Channel**, New Zealand
38 D 10 **Colville Lake**, NT, Canada
63 N 4 **Colwyn Bay**, U.K.
76 G 8 **Comacchio**, Italy

Country · Internal administrative region: State/Province/Territory/Dependent territory · Capital city · Mountain range/Undersea ridge · Mountain peak/Volcano/Seamount · Geographic feature · Headland/Point/Cape/Peninsula · Desert · Island/Island group · Antarctic base · Ocean · Sea · Bay/Gulf/Channel/Strait · Lake · Salt pan/Dry/Intermittent lake · R

□ Internal administrative region: State/Province/Territory/Dependent territory   ■ Capital city   ▲▲ Mountain range/ Undersea ridge   ▲ Mountain peak/ Volcano/Seamount   ◇ Geographic feature   ▶ Headland/Point/ Cape/Peninsula   ■ Desert   ▥ Island/Island group   ⬚ Antarctic base   ⊗ Ocean   ▤ Sea   ≈ Bay/Gulf/Channel/Strait   ᔐ Lake   ▨ Salt pan/Dry/ Intermittent lake   ᔐ River

Daudnagar – Drogheda

107 P 12 **Daudnagar**, India
85 F 16 **Daugai**, Lithuania
84 H 13 **Daugavpils**, Latvia
105 C 17 **Daund**, India
115 F 20 **Daung Kyun**, Myanmar
40 H 9 **Dauphin**, MB, Canada
19 O 8 **Dauphin Island**, AL, U.S.A.
129 R 9 **Daura**, Nigeria
95 Y 7 **Däväşşi**, Azerbaijan
105 D 20 **Davangere**, India
121 N 22 **Davao**, Philippines
117 R 7 **Davao Gulf**, Philippines
23 W 13 **Davenport**, IA, U.S.A.
32 K 7 **Davenport**, WA, U.S.A.
63 T 8 **Daventry**, U.K.
47 S 14 **David**, Panama
39 M 19 **Davidson**, SK, Canada
25 N 12 **Davis**, OK, U.S.A.
33 G 18 **Davis**, CA, U.S.A.
145 X 6 **Davis**, Antarctica
30 G 10 **Davis Dam**, AZ, U.S.A.
41 V 7 **Davis Inlet**, NL, Canada
26 H 9 **Davis Mountains**, TX, U.S.A.
145 Y 8 **Davis Sea**, Antarctica
41 T 1 **Davis Strait**, NU, Canada
93 U 2 **Davlekanovo**, Russian Federation
74 J 8 **Davos**, Switzerland
39 K 14 **Davy Lake**, SK, Canada
87 S 8 **Davydiv Brid**, Ukraine
111 H 16 **Dawa**, China
99 Y 10 **Dawḩat Şawqirah**, Oman
85 I 16 **Dawhinava**, Belarus
98 M 9 **Dawqah**, Saudi Arabia
99 W 10 **Dawqah**, Oman
124 D 10 **Dawra**, Western Sahara
19 S 5 **Dawson**, GA, U.S.A.
22 K 5 **Dawson**, ND, U.S.A.
38 A 12 **Dawson**, YT, Canada
39 G 17 **Dawson Creek**, BC, Canada
16 E 6 **Dawson Springs**, KY, U.S.A.
112 K 6 **Dawu**, China
113 U 6 **Dawu**, China
99 Z 8 **Dawwah**, Oman
64 L 13 **Dax**, France
113 P 12 **Daxin**, China
111 D 17 **Daxing**, China
112 L 6 **Daxue Shan**, China
118 A 5 **Dayang Bunting**, Malaysia
109 W 2 **Dayangshu**, China
110 J 7 **Dayangshu**, China
112 K 10 **Dayao**, China
112 M 6 **Dayi**, China
99 Y 6 **Dayl**, Oman
97 N 4 **Dayr az Zawr**, Syria
96 J 2 **Dayr Ḩāfir**, Syria
16 H 10 **Dayton**, TN, U.S.A.
21 L 19 **Dayton**, OH, U.S.A.
27 T 10 **Dayton**, TX, U.S.A.
32 K 9 **Dayton**, WA, U.S.A.
19 X 9 **Daytona Beach**, FL, U.S.A.
113 U 10 **Dayu**, China
32 J 11 **Dayville**, OR, U.S.A.
113 P 6 **Dazhu**, China
132 M 13 **De Aar**, Republic of South Africa
68 H 7 **De Cocksdorp**, Netherlands
19 Q 7 **De Funiak Springs**, FL, U.S.A.
69 B 16 **De Haan**, Belgium
21 G 16 **De Kalb**, IL, U.S.A.
27 T 4 **De Kalb**, TX, U.S.A.
89 W 13 **De-Kastri-Nysh**, Russian Federation
68 H 7 **De Koog**, Netherlands
35 N 4 **De Long Mountains**, AK, U.S.A.
68 O 11 **De Lutte**, Netherlands
69 A 17 **De Panne**, Belgium
20 G 12 **De Pere**, WI, U.S.A.
25 S 13 **De Queen**, AR, U.S.A.
18 H 7 **De Ridder**, LA, U.S.A.
23 S 13 **De Soto**, IA, U.S.A.
20 L 9 **De Tour Village**, MI, U.S.A.
23 W 12 **De Witt**, IA, U.S.A.
25 X 12 **De Witt**, AR, U.S.A.
96 G 10 **Dead Sea**, Israel
48 M 4 **Deadman's Cay**, The Bahamas
63 Z 11 **Deal**, U.K.
21 M 15 **Dearborn**, MI, U.S.A.
39 D 16 **Dease Lake**, BC, Canada
38 I 8 **Dease Strait**, NU, Canada
33 L 21 **Death Valley**, CA, U.S.A.
33 K 21 **Death Valley**, CA, U.S.A.
119 O 10 **Debak**, Malaysia
87 Y 6 **Debal'tseve**, Ukraine
82 B 12 **Debar**, Macedonia (F.Y.R.O.M.)
79 L 17 **Dębica**, Poland
89 X 9 **Debin**, Russian Federation
79 M 14 **Dęblin**, Poland
78 D 11 **Dębno**, Poland
127 I 20 **Debre Birhan**, Ethiopia
127 H 19 **Debre Markos**, Ethiopia
127 I 19 **Debre Werk'**, Ethiopia
79 M 22 **Debrecen**, Hungary
81 K 15 **Dečani**, Serbia and Montenegro
19 P 2 **Decatur**, AL, U.S.A.
19 S 3 **Decatur**, GA, U.S.A.
21 F 19 **Decatur**, IL, U.S.A.
21 K 17 **Decatur**, IN, U.S.A.
23 P 12 **Decatur**, NE, U.S.A.
27 P 5 **Decatur**, TX, U.S.A.
105 E 18 **Deccan Plateau**, India
144 H 3 **Deception Island**, Antarctica
77 C 19 **Decimomannu**, Italy
65 R 8 **Decize**, France
23 U 10 **Decorah**, IA, U.S.A.
68 M 9 **Dedemsvaart**, Netherlands
127 J 20 **Deder**, Ethiopia
58 K 8 **Dedo de Deus**, Brazil
95 V 7 **Dedop'listsqaro**, Georgia
128 L 10 **Dédougou**, Burkina Faso
133 R 5 **Dedza**, Malawi
60 I 11 **Dee**, U.K.
42 H 10 **Deep River**, ON, Canada
43 S 11 **Deer Island**, NB, Canada
15 R 6 **Deer Isle**, ME, U.S.A.
41 X 10 **Deer Lake**, NL, Canada
32 K 6 **Deer Park**, WA, U.S.A.
19 Y 12 **Deerfield Beach**, FL, U.S.A.
127 M 23 **Deeri**, Somalia
35 N 6 **Deering**, AK, U.S.A.
21 K 17 **Defiance**, OH, U.S.A.
112 I 5 **Dêgê**, China
127 L 21 **Degeh Bur**, Ethiopia
43 P 7 **Dégelis**, QC, Canada
129 R 14 **Degema**, Nigeria
73 L 22 **Deggendorf**, Germany
92 M 8 **Degtevo**, Russian Federation
100 J 10 **Deh Bīd**, Iran
101 Q 10 **Deh Shū**, Afghanistan
125 Q 8 **Dehiba**, Tunisia
100 F 7 **Dehlorān**, Iran
106 J 7 **Dehra Dun**, India
107 O 12 **Dehri**, India
113 X 10 **Dehua**, China
110 K 12 **Dehui**, China
127 B 21 **Deim Zubeir**, Sudan
69 D 18 **Deinze**, Belgium
86 I 8 **Dej**, Romania
127 I 19 **Dejen**, Ethiopia
113 P 8 **Dejiang**, China
127 I 17 **Dekemhare**, Eritrea
130 L 10 **Dekese**, Democratic Republic of Congo
130 J 4 **Dékoa**, Central African Republic
26 L 11 **Del Rio**, TX, U.S.A.
33 I 22 **Delano**, CA, U.S.A.
101 Q 9 **Delārām**, Afghanistan
132 M 11 **Delareyville**, Republic of South Africa
14 I 10 **Delaware**, NY, U.S.A.
17 W 3 **Delaware**, U.S.A.
21 M 18 **Delaware**, OH, U.S.A.
17 X 2 **Delaware Bay**, DE, U.S.A.
26 G 7 **Delaware Mountains**, TX, U.S.A.
82 E 11 **Delčevo**, Macedonia (F.Y.R.O.M.)
17 S 12 **Delco**, NC, U.S.A.
74 D 6 **Delémont**, Switzerland
129 X 9 **Délép**, Chad
68 F 13 **Delft**, Netherlands
68 N 6 **Delfzijl**, Netherlands
127 E 14 **Delgo**, Sudan
106 J 8 **Delhi**, India
106 J 8 **Delhi**, India
100 I 7 **Delījān**, Iran
38 E 11 **Déline**, NT, Canada
73 K 15 **Delitzsch**, Germany
125 N 5 **Dellys**, Algeria
72 E 12 **Delmenhorst**, Germany
80 C 9 **Delnice**, Croatia
135 S 15 **Deloraine**, TAS, Australia
83 J 21 **Delos**, Greece
19 Y 12 **Delray Beach**, FL, U.S.A.
30 J 4 **Delta**, UT, U.S.A.
31 O 5 **Delta**, CO, U.S.A.
129 Q 13 **Delta**, Nigeria
51 S 3 **Delta Amacuro**, Venezuela
35 S 7 **Delta Junction**, AK, U.S.A.
19 X 9 **Deltona**, FL, U.S.A.
105 B 16 **Delvada**, India
130 L 11 **Demba**, Democratic Republic of Congo
127 G 20 **Dembī Dolo**, Ethiopia
131 N 5 **Dembia**, Central African Republic
92 H 1 **Demidov**, Russian Federation
31 O 14 **Deming**, NM, U.S.A.
94 D 10 **Demirci**, Turkey
94 C 10 **Demirköprü Baraji**, Turkey
82 N 11 **Demirköy**, Turkey
72 L 9 **Demmin**, Germany
130 M 9 **Democratic Republic Of Congo**, Africa
19 O 4 **Demopolis**, AL, U.S.A.
117 Y 12 **Demta**, Indonesia
90 F 13 **Demyansk**, Russian Federation
68 H 7 **Den Burg**, Netherlands
115 H 15 **Den Chai**, Thailand
68 H 8 **Den Helder**, Netherlands
68 I 8 **Den Oever**, Netherlands
127 J 18 **Denakil Desert**, Ethiopia
35 R 8 **Denali**, AK, U.S.A.
127 L 22 **Denan**, Ethiopia
103 Q 14 **Denau**, Uzbekistan
42 H 11 **Denbigh**, ON, Canada
63 O 4 **Denbigh**, U.K.
116 H 12 **Dendang**, Indonesia
128 J 8 **Dendâra**, Mauritania
69 E 19 **Denderleeuw**, Belgium
69 F 18 **Dendermonde**, Belgium
144 J 8 **Dendtler Island**, Antarctica
68 N 11 **Denekamp**, Netherlands
129 S 9 **Dengas**, Niger
129 Q 10 **Denge**, Nigeria
113 T 3 **Dengfeng**, China
129 S 11 **Dengi**, Nigeria
113 S 5 **Dengzhou**, China
134 E 8 **Denham**, WA, Australia
67 U 9 **Denia**, Spain
141 U 1 **Denig**, Nauru
135 S 12 **Deniliquin**, NSW, Australia
33 J 14 **Denio**, NV, U.S.A.
23 Q 12 **Denison**, IA, U.S.A.
27 Q 4 **Denison**, TX, U.S.A.
94 D 12 **Denizli**, Turkey
17 N 13 **Denmark**, SC, U.S.A.
71 C 25 **Denmark**, Europe
134 G 12 **Denmark**, WA, Australia
143 O 14 **Denmark Strait**, Arctic Ocean
63 Z 8 **Dennington**, U.K.
116 L 15 **Denpasar**, Indonesia
17 V 3 **Denton**, MD, U.S.A.
27 Q 5 **Denton**, TX, U.S.A.
138 G 6 **D'Entrecasteaux Islands**, Papua New Guinea
31 R 4 **Denver**, CO, U.S.A.
104 C 13 **Deogarh**, India
107 R 12 **Deoghar**, India
105 F 16 **Deoli**, India
105 F 14 **Deori**, India
107 P 10 **Deoria**, India
107 N 13 **Deosil**, India
42 H 8 **Depot-Forbes**, QC, Canada
145 W 5 **Depot Peak**, Antarctica
129 Y 6 **Dépression Du Mourdi**, Chad
89 U 8 **Deputatskiy**, Russian Federation
112 J 8 **Dêqên**, China
113 S 12 **Deqing**, China
101 W 11 **Dera Ghazi Khan**, Pakistan
101 V 9 **Dera Ismail Khan**, Pakistan
86 M 5 **Derazhnya**, Ukraine
93 S 15 **Derbent**, Russian Federation
103 Q 14 **Derbent**, Uzbekistan
43 V 10 **Derbert**, NS, Canada
110 H 6 **Derbur**, China
25 N 6 **Derby**, KS, U.S.A.
63 S 5 **Derby**, U.K.
134 I 4 **Derby**, WA, Australia
129 Y 9 **Déréssa**, Chad
87 T 6 **Deriyivka**, Ukraine
87 Z 6 **Derkul**, Ukraine
112 J 8 **Dêrong**, China
133 S 6 **Derre**, Mozambique
15 N 8 **Derry**, NH, U.S.A.
63 X 6 **Dersingham**, U.K.
111 B 14 **Derst**, China
127 H 15 **Derudeb**, Sudan
80 H 10 **Derventa**, Bosnia and Herzegovina
103 P 4 **Derzhavinsk**, Kazakhstan
21 H 16 **Des Plains**, IL, U.S.A.
23 S 13 **Des Moines**, IA, U.S.A.
23 S 12 **Des Moines**, IA/MO, U.S.A.
31 T 8 **Des Moines**, NM, U.S.A.
56 H 11 **Desaguadero**, Argentina
44 E 2 **Descanso**, Mexico
127 I 19 **Desē**, Ethiopia
57 I 21 **Deseado**, Argentina
57 H 20 **Deseado**, Argentina
44 H 3 **Desemboque**, Mexico
30 I 3 **Deseret Peak**, UT, U.S.A.
33 M 25 **Desert Center**, CA, U.S.A.
30 I 2 **Desert Peak**, UT, U.S.A.
30 K 9 **Desert View**, AZ, U.S.A.
56 I 10 **Desiderio Tello**, Argentina
83 D 15 **Deskati**, Greece
87 Q 3 **Desna**, Ukraine
121 M 17 **Desolation Point**, Philippines
80 M 12 **Despotovac**, Serbia and Montenegro
73 K 15 **Dessau**, Germany
69 E 18 **Destelbergen**, Belgium
86 E 11 **Deta**, Romania
133 N 7 **Dete**, Zimbabwe
73 F 14 **Detmold**, Germany
21 M 15 **Detroit**, MI, U.S.A.
43 S 4 **Détroit de Jacques-Cartier**, QC, Canada
43 T 4 **Détroit d'Honguedo**, QC, Canada
23 P 5 **Detroit Lakes**, MN, U.S.A.
69 K 16 **Deurne**, Netherlands
75 Y 5 **Deutschkreutz**, Austria
75 V 8 **Deutschlandsberg**, Austria
86 H 10 **Deva**, Romania
94 K 9 **Deveci Dağlari**, Turkey
94 K 11 **Develi**, Turkey
68 L 11 **Deventer**, Netherlands
104 B 12 **Devikot**, India
137 H 15 **Devil River Peak**, New Zealand
20 D 8 **Devil's Island**, WI, U.S.A.
22 L 3 **Devil's Lake**, ND, U.S.A.
22 L 3 **Devil's Lake**, ND, U.S.A.
29 Y 8 **Devil's Tower**, WY, U.S.A.
82 H 11 **Devin**, Bulgaria
27 O 11 **Devine**, TX, U.S.A.
135 S 15 **Deviot**, TAS, Australia
63 R 11 **Devizes**, U.K.
82 M 8 **Devnya**, Bulgaria
37 P 4 **Devon Island**, NU, Canada
135 S 15 **Devonport**, TAS, Australia
94 G 7 **Devrek**, Turkey
105 E 15 **Dewas**, India
63 S 3 **Dewsbury**, U.K.
113 N 6 **Deyang**, China
100 M 8 **Deyhuk**, Iran
100 I 12 **Deyyer**, Iran
100 G 8 **Dezfūl**, Iran
111 D 19 **Dezhou**, China
99 T 5 **Dhahran**, Saudi Arabia
107 U 12 **Dhaka**, Bangladesh
99 P 13 **Dhamār**, Yemen
105 G 16 **Dhamtari**, India
107 R 13 **Dhanbad**, India
106 M 8 **Dhangadhi**, Nepal
107 R 10 **Dhankuta**, Nepal
105 D 15 **Dhar**, India
107 R 10 **Dharan Bazar**, Nepal
107 W 12 **Dharmanagar**, India
105 C 19 **Dharwad**, India
107 O 8 **Dhaulagiri**, Nepal
107 Y 9 **Dhemaji**, India
96 G 10 **Dhībān**, Jordan
99 O 14 **Dhubāb**, Yemen
107 U 11 **Dhuburi**, India
105 D 16 **Dhule**, India
127 O 20 **Dhuudo**, Somalia
115 O 21 **Di Linh**, Vietnam
83 J 26 **Dia**, Greece
33 G 21 **Diablo Range**, CA, U.S.A.
133 U 3 **Diaca**, Mozambique
128 K 9 **Diafarabé**, Mali
128 G 9 **Dialafara**, Mali
128 F 9 **Dialakoto**, Senegal
59 C 14 **Diamante**, Argentina
135 Q 7 **Diamantina**, QLD, Australia
107 S 14 **Diamond Harbour**, India
31 N 2 **Diamond Peak**, CO, U.S.A.
29 R 14 **Diamondville**, WY, U.S.A.
128 F 8 **Diamounguél**, Senegal
113 S 13 **Dianbai**, China
112 K 10 **Diancang Shan**, China
113 P 6 **Dianjiang**, China
110 M 11 **Diaoling**, China
129 O 10 **Diapaga**, Burkina Faso
132 H 11 **Diaz Point**, Namibia
99 X 5 **Dibā al Ḩişn**, Oman
130 M 11 **Dibaya**, Democratic Republic of Congo
130 K 10 **Dibaya-Lubwe**, Democratic Republic of Congo
127 A 18 **Dibbis**, Sudan
132 L 12 **Dibeng**, Republic of South Africa
107 X 9 **Dibrugarh**, India
96 K 3 **Dibsī**, Syria
26 L 5 **Dickens**, TX, U.S.A.
22 H 5 **Dickinson**, ND, U.S.A.
16 E 8 **Dickson**, TN, U.S.A.
95 P 11 **Dicle Baraji**, Turkey
68 L 13 **Didam**, Netherlands
63 T 10 **Didcot**, U.K.
128 I 9 **Didiéni**, Mali
104 D 12 **Didwana**, India
82 L 12 **Didymoteicho**, Greece
65 U 12 **Die**, France
128 L 10 **Diébougou**, Burkina Faso
73 F 20 **Dieburg**, Germany
128 H 12 **Diéké**, Guinea
69 K 23 **Diekirch**, Luxembourg
69 L 24 **Diekirch**, Luxembourg
128 I 9 **Diéma**, Mali
68 H 11 **Diemen**, Netherlands
114 J 12 **Điên Biên Phu**, Vietnam
115 L 14 **Diên Châu**, Vietnam
84 G 12 **Dienvidsusēja**, Latvia
72 E 13 **Diepholz**, Germany
65 O 2 **Dieppe**, France
68 L 12 **Dieren**, Netherlands
25 S 12 **Dierks**, AR, U.S.A.
69 I 18 **Diest**, Belgium
129 U 9 **Diffa**, Niger
129 U 8 **Diffa**, Niger
131 O 5 **Digba**, Democratic Republic of Congo
43 T 11 **Digby**, NS, Canada
24 I 4 **Dighton**, KS, U.S.A.
65 V 13 **Digne-les-Baines**, France
65 S 9 **Digoin**, France
121 M 23 **Digos**, Philippines
101 V 14 **Digri**, Pakistan
127 K 24 **Diinsoor**, Somalia
65 T 7 **Dijon**, France
70 G 13 **Dikanäs**, Sweden
127 K 19 **Dikhil**, Djibouti
94 B 10 **Dikili**, Turkey
89 S 11 **Dikimdya**, Russian Federation
128 J 12 **Dikodougou**, Côte d'Ivoire
69 B 18 **Diksmuide**, Belgium
89 N 6 **Dikson**, Russian Federation
129 V 10 **Dikwa**, Nigeria
127 I 22 **Dīla**, Ethiopia
117 Q 15 **Dili**, East Timor
131 O 5 **Dili**, Democratic Republic of Congo
95 U 8 **Dilijan**, Armenia
27 N 12 **Dilley**, TX, U.S.A.
73 C 21 **Dilligen**, Germany
127 D 18 **Dilling**, Sudan
73 I 23 **Dillingen**, Germany
35 N 11 **Dillingham**, AK, U.S.A.
17 R 11 **Dillon**, SC, U.S.A.
29 O 8 **Dillon**, MT, U.S.A.
130 L 14 **Dilolo**, Democratic Republic of Congo
69 K 18 **Dilsen**, Belgium
97 T 6 **Diltāwa**, Iraq
107 X 11 **Dimapur**, India
130 M 11 **Dimbelenge**, Democratic Republic of Congo
128 K 13 **Dimbokro**, Côte d'Ivoire
81 O 14 **Dimitrovgrad**, Serbia and Montenegro
82 J 10 **Dimitrovgrad**, Bulgaria
93 S 2 **Dimitrovgrad**, Russian Federation
26 J 3 **Dimmit**, TX, U.S.A.
121 M 18 **Dinagat**, Philippines
121 M 18 **Dinagat**, Philippines
107 T 11 **Dinajpur**, Bangladesh
64 K 5 **Dinan**, France
69 H 22 **Dinant**, Belgium
107 P 11 **Dinapur**, India
94 E 11 **Dinar**, Turkey
80 E 12 **Dinara**, Croatia
80 E 11 **Dinaric Alps**, Bosnia and Herzegovina
127 G 18 **Dinder**, Sudan
105 E 23 **Dindigul**, India
105 G 15 **Dindori**, India
130 I 11 **Dinga**, Democratic Republic of Congo
120 G 10 **Dingalan Bay**, Philippines
113 P 1 **Dingbian**, China
113 Q 1 **Dingbian**, China
132 F 1 **Dinge**, Angola
107 R 10 **Dingla**, Nepal
61 A 20 **Dingle**, Republic of Ireland
61 A 20 **Dingle Bay**, Republic of Ireland
14 I 11 **Dingmans Ferry**, PA, U.S.A.
113 U 11 **Dingnan**, China
73 L 23 **Dingolfing**, Germany
113 V 3 **Dingtao**, China
128 G 10 **Dinguiraye**, Guinea
43 Y 7 **Dingwall**, NS, Canada
113 N 2 **Dingxi**, China
111 D 17 **Dingxing**, China
111 C 18 **Dingzhou**, China
114 N 12 **Dinh Lâp**, Vietnam
107 T 10 **Dinhata**, India
73 H 22 **Dinkelsbühl**, Germany
31 N 3 **Dinosaur**, CO, U.S.A.
69 F 15 **Dinteloord**, Netherlands
68 M 13 **Dinxperlo**, Netherlands
128 J 10 **Dioïla**, Mali
58 G 9 **Dionísio Cerqueira**, Brazil
55 I 20 **Dioníso Cerqueira**, Brazil
128 D 9 **Diouloulou**, Senegal
128 I 8 **Dioumara**, Mali
129 P 10 **Dioundiou**, Niger
128 E 8 **Diourbel**, Senegal
106 M 8 **Dipayal**, Nepal
107 W 11 **Diphu**, India
121 J 20 **Dipolog**, Philippines
69 L 25 **Dippach**, Luxembourg
128 L 8 **Diré**, Mali
127 K 20 **Dirē Dawa**, Ethiopia
47 N 9 **Diriamba**, Nicaragua
132 K 7 **Dirico**, Angola
134 E 8 **Dirk Hartog Island**, WA, Australia
129 U 6 **Dirkou**, Niger
135 U 9 **Dirranbandi**, QLD, Australia
99 N 10 **Ḑirs**, Saudi Arabia
135 Q 13 **Discovery Bay**, SA, Australia
74 H 9 **Disentis**, Switzerland
143 N 11 **Disko**, Greenland
145 W 4 **Dismal Mountains**, Antarctica
107 V 10 **Dispur**, India
43 N 10 **Disraëli**, QC, Canada
63 Y 7 **Diss**, U.K.
17 U 3 **District of Columbia**, U.S.A.
121 G 16 **Dit**, Philippines
105 A 16 **Diu**, India
121 M 19 **Diuata Mountains**, Philippines
121 L 19 **Diuata Point**, Philippines
100 G 5 **Dīvān Derreh**, Iran
130 F 9 **Divénié**, Congo
29 O 7 **Divide**, MT, U.S.A.
120 I 7 **Divilacan Bay**, Philippines
55 K 18 **Divinópolis**, Brazil
47 V 15 **Divisa**, Panama
93 N 11 **Divnoye**, Russian Federation
128 J 13 **Divo**, Côte d'Ivoire
95 N 10 **Divriği**, Turkey
101 T 14 **Diwana**, Pakistan
21 F 16 **Dixon**, IL, U.S.A.
39 B 18 **Dixon Entrance**, BC, Canada
49 N 3 **Dixon's**, The Bahamas
95 S 9 **Diyadin**, Turkey
95 P 12 **Diyarbakir**, Turkey
129 T 5 **Djado**, Niger
125 O 7 **Djamâa**, Algeria
130 H 9 **Djambala**, Congo
130 J 9 **Djampie**, Democratic Republic of Congo
125 Q 12 **Djanet**, Algeria
138 G 3 **Djaul Island**, Papua New Guinea
124 L 7 **Djebel Aïssa**, Algeria
125 P 12 **Djebel Ounane**, Algeria
125 P 13 **Djebel Telerhteba**, Algeria
125 N 12 **Djebr**, Algeria
129 X 10 **Djébrène**, Chad
129 X 9 **Djédaa**, Chad
124 K 11 **Djedid**, Algeria
124 M 6 **Djelfa**, Algeria
131 N 4 **Djéma**, Central African Republic
128 K 9 **Djenné**, Mali
130 L 9 **Djia**, Democratic Republic of Congo
128 M 9 **Djibo**, Burkina Faso
127 K 19 **Djibouti**, Djibouti
127 L 18 **Djibouti**, Africa
128 I 8 **Djiguéni**, Mauritania
130 L 7 **Djolu**, Democratic Republic of Congo
129 O 11 **Djougou**, Benin
129 U 15 **Djoum**, Cameroon
70 D 11 **Djúpivogur**, Iceland
70 I 7 **Djupvik**, Norway
87 U 7 **Dmytrivka**, Ukraine
87 W 6 **Dmytrivka**, Ukraine
87 Q 4 **Dnieper**, Europe
86 K 6 **Dniester**, Moldova/Ukraine
87 U 6 **Dniprodzerzhyns'k**, Ukraine
87 U 6 **Dnipropetrovs'k**, Ukraine
87 Q 9 **Dniprovs'kyy Lyman**, Ukraine
87 P 10 **Dnistrov'ky Lyman**, Ukraine
90 E 12 **Dno**, Russian Federation
85 F 21 **Dnyaprowski Buhski Kanal**, Belarus
115 L 14 **Đô Luong**, Vietnam
114 M 12 **Đo Son**, Vietnam
43 S 8 **Doaktown**, NB, Canada
116 M 13 **Doangdoangan Kecil**, Indonesia
129 W 12 **Doba**, Chad
85 L 19 **Dobasna**, Belarus
84 E 11 **Dobele**, Latvia
73 L 16 **Döbeln**, Germany
75 V 1 **Dobersberg**, Austria
78 E 11 **Dobiegniew**, Poland
117 V 13 **Dobo**, Indonesia
80 H 10 **Doboj**, Bosnia and Herzegovina
78 K 9 **Dobre Miasto**, Poland
82 N 6 **Dobrich**, Bulgaria
82 N 7 **Dobrich**, Bulgaria
92 M 5 **Dobrinka**, Russian Federation
85 D 15 **Dobrovol'sk**, Russian Federation
85 N 20 **Dobrush**, Belarus
87 Q 1 **Dobryanka**, Ukraine
91 T 12 **Dobryanka**, Russian Federation
121 E 24 **Doc Can**, Philippines
134 L 7 **Docker River**, NT, Australia
106 I 4 **Doda**, India
105 D 22 **Dodda Betta**, India
83 L 21 **Dodecanese**, Greece
24 J 6 **Dodge City**, KS, U.S.A.
21 E 14 **Dodgeville**, WI, U.S.A.
62 K 15 **Dodman Point**, U.K.
131 U 11 **Dodoma**, Tanzania
131 U 12 **Dodoma**, Tanzania
29 U 2 **Dodson**, MT, U.S.A.
68 L 13 **Doesburg**, Netherlands
68 L 13 **Doetinchem**, Netherlands
19 S 8 **Dog Island**, FL, U.S.A.
42 B 6 **Dog Lake**, ON, Canada
108 K 8 **Dogai Coring**, China
123 D 17 **Dōgo**, Japan
129 P 9 **Dogondoutchi**, Niger
129 W 11 **Dogoumbo**, Chad
95 O 8 **Doğu Karadeniz Dağlari**, Turkey
95 T 10 **Doğubeyazit**, Turkey
99 U 5 **Doha**, Qatar
107 W 14 **Dohazari**, Bangladesh
115 F 14 **Doi Inthanon**, Thailand
71 D 18 **Dokka**, Norway
68 K 6 **Dokkum**, Netherlands
85 J 15 **Dokshytsy**, Belarus
87 X 7 **Dokuchayevs'k**, Ukraine
57 I 18 **Dolavón**, Argentina
42 M 6 **Dolbeau**, QC, Canada
65 U 7 **Dôle**, France
47 S 14 **Dolega**, Panama
63 N 6 **Dolgellau**, U.K.
89 X 14 **Dolinsk**, Russian Federation
81 N 14 **Doljevac**, Serbia and Montenegro
72 D 11 **Dollart**, Germany
72 J 13 **Dolle**, Germany
144 J 4 **Dolleman Island**, Antarctica
79 J 19 **Dolný Kubín**, Slovakia
127 K 23 **Dolo Odo**, Ethiopia
76 F 5 **Dolomites**, Italy
109 Q 5 **Doloon**, Mongolia
46 J 3 **Dolores**, Guatemala
59 D 15 **Dolores**, Uruguay
59 D 17 **Dolores**, Argentina
38 F 8 **Dolphin and Union Strait**, NU, Canada
132 H 11 **Dolphin Head**, Namibia
86 I 6 **Dolyna**, Ukraine
87 S 7 **Dolyns'ka**, Ukraine
58 F 13 **Dom Pedrito**, Brazil
107 T 11 **Domar**, Bangladesh
79 M 18 **Domaradz**, Poland
79 B 18 **Domažlice**, Czech Republic
71 C 17 **Dombås**, Norway
133 Q 8 **Dombe**, Mozambique
79 H 25 **Dombóvár**, Hungary
39 G 19 **Dome Creek**, BC, Canada
56 F 9 **Domeyko**, Chile
64 M 5 **Domfront**, France
49 Y 10 **Dominica**, North America
47 Q 13 **Dominical**, Costa Rica
49 R 8 **Dominican Republic**, North America
127 M 21 **Domo**, Ethiopia
76 B 5 **Domodossola**, Italy
83 E 17 **Domokos**, Greece
117 N 15 **Dompu**, Indonesia
80 C 7 **Domžale**, Slovenia
44 K 6 **Don**, Mexico
60 I 10 **Don**, U.K.
92 M 9 **Don**, Russian Federation
18 K 8 **Donaldsonville**, LA, U.S.A.
19 S 6 **Donalsonville**, GA, U.S.A.
73 E 25 **Donaueschingen**, Germany
73 I 23 **Donauwörth**, Germany
63 T 3 **Doncaster**, U.K.
132 G 3 **Dondo**, Angola
133 R 7 **Dondo**, Mozambique
121 G 19 **Dondonay**, Philippines
61 D 15 **Donegal**, Republic of Ireland
61 C 15 **Donegal Bay**, Republic of Ireland
87 X 7 **Donets'k**, Ukraine
115 N 16 **Đông Ha**, Vietnam
115 M 15 **Dông Hôi**, Vietnam
129 S 12 **Donga**, Nigeria
113 R 10 **Dong'an**, China
134 F 10 **Dongara**, WA, Australia
112 M 10 **Dongchuan**, China
108 J 9 **Dongco**, China
113 Q 15 **Dongfang**, China
110 O 10 **Dongfanghong**, China
111 K 14 **Dongfeng**, China
117 N 11 **Donggala**, Indonesia
111 J 17 **Donggang**, China
113 U 12 **Dongguan**, China
113 R 14 **Donghai Dao**, China
113 R 9 **Dongkou**, China
113 P 11 **Donglan**, China
110 N 12 **Dongning**, China
112 K 8 **Dongnyi**, China
130 J 6 **Dongo**, Democratic Republic of Congo
132 H 5 **Dongo**, Angola
127 E 14 **Dongola**, Sudan
127 E 23 **Dongotona Mountains**, Sudan
130 J 6 **Dongou**, Congo
113 S 13 **Dongping**, China
113 V 2 **Dongping**, China
113 R 14 **Dongshan**, China
113 W 12 **Dongshan Dao**, China
109 S 7 **Dongsheng**, China
113 Y 4 **Dongtai**, China
113 T 8 **Dongting Hu**, China
113 Y 7 **Dongyang**, China
111 F 19 **Dongying**, China
113 W 7 **Dongzhi**, China
68 L 7 **Donkerbroek**, Netherlands
70 F 11 **Dønna**, Norway
42 M 9 **Donnacona**, QC, Canada
76 B 6 **Donnas**, Italy
39 H 17 **Donnelly**, AB, Canada
75 T 6 **Donnersbach**, Austria
67 Q 1 **Donostia-San Sebastián**, Spain
83 K 22 **Donoussa**, Greece
93 N 12 **Donskoye**, Russian Federation
121 J 14 **Donsol**, Philippines
20 H 11 **Door Peninsula**, WI, U.S.A.
63 Q 13 **Dorchester**, U.K.
132 I 9 **Dordabis**, Namibia
65 N 12 **Dordogne**, France
69 G 14 **Dordrecht**, Netherlands
129 N 9 **Dori**, Burkina Faso
63 V 11 **Dorking**, U.K.
74 J 6 **Dornbirn**, Austria
60 H 9 **Dornoch Firth**, U.K.
109 T 3 **Dornod**, Mongolia
109 R 5 **Dornogovi**, Mongolia
128 M 8 **Doro**, Mali
79 I 22 **Dorog**, Hungary
71 H 14 **Dorotea**, Sweden
134 E 8 **Dorre Island**, WA, Australia
135 V 10 **Dorrigo**, NSW, Australia
129 S 13 **Dorsale Camerounaise**, Cameroon
73 D 15 **Dortmund**, Germany
94 L 13 **Dörtyol**, Turkey
131 P 5 **Doruma**, Democratic Republic of Congo
100 M 7 **Dorūneh**, Iran
66 K 12 **Dos Hermanas**, Spain
46 I 1 **Dos Lagunos**, Guatemala
57 I 18 **Dos Pozos**, Argentina
82 H 11 **Dospat**, Bulgaria
129 O 9 **Dosso**, Niger
129 O 10 **Dosso**, Niger
102 I 6 **Dossor**, Kazakhstan
103 Y 8 **Dostyk**, Kazakhstan
35 S 7 **Dot Lake**, AK, U.S.A.
19 R 6 **Dothan**, AL, U.S.A.
65 R 2 **Douai**, France
129 S 14 **Douala**, Cameroon
64 H 5 **Douarnenez**, France
137 D 23 **Double Cone**, New Zealand
19 P 2 **Double Springs**, AL, U.S.A.
137 A 23 **Doubtful Sound**, New Zealand
136 I 5 **Doubtless Bay**, New Zealand
64 M 7 **Doué-la Fontaine**, France
128 L 8 **Douentza**, Mali
19 U 6 **Douglas**, GA, U.S.A.
29 Y 12 **Douglas**, WY, U.S.A.
30 M 15 **Douglas**, AZ, U.S.A.
61 G 16 **Douglas**, U.K.
132 M 12 **Douglas**, Republic of South Africa
16 K 9 **Douglas Lake**, TN, U.S.A.
65 Q 2 **Doullens**, France
55 H 18 **Dourados**, Brazil
129 W 10 **Dourbali**, Chad
125 P 7 **Douz**, Tunisia
14 J 12 **Dover**, NJ, U.S.A.
15 O 8 **Dover**, NH, U.S.A.
16 D 8 **Dover**, TN, U.S.A.
17 W 2 **Dover**, DE, U.S.A.
63 Z 12 **Dover**, U.K.
100 H 7 **Dow Rūd**, Iran
101 S 7 **Dowl at Yār**, Afghanistan
101 Q 8 **Dowlatābād**, Afghanistan
101 R 6 **Dowlatābād**, Afghanistan
29 P 13 **Downey**, ID, U.S.A.
63 X 6 **Downham Market**, U.K.
14 I 10 **Downsville**, NY, U.S.A.
101 U 6 **Dowshī**, Afghanistan
85 M 19 **Dowsk**, Belarus
123 D 17 **Dōzen**, Japan
87 R 4 **Drabiv**, Ukraine
58 H 5 **Dracena**, Brazil
68 L 7 **Drachten**, Netherlands
86 M 13 **Dragalina**, Romania
86 J 13 **Drăgănești-Vlașca**, Romania
83 K 26 **Dragonada**, Greece
85 G 21 **Drahichyn**, Belarus
57 G 26 **Drake Passage**, Chile
133 N 14 **Drakensberg**, Republic of South Africa
82 H 12 **Drama**, Greece
71 D 20 **Drammen**, Norway
79 F 25 **Dráva**, Hungary
80 F 7 **Drava**, Croatia
80 C 6 **Dravograd**, Slovenia
78 E 10 **Drawa**, Poland
39 I 19 **Drayton Valley**, AB, Canada
68 M 9 **Drenthe**, Netherlands
16 C 8 **Dresden**, TN, U.S.A.
73 N 17 **Dresden**, Germany
84 K 13 **Dretun'**, Belarus
65 O 4 **Dreux**, France
71 E 17 **Drevsjø**, Norway
32 K 12 **Drewsey**, OR, U.S.A.
137 L 15 **Dreyers Rock**, New Zealand
81 K 16 **Drin**, Albania
80 I 11 **Drina**, Bosnia and Herzegovina
81 K 17 **Drini i Zi**, Albania
18 I 5 **Driskill Mountain**, LA, U.S.A.
80 E 12 **Drniš**, Croatia
86 G 12 **Drobeta-Turnu Severin**, Romania
61 E 17 **Drogheda**, Republic of Ireland

Country · Internal administrative region: State/Province/Territory/Dependent territory · Capital city · Mountain range/Undersea ridge · Mountain peak/Volcano/Seamount · Geographic feature · Headland/Point/Cape/Peninsula · Desert · Island/Island group · Antarctic base · Ocean · Sea · Bay/Gulf/Channel/Strait · Lake · Salt pan/Dry/Intermittent lake

Drohobych – Ephrata

I 5 Drohobych, Ukraine
R 8 Droitwich, U.K.
A 9 Dronero, Italy
N 12 Dronning Ingrid Land, Greenland
K 10 Dronten, Netherlands
V 2 Drosendorf, Austria
W 6 Drosh, Pakistan
K 19 Drumheller, AB, Canada
L 9 Drummond, MI, U.S.A.
N 5 Drummond, MT, U.S.A.
L 9 Drummond Island, MI, U.S.A.
M 10 Drummondville, QC, Canada
E 17 Druskininkai, Lithuania
L 17 Druts', Belarus
I 13 Druya, Belarus
V 8 Druzhina, Russian Federation
I 11 Drwęca, Poland
V 15 Dry Tortugas, FL, U.S.A.
J 8 Dryanovo, Bulgaria
J 11 Dryden, ON, Canada
K 13 Drysa, Belarus
C 12 Du Bois, PA, U.S.A.
F 22 Du Quoin, IL, U.S.A.
O 10 Duanshan, China
U 7 Duaringa, QLD, Australia
J 4 Ḑubā, Saudi Arabia
X 5 Dubai, United Arab Emirates
O 8 Dubăsari, Moldova
O 8 Dubăsari Reservoir, Moldova
J 3 Dubawnt Lake, NU, Canada
U 11 Dubbo, NSW, Australia
U 4 Dublin, GA, U.S.A.
F 18 Dublin, Republic of Ireland
I 14 Dubna, Russian Federation
K 3 Dubno, Ukraine
P 10 Dubois, ID, U.S.A.
S 11 Dubois, WY, U.S.A.
P 8 Dubovka, Russian Federation
H 15 Dubrovnik, Croatia
L 2 Dubrovytsya, Ukraine
M 16 Dubrowna, Belarus
W 11 Dubuque, IA, U.S.A.
O 18 Đuc Pho, Vietnam
O 21 Đuc Trong, Vietnam
L 3 Duchesne, UT, U.S.A.
Q 5 Duchess, QLD, Australia
I 10 Ducktown, TN, U.S.A.
T 8 Dudchany, Ukraine
L 26 Dudelange, Luxembourg
E 18 Dudhani, India
O 12 Dudhi, India
N 8 Dudinka, Russian Federation
R 7 Dudley, U.K.
I 13 Duékoué, Côte d'Ivoire
N 4 Dueñas, Spain
L 4 Duero, Spain
P 10 Dufek Coast, Antarctica
Q 7 Duff Islands, Solomon Islands
B 6 Dufourspitze, Italy/Switzerland
C 12 Dugi Otok, Croatia
C 16 Duisburg, Germany
E 21 Duk Faiwil, Sudan
J 21 Dukat i Ri, Albania
N 13 Dukathole, Republic of South Africa
U 5 Dukhān, Qatar
O 5 Dukhnah, Saudi Arabia
U 11 Duki, Pakistan
H 14 Dūkštas, Lithuania
O 8 Dulan, China
P 8 Dulce, NM, U.S.A.
K 9 Dulce, Argentina
O 5 Dulce Nombre de Culmi, Honduras
M 8 Dŭlgopol, Bulgaria
E 18 Duliu, China
K 17 Duljugan Point, Philippines
D 15 Dülmen, Germany
M 6 Dulovo, Bulgaria
V 7 Dululu, QLD, Australia
T 5 Duluth, MN, U.S.A.
N 12 Dulverton, U.K.
H 6 Dūmā, Syria
J 19 Dumaguete, Philippines
E 10 Dumai, Indonesia
E 17 Dumaran, Philippines
W 13 Dumas, AR, U.S.A.
J 1 Dumas, TX, U.S.A.
I 6 Ḑumayr, Syria
G 13 Dumbarton, U.K.
I 11 Dumbrăveni, Romania
K 4 Dumchele, India
T 4 Dumfries, VA, U.S.A.
H 15 Dumfries, U.K.
R 12 Dumka, India
V 14 Dumont d'Urville, Antarctica
U 15 Dumont d'Urville Sea, Antarctica
F 7 Dumyāt, Egypt
H 22 Dunajská Streda, Slovakia
I 26 Dunaszekcső, Hungary
I 24 Dunaújváros, Hungary
F 6 Dunavtsi, Bulgaria
L 6 Dunayivtsi, Ukraine
M 12 Duncan, OK, U.S.A.
N 13 Duncan, AZ, U.S.A.
N 22 Duncan Passage, India
J 7 Duncansby Head, U.K.
D 9 Dundaga, Latvia
V 2 Dundalk, MD, U.S.A.
E 17 Dundalk, Republic of Ireland
E 17 Dundalk Bay, Republic of Ireland
E 13 Dundas, ON, Canada
M 1 Dundas Strait, NT, Australia
I 12 Dundee, U.K.
P 12 Dundee, Republic of South Africa
H 3 Dundee Island, Antarctica
Q 4 Dundgovi, Mongolia
E 24 Dunedin, New Zealand
C 14 Dungarpur, India
D 20 Dungarvan, Republic of Ireland
Y 13 Dungeness, U.K.
P 5 Dungu, Democratic Republic of Congo
E 6 Dungun, Malaysia
H 13 Dungunab, Sudan
L 3 Dunhua, China
N 6 Dunhuang, China
E 10 Dunilupinar, Turkey
Q 1 Dunkerque, France
N 12 Dunkery Beacon, U.K.
C 9 Dunkirk, NY, U.S.A.
M 13 Dunkwa, Ghana
Q 13 Dunlap, IA, U.S.A.
N 3 Dunmarra, NT, Australia
H 11 Dunmore, PA, U.S.A.
R 10 Dunn, NC, U.S.A.
19 V 9 Dunnellon, FL, U.S.A.
22 K 13 Dunning, NE, U.S.A.
137 D 24 Dunrobin, New Zealand
22 K 2 Dunseith, ND, U.S.A.
33 G 15 Dunsmuir, CA, U.S.A.
63 U 9 Dunstable, U.K.
137 D 23 Dunstan Mountains, New Zealand
84 F 10 Dunte, Latvia
38 K 13 Dunvegan Lake, NT, Canada
111 E 14 Duolun, China
82 F 10 Dupnista, Bulgaria
22 I 8 Dupree, SD, U.S.A.
29 O 3 Dupuyer, MT, U.S.A.
20 C 11 Durand, WI, U.S.A.
21 L 14 Durand, MI, U.S.A.
31 O 7 Durango, CO, U.S.A.
44 M 7 Durango, Mexico
45 N 8 Durango, Mexico
47 O 4 Durango, Honduras
67 P 1 Durango, Spain
82 O 6 Durankulak, Bulgaria
25 O 13 Durant, OK, U.S.A.
59 E 15 Durazno, Uruguay
59 E 15 Durazno, Uruguay
133 P 13 Durban, Republic of South Africa
67 O 13 Dúrcal, Spain
73 B 17 Düren, Germany
105 G 16 Durg, India
107 R 13 Durgapur, India
17 R 9 Durham, NC, U.S.A.
61 J 15 Durham, U.K.
116 E 10 Duri, Indonesia
87 N 9 Durleşti, Moldova
81 J 14 Durmitor, Serbia and Montenegro
60 G 8 Durness, U.K.
75 Y 3 Dürnkrut, Austria
81 J 18 Durrës, Albania
63 Q 10 Dursley, U.K.
94 D 9 Dursunbey, Turkey
138 A 6 Duru, Papua New Guinea
127 M 20 Durukhsi, Somalia
82 O 12 Durusu Gölü, Turkey
137 I 15 D'Urville Island, New Zealand
101 S 11 Dushai, Pakistan
102 M 14 Dushak, Turkmenistan
113 P 10 Dushan, China
103 R 13 Dushanbe, Tajikistan
14 G 11 Dushore, PA, U.S.A.
137 A 24 Dusky Sound, New Zealand
73 C 16 Düsseldorf, Germany
144 J 8 Dustin Island, Antarctica
116 F 11 Dusunmudo, Indonesia
34 K 14 Dutch Harbor, AK, U.S.A.
91 S 7 Dutovo, Russian Federation
129 S 10 Dutse, Nigeria
129 R 10 Dutsin-Ma, Nigeria
105 F 20 Duttaluru, India
91 U 14 Duvan, Russian Federation
135 R 1 Duyfken Point, QLD, Australia
113 P 10 Duyun, China
79 M 15 Duża, Poland
94 G 8 Düzce, Turkey
82 K 7 Dve Mogili, Bulgaria
90 K 6 Dvinskaya Guba, Russian Federation
87 X 4 Dvorichna, Ukraine
105 A 15 Dwarka, India
21 G 17 Dwight, IL, U.S.A.
28 K 5 Dworshak Reservoir, ID, U.S.A.
87 Z 7 Dyakove, Ukraine
16 B 8 Dyersburg, TN, U.S.A.
89 T 10 Dyeundyu, Russian Federation
87 U 4 Dykan'ka, Ukraine
63 Y 12 Dymchurch, U.K.
87 P 3 Dymer, Ukraine
87 X 6 Dymytrov, Ukraine
79 M 18 Dynów, Poland
135 U 6 Dysart, QLD, Australia
83 D 20 Dytiki Ellas, Greece
83 D 14 Dytiki Makedonia, Greece
93 V 1 Dyurtyuli, Russian Federation
133 X 4 Dzaoudzi, France
95 Z 10 Džarskij, Azerbaijan
109 N 3 Dzavhan, Mongolia
93 O 1 Dzerzhinsk, Russian Federation
87 X 6 Dzerzhyns'k, Ukraine
103 O 9 Dzhalagash, Kazakhstan
103 T 11 Dzhalal-Abadskaya Oblast', Kyrgyzstan
102 H 5 Dzhangala, Kazakhstan
87 U 11 Dzhankoy, Ukraine
102 X 8 Dzhansugurov, Kazakhstan
102 F 5 Dzhanybek, Kazakhstan
87 S 10 Dzharylhats'ka Zatoka, Ukraine
102 I 12 Dzhebel, Turkmenistan
103 T 14 Dzhilandy, Tajikistan
103 Q 12 Dzhizak, Uzbekistan
92 K 13 Dzhubga, Russian Federation
87 O 6 Dzhuryn, Ukraine
103 O 8 Dzhusaly, Kazakhstan
78 K 10 Działdowo, Poland
45 Y 10 Dzilam de Bravo, Mexico
125 O 7 Dzioua, Algeria
85 J 14 Dzisna, Belarus
85 F 21 Dzivin, Belarus
109 N 2 Dzur, Mongolia
109 R 3 Dzuunmod, Mongolia
85 I 18 Dzyarzhynsk, Belarus
85 J 22 Dzyarzhynsk, Belarus
85 I 17 Dzyarzhynskaya Hara, Belarus

E

115 O 19 Ea Hleo, Vietnam
31 U 5 Eads, CO, U.S.A.
30 M 11 Eagar, AZ, U.S.A.
35 T 6 Eagle, AK, U.S.A.
41 W 8 Eagle, NL, Canada
15 Q 2 Eagle Lake, ME, U.S.A.
15 R 1 Eagle Lake, ME, U.S.A.
33 H 16 Eagle Lake, CA, U.S.A.
26 M 12 Eagle Pass, TX, U.S.A.
20 F 9 Eagle River, WI, U.S.A.
63 W 3 Easington, U.K.
63 T 1 Easingwold, U.K.
16 L 11 Easley, SC, U.S.A.
63 X 6 East Anglia, U.K.
145 R 4 East Antarctica, Antarctica
14 D 9 East Aurora, NY, U.S.A.
18 M 9 East Bay, LA, U.S.A.
138 E 5 East Bay, Papua New Guinea
49 Q 5 East Caicos, Turks and Caicos Islands
136 O 10 East Cape, New Zealand
109 X 12 East China Sea, China/Japan
63 Y 6 East Dereham, U.K.
57 L 24 East Falkland, Falkland Islands
63 W 12 East Grinstead, U.K.
14 M 12 East Hampton, NY, U.S.A.
60 H 13 East Kilbride, U.K.
21 O 17 East Liverpool, OH, U.S.A.
133 O 14 East London, Republic of South Africa
62 L 14 East Looe, U.K.
138 H 4 East New Britain, Papua New Guinea
19 S 3 East Point, GA, U.S.A.
138 C 4 East Sepik, Papua New Guinea
89 V 5 East Siberian Sea, Russian Federation
21 E 21 East St Louis, IL, U.S.A.
117 R 15 East Timor, Asia
63 X 13 Eastbourne, U.K.
10 E 12 Easter Island, Chile
105 G 24 Eastern, Sri Lanka
107 R 10 Eastern, Nepal
128 G 12 Eastern, Sierra Leone
128 M 13 Eastern, Ghana
131 W 7 Eastern, Kenya
133 P 6 Eastern, Zambia
133 N 14 Eastern Cape, Republic of South Africa
126 F 9 Eastern Desert, Egypt
127 F 22 Eastern Equatoria, Sudan
105 F 20 Eastern Ghats, India
138 D 5 Eastern Highlands, Papua New Guinea
63 T 12 Eastleigh, U.K.
41 Q 10 Eastmain, QC, Canada
41 P 10 Eastmain, QC, Canada
19 U 5 Eastman, GA, U.S.A.
14 I 12 Easton, PA, U.S.A.
17 V 3 Easton, MD, U.S.A.
63 Q 14 Easton, U.K.
63 T 5 Eastwood, U.K.
19 T 3 Eatonton, GA, U.S.A.
20 D 11 Eau Claire, WI, U.S.A.
140 L 15 Eauripik, Federated States of Micronesia
129 P 11 Eban, Nigeria
45 R 10 Ebano, Mexico
63 O 9 Ebbw Vale, U.K.
129 T 15 Ebebiyin, Equatorial Guinea
75 S 5 Ebensee, Austria
94 G 11 Eber Gölü, Turkey
72 M 12 Eberswalde-Finow, Germany
122 J 5 Ebetsu, Japan
112 M 7 Ebian, China
123 C 23 Ebino, Japan
108 J 4 Ebinur Hu, China
77 K 16 Eboli, Italy
129 T 15 Ebolowa, Cameroon
141 Y 5 Ebon, Marshall Islands
132 H 9 Ebony, Namibia
129 R 13 Ebonyi, Nigeria
67 T 5 Ebro, Spain
94 A 8 Eceabat, Turkey
124 L 6 Ech Chélif, Algeria
74 B 9 Echallens, Switzerland
82 I 12 Echinos, Greece
123 G 16 Echizen-misaki, Japan
32 J 9 Echo, OR, U.S.A.
38 G 10 Echo Bay, NT, Canada
42 A 8 Echo Bay, ON, Canada
69 K 17 Echt, Netherlands
69 M 24 Echternach, Luxembourg
135 S 12 Echuca, VIC, Australia
66 M 12 Écija, Spain
20 K 9 Eckermann, MI, U.S.A.
72 H 8 Eckernförde, Germany
52 A 9 Ecuador, South America
127 J 17 Ed, Eritrea
127 B 19 Ed Da'ein, Sudan
127 G 19 Ed Damazin, Sudan
127 F 15 Ed Damer, Sudan
127 E 15 Ed Debba, Sudan
127 E 17 Ed Dueim, Sudan
68 I 10 Edam, Netherlands
60 I 7 Eday, U.K.
16 D 7 Eddyville, KY, U.S.A.
68 K 13 Ede, Netherlands
129 P 12 Ede, Nigeria
129 S 14 Edéa, Cameroon
26 M 8 Eden, TX, U.S.A.
61 I 15 Eden, U.K.
135 U 13 Eden, NSW, Australia
137 C 25 Edendale, New Zealand
17 V 8 Edenton, NC, U.S.A.
82 D 13 Edessa, Greece
136 M 10 Edgecumbe, New Zealand
22 M 6 Edgeley, ND, U.S.A.
22 G 11 Edgemont, SD, U.S.A.
143 U 11 Edgeøya, Svalbard
27 P 15 Edinburg, TX, U.S.A.
60 I 13 Edinburgh, U.K.
86 M 7 Edineţ, Moldova
82 M 11 Edirne, Turkey
94 B 6 Edirne, Turkey
125 Q 10 Edjeleh, Algeria
16 H 7 Edmonton, KY, U.S.A.
39 J 18 Edmonton, AB, Canada
43 Q 7 Edmundston, NB, Canada
27 R 11 Edna, TX, U.S.A.
129 Q 13 Edo, Nigeria
76 E 5 Edolo, Italy
94 B 9 Edremit, Turkey
94 A 9 Edremit Körfezi, Turkey
39 I 18 Edson, AB, Canada
56 J 13 Eduardo Castex, Argentina
145 N 11 Edward VII Peninsula, Antarctica
145 X 4 Edward VIII Gulf, Antarctica
26 K 8 Edwards Plateau, TX, U.S.A.
21 F 20 Edwardsville, IL, U.S.A.
130 H 9 Edzouga, Congo
34 M 10 Eek, AK, U.S.A.
69 D 17 Eeklo, Belgium
68 N 5 Eemshaven, Netherlands
139 R 11 Éfaté, Vanuatu
75 S 3 Eferding, Austria
21 G 20 Effingham, IL, U.S.A.
117 T 11 Eftorobi, Indonesia
109 S 3 Eg, Mongolia
35 N 11 Egegik, AK, U.S.A.
79 K 22 Eger, Hungary
75 W 2 Eggenburg, Austria
73 L 24 Eggenfelden, Germany
69 H 20 Eghezée, Belgium
70 D 10 Egilsstaðir, Iceland
94 F 12 Eğirdir, Turkey
94 F 11 Eğirdir Gölü, Turkey
65 P 10 Égletons, France
36 M 3 Eglinton Island, NT, Canada
89 Z 6 Egvekinot, Russian Federation
126 C 10 Egypt, Africa
73 G 24 Ehingen, Germany
123 C 24 Ei, Japan
68 M 12 Eibergen, Netherlands
75 V 8 Eibiswald, Austria
71 B 19 Eidfjord, Norway
73 B 19 Eifel, Germany
74 F 9 Eiger, Switzerland
60 F 11 Eigg, U.K.
105 B 25 Eight Degree Channel, Maldives
144 J 8 Eights Coast, Antarctica
134 H 5 Eighty Mile Beach, WA, Australia
73 L 16 Eilenburg, Germany
96 F 11 Ein Yahav, Israel
135 S 4 Einasleigh, QLD, Australia
73 H 15 Einbeck, Germany
69 J 16 Eindhoven, Netherlands
70 B 11 Eiriksjökull, Iceland
54 B 12 Eirunepé, Brazil
73 H 17 Eisenach, Germany
75 U 6 Eisenerz, Austria
75 U 9 Eisenkappel, Austria
75 Y 5 Eisenstadt, Austria
73 I 18 Eisfeld, Germany
85 F 17 Eišiškės, Lithuania
73 J 15 Eisleben Lutherstadt, Germany
67 W 9 Eivissa, Spain
67 S 3 Ejea de los Caballeros, Spain
133 W 10 Ejeda, Madgascar
109 P 6 Ejin Qi, China
95 T 9 Ejmiatsin, Armenia
128 M 12 Ejura, Ghana
45 T 12 Ejutla, Mexico
29 Y 6 Ekalaka, MT, U.S.A.
137 K 15 Eketahuna, New Zealand
103 U 3 Ekibastuz, Kazakhstan
89 Q 9 Ekonda, Russian Federation
130 I 7 Ekouamou, Congo
71 F 23 Eksjö, Sweden
35 O 11 Ekuk, AK, U.S.A.
130 L 8 Ekuku, Democratic Republic of Congo
41 N 9 Ekwan, ON, Canada
125 Q 11 El Adeb Larache, Algeria
126 D 8 El 'Alamein, Egypt
125 O 8 El Alia, Algeria
66 L 12 El Arahal, Spain
44 H 5 El Arco, Mexico
124 K 7 El Aricha, Algeria
126 G 7 El 'Arîsh, Egypt
126 F 10 El Balyana, Egypt
44 L 3 El Barreal, Mexico
127 F 19 El Barun, Sudan
51 N 4 El Baúl, Venezuela
124 L 7 El Bayadh, Algeria
127 J 24 El Beru Hagia, Somalia
47 R 9 El Bluff, Nicaragua
57 G 17 El Bolsón, Argentina
125 Q 8 El Borma, Tunisia
127 D 22 El Buheyrat, Sudan
57 H 17 El Cain, Argentina
33 K 26 El Cajon, CA, U.S.A.
50 K 6 El Campin, Colombia
27 R 11 El Campo, TX, U.S.A.
52 B 8 El Carmen, Ecuador
53 L 18 El Carmen, Bolivia
45 N 7 El Casco, Mexico
33 M 26 El Centro, CA, U.S.A.
53 M 20 El Cerro, Bolivia
45 W 13 El Chichónal, Mexico
44 G 2 El Chinero, Mexico
45 Z 10 El Cuyo, Mexico
50 F 9 El Diviso, Colombia
25 O 6 El Dorado, KS, U.S.A.
25 V 14 El Dorado, AR, U.S.A.
44 L 8 El Dorado, Mexico
50 K 9 El Dorado, Colombia
50 J 11 El Encanto, Colombia
46 J 4 El Estor, Guatemala
126 E 9 El Faiyûm, Egypt
127 B 17 El Fasher, Sudan
126 E 9 El Fashn, Egypt
127 K 21 El Fud, Ethiopia
44 K 6 El Fuerte, Mexico
127 A 17 El Geneina, Sudan
127 F 17 El Geteina, Sudan
127 F 17 El Gezira, Sudan
126 E 8 El Gîza, Egypt
124 M 9 El Goléa, Algeria
46 J 4 El Golfete, Guatemala
44 G 2 El Golfo de Santa Clara, Mexico
128 G 4 El Hammâmi, Mauritania
128 J 4 El Hank, Mauritania
47 S 14 El Hato del Volcán, Panama
127 G 18 El Hawata, Sudan
127 C 18 El Hilla, Sudan
124 M 9 El Homr, Algeria
124 G 7 El Jadida, Morocco
125 Q 6 El Jem, Tunisia
124 G 8 El Kelaâ des Srarhna, Morocco
127 K 22 Ēl Kerē, Ethiopia
127 E 15 El Khandaq, Sudan
126 E 11 El Khârga, Egypt
128 K 5 El Khnâchich, Mali
127 L 22 Ēl K'oran, Ethiopia
127 D 19 El Lagowa, Sudan
47 X 13 El Llano, Panama
49 S 7 El Macao, Dominican Republic
126 E 8 El Mansûra, Egypt
51 R 5 El Manteco, Venezuela
125 O 7 El Meghaïer, Algeria
126 E 9 El Minya, Egypt
67 O 6 El Molar, Spain
128 I 6 El Mreyyé, Mauritania
127 C 19 El Muglad, Sudan
46 L 5 El Negrito, Honduras
121 E 16 El Nido, Philippines
127 D 18 El Obeid, Sudan
127 C 18 El Odaiya, Sudan
45 O 6 El Oro, Mexico
52 A 11 El Oro, Ecuador
125 O 7 El Oued, Algeria
21 F 17 El Paso, IL, U.S.A.
26 E 7 El Paso, TX, U.S.A.
67 U 6 El Perelló, Spain
47 X 13 El Porvenir, Panama
46 I 5 El Progreso, Guatemala
46 I 6 El Progreso, Guatemala
46 M 8 El Puente, Nicaragua
53 L 19 El Puente, Bolivia
66 K 13 El Puerto de Santa María, Spain
126 D 11 El Qasr, Egypt
47 Z 15 El Real, Panama
24 M 10 El Reno, OK, U.S.A.
126 F 11 El Ridisiya Bahari, Egypt
66 K 11 El Ronquillo, Spain
126 E 8 El Saff, Egypt
44 H 3 El Sahuaro, Mexico
57 H 21 El Salado, Argentina
44 M 8 El Salto, Mexico
46 J 7 El Salvador, North America
56 G 7 El Salvador, Chile
121 L 20 El Salvador, Philippines
49 S 7 El Seibo, Dominican Republic
56 G 13 El Sosneado, Argentina
44 M 4 El Sueco, Mexico
66 K 3 El Teleno, Spain
51 Q 4 El Tigre, Venezuela
56 F 9 El Toro, Chile
59 B 14 El Trebol, Argentina
126 F 9 El Tûr, Egypt
57 G 24 El Turbio, Argentina
47 W 14 El Valle, Panama
67 W 5 El Vendrell, Spain
46 M 8 El Viejo, Nicaragua
50 K 4 El Vigia, Venezuela
131 X 6 El Wak, Kenya
127 D 17 El Wuz, Sudan
83 F 23 Elafonisos, Greece
83 L 26 Elasa, Greece
83 E 15 Elassona, Greece
96 F 13 Elat, Israel
140 M 15 Elato, Federated States of Micronesia
95 O 11 Elazığ, Turkey
19 Q 6 Elba, AL, U.S.A.
81 K 19 Elbasan, Albania
32 H 8 Elbe, WA, U.S.A.
72 I 11 Elbe, Czech Republic/Germany
19 U 2 Elberton, GA, U.S.A.
94 M 11 Elbistan, Turkey
78 J 8 Elbląg, Poland
39 M 19 Elbow, SK, Canada
93 N 14 Elbrus, Russian Federation
68 K 10 Elburg, Netherlands
100 I 5 Elburz Mountains, Iran
67 S 10 Elche, Spain
67 R 10 Elche de la Sierra, Spain
67 S 10 Elda, Spain
89 U 11 El'dikan, Russian Federation
25 U 5 Eldon, MO, U.S.A.
21 G 22 Eldorado, IL, U.S.A.
26 L 9 Eldorado, TX, U.S.A.
58 F 9 Eldorado, Argentina
54 J 12 Eldorado dos Carajás, Brazil
131 U 7 Eldoret, Kenya
83 G 20 Elefsina, Greece
84 E 12 Eleja, Latvia
131 U 4 Elemi Triangle, Kenya
82 K 8 Elena, Bulgaria
31 P 13 Elephant Butte Reservoir, NM, U.S.A.
144 G 2 Elephant Island, Antarctica
48 L 2 Eleuthera, The Bahamas
21 G 16 Elgin, IL, U.S.A.
22 I 6 Elgin, ND, U.S.A.
27 Q 9 Elgin, TX, U.S.A.
32 K 10 Elgin, OR, U.S.A.
60 I 9 Elgin, U.K.
131 T 7 Elgon, Kenya
117 T 15 Eliase, Indonesia
31 T 12 Elida, NM, U.S.A.
82 G 9 Elin Pelin, Bulgaria
131 N 8 Elipa, Democratic Republic of Congo
54 L 13 Eliseu Martins, Brazil
93 O 11 Elista, Russian Federation
14 J 13 Elizabeth, NJ, U.S.A.
17 W 8 Elizabeth City, NC, U.S.A.
16 L 8 Elizabethton, TN, U.S.A.
16 G 6 Elizabethtown, KY, U.S.A.
17 S 11 Elizabethtown, NC, U.S.A.
78 M 9 Ełk, Poland
24 J 10 Elk City, OK, U.S.A.
28 L 7 Elk City, ID, U.S.A.
39 K 18 Elk Point, AB, Canada
23 S 7 Elk River, MN, U.S.A.
21 J 16 Elkhart, IN, U.S.A.
24 G 7 Elkhart, KS, U.S.A.
21 G 14 Elkhorn, WI, U.S.A.
82 L 10 Elkhovo, Bulgaria
17 O 8 Elkin, NC, U.S.A.
17 P 3 Elkins, WV, U.S.A.
33 M 16 Elko, NV, U.S.A.
39 J 21 Elko, BC, Canada
16 F 10 Elkton, TN, U.S.A.
17 R 4 Elkton, VA, U.S.A.
19 S 5 Ellaville, GA, U.S.A.
37 N 2 Ellef Ringnes Island, NU, Canada
22 M 6 Ellendale, ND, U.S.A.
32 I 8 Ellensburg, WA, U.S.A.
63 P 6 Ellesmere, U.K.
37 P 1 Ellesmere Island, NU, Canada
63 P 4 Ellesmere Port, U.K.
19 S 1 Ellijay, GA, U.S.A.
133 O 14 Elliot, Republic of South Africa
42 C 9 Elliot Lake, ON, Canada
135 N 3 Elliott, NT, Australia
17 Q 5 Elliott Knob, VA, U.S.A.
133 N 10 Ellisras, Republic of South Africa
135 O 11 Elliston, SA, Australia
60 J 10 Ellon, U.K.
15 R 5 Ellsworth, ME, U.S.A.
20 C 11 Ellsworth, WI, U.S.A.
144 J 8 Ellsworth Land, Antarctica
144 L 8 Ellsworth Mountains, Antarctica
73 H 22 Ellwangen, Germany
32 G 7 Elma, WA, U.S.A.
94 E 13 Elmalı, Turkey
74 K 7 Elmen, Austria
14 F 10 Elmira, NY, U.S.A.
43 W 8 Elmira, PE, Canada
72 G 10 Elmshorn, Germany
24 I 8 Elmwood, OK, U.S.A.
30 K 13 Eloy, AZ, U.S.A.
68 K 13 Elst, Netherlands
73 M 16 Elsterwerda, Germany
136 J 13 Eltham, New Zealand
93 Q 8 El'ton, Russian Federation
105 G 19 Eluru, India
84 H 8 Elva, Estonia
66 J 9 Elvas, Portugal
71 E 18 Elverum, Norway
54 A 12 Elvira, Brazil
21 J 18 Elwood, IN, U.S.A.
33 N 18 Ely, NV, U.S.A.
63 W 7 Ely, U.K.
21 N 16 Elyria, OH, U.S.A.
73 G 14 Elze, Germany
139 R 11 Émaé, Vanuatu
101 U 5 Emām Şaḩēb, Afghanistan
102 K 7 Emba, Kazakhstan
102 L 6 Emba, Kazakhstan
46 J 7 Embalse Cerrón Grande, El Salvador
57 H 15 Embalse Cerros Colorados, Argentina
46 H 5 Embalse Chixoy, Guatemala
67 Q 8 Embalse de Alarcón, Spain
66 L 5 Embalse de Almendra, Spain
67 Q 6 Embalse de Buendia, Spain
66 M 8 Embalse de Cíjara, Spain
66 M 8 Embalse de Garcia Sola, Spain
51 R 4 Embalse de Guri, Venezuela
67 N 12 Embalse de Iznajar, Spain
66 L 9 Embalse de Orellana, Spain
66 K 8 Embalse de Valdecañas, Spain
66 M 9 Embalse del Zújar, Spain
57 H 15 Embalse Ezequiel Ramos Mexia, Argentina
57 H 18 Embalse Florentino Ameghino, Argentina
56 J 5 Embarcación, Argentina
130 K 8 Embondo, Democratic Republic of Congo
64 K 7 Embouchure de la Loire, France
131 V 8 Embu, Kenya
72 D 10 Emden, Germany
112 M 7 Emei, China
135 U 6 Emerald, QLD, Australia
30 K 5 Emery, UT, U.S.A.
94 D 10 Emet, Turkey
138 B 6 Emeti, Papua New Guinea
129 X 6 Emi Koussi, Chad
76 F 9 Emilia-Romagna, Italy
45 X 13 Emiliano Zapata, Mexico
108 J 3 Emin, China
138 F 2 Emirau Island, Papua New Guinea
94 F 10 Emirdağ, Turkey
135 T 14 Emita, TAS, Australia
72 C 13 Emlichheim, Germany
84 D 7 Emmaste, Estonia
68 K 9 Emmeloord, Netherlands
68 N 9 Emmen, Netherlands
73 B 14 Emmerich, Germany
135 S 7 Emmet, QLD, Australia
23 R 11 Emmetsburg, IA, U.S.A.
34 L 8 Emmonak, AK, U.S.A.
26 I 11 Emory Peak, TX, U.S.A.
44 I 5 Empalme, Mexico
58 C 10 Empedrado, Argentina
76 E 10 Empoli, Italy
17 T 7 Emporia, VA, U.S.A.
25 P 5 Emporia, KS, U.S.A.
14 D 11 Emporium, PA, U.S.A.
72 D 12 Ems, Germany
42 F 10 Emsdale, ON, Canada
133 P 11 Emzinoni, Republic of South Africa
96 F 10 En Gedi, Israel
97 F 11 'En Hazeva, Israel
127 C 18 En Nahud, Sudan
117 W 12 Enarotali, Indonesia
55 G 20 Encarnación, Paraguay
27 N 13 Encinal, TX, U.S.A.
33 K 26 Encinitas, CA, U.S.A.
31 R 11 Encino, NM, U.S.A.
56 H 11 Encón, Argentina
58 H 12 Encruzilhada do Sul, Brazil
79 L 21 Encs, Hungary
118 E 9 Endau, Malaysia
117 O 15 Endeh, Indonesia
140 K 4 Enderbury, Kiribati
145 U 3 Enderby Land, Antarctica
14 H 10 Endicott, NY, U.S.A.
35 P 4 Endicott Mountains, AK, U.S.A.
134 F 10 Eneabba, WA, Australia
59 D 19 Energia, Argentina
82 K 13 Enez, Turkey
94 A 7 Enez, Turkey
14 L 10 Enfield, CT, U.S.A.
17 T 8 Enfield, NC, U.S.A.
43 V 10 Enfield, NS, Canada
63 W 10 Enfield, U.K.
138 B 4 Enga, Papua New Guinea
20 J 9 Engadine, MI, U.S.A.
71 C 15 Engan, Norway
122 L 4 Engaru, Japan
74 G 8 Engelberg, Switzerland
75 R 3 Engelhartszell, Austria
93 Q 5 Engel's, Russian Federation
68 H 6 Engelschmangat, Netherlands
68 L 5 Engelsmanplaat, Netherlands
116 E 13 Enggano, Indonesia
69 E 20 Enghien, Belgium
25 W 12 England, AR, U.S.A.
61 I 19 England, U.K.
41 X 9 Englee, NL, Canada
42 E 7 Englehart, ON, Canada
63 Q 14 English Channel, France/United Kingdom
144 J 6 English Coast, Antarctica
84 E 10 Engure, Latvia
84 E 10 Engures ezers, Latvia
24 M 8 Enid, OK, U.S.A.
122 J 6 Eniwa, Japan
68 I 9 Enkhuizen, Netherlands
77 J 22 Enna, Italy
38 L 12 Ennadai Lake, NU, Canada
29 P 8 Ennis, MT, U.S.A.
61 B 19 Ennis, Republic of Ireland
61 E 19 Enniscorthy, Republic of Ireland
61 D 16 Enniskillen, U.K.
75 T 4 Enns, Austria
113 S 13 Enping, China
64 L 5 Enree, France
68 N 11 Enschede, Netherlands
44 F 2 Ensenada, Mexico
113 Q 7 Enshi, China
123 I 18 Enshū-nada, Japan
131 S 8 Entebbe, Uganda
19 R 6 Enterprise, AL, U.S.A.
30 H 7 Enterprise, UT, U.S.A.
32 L 10 Enterprise, OR, U.S.A.
39 H 14 Enterprise, NT, Canada
121 D 17 Enterprise Point, Philippines
39 H 19 Entrance, AB, Canada
59 C 14 Entre Ríos, Argentina
66 H 8 Entroncamento, Portugal
129 R 13 Enugu, Nigeria
129 R 13 Enugu, Nigeria
89 Z 5 Enurmino, Russian Federation
54 B 12 Envira, Brazil
68 K 11 Epe, Netherlands
130 I 7 Epéna, Congo
65 S 4 Épernay, France
14 G 13 Ephrata, PA, U.S.A.
32 J 7 Ephrata, WA, U.S.A.

Country · Internal administrative region: State/Province/Territory/Dependent territory · Capital city · Mountain range/Undersea ridge · Mountain peak/Volcano/Seamount · Geographic feature · Headland/Point/Cape/Peninsula · Desert · Island/Island group · Antarctic base · Ocean · Sea · Bay/Gulf/Channel/Strait · Lake · Salt pan/Dry/Intermittent lake · River

139 R 11 Epi, Vanuatu
65 V 5 Épinal, France
94 H 15 Episkopi, Cyprus
63 W 10 Epping, U.K.
63 V 11 Epsom, U.K.
57 J 14 Epu-pel, Argentina
63 U 3 Epworth, U.K.
130 K 8 Equateur, Democratic Republic of Congo
105 L 20 Equatorial Channel, Maldives
129 R 15 Equatorial Guinea, Africa
124 I 8 Er Rachidia, Morocco
127 E 18 Er Rahad, Sudan
124 J 9 Er Raoui, Algeria
127 F 19 Er Renk, Sudan
138 C 5 Erave, Papua New Guinea
94 L 8 Erbaa, Turkey
95 T 11 Erşşek, Turkey
95 S 10 Erciş, Turkey
94 K 11 Erciyes Dağl, Turkey
79 I 23 Érd, Hungary
94 C 8 Erdek, Turkey
94 J 13 Erdemli, Turkey
109 Q 3 Erdenet, Mongolia
109 Q 5 Erdenetsogt, Mongolia
73 K 24 Erding, Germany
58 H 10 Erechim, Brazil
109 T 2 Ereentsav, Mongolia
94 I 12 Ereğli, Turkey
94 G 7 Ereğli, Turkey
110 B 13 Erenhot, China
124 I 8 Erfoud, Morocco
73 I 17 Erfurt, Germany
128 K 5 Erg Atouila, Mali
124 H 13 'Erg Chech, Algeria
129 W 8 Erg du Djourab, Chad
124 I 10 Erg Iabès, Algeria
124 G 11 Erg Iguidi, Algeria
95 O 11 Ergani, Turkey
109 S 5 Ergel, Mongolia
82 L 13 Ergene, Turkey
84 G 11 Ērgli, Latvia
111 J 15 Erhulai, China
138 C 5 Eri, Papua New Guinea
66 F 9 Ericeira, Portugal
14 B 10 Erie, PA, U.S.A.
83 A 15 Eriekoussa, Greece
128 K 5 'Erigât, Mali
40 I 10 Eriksdale, MB, Canada
122 L 6 Erimo, Japan
122 L 7 Erimo-misaki, Japan
60 E 11 Eriskay, U.K.
127 H 16 Eritrea, Africa
72 M 13 Erkner, Germany
73 I 20 Erlangen, Germany
135 N 7 Erldunda, NT, Australia
68 J 11 Ermelo, Netherlands
133 P 11 Ermelo, Republic of South Africa
94 H 13 Ermenek, Turkey
83 F 21 Ermioni, Greece
83 I 21 Ermoupoli, Greece
73 E 17 Erndtebrück, Germany
75 X 3 Ernstbrunn, Austria
105 E 22 Erode, India
135 R 8 Eromanga, QLD, Australia
132 H 9 Erongo, Namibia
69 F 22 Erquelinnes, Belgium
61 B 16 Erris Head, Republic of Ireland
15 N 5 Errol, NH, U.S.A.
139 R 12 Erromango, Vanuatu
81 L 20 Ersekë, Albania
110 I 4 Ershiwuzhan, China
110 J 4 Ershizhan, China
23 P 4 Erskine, MN, U.S.A.
108 L 4 Ertai, China
95 R 12 Eruh, Turkey
58 G 13 Erval, Brazil
73 F 15 Erwitte, Germany
83 F 19 Erythres, Greece
112 J 10 Eryuan, China
110 K 7 Erzhan, China
89 O 14 Erzin, Russian Federation
94 L 13 Erzin, Turkey
95 O 9 Erzincan, Turkey
95 Q 9 Erzurum, Turkey
85 D 14 Eržvilkas, Lithuania
124 E 11 Es Semara, Western Sahara
127 F 18 Es Suki, Sudan
138 G 7 Esa-ala, Papua New Guinea
122 J 7 Esan-misaki, Japan
122 I 8 Esashi, Japan
122 K 3 Esashi, Japan
71 B 25 Esbjerg, Denmark
30 K 7 Escalante, UT, U.S.A.
121 J 17 Escalante, Philippines
45 N 6 Escalón, Mexico
20 H 10 Escanaba, MI, U.S.A.
45 X 12 Escárcega, Mexico
120 I 5 Escarpada Point, Philippines
69 F 16 Escaut, Belgium
69 K 26 Esch-sur-Alzette, Luxembourg
73 H 16 Eschwege, Germany
53 H 19 Escoma, Bolivia
33 K 26 Escondido, CA, U.S.A.
47 Q 9 Escondido, Nicaragua
44 M 9 Escuinapa, Mexico
46 H 6 Escuintla, Guatemala
129 T 14 Eséka, Cameroon
94 D 13 Esen, Turkey
102 I 14 Esenguly, Turkmenistan
100 I 7 Eşfahān, Iran
100 J 8 Eşfahān, Iran
100 M 5 Esfarāyen, Iran
41 T 8 Esker, NL, Canada
71 G 21 Eskilstuna, Sweden
94 F 9 Eskişehir, Turkey
100 F 6 Eslāmābād-e Gharb, Iran
48 K 5 Esmeralda, Cuba
52 B 7 Esmeraldas, Ecuador
52 A 8 Esmeraldas, Ecuador
101 O 13 Espakeh, Iran
65 Q 12 Espalion, France
31 Q 9 Espanola, NM, U.S.A.
42 C 9 Espanola, ON, Canada
72 F 13 Espelkamp, Germany
134 I 12 Esperance, WA, Australia
44 J 5 Esperanza, Mexico
53 F 16 Esperanza, Peru
57 G 23 Esperanza, Argentina
144 H 3 Esperanza, Antarctica
66 M 10 Espiel, Spain
50 I 7 Espinal, Colombia
66 G 5 Espinho, Portugal
55 M 17 Espírito Santo, Brazil
139 P 10 Espiritu Santo, Vanuatu
55 N 14 Esplanada, Brazil
71 L 19 Espoo, Finland
66 H 4 Esposende, Portugal
57 G 18 Esquel, Argentina
58 C 12 Esquina, Argentina
124 F 8 Essaouira, Morocco
73 C 15 Essen, Germany
51 U 6 Essequibo, Guyana
42 B 14 Essex, ON, Canada
89 Y 10 Esso, Russian Federation
129 V 15 Est, Cameroon
120 I 7 Estagno Point, Philippines
55 N 14 Estância, Brazil
76 G 7 Este, Italy
56 K 9 Esteban Rams, Argentina
47 N 8 Estelí, Nicaragua
67 Q 2 Estella, Spain
26 L 3 Estelline, TX, U.S.A.
66 M 14 Estepona, Spain
35 R 7 Ester, AK, U.S.A.
23 Q 10 Estherville, IA, U.S.A.
17 N 15 Estill, SC, U.S.A.
84 F 7 Estonia, Europe
57 I 26 Estrecho de Le Maire, Argentina
57 E 22 Estrecho Nelson, Chile
66 I 9 Estremoz, Portugal
130 D 7 Estuaire, Gabon
106 K 9 Etah, India
65 U 3 Étain, France
37 Y 9 Etamamiou, QC, Canada
41 W 10 Etamamiou, QC, Canada
65 P 5 Étampes, France
106 K 10 Etawah, India
127 G 21 Ethiopia, Africa
127 G 20 Ethiopian Highlands, Ethiopia
94 H 9 Etimesğut, Turkey
34 K 9 Etolin Strait, AK, U.S.A.
130 H 7 Etoumbi, Congo
65 N 3 Étretat, France
82 H 9 Etropole, Bulgaria
64 M 15 Etsaut, France
69 L 24 Ettelbruck, Luxembourg
140 I 11 Eua, Tonga
134 L 10 Eucla, WA, Australia
21 N 16 Euclid, OH, U.S.A.
19 R 5 Eufaula, AL, U.S.A.
25 Q 11 Eufaula, OK, U.S.A.
25 P 10 Eufaula Lake, OK, U.S.A.
32 F 11 Eugene, OR, U.S.A.
135 S 9 Eulo, QLD, Australia
18 J 7 Eunice, LA, U.S.A.
31 U 14 Eunice, NM, U.S.A.
69 L 20 Eupen, Belgium
96 L 3 Euphrates, Syria/Iraq
18 M 3 Eupora, MS, U.S.A.
28 M 2 Eureka, MT, U.S.A.
30 J 4 Eureka, UT, U.S.A.
33 E 15 Eureka, CA, U.S.A.
33 M 17 Eureka, NV, U.S.A.
68 F 13 Europoort, Netherlands
73 C 18 Euskirchen, Germany
19 W 9 Eustis, FL, U.S.A.
19 O 4 Eutaw, AL, U.S.A.
39 E 19 Eutsuk Lake, BC, Canada
41 O 4 Evans Strait, NU, Canada
21 H 15 Evanston, IL, U.S.A.
29 Q 15 Evanston, WY, U.S.A.
21 H 22 Evansville, IN, U.S.A.
27 O 8 Evant, TX, U.S.A.
133 O 11 Evaton, Republic of South Africa
100 J 12 Evaz, Iran
89 Y 9 Evensk, Russian Federation
14 D 13 Everett, PA, U.S.A.
32 H 6 Everett, WA, U.S.A.
19 X 14 Everglades, FL, U.S.A.
19 P 6 Evergreen, AL, U.S.A.
63 R 8 Evesham, U.K.
71 K 15 Evijärvi, Finland
71 B 21 Evje, Norway
66 I 10 Évora, Portugal
66 I 9 Évora, Portugal
65 O 4 Évreux, France
82 K 13 Evros, Greece
83 H 19 Evvoia, Greece
34 B 7 Ewa Beach, HI, U.S.A.
130 G 8 Ewo, Congo
25 S 3 Excelsior Springs, MO, U.S.A.
63 N 13 Exe, U.K.
144 L 11 Executive Committee Range, Antarctica
33 J 21 Exeter, CA, U.S.A.
63 N 13 Exeter, U.K.
23 R 13 Exira, IA, U.S.A.
63 O 14 Exminster, U.K.
63 N 12 Exmoor, U.K.
17 W 5 Exmore, VA, U.S.A.
63 O 14 Exmouth, U.K.
134 E 6 Exmouth, WA, Australia
64 H 14 Exton, PA, U.S.A.
66 K 8 Extremadura, Spain
129 V 11 Extrême-Nord, Cameroon
48 L 3 Exuma Cays, The Bahamas
63 Y 7 Eye, U.K.
127 O 21 Eyl, Somalia
65 P 10 Eymoutiers, France
135 O 11 Eyre Peninsula, SA, Australia
137 H 20 Eyreton, New Zealand
84 J 12 Ezernieki, Latvia
113 U 7 Ezhou, China
94 A 9 Ezine, Turkey

F

105 L 17 Faadhippolhu Atoll, Maldives
127 J 24 Faafxadhuun, Somalia
26 E 7 Fabens, TX, U.S.A.
129 T 7 Fachi, Niger
57 G 19 Facundo, Argentina
129 Y 7 Fada, Chad
129 N 10 Fada-Ngourma, Burkina Faso
76 G 9 Faenza, Italy
86 J 10 Făgăraş, Romania
71 G 20 Fagersta, Sweden
86 G 10 Făget, Romania
70 C 11 Fagurhólsmýri, Iceland
74 G 9 Faido, Switzerland
60 J 6 Fair Isle, U.K.
35 R 7 Fairbanks, AK, U.S.A.
21 G 21 Fairfield, IL, U.S.A.
27 R 7 Fairfield, TX, U.S.A.
28 L 11 Fairfield, ID, U.S.A.
33 G 19 Fairfield, CA, U.S.A.
137 F 21 Fairlie, New Zealand
17 P 2 Fairmont, WV, U.S.A.
23 N 15 Fairmont, NE, U.S.A.
23 R 10 Fairmont, MN, U.S.A.
31 Q 5 Fairplay, CO, U.S.A.
20 I 10 Fairport, MI, U.S.A.
24 L 9 Fairview, OK, U.S.A.
101 X 9 Faisalabad, Pakistan
22 I 8 Faith, SD, U.S.A.
107 N 10 Faizabad, India
49 U 8 Fajardo, Puerto Rico
97 W 9 Fajir, Iraq
140 J 6 Fakaofo, Tokelau Islands
63 Y 6 Fakenham, U.K.
117 U 12 Fakfak, Indonesia
82 M 10 Fakiya, Bulgaria
71 D 26 Fakse Bugt, Denmark
111 I 14 Faku, China
64 M 4 Falaise, France
129 R 7 Falaise de Tiguidit, Niger
107 T 10 Falakata, India
50 M 2 Falcón, Venezuela
76 I 10 Falconara Marittima, Italy
86 M 8 Fălești, Moldova
27 P 14 Falfurrias, TX, U.S.A.
72 L 13 Falkensee, Germany
60 H 13 Falkirk, U.K.
57 J 24 Falkland Islands, U.K.
57 K 24 Falkland Sound, Falkland Islands
83 G 23 Falkonera, Greece
71 E 22 Falköping, Sweden
15 O 11 Fall River, MA, U.S.A.
33 J 17 Fallon, NV, U.S.A.
23 Q 15 Falls City, NE, U.S.A.
17 S 8 Falls Lake Reserve, NC, U.S.A.
16 J 4 Falmouth, KY, U.S.A.
17 T 4 Falmouth, VA, U.S.A.
48 K 8 Falmouth, Jamaica
62 J 15 Falmouth, U.K.
62 J 15 Falmouth Bay, U.K.
132 J 15 False Bay, Republic of South Africa
34 L 13 False Pass, AK, U.S.A.
105 J 16 False Point, India
71 D 26 Falster, Denmark
86 L 8 Fălticeni, Romania
71 G 19 Falun, Sweden
56 H 9 Famatina, Argentina
100 H 6 Famenin, Iran
114 J 11 Fan Si Pan, Vietnam
113 X 6 Fanchang, China
133 Y 8 Fandriana, Madgascar
114 G 13 Fang, Thailand
127 E 20 Fangak, Sudan
113 T 4 Fangcheng, China
113 Z 12 Fangshan, Taiwan
113 R 5 Fangxian, China
110 M 11 Fangzheng, China
110 J 13 Fanjiatun, China
101 N 13 Fannūj, Iran
71 B 25 Fanø, Denmark
76 H 10 Fano, Italy
113 Y 8 Fanshan, China
111 B 17 Fanshi, China
106 M 8 Far Western, Nepal
144 H 4 Faraday, Antarctica
131 Q 5 Faradje, Democratic Republic of Congo
133 Y 10 Farafangana, Madgascar
101 Q 8 Farāh, Afghanistan
101 P 9 Farāh, Afghanistan
140 A 8 Farallon de Medinilla, Northern Mariana Islands
140 A 5 Farallon de Pajaros, Northern Mariana Islands
128 H 11 Faranah, Guinea
99 X 10 Fararah, Oman
140 M 14 Faraulep, Federated States of Micronesia
63 T 13 Fareham, U.K.
35 P 8 Farewell, AK, U.S.A.
137 H 15 Farewell Spit, New Zealand
103 S 12 Farghona Wiloyati, Uzbekistan
19 V 7 Fargo, GA, U.S.A.
23 O 5 Fargo, ND, U.S.A.
23 S 9 Faribault, MN, U.S.A.
106 J 9 Faridabad, India
106 H 6 Faridkot, India
107 T 13 Faridpur, Bangladesh
101 O 6 Farīmān, Iran
63 S 10 Faringdon, U.K.
71 G 24 Färjestaden, Sweden
15 P 5 Farmington, ME, U.S.A.
31 O 8 Farmington, NM, U.S.A.
17 R 6 Farmville, VA, U.S.A.
63 U 11 Farnborough, U.K.
63 T 11 Farnham, U.K.
38 C 13 Faro, YT, Canada
66 H 12 Faro, Portugal
66 H 12 Faro, Portugal
143 R 15 Faroe Islands, Denmark
143 Q 15 FaroeŠIceland Ridge, Arctic Ocean
71 I 22 Fårösund, Sweden
71 I 22 Fårösund, Sweden
25 X 5 Farrington, MO, U.S.A.
100 J 10 Fārs, Iran
83 E 17 Farsala, Greece
29 S 13 Farson, WY, U.S.A.
26 I 3 Farwell, TX, U.S.A.
144 J 8 Farwell Island, Antarctica
101 R 6 Fāryāb, Afghanistan
100 J 11 Fasā, Iran
77 N 16 Fasano, Italy
87 P 4 Fastiv, Ukraine
131 R 6 Fataki, Democratic Republic of Congo
106 I 7 Fatehabad, India
106 L 9 Fatehgarh, India
106 M 11 Fatehpur, India
92 J 4 Fatezh, Russian Federation
128 D 8 Fatick, Senegal
130 I 10 Fatundu, Democratic Republic of Congo
139 S 8 Fatutaka, Solomon Islands
70 G 10 Fauske, Norway
63 Y 11 Faversham, U.K.
70 A 11 Faxaflói, Iceland
129 X 7 Faya, Chad
139 Q 13 Fayaoué, New Caledonia
18 K 5 Fayette, MS, U.S.A.
19 O 3 Fayette, AL, U.S.A.
16 F 10 Fayetteville, TN, U.S.A.
17 R 10 Fayetteville, NC, U.S.A.
21 L 20 Fayetteville, OH, U.S.A.
25 S 9 Fayetteville, AR, U.S.A.
141 N 14 Fayu, Federated States of Micronesia
128 G 4 Fdérik, Mauritania
65 N 3 Fécamp, France
80 H 13 Federacija Bosna Hercegovina, Bosnia and Herzegovina
58 D 13 Federación, Argentina
58 D 13 Federal, Argentina
129 R 12 Federal Capital Territory, Nigeria
141 Q 14 Federated States of Micronesia, Oceania
97 O 3 Fedghāmi, Syria
103 O 2 Fedorovka, Kazakhstan
72 I 8 Fehmarn, Germany
72 I 7 Fehmarnbelt, Germany
75 X 8 Fehring, Austria
54 B 13 Feijó, Brazil
55 N 14 Feira de Santana, Brazil
94 K 12 Feke, Turkey
67 Y 8 Felanitx, Spain
75 X 8 Feldbach, Austria
74 I 7 Feldkirch, Austria
75 S 8 Feldkirchen in Kärnten, Austria
105 L 18 Felidhu Atoll, Maldives
45 Z 11 Felipe Carrillo Puerto, Mexico
63 Z 9 Felixstowe, U.K.
76 G 6 Feltre, Italy
71 E 17 Femunden, Norway
95 O 8 Fener Burnu, Turkey
83 J 14 Fengari, Greece
111 I 16 Fengcheng, China
113 U 8 Fengcheng, China
113 P 7 Fengdu, China
113 P 8 Fenggang, China
113 Z 7 Fenghua, China
113 Q 8 Fenghuang, China
113 W 11 Fenghuang, China
113 Q 6 Fengjie, China
113 Z 11 Fenglin, Taiwan
111 E 15 Fengning, China
112 J 11 Fengqing, China
113 Q 9 Fengqiu, China
71 F 17 Fengrun, China
110 I 4 Fengshui Shan, China
113 V 11 Fengshun, China
113 V 5 Fengtai, China
113 O 4 Fengxian, China
113 U 4 Fengxian, China
113 Z 6 Fengxian, China
113 P 3 Fengxiang, China
113 V 8 Fengxin, China
113 W 4 Fengyang, China
113 Z 11 Fengyüan, Taiwan
111 B 16 Fengzhen, China
107 V 13 Feni, Bangladesh
138 I 3 Feni Islands, Papua New Guinea
21 E 14 Fennimore, WI, U.S.A.
133 Z 7 Fenoarivo Atsinanana, Madgascar
113 S 1 Fenyang, China
87 V 12 Feodosiya, Ukraine
21 I 21 Ferdinand, IN, U.S.A.
101 N 7 Ferdows, Iran
82 K 13 Feres, Greece
127 L 22 Fērfēr, Ethiopia
103 T 12 Fergana, Uzbekistan
103 S 12 Fergana Valley, Uzbekistan
23 P 6 Fergus Falls, MN, U.S.A.
138 G 6 Fergusson Island, Papua New Guinea
125 P 6 Fériana, Tunisia
128 K 11 Ferkessédougou, Côte d'Ivoire
76 I 11 Fermo, Italy
66 K 5 Fermoselle, Spain
61 C 20 Fermoy, Republic of Ireland
56 J 8 Fernández, Argentina
19 W 7 Fernandina Beach, FL, U.S.A.
58 I 4 Fernandópolis, Brazil
33 I 17 Fernley, NV, U.S.A.
77 M 16 Ferrandina, Italy
76 G 8 Ferrara, Italy
66 H 10 Ferreira do Alentejo, Portugal
18 K 6 Ferriday, LA, U.S.A.
66 I 1 Ferrol, Spain
124 I 7 Fès, Morocco
130 J 11 Feshi, Democratic Republic of Congo
22 K 4 Fessenden, ND, U.S.A.
25 Y 5 Festus, MO, U.S.A.
86 M 13 Feteşti-Gara, Romania
94 D 13 Fethiye, Turkey
102 I 10 Fetisovo, Kazakhstan
60 K 4 Fetlar, U.K.
73 H 22 Feuchtwangen, Germany
65 S 10 Feurs, France
101 V 5 Feyzābād, Afghanistan
63 N 5 Ffestiniog, U.K.
56 H 8 Fiambalá, Argentina
133 X 9 Fianarantsoa, Madgascar
133 X 9 Fianarantsoa, Madgascar
129 V 11 Fianga, Chad
127 I 20 Fiché, Ethiopia
73 J 20 Fichtelgebirge, Germany
76 G 12 Ficulle, Italy
76 E 8 Fidenza, Italy
81 J 20 Fier, Albania
74 F 10 Fiesch, Switzerland
20 J 12 Fife Lake, MI, U.S.A.
60 I 12 Fife Ness, U.K.
65 P 12 Figeac, France
66 G 7 Figueira da Foz, Portugal
67 Y 3 Figueres, Spain
124 K 8 Figuig, Morocco
129 V 11 Figuil, Cameroon
139 W 12 Fiji, Oceania
127 K 21 Fīk', Ethiopia
133 O 8 Filabusi, Zimbabwe
47 O 10 Filadelfia, Costa Rica
55 F 18 Filadélfia, Paraguay
79 K 21 Fil'akovo, Slovakia
145 N 5 Filchner Ice Shelf, Antarctica
63 O 7 Filey, U.K.
63 V 1 Filey Head, U.K.
86 H 12 Filiaşi, Romania
83 C 22 Filiatra, Greece
129 P 9 Filingué, Niger
83 B 17 Filippiada, Greece
30 I 5 Fillmore, UT, U.S.A.
33 J 24 Fillmore, CA, U.S.A.
127 J 23 Filtu, Ethiopia
145 P 1 Fimbul Ice Shelf, Antarctica
145 P 2 Fimbulheimen, Antarctica
67 P 12 Fiñana, Spain
21 L 17 Findlay, OH, U.S.A.
14 F 9 Finger Lakes, NY, U.S.A.
133 P 5 Fingoè, Mozambique
94 E 14 Finike, Turkey
138 D 4 Finisterre Range, Papua New Guinea
135 O 7 Finke, NT, Australia
71 L 18 Finland, Europe
39 E 16 Finlay, BC, Canada
23 N 4 Finley, ND, U.S.A.
135 S 12 Finley, NSW, Australia
99 Z 7 Fins, Oman
138 E 5 Finschhafen, Papua New Guinea
74 F 9 Finsteraarhorn, Switzerland
137 A 25 Fiordland, New Zealand
39 J 15 Firebag, AB, Canada
76 F 9 Firenzuola, Italy
59 B 15 Firmat, Argentina
65 S 11 Firminy, France
90 G 13 Firovo, Russian Federation
106 K 10 Firozabad, India
106 H 6 Firozpur, India
61 G 14 Firth of Clyde, U.K.
60 I 12 Firth of Forth, U.K.
60 F 12 Firth of Lorn, U.K.
136 L 8 Firth of Thames, New Zealand
100 J 11 Fīrūzābād, Iran
100 J 6 Fīrūzkūh, Iran
41 N 4 Fisher Strait, NU, Canada
62 K 9 Fishguard, U.K.
62 J 8 Fishguard Bay, U.K.
65 R 3 Fismes, France
60 J 5 Fitful Head, U.K.
57 H 20 Fitz Roy, Argentina
53 F 16 Fitzcarrald, Peru
134 J 4 Fitzroy, WA, Australia
134 J 4 Fitzroy Crossing, WA, Australia
42 C 10 Fitzwilliam Island, ON, Canada
77 G 14 Fiumicino, Italy
76 D 9 Fivizzano, Italy
131 Q 10 Fizi, Democratic Republic of Congo
71 C 19 Flå, Norway
70 C 12 Flaga, Iceland
36 K 10 Flagstaff, AZ, U.S.A.
15 O 4 Flagstaff Lake, ME, U.S.A.
41 P 8 Flaherty Island, ON, Canada
63 V 1 Flamborough, U.K.
63 V 1 Flamborough Head, U.K.
73 K 14 Fläming, Germany
30 M 2 Flaming Gorge Reservoir, UT/WY, U.S.A.
19 X 14 Flamingo, FL, U.S.A.
69 C 19 Flanders, Belgium
71 G 14 Flåsjön, Sweden
29 N 3 Flathead Lake, MT, U.S.A.
75 S 8 Flattnitz, Austria
63 O 2 Fleetwood, U.K.
71 A 21 Flekkefjord, Norway
71 B 26 Flensburg, Denmark
72 G 7 Flensburg, Germany
64 M 4 Flers, France
144 I 8 Fletcher Peninsula, Antarctica
74 B 8 Fleurier, Switzerland
68 I 10 Flevoland, Netherlands
40 H 7 Flin Flon, MB, Canada
135 R 5 Flinders, QLD, Australia
135 T 14 Flinders Island, TAS, Australia
135 P 10 Flinders Ranges, SA, Australia
21 L 14 Flint, MI, U.S.A.
63 O 4 Flint, U.K.
141 S 7 Flint, Kiribati
25 O 7 Flint Hills, KS, U.S.A.
71 E 18 Flisa, Norway
71 E 19 Flisa, Norway
21 G 21 Flora, IL, U.S.A.
65 S 12 Florac, France
19 Q 6 Florala, AL, U.S.A.
14 A 13 Florence, PA, U.S.A.
17 P 12 Florence, SC, U.S.A.
19 O 1 Florence, AL, U.S.A.
25 O 5 Florence, KS, U.S.A.
30 K 13 Florence, AZ, U.S.A.
32 F 11 Florence, OR, U.S.A.
76 F 10 Florence, Italy
50 H 9 Florencia, Colombia
69 G 22 Florennes, Belgium
69 J 25 Florenville, Belgium
46 I 3 Flores, Guatemala
59 E 15 Flores, Uruguay
117 O 15 Flores, Indonesia
117 N 15 Flores Sea, Indonesia
54 N 13 Floresta, Brazil
81 N 7 Floreşti, Moldova
27 P 11 Floresville, TX, U.S.A.
54 L 12 Floriano, Brazil
58 J 10 Florianópolis, Brazil
19 W 10 Florida, U.S.A.
59 E 15 Florida, Uruguay
59 E 15 Florida, Uruguay
19 X 14 Florida Bay, FL, U.S.A.
138 L 6 Florida Islands, Solomon Islands
19 W 15 Florida Keys, FL, U.S.A.
82 C 13 Florina, Greece
25 Y 4 Florissant, MO, U.S.A.
71 A 17 Florø, Norway
26 K 4 Floydada, TX, U.S.A.
68 J 8 Fluessen, Netherlands
117 S 11 Fluk, Indonesia
138 A 5 Fly, Papua New Guinea
140 I 10 Foa, Tonga
80 I 13 Foča, Bosnia and Herzegovina
86 L 11 Focşani, Romania
130 M 4 Fodé, Central African Republic
113 T 12 Fogang, China
124 M 11 Foggâret ez Zoûa, Algeria
77 L 15 Foggia, Italy
41 Y 9 Fogo Island, NL, Canada
117 Q 15 Foho Tatamailau, East Timor
72 F 7 Föhr, Germany
72 P 15 Foix, France
70 G 10 Folda, Norway
83 I 23 Folegandros, Greece
19 O 7 Foley, AL, U.S.A.
41 P 1 Foley Island, NU, Canada
42 C 6 Foleyet, ON, Canada
76 H 12 Foligno, Italy
63 Z 12 Folkestone, U.K.
76 E 12 Follonica, Italy
17 Q 15 Folly Beach, SC, U.S.A.
133 W 4 Fomboni, Comoros
20 G 13 Fond du Lac, WI, U.S.A.
77 I 15 Fondi, Italy
77 C 17 Fonni, Italy
30 J 2 Fonseca, Colombia
69 F 21 Fontaine-l'Eveque, Belgium
65 Q 5 Fontainebleau, France
54 D 10 Fonte Boa, Brazil
65 O 4 Fontenay-Trésigny, France
70 D 9 Fontur, Iceland
140 I 10 Fonualei, Tonga
79 G 24 Fonyód, Hungary
135 T 11 Forbes, NSW, Australia
71 A 17 Førde, Norway
71 A 19 Førde, Norway
63 R 13 Fordingbridge, U.K.
14 J 13 Fords, NJ, U.S.A.
25 V 13 Fordyce, AR, U.S.A.
128 F 11 Forécariah, Guinea
18 M 5 Forest, MS, U.S.A.
63 Q 1 Forest of Bowland, U.K.
63 Q 9 Forest of Dean, U.K.
43 P 6 Forestville, QC, Canada
60 I 11 Forfar, U.K.
24 I 7 Forgan, OK, U.S.A.
32 F 6 Forks, WA, U.S.A.
76 G 9 Forlì, Italy
63 O 3 Formby, U.K.
67 W 9 Formentera, Spain
77 I 15 Formia, Italy
55 K 18 Formiga, Brazil
55 K 16 Formosa, Brazil
56 M 7 Formosa, Argentina
56 L 6 Formosa, Argentina
55 K 14 Formosa do Rio Preto, Brazil
67 Z 7 Fornells, Spain
76 D 8 Fornovo di Taro, Italy
71 D 16 Forolshogna, Norway
134 K 11 Forrest, WA, Australia
25 X 11 Forrest City, AR, U.S.A.
135 S 4 Forsayth, QLD, Australia
70 H 8 Forsbakken, Norway
71 L 18 Forssa, Finland
73 O 15 Forst, Germany
135 V 11 Forster, NSW, Australia
19 T 4 Forsyth, GA, U.S.A.
29 W 6 Forsyth, MT, U.S.A.
101 X 11 Fort Abbas, Pakistan
41 O 10 Fort Albany, ON, Canada
60 G 10 Fort Augustus, U.K.
133 N 14 Fort Beaufort, Republic of South Africa
29 R 4 Fort Benton, MT, U.S.A.
33 E 17 Fort Bragg, CA, U.S.A.
29 R 14 Fort Bridger, WY, U.S.A.
39 J 14 Fort Chipewyan, AB, Canada
31 R 3 Fort Collins, CO, U.S.A.
42 I 10 Fort Coulonge, QC, Canada
49 Y 11 Fort-de-France, Martinique
23 S 11 Fort Dodge, IA, U.S.A.
40 J 11 Fort Frances, ON, Canada
31 R 7 Fort Garland, CO, U.S.A.
38 D 10 Fort Good Hope, NT, Canada
26 E 8 Fort Hancock, TX, U.S.A.
19 Y 13 Fort Lauderdale, FL, U.S.A.
39 F 14 Fort Liard, NT, Canada
49 P 7 Fort Liberté, Haiti
39 J 15 Fort MacKay, AB, Canada
39 J 16 Fort McMurray, AB, Canada
38 B 9 Fort McPherson, NT, Canada
19 W 12 Fort Myers, FL, U.S.A.
19 W 12 Fort Myers Beach, FL, U.S.A.
39 F 15 Fort Nelson, BC, Canada
19 R 2 Fort Payne, AL, U.S.A.
29 W 3 Fort Peck, MT, U.S.A.
29 W 4 Fort Peck Reservoir, MT, U.S.A.
19 Y 11 Fort Pierce, FL, U.S.A.
131 R 7 Fort Portal, Uganda
38 H 13 Fort Providence, NT, Canada
38 I 13 Fort Resolution, NT, Canada
133 O 8 Fort Rixon, Zimbabwe
25 R 6 Fort Scott, KS, U.S.A.
40 M 7 Fort Severn, ON, Canada
102 G 8 Fort-Shevchenko, Kazakhstan
38 F 13 Fort Simpson, NT, Canada
25 S 10 Fort Smith, AR, U.S.A.
29 U 8 Fort Smith, MT, U.S.A.
39 I 14 Fort Smith, NT, Canada
39 F 18 Fort St James, BC, Canada
39 G 17 Fort St John, BC, Canada
26 I 8 Fort Stockton, TX, U.S.A.
31 T 11 Fort Sumner, NM, U.S.A.
24 K 8 Fort Supply, OK, U.S.A.
19 T 4 Fort Valley, GA, U.S.A.
19 Q 7 Fort Walton Beach, FL, U.S.A.
21 J 17 Fort Wayne, IN, U.S.A.
60 G 11 Fort William, U.K.
27 P 6 Fort Worth, TX, U.S.A.
35 S 5 Fort Yukon, AK, U.S.A.
54 N 11 Fortaleza, Brazil
53 O 22 Forte Coimbra, Bolivia
76 E 10 Forte dei Marmi, Italy
60 H 12 Forth, U.K.
53 N 21 Fortín, Bolivia
55 F 18 Fortín Carlos Antonio López, Paraguay
55 E 18 Fortín Coronel Eugenio Garay, Paraguay
55 F 17 Fortín Galpón, Paraguay
55 E 18 Fortín Infante Rivarola, Paraguay
55 F 18 Fortín Madrejón, Paraguay
56 L 5 Fortín Pilcomayo, Argentina
53 M 21 Fortín Ravelo, Bolivia
137 D 26 Fortrose, New Zealand
22 G 2 Fortuna, ND, U.S.A.
33 E 16 Fortuna, CA, U.S.A.
41 Y 11 Fortune Bay, NL, Canada
63 Q 14 Fortuneswell, U.K.
100 J 13 Forūr, Iran
65 T 14 Fos-sur-Mer, France
63 W 5 Fosdyke, U.K.
113 T 12 Foshan, China
70 C 12 Foss, Iceland
76 A 8 Fossano, Italy
69 G 21 Fosses-la-Ville, Belgium
76 H 10 Fossombrone, Italy
130 E 8 Fougamou, Gabon
64 L 5 Fougères, France
126 G 12 Foul Bay, Egypt
60 J 5 Foula, U.K.
130 D 8 Foulenzem, Gabon
63 Y 10 Foulness Island, U.K.
63 Y 10 Foulness Point, U.K.
124 H 9 Foum Zguid, Morocco
129 T 13 Foumban, Cameroon
29 Z 9 Four Corners, WY, U.S.A.
83 L 21 Fournoi, Greece
128 G 10 Fouta Djallon, Guinea
137 B 26 Foveaux Strait, New Zealand
135 N 10 Fowlers Bay, SA, Australia
39 I 18 Fox Creek, AB, Canada
137 D 20 Fox Glacier, New Zealand
34 I 14 Fox Islands, AK, U.S.A.
39 I 15 Fox Lake, AB, Canada
33 I 15 Fox Mountain, NV, U.S.A.
137 F 20 Fox Peak, New Zealand
41 P 2 Foxe Basin, NU, Canada
41 O 2 Foxe Channel, NU, Canada

Country · Internal administrative region: State/Province/Territory/Dependent territory · Capital city · Mountain range/Undersea ridge · Mountain peak/Volcano/Seamount · Geographic feature · Headland/Point/Cape/Peninsula · Desert · Island/Island group · Antarctic base · Ocean · Sea · Bay/Gulf/Channel/Strait · Lake · Salt pan/Dry/Intermittent lake · R

Country ■ Internal administrative region: State/Province/Territory/Dependent territory □ | Capital city ▮ | Mountain range/Undersea ridge ▲▲ | Mountain peak/Volcano/Seamount ▲ | Geographic feature ◇ | Headland/Point/Cape/Peninsula ▶ | Desert ▲ | Island/Island group ⬚ | Antarctic base ⊞ | Ocean ≋ | Sea ≈ | Bay/Gulf/Channel/Strait ≈ | Lake ⬚ | Salt pan/Dry/Intermittent lake ▬ | River ∿

Golden Meadow – Gürün

18 L 9 Golden Meadow, LA, U.S.A.
32 I 9 Goldendale, WA, U.S.A.
34 K 20 Goldfield, NV, U.S.A.
17 T 10 Goldsboro, NC, U.S.A.
27 O 8 Goldthwaite, TX, U.S.A.
95 R 8 Göle, Turkey
78 D 10 Goleniów, Poland
100 L 4 Golestān, Iran
33 I 24 Goleta, CA, U.S.A.
67 W 5 Golf de Sant Jordi, Spain
125 Q 7 Golfe de Gabès, Tunisia
125 R 5 Golfe de Hammamet, Tunisia
49 O 7 Golfe de la Gonâve, Haiti
64 J 4 Golfe de St-Malo, France
127 L 19 Golfe de Tadjoura, Djibouti
125 Q 5 Golfe de Tunis, Tunisia
47 R 14 Golfito, Costa Rica
67 Q 13 Golfo de Almería, Spain
57 F 17 Golfo de Ancud, Chile
57 E 14 Golfo de Arauco, Chile
48 G 4 Golfo de Batabanó, Cuba
66 J 12 Golfo de Cádiz, Portugal/Spain
47 T 15 Golfo de Chiriquí, Panama
57 E 18 Golfo de Corcovado, Chile
46 L 8 Golfo de Fonseca, Honduras
48 K 6 Golfo de Guacanayabo, Cuba
47 U 13 Golfo de los Mosquitos, Panama
67 S 12 Golfo de Mazarrón, Spain
47 U 15 Golfo de Montijo, Panama
47 P 13 Golfo de Nicoya, Costa Rica
57 E 21 Golfo de Penas, Chile
57 I 20 Golfo de San Jorge, Argentina
47 Y 14 Golfo de San Miguel, Panama
45 U 14 Golfo de Tehuantepec, Mexico
50 G 4 Golfo de Urabá, Colombia
67 U 8 Golfo de Valencia, Spain
77 C 19 Golfo di Cagliari, Italy
77 H 21 Golfo di Castellammare, Italy
77 L 22 Golfo di Catania, Italy
77 B 15 Golfo di dell'Asinara, Italy
77 I 15 Golfo di Gaeta, Italy
77 L 20 Golfo di Gioia, Italy
77 M 14 Golfo di Manfredonia, Italy
77 I 16 Golfo di Napoli, Italy
77 L 24 Golfo di Noto, Italy
77 B 18 Golfo di Oristano, Italy
77 D 17 Golfo di Orosei, Italy
77 B 19 Golfo di Palmas, Italy
77 L 18 Golfo di Policastro, Italy
77 K 17 Golfo di Salerno, Italy
77 M 20 Golfo di Santa Eufemia, Italy
77 D 20 Golfo di Squillace, Italy
77 N 18 Golfo di Taranto, Italy
76 I 7 Golfo di Trieste, Italy
47 R 14 Golfo Dulce, Costa Rica
57 J 17 Golfo Nuevo, Argentina
57 J 17 Golfo San José, Argentina
57 J 17 Golfo San Matías, Argentina
57 E 23 Golfo Trinidad, Chile
110 H 12 Golin Baixing, China
109 N 8 Golmud, China
120 F 12 Golo, Philippines
100 H 7 Golpāyegān, Iran
60 H 9 Golspie, U.K.
103 T 3 Golubovka, Kazakhstan
82 H 11 Golyam Perelik, Bulgaria
82 I 11 Golyam Persenk, Bulgaria
131 Q 9 Goma, Democratic Republic of Congo
104 G 12 Gomati, India
129 T 11 Gombe, Nigeria
129 T 11 Gombe, Nigeria
129 U 11 Gombi, Nigeria
44 L 4 Gómez Farías, Mexico
45 N 7 Gómez Palacio, Mexico
49 O 7 Gonaïves, Haiti
100 L 5 Gonbad-e Kavus, Iran
107 N 10 Gonda, India
127 H 18 Gonder, Ethiopia
105 F 15 Gondia, India
113 S 7 Gong'an, China
113 R 11 Gongcheng, China
112 L 7 Gongga Shan, China
108 L 11 Gonggar, China
109 P 8 Gonghe, China
111 C 15 Gonghui, China
108 J 4 Gongliu, China
109 N 6 Gongpoquan, China
113 T 3 Gongyi, China
110 J 13 Gongzhuling, China
129 T 10 Goniri, Nigeria
123 A 21 Gōnoura, Japan
120 H 6 Gonzaga, Philippines
27 Q 10 Gonzales, TX, U.S.A.
33 G 21 Gonzales, CA, U.S.A.
47 Y 14 Gonzalo Vásquez, Panama
17 T 5 Goochland, VA, U.S.A.
138 G 6 Goodenough Island, Papua New Guinea
28 L 12 Gooding, ID, U.S.A.
24 G 3 Goodland, KS, U.S.A.
34 M 10 Goodnews, AK, U.S.A.
135 S 11 Goolgowi, NSW, Australia
134 G 11 Goomalling, WA, Australia
135 U 9 Goondiwindi, QLD, Australia
58 M 11 Goor, Netherlands
57 L 24 Goose Green, Falkland Islands
33 I 14 Goose Lake, CA, U.S.A.
107 P 10 Gopalganj, India
106 K 7 Gopeshwar, India
79 F 14 Góra, Poland
102 J 12 Gora Arlang, Turkmenistan
103 P 14 Gora Ayribaba, Turkmenistan
88 M 14 Gora Belukha, Russian Federation
102 I 9 Gora Besshoky, Kazakhstan
91 U 10 Gora Denezhkin Kamen', Russian Federation
91 U 9 Gora Isherim, Russian Federation
102 J 13 Gora Khasardag, Turkmenistan
103 P 12 Gora Khayatbashi, Uzbekistan
91 U 11 Gora Konzhakovskiy Kamen', Russian Federation
103 V 7 Gora Kotanemel', Kazakhstan
91 S 7 Gora Kozhim-Iz, Russian Federation
89 Z 8 Gora Ledyanaya, Russian Federation
89 X 13 Gora Lopatina, Russian Federation
103 S 10 Gora Manas, Kyrgyzstan
89 O 13 Gora Munku Sardyk, Russian Federation
108 K 3 Gora Mustau, China
91 T 5 Gora Narodnaya, Russian Federation
89 X 10 Gora Nukh Yablonevyy, Russian Federation
91 U 3 Gora Payyer, Russian Federation
89 W 9 Gora Pobeda, Russian Federation
103 T 7 Gora Shunak, Kazakhstan
102 K 13 Gora Tagarev, Turkmenistan
89 V 14 Gora Tardoki-Yani, Russian Federation
91 T 6 Gora Tel'pos-Iz, Russian Federation
88 J 8 Gora Telposiz, Russian Federation
107 O 10 Gorakhpur, India
80 I 13 Goražde, Bosnia and Herzegovina
17 S 5 Gordonsville, VA, U.S.A.
129 W 12 Goré, Chad
137 D 25 Gore, New Zealand
42 B 9 Gore Bay, ON, Canada
14 M 5 Gore Mountain, VT, U.S.A.
94 J 11 Göreme, Turkey
61 E 19 Gorey, Republic of Ireland
100 K 5 Gorgān, Iran
137 D 23 Gorge Creek, New Zealand
128 F 7 Gorgol, Mauritania
127 H 18 Gorgora, Ethiopia
95 T 6 Gori, Georgia
69 H 14 Gorinchem, Netherlands
95 V 9 Goris, Armenia
90 I 14 Goritsy, Russian Federation
76 I 6 Gorizia, Italy
107 P 9 Gorkha, Nepal
90 M 14 Gor'kovskoye Vodokhranilishche, Russian Federation
79 L 18 Gorlice, Poland
73 O 16 Görlitz, Germany
82 H 7 Gorni Dŭbnik, Bulgaria
80 L 12 Gornji Milanovac, Serbia and Montenegro
88 M 13 Gorno Altaysk, Russian Federation
88 L 13 Gornyak, Russian Federation
93 R 5 Gornyy, Russian Federation
93 P 7 Gornyy Balykley, Russian Federation
90 L 14 Gorodets, Russian Federation
93 P 3 Gorodishche, Russian Federation
93 N 11 Gorodovikovsk, Russian Federation
138 D 4 Goroka, Papua New Guinea
133 R 7 Gorongosa, Mozambique
117 P 10 Gorontalo, Indonesia
68 L 12 Gorssel, Netherlands
102 I 11 Gory Akkyr, Turkmenistan
103 N 12 Gory Auminzatau, Uzbekistan
103 Q 14 Gory Baysuntau, Uzbekistan
103 N 10 Gory Bukantau, Uzbekistan
89 P 7 Gory Byrranga, Russian Federation
103 O 11 Gory Dzhetymtau, Uzbekistan
89 P 8 Gory Kamen', Russian Federation
102 J 11 Gory Koymatdag, Turkmenistan
102 L 7 Gory Mugodzhary, Kazakhstan
89 O 9 Gory Putorana, Russian Federation
79 K 15 Góry Świętokrzyskie, Poland
78 E 11 Gorzów Wielkopolski, Poland
135 V 11 Gosford, NSW, Australia
122 J 9 Goshogawara, Japan
73 H 14 Goslar, Germany
80 D 11 Gospić, Croatia
63 T 13 Gosport, U.K.
69 G 21 Gosselies, Belgium
71 B 15 Gossen, Norway
128 M 8 Gossi, Mali
82 C 11 Gostivar, Macedonia (F.Y.R.O.M.)
78 G 13 Gostyń, Poland
78 J 12 Gostynin, Poland
123 J 17 Gotemba, Japan
73 I 17 Gotha, Germany
22 K 14 Gothenburg, NE, U.S.A.
71 D 22 Gothenburg, Sweden
129 O 9 Gothèye, Niger
71 I 23 Gotland, Sweden
123 A 23 Gotō-rettō, Japan
82 G 12 Gotse Delchev, Bulgaria
71 I 22 Gotska Sandön, Sweden
123 D 19 Gōtsu, Japan
73 H 15 Göttingen, Germany
68 G 13 Gouda, Netherlands
128 F 9 Goudiri, Senegal
129 T 9 Goudoumaria, Niger
135 U 12 Goulburn, NSW, Australia
135 N 1 Goulburn Islands, NT, Australia
145 O 9 Gould Coast, Antarctica
129 V 10 Goulfey, Cameroon
128 I 8 Goumbou, Mali
128 L 8 Goundam, Mali
129 X 11 Goundi, Chad
128 L 9 Gourcy, Burkina Faso
129 S 9 Gouré, Niger
65 P 3 Gournay-en-Bray, France
129 Y 6 Gouro, Chad
14 H 6 Gouverneur, NY, U.S.A.
55 M 17 Governador Valadares, Brazil
109 N 4 Govi-Altay, Mongolia
109 O 5 Govi Altayn Nuruu, Mongolia
107 N 12 Govind Ballash Pant Sagar, India
103 P 14 Govurdak, Turkmenistan
14 C 9 Gowanda, NY, U.S.A.
42 D 7 Gowganda, ON, Canada
58 C 11 Goya, Argentina
95 X 8 Göyçay, Azerbaijan
94 F 8 Göynük, Turkey
95 Q 10 Göynük, Turkey
129 U 14 Goyoum, Cameroon
95 Y 10 Göytäpä, Azerbaijan
129 Z 10 Goz-Beïda, Chad
127 G 16 Goz Regeb, Sudan
108 I 8 Gozha Co, China
77 J 25 Gozo, Malta
132 M 14 Graaf-Reinet, Republic of South Africa
128 I 14 Grabo, Côte d'Ivoire
80 D 11 Gračac, Croatia
42 I 9 Gracefield, QC, Canada
23 O 7 Graceville, MN, U.S.A.
46 K 6 Gracias, Honduras
80 H 10 Gradačac, Bosnia and Herzegovina
82 L 9 Gradets, Bulgaria
66 L 1 Grado, Spain
76 I 6 Grado, Italy
31 T 10 Grady, NM, U.S.A.
17 P 2 Grafton, WV, U.S.A.
23 N 2 Grafton, ND, U.S.A.
135 W 10 Grafton, NSW, Australia
37 O 3 Graham Island, NU, Canada
39 C 19 Graham Island, BC, Canada
144 H 3 Graham Land, Antarctica
133 N 15 Grahamstown, Republic of South Africa
54 K 12 Grajaú, Brazil
78 M 9 Grajewo, Poland
82 N 10 Gramatikovo, Bulgaria
60 H 11 Grampian Mtns, U.K.
72 N 11 Gramzow, Germany
57 G 21 Gran Altiplanicie Central, Argentina
56 K 6 Gran Chaco, Argentina/Paraguay
53 E 15 Gran Pajonal, Peru
31 U 6 Granada, CO, U.S.A.
47 N 9 Granada, Nicaragua
50 J 7 Granada, Colombia
67 O 12 Granada, Spain
42 M 10 Granby, QC, Canada
22 H 7 Grand, SD, U.S.A.
48 K 1 Grand Bahama, The Bahamas
128 K 14 Grand-Bassam, Côte d'Ivoire
43 S 10 Grand Bay, NB, Canada
42 C 13 Grand Bend, ON, Canada
49 P 5 Grand Caicos, Turks and Caicos Islands
30 J 9 Grand Canyon, AZ, U.S.A.
30 H 9 Grand Canyon, AZ, U.S.A.
48 H 7 Grand Cayman, Cayman Islands
128 I 14 Grand Cess, Liberia
32 J 6 Grand Coulee, WA, U.S.A.
129 T 7 Grand Erg de Bilma, Niger
124 J 9 Grand Erg Occidental, Algeria
125 N 10 Grand Erg Oriental, Algeria
43 Q 8 Grand Falls, NB, Canada
23 N 3 Grand Forks, ND, U.S.A.
21 I 14 Grand Haven, MI, U.S.A.
20 I 8 Grand Island, MI, U.S.A.
22 M 14 Grand Island, NE, U.S.A.
16 B 10 Grand Junction, TN, U.S.A.
31 N 5 Grand Junction, CO, U.S.A.
18 I 8 Grand Lake, LA, U.S.A.
21 K 18 Grand Lake, OH, U.S.A.
41 X 10 Grand Lake, NL, Canada
43 S 9 Grand Lake, NB, Canada
22 J 8 Grand Lake o' the Cherokees, OK, U.S.A.
15 T 5 Grand Manan Channel, ME, U.S.A.
43 S 11 Grand Manan Island, NB, Canada
20 J 8 Grand Marais, MI, U.S.A.
23 V 3 Grand Marais, MN, U.S.A.
42 L 9 Grand-Mère, QC, Canada
23 V 2 Grand Portage, MN, U.S.A.
21 J 14 Grand Rapids, MI, U.S.A.
23 R 4 Grand Rapids, MN, U.S.A.
40 I 8 Grand Rapids, MB, Canada
42 I 9 Grand-Remous, QC, Canada
29 R 10 Grand Teton, WY, U.S.A.
20 J 11 Grand Traverse Bay, MI, U.S.A.
49 Q 5 Grand Turk, Turks and Caicos Islands
28 J 11 Grand View, ID, U.S.A.
47 Q 8 Grande, Nicaragua
53 L 21 Grande, Bolivia/Brazil
39 H 18 Grande Cache, AB, Canada
133 W 4 Grande Comore, Comoros
43 W 6 Grande-Entrée, QC, Canada
39 H 18 Grande Prairie, AB, Canada
43 T 5 Grande-Vallée, QC, Canada
26 J 8 Grandfalls, TX, U.S.A.
24 L 12 Grandfield, OK, U.S.A.
66 G 10 Grândola, Portugal
32 I 9 Grandview, WA, U.S.A.
29 S 14 Granger, WY, U.S.A.
28 K 6 Grangeville, ID, U.S.A.
21 E 21 Granite City, IL, U.S.A.
23 P 8 Granite Falls, MN, U.S.A.
29 S 7 Granite Peak, MT, U.S.A.
30 I 3 Granite Peak, UT, U.S.A.
22 I 14 Grant, NE, U.S.A.
144 L 11 Grant Island, Antarctica
63 U 5 Grantham, U.K.
31 O 10 Grants, NM, U.S.A.
32 F 13 Grants Pass, OR, U.S.A.
30 J 3 Grantsville, UT, U.S.A.
64 L 4 Granville, France
28 J 12 Grasmere, ID, U.S.A.
71 I 19 Gräsö, Sweden
33 H 17 Grass Valley, CA, U.S.A.
77 M 16 Grassano, Italy
65 W 13 Grasse, France
29 S 5 Grassrange, MT, U.S.A.
22 G 4 Grassy Butte, ND, U.S.A.
74 H 9 Graubünden, Switzerland
67 U 3 Graus, Spain
58 H 12 Gravataí, Brazil
69 K 14 Grave, Netherlands
28 L 6 Grave Peak, ID, U.S.A.
76 D 5 Gravedona, Italy
42 F 11 Gravenhurst, ON, Canada
63 X 11 Gravesend, U.K.
19 T 4 Gray, GA, U.S.A.
65 U 7 Gray, France
20 K 11 Grayling, MI, U.S.A.
21 G 21 Grayville, IL, U.S.A.
92 I 6 Grayvoron, Russian Federation
75 W 7 Graz, Austria
48 L 1 Great Abaco, The Bahamas
134 K 11 Great Australian Bight, WA, Australia
48 J 2 Great Bahama Bank, The Bahamas
136 L 7 Great Barrier Island, New Zealand
135 S 1 Great Barrier Reef, QLD, Australia
14 L 10 Great Barrington, MA, U.S.A.
33 M 17 Great Basin, NV/UT, U.S.A.
38 F 10 Great Bear Lake, NT, Canada
24 L 5 Great Bend, KS, U.S.A.
61 J 14 Great Britain, U.K.
105 N 25 Great Channel, India
115 B 19 Great Coco Island, Myanmar
29 U 13 Great Divide Basin, WY, U.S.A.
135 T 13 Great Dividing Range, VIC, Australia
63 X 9 Great Dunmow, U.K.
136 I 4 Great Exhibition Bay, New Zealand
48 L 3 Great Exuma Island, The Bahamas
29 Q 4 Great Falls, MT, U.S.A.
107 P 10 Great Gandak, India
63 Q 12 Great Harwood, U.K.
79 L 24 Great Hungarian Plain, Hungary
49 N 5 Great Inagua Island, The Bahamas
132 K 14 Great Karoo, Republic of South Africa
63 Q 8 Great Malvern, U.K.
136 L 8 Great Mercury Island, New Zealand
105 O 25 Great Nicobar, India
63 X 7 Great Ouse, U.K.
41 Q 2 Great Plain of the Koukdjuak, NU, Canada
12 M 5 Great Plains, U.S.A., U.S.A.
96 F 12 Great Rift Valley, Jordan
127 H 22 Great Rift Valley, Africa
14 J 8 Great Sacandaga Lake, NY, U.S.A.
30 J 2 Great Salt Lake, UT, U.S.A.
30 I 3 Great Salt Lake Desert, UT, U.S.A.
24 M 7 Great Salt Plains Lake, OK, U.S.A.
126 B 9 Great Sand Sea, Egypt/Libya
134 J 5 Great Sandy Desert, WA, Australia
38 H 13 Great Slave Lake, NT, Canada
16 J 10 Great Smoky Mountains, NC, U.S.A.
39 F 16 Great Snow Mountain, BC, Canada
62 M 12 Great Torrington, U.K.
134 L 8 Great Victoria Desert, WA, Australia
15 S 5 Great Wass Island, ME, U.S.A.
115 E 21 Great West Torres Islands, Myanmar
63 Z 6 Great Yarmouth, U.K.
97 S 2 Great Zab, Iraq
129 N 13 Greater Accra, Ghana
48 I 5 Greater Antilles, Cuba
57 H 24 Greec, Chile
14 E 8 Greece, NY, U.S.A.
83 C 17 Greece, Europe
31 S 3 Greeley, CO, U.S.A.
17 P 13 Greeleyville, SC, U.S.A.
30 L 4 Green, UT, U.S.A.
20 H 11 Green Bay, WI, U.S.A.
20 H 12 Green Bay, WI, U.S.A.
19 W 8 Green Cove Springs, FL, U.S.A.
138 I 4 Green Islands, Papua New Guinea
39 L 17 Green Lake, SK, Canada
14 L 8 Green Mountains, VT, U.S.A.
30 L 5 Green River, UT/WY, U.S.A.
138 A 3 Green River, Papua New Guinea
16 H 6 Green River Lake, KY, U.S.A.
21 I 19 Greencastle, IN, U.S.A.
16 L 8 Greeneville, TN, U.S.A.
14 L 9 Greenfield, MA, U.S.A.
25 S 6 Greenfield, MO, U.S.A.
31 R 6 Greenhorn Mountain, CO, U.S.A.
143 P 11 Greenland, Denmark
143 S 12 Greenland Plain, Arctic Ocean
143 R 13 Greenland Sea, Arctic Ocean
14 M 12 Greenport, NY, U.S.A.
17 P 8 Greensboro, NC, U.S.A.
14 B 13 Greensburg, PA, U.S.A.
18 L 7 Greensburg, LA, U.S.A.
21 J 20 Greensburg, IN, U.S.A.
24 K 6 Greensburg, KS, U.S.A.
14 A 11 Greenville, PA, U.S.A.
15 Q 4 Greenville, ME, U.S.A.
16 M 11 Greenville, SC, U.S.A.
17 T 9 Greenville, NC, U.S.A.
18 K 3 Greenville, MS, U.S.A.
19 Q 5 Greenville, AL, U.S.A.
19 T 7 Greenville, FL, U.S.A.
21 K 18 Greenville, OH, U.S.A.
25 Y 7 Greenville, MO, U.S.A.
27 R 5 Greenville, TX, U.S.A.
33 H 16 Greenville, CA, U.S.A.
128 H 14 Greenville, Liberia
21 N 17 Greenwich, OH, U.S.A.
63 W 10 Greenwich, U.K.
16 M 12 Greenwood, SC, U.S.A.
18 H 4 Greenwood, LA, U.S.A.
18 M 3 Greenwood, MS, U.S.A.
25 V 10 Greers Ferry Lake, AR, U.S.A.
22 L 11 Gregory, SD, U.S.A.
135 R 4 Gregory Range, QLD, Australia
72 M 9 Greifswald, Germany
72 M 8 Greifswalder Bodden, Germany
75 U 4 Grein, Austria
73 K 18 Greiz, Germany
90 K 3 Gremikha, Russian Federation
71 D 24 Grenå, Denmark
18 M 3 Grenada, MS, U.S.A.
49 Y 13 Grenada, North America
18 M 2 Grenada Lake, MS, U.S.A.
74 D 7 Grenchen, Switzerland
65 U 11 Grenoble, France
49 Y 13 Grenville, Grenada
69 E 14 Grevelingen, Netherlands
73 D 14 Greven, Germany
83 C 15 Grevena, Greece
73 B 16 Grevenbroich, Germany
69 L 24 Grevenmacher, Luxembourg
69 M 25 Grevenmacher, Luxembourg
72 I 9 Grevesmühlen, Germany
137 F 18 Grey, New Zealand
41 X 9 Grey Islands, NL, Canada
29 V 9 Greybull, WY, U.S.A.
137 F 18 Greymouth, New Zealand
133 P 12 Greytown, Republic of South Africa
137 L 16 Greytown, New Zealand
93 N 5 Gribanovskiy, Russian Federation
75 S 4 Grieskirchen, Austria
19 S 3 Griffin, GA, U.S.A.
135 S 11 Griffith, NSW, Australia
95 Q 6 Grigoleti, Georgia
87 O 9 Grigoriopol, Moldova
130 K 4 Grimari, Central African Republic
73 L 16 Grimma, Germany
72 L 9 Grimmen, Germany
63 V 3 Grimsby, U.K.
70 C 9 Grimsey, Iceland
70 C 10 Grímsstaðir, Iceland
70 A 12 Grindavík, Iceland
74 F 9 Grindelwald, Switzerland
80 C 6 Grintovec, Slovenia
132 L 12 Griquatown, Republic of South Africa
37 P 3 Grise Fiord, NU, Canada
80 E 10 Grmeč, Bosnia and Herzegovina
69 H 17 Grobbendonk, Belgium
84 B 11 Grobiņa, Latvia
75 S 6 Gröbming, Austria
79 G 16 Grodków, Poland
68 M 12 Groenlo, Netherlands
78 L 13 Grójec, Poland
71 E 14 Grong, Norway
68 M 6 Groningen, Netherlands
68 M 6 Groningen, Netherlands
26 L 2 Groom, TX, U.S.A.
132 I 12 Groot Karas Berg, Namibia
135 P 2 Groote Eylandt, NT, Australia
132 J 8 Grootfontein, Namibia
132 J 9 Gross Ums, Namibia
76 F 12 Grosseto, Italy
75 P 7 Grossglockner, Austria
41 W 7 Groswater Bay, NL, Canada
14 B 11 Grove City, PA, U.S.A.
19 O 6 Grove Hill, AL, U.S.A.
15 N 5 Groveton, NH, U.S.A.
93 Q 14 Groznyy, Russian Federation
82 M 10 Grudovo, Bulgaria
78 I 10 Grudziądz, Poland
132 J 12 Grünau, Namibia
84 E 12 Gruzdžiai, Lithuania
92 M 4 Gryazi, Russian Federation
90 K 12 Gryazovets, Russian Federation
74 D 9 Gstaad, Switzerland
118 C 6 Gua Musang, Malaysia
47 S 13 Guabito, Panama
56 I 7 Guachipas, Argentina
45 O 11 Guadalajara, Mexico
67 P 6 Guadalajara, Spain
138 K 7 Guadalcanal, Solomon Islands
138 M 7 Guadalcanal, Solomon Islands
56 H 12 Guadalcanal, Argentina
66 L 12 Guadalquivir, Spain
45 Q 7 Guadalupe, Mexico
45 N 8 Guadalupe, Mexico
66 M 8 Guadalupe, Spain
26 F 7 Guadalupe Mountains, TX, U.S.A.
26 G 7 Guadalupe Peak, TX, U.S.A.
49 Y 9 Guadeloupe, France
49 X 9 Guadeloupe Passage, Montserrat
67 N 9 Guadiana, Spain
67 P 12 Guadix, Spain
58 H 12 Guaíba, Brazil
50 M 8 Guainía, Colombia
50 M 8 Guainía, Colombia
58 F 7 Guaíra, Brazil
55 D 14 Guajará-Mirim, Brazil
58 C 13 Gualeguay, Argentina
59 C 15 Gualeguay, Argentina
55 L 11 Gualeguaychú, Argentina
57 D 14 Gualeguaychú, Argentina
57 G 18 Gualjaina, Argentina
140 A 9 Guam, Guam
140 A 9 Guam, U.S.A.
59 B 18 Guaminí, Argentina
44 K 7 Guamúchil, Mexico
112 M 6 Guan Xian, China
48 H 4 Guanabacoa, Cuba
47 N 3 Guanaja, Honduras
45 P 11 Guanajuato, Mexico
45 P 10 Guanajuato, Mexico
55 L 15 Guanambi, Brazil
50 M 4 Guanare, Venezuela
56 G 9 Guandacol, Argentina
113 S 1 Guandi Shan, China
48 F 4 Guane, Cuba
113 V 9 Guangchang, China
113 X 6 Guangde, China
113 U 11 Guangdong, China
113 X 8 Guangfeng, China
113 T 13 Guanghai, China
112 K 9 Guangmao Shan, China
113 N 11 Guangnan, China
113 T 12 Guangning, China
111 F 19 Guangrao, China
113 U 5 Guangshui, China
113 Q 12 Guangxi Zhuangzu, China
113 O 5 Guangyuan, China
113 W 9 Guangze, China
113 T 12 Guangzhou, China
113 W 3 Guanhu, China
48 M 6 Guantánamo, Cuba
48 M 6 Guantánamo Bay Naval Base, U.S.A., U.S.A.
113 X 3 Guanyun, China
47 R 12 Guápiles, Costa Rica
55 E 15 Guaporé, Brazil
53 H 19 Guaqui, Bolivia
58 O 5 Guarapari, Brazil
58 H 10 Guarapuava, Brazil
58 J 8 Guaraqueçaba, Brazil
58 J 9 Guaratuba, Brazil
53 I 17 Guarayos, Bolivia
66 J 5 Guarda, Portugal
66 J 6 Guarda, Portugal
51 O 4 Guárico, Venezuela
58 L 7 Guarujá, Brazil
44 K 7 Guasave, Mexico
46 H 6 Guatemala, Guatemala
46 I 4 Guatemala, North America
51 O 2 Guatire, Venezuela
50 K 9 Guaviare, Colombia
50 M 7 Guaviare, Colombia
49 U 8 Guayama, Puerto Rico
52 A 10 Guayaquil, Ecuador
53 K 15 Guayaramerín, Bolivia
52 A 10 Guayas, Ecuador
44 I 5 Guaymas, Mexico
46 H 6 Guazacapán, Guatemala
88 M 8 Guba, Russian Federation
127 G 19 Guba, Ethiopia
91 R 1 Guba Dolgaya, Russian Federation
91 T 11 Gubakha, Russian Federation
78 D 13 Gubin, Poland
129 U 10 Gubio, Nigeria
95 P 5 Gudaut'a, Georgia
99 O 1 Gudayyidat 'Ar'ar, Saudi Arabia
93 Q 14 Gudermes, Russian Federation
105 G 19 Gudivada, India
105 F 20 Gudur, India
128 H 12 Guéckédou, Guinea
129 V 10 Guélengdeng, Chad
125 P 5 Guelma, Algeria
124 F 9 Guelmine, Morocco
42 E 13 Guelph, ON, Canada
45 R 8 Güémez, Mexico
129 O 10 Guéné, Benin
129 X 10 Guéra, Chad
125 N 8 Guerara, Algeria
124 J 7 Guercif, Morocco
65 P 9 Guéret, France
29 Z 12 Guernsey, WY, U.S.A.
61 J 25 Guernsey, U.K.
128 G 7 Guérou, Mauritania
45 Q 6 Guerrero, Mexico
45 Q 13 Guerrero, Mexico
44 G 5 Guerrero Negro, Mexico
128 J 13 Guéyo, Côte d'Ivoire
127 H 22 Gugë, Ethiopia
140 A 7 Guguan, Northern Mariana Islands
51 O 6 Guiana Highlands, South America
113 W 6 Guichi, China
59 E 14 Guichón, Uruguay
129 W 11 Guidari, Chad
129 V 11 Guider, Cameroon
128 G 8 Guidimaka, Mauritania
113 P 10 Guiding, China
113 Q 12 Guigang, China
128 I 13 Guiglo, Côte d'Ivoire
66 L 6 Guijuelo, Spain
63 U 11 Guildford, U.K.
110 H 11 Guiler, China
15 Q 4 Guilford, ME, U.S.A.
113 R 11 Guilin, China
65 W 12 Guillestre, France
121 I 17 Guimaras, Philippines
19 O 2 Guin, AL, U.S.A.
121 L 18 Guindulman, Philippines
128 F 10 Guinea, Africa
128 E 10 Guinea-Bissau, Africa
128 I 12 Guinée-Forestière, Guinea
128 F 10 Guinée-Maritime, Guinea
48 H 4 Güines, Cuba
64 J 5 Guingamp, France
113 R 12 Guiping, China
63 Y 6 Guist, U.K.
66 I 1 Guitiriz, Spain
121 M 16 Guiuan, Philippines
113 O 9 Guiyang, China
113 T 10 Guiyang, China
113 O 9 Guizhou, China
105 B 14 Gujarat, India
101 Y 9 Gujranwala, Pakistan
101 Y 8 Gujrat, Pakistan
109 P 8 Gulang, China
105 E 18 Gulbarga, India
84 I 10 Gulbene, Latvia
103 U 12 Gülchö, Kyrgyzstan
138 C 6 Gulf, Papua New Guinea
115 I 22 Gulf of Thailand, Thailand
127 M 18 Gulf of Aden, Africa/Asia
35 Q 11 Gulf of Alaska, AK, U.S.A.
89 Z 6 Gulf of Anadyr, Russian Federation
98 I 3 Gulf of Aqaba, Asia
38 L 4 Gulf of Boothia, NU, Canada
71 I 19 Gulf of Bothnia, Sweden
44 G 3 Gulf of California, Mexico
135 Q 2 Gulf of Carpentaria, QLD, Australia
83 E 19 Gulf of Corinth, Greece
50 G 3 Gulf of Darién, Colombia
71 L 20 Gulf of Finland, Europe
78 J 7 Gulf of Gdańsk, Europe
76 C 10 Gulf of Genoa, Italy
52 A 10 Gulf of Guayaquil, Ecuador
129 R 15 Gulf of Guinea, Africa
46 M 3 Gulf of Honduras, Honduras
105 A 14 Gulf of Kachchh, India
105 B 16 Gulf of Khambhat, India
15 P 9 Gulf of Maine, ME, U.S.A.
105 F 24 Gulf of Mannar, Sri Lanka
115 E 17 Gulf of Martaban, Myanmar
13 R 15 Gulf of Mexico, North America
99 Y 5 Gulf of Oman, Asia
47 X 15 Gulf of Panama, Panama
138 C 6 Gulf of Papua, Papua New Guinea
51 R 3 Gulf of Paria, Venezuela
84 E 9 Gulf of Riga, Estonia/Latvia
126 C 7 Gulf of Salûm, Egypt/Libya
125 V 8 Gulf of Sirte, Libya
43 W 5 Gulf of St Lawrence, QC, Canada
126 F 8 Gulf of Suez, Egypt
87 Y 9 Gulf of Taganrog, Russian Federation/Ukraine
113 Q 14 Gulf of Tongking, China
80 A 8 Gulf of Trieste, Slovenia
50 K 2 Gulf of Venezuela, Venezuela
76 H 7 Gulf of Venice, Italy
19 O 8 Gulf Shores, AL, U.S.A.
135 P 12 Gulf St Vincent, SA, Australia
13 T 13 Gulfport, MS, U.S.A.
113 O 8 Gulin, China/Vietnam
113 V 7 Guling, China
103 R 12 Gulistan, Uzbekistan
94 B 12 Güllük Körfezi, Turkey
94 A 9 Gülpinar, Turkey
95 Q 5 Gulrip'shi, Georgia
103 U 7 Gul'shad, Kazakhstan
131 S 6 Gulu, Uganda
82 K 10 Gŭlŭbovo, Bulgaria
82 I 7 Gulyantsi, Bulgaria
132 L 7 Gumare, Botswana
102 I 13 Gumdag, Turkmenistan
129 S 10 Gumel, Nigeria
105 I 15 Gumla, India
104 E 13 Guna, India
127 I 19 Guna Terara, Ethiopia
75 Q 4 Gundertshausen, Austria
94 L 12 Güney Doğu Toroslar, Turkey
130 J 11 Gungu, Democratic Republic of Congo
93 R 15 Gunib, Russian Federation
80 I 10 Gunja, Croatia
143 P 13 Gunnbjørn Fjeld, Greenland
135 U 10 Gunnedah, NSW, Australia
30 K 5 Gunnison, UT, U.S.A.
31 P 5 Gunnison, CO, U.S.A.
105 E 19 Guntakal, India
19 Q 2 Guntersville Lake, AL, U.S.A.
105 G 19 Guntur, India
116 B 8 Gunung Abongabong, Indonesia
119 O 10 Gunung Ayer, Malaysia
118 C 7 Gunung Batu Puteh, Malaysia
118 E 10 Gunung Belumut, Malaysia
118 C 7 Gunung Benum, Malaysia
118 A 6 Gunung Bintang, Malaysia
117 Q 10 Gunung Bulawa, Indonesia
118 C 6 Gunung Camah, Malaysia
117 W 12 Gunung Dom, Indonesia
116 D 11 Gunung Kerinci, Indonesia
117 U 11 Gunung Kwoka, Indonesia
118 D 5 Gunung Lawit, Malaysia
118 D 9 Gunung Ledang, Malaysia
118 C 7 Gunung Liang Timur, Malaysia
119 X 7 Gunung Magdaline, Malaysia
119 O 10 Gunung Malino, Indonesia
118 D 6 Gunung Mandi Angin, Malaysia
117 V 11 Gunung Mebo, Indonesia
119 W 4 Gunung Menapod, Malaysia
119 T 7 Gunung Murud, Malaysia
117 Q 15 Gunung Mutis, Indonesia
118 C 5 Gunung Noring, Malaysia
119 T 7 Gunung Pagon, Malaysia
116 K 15 Gunung Semeru, Indonesia
116 I 14 Gunung Slamet, Indonesia
118 D 6 Gunung Tahan, Malaysia
118 D 7 Gunung Tapis, Malaysia
119 X 6 Gunung Tribulation, Malaysia
119 U 5 Gunung Trus Madi, Malaysia
117 P 11 Gunung Tumpu, Indonesia
117 R 14 Gunungapi, Indonesia
116 C 10 Gunungsitoli, Indonesia
105 I 17 Gunupur, India
73 H 23 Günzburg, Germany
111 E 15 Guojiatun, China
113 V 4 Guoyang, China
86 K 8 Gura Humorului, Romania
106 H 3 Gurais, India
110 A 13 Gurban Obo, China
101 O 14 Gurdim, Iran
104 B 13 Gurha, India
58 I 4 Gurinhatã, Brazil
75 T 8 Gurk, Austria
133 Q 6 Guro, Mozambique
133 S 5 Guruè, Mozambique
94 M 11 Gürün, Turkey

Country | Internal administrative region: State/Province/Territory/Dependent territory | Capital city | Mountain range/Undersea ridge | Mountain peak/Volcano/Seamount | Geographic feature | Headland/Point/Cape/Peninsula | Desert | Island/Island group | Antarctic base | Ocean | Sea | Bay/Gulf/Channel/Strait | Lake | Salt pan/Dry/Intermittent lake

□ Country ▣ Internal administrative region: State/Province/Territory/Dependent territory ▲ Capital city ▲▲ Mountain range/Undersea ridge ▲ Mountain peak/Volcano/Seamount ◇ Geographic feature ▶ Headland/Point/Cape/Peninsula ▦ Desert ⌖ Island/Island group ⛨ Antarctic base ～ Ocean ⌇ Sea ≈ Bay/Gulf/Channel/Strait ◣ Lake ⚐ Salt pan/Dry/Intermittent lake

Imi-n-Tanoute – Jazā'ir Farasān

G 8 Imi-n-Tanoute, Morocco
X 9 Imişli, Azerbaijan
K 16 Imlay, NV, U.S.A.
B 12 Imlili, Western Sahara
H 26 Immenstadt, Germany
T 4 Immingham, U.K.
X 12 Immokalee, FL, U.S.A.
R 13 Imo, Nigeria
G 9 Imola, Italy
A 3 Imonda, Papua New Guinea
K 11 Imperatriz, Brazil
B 10 Imperia, Italy
I 15 Imperial, NE, U.S.A.
D 17 Imperial, Peru
J 7 Impfondo, Congo
X 12 Imphal, India
D 8 Imrali, Turkey
A 8 Imroz, Turkey
L 7 Imst, Austria
I 8 Imtān, Syria
I 3 Imuris, Mexico
D 17 Imuruan Bay, Philippines
Q 10 In Aménas, Algeria
O 13 In Amguel, Algeria
O 13 In Ekker, Algeria
M 11 In Salah, Algeria
I 16 Ina, Japan
G 17 Inangahua Junction, New Zealand
U 12 Inanwatan, Indonesia
H 16 Iñapari, Peru
L 8 Inari, Finland
Q 10 Inarigda, Russian Federation
M 8 Inarijärvi, Finland
J 13 Inawashiro-ko, Japan
G 7 Inca de Oro, Chile
J 6 Ince Burun, Turkey
I 14 Incekum Burnu, Turkey
F 5 Inchiri, Mauritania
N 12 Inch'ŏn, South Korea
H 20 Incourt, Belgium
F 11 Inčukalns, Latvia
I 17 Inda Silasē, Ethiopia
F 15 Indalsälven, Sweden
E 12 Indaw, Myanmar
S 3 Independence, MO, U.S.A.
R 10 Independence Fjord, Greenland
P 7 Indepenence, KS, U.S.A.
I 10 Inder, China
I 6 Inderborskiy, Kazakhstan
O 11 India, Asia
W 7 Indian Harbour, NL, Canada
U 4 Indian Head, MD, U.S.A.
L 18 Indian Lake, OH, U.S.A.
S 11 Indian Ocean, 0
M 21 Indian Springs, NV, U.S.A.
M 10 Indian Wells, AZ, U.S.A.
C 12 Indiana, PA, U.S.A.
H 18 Indiana, U.S.A.
I 19 Indianapolis, IN, U.S.A.
L 3 Indianola, MS, U.S.A.
S 13 Indianola, IA, U.S.A.
O 3 Indiga, Russian Federation
U 7 Indigirka, Russian Federation
L 5 Indio, CA, U.S.A.
M 6 Indispensable Strait, Solomon Islands
M 19 Indochina Peninsula, Cambodia
H 13 Indonesia, Asia
D 15 Indore, India
G 17 Indravati, India
E 18 Indura, Belarus
W 9 Indus, India/Pakistan
I 6 Inebolu, Turkey
E 9 İnegöl, Turkey
H 11 Infanta, Philippines
M 1 Infiesto, Spain
Q 7 Ingal, Niger
J 8 Ingende, Democratic Republic of Congo
K 5 Ingeniero Guillermo Neuva Juárez, Argentina
G 17 Ingeniero Jacobacci, Argentina
T 4 Ingham, QLD, Australia
Q 1 Ingleborough, U.K.
Q 1 Ingleton, U.K.
J 12 Inglewood, New Zealand
W 4 Ingoldmells, U.K.
J 22 Ingolstadt, Germany
V 5 Ingomar, MT, U.S.A.
Y 7 Ingonish, NS, Canada
S 11 Ingraj Bazar, India
W 6 Ingrid Christensen Coast, Antarctica
R 10 Inhambane, Mozambique
Q 9 Inhambane, Mozambique
R 7 Inhaminga, Mozambique
R 10 Inharrime, Mozambique
R 8 Inhul, Ukraine
S 8 Inhulets, Ukraine
A 17 Inishbofin, Republic of Ireland
B 18 Inisheer, Republic of Ireland
B 18 Inishmore, Republic of Ireland
A 17 Inishturk, Republic of Ireland
F 12 Injgan Sum, China
H 19 Injibara, Ethiopia
U 8 Injune, QLD, Australia
I 18 Inland Kaikoura Range, New Zealand
M 10 Inman, SC, U.S.A.
K 24 Inn, Germany
Q 8 Innamincka, SA, Australia
E 13 Inner Hebrides, U.K.
E 12 Inner Mongolia, China
F 9 Innertkirchen, Switzerland
T 4 Innisfail, QLD, Australia
M 7 Innsbruck, Austria
J 9 Inongo, Democratic Republic of Congo
H 11 Inowrocław, Poland
J 20 Inquisivi, Bolivia
C 7 Ins, Switzerland
M 12 Insurăţei, Romania
T 4 Inta, Russian Federation
E 9 Interlaken, Switzerland
S 2 International Falls, MN, U.S.A.
N 21 Interview Island, India
C 11 Intiyaco, Argentina
K 11 Întorsura Buzăului, Romania
K 5 Intsy, Russian Federation
E 10 Intutu, Peru
L 15 Inubō-zaki, Japan
P 6 Inukjuak, QC, Canada
C 9 Inuvik, NT, Canada
G 12 Inveraray, U.K.
C 25 Invercargill, New Zealand
V 10 Inverell, NSW, Australia
V 9 Inverness, FL, U.S.A.
X 8 Inverness, NS, Canada
60 H 10 Inverness, U.K.
88 M 13 Inya, Russian Federation
133 Q 7 Inyangani, Zimbabwe
33 K 22 Inyocern, CA, U.S.A.
131 S 12 Inyonga, Tanzania
93 Q 3 Inza, Russian Federation
93 X 2 Inzer, Russian Federation
123 C 25 Iō-jima, Japan
123 N 23 Iō-Tori-jima, Japan
83 B 16 Ioannina, Greece
25 Q 6 Iola, KS, U.S.A.
43 Y 8 Iona, NS, Canada
60 E 12 Iona, U.K.
132 G 6 Iona, Angola
86 I 12 Ioneşti, Romania
21 K 14 Ionia, MI, U.S.A.
83 A 17 Ionian Islands, Greece
83 B 17 Ionioi Nisoi, Greece
83 J 23 Ios, Greece
18 I 7 Iowa, LA, U.S.A.
23 R 12 Iowa, U.S.A.
23 N 13 Iowa City, IA, U.S.A.
23 T 11 Iowa Falls, IA, U.S.A.
46 I 6 Ipala, Guatemala
55 L 17 Ipatinga, Brazil
93 N 11 Ipatovo, Russian Federation
83 B 16 Ipeiros, Greece
79 I 21 Ipel, Slovakia
50 G 9 Ipiales, Colombia
121 I 21 Ipil, Philippines
58 I 8 Ipiranga, Brazil
54 A 13 Ipixuna, Brazil
118 B 7 Ipoh, Malaysia
130 L 4 Ippy, Central African Republic
94 B 7 Ipsala, Turkey
63 Z 8 Ipswich, U.K.
135 W 9 Ipswich, QLD, Australia
54 M 11 Ipu, Brazil
41 R 3 Iqaluit, NU, Canada
109 N 7 Iqe, China
53 F 19 Iquipi, Peru
56 F 3 Iquique, Chile
52 F 11 Iquitos, Peru
130 L 4 Ira Banda, Central African Republic
123 N 26 Irabu-jima, Japan
123 I 18 Irago-misaki, Japan
58 G 10 Irai, Brazil
82 F 13 Irakleia, Greece
83 J 23 Irakleia, Greece
83 J 26 Irakleiou, Greece
55 M 15 Iramaia, Brazil
100 K 7 Iran, Asia
100 K 9 Iranian Plateau, Iran
101 O 13 Īrānshahr, Iran
45 P 11 Irapuato, Mexico
97 R 8 Iraq, Asia
58 I 9 Irati, Brazil
91 R 6 Irayel', Russian Federation
84 C 9 Irbe Strait, Estonia/Latvia
96 H 8 Irbid, Jordan
55 M 14 Irecê, Brazil
61 D 17 Ireland, Republic of, Europe
103 N 6 Irgiz, Kazakhstan
124 H 8 Irhil M'Goun, Morocco
94 F 4 İri Dağh, Iran
117 W 12 Irian Jaya, Indonesia
129 Z 8 Iriba, Chad
120 J 13 Iriga, Philippines
131 U 12 Iringa, Tanzania
131 U 12 Iringa, Tanzania
123 M 26 Iriomote-jima, Japan
47 O 4 Iriona, Honduras
54 H 11 Iriri, Brazil
61 G 17 Irish Sea, Republic of Ireland/United Kingdom
54 K 10 Irituia, Brazil
89 P 14 Irkutsk, Russian Federation
103 N 10 Irlir Toghi, Uzbekistan
94 I 9 Irmak, Turkey
123 J 18 Irō-zaki, Japan
20 H 9 Iron Mountain, MI, U.S.A.
20 G 9 Iron River, MI, U.S.A.
21 M 21 Ironton, OH, U.S.A.
20 E 8 Ironwood, MI, U.S.A.
42 E 6 Iroquois Falls, ON, Canada
87 P 3 Irpin', Ukraine
99 R 14 Irqah, Yemen
114 C 13 Irrawaddy, Myanmar
115 C 17 Irrawaddy, Myanmar
87 N 3 Irsha, Ukraine
88 K 10 Irtysh, Russian Federation
103 U 2 Irtyshsk, Kazakhstan
123 K 16 Iruma, Japan
53 I 19 Irupana, Bolivia
27 Q 5 Irving, TX, U.S.A.
16 F 5 Irvington, KY, U.S.A.
137 G 20 Irwell, New Zealand
129 Q 9 Isa, Nigeria
22 I 7 Isabel, SD, U.S.A.
138 L 5 Isabel, Solomon Islands
121 H 23 Isabela, Philippines
87 N 11 Isaccea, Romania
70 A 10 Ísafjörður, Iceland
123 B 22 Isahaya, Japan
130 L 8 Isanga, Democratic Republic of Congo
129 Q 12 Isanlu, Nigeria
74 K 8 Ischgl, Austria
77 J 16 Ischia, Italy
123 H 18 Ise, Japan
123 H 18 Ise-wan, Japan
131 N 7 Isengi, Democratic Republic of Congo
77 J 14 Isernia, Italy
129 P 12 Iseyin, Nigeria
103 R 12 Isfana, Kyrgyzstan
97 U 9 Ishaq, Iraq
123 N 26 Ishigaki, Japan
123 N 26 Ishigaki-jima, Japan
122 J 5 Ishikari-wan, Japan
123 N 24 Ishikawa, Japan
88 K 11 Ishim, Russian Federation
122 L 12 Ishinomaki, Japan
123 E 20 Ishizuchi-san, Japan
103 Q 12 Ishtykhan, Uzbekistan
107 T 12 Ishurdi, Bangladesh
88 K 11 Isil'kul', Russian Federation
131 V 7 Isiolo, Kenya
131 P 6 Isiro, Democratic Republic of Congo
135 S 7 Isisford, QLD, Australia
94 L 13 Iskenderun, Turkey
94 K 13 Iskenderun Körfezi, Turkey
94 J 8 Iskilip, Turkey
82 H 7 Iskŭr, Bulgaria
127 O 19 Iskushuban, Somalia
44 H 4 Isla Ángel de la Guarda, Mexico
57 G 25 Isla Aracena, Chile
53 B 18 Isla Baltra, Ecuador
49 P 8 Isla Beata, Dominican Republic
51 P 1 Isla Blanquilla, Venezuela
57 E 21 Isla Campana, Chile
44 I 7 Isla Carmen, Mexico
44 F 5 Isla Cedros, Mexico
44 J 8 Isla Cerralvo, Mexico
57 F 23 Isla Chatham, Chile
57 G 25 Isla Clarence, Chile
51 Q 2 Isla Coche, Venezuela
47 T 15 Isla Coiba, Panama
57 F 24 Isla Contreras, Chile
45 W 12 Isla de Aguada, Mexico
67 P 15 Isla de Alborán, Spain
44 K 8 Isla de Altamura, Mexico
129 R 15 Isla de Bioco, Equatorial Guinea
47 Q 14 Isla de Caño, Costa Rica
57 E 18 Isla de Chiloé, Chile
47 T 13 Isla de Colón, Panama
45 Z 11 Isla de Cozumel, Mexico
47 N 3 Isla de Guanaja, Honduras
48 G 5 Isla de la Juventud, Cuba
57 J 26 Isla de los Estados, Argentina
51 Q 2 Isla de Margarita, Venezuela
47 O 10 Isla de Ometepe, Nicaragua
47 N 3 Isla de Roatán, Honduras
46 M 4 Isla de Utila, Honduras
47 Y 14 Isla del Rey, Panama
47 R 9 Isla del Venado, Nicaragua
57 F 25 Isla Desolación, Chile
57 E 23 Isla Duque de York, Chile
57 E 22 Isla Esmeralda, Chile
53 C 19 Isla Española, Ecuador
44 J 8 Isla Espíritu Santo, Mexico
53 A 19 Isla Fernandina, Ecuador
59 B 20 Isla Flamenco, Argentina
59 B 20 Isla Gama, Argentina
53 C 18 Isla Genovesa, Ecuador
57 H 26 Isla Gordon, Chile
57 H 25 Isla Grande de Tierra del Fuego, Chile
44 E 4 Isla Guadalupe, Mexico
57 E 18 Isla Guafo, Chile
57 E 19 Isla Guamblin, Chile
57 F 23 Isla Hanover, Chile
57 H 26 Isla Hoste, Chile
53 A 19 Isla Isabela, Ecuador
57 F 19 Isla James, Chile
57 F 21 Isla Javier, Chile
47 T 15 Isla Jicarón, Panama
57 F 23 Isla Jorge Montt, Chile
51 P 2 Isla La Tortuga, Venezuela
57 I 26 Isla Lennox, Chile
57 G 26 Isla Londonderry, Chile
57 E 23 Isla Madre de Dios, Chile
57 F 19 Isla Magdalena, Chile
53 A 18 Isla Marchena, Ecuador
44 L 10 Isla Maria Cleofas, Mexico
44 L 10 Isla Maria Madre, Mexico
44 L 10 Isla Maria Magdelena, Mexico
57 F 19 Isla Melchor, Chile
57 E 15 Isla Mocha, Chile
49 T 8 Isla Mona, Puerto Rico
47 T 15 Isla Montuosa, Panama
57 E 22 Isla Mornington, Chile
57 H 26 Isla Navarino, Chile
57 I 26 Isla Nueva, Chile
51 O 2 Isla Orchila, Venezuela
47 T 15 Isla Parida, Panama
57 E 22 Isla Patricio Lynch, Chile
57 I 26 Isla Picton, Chile
53 B 17 Isla Pinta, Ecuador
57 E 21 Isla Prat, Chile
52 A 10 Isla Puná, Ecuador
57 G 24 Isla Riesco, Chile
53 C 19 Isla San Cristóbal, Ecuador
44 H 5 Isla San Esteban, Mexico
44 I 7 Isla San José, Mexico
47 X 14 Isla San José, Panama
44 L 10 Isla San Juanito, Mexico
44 H 4 Isla San Lorenzo, Mexico
53 B 18 Isla San Salvador, Ecuador
44 I 7 Isla Santa Catalina, Mexico
53 B 18 Isla Santa Cruz, Ecuador
53 B 19 Isla Santa Fé, Ecuador
57 G 25 Isla Santa Inés, Chile
44 H 8 Isla Santa Margarita, Mexico
53 B 19 Isla Santa Maria, Ecuador
49 S 8 Isla Saona, Dominican Republic
47 S 14 Isla Sevilla, Panama
57 G 26 Isla Stewart, Chile
44 H 4 Isla Tiburón, Mexico
59 B 19 Isla Trinidad, Argentina
57 F 20 Isla Victoria, Chile
57 F 24 Isla Vidal, Chile
57 F 22 Isla Wellington, Chile
47 O 10 Isla Zapatera, Nicaragua
94 L 13 Islahiye, Turkey
101 Y 8 Islamabad, Pakistan
19 Y 14 Islamorada, FL, U.S.A.
121 C 19 Island Bay, Philippines
40 J 8 Island Lake, MB, Canada
40 J 8 Island Lake, MB, Canada
29 Q 9 Island Park, ID, U.S.A.
34 I 14 Islands of The Four Mountains, AK, U.S.A.
67 V 7 Islas Columbretes, Spain
46 M 4 Islas de la Bahía, Honduras
47 S 9 Islas del Maíz, Nicaragua
57 H 26 Islas Diego Ramirez, Chile
51 O 2 Islas Los Roques, Venezuela
44 L 10 Islas Marías, Mexico
47 T 15 Islas Secas, Panama
57 I 26 Islas Wollaston, Chile
60 E 13 Islay, U.K.
15 R 6 Isle au Haut, ME, U.S.A.
60 E 8 Isle of Lewis, U.K.
61 H 16 Isle of Man, U.K.
63 Q 14 Isle of Portland, U.K.
63 Y 11 Isle of Sheppey, U.K.
63 O 1 Isle of Walney, U.K.
63 S 14 Isle of Wight, U.K.
20 G 6 Isle Royale, MI, U.S.A.
18 K 9 Isles Dernieres, LA, U.S.A.
61 E 24 Isles of Scilly, U.K.
126 F 8 Ismâ'iliya, Egypt
95 X 7 Ismayilli, Azerbaijan
126 F 11 Isna, Egypt
133 Q 3 Isoka, Zambia
77 J 20 Isola Alicudi, Italy
77 B 15 Isola Asinara, Italy
77 C 15 Isola Caprera, Italy
76 D 12 Isola d'Elba, Italy
77 I 16 Isola d'Ischia, Italy
76 E 13 Isola del Giglio, Italy
76 D 12 Isola di Capraia, Italy
77 J 16 Isola di Capri, Italy
76 D 11 Isola di Gorgona, Italy
77 H 26 Isola di Lampedusa, Italy
77 G 26 Isola di Lampione, Italy
77 H 26 Isola di Linosa, Italy
76 E 13 Isola di Montecristo, Italy
77 G 24 Isola di Pantelleria, Italy
77 B 19 Isola di San Pietro, Italy
77 B 19 Isola di Sant'Antioco, Italy
77 I 20 Isola di Ustica, Italy
77 G 22 Isola Favignana, Italy
77 J 20 Isola Filicudi, Italy
77 G 21 Isola Levanzo, Italy
77 K 20 Isola Lipari, Italy
77 C 15 Isola Maddalena, Italy
77 G 21 Isola Marettimo, Italy
77 K 20 Isola Panarea, Italy
76 D 12 Isola Pianosa, Italy
77 K 20 Isola Salina, Italy
77 K 20 Isola Stromboli, Italy
77 K 21 Isola Vulcano, Italy
77 F 21 Isole Egadi, Italy
77 G 26 Isole Pelagie, Italy
76 L 13 Isole Pianosa, Italy
77 H 16 Isole Ponziane, Italy
76 L 13 Isole Tremiti, Italy
94 F 12 Isparta, Turkey
82 L 7 Isperikh, Bulgaria
96 F 11 Israel, Asia
134 J 11 Israelite Bay, WA, Australia
128 J 13 Issia, Côte d'Ivoire
103 W 10 Issyk-Kul'skaya Oblast', Kyrgyzstan
79 K 21 Istállós-kő, Hungary
82 O 12 Istanbul, Turkey
94 D 7 Istanbul, Turkey
100 H 7 Īstgāh-e Eznā, Iran
115 F 23 Isthmus of Kra, Thailand
47 W 13 Isthmus of Panama, Panama
83 F 18 Istiaia, Greece
95 V 9 Istisu, Azerbaijan
45 V 13 Istmo de Tehuantepec, Mexico
80 A 9 Istra, Croatia
107 T 14 Iswaripur, Bangladesh
103 W 9 Isyk, Kazakhstan
55 N 15 Itabuna, Brazil
54 F 10 Itacoatiara, Brazil
58 H 6 Itaguajé, Brazil
55 K 15 Itaguari, Brazil
54 G 11 Itaituba, Brazil
58 J 10 Itajaí, Brazil
58 L 6 Itajubá, Brazil
76 F 10 Italy, Europe
133 W 10 Itampolo, Madgascar
107 X 9 Itanagar, India
55 M 16 Itaobim, Brazil
58 I 4 Itapagipe, Brazil
55 N 16 Itapebi, Brazil
54 L 11 Itapecuru Mirim, Brazil
58 O 6 Itaperuna, Brazil
58 J 7 Itapetininga, Brazil
58 J 7 Itapeva, Brazil
54 B 12 Itapiranga, Brazil
58 E 11 Itaqui, Brazil
58 J 7 Itararé, Brazil
105 E 15 Itarsi, India
58 H 3 Itarumã, Brazil
54 I 9 Itaupā, Brazil
120 H 2 Itbayat, Philippines
53 G 20 Ite, Peru
83 E 19 Itea, Greece
131 P 9 Itebero, Democratic Republic of Congo
14 G 9 Ithaca, NY, U.S.A.
83 B 19 Ithaki, Greece
83 B 19 Ithaki, Greece
55 M 16 Itinga, Brazil
55 G 16 Itiquira, Brazil
123 K 17 Itō, Japan
123 I 15 Itoigawa, Japan
130 L 8 Itoko, Democratic Republic of Congo
143 Q 13 Ittoqqortoormiit, Greenland
58 K 7 Itu, Brazil
54 B 11 Itui, Brazil
58 J 3 Ituitaba, Brazil
55 J 17 Ituiutaba, Brazil
131 P 10 Itula, Democratic Republic of Congo
55 J 17 Itumbiara, Brazil
51 U 6 Ituni, Guyana
58 I 10 Ituporanga, Brazil
58 I 4 Iturama, Brazil
56 N 8 Ituzaingó, Argentina
58 E 10 Ituzaingo, Argentina
72 G 9 Itzehoe, Germany
89 Z 6 Iul'tin, Russian Federation
58 G 7 Ivai, Brazil
70 M 8 Ivalo, Finland
85 G 21 Ivanava, Belarus
80 E 7 Ivanec, Croatia
135 S 11 Ivanhoe, NSW, Australia
80 E 8 Ivanić Grad, Croatia
80 K 13 Ivanjica, Serbia and Montenegro
80 F 10 Ivanjska, Bosnia and Herzegovina
87 P 3 Ivankiv, Ukraine
86 J 6 Ivano-Frankivs'k, Ukraine
93 V 4 Ivanovka, Russian Federation
90 K 14 Ivanovo, Russian Federation
90 K 14 Ivanovskaya Oblast', Russian Federation
93 S 4 Ivanteyevka, Russian Federation
87 S 3 Ivanytsya, Ukraine
85 G 20 Ivatsevichy, Belarus
82 K 12 Ivaylovgrad, Bulgaria
88 J 9 Ivdel', Russian Federation
86 M 11 Iveşti, Romania
58 G 6 Ivinheima, Brazil
142 L 13 Ivittuut, Greenland
133 X 9 Ivohibe, Madgascar
128 J 14 Ivory Coast, Côte d'Ivoire
76 B 7 Ivrea, Italy
41 P 4 Ivujivik, QC, Canada
85 I 17 Ivyanyets, Belarus
17 O 4 Ivydale, WV, U.S.A.
122 L 10 Iwaizumi, Japan
123 L 14 Iwaki, Japan
122 J 9 Iwaki-san, Japan
123 D 20 Iwakuni, Japan
122 J 5 Iwamizawa, Japan
122 I 6 Iwanai, Japan
122 K 10 Iwate-san, Japan
129 P 12 Iwo, Nigeria
85 G 17 Iwye, Belarus
53 I 17 Ixiamas, Bolivia
45 N 10 Ixtlán, Mexico
45 T 13 Ixtlán, Mexico
63 Y 8 Ixworth, U.K.
123 E 20 Iyomishima, Japan
131 U 12 Izazi, Tanzania
93 R 15 Izberbash, Russian Federation
69 C 18 Izegem, Belgium
123 N 24 Izena-jima, Japan
91 R 14 Izhevsk, Russian Federation
87 N 11 Izmayil, Ukraine
94 B 10 Izmir, Turkey
94 A 10 Izmir Körfezi, Turkey
94 E 8 Iznik Gölü, Turkey
92 M 12 Izobil'nyy, Russian Federation
45 R 12 Iztaccihuatl, Mexico
46 H 7 Iztapa, Guatemala
123 K 17 Izu-hantō, Japan
123 K 18 Izu-shotō, Japan
45 R 12 Izúcar de Matamoros, Mexico
123 A 20 Izuhara, Japan
123 B 23 Izumi, Japan
123 D 18 Izumo, Japan
86 L 4 Izyaslav, Ukraine
87 X 5 Izyum, Ukraine

J

142 M 13 J.A.D. Jenson Nunatakker, Greenland
97 N 2 Jabal 'Abd al 'Azīz, Syria
97 N 2 Jabal Abd al Aziz, Syria
96 K 4 Jabal Abū Raḩbah, Syria
98 J 3 Jabal ad Dubbagh, Saudi Arabia
96 I 8 Jabal ad Duruz, Syria
96 J 3 Jabal Aḩaş, Syria
96 H 11 Jabal al 'Adhiriyāt, Jordan
96 I 2 Jabal al Akr, Syria
99 P 10 Jabal al Amlaḩ, Saudi Arabia
96 I 8 Jabal al 'Arab, Syria
96 F 13 Jabal al Khashsh, Jordan
98 J 3 Jabal al Lawz, Saudi Arabia
99 V 11 Jabal al Qamar, Oman
99 O 13 Jabal an Nabi Shu'ayb, Yemen
96 J 6 Jabal an Niqniqīyah, Syria
96 H 4 Jabal an Nuşayrīyah, Syria
99 P 10 Jabal ar Rubūţ, Saudi Arabia
125 Z 13 Jabal Arkenu, Libya
125 S 9 Jabal as Sawdā', Libya
99 Y 7 Jabal ash Shām, Oman
96 H 6 Jabal ash Sharqī, Lebanon
96 I 5 Jabal ash Shawmarīyah, Syria
98 J 3 Jabal ash Shifa, Saudi Arabia
96 L 7 Jabal aţ Ţanf, Syria
96 F 13 Jabal Bāqir, Jordan
125 U 13 Jabal Bin Ghanīmah, Libya
96 L 4 Jabal Bishrī, Syria
99 X 6 Jabal Ḩafīt, United Arab Emirates
99 W 15 Jabal Ḩajhir, Yemen
97 S 4 Jabal Hamrin, Iraq
99 Z 7 Jabal Khadar, Oman
125 R 8 Jabal Nafūsah, Libya
98 L 5 Jabal Nahr, Saudi Arabia
125 W 14 Jabal Nuqayy, Libya
98 M 8 Jabal Qarnayţ, Saudi Arabia
98 L 6 Jabal Raḑwá, Saudi Arabia
98 M 2 Jabal Rāf, Saudi Arabia
96 G 13 Jabal Ramm, Jordan
99 Z 7 Jabal Salakh, Oman
99 N 10 Jabal Sawdā', Saudi Arabia
96 K 4 Jabal Shā'ir, Syria
97 O 2 Jabal Sinjār, Iraq
99 O 13 Jabal Taqar, Yemen
99 P 13 Jabal Thamar, Yemen
96 L 4 Jabal Thulaythawat Gharbī, Syria
99 Q 9 Jabal Tuwayq, Saudi Arabia
125 U 8 Jabal Waddān, Libya
125 V 9 Jabal Zaltan, Libya
105 G 15 Jabalpur, India
69 B 17 Jabbeke, Belgium
135 N 1 Jabiru, NT, Australia
96 H 3 Jablah, Syria
80 G 13 Jablanica, Bosnia and Herzegovina
79 E 16 Jablonec nad Nisou, Czech Republic
58 J 5 Jaboticabal, Brazil
141 Y 3 Jabwat, Marshall Islands
67 T 2 Jaca, Spain
45 R 11 Jacala, Mexico
46 F 4 Jacaltenango, Guatemala
54 G 12 Jacareacanga, Brazil
58 L 7 Jacareí, Brazil
56 H 9 Jáchal, Argentina
54 D 13 Jaciparaná, Brazil
15 P 3 Jackman, ME, U.S.A.
27 O 5 Jacksboro, TX, U.S.A.
16 C 9 Jackson, TN, U.S.A.
18 L 5 Jackson, MS, U.S.A.
19 O 6 Jackson, AL, U.S.A.
19 T 3 Jackson, GA, U.S.A.
21 K 15 Jackson, MI, U.S.A.
21 N 20 Jackson, OH, U.S.A.
29 R 11 Jackson, WY, U.S.A.
33 H 19 Jackson, CA, U.S.A.
137 C 21 Jackson Bay, New Zealand
137 C 21 Jackson Bay, New Zealand
29 R 10 Jackson Lake, WY, U.S.A.
137 G 19 Jacksons, New Zealand
17 T 11 Jacksonville, NC, U.S.A.
19 W 7 Jacksonville, FL, U.S.A.
21 E 19 Jacksonville, IL, U.S.A.
25 V 11 Jacksonville, AR, U.S.A.
27 S 7 Jacksonville, TX, U.S.A.
19 W 7 Jacksonville Beach, FL, U.S.A.
49 P 8 Jacmel, Haiti
47 P 13 Jacó, Costa Rica
101 U 12 Jacobabad, Pakistan
54 J 11 Jacunda, Brazil
58 J 8 Jacupiranga, Brazil
72 E 10 Jadebusen, Germany
99 V 12 Jādib, Yemen
67 P 6 Jadraque, Spain
52 B 12 Jaén, Peru
67 O 11 Jaén, Spain
105 F 23 Jaffna, Sri Lanka
14 M 9 Jaffrey, NH, U.S.A.
105 H 17 Jagdalpur, India
110 I 6 Jagdaqi, China
97 O 1 Jāghir Bāzār, Syria
80 M 12 Jagodina, Serbia and Montenegro
106 H 6 Jagraon, India
105 F 17 Jagtial, India
59 G 14 Jaguarão, Brazil
59 G 14 Jaguarão, Uruguay
56 H 8 Jagüé, Argentina
48 H 4 Jagüey Grande, Cuba
107 P 11 Jahanabad, India
100 J 11 Jahrom, Iran
54 M 12 Jaicós, Brazil
107 W 11 Jaintiapur, Bangladesh
104 D 12 Jaipur, India
104 B 12 Jaisalmer, India
107 N 8 Jajarkot, Nepal
80 G 11 Jajce, Bosnia and Herzegovina
107 U 9 Jakar, Bhutan
116 H 13 Jakarta, Indonesia
116 H 13 Jakarta Raya, Indonesia
39 B 14 Jakes Corner, YT, Canada
101 P 13 Jakki, Iran
70 H 11 Jäkkvik, Sweden
71 K 15 Jakobstad, Finland
110 E 7 Jalai Nur, China
99 Q 5 Jalājil, Saudi Arabia
103 T 11 Jalal-Abad, Kyrgyzstan
101 V 7 Jalālābād, Afghanistan
106 I 6 Jalandhar, India
46 I 6 Jalapa, Guatemala
47 N 7 Jalapa, Nicaragua
45 T 12 Jalapa Enriquez, Mexico
106 K 11 Jalaun, India
97 U 5 Jalawlā, Iraq
58 I 4 Jales, Brazil
107 R 15 Jaleshwar, India
105 D 16 Jalgaon, India
97 X 11 Jalībah, Iraq
129 T 12 Jalingo, Nigeria
44 M 11 Jalisco, Mexico
105 D 17 Jalna, India
106 C 13 Jalor, India
45 O 10 Jalostotitlán, Mexico
45 O 10 Jalpa, Mexico
107 S 10 Jalpaiguri, India
125 X 9 Jālū, Libya
141 Y 4 Jaluit, Marshall Islands
127 K 25 Jamaame, Somalia
48 K 8 Jamaica, North America
48 L 7 Jamaica Channel, Jamaica
107 U 12 Jamalpur, Bangladesh
116 F 9 Jamaluang, Malaysia
116 F 11 Jambi, Indonesia
116 E 11 Jambi, Indonesia
119 W 4 Jambongan, Malaysia
22 M 5 James, ND/SD, U.S.A.
37 T 10 James Bay, NU, Canada
144 H 3 James Ross Island, Antarctica
14 C 10 Jamestown, NY, U.S.A.
22 M 5 Jamestown, ND, U.S.A.
106 H 4 Jammu, India
106 I 3 Jammu and Kashmir, India/Pakistan
105 A 15 Jamnagar, India
69 J 25 Jamoigne, Belgium
101 V 11 Jampur, Pakistan
71 L 17 Jämsä, Finland
105 J 15 Jamshedpur, India
129 T 12 Jamtari, Nigeria
107 Q 12 Jamui, India
107 T 12 Jamuna, Bangladesh
143 R 13 Jan Mayen, Norway
107 Q 10 Janakpur, Nepal
55 L 16 Janaúba, Brazil
101 W 8 Jand, Pakistan
100 K 7 Jandaq, Iran
95 U 7 Jandari, Georgia
21 F 14 Janesville, WI, U.S.A.
116 M 12 Jangeru, Indonesia
107 R 12 Jangipur, India
103 S 11 Jangy-Bazar, Kyrgyzstan
44 K 3 Janos, Mexico
79 N 15 Janów Lubelski, Poland
79 N 12 Janów Podlaski, Poland
55 L 16 Januária, Brazil
122 I 11 Japan, Asia
72 E 7 Japsand, Germany
54 B 10 Japurá, Brazil
107 X 11 Japvo Mount, India
47 Z 15 Jaqué, Panama
96 K 1 Jarābulus, Syria
58 J 9 Jaraguá do Sul, Brazil
66 L 8 Jaraicejo, Spain
96 H 9 Jarash, Jordan
55 G 18 Jardim, Brazil
54 H 9 Jari, Brazil
107 R 13 Jarkhand, India
78 G 13 Jarocin, Poland
79 N 17 Jarosław, Poland
105 I 15 Jashpurnagar, India
85 G 16 Jāšiūnai, Lithuania
100 M 14 Jāsk, Iran
79 M 18 Jasło, Poland
144 I 4 Jason Peninsula, Antarctica
19 P 3 Jasper, AL, U.S.A.
19 S 2 Jasper, GA, U.S.A.
19 U 7 Jasper, FL, U.S.A.
21 I 21 Jasper, IN, U.S.A.
25 U 9 Jasper, AR, U.S.A.
27 U 8 Jasper, TX, U.S.A.
39 H 19 Jasper, AB, Canada
97 W 7 Jaşşān, Iraq
78 G 10 Jastrowie, Poland
79 I 18 Jastrzębie-Zdrój, Poland
79 K 23 Jászberény, Hungary
55 I 17 Jataí, Brazil
54 F 9 Jatapu, Brazil
101 U 15 Jati, Pakistan
58 J 6 Jaú, Brazil
53 D 16 Jauja, Peru
84 G 12 Jaunjelgava, Latvia
84 H 10 Jaunpiebalga, Latvia
84 D 11 Jaunpils, Latvia
107 N 11 Jaunpur, India
116 H 15 Java, Indonesia
116 I 13 Java Sea, Indonesia
101 R 7 Javand, Afghanistan
109 S 3 Javarthushuu, Mongolia
79 E 19 Javořice, Czech Republic
79 H 19 Javorníky, Slovakia
116 G 14 Jawa Barat, Indonesia
116 I 14 Jawa Tengah, Indonesia
116 K 15 Jawa Timur, Indonesia
127 M 24 Jawhar, Somalia
52 B 13 Jayanca, Peru
117 Y 12 Jayapura, Indonesia
107 Q 10 Jaynagar, India
105 H 17 Jaypur, India
96 I 6 Jayrūd, Syria
99 N 11 Jazā'ir Farasān, Saudi Arabia

ountry · Internal administrative region: State/Province/Territory/Dependent territory · Capital city · Mountain range/Undersea ridge · Mountain peak/Volcano/Seamount · Geographic feature · Headland/Point/Cape/Peninsula · Desert · Island/Island group · Antarctic base · Ocean · Sea · Bay/Gulf/Channel/Strait · Lake · Salt pan/Dry/Intermittent lake · River

Jazirah Doberai – Kapellskär

117 U 11 Jazirah Doberai, Indonesia
99 Z 8 Jazîrat Maşîrah, Oman
97 N 3 Jazrah, Syria
96 G 5 Jbail, Lebanon
124 J 7 Jbel Bou Naceur, Morocco
124 F 10 Jdiriya, Western Sahara
96 J 2 Jebal Aḩaş, Syria
129 P 12 Jebba, Nigeria
86 E 10 Jebel, Romania
127 C 15 Jebel Abyad Plateau, Sudan
125 P 6 Jebel Chambi, Tunisia
96 G 6 Jebel Libnan, Lebanon
127 B 18 Jebel Marra, Sudan
127 H 14 Jebel Oda, Sudan
127 B 17 Jebel Teljo, Sudan
127 B 13 Jebel Uweinat, Sudan
101 S 5 Jebri, Pakistan
98 L 8 Jeddah, Saudi Arabia
79 K 16 Jędrzejów, Poland
23 R 12 Jefferson, IA, U.S.A.
25 V 4 Jefferson City, MO, U.S.A.
29 U 12 Jeffrey City, WY, U.S.A.
132 M 15 Jeffrey's Bay, Republic of South Africa
129 P 10 Jega, Nigeria
84 H 12 Jēkabpils, Latvia
127 K 20 Jeldēsa, Ethiopia
79 E 15 Jelenia Góra, Poland
84 E 11 Jelgava, Latvia
118 C 5 Jeli, Malaysia
40 L 11 Jellicoe, ON, Canada
136 K 7 Jellicoe Channel, New Zealand
116 G 9 Jemaja, Indonesia
116 K 15 Jember, Indonesia
69 G 21 Jemeppe, Belgium
103 Z 6 Jeminay, Kazakhstan
18 J 6 Jena, LA, U.S.A.
73 J 17 Jena, Germany
125 P 5 Jendouba, Tunisia
103 Y 10 Jengish Chokusu, Kyrgyzstan
95 Y 9 Jenikand, Azerbaijan
96 G 8 Jenin, Israel
16 L 6 Jenkins, KY, U.S.A.
39 K 20 Jenner, AB, Canada
18 I 8 Jennings, LA, U.S.A.
30 M 3 Jensen, UT, U.S.A.
116 I 13 Jepara, Indonesia
55 M 15 Jequié, Brazil
127 E 22 Jerbar, Sudan
49 N 7 Jérémie, Haiti
45 O 9 Jerez, Mexico
66 K 13 Jerez de la Frontera, Spain
66 J 10 Jerez de los Caballeros, Spain
81 L 21 Jergucat, Albania
96 G 9 Jericho, Israel
135 T 6 Jericho, QLD, Australia
135 S 12 Jerilderie, NSW, Australia
134 H 12 Jerramungup, WA, Australia
101 U 14 Jerruck, Pakistan
61 J 26 Jersey, U.K.
14 J 13 Jersey City, NJ, U.S.A.
21 E 20 Jerseyville, IL, U.S.A.
96 G 9 Jerusalem, Israel
76 I 11 Jesi, Italy
107 T 13 Jessore, Bangladesh
19 W 5 Jesup, GA, U.S.A.
56 J 10 Jesús María, Argentina
24 J 5 Jetmore, KS, U.S.A.
72 E 10 Jever, Germany
78 J 9 Jezioro Jeziorak, Poland
78 G 7 Jezioro Łebsko, Poland
78 L 9 Jezioro Mamry, Poland
78 L 9 Jezioro Śniardwy, Poland
78 J 12 Jezioro Włocławskie, Poland
78 L 12 Jezioro Zegrzyńskie, Poland
96 G 7 Jezzine, Lebanon
105 D 15 Jhabua, India
101 T 12 Jhal, Pakistan
101 R 14 Jhal Jhao, Pakistan
101 X 9 Jhang, Pakistan
104 F 13 Jhansi, India
105 I 15 Jharkhand, India
105 I 15 Jharsuguda, India
101 U 12 Jhatpat, Pakistan
101 X 8 Jhelum, Pakistan
107 T 13 Jhenida, Bangladesh
101 V 14 Jhudo, Pakistan
55 E 14 Ji-Paraná, Brazil
111 E 17 Ji Xian, China
113 T 10 Jiahe, China
113 O 5 Jialing, China
110 M 10 Jiamusi, China
111 K 15 Ji'an, China
113 U 9 Ji'an, China
112 J 9 Jianchuan, China
113 X 7 Jiande, China
113 O 5 Jiange, China
113 S 11 Jianghua, China
113 W 9 Jiangle, China
113 T 12 Jiangmen, China
113 X 4 Jiangsu, China
113 V 9 Jiangxi, China
113 Y 5 Jiangyin, China
113 N 5 Jiangyou, China
113 X 4 Jianhu, China
113 T 7 Jianli, China
113 W 9 Jianning, China
113 X 9 Jian'ou, China
113 R 6 Jianshi, China
112 L 12 Jianshui, China
113 N 6 Jianyang, China
113 X 9 Jianyang, China
113 S 1 Jiaocheng, China
110 L 13 Jiaohe, China
111 D 19 Jiaohe, China
113 S 1 Jiaokou, China
113 V 11 Jiaoling, China
111 G 21 Jiaonan, China
113 X 2 Jiaonan, China
111 F 20 Jiaozhou, China
113 T 3 Jiaozuo, China
112 K 11 Jiasa, China
113 W 5 Jiashan, China
113 W 3 Jiawang, China
113 Y 6 Jiaxing, China
110 M 8 Jiayin, China
109 O 6 Jiayuguan, China
113 V 12 Jiazi, China
86 H 8 Jibou, Romania
99 X 10 Jiddat al Ḩarāsīs, Oman
113 U 4 Jieshou, China
113 S 1 Jiexiu, China
113 W 12 Jieyang, China
85 F 16 Jieznas, Lithuania
129 S 10 Jigawa, Nigeria
112 L 4 Jigzhi, China
79 E 19 Jihlava, Czech Republic
125 O 5 Jijel, Algeria
127 K 20 Jijiga, Ethiopia
127 K 25 Jilib, Somalia
110 K 13 Jilin, China
110 L 13 Jilin, China
127 H 21 Jīma, Ethiopia
86 E 10 Jimbolia, Romania
45 N 6 Jiménez, Mexico
121 K 20 Jimenez, Philippines
111 G 20 Jimo, China
113 V 2 Jinan, China
113 Q 11 Jinchai, China
109 P 7 Jinchang, China
113 T 3 Jincheng, China
112 L 5 Jinchuan, China
106 I 8 Jind, India
135 T 13 Jindabyne, NSW, Australia
79 D 19 Jindřichův Hradec, Czech Republic
113 R 5 Jing Shan, China
113 P 3 Jingchuan, China
113 X 6 Jingde, China
113 W 7 Jingdezhen, China
112 J 12 Jinggu, China
111 D 18 Jinghai, China
113 W 12 Jinghai, China
108 J 4 Jinghe, China
112 K 13 Jinghong, China
113 T 6 Jingmen, China
113 O 3 Jingning, China
110 E 13 Jingpeng, China
110 M 13 Jingpo, China
110 M 12 Jingpo Hu, China
113 S 7 Jingsha, China
109 Q 8 Jingtai, China
113 O 12 Jingxi, China
113 X 6 Jingxian, China
111 K 16 Jingyu, China
109 Q 8 Jingyuan, China
113 T 6 Jingzhou, China
113 Q 9 Jingzhou, China
110 H 6 Jinhe, China
113 X 7 Jinhua, China
111 B 15 Jining, China
113 V 3 Jining, China
131 S 7 Jinja, Uganda
112 K 10 Jinjiang, China
113 X 11 Jinjiang, China
127 H 22 Jinka, Ethiopia
112 L 7 Jinkouhe, China
47 N 8 Jinotega, Nicaragua
47 N 10 Jinotepe, Nicaragua
113 O 9 Jinsha, China
111 F 15 Jinshan, China
113 Z 6 Jinshan, China
113 S 7 Jinshi, China
113 N 6 Jintang, China
121 J 15 Jintotolo, Philippines
113 W 8 Jinxi, China
113 V 3 Jinxiang, China
111 H 16 Jinzhou, China
111 I 17 Jinzhou, China
52 A 9 Jipijapa, Ecuador
110 E 12 Jirin Gol, China
100 M 11 Jīroft, Iran
127 N 21 Jirriiban, Somalia
113 Q 8 Jishou, China
96 H 2 Jisr Ash Shughūr, Syria
118 A 5 Jitra, Malaysia
86 H 12 Jiu, Romania
113 S 10 Jiucai Ling, China
113 V 7 Jiujiang, China
113 U 8 Jiuling Shan, China
112 L 7 Jiulong, China
109 O 7 Jiuquan, China
113 Q 15 Jiusuo, China
110 K 12 Jiutai, China
113 O 11 Jiuzhou, China
101 P 14 Jiwani, Pakistan
110 I 6 Jiwen, China
110 N 11 Jixi, China
113 X 7 Jixi, China
110 N 10 Jixian, China
113 R 2 Jixian, China
99 O 11 Jīzān, Saudi Arabia
123 E 18 Jizō-zaki, Japan
103 Q 12 Jizzakh Wiloyati, Uzbekistan
58 H 10 Joaçaba, Brazil
54 O 12 João Pessoa, Brazil
55 K 17 João Pinheiro, Brazil
56 J 6 Joaquín V. González, Argentina
121 N 20 Jobo Point, Philippines
104 C 12 Jodhpur, India
71 O 16 Joensuu, Finland
31 U 4 Joes, CO, U.S.A.
123 I 14 Jōetsu, Japan
133 R 8 Jofane, Mozambique
107 R 10 Jogbani, India
106 L 8 Jogbura, Nepal
84 H 7 Jõgeva, Estonia
84 I 6 Jõgua, Estonia
33 K 23 Johannesburg, CA, U.S.A.
133 O 11 Johannesburg, Republic of South Africa
32 J 11 John Day, OR, U.S.A.
17 S 8 John H. Kerr Reservoir, NC, U.S.A.
31 U 6 John Martin Reservoir, CO, U.S.A.
60 I 8 John o'Groats, U.K.
24 G 6 Johnson, KS, U.S.A.
16 M 8 Johnson City, TN, U.S.A.
27 O 9 Johnson City, TX, U.S.A.
118 E 10 Johor, Malaysia
118 E 9 Johor, Malaysia
118 E 10 Johor Bahru, Malaysia
84 I 6 Jõhvi, Estonia
58 J 9 Joinville, Brazil
65 T 5 Joinville, France
144 H 2 Joinville Island, Antarctica
70 I 11 Jokkmokk, Sweden
70 B 9 Jökulbunga, Iceland
100 F 3 Jolfa, Iran
21 G 16 Joliet, IL, U.S.A.
42 L 10 Joliette, QC, Canada
121 G 24 Jolo, Philippines
121 G 24 Jolo, Philippines
120 I 11 Jomalig, Philippines
107 O 8 Jomsom, Nepal
46 K 3 Jonathan Point, Belize
85 F 15 Jonava, Lithuania
37 P 3 Jones Sound, NU, Canada
18 I 5 Jonesboro, LA, U.S.A.
19 S 3 Jonesboro, GA, U.S.A.
25 X 9 Jonesboro, AR, U.S.A.
17 N 11 Jonesville, SC, U.S.A.
18 J 6 Jonesville, LA, U.S.A.
127 E 21 Jonglei, Sudan
127 F 21 Jonglei, Sudan
84 E 12 Joniškis, Lithuania
71 F 22 Jönköping, Sweden
43 N 6 Jonquière, QC, Canada
25 R 7 Joplin, MO, U.S.A.
104 E 12 Jora, India
29 V 4 Jordan, MT, U.S.A.
96 H 11 Jordan, Asia
96 G 9 Jordan, Israel
32 L 13 Jordan Valley, OR, U.S.A.
107 X 10 Jorhat, India
47 U 15 Jorones, Panama
129 S 11 Jos, Nigeria
53 J 17 José Agustín Palacios, Bolivia
57 G 18 José de San Martín, Argentina
120 I 12 José Pañganiban, Philippines
59 G 15 José Pedro Varela, Uruguay
134 L 2 Joseph Bonaparte Gulf, WA, Australia
138 C 4 Josephstaal, Papua New Guinea
96 G 7 Jouaiya, Lebanon
133 N 11 Jouberton, Republic of South Africa
68 K 8 Joure, Netherlands
70 M 11 Joutsijärvi, Finland
107 W 11 Jowai, India
101 S 5 Jowzjān, Afghanistan
32 F 6 Joyce, WA, U.S.A.
128 E 6 Jreïda, Mauritania
32 E 5 Juan de Fuca Strait, WA, U.S.A.
133 V 6 Juan de Nova, France
10 G 12 Juan Fernández Islands, Chile
52 D 13 Juanjuí, Peru
54 M 13 Juàzeiro, Brazil
54 N 12 Juàzeiro do Norte, Brazil
128 I 13 Juazohn, Liberia
127 E 23 Juba, Sudan
127 K 24 Juba, Somalia
127 K 25 Jubbada Dhexe, Somalia
127 K 26 Jubbada Hoose, Somalia
134 K 9 Jubilee Lake, WA, Australia
107 R 9 Jubing, Nepal
67 Q 8 Júcar, Spain
45 U 14 Juchitán, Mexico
45 N 11 Juchitlán, Mexico
97 P 10 Judaidat al Hamir, Iraq
75 U 7 Judenburg, Austria
112 J 9 Judian, China
47 O 9 Juigalpa, Nicaragua
55 F 14 Juína, Brazil
72 C 10 Juist, Germany
58 N 6 Juiz de Fora, Brazil
56 I 5 Jujuy, Argentina
53 I 22 Julaca, Bolivia
119 P 10 Julau, Malaysia
53 H 19 Juli, Peru
135 R 5 Julia Creek, QLD, Australia
53 H 19 Juliaca, Peru
80 A 6 Julian Alps, Slovenia
51 W 7 Juliana Top, Suriname
68 H 8 Julianadorp, Netherlands
73 B 17 Jülich, Germany
67 S 10 Jumilla, Spain
107 N 8 Jumla, Nepal
110 F 11 Jun Bulen, China
105 A 15 Junagadh, India
105 H 17 Junagarh, India
113 X 3 Junan, China
26 M 9 Junction, TX, U.S.A.
30 J 6 Junction, UT, U.S.A.
18 I 4 Junction City, LA, U.S.A.
25 O 4 Junction City, KS, U.S.A.
32 F 11 Junction City, OR, U.S.A.
135 R 7 Jundah, QLD, Australia
58 K 7 Jundiaí, Brazil
35 X 10 Juneau, AK, U.S.A.
74 F 9 Jungfrau, Switzerland
108 K 4 Junggar Desert, China
53 D 16 Junín, Peru
59 B 16 Junín, Argentina
113 N 8 Junlian, China
71 H 15 Junsele, Sweden
32 K 12 Juntura, OR, U.S.A.
85 G 16 Juozapinės kalnas, Lithuania
58 K 8 Juquiá, Brazil
58 K 8 Juquiá, Brazil
60 F 12 Jura, U.K.
65 U 9 Jura, France/Switzerland
50 F 5 Juradó, Colombia
85 D 15 Jurbarkas, Lithuania
96 G 11 Jurf ad Darāwish, Jordan
110 G 12 Jurh, China
134 F 10 Jurien, WA, Australia
87 N 12 Jurilovca, Romania
84 E 11 Jūrmala, Latvia
118 A 14 Jurong, Singapore
118 A 14 Jurong Island, Singapore
54 C 11 Juruá, Brazil
54 C 11 Juruá, Brazil
54 F 13 Juruena, Brazil
110 F 11 Jus Hua, China
56 I 12 Justo Daract, Argentina
54 C 10 Jutaí, Brazil
54 C 11 Jutaí, Brazil
73 L 14 Jüterbog, Germany
58 F 6 Juti, Brazil
46 I 6 Jutiapa, Guatemala
47 N 4 Jutiapa, Honduras
47 N 6 Juticalpa, Honduras
71 N 17 Juva, Finland
101 P 9 Juwain, Afghanistan
113 X 2 Juxian, China
113 V 3 Juye, China
100 J 12 Jūyom, Iran
71 C 24 Jylland, Denmark
71 M 16 Jyväskylä, Finland

K

101 Z 5 K2, Pakistan
34 E 9 Ka Lae, HI, U.S.A.
70 L 8 Kaamanen, Finland
127 K 26 Kaambooni, Somalia
131 Y 9 Kaambooni, Kenya
117 O 13 Kabaena, Indonesia
103 N 12 Kabakly, Turkmenistan
128 G 11 Kabala, Sierra Leone
131 Q 8 Kabale, Uganda
131 O 11 Kabalo, Democratic Republic of Congo
131 P 10 Kabambare, Democratic Republic of Congo
116 C 9 Kabanjahe, Indonesia
121 I 18 Kabankalan, Philippines
139 Y 12 Kabara, Fiji
93 O 14 Kabardino Balkarskaya Respublika, Russian Federation
131 P 9 Kabare, Democratic Republic of Congo
121 I 21 Kabasalan, Philippines
70 I 12 Kåbdalis, Sweden
115 I 19 Kabin Buri, Thailand
42 B 5 Kabinakagami Lake, ON, Canada
131 N 11 Kabinda, Democratic Republic of Congo
123 M 26 Kabira, Japan
119 O 10 Kabong, Malaysia
131 N 12 Kabongo, Democratic Republic of Congo
115 F 20 Kabosa Island, Myanmar
101 O 5 Kabūd Gonbad, Iran
100 G 6 Kabūd Rāhang, Iran
101 U 7 Kābul, Afghanistan
101 U 7 Kabul, Afghanistan
131 Q 15 Kabunda, Democratic Republic of Congo
117 R 9 Kaburuang, Indonesia
127 F 16 Kabushiya, Sudan
133 O 5 Kabwe, Zambia
81 M 16 Kačanik, Serbia and Montenegro
129 R 11 Kachia, Nigeria
114 E 8 Kachin, Myanmar
103 U 2 Kachiry, Kazakhstan
133 P 5 Kacholola, Zambia
89 Q 13 Kachug, Russian Federation
115 F 20 Kadan Kyun, Myanmar
139 W 12 Kadavu, Fiji
139 W 12 Kadavu Passage, Fiji
97 T 7 Kādhimain, Iraq
94 D 7 Kadıköy, Turkey
94 G 11 Kadinhani, Turkey
128 J 11 Kadiolo, Mali
105 E 20 Kadiri, India
94 L 12 Kadirli, Turkey
105 B 22 Kadmat, India
22 I 10 Kadoka, SD, U.S.A.
133 P 7 Kadoma, Zimbabwe
127 D 19 Kadugli, Sudan
129 R 11 Kaduna, Nigeria
129 R 11 Kaduna, Nigeria
90 I 11 Kaduy, Russian Federation
95 V 10 Kadžaran, Armenia
128 F 7 Kaédi, Mauritania
129 V 11 Kaélé, Cameroon
136 J 5 Kaeo, New Zealand
111 K 18 Kaesŏng, North Korea
98 K 1 Kāf, Saudi Arabia
130 M 13 Kafakumba, Democratic Republic of Congo
128 E 9 Kaffrine, Senegal
127 A 20 Kafia Kingi, Sudan
133 O 5 Kafue, Zambia
123 H 16 Kaga, Japan
130 K 3 Kaga Bandoro, Central African Republic
101 X 7 Kagan, Pakistan
103 O 13 Kagan, Uzbekistan
131 R 9 Kagera, Tanzania
95 S 9 Kağizman, Turkey
127 E 17 Kagmar, Sudan
123 C 24 Kagoshima, Japan
100 M 5 Kāhak, Iran
131 S 10 Kahama, Tanzania
87 Q 4 Kaharlyk, Ukraine
130 J 12 Kahemba, Democratic Republic of Congo
100 M 12 Kahnūj, Iran
128 I 14 Kahnwia, Liberia
136 I 5 Kahoe, New Zealand
25 V 1 Kahoka, MO, U.S.A.
34 C 8 Kahoolawe, HI, U.S.A.
94 L 12 Kahramanmaraş, Turkey
95 N 12 Kahta, Turkey
117 U 13 Kai Besar, Indonesia
117 U 13 Kai Kecil, Indonesia
129 P 11 Kaiama, Nigeria
137 H 20 Kaiapoi, New Zealand
30 K 8 Kaibito, AZ, U.S.A.
113 T 3 Kaifeng, China
136 J 6 Kaikohe, New Zealand
137 I 18 Kaikoura, New Zealand
137 I 18 Kaikoura Peninsula, New Zealand
113 P 9 Kaili, China
110 H 13 Kailu, China
34 D 7 Kailua, HI, U.S.A.
117 V 12 Kaimana, Indonesia
84 D 7 Käina, Estonia
123 F 20 Kainan, Japan
138 D 5 Kainantu, Papua New Guinea
75 X 7 Kaindorf, Austria
129 P 11 Kainji Reservoir, Nigeria
70 K 10 Kainulasjärvi, Sweden
136 I 7 Kaipara Harbour, New Zealand
113 S 13 Kaiping, China
137 N 14 Kairakau Beach, New Zealand
138 B 3 Kairiru, Papua New Guinea
125 Q 6 Kairouan, Tunisia
138 D 6 Kairuku, Papua New Guinea
145 W 7 Kaiser Wilhelm II Land, Antarctica
73 D 21 Kaiserslautern, Germany
85 F 15 Kaišiadorys, Lithuania
137 E 25 Kaitangata, New Zealand
70 I 10 Kaitumälven, Sweden
34 C 7 Kaiwi Channel, HI, U.S.A.
113 Q 6 Kaixian, China
111 J 14 Kaiyuan, China
112 M 13 Kaiyuan, China
71 M 14 Kajaani, Finland
135 Q 5 Kajabbi, QLD, Australia
101 R 9 Kajaki, Afghanistan
118 C 8 Kajang, Malaysia
129 R 11 Kajuru, Nigeria
127 C 19 Kaka, Sudan
137 E 25 Kaka Point, New Zealand
117 P 14 Kakabia, Indonesia
121 K 23 Kakal, Philippines
132 K 12 Kakamas, Republic of South Africa
131 T 7 Kakamega, Kenya
105 N 23 Kakana, India
136 K 13 Kakaramea, New Zealand
128 H 13 Kakata, Liberia
136 K 13 Kakatahi, New Zealand
107 X 12 Kakching, India
123 D 19 Kake, Japan
130 L 10 Kakenge, Democratic Republic of Congo
87 T 9 Kakhovka Tavriys'k, Ukraine
87 T 8 Kakhovs'ke Vodoskhovyshche, Ukraine
100 I 11 Kākī, Iran
105 H 18 Kakinada, India
128 K 12 Kakpin, Côte d'Ivoire
35 S 3 Kaktovik, AK, U.S.A.
122 K 12 Kakuda, Japan
119 Q 9 Kakus, Malaysia
101 O 8 Kāl-e Namakasār, Afghanistan
131 R 12 Kala, Tanzania
101 V 8 Kalabagh, Pakistan
117 Q 15 Kalabahi, Indonesia
119 W 7 Kalabakan, Malaysia
132 L 5 Kalabo, Zambia
92 M 7 Kalach, Russian Federation
93 O 8 Kalach-na-Donu, Russian Federation
42 H 12 Kaladar, ON, Canada
132 K 9 Kalahari Desert, Botswana
71 L 14 Kalajoki, Finland
71 K 14 Kalajoki, Finland
129 P 11 Kalalé, Benin
101 W 6 Kalam, Pakistan
83 F 14 Kalamaria, Greece
83 D 22 Kalamata, Greece
21 J 15 Kalamazoo, MI, U.S.A.
105 E 17 Kalamnuri, India
83 B 18 Kalamos, Greece
83 D 16 Kalampaka, Greece
87 T 12 Kalamyts'ka Zatoka, Ukraine
128 I 10 Kalana, Mali
87 S 10 Kalanchak, Ukraine
131 T 11 Kalangali, Tanzania
117 O 14 Kalao, Indonesia
117 O 14 Kalaotoa, Indonesia
97 V 5 Kalār, Iraq
115 K 16 Kalasin, Thailand
101 T 11 Kalat, Pakistan
121 K 21 Kalatungan Mountains, Philippines
83 D 20 Kalavryta, Greece
134 F 9 Kalbarri, WA, Australia
94 I 9 Kalecik, Turkey
117 Q 13 Kaledupa, Indonesia
131 N 10 Kalema, Democratic Republic of Congo
131 Q 11 Kalémié, Democratic Republic of Congo
114 C 10 Kalemyo, Myanmar
90 G 5 Kalevala, Russian Federation
114 C 10 Kalewa, Myanmar
93 X 2 Kalga, Russian Federation
134 I 10 Kalgoorlie, WA, Australia
121 H 15 Kalibo, Philippines
131 O 9 Kalima, Democratic Republic of Congo
116 I 11 Kalimantan Barat, Indonesia
116 M 12 Kalimantan Selatan, Indonesia
116 J 12 Kalimantan Tengah, Indonesia
116 L 10 Kalimantan Timur, Indonesia
107 S 10 Kalimpang, India
105 I 16 Kalinga, India
85 B 15 Kaliningrad, Russian Federation
85 B 15 Kaliningradskaya Oblast', Russian Federation
103 R 14 Kalininobod, Tajikistan
93 O 5 Kalininsk, Russian Federation
85 L 21 Kalinkavichy, Belarus
28 M 3 Kalispell, MT, U.S.A.
79 H 14 Kalisz, Poland
78 F 10 Kalisz Pomorski, Poland
131 R 11 Kaliua, Tanzania
94 D 11 Kalkan, Turkey
134 M 4 Kalkarindji, NT, Australia
20 J 11 Kalkaska, MI, U.S.A.
132 I 8 Kalkfeld, Namibia
71 F 15 Kallsjön, Sweden
71 G 24 Kalmar, Sweden
84 F 11 Kalnciems, Latvia
79 I 25 Kalocsa, Hungary
133 N 6 Kalomo, Zambia
114 D 9 Kalon, Myanmar
106 K 6 Kalpa, India
105 C 23 Kalpeni, India
106 L 11 Kalpi, India
129 S 9 Kalguéri, Niger
85 H 14 Kaltanėnai, Lithuania
92 J 2 Kaluga, Russian Federation
134 K 2 Kalumburu, WA, Australia
71 D 25 Kalundborg, Denmark
86 I 5 Kalush, Ukraine
105 F 25 Kalutara, Sri Lanka
92 I 2 Kaluzhskaya Oblast', Russian Federation
85 E 16 Kalvarija, Lithuania
90 I 14 Kalyazin, Russian Federation
83 M 22 Kalymnos, Greece
83 M 22 Kalymnos, Greece
87 N 5 Kalynivka, Ukraine
91 S 10 Kama, Russian Federation
115 C 14 Kama, Myanmar
131 O 10 Kama, Democratic Republic of Congo
122 L 10 Kamaishi, Japan
123 J 16 Kamakura, Japan
128 G 11 Kamakwie, Sierra Leone
94 I 10 Kaman, Turkey
132 G 8 Kamanjab, Namibia
99 O 12 Kamarān, Yemen
128 G 11 Kamaron, Sierra Leone
134 I 10 Kambalda, WA, Australia
131 O 14 Kambove, Democratic Republic of Congo
89 Y 9 Kamchatka Peninsula, Russian Federation
82 K 7 Kamen, Bulgaria
88 M 12 Kamen'-na-Obi, Russian Federation
131 N 11 Kamende, Democratic Republic of Congo
90 M 5 Kamenka, Russian Federation
93 O 4 Kamenka, Russian Federation
102 H 4 Kamenka, Kazakhstan
92 L 13 Kamennomostskiy, Russian Federation
92 L 9 Kamenolomni, Russian Federation
92 M 8 Kamensk-Shakhtinskiy, Russian Federation
88 J 10 Kamensk-Ural'skiy, Russian Federation
122 H 18 Kameyama, Japan
123 B 23 Kami-Koshiki-jima, Japan
78 D 9 Kamień Pomorski, Poland
79 J 15 Kamieńsk, Poland
122 K 4 Kamikawa, Japan
38 L 11 Kamilukuak Lake, NU, Canada
86 K 1 Kamin'-Kashyrs'kyy, Ukraine
131 N 13 Kamina, Democratic Republic of Congo
123 H 16 Kamioka, Japan
123 A 20 Kamitsushima, Japan
39 H 21 Kamloops, BC, Canada
95 U 8 Kamo, Armenia
123 L 16 Kamogawa, Japan
131 S 7 Kampala, Uganda
116 E 8 Kampar, Malaysia
68 K 10 Kampen, Netherlands
131 O 10 Kampene, Democratic Republic of Congo
115 G 16 Kamphaeng Phet, Thailand
115 M 20 Kâmpóng Cham, Cambodia
115 L 20 Kâmpóng Chhnăng, Cambodia
115 K 19 Kâmpóng Khleăng, Cambodia
115 K 22 Kâmpóng Saôm, Cambodia
118 F 10 Kampong Sedili Kechil, Malaysia
115 K 21 Kâmpóng Spoe, Cambodia
115 L 20 Kâmpóng Thum, Cambodia
115 K 22 Kâmpôt, Cambodia
128 L 11 Kampti, Burkina Faso
118 A 7 Kampung Koh, Malaysia
128 E 10 Kamsar, Guinea
93 R 1 Kamskoye Ust'ye, Russian Federatio
91 S 11 Kamskoye Vodokhranilishche, Russian Federation
127 K 25 Kamsuuma, Somalia
122 L 6 Kamui-dake, Japan
122 I 6 Kamui-misaki, Japan
131 S 7 Kamuli, Uganda
86 M 2 Kam"yane, Ukraine
86 L 6 Kam"yanets'-Podil's'kyy, Ukraine
87 U 8 Kam"yanka, Ukraine
85 E 20 Kamyanyets, Belarus
100 F 6 Kāmyārān, Iran
85 K 15 Kamyen', Belarus
93 P 7 Kamyshin, Russian Federation
103 N 8 Kamyshlybash, Kazakhstan
93 R 11 Kamyzyak, Russian Federation
114 C 11 Kan, Myanmar
30 J 7 Kanab, UT, U.S.A.
34 E 14 Kanaga Island, AK, U.S.A.
41 U 8 Kanairiktok, NL, Canada
83 B 17 Kanallaki, Greece
130 L 11 Kananga, Democratic Republic of C
93 Q 1 Kanash, Russian Federation
123 H 15 Kanazawa, Japan
114 D 10 Kanbalu, Myanmar
123 J 17 Kanbara, Japan
115 G 19 Kanchanaburi, Thailand
105 F 21 Kanchipuram, India
101 S 10 Kandahār, Afghanistan
101 S 9 Kandahār, Afghanistan
90 H 3 Kandalaksha, Russian Federation
90 H 4 Kandalakshskiy Zaliv, Russian Federation
129 N 11 Kandé, Togo
101 V 12 Kandhkot, Pakistan
129 O 10 Kandi, Benin
101 U 13 Kandiaro, Pakistan
83 B 18 Kandila, Greece
94 F 7 Kandira, Turkey
105 A 14 Kandla, India
133 W 7 Kandreho, Madgascar
138 F 5 Kandrian, Papua New Guinea
105 G 25 Kandy, Sri Lanka
102 L 5 Kandyagash, Kazakhstan
14 C 11 Kane, PA, U.S.A.
129 W 8 Kanem, Chad
34 C 7 Kaneohe, HI, U.S.A.
84 I 9 Kanepi, Estonia
132 L 10 Kang, Botswana
121 F 24 Kang Tipayan Dakula, Philippines
142 M 12 Kangaamiut, Greenland
128 I 10 Kangaba, Mali
94 M 10 Kangal, Turkey
100 M 14 Kangān, Iran
118 A 4 Kangar, Malaysia
135 P 12 Kangaroo Island, SA, Australia
71 M 17 Kangasniemi, Finland
107 S 9 Kangchenjunga, India/Nepal
112 L 6 Kangding, China
111 K 17 Kangdong, North Korea
41 S 1 Kangeeak Point, NU, Canada
143 N 12 Kangerlussuaq, Greenland
143 O 11 Kangersuatsiaq, Greenland
131 U 6 Kangetet, Kenya
111 L 16 Kanggye, North Korea
41 T 6 Kangiqsualujjuaq, QC, Canada
41 R 4 Kangiqsujuaq, QC, Canada
41 R 5 Kangirsuk, QC, Canada
111 M 18 Kangnŭng, South Korea
130 E 7 Kango, Gabon
111 I 14 Kangping, China
106 I 5 Kangra, India
107 W 9 Kangto, India
115 C 16 Kangyidaung, Myanmar
114 C 11 Kani, Myanmar
128 J 12 Kani, Côte d'Ivoire
119 W 4 Kanibongan, Malaysia
90 M 2 Kanin Kamen', Russian Federation
90 L 2 Kanin Nos, Russian Federation
87 Q 4 Kaniv, Ukraine
105 F 15 Kaniwara, India
80 K 7 Kanjiža, Serbia and Montenegro
21 H 17 Kankakee, IL, U.S.A.
128 H 11 Kankan, Guinea
105 G 16 Kanker, India
115 F 21 Kanmaw Kyun, Myanmar
17 O 10 Kannapolis, NC, U.S.A.
106 K 10 Kannauj, India
129 R 10 Kano, Nigeria
129 S 10 Kano, Nigeria
123 C 24 Kanoya, Japan
106 M 10 Kanpur, India
24 L 5 Kansas, U.S.A.
25 O 3 Kansas, KS, U.S.A.
25 R 3 Kansas City, MO, U.S.A.
89 O 12 Kansk, Russian Federation
115 G 25 Kantang, Thailand
129 N 10 Kantchari, Burkina Faso
92 L 7 Kantemirovka, Russian Federation
107 S 15 Kanthi, India
140 J 4 Kanton, Kiribati
123 K 15 Kanuma, Japan
106 H 9 Kanwat, India
132 M 10 Kanye, Botswana
117 S 10 Kao, Indonesia
140 I 10 Kao, Tonga
115 J 21 Kaôh Kŏng, Cambodia
115 J 22 Kaôh Rŭng, Cambodia
113 Z 12 Kaohsiung, Taiwan
132 G 7 Kaokoveld, Namibia
128 E 8 Kaolack, Senegal
132 M 5 Kaoma, Zambia
130 M 3 Kaouadja, Central African Republic
72 M 7 Kap Arkona, Germany
143 Q 13 Kap Brewster, Greenland
142 M 14 Kap Farvel, Greenland
143 R 9 Kap Morris Jesup, Greenland
95 V 10 Kapan, Armenia
130 M 13 Kapanga, Democratic Republic of C
133 P 2 Kapatu, Zambia
103 V 9 Kapchagay, Kazakhstan
103 W 9 Kapchagayskoye Vodokhranilishche, Kazakhstan
69 E 16 Kapelle, Netherlands
69 G 16 Kapellen, Belgium
71 I 20 Kapellskär, Sweden

Country · Internal administrative region: State/Province/Territory/Dependent territory · Capital city · Mountain range/Undersea ridge · Mountain peak/Volcano/Seamount · Geographic feature · Headland/Point/Cape/Peninsula · Desert · Island/Island group · Antarctic base · Ocean · Sea · Bay/Gulf/Channel/Strait · Lake · Salt pan/Dry/Intermittent lake

untry ☐ Internal administrative region: State/Province/Territory/Dependent territory   ★ Capital city   ▲▲ Mountain range/Undersea ridge   ▲ Mountain peak/Volcano/Seamount   ◇ Geographic feature   ▶ Headland/Point/Cape/Peninsula   ☀ Desert   ☲ Island/Island group   ⊞ Antarctic base   ⊇ Ocean   ⊇ Sea   ≈ Bay/Gulf/Channel/Strait   ◡ Lake   ⤸ Salt pan/Dry/Intermittent lake   ⤳ River

Kiel – Kreuzlingen

72 H 8 **Kiel**, Germany
79 K 15 **Kielce**, Poland
72 H 8 **Kieler Bucht**, Germany
131 P 14 **Kienge**, Democratic Republic of Congo
138 J 5 **Kieta**, Papua New Guinea
87 P 3 **Kiev**, Ukraine
87 P 3 **Kiev Reservoir**, Ukraine
128 G 7 **Kiffa**, Mauritania
81 H 14 **Kifino Selo**, Bosnia and Herzegovina
83 G 20 **Kifisia**, Greece
83 E 18 **Kifisos**, Greece
97 U 5 **Kifrī**, Iraq
131 Q 9 **Kigali**, Rwanda
128 J 10 **Kignan**, Mali
131 Q 10 **Kigoma**, Tanzania
131 Q 11 **Kigoma**, Tanzania
34 D 8 **Kihei**, HI, U.S.A.
136 L 10 **Kihikihi**, New Zealand
84 F 8 **Kihnu**, Estonia
123 H 19 **Kii-nagashima**, Japan
123 G 19 **Kii-sanchi**, Japan
123 G 19 **Kii-suidō**, Japan
103 T 7 **Kiik**, Kazakhstan
123 O 21 **Kikai**, Japan
123 O 21 **Kikai-jima**, Japan
80 L 8 **Kikinda**, Serbia and Montenegro
101 Q 14 **Kikki**, Pakistan
91 O 14 **Kiknur**, Russian Federation
131 O 12 **Kikondja**, Democratic Republic of Congo
138 C 5 **Kikori**, Papua New Guinea
138 C 5 **Kikori**, Papua New Guinea
130 J 11 **Kikwit**, Democratic Republic of Congo
34 A 6 **Kilauea**, HI, U.S.A.
34 E 9 **Kilauea**, HI, U.S.A.
111 M 15 **Kilchu**, North Korea
61 E 18 **Kilcock**, Republic of Ireland
61 E 18 **Kildare**, Republic of Ireland
130 K 11 **Kilembe**, Democratic Republic of Congo
27 T 6 **Kilgore**, TX, U.S.A.
141 Y 4 **Kili Island**, Marshall Islands
131 Q 10 **Kiliba**, Democratic Republic of Congo
131 X 10 **Kilifi**, Kenya
131 V 9 **Kilimanjaro**, Tanzania
131 V 10 **Kilimanjaro**, Tanzania
131 X 12 **Kilindoni**, Tanzania
84 F 8 **Kilingi-Nõmme**, Estonia
94 M 13 **Kilis**, Turkey
96 J 1 **Kilis**, Syria
61 B 19 **Kilkee**, Republic of Ireland
61 D 19 **Kilkenny**, Republic of Ireland
62 K 13 **Kilkhampton**, U.K.
82 F 13 **Kilkis**, Greece
42 D 9 **Killarney**, ON, Canada
61 B 20 **Killarney**, Republic of Ireland
22 H 4 **Killdeer**, ND, U.S.A.
27 P 8 **Killeen**, TX, U.S.A.
41 T 5 **Killiniq**, QC, Canada
60 G 13 **Kilmarnock**, U.K.
91 Q 14 **Kil'mez'**, Russian Federation
131 V 12 **Kilosa**, Tanzania
61 B 19 **Kilrush**, Republic of Ireland
105 B 22 **Kilttan**, India
131 P 13 **Kilwa**, Democratic Republic of Congo
131 W 13 **Kilwa Kivinje**, Tanzania
117 T 12 **Kilwo**, Indonesia
31 T 7 **Kim**, CO, U.S.A.
129 W 11 **Kim**, Chad
117 X 14 **Kimaan**, Indonesia
131 W 13 **Kimambi**, Tanzania
130 G 10 **Kimba**, Congo
135 O 11 **Kimba**, SA, Australia
22 G 14 **Kimball**, NE, U.S.A.
138 G 4 **Kimbe**, Papua New Guinea
132 M 12 **Kimberley**, Republic of South Africa
134 K 3 **Kimberley**, WA, Australia
111 M 16 **Kimch'aek**, North Korea
41 R 4 **Kimmirut**, NU, Canada
83 I 23 **Kimolos**, Greece
128 K 10 **Kimparana**, Mali
130 G 11 **Kimpese**, Democratic Republic of Congo
122 I 13 **Kimpoku-san**, Japan
130 H 11 **Kimvula**, Democratic Republic of Congo
119 V 6 **Kinabatangan**, Malaysia
131 W 10 **Kinango**, Kenya
83 L 22 **Kinaros**, Greece
42 C 12 **Kincardine**, ON, Canada
131 N 13 **Kinda**, Democratic Republic of Congo
18 I 7 **Kinder**, LA, U.S.A.
39 L 19 **Kindersley**, SK, Canada
128 F 11 **Kindia**, Guinea
131 O 9 **Kindu**, Democratic Republic of Congo
93 T 3 **Kinel'-Cherkasy**, Russian Federation
90 L 13 **Kineshma**, Russian Federation
33 H 21 **King City**, CA, U.S.A.
57 K 23 **King George Bay**, Falkland Islands
144 G 3 **King George Island**, Antarctica
37 S 9 **King George Islands**, NU, Canada
135 R 14 **King Island**, TAS, Australia
145 X 7 **King Leopold and Queen Astrid Coast**, Antarctica
134 I 3 **King Leopold Ranges**, WA, Australia
39 D 16 **King Mountain**, BC, Canada
144 J 9 **King Peninsula**, Antarctica
134 I 3 **King Sound**, WA, Australia
40 L 1 **King William Island**, NU, Canada
135 W 8 **Kingaroy**, QLD, Australia
24 M 9 **Kingfisher**, OK, U.S.A.
90 D 11 **Kingisepp**, Russian Federation
24 M 6 **Kingman**, KS, U.S.A.
30 G 10 **Kingman**, AZ, U.S.A.
101 V 10 **Kingri**, Pakistan
61 M 19 **King's**, U.K.
63 X 6 **King's Lynn**, U.K.
14 L 12 **Kings Park**, NY, U.S.A.
30 L 2 **Kings Peak**, UT, U.S.A.
63 T 12 **King's Worthy**, U.K.
63 N 15 **Kingsbridge**, U.K.
63 T 11 **Kingsclere**, U.K.
135 P 12 **Kingscote**, SA, Australia
19 W 6 **Kingsland**, GA, U.S.A.
16 L 8 **Kingsport**, TN, U.S.A.
14 J 10 **Kingston**, NY, U.S.A.
15 N 11 **Kingston**, RI, U.S.A.
21 D 19 **Kingston**, IL, U.S.A.
42 I 12 **Kingston**, ON, Canada
48 L 8 **Kingston**, Jamaica
137 C 23 **Kingston**, New Zealand
135 Q 13 **Kingston S.E.**, SA, Australia
63 V 2 **Kingston upon Hull**, U.K.
63 V 11 **Kingston upon Thames**, U.K.
49 Y 12 **Kingstown**, St Vincent and the Grenadines
27 P 13 **Kingsville**, TX, U.S.A.
63 Q 11 **Kingswood**, U.K.
63 P 8 **Kington**, U.K.
130 J 11 **Kingungi**, Democratic Republic of Congo
122 L 12 **Kinka-san**, Japan
130 G 10 **Kinkala**, Congo
136 L 11 **Kinloch**, New Zealand
71 E 23 **Kinna**, Sweden
69 K 17 **Kinrooi**, Belgium
130 H 10 **Kinshasa**, Democratic Republic of Congo
130 H 10 **Kinshasa**, Democratic Republic of Congo
24 K 5 **Kinsley**, KS, U.S.A.
17 T 10 **Kinston**, NC, U.S.A.
128 M 12 **Kintampo**, Ghana
128 H 10 **Kintinian**, Guinea
117 P 11 **Kintom**, Indonesia
116 L 12 **Kintop**, Indonesia
61 F 14 **Kintyre**, U.K.
114 D 10 **Kinu**, Myanmar
131 T 10 **Kinyangiri**, Tanzania
127 F 23 **Kinyeti**, Sudan
131 T 12 **Kipembawe**, Tanzania
131 R 12 **Kipili**, Tanzania
34 L 10 **Kipnuk**, AK, U.S.A.
131 P 15 **Kipushi**, Democratic Republic of Congo
131 Q 15 **Kipushia**, Democratic Republic of Congo
139 N 7 **Kirakira**, Solomon Islands
105 G 17 **Kirandul**, India
128 H 8 **Kirané**, Mali
105 F 23 **Kiranur**, India
85 L 18 **Kirawsk**, Belarus
27 U 8 **Kirbyville**, TX, U.S.A.
75 T 5 **Kirchdorf**, Austria
73 G 23 **Kirchheim**, Germany
89 Q 13 **Kirenga**, Russian Federation
89 Q 12 **Kirensk**, Russian Federation
103 T 10 **Kirghiz Range**, Kyrgyzstan
130 J 8 **Kiri**, Democratic Republic of Congo
140 I 4 **Kiribati**, Oceania
95 Q 8 **Kirik**, Turkey
94 L 13 **Kirikhan**, Turkey
94 I 9 **Kirikkale**, Turkey
90 J 11 **Kirillov**, Russian Federation
90 F 11 **Kirishi**, Russian Federation
123 C 23 **Kirishima-yama**, Japan
136 K 11 **Kiritehere**, New Zealand
138 G 6 **Kiriwina Island**, Papua New Guinea
63 Q 1 **Kirkby Lonsdale**, U.K.
63 U 1 **Kirkbymoorside**, U.K.
60 I 12 **Kirkcaldy**, U.K.
70 M 6 **Kirkenes**, Norway
63 P 2 **Kirkham**, U.K.
71 L 19 **Kirkkonummi**, Finland
42 E 6 **Kirkland Lake**, ON, Canada
82 M 11 **Kirklareli**, Turkey
94 C 6 **Kirklareli**, Turkey
25 U 1 **Kirksville**, MO, U.S.A.
97 T 3 **Kirkūk**, Iraq
60 I 7 **Kirkwall**, U.K.
25 X 4 **Kirkwood**, MO, U.S.A.
73 D 20 **Kirn**, Germany
91 P 12 **Kirov**, Russian Federation
92 I 2 **Kirov**, Russian Federation
87 V 8 **Kirove**, Ukraine
91 P 12 **Kirovo-Chepetsk**, Russian Federation
87 R 6 **Kirovohrad**, Ukraine
91 P 13 **Kirovskaya Oblast'**, Russian Federation
87 V 11 **Kirovs'ke**, Ukraine
91 Q 11 **Kirs**, Russian Federation
94 J 10 **Kirşehir**, Turkey
101 T 12 **Kirthar Range**, Pakistan
70 I 9 **Kiruna**, Sweden
131 N 8 **Kirundu**, Democratic Republic of Congo
92 L 1 **Kirzhach**, Russian Federation
71 G 22 **Kisa**, Sweden
131 N 7 **Kisangani**, Democratic Republic of Congo
117 R 14 **Kisar**, Indonesia
131 W 12 **Kisarawe**, Tanzania
123 K 16 **Kisarazu**, Japan
88 M 12 **Kiselevsk**, Russian Federation
80 H 12 **Kiseljak**, Bosnia and Herzegovina
107 R 11 **Kishanganj**, India
123 C 24 **Kishika-zaki**, Japan
123 G 19 **Kishiwada**, Japan
103 S 2 **Kishkenekol'**, Kazakhstan
107 U 12 **Kishorganj**, Bangladesh
106 I 4 **Kishtwar**, India
129 P 12 **Kisi**, Nigeria
131 T 8 **Kisii**, Kenya
34 C 12 **Kiska Island**, AK, U.S.A.
79 J 25 **Kiskőrös**, Hungary
79 K 24 **Kiskunfélegyháza**, Hungary
79 J 25 **Kiskunhalas**, Hungary
93 O 13 **Kislovodsk**, Russian Federation
127 K 26 **Kismaayo**, Somalia
123 I 17 **Kiso-sanmyaku**, Japan
128 H 11 **Kissidougou**, Guinea
19 W 10 **Kissimmee**, FL, U.S.A.
131 T 8 **Kisumu**, Kenya
79 N 21 **Kisvárda**, Hungary
31 U 5 **Kit Carson**, CO, U.S.A.
128 H 9 **Kita**, Mali
123 B 20 **Kita-Kyūshū**, Japan
123 L 14 **Kitaibaraki**, Japan
122 K 11 **Kitakami**, Japan
122 K 13 **Kitakata**, Japan
131 U 7 **Kitale**, Kenya
122 L 4 **Kitami**, Japan
122 J 3 **Kitami-sanchi**, Japan
131 O 11 **Kitanda**, Democratic Republic of Congo
123 D 22 **Kitaura**, Japan
42 D 13 **Kitchener**, ON, Canada
131 S 6 **Kitgum**, Uganda
39 D 19 **Kitimat**, BC, Canada
70 L 10 **Kitinen**, Finland
83 E 14 **Kitros**, Greece
86 K 6 **Kitsman'**, Ukraine
14 B 12 **Kittanning**, PA, U.S.A.
70 K 10 **Kittilä**, Finland
17 W 8 **Kitty Hawk**, NC, U.S.A.
131 S 12 **Kitunda**, Tanzania
133 O 4 **Kitwe**, Zambia
75 P 6 **Kitzbühel**, Austria
75 O 7 **Kitzbüheler Alpen**, Austria
138 A 5 **Kiunga**, Papua New Guinea
71 L 15 **Kivijärvi**, Finland
84 I 6 **Kiviõli**, Estonia
138 C 6 **Kiwai Island**, Papua New Guinea
35 N 6 **Kiwalik**, AK, U.S.A.
103 S 5 **Kiyevka**, Kazakhstan
94 C 6 **Kiyiköy**, Turkey
91 T 11 **Kizel**, Russian Federation
90 M 10 **Kizema**, Russian Federation
94 I 9 **Kizilirmak**, Turkey
94 G 12 **Kizilören**, Turkey
95 P 13 **Kiziltepe**, Turkey
93 Q 13 **Kizlyar**, Russian Federation
69 G 14 **Klaaswaal**, Netherlands
117 X 15 **Kladar**, Indonesia
79 C 17 **Kladno**, Czech Republic
80 O 10 **Kladovo**, Serbia and Montenegro
115 I 20 **Klaeng**, Thailand
119 W 5 **Klagan**, Malaysia
75 T 9 **Klagenfurt**, Austria
84 B 13 **Klaipėda**, Lithuania
33 E 14 **Klamath**, CA, U.S.A.
33 H 14 **Klamath Falls**, OR, U.S.A.
79 B 18 **Klatovy**, Czech Republic
68 N 9 **Klazienaveen**, Netherlands
132 I 13 **Kleinsee**, Republic of South Africa
80 E 11 **Klekovača**, Bosnia and Herzegovina
87 N 7 **Klembivka**, Ukraine
133 N 11 **Klerksdorp**, Republic of South Africa
78 N 12 **Kleszczele**, Poland
92 H 3 **Kletnya**, Russian Federation
86 L 3 **Klevan**, Ukraine
73 B 15 **Kleve**, Germany
85 L 18 **Klichaw**, Belarus
85 O 17 **Klimavichy**, Belarus
82 L 7 **Kliment**, Bulgaria
90 H 14 **Klin**, Russian Federation
71 H 23 **Klintehamn**, Sweden
93 S 5 **Klintsovka**, Russian Federation
92 G 3 **Klintsy**, Russian Federation
81 O 15 **Klisura**, Serbia and Montenegro
80 F 11 **Ključ**, Bosnia and Herzegovina
79 I 15 **Kłobuck**, Poland
79 F 17 **Kłodzko**, Poland
71 D 19 **Kløfta**, Norway
69 E 16 **Kloosterzande**, Netherlands
74 J 8 **Klosters**, Switzerland
79 H 15 **Kluczbork**, Poland
85 I 19 **Klyetsk**, Belarus
89 Y 10 **Klyuchi**, Russian Federation
63 S 1 **Knaresborough**, U.K.
71 A 18 **Knarvik**, Norway
82 H 7 **Knezha**, Bulgaria
80 L 12 **Knić**, Serbia and Montenegro
63 O 7 **Knighton**, U.K.
80 E 12 **Knin**, Croatia
75 U 7 **Knittelfeld**, Austria
19 V 12 **Knob Island**, FL, U.S.A.
69 C 16 **Knokke-Heist**, Belgium
63 T 2 **Knottingley**, U.K.
21 I 17 **Knox**, IN, U.S.A.
141 Z 4 **Knox**, Marshall Islands
145 X 10 **Knox Coast**, Antarctica
16 J 9 **Knoxville**, TN, U.S.A.
19 T 4 **Knoxville**, GA, U.S.A.
23 T 13 **Knoxville**, IA, U.S.A.
143 P 10 **Knud Rasmussen Land**, Greenland
63 Q 4 **Knutsford**, U.K.
132 L 15 **Knysna**, Republic of South Africa
115 F 23 **Ko Chan**, Thailand
115 J 21 **Ko Chang**, Thailand
122 I 8 **Ko-jima**, Japan
115 J 21 **Ko Kut**, Thailand
115 F 25 **Ko Lanta**, Thailand
115 G 25 **Ko Lanta**, Thailand
115 G 25 **Ko Libong**, Thailand
115 H 23 **Ko Phangan**, Thailand
115 F 23 **Ko Phra Thong**, Thailand
115 F 25 **Ko Phuket**, Thailand
115 H 23 **Ko Samui**, Thailand
115 G 23 **Ko Tao**, Thailand
115 G 25 **Ko Yao Yai**, Thailand
131 W 11 **Koani**, Tanzania
116 G 12 **Koba**, Indonesia
80 A 7 **Kobarid**, Slovenia
117 R 10 **Kobe**, Indonesia
123 F 18 **Kōbe**, Japan
87 T 5 **Kobelyaky**, Ukraine
128 H 8 **Kobenni**, Mauritania
73 D 18 **Koblenz**, Germany
87 Q 9 **Kobleve**, Ukraine
127 I 18 **K'obo**, Ethiopia
131 R 6 **Koboko**, Uganda
117 V 13 **Kobroör**, Indonesia
85 F 21 **Kobryn**, Belarus
35 O 5 **Kobuk**, AK, U.S.A.
35 O 5 **Kobuk**, AK, U.S.A.
95 Q 7 **K'obulet'i**, Georgia
94 E 8 **Kocaeli**, Turkey
82 E 11 **Kočani**, Macedonia (F.Y.R.O.M.)
80 K 11 **Koceljevo**, Serbia and Montenegro
80 C 8 **Kočevje**, Slovenia
107 T 10 **Koch Bihar**, India
123 E 20 **Kōchi**, Japan
103 V 10 **Kochkor**, Kyrgyzstan
93 R 13 **Kochubey**, Russian Federation
79 N 14 **Kock**, Poland
123 B 26 **Kodakara-jima**, Japan
107 Q 9 **Kodari**, Nepal
107 Q 12 **Kodarma**, India
35 Q 11 **Kodiak**, AK, U.S.A.
35 P 12 **Kodiak Island**, AK, U.S.A.
105 A 16 **Kodinar**, India
90 K 7 **Kodino**, Russian Federation
89 P 12 **Kodinsk**, Russian Federation
127 E 20 **Kodok**, Sudan
122 J 8 **Kodomari-misaki**, Japan
82 K 12 **Kodzhaele**, Greece
132 J 11 **Koës**, Namibia
82 M 11 **Kofşşaz**, Turkey
94 H 15 **Kofinou**, Cyprus
75 V 7 **Köflach**, Austria
128 M 13 **Koforidua**, Ghana
123 J 16 **Kōfu**, Japan
123 E 18 **Kōfu**, Japan
41 P 6 **Kogaluk**, QC, Canada
88 L 10 **Kogalym**, Russian Federation
71 D 25 **Køge**, Denmark
129 Q 12 **Kogi**, Nigeria
101 R 8 **Koh-i-Sangān**, Afghanistan
101 S 13 **Kohan**, Pakistan
101 W 8 **Kohat**, Pakistan
84 G 6 **Kohila**, Estonia
107 X 11 **Kohima**, India
100 H 9 **Kohkīlūyeh Va Būyeraḥmadī**, Iran
101 P 7 **Kohsan**, Afghanistan
84 I 5 **Kohtla-Järve**, Estonia
97 T 2 **Koi Sanjaq**, Iraq
70 L 11 **Koivu**, Finland
111 N 21 **Kōje-do**, South Korea
134 G 12 **Kojonup**, WA, Australia
103 V 12 **Kök-Aygy**, Kyrgyzstan
103 S 12 **Kokand**, Uzbekistan
128 E 8 **Koki**, Senegal
71 K 14 **Kokkola**, Finland
129 P 10 **Koko**, Nigeria
138 E 6 **Kokoda**, Papua New Guinea
128 H 9 **Kokofata**, Mali
21 I 18 **Kokomo**, IN, U.S.A.
137 E 23 **Kokonga**, New Zealand
138 H 4 **Kokopo**, Papua New Guinea
129 O 12 **Kokoro**, Benin
103 X 5 **Kokpekti**, Kazakhstan
103 Q 10 **Koksaray**, Kazakhstan
103 R 3 **Kokshetau**, Kazakhstan
69 A 17 **Koksijde**, Belgium
133 O 13 **Kokstad**, Republic of South Africa
103 X 9 **Koktal**, Kazakhstan
103 Y 7 **Koktuma**, Kazakhstan
123 C 23 **Kokubu**, Japan
90 J 4 **Kola Peninsula**, Russian Federation
117 O 13 **Kolaka**, Indonesia
105 E 21 **Kolar**, India
104 E 13 **Kolaras**, India
70 K 10 **Kolari**, Finland
81 J 15 **Kolašin**, Serbia and Montenegro
104 C 11 **Kolayat**, India
128 E 9 **Kolda**, Senegal
130 M 10 **Kole**, Democratic Republic of Congo
131 N 6 **Kole**, Democratic Republic of Congo
84 H 7 **Kolga-Jaani**, Estonia
84 G 5 **Kolga laht**, Estonia
105 C 18 **Kolhapur**, India
105 L 19 **Kolhumadulu Atoll**, Maldives
35 O 10 **Koliganek**, AK, U.S.A.
71 O 15 **Kolin**, Finland
79 E 17 **Kolín**, Czech Republic
127 I 21 **K'olīto**, Ethiopia
140 H 8 **Koliu**, Wallis and Futuna Islands
84 D 9 **Kolkasrags**, Latvia
103 R 14 **Kolkhozobod**, Tajikistan
86 K 2 **Kolky**, Ukraine
75 S 3 **Kollerschlag**, Austria
78 M 10 **Kolno**, Poland
78 I 13 **Koło**, Poland
78 E 8 **Kołobrzeg**, Poland
128 I 9 **Kolokani**, Mali
138 K 6 **Kolombangara**, Solomon Islands
92 L 2 **Kolomna**, Russian Federation
86 J 6 **Kolomyya**, Ukraine
128 J 10 **Kolondiéba**, Mali
141 Q 15 **Kolonia**, Federated States of Micronesia
117 P 13 **Kolono**, Indonesia
88 M 11 **Kolpashevo**, Russian Federation
90 F 10 **Kolpino**, Russian Federation
83 H 15 **Kolpos Agiou Orous**, Greece
83 H 25 **Kolpos Chanion**, Greece
83 G 14 **Kolpos Ierissou**, Greece
83 G 15 **Kolpos Kassandras**, Greece
82 H 13 **Kolpos Kavalas**, Greece
83 G 25 **Kolpos Kissamou**, Greece
103 X 9 **Kol'shat**, Kazakhstan
93 T 3 **Koltubanovskiy**, Russian Federation
103 R 4 **Koluton**, Kazakhstan
131 N 14 **Kolwezi**, Democratic Republic of Congo
85 M 22 **Kolyban**, Belarus
89 W 8 **Kolyma**, Russian Federation
126 F 11 **Kôm Ombo**, Egypt
123 H 17 **Komaki**, Japan
131 Q 8 **Komanda**, Democratic Republic of Congo
79 H 22 **Komárno**, Slovakia
123 H 16 **Komatsu**, Japan
117 P 11 **Kombakomba**, Indonesia
128 M 10 **Kombissiri**, Burkina Faso
91 R 10 **Komi-Permyatskiy Avtonomnyy Okrug**, Russian Federation
87 Q 9 **Kominternivs'ke**, Ukraine
79 H 25 **Komló**, Hungary
117 N 15 **Komodo**, Indonesia
128 H 11 **Komodou**, Guinea
123 J 15 **Komoro**, Japan
83 J 13 **Komotini**, Greece
87 R 7 **Kompaniyivka**, Ukraine
132 M 14 **Kompasberg**, Republic of South Africa
103 N 2 **Komsomolets**, Kazakhstan
89 W 13 **Komsomol'sk-na-Amure**, Russian Federation
89 Y 6 **Komsomol'skiy**, Russian Federation
102 M 5 **Komsomol'skoye**, Kazakhstan
82 J 11 **Komuniga**, Bulgaria
115 O 18 **Kon Plong**, Vietnam
115 O 18 **Kon Tum**, Vietnam
105 J 17 **Konarka**, India
106 K 11 **Konch**, India
105 H 17 **Kondagaon**, India
131 U 11 **Kondoa**, Tanzania
93 P 4 **Kondol**, Russian Federation
101 U 5 **Kondūz**, Afghanistan
139 P 13 **Koné**, New Caledonia
143 O 13 **Kong Christian IX Land**, Greenland
143 P 12 **Kong Christian X Land**, Greenland
143 N 12 **Kong Frederik IX Land**, Greenland
143 Q 11 **Kong Frederik VIII Land**, Greenland
143 Q 12 **Kong Wilhelm Land**, Greenland
132 L 7 **Kongola**, Namibia
131 O 11 **Kongolo**, Democratic Republic of Congo
128 M 9 **Kongoussi**, Burkina Faso
71 D 20 **Kongsberg**, Norway
71 E 19 **Kongsvinger**, Norway
108 G 6 **Kongur Shan**, China
131 U 11 **Kongwa**, Tanzania
73 M 25 **Königssee**, Germany
78 H 13 **Konin**, Poland
137 L 15 **Konini**, New Zealand
83 B 15 **Konitsa**, Greece
80 H 13 **Konjic**, Bosnia and Herzegovina
70 J 8 **Könkämäeno**, Finland
128 K 8 **Konna**, Mali
128 M 13 **Konongo**, Ghana
138 G 3 **Konos**, Papua New Guinea
90 K 10 **Konosha**, Russian Federation
87 S 2 **Konotop**, Ukraine
79 K 15 **Końskie**, Poland
127 H 22 **Konso**, Ethiopia
73 F 25 **Konstanz**, Germany
105 G 18 **Konta**, India
129 Q 11 **Kontagora**, Nigeria
71 N 14 **Kontiomäki**, Finland
94 H 12 **Konya**, Turkey
117 U 11 **Koor**, Indonesia
134 G 10 **Koorda**, WA, Australia
28 K 6 **Kooskia**, ID, U.S.A.
136 K 11 **Kopaki**, New Zealand
81 L 14 **Kopaonik**, Serbia and Montenegro
70 C 9 **Kópasker**, Iceland
103 V 7 **Kopbirlik**, Kazakhstan
80 A 8 **Koper**, Slovenia
102 J 13 **Kopet Dag**, Turkmenistan
81 J 16 **Koplik**, Albania
105 D 21 **Koppa**, India
71 D 17 **Koppang**, Norway
80 F 7 **Koprivnica**, Croatia
86 L 5 **Kopychyntsi**, Ukraine
81 L 17 **Korab**, Albania
81 L 17 **Korab**, Albania
92 M 3 **Korablino**, Russian Federation
127 L 22 **K'orahē**, Ethiopia
105 E 18 **Korangal**, India
105 H 15 **Korba**, India
73 F 16 **Korbach**, Germany
129 X 11 **Korbol**, Chad
81 L 20 **Korşşë**, Albania
81 F 15 **Korčula**, Croatia
81 E 15 **Korčula**, Croatia
81 E 14 **Korčulanski Kanal**, Croatia
103 U 10 **Korday**, Kazakhstan
100 F 5 **Kordestān**, Iran
111 I 18 **Korea Bay**, China/North Korea
111 M 22 **Korea Strait**, Japan/South Korea
127 I 18 **Korem**, Ethiopia
136 J 7 **Koremoa**, New Zealand
92 I 5 **Korenevo**, Russian Federation
92 L 11 **Korenovsk**, Russian Federation
86 L 3 **Korets'**, Ukraine
89 Z 9 **Korf**, Russian Federation
94 E 8 **Körfez**, Turkey
108 I 4 **Korgas**, China
128 J 11 **Korhogo**, Côte d'Ivoire
83 F 20 **Korinthos**, Greece
79 H 23 **Kőris-hegy**, Hungary
122 K 13 **Kōriyama**, Japan
94 E 12 **Korkuteli**, Turkey
108 K 5 **Korla**, China
79 F 24 **Körmend**, Hungary
80 C 12 **Kornat**, Croatia
75 X 3 **Korneuburg**, Austria
128 L 9 **Koro**, Mali
139 Y 11 **Koro**, Fiji
139 X 12 **Koro Sea**, Fiji
129 X 8 **Koro Toro**, Chad
94 F 8 **Köroğlu Dağlari**, Turkey
94 G 8 **Köroğlu Tepesi**, Turkey
131 W 11 **Korogwe**, Tanzania
121 L 23 **Koronadal**, Philippines
83 D 23 **Koroni**, Greece
140 I 15 **Koror**, Palau
79 K 24 **Körös**, Hungary
87 N 3 **Korosten'**, Ukraine
87 O 4 **Korostyshiv**, Ukraine
71 M 17 **Korpilahti**, Finland
87 Q 5 **Korsun'-Shevchenkivs'kyy**, Ukraine
69 B 18 **Kortemark**, Belgium
127 E 15 **Korti**, Sudan
69 C 19 **Kortrijk**, Belgium
89 Y 9 **Koryakskiy Khrebet**, Russian Federation
91 N 10 **Koryazhma**, Russian Federation
78 N 10 **Korycin**, Poland
87 R 1 **Koryukivka**, Ukraine
83 M 22 **Kos**, Greece
83 M 23 **Kos**, Greece
87 U 10 **Kosa Arabats'ka Strilka**, Ukraine
87 V 10 **Kosa Biryuchyy Ostriv**, Ukraine
111 L 17 **Kosan**, North Korea
78 F 13 **Kościan**, Poland
78 H 9 **Kościerzyna**, Poland
18 M 4 **Kosciusko**, MS, U.S.A.
84 G 6 **Kose**, Estonia
88 M 14 **Kosh-Agach**, Russian Federation
103 U 11 **Kosh-Döbö**, Kyrgyzstan
123 B 23 **Koshiki-kaikyō**, Japan
123 A 23 **Koshikijima-rettō**, Japan
101 P 7 **Koshk**, Afghanistan
107 R 10 **Kosi Reservoir**, Nepal
79 L 20 **Košice**, Slovakia
86 J 7 **Kosiv**, Ukraine
80 K 12 **Kosjerić**, Serbia and Montenegro
103 Q 5 **Koskol'**, Kazakhstan
111 M 18 **Kosŏng**, North Korea
81 L 15 **Kosovo**, Serbia and Montenegro
81 L 15 **Kosovska Mitrovica**, Serbia and Montenegro
141 R 15 **Kosrae**, Federated States of Micronesia
141 R 15 **Kosrae**, Federated States of Micronesia
75 P 6 **Kössen**, Austria
103 O 4 **Kostanay**, Kazakhstan
103 O 3 **Kostanay**, Kazakhstan
82 H 10 **Kostenets**, Bulgaria
127 F 18 **Kosti**, Sudan
82 F 9 **Kostinbrod**, Bulgaria
86 L 3 **Kostopil'**, Ukraine
90 K 13 **Kostroma**, Russian Federation
90 L 12 **Kostromskaya Oblast'**, Russian Federation
78 D 12 **Kostrzyn**, Poland
87 X 6 **Kostyantynivka**, Ukraine
91 S 4 **Kos'yu**, Russian Federation
78 F 8 **Koszalin**, Poland
79 K 17 **Koszyce**, Poland
101 U 13 **Kot Diji**, Pakistan
106 I 9 **Kot Putli**, India
104 D 13 **Kota**, India
119 V 4 **Kota Belud**, Malaysia
118 C 5 **Kota Bharu**, Malaysia
119 U 5 **Kota Kinabalu**, Malaysia
118 F 10 **Kota Tinggi**, Malaysia
116 F 13 **Kotaagung**, Indonesia
116 M 12 **Kotabaru**, Indonesia
116 F 13 **Kotabumi**, Indonesia
117 Q 10 **Kotamobagu**, Indonesia
116 D 10 **Kotapinang**, Indonesia
136 K 12 **Kotare**, New Zealand
82 L 8 **Kotel**, Bulgaria
91 O 13 **Kotel'nich**, Russian Federation
93 O 9 **Kotel'nikovo**, Russian Federation
87 U 4 **Kotel'va**, Ukraine
131 T 6 **Kotido**, Uganda
71 N 18 **Kotka**, Finland
91 N 10 **Kotlas**, Russian Federation
106 G 4 **Kotli**, India
81 I 16 **Kotor**, Serbia and Montenegro
80 G 10 **Kotor Varoš**, Bosnia and Herzegovina
129 R 10 **Kotorkoshi**, Nigeria
128 L 12 **Kotouba**, Côte d'Ivoire
87 O 8 **Kotovs'k**, Ukraine
85 F 18 **Kotra**, Belarus
101 U 14 **Kotri**, Pakistan
75 Q 9 **Kötschach**, Austria
105 G 18 **Kottagudem**, India
105 G 19 **Kottapatnam**, India
130 L 4 **Kotto**, Central African Republic
89 R 8 **Kotuy**, Russian Federation
35 N 5 **Kotzebue**, AK, U.S.A.
34 M 5 **Kotzebue Sound**, AK, U.S.A.
130 K 4 **Kouango**, Central African Republic
128 G 10 **Koubia**, Guinea
130 E 10 **Kouilou**, Congo
94 G 15 **Koúklia**, Cyprus
130 E 8 **Koulamoutou**, Gabon
128 I 9 **Koulikoro**, Mali
128 I 9 **Koulikoro**, Mali
139 O 13 **Koumac**, New Caledonia
128 F 10 **Koumbia**, Guinea
129 X 11 **Koumra**, Chad
128 F 9 **Koûndâra**, Guinea
128 E 9 **Koungheul**, Senegal
128 M 10 **Koupéla**, Burkina Faso
51 Y 6 **Kourou**, French Guiana
128 H 11 **Kouroussa**, Guinea
128 F 9 **Koussanar**, Senegal
129 V 10 **Kousséri**, Chad
128 J 10 **Koutiala**, Mali
83 D 16 **Koutsochero**, Greece
71 N 18 **Kouvola**, Finland
90 G 3 **Kovdor**, Russian Federation
86 J 2 **Kovel'**, Ukraine
93 N 1 **Kovrov**, Russian Federation
93 O 3 **Kovylkino**, Russian Federation
135 R 3 **Kowanyama**, QLD, Australia
113 U 13 **Kowloon**, China
111 L 17 **Kowŏn**, North Korea
94 C 12 **Köycegiz**, Turkey
90 L 5 **Koyda**, Russian Federation
35 O 6 **Koykuyuk**, AK, U.S.A.
105 C 18 **Koyna Reservoir**, India
82 G 7 **Koynare**, Bulgaria
35 N 6 **Koyuk**, AK, U.S.A.
94 M 9 **Koyulhisar**, Turkey
94 K 12 **Kozan**, Turkey
83 D 15 **Kozani**, Greece
80 F 9 **Kozara**, Bosnia and Herzegovina
87 Q 3 **Kozelets'**, Ukraine
92 J 3 **Kozel'sk**, Russian Federation
89 R 7 **Kozhevnikovo**, Russian Federation
79 L 14 **Kozienice**, Poland
82 G 6 **Kozloduy**, Bulgaria
93 Q 1 **Koz'modem'yansk**, Russian Federati
123 K 18 **Kōzu-shima**, Japan
87 O 5 **Kozyatyn**, Ukraine
129 N 13 **Kpalimé**, Togo
115 F 22 **Kra Buri**, Thailand
115 G 25 **Krabi**, Thailand
115 M 20 **Krâchéh**, Cambodia
80 L 12 **Kragujevac**, Serbia and Montenegro
116 G 14 **Krakatau**, Indonesia
79 K 17 **Kraków**, Poland
115 K 19 **Krâlănh**, Cambodia
49 S 13 **Kralendijk**, Netherlands Antilles
80 B 9 **Kraljevića**, Croatia
80 L 12 **Kraljevo**, Serbia and Montenegro
79 B 17 **Kralovice**, Czech Republic
87 X 6 **Kramators'k**, Ukraine
69 F 15 **Krammer**, Netherlands
83 F 21 **Kranidi**, Greece
80 B 7 **Kranj**, Slovenia
118 A 13 **Kranji Reservoir**, Singapore
102 K 4 **Kransoyar**, Kazakhstan
80 D 7 **Krapina**, Croatia
79 H 16 **Krapkowice**, Poland
88 K 6 **Krasino**, Russian Federation
84 I 13 **Krāslava**, Latvia
85 N 18 **Krasnapollye**, Belarus
93 N 1 **Krasnaya**, Russian Federation
92 L 13 **Krasnaya Polyana**, Russian Federatio
85 I 19 **Krasnaya Slabada**, Belarus
87 O 8 **Krasni Okny**, Ukraine
79 M 15 **Kraśnik**, Poland
93 Q 6 **Krasnoarmeysk**, Russian Federation
87 X 7 **Krasnoarmiys'k**, Ukraine
91 N 9 **Krasnoborsk**, Russian Federation
92 K 12 **Krasnodar**, Russian Federation
92 L 11 **Krasnodarskiy Kray**, Russian Federation
92 M 11 **Krasnogvardeyskoye**, Russian Feder
87 V 5 **Krasnohrad**, Ukraine
91 S 12 **Krasnokamsk**, Russian Federation
93 U 5 **Krasnokholm**, Russian Federation
87 W 5 **Krasnopavlivka**, Ukraine
87 T 10 **Krasnoperekops'k**, Ukraine
87 U 3 **Krasnopillya**, Ukraine
89 N 9 **Krasnosel'kup**, Russian Federation
90 J 4 **Krasnoshchel'ye**, Russian Federation
87 S 6 **Krasnosillya**, Ukraine
93 O 2 **Krasnoslobodsk**, Russian Federation
91 U 13 **Krasnoufimsk**, Russian Federation
93 W 2 **Krasnousol'skiy**, Russian Federation
91 T 10 **Krasnovishersk**, Russian Federation
102 H 12 **Krasnovodskiy Zaliv**, Turkmenistan
89 N 12 **Krasnoyarsk**, Russian Federation
92 H 2 **Krasnoye**, Russian Federation
79 O 15 **Krasnystaw**, Poland
92 G 2 **Krasnyy**, Russian Federation
90 I 13 **Krasnyy Kholm**, Russian Federation
93 Q 6 **Krasnyy Kut**, Russian Federation
87 Z 6 **Krasnyy Luch**, Ukraine
87 X 5 **Krasnyy Lyman**, Ukraine
93 P 6 **Krasnyy Yar**, Russian Federation
93 S 10 **Krasnyy Yar**, Russian Federation
93 R 11 **Krasnyye Barrikady**, Russian Federa
82 E 10 **Kratovo**, Macedonia (F.Y.R.O.M.)
117 Y 12 **Krau**, Indonesia
93 R 13 **Kraynovka**, Russian Federation
73 B 16 **Krefeld**, Germany
87 T 6 **Kremenchuk**, Ukraine
87 S 5 **Kremenchuts'ka Vodoskhovyshche**, Ukraine
86 K 4 **Kremenets'**, Ukraine
87 Y 5 **Kreminna**, Ukraine
86 J 6 **Kremintsi**, Ukraine
31 Q 3 **Kremmling**, CO, U.S.A.
75 V 3 **Krems an der Donau**, Austria
82 F 11 **Kresna**, Bulgaria
83 D 21 **Krestena**, Greece
91 Q 4 **Krestovka**, Russian Federation
89 R 11 **Krestyakh**, Russian Federation
84 B 13 **Kretinga**, Lithuania
75 Q 8 **Kreuzeck**, Austria
74 H 6 **Kreuzlingen**, Switzerland

Country · Internal administrative region: State/Province/Territory/Dependent territory · Capital city · Mountain range/Undersea ridge · Mountain peak/Volcano/Seamount · Geographic feature · Headland/Point/Cape/Peninsula · Desert · Island/Island group · Antarctic base · Ocean · Sea · Bay/Gulf/Channel/Strait · Lake · Salt pan/Dry/Intermittent lake

Kribi – Lake Meredith

S 15 **Kribi**, Cameroon
W 6 **Krieglach**, Austria
C 18 **Krikellos**, Greece
O 7 **Krimml**, Austria
E 19 **Krishna**, India
E 21 **Krishnagiri**, India
S 13 **Krishnanagar**, India
D 21 **Krishnaraja Sagara**, India
B 22 **Kristiansand**, Norway
F 25 **Kristianstad**, Sweden
C 15 **Kristiansund**, Norway
J 17 **Kristinestad**, Finland
J 26 **Kríti**, Greece
E 10 **Kriva Palanka**, Macedonia (F.Y.R.O.M.)
F 7 **Križevci**, Croatia
B 9 **Krk**, Croatia
B 9 **Krk**, Croatia
E 12 **Krka**, Croatia
U 11 **Krms'kyy Pivostriv**, Ukraine
H 7 **Krokowa**, Poland
B 10 **Króksfjarðarnes**, Iceland
S 2 **Krolevets'**, Ukraine
J 4 **Kromy**, Russian Federation
J 19 **Kronach**, Germany
J 21 **Krŏng Kaôh Kŏng**, Cambodia
Z 10 **Kronotskiy Poluostrov**, Russian Federation
Z 11 **Kronotskiy Zaliv**, Russian Federation
N 12 **Kroonstad**, Republic of South Africa
L 11 **Kropotkin**, Russian Federation
M 18 **Krosno**, Poland
G 14 **Krotoszyn**, Poland
J 7 **Krotz Springs**, LA, U.S.A.
D 7 **Krško**, Slovenia
J 12 **Krumovgrad**, Bulgaria
J 11 **Krupanj**, Serbia and Montenegro
I 21 **Krupina**, Slovakia
M 13 **Kruševac**, Serbia and Montenegro
N 17 **Kryichaw**, Belarus
J 12 **Krymsk**, Russian Federation
T 13 **Krymski Hori**, Ukraine
L 18 **Krynica**, Poland
P 7 **Kryve Ozero**, Ukraine
T 7 **Kryvyy Rih**, Ukraine
N 7 **Kryzhopil'**, Ukraine
I 15 **Krzepice**, Poland
K 10 **Ksabi**, Algeria
M 6 **Ksar Chellala**, Algeria
M 6 **Ksar el Boukhari**, Algeria
I 6 **Ksar el Kebir**, Morocco
O 1 **Kstovo**, Russian Federation
S 6 **Kuala Belait**, Brunei
B 6 **Kuala Kangsar**, Malaysia
C 5 **Kuala Kerai**, Malaysia
Y 5 **Kuala Kinabatangan**, Malaysia
C 7 **Kuala Lipis**, Malaysia
C 8 **Kuala Lumpur**, Malaysia
C 8 **Kuala Lumpur**, Malaysia
U 5 **Kuala Penyu**, Malaysia
B 8 **Kuala Selangor**, Malaysia
E 6 **Kuala Terengganu**, Malaysia
K 11 **Kualakurun**, Indonesia
W 6 **Kuamut**, Malaysia
F 16 **Kuancheng**, China
J 16 **Kuandian**, China
Z 12 **Kuanshan**, Taiwan
E 8 **Kuantan**, Malaysia
O 1 **Kubaybāt**, Syria
R 7 **Kubaysah**, Iraq
A 18 **Kubbum**, Sudan
B 5 **Kubeai**, Papua New Guinea
L 6 **Kubrat**, Bulgaria
M 11 **Kučevo**, Serbia and Montenegro
J 15 **Kuchaiburi**, India
N 10 **Kuching**, Malaysia
B 25 **Kuchino-Erabu-shima**, Japan
B 26 **Kuchino-shima**, Japan
B 22 **Kuchinotsu**, Japan
L 19 **Kuda Huvadu Channel**, Maldives
C 19 **Kudal**, India
N 10 **Kudayd**, Saudi Arabia
F 16 **Kudowa-Zdrój**, Poland
J 14 **Kudus**, Indonesia
S 11 **Kudymkar**, Russian Federation
O 6 **Kufstein**, Austria
G 9 **Kugluktuk**, NU, Canada
C 8 **Kugmallit Bay**, NT, Canada
N 12 **Kūh-e Bazmān**, Iran
F 5 **Kūh-e Chehel Chashmeh**, Iran
L 12 **Kūh-e Fūrgun**, Iran
H 8 **Kūh-e Garbosh**, Iran
T 2 **Kūh-e Ḩājī Ebrāhīm**, Iraq
F 5 **Kūh-e-Haji Ebrahim**, Iran
K 12 **Kūh-e Hormoz**, Iran
L 11 **Kūh-e Ilazārān**, Iran
M 8 **Kūh-e Nāy Band**, Iran
O 13 **Kūh-e Nokhowch**, Iran
O 9 **Kūh-e Palangān**, Iran
I 11 **Kūh-e Shīb**, Iran
P 12 **Kūh-e Taftān**, Iran
Q 13 **Kūhak**, Iran
H 3 **Kuhha-ye Sabalan**, Iran
N 14 **Kuhmo**, Finland
V 12 **Kuitan**, China
I 4 **Kuito**, Angola
L 9 **Kuji**, Japan
K 14 **Kuji**, Japan
C 21 **Kujū-san**, Japan
U 9 **Kukawa**, Nigeria
L 16 **Kukës**, Albania
E 10 **Kukup**, Malaysia
J 8 **Kula**, Serbia and Montenegro
E 6 **Kula**, Bulgaria
C 10 **Kula**, Turkey
K 11 **Kula Kangri**, China
F 23 **Kulassein**, Philippines
V 12 **Kulaura**, Bangladesh
C 11 **Kuldīga**, Latvia
N 1 **Kulebaki**, Russian Federation
N 7 **Kulgera**, NT, Australia
O 10 **Kulkuduk**, Uzbekistan
J 5 **Kullu**, India
J 19 **Kulmbach**, Germany
S 14 **Kŭlob**, Tajikistan
Q 11 **Kulp**, Turkey
J 7 **Kul'sary**, Kazakhstan
R 13 **Kulti**, India
H 10 **Kulu**, Turkey
H 6 **Kulumadau**, Papua New Guinea
L 12 **Kulunda**, Russian Federation
O 12 **Kuma**, Russian Federation
K 15 **Kumagaya**, Japan
I 7 **Kumaishi**, Japan

123 C 22 **Kumamoto**, Japan
123 H 19 **Kumano**, Japan
82 D 10 **Kumanovo**, Macedonia (F.Y.R.O.M.)
137 E 18 **Kumara Junction**, New Zealand
134 H 7 **Kumarina Roadhouse**, WA, Australia
128 L 13 **Kumasi**, Ghana
129 S 14 **Kumba**, Cameroon
105 F 22 **Kumbakonam**, India
117 Y 14 **Kumbe**, Indonesia
94 F 10 **Kümbet**, Turkey
99 P 9 **Kumdah**, Saudi Arabia
123 M 25 **Kume-jima**, Japan
93 W 3 **Kumertau**, Russian Federation
111 M 20 **Kumi**, South Korea
131 T 7 **Kumi**, Uganda
71 G 21 **Kumla**, Sweden
72 L 9 **Kummerower See**, Germany
129 T 11 **Kumo**, Nigeria
115 J 16 **Kumphawapi**, Thailand
105 C 20 **Kumta**, India
131 N 6 **Kumu**, Democratic Republic of Congo
108 L 5 **Kümüx**, China
119 X 6 **Kunak**, Malaysia
101 V 6 **Kunar**, Afghanistan
84 H 5 **Kunda**, Estonia
106 M 11 **Kunda**, India
132 I 2 **Kunda-dia-Baze**, Angola
119 V 4 **Kundat**, Malaysia
138 C 4 **Kundiawa**, Papua New Guinea
116 F 10 **Kundur**, Indonesia
101 U 5 **Kunduz**, Afghanistan
132 G 8 **Kunene**, Namibia
132 F 7 **Kunene**, Namibia
103 V 10 **Kungei Alatau**, Kyrgyzstan
39 C 20 **Kunghit Island**, BC, Canada
102 L 10 **Kungrad**, Uzbekistan
71 D 23 **Kungsbacka**, Sweden
130 J 6 **Kungu**, Democratic Republic of Congo
91 T 13 **Kungur**, Russian Federation
114 F 12 **Kunhing**, Myanmar
123 D 21 **Kunisaki**, Japan
114 F 10 **Kunlong**, Myanmar
108 H 7 **Kunlun Shan**, China
112 L 11 **Kunming**, China
111 L 20 **Kunsan**, South Korea
113 Y 5 **Kunshan**, China
79 K 24 **Kunszentmárton**, Hungary
138 I 4 **Kunua**, Papua New Guinea
134 K 3 **Kununurra**, WA, Australia
130 H 10 **Kunzulu**, Democratic Republic of Congo
90 G 3 **Kuolayarvi**, Russian Federation
71 N 15 **Kuopio**, Finland
117 P 15 **Kupang**, Indonesia
138 E 7 **Kupiano**, Papua New Guinea
84 G 13 **Kupiškis**, Lithuania
35 X 11 **Kupreanof Island**, AK, U.S.A.
87 X 4 **Kup''yans'k**, Ukraine
108 J 5 **Kuqa**, China
95 V 7 **Kür**, Azerbaijan/Turkey
89 N 13 **Kuragino**, Russian Federation
123 E 19 **Kurashiki**, Japan
123 E 18 **Kurayoshi**, Japan
103 Y 5 **Kurchum**, Kazakhstan
100 E 2 **Kurdistan**, Iran
82 J 12 **Kŭrdzhali**, Bulgaria
82 J 11 **Kŭrdzhali**, Bulgaria
94 I 7 **Küre**, Turkey
123 D 20 **Kure**, Japan
94 H 7 **Küre Dağlari**, Turkey
84 D 8 **Kuressaare**, Estonia
103 R 5 **Kurgal'dzhinskiy**, Kazakhstan
88 J 11 **Kurgan**, Russian Federation
92 M 12 **Kurganinsk**, Russian Federation
140 D 2 **Kuria**, Kiribati
99 Y 11 **Kuria Muria**, Oman
71 K 16 **Kurikka**, Finland
89 Y 14 **Kuril Islands**, Russian Federation
93 R 6 **Kurilovka**, Russian Federation
89 Y 14 **Kuril'sk**, Russian Federation
47 Q 8 **Kurinwás**, Nicaragua
92 M 1 **Kurlovskiy**, Russian Federation
127 G 19 **Kurmuk**, Sudan
105 E 19 **Kurnool**, India
123 N 26 **Kuro-shima**, Japan
123 H 15 **Kurobe**, Japan
123 K 14 **Kuroiso**, Japan
79 M 14 **Kurów**, Poland
137 E 22 **Kurow**, New Zealand
93 N 13 **Kursavka**, Russian Federation
84 E 13 **Kuršėnai**, Lithuania
84 D 12 **Kursīši**, Latvia
92 J 5 **Kursk**, Russian Federation
85 B 15 **Kurskaya Kosa**, Russian Federation
92 I 5 **Kurskaya Oblast'**, Russian Federation
94 H 8 **Kurşunlu**, Turkey
95 R 12 **Kurtalan**, Turkey
108 K 5 **Kuruktag**, China
132 L 11 **Kuruman**, Republic of South Africa
123 B 21 **Kurume**, Japan
89 R 13 **Kurumkan**, Russian Federation
105 F 25 **Kurunegala**, Sri Lanka
51 U 7 **Kurupukari**, Guyana
91 S 8 **Kur'ya**, Russian Federation
102 H 10 **Kuryk**, Kazakhstan
94 C 8 **Kuş Gölü**, Turkey
94 B 11 **Kuşadasi**, Turkey
83 M 20 **Kuşadasi Körfezi**, Greece
94 B 11 **Kusadasi Körfezi**, Turkey
39 B 14 **Kusawa Lake**, YT, Canada
92 L 10 **Kushchevskaya**, Russian Federation
123 C 24 **Kushima**, Japan
123 H 20 **Kushimoto**, Japan
122 M 5 **Kushiro**, Japan
103 O 3 **Kushmurun**, Kazakhstan
93 V 1 **Kushnarenkovo**, Russian Federation
105 D 19 **Kushtagi**, India
107 T 13 **Kushtia**, Bangladesh
102 I 4 **Kushum**, Kazakhstan
34 M 9 **Kuskokwim**, AK, U.S.A.
34 L 10 **Kuskokwim Bay**, AK, U.S.A.
35 O 10 **Kuskokwim Mountains**, AK, U.S.A.
122 M 4 **Kussharo-ko**, Japan
94 E 9 **Kütahya**, Turkey
95 R 6 **K'ut'aisi**, Georgia
136 N 10 **Kutarere**, New Zealand
122 J 6 **Kutchan**, Japan
80 F 8 **Kutina**, Croatia
114 F 10 **Kutkai**, Myanmar
78 J 13 **Kutno**, Poland
130 J 9 **Kutu**, Democratic Republic of Congo
127 B 17 **Kutum**, Sudan
41 S 6 **Kuujjuaq**, QC, Canada
41 P 8 **Kuujjuaraapik**, QC, Canada

84 G 5 **Kuusalu**, Estonia
70 N 11 **Kuusamo**, Finland
93 Y 4 **Kuvandyk**, Russian Federation
132 H 5 **Kuvango**, Angola
90 G 13 **Kuvshinovo**, Russian Federation
99 S 3 **Kuwait**, Kuwait
99 R 2 **Kuwait**, Asia
90 K 6 **Kuya**, Russian Federation
87 Q 9 **Kuyal'nyts'kyy Lyman**, Ukraine
88 L 12 **Kuybyshev**, Russian Federation
93 S 2 **Kuybyshev Reservoir**, Russian Federation
87 W 8 **Kuybysheve**, Ukraine
103 Q 3 **Kuybyshevskiy**, Kazakhstan
91 T 14 **Kuyeda**, Russian Federation
103 U 8 **Kuygan**, Kazakhstan
108 K 4 **Kuytun**, China
47 Q 6 **Kuyu Tingni**, Nicaragua
93 Q 4 **Kuznetsk**, Russian Federation
86 K 2 **Kuznetsovs'k**, Ukraine
90 J 5 **Kuzomen'**, Russian Federation
122 K 10 **Kuzumaki**, Japan
70 H 7 **Kvaløya**, Norway
70 K 5 **Kvaløya**, Norway
70 K 6 **Kvalsund**, Norway
80 B 10 **Kvarner**, Croatia
80 B 10 **Kvarnerić**, Croatia
35 O 11 **Kvichak Bay**, AK, U.S.A.
133 P 13 **Kwa Mashu**, Republic of South Africa
131 U 11 **Kwa Mtoro**, Tanzania
115 F 18 **Kwai**, Thailand
141 X 2 **Kwajalein**, Marshall Islands
129 Q 13 **Kwale**, Nigeria
130 H 9 **Kwamouth**, Democratic Republic of Congo
111 L 21 **Kwangju**, South Korea
111 M 14 **Kwanmo-bong**, North Korea
129 P 11 **Kwara**, Nigeria
133 P 12 **Kwazulu-Natal**, Republic of South Africa
133 P 7 **Kwekwe**, Zimbabwe
132 M 9 **Kweneng**, Botswana
78 I 9 **Kwidzyn**, Poland
34 M 10 **Kwigillingok**, AK, U.S.A.
138 E 7 **Kwikila**, Papua New Guinea
129 X 11 **Kyabé**, Chad
115 E 16 **Kyaikto**, Myanmar
89 P 14 **Kyakhta**, Russian Federation
135 N 11 **Kyancutta**, SA, Australia
115 C 15 **Kyangin**, Myanmar
114 E 11 **Kyaukme**, Myanmar
115 F 20 **Kyaukpya**, Myanmar
114 B 12 **Kyauktaw**, Myanmar
115 C 15 **Kyeintali**, Myanmar
131 T 13 **Kyela**, Tanzania
60 F 10 **Kyle of Lochalsh**, U.K.
73 B 19 **Kyll**, Germany
83 E 20 **Kyllini**, Greece
83 H 18 **Kymi**, Greece
135 R 5 **Kynuna**, QLD, Australia
123 G 17 **Kyōga-misaki**, Japan
111 N 20 **Kyŏngju**, South Korea
123 G 18 **Kyōto**, Japan
122 J 10 **Kyowa**, Japan
83 C 21 **Kyparissia**, Greece
83 C 21 **Kyparissiakos Kolpos**, Greece
89 R 14 **Kyra**, Russian Federation
83 H 17 **Kyra Panagia**, Greece
103 V 11 **Kyrgyzstan**, Asia
72 K 12 **Kyritz**, Germany
87 O 11 **Kyrnychky**, Ukraine
87 Q 2 **Kyselivka**, Ukraine
89 U 8 **Kytalyktakh**, Russian Federation
83 F 24 **Kythira**, Greece
83 F 24 **Kythira**, Greece
83 H 21 **Kythnos**, Greece
115 F 22 **Kyun Pila**, Myanmar
102 K 8 **Kyushe**, Kazakhstan
123 C 22 **Kyūshū**, Japan
82 F 10 **Kyustendil**, Bulgaria
82 F 10 **Kyustendil**, Bulgaria
71 L 15 **Kyyjärvi**, Finland
89 O 13 **Kyzyl**, Russian Federation
103 S 10 **Kyzyl-Adyr**, Kyrgyzstan
103 T 12 **Kyzyl-Kyya**, Kyrgyzstan
103 O 10 **Kyzylkum Desert**, Kazakhstan
103 O 9 **Kyzylorda**, Kazakhstan
103 P 9 **Kyzylorda**, Kazakhstan
102 I 9 **Kyzylsay**, Kazakhstan
103 R 6 **Kyzylzhar**, Kazakhstan

L

66 J 9 **La Albuera**, Spain
67 S 4 **La Almunia de Doña Godina**, Spain
51 Q 2 **La Asunción**, Venezuela
43 N 6 **La Baie**, QC, Canada
56 J 8 **La Banda**, Argentina
66 L 3 **La Bañeza**, Spain
29 R 13 **La Barge**, WY, U.S.A.
64 J 7 **La Baule-Escoublac**, France
19 W 12 **La Belle**, FL, U.S.A.
65 Q 10 **La Bourboule**, France
45 S 8 **La Carbonera**, Mexico
59 A 15 **La Carlota**, Argentina
67 O 10 **La Carolina**, Spain
46 M 4 **La Ceiba**, Honduras
65 R 7 **La Charité-sur-Loire**, France
65 P 8 **La Châtre**, France
74 C 7 **La-Chaux-de-Fonds**, Switzerland
47 W 14 **La Chorrera**, Panama
44 M 8 **La Ciudad**, Mexico
56 I 8 **La Cocha**, Argentina
45 X 11 **La Costa**, Mexico
20 D 13 **La Crosse**, WI, U.S.A.
24 K 4 **La Crosse**, KS, U.S.A.
44 L 8 **La Cruz**, Mexico
47 N 11 **La Cruz**, Costa Rica
58 E 11 **La Cruz**, Argentina
46 G 6 **La Democracia**, Guatemala
51 O 8 **La Esmeralda**, Venezuela
53 L 23 **La Esmeralda**, Bolivia
46 K 6 **La Esperanza**, Honduras
57 G 16 **La Esperanza**, Argentina
53 L 19 **La Estrella**, Bolivia
65 N 6 **La Flèche**, France
139 P 14 **La Foa**, New Caledonia
66 K 5 **La Fuente de San Esteban**, Spain
125 P 5 **La Galite**, Tunisia
51 S 6 **La Gran Sabana**, Venezuela
32 K 10 **La Grande**, OR, U.S.A.
19 S 4 **La Grange**, GA, U.S.A.
27 Q 10 **La Grange**, TX, U.S.A.
43 N 10 **La Guadeloupe**, QC, Canada
50 K 1 **La Guajira**, Colombia

31 T 6 **La Junta**, CO, U.S.A.
59 A 14 **La Laguna**, Argentina
57 F 14 **La Laja**, Chile
46 I 3 **La Libertad**, Guatemala
46 L 6 **La Libertad**, Honduras
46 I 7 **La Libertad**, El Salvador
52 B 13 **La Libertad**, Peru
56 G 11 **La Ligua**, Chile
46 L 5 **La Lima**, Honduras
66 M 14 **La Línea de la Concepción**, Spain
59 A 21 **La Lobería**, Argentina
39 K 16 **La Loche**, SK, Canada
69 F 21 **La Louvière**, Belgium
77 D 15 **La Maddalena**, Italy
43 O 7 **La Malbaie**, QC, Canada
53 E 17 **La Mejorada**, Peru
53 E 16 **La Merced**, Peru
45 O 5 **La Mora**, Mexico
65 V 11 **La Mure**, France
66 M 8 **La Nava de Ricomalillo**, Spain
56 F 6 **La Negra**, Chile
53 D 16 **La Oroya**, Peru
46 I 2 **La Palma**, Guatemala
47 Z 14 **La Palma**, Panama
59 G 15 **La Paloma**, Uruguay
57 I 14 **La Pampa**, Argentina
44 J 8 **La Paz**, Mexico
46 L 6 **La Paz**, Honduras
46 M 9 **La Paz**, Nicaragua
53 I 19 **La Paz**, Bolivia
53 H 18 **La Paz**, Bolivia
56 H 12 **La Paz**, Argentina
58 C 13 **La Paz**, Argentina
50 M 11 **La Pedrera**, Colombia
47 U 15 **La Pena**, Panama
45 N 5 **La Perla**, Mexico
122 I 2 **La Pérouse Strait**, Japan
45 S 8 **La Pesca**, Mexico
45 P 11 **La Piedad**, Mexico
32 H 12 **La Pine**, OR, U.S.A.
47 V 14 **La Pintada**, Panama
22 J 8 **La Plant**, SD, U.S.A.
59 D 16 **La Plata**, Argentina
21 I 16 **La Porte**, IN, U.S.A.
26 M 11 **La Pryor**, TX, U.S.A.
56 I 4 **La Quiaca**, Argentina
56 H 9 **La Rioja**, Argentina
56 I 9 **La Rioja**, Argentina
67 Q 3 **La Rioja**, Spain
66 L 2 **La Robla**, Spain
66 K 9 **La Roca de la Sierra**, Spain
69 J 22 **La Roche-en-Ardenne**, Belgium
64 L 8 **La Roche-sur-Yon**, France
64 L 9 **La Rochelle**, France
67 Q 9 **La Roda**, Spain
49 S 8 **La Romana**, Dominican Republic
39 M 16 **La Ronge**, SK, Canada
45 P 5 **La Rosita**, Mexico
58 C 11 **La Sabana**, Argentina
21 F 16 **La Salle**, IL, U.S.A.
42 F 6 **La Sarre**, QC, Canada
56 F 9 **La Serena**, Chile
67 W 3 **La Seu d'Urgell**, Spain
67 P 9 **La Solana**, Spain
76 D 9 **La Spezia**, Italy
50 I 10 **La Tagua**, Colombia
56 I 11 **La Toma**, Argentina
42 L 8 **La Tuque**, QC, Canada
45 P 13 **La Unión**, Mexico
46 L 8 **La Unión**, El Salvador
53 M 19 **La Unión**, Bolivia
67 S 12 **La Unión**, Spain
27 P 11 **La Vernia**, TX, U.S.A.
45 O 6 **La Vibora**, Mexico
53 G 20 **La Yarada**, Peru
75 X 2 **Laa an der Thaya**, Austria
72 K 9 **Laage**, Germany
127 N 20 **Laascaanood**, Somalia
127 N 19 **Laasgoray**, Somalia
124 D 10 **Laâyoune**, Western Sahara
119 R 8 **Labang**, Malaysia
139 X 11 **Labasa**, Fiji
128 G 10 **Labé**, Guinea
42 J 9 **Labelle**, QC, Canada
119 S 7 **Labi**, Brunei
80 B 9 **Labin**, Croatia
92 M 12 **Labinsk**, Russian Federation
118 D 9 **Labis**, Malaysia
120 I 12 **Labo**, Philippines
64 L 13 **Labouheyre**, France
59 A 16 **Laboulaye**, Argentina
41 U 7 **Labrador**, NL, Canada
142 L 13 **Labrador Basin**, Arctic Ocean
41 T 9 **Labrador City**, NL, Canada
142 L 12 **Labrador Sea**, Arctic Ocean
54 D 12 **Lábrea**, Brazil
116 F 11 **Labu**, Indonesia
119 T 6 **Labuan**, Malaysia
110 G 7 **Labudalin**, China
117 N 15 **Labuhanbajo**, Indonesia
116 D 9 **Labuhanbilik**, Indonesia
116 B 9 **Labuhanhaji**, Indonesia
116 G 13 **Labuhanmeringgai**, Indonesia
88 L 8 **Labytnangi**, Russian Federation
81 K 17 **Laş**, Albania
129 V 9 **Lac**, Chad
41 Q 8 **Lac à l'Eau Claire**, QC, Canada
41 R 8 **Lac Bienville**, QC, Canada
41 P 8 **Lac Burton**, QC, Canada
41 S 8 **Lac Caniapiscau**, QC, Canada
129 T 13 **Lac de Bamendjing**, Cameroon
128 I 13 **Lac de Buyo**, Côte d'Ivoire
128 J 12 **Lac de Kossou**, Côte d'Ivoire
129 V 12 **Lac de Ladgo**, Cameroon
128 H 9 **Lac de Manantali**, Mali
129 U 13 **Lac de Mbakaou**, Cameroon
74 C 8 **Lac de Neuchâtel**, Switzerland
42 G 7 **Lac Decelles**, QC, Canada
42 F 7 **Lac des Quinze**, QC, Canada
41 Q 10 **Lac Evans**, QC, Canada
128 K 7 **Lac Faguibine**, Mali
128 L 8 **Lac Garou**, Mali
41 Q 7 **Lac Guillaume-Delisle**, QC, Canada
41 U 9 **Lac Joseph**, NL, Canada
42 K 7 **Lac Kempt**, QC, Canada
42 F 8 **Lac Kipawa**, QC, Canada
23 T 2 **Lac la Croix**, MN, U.S.A.
38 G 12 **Lac la Martre**, NT, Canada
39 M 16 **Lac la Ronge**, SK, Canada
130 J 9 **Lac Mai- Ndombe**, Democratic Republic of Congo
41 S 10 **Lac Manouane**, QC, Canada
43 N 10 **Lac-Mégantic**, QC, Canada

41 Q 7 **Lac Minto**, QC, Canada
41 Q 10 **Lac Mistassini**, QC, Canada
128 L 8 **Lac Niangay**, Mali
130 J 8 **Lac Ntomba**, Democratic Republic of Congo
130 D 8 **Lac Onangue**, Gabon
41 Q 5 **Lac Payne**, QC, Canada
43 Q 3 **Lac Sainte Anne**, QC, Canada
40 K 10 **Lac Seul**, ON, Canada
42 G 7 **Lac Simàrd**, QC, Canada
42 M 6 **Lac St-Jean**, QC, Canada
115 O 20 **Lac Thiên**, Vietnam
131 O 13 **Lac Upemba**, Democratic Republic of Congo
64 L 11 **Lacanau**, France
45 X 14 **Lacanja**, Mexico
80 J 10 **Lacarak**, Serbia and Montenegro
65 Q 14 **Lacaune**, France
105 A 22 **Laccadive Islands**, India
74 H 7 **Lachen**, Switzerland
135 S 11 **Lachlan**, NSW, Australia
107 S 9 **Lachung**, India
42 K 10 **Lachute**, QC, Canada
95 W 9 **Laşşin**, Azerbaijan
14 D 8 **Lackawanna**, NY, U.S.A.
77 C 18 **Laconi**, Italy
15 N 7 **Laconia**, NH, U.S.A.
87 N 12 **Lacul Razim**, Romania
87 N 13 **Lacul Sinoie**, Romania
106 I 3 **Ladakh Range**, India
85 A 16 **Ladushkin**, Russian Federation
135 T 14 **Lady Barron**, TAS, Australia
20 D 10 **Ladysmith**, WI, U.S.A.
133 P 12 **Ladysmith**, Republic of South Africa
87 P 6 **Ladyzhynka**, Ukraine
138 E 5 **Lae**, Papua New Guinea
141 W 2 **Lae**, Marshall Islands
71 D 23 **Laesø**, Denmark
70 L 7 **Laevvajåk**, Norway
16 G 8 **Lafayette**, TN, U.S.A.
18 J 7 **Lafayette**, LA, U.S.A.
48 F 4 **Lafé**, Cuba
129 S 12 **Lafia**, Nigeria
129 Q 12 **Lafiagi**, Nigeria
93 R 12 **Lagan'**, Russian Federation
128 E 8 **Lagbar**, Senegal
71 C 17 **Lågen**, Norway
101 V 6 **Laghmān**, Afghanistan
124 M 7 **Laghouat**, Algeria
82 F 13 **Lagkadas**, Greece
57 F 22 **Lago Argentino**, Argentina
59 F 14 **Lago Artificial de Rincón del Bonete**, Uruguay
47 Y 13 **Lago Bayano**, Panama
57 G 20 **Lago Buenos Aires**, Argentina
57 G 22 **Lago Cardiel**, Argentina
46 I 7 **Lago Coatepeque**, El Salvador
57 H 19 **Lago Colhué Huapi**, Argentina
46 H 6 **Lago de Amatitlán**, Guatemala
47 N 8 **Lago de Apanás**, Nicaragua
46 G 6 **Lago de Atitlán**, Guatemala
133 Q 5 **Lago de Cahora Bassa**, Mozambique
46 I 6 **Lago de Guija**, El Salvador
46 J 4 **Lago de Izabal**, Guatemala
46 L 4 **Lago de Los Micos**, Honduras
47 N 9 **Lago de Managua**, Nicaragua
53 I 21 **Lago de Poopó**, Bolivia
76 G 12 **Lago di Bolsena**, Italy
76 H 13 **Lago di Bracciano**, Italy
76 D 6 **Lago di Como**, Italy
76 E 7 **Lago di Garda**, Italy
77 L 14 **Lago di Lesina**, Italy
74 H 11 **Lago di Lugano**, Switzerland
77 L 14 **Lago di Varano**, Italy
76 E 6 **Lago d'Iseo**, Italy
57 H 25 **Lago Fagnano**, Argentina
47 W 13 **Lago Gatún**, Panama
57 G 20 **Lago General Carrera**, Chile
46 J 7 **Lago Ilopango**, El Salvador
57 E 17 **Lago Llanquihué**, Chile
76 C 6 **Lago Maggiore**, Italy
59 G 14 **Lago Mangueira**, Brazil
58 A 13 **Lago Mar Chiquita**, Argentina
57 H 19 **Lago Musters**, Argentina
57 F 16 **Lago Nahuel Huapi**, Argentina
57 F 22 **Lago O'Higgins**, Chile
77 C 17 **Lago Omodeo**, Italy
57 H 15 **Lago Pellegrini**, Argentina
46 I 3 **Lago Petén Itzá**, Guatemala
57 F 16 **Lago Ranco**, Chile
57 F 16 **Lago Rupanco**, Chile
57 F 22 **Lago San Martin**, Argentina
76 G 11 **Lago Trasimeno**, Italy
57 G 22 **Lago Viedma**, Argentina
57 F 22 **Lago Viedma**, Argentina
66 G 12 **Lagoa**, Portugal
58 H 12 **Lagoa dos Patos**, Brazil
55 I 23 **Lagoa Mangueira**, Brazil
59 G 14 **Lagoa Mirim**, Brazil/Uruguay
58 H 10 **Lagoa Vermelha**, Brazil
95 V 6 **Lagodekhi**, Georgia
120 J 12 **Lagonoy**, Philippines
120 K 13 **Lagonoy Gulf**, Philippines
66 G 12 **Lagos**, Portugal
129 O 13 **Lagos**, Nigeria
129 P 13 **Lagos**, Nigeria
45 P 10 **Lagos de Moreno**, Mexico
131 Q 11 **Lagosa**, Tanzania
134 H 4 **Lagrange**, WA, Australia
31 P 10 **Laguna**, NM, U.S.A.
58 J 11 **Laguna**, Brazil
47 R 6 **Laguna Bismuna**, Nicaragua
120 G 11 **Laguna de Bay**, Philippines
47 Q 5 **Laguna de Caratasca**, Honduras
45 O 11 **Laguna de Chapala**, Mexico
47 T 13 **Laguna de Chiriqui**, Panama
47 Q 7 **Laguna de Huaunta**, Nicaragua
47 R 9 **Laguna de Perlas**, Nicaragua
47 R 9 **Laguna de Perlas**, Nicaragua
53 K 17 **Laguna de San Luis**, Bolivia
45 X 12 **Laguna de Términos**, Mexico
81 J 19 **Laguna e Karavastasé**, Albania
47 P 4 **Laguna Ibans**, Honduras
47 R 7 **Laguna Karatá**, Nicaragua
27 Q 14 **Laguna Madre**, TX, U.S.A.
45 S 8 **Laguna Madre**, Mexico
53 J 17 **Laguna Rogaguado**, Bolivia
45 U 14 **Laguna Superior**, Mexico
47 R 6 **Laguna Taberis**, Nicaragua
76 G 7 **Laguna Veneta**, Italy
56 G 4 **Lagunas**, Chile
110 J 9 **Laha**, China
119 X 6 **Lahad Datu**, Malaysia
34 D 7 **Lahaina**, HI, U.S.A.

116 F 12 **Lahat**, Indonesia
114 D 7 **Lahe**, Myanmar
116 B 10 **Lahewa**, Indonesia
99 P 14 **Laḩij**, Yemen
73 E 18 **Lahn**, Germany
71 E 24 **Laholmsbukten**, Sweden
101 Y 9 **Lahore**, Pakistan
71 M 18 **Lahti**, Finland
129 W 11 **Laï**, Chad
114 J 11 **Lai Chau**, Vietnam
113 Q 7 **Laifeng**, China
65 O 4 **L'Aigle**, France
132 L 15 **Laingsburg**, Republic of South Africa
70 J 8 **Lainioälven**, Sweden
116 E 12 **Lais**, Indonesia
93 S 1 **Laishevo**, Russian Federation
113 W 2 **Laiwu**, China
111 G 20 **Laixi**, China
111 G 20 **Laiyang**, China
111 C 17 **Laiyuan**, China
111 G 19 **Laizhou**, China
111 G 19 **Laizhou Wan**, China
95 S 6 **Lajanurpekhi**, Georgia
58 H 12 **Lajeado**, Brazil
58 I 10 **Lajes**, Brazil
80 K 11 **Lajkovac**, Serbia and Montenegro
127 J 19 **Lake Abbe**, Ethiopia
32 I 13 **Lake Abert**, OR, U.S.A.
42 F 6 **Lake Abitibi**, ON, Canada
131 R 6 **Lake Albert**, Uganda/Democratic Republic of Congo
134 M 7 **Lake Amadeus**, NT, Australia
134 L 3 **Lake Argyle**, WA, Australia
18 I 8 **Lake Arthur**, LA, U.S.A.
36 M 9 **Lake Athabasca**, AB/SK, Canada
134 J 6 **Lake Auld**, WA, Australia
134 G 9 **Lake Austin**, WA, Australia
89 Q 13 **Lake Baikal**, Russian Federation
103 T 8 **Lake Balkhash**, Kazakhstan
134 I 9 **Lake Ballard**, WA, Australia
133 O 3 **Lake Bangweulu**, Zambia
134 H 9 **Lake Barlee**, WA, Australia
137 E 22 **Lake Benmore**, New Zealand
23 P 9 **Lake Benton**, MN, U.S.A.
19 T 5 **Lake Blackshear**, GA, U.S.A.
135 Q 9 **Lake Blanche**, SA, Australia
80 B 6 **Lake Bled**, Slovenia
121 L 23 **Lake Buluan**, Philippines
134 I 9 **Lake Carey**, WA, Australia
135 T 11 **Lake Cargelligo**, NSW, Australia
134 I 8 **Lake Carnegie**, WA, Australia
129 V 9 **Lake Chad**, Chad
14 L 5 **Lake Champlain**, VT, U.S.A.
18 H 7 **Lake Charles**, LA, U.S.A.
32 I 6 **Lake Chelan**, WA, U.S.A.
20 E 9 **Lake Chippewa**, WI, U.S.A.
16 J 8 **Lake City**, TN, U.S.A.
17 Q 12 **Lake City**, SC, U.S.A.
19 V 7 **Lake City**, FL, U.S.A.
20 K 12 **Lake City**, MI, U.S.A.
39 I 15 **Lake Claire**, AB, Canada
137 G 19 **Lake Coleridge**, New Zealand
27 S 9 **Lake Conroe**, TX, U.S.A.
74 H 5 **Lake Constance**, Switzerland
134 I 10 **Lake Cowan**, WA, Australia
16 I 7 **Lake Cumberland**, KY, U.S.A.
135 T 5 **Lake Dalrymple**, QLD, Australia
134 I 7 **Lake Disappointment**, WA, Australia
63 P 1 **Lake District**, U.K.
134 I 6 **Lake Dora**, WA, Australia
134 I 11 **Lake Dundas**, WA, Australia
131 Q 8 **Lake Edward**, Democratic Republic of Congo/Uganda
137 H 21 **Lake Ellesmere**, New Zealand
14 A 9 **Lake Erie**, PA, U.S.A.
21 M 16 **Lake Erie**, OH, U.S.A.
42 C 15 **Lake Erie**, ON, Canada
131 U 10 **Lake Eyasi**, Tanzania
135 O 8 **Lake Eyre North**, SA, Australia
135 O 9 **Lake Eyre South**, SA, Australia
27 S 5 **Lake Fork Reservoir**, TX, U.S.A.
135 Q 10 **Lake Frome**, SA, Australia
135 O 10 **Lake Gairdner**, SA, Australia
65 V 9 **Lake Geneva**, France/Switzerland
14 K 7 **Lake George**, NY, U.S.A.
19 W 9 **Lake George**, FL, U.S.A.
20 F 8 **Lake Gogebic**, MI, U.S.A.
135 S 15 **Lake Gordon**, TAS, Australia
134 H 11 **Lake Grace**, WA, Australia
134 K 5 **Lake Gregory**, WA, Australia
137 B 25 **Lake Hauroko**, New Zealand
30 H 11 **Lake Havasu City**, AZ, U.S.A.
137 D 22 **Lake Hawea**, New Zealand
134 I 11 **Lake Hope**, WA, Australia
134 L 7 **Lake Hopkins**, WA, Australia
20 L 10 **Lake Huron**, MI, U.S.A.
42 A 10 **Lake Huron**, ON, Canada
27 T 11 **Lake Jackson**, TX, U.S.A.
133 O 6 **Lake Kariba**, Zimbabwe
27 N 4 **Lake Kemp**, TX, U.S.A.
16 L 11 **Lake Keowee**, SC, U.S.A.
110 O 11 **Lake Khanka**, China
134 H 11 **Lake King**, WA, Australia
131 Q 9 **Lake Kivu**, Rwanda/Democratic Republic of Congo
28 L 2 **Lake Koocanusa**, MT, U.S.A.
131 S 7 **Lake Kyoga**, Uganda
90 F 9 **Lake Ladoga**, Russian Federation
121 K 21 **Lake Lanao**, Philippines
134 I 10 **Lake Lefroy**, WA, Australia
27 Q 5 **Lake Lewisville**, TX, U.S.A.
27 R 7 **Lake Limestone**, TX, U.S.A.
20 G 7 **Lake Linden**, MI, U.S.A.
27 S 9 **Lake Livingston**, TX, U.S.A.
39 I 20 **Lake Louise**, AB, Canada
134 L 6 **Lake MacDonald**, WA, Australia
134 L 6 **Lake Mackay**, WA, Australia
134 E 7 **Lake MacLeod**, WA, Australia
121 M 19 **Lake Mainit**, Philippines
133 R 4 **Lake Malawi**, Malawi
137 B 24 **Lake Manapouri**, New Zealand
40 I 10 **Lake Manitoba**, MB, Canada
131 U 10 **Lake Manyara**, Tanzania
50 K 3 **Lake Maracaibo**, Venezuela
17 P 13 **Lake Marion**, SC, U.S.A.
134 I 10 **Lake Marmion**, WA, Australia
19 Q 4 **Lake Martin**, AL, U.S.A.
17 W 9 **Lake Mattamuskeet**, NC, U.S.A.
134 M 9 **Lake Maurice**, SA, Australia
22 I 14 **Lake McConaughy**, NE, U.S.A.
30 G 9 **Lake Mead**, AZ/NV, U.S.A.
41 V 8 **Lake Melville**, NL, Canada
14 L 4 **Lake Memphremagog**, VT, U.S.A.
26 K 2 **Lake Meredith**, TX, U.S.A.

ountry | Internal administrative region: State/Province/Territory/Dependent territory | Capital city | Mountain range/Undersea ridge | Mountain peak/Volcano/Seamount | Geographic feature | Headland/Point/Cape/Peninsula | Desert | Island/Island group | Antarctic base | Ocean | Sea | Bay/Gulf/Channel/Strait | Lake | Salt pan/Dry/Intermittent lake | River

□ Country   ▣ Internal administrative region: State/Province/Territory/Dependent territory   ● Capital city   ▲ Mountain range/Undersea ridge   ▲ Mountain peak/Volcano/Seamount   ◇ Geographic feature   ▶ Headland/Point/Cape/Peninsula   ▲ Desert   ⊞ Island/Island group   ▦ Antarctic base   ⊃ Ocean   ⊋ Sea   ≈ Bay/Gulf/Channel/Strait   ↘ Lake   Salt pan/Dry/Intermittent lake

Lincoln – Mabalacat

F 18 Lincoln, IL, U.S.A.
P 14 Lincoln, NE, U.S.A.
B 16 Lincoln, Argentina
U 4 Lincoln, U.K.
H 20 Lincoln, New Zealand
F 10 Lincoln City, OR, U.S.A.
V 3 Lincolnshire Wolds, U.K.
G 26 Lindau, Germany
D 9 Linden, TN, U.S.A.
O 5 Linden, AL, U.S.A.
U 5 Linden, TX, U.S.A.
U 5 Linden, Guyana
W 13 Lindi, Tanzania
X 14 Lindi, Tanzania
J 9 Lindian, China
O 24 Lindos, Greece
G 12 Lindsay, ON, Canada
Q 1 Line Islands, Kiribati
S 2 Linfen, China
F 9 Lingayen, Philippines
F 9 Lingayen Gulf, Philippines
R 3 Lingbao, China
W 4 Lingbi, China
D 13 Lingen, Germany
W 12 Lingfield, U.K.
F 11 Lingga, Indonesia
M 7 Lingkabau, Malaysia
L 7 Lingomo, Democratic Republic of Congo
C 17 Lingqiu, China
U 3 Lingshan, China
S 2 Lingshi, China
R 15 Lingshui, China
P 3 Lingtai, China
E 8 Linguère, Senegal
G 15 Lingyuan, China
I 5 Linhai, China
Z 7 Linhai, China
M 17 Linhares, Brazil
R 6 Linhe, China
L 15 Linjiang, China
G 22 Linköping, Sweden
M 11 Linkou, China
F 12 Linkuva, Lithuania
T 2 Linlü Shan, China
P 15 Linn, TX, U.S.A.
B 17 Linnich, Germany
V 1 Linqing, China
U 4 Linquan, China
I 6 Lins, Brazil
X 3 Linshu, China
O 7 Linshui, China
H 8 Linthal, Switzerland
H 20 Linton, IN, U.S.A.
K 6 Linton, ND, U.S.A.
Q 3 Lintong, China
F 13 Linxi, China
M 2 Linxia, China
E 19 Linyi, China
W 3 Linyi, China
R 3 Linyi, China
P 3 Linyou, China
T 3 Linz, Austria
T 8 Lio Matoh, Malaysia
J 2 Lioboml', Ukraine
L 16 Lioni, Italy
U 9 Lioua, Chad
H 7 Liouesso, Congo
G 12 Lipa, Philippines
L 7 Lipcani, Moldova
L 4 Lipetsk, Russian Federation
L 4 Lipetskaya Oblast', Russian Federation
D 11 Lipiany, Poland
Q 10 Liping, China
I 11 Lipno, Poland
F 10 Lipova, Romania
C 15 Lippe, Germany
E 15 Lippstadt, Germany
N 9 Lipsk, Poland
N 9 Liptougou, Burkina Faso
J 19 Liptovský Mikuláš, Slovakia
R 11 Lipu, China
S 6 Lira, Uganda
I 8 Liranga, Congo
N 3 Lisakovsk, Kazakhstan
L 6 Lisala, Democratic Republic of Congo
F 9 Lisboa, Portugal
N 6 Lisbon, ND, U.S.A.
G 9 Lisbon, Portugal
P 6 Lisbon Falls, ME, U.S.A.
E 11 Lisec, Macedonia (F.Y.R.O.M.)
R 1 Lishi, China
J 13 Lishu, China
Y 8 Lishui, China
N 4 Lisieux, France
L 14 Liskeard, U.K.
L 6 Liski, Russian Federation
W 9 Lismore, NSW, Australia
T 12 Liss, U.K.
B 19 Listowel, Republic of Ireland
K 7 Litang, China
Q 12 Litang, China
F 20 Litchfield, IL, U.S.A.
B 21 Lithakia, Greece
U 11 Lithgow, NSW, Australia
C 14 Lithuania, Europe
U 1 Litschau, Austria
N 22 Little Andaman, India
U 8 Little Bighorn, MT, U.S.A.
I 7 Little Cayman, Cayman Islands
B 19 Little Coco Island, Myanmar
K 9 Little Colorado, AZ, U.S.A.
C 9 Little Current, ON, Canada
I 8 Little Falls, NY, U.S.A.
P 6 Little Falls, MN, U.S.A.
Q 6 Little Falls, MN, U.S.A.
J 9 Little Grand Rapids, MB, Canada
O 5 Little Inagua Island, The Bahamas
K 15 Little Karoo, Republic of South Africa
G 4 Little Missouri, ND, U.S.A.
O 24 Little Nicobar, India
V 11 Little Rock, AR, U.S.A.
I 13 Little Sable Point, MI, U.S.A.
I 7 Little Sandy Desert, WA, Australia
D 13 Little Sitkin Island, AK, U.S.A.
S 3 Little Zab, Iraq
R 3 Littleborough, U.K.
I 4 Littlefield, TX, U.S.A.
V 13 Littlehampton, U.K.
X 7 Littleport, U.K.
S 14 Littoral, Cameroon
N 5 Lityn, Ukraine
P 4 Liuba, China
111 K 14 Liuhe, China
110 H 11 Liuhu, China
113 Q 11 Liujiang, China
113 R 1 Liulin, China
113 T 8 Liuyang, China
110 J 7 Liuzhan, China
113 Q 11 Liuzhou, China
86 H 7 Livada, Romania
84 H 12 Līvāni, Latvia
103 N 4 Livanovka, Kazakhstan
19 U 7 Live Oak, FL, U.S.A.
16 E 6 Livermore, KY, U.S.A.
43 U 12 Liverpool, NS, Canada
63 O 4 Liverpool, U.K.
63 O 3 Liverpool Bay, U.K.
27 T 9 Livingston, TX, U.S.A.
29 R 7 Livingston, MT, U.S.A.
46 J 4 Livingston, Guatemala
144 G 3 Livingston Island, Antarctica
18 L 7 Livingstone, LA, U.S.A.
133 N 7 Livingstone, Zambia
133 R 3 Livingstonia, Malawi
80 F 12 Livno, Bosnia and Herzegovina
92 K 4 Livny, Russian Federation
76 E 11 Livorno, Italy
131 V 13 Liwale, Tanzania
78 M 12 Liwiec, Poland
113 O 4 Lixan, China
112 L 9 Lixi, China
113 S 7 Lixian, China
83 A 19 Lixouri, Greece
113 X 5 Liyang, China
62 J 15 Lizard, U.K.
62 J 15 Lizard Point, U.K.
80 K 12 Ljig, Serbia and Montenegro
80 B 7 Ljubljana, Slovenia
80 J 11 Ljubovija, Serbia and Montenegro
71 I 23 Ljugarn, Sweden
71 G 16 Ljungan, Sweden
71 F 24 Ljungby, Sweden
71 G 17 Ljusdal, Sweden
71 G 17 Ljusnan, Sweden
62 L 5 Llanaelhaearn, U.K.
62 M 5 Llanberis, U.K.
63 O 5 Llandderfel, U.K.
62 M 9 Llandeilo, U.K.
62 L 9 Llandissilio, U.K.
63 N 9 Llandovery, U.K.
63 O 8 Llandrindod Wells, U.K.
63 N 4 Llandudno, U.K.
63 M 5 Llandwrog, U.K.
62 M 10 Llanelli, U.K.
62 M 4 Llanerchymedd, U.K.
67 N 1 Llanes, Spain
62 M 4 Llanfairpwllgwyngyll, U.K.
63 O 6 Llangadfan, U.K.
62 M 6 Llangelynin, U.K.
63 O 5 Llangollen, U.K.
63 N 7 Llangurig, U.K.
62 L 5 Llanllyfni, U.K.
27 O 9 Llano, TX, U.S.A.
45 N 5 Llano de los Caballos Mesteños, Mexico
26 I 5 Llano Estacado, TX, U.S.A.
50 K 9 Llanos, Colombia
62 M 8 Llanrhystud, U.K.
63 N 5 Llanrwst, U.K.
63 O 10 Llantrisant, U.K.
63 N 11 Llantwit Major, U.K.
67 U 4 Lleida, Spain
66 K 10 Llerena, Spain
62 L 5 Lleyn Peninsula, U.K.
53 I 22 Llica, Bolivia
67 T 8 Lliria, Spain
67 W 3 Llivia, Spain
121 M 16 Llorente, Philippines
39 K 18 Lloydminster, SK, Canada
67 Y 8 Llucmajor, Spain
30 K 6 Loa, UT, U.S.A.
76 B 9 Loano, Italy
73 O 16 Löbau, Germany
130 I 5 Lobaye, Central African Republic
57 L 15 Loberia, Argentina
59 D 18 Lobería, Argentina
78 E 10 Łobez, Poland
132 G 4 Lobito, Angola
120 G 12 Lobo, Philippines
66 K 9 Lobón, Spain
59 D 16 Lobos, Argentina
115 M 21 Lôc Ninh, Vietnam
74 G 10 Locarno, Switzerland
60 G 12 Loch Lomond, U.K.
60 H 10 Loch Ness, U.K.
60 H 11 Loch Rannoch, U.K.
60 G 9 Loch Shin, U.K.
68 M 12 Lochem, Netherlands
65 O 7 Loches, France
60 F 13 Lochgilphead, U.K.
60 G 9 Lochinver, U.K.
78 M 12 Łochów, Poland
135 O 11 Lock, SA, Australia
14 E 12 Lock Haven, PA, U.S.A.
61 I 14 Lockerbie, U.K.
135 S 1 Lockhart River, QLD, Australia
77 M 21 Locri, Italy
96 F 9 Lod, Israel
63 Z 7 Loddon, U.K.
65 R 13 Lodève, France
90 G 10 Lodeynoye Pole, Russian Federation
29 V 8 Lodge Grass, MT, U.S.A.
101 W 11 Lodhran, Pakistan
33 H 19 Lodi, CA, U.S.A.
76 D 7 Lodi, Italy
70 G 9 Lødingen, Norway
130 M 10 Lodja, Democratic Republic of Congo
131 U 6 Lodwar, Kenya
79 J 14 Łódź, Poland
115 I 15 Loei, Thailand
75 P 6 Lofer, Austria
70 F 9 Lofoten, Norway
93 O 7 Log, Russian Federation
16 M 5 Logan, WV, U.S.A.
30 K 1 Logan, UT, U.S.A.
31 T 10 Logan, NM, U.S.A.
21 I 18 Logansport, IN, U.S.A.
129 V 10 Logone Birni, Cameroon
129 W 11 Logone Occidental, Chad
129 W 12 Logone Oriental, Chad
67 Q 3 Logroño, Spain
106 H 8 Loharu, India
133 Y 5 Lohatanjona Angadoka, Madgascar
104 C 12 Lohawat, India
114 E 12 Loi-lem, Myanmar
114 E 11 Loi Sang, Myanmar
114 E 13 Loikaw, Myanmar
64 L 7 Loire, France
52 B 11 Loja, Ecuador
52 A 11 Loja, Ecuador
67 N 12 Loja, Spain
119 W 5 Lokan, Malaysia
70 M 9 Lokan tekojärvi, Finland
69 E 17 Lokeren, Belgium
87 S 4 Lokhvytsya, Ukraine
131 U 6 Lokichar, Kenya
131 T 5 Lokichokio, Kenya
90 E 13 Loknya, Russian Federation
129 R 12 Loko, Nigeria
130 M 8 Lokofe, Democratic Republic of Congo
129 R 12 Lokoja, Nigeria
130 K 9 Lokolama, Democratic Republic of Congo
129 V 15 Lokomo, Cameroon
41 T 4 Loks Land, NU, Canada
132 G 5 Lola, Angola
71 D 26 Lolland, Denmark
131 U 9 Lollondo, Tanzania
29 N 5 Lolo, MT, U.S.A.
28 M 5 Lolo Hot Springs, MT, U.S.A.
138 G 4 Lolobau Island, Papua New Guinea
129 T 15 Lolodorf, Cameroon
71 C 17 Lom, Norway
82 F 6 Lom, Bulgaria
115 I 16 Lom Sak, Thailand
128 H 11 Loma Mountains, Sierra Leone
53 E 19 Lomas, Peru
59 C 16 Lomas de Zamora, Argentina
134 I 3 Lombadina, WA, Australia
76 E 6 Lombardia, Italy
117 P 15 Lomblen, Indonesia
116 L 15 Lombok, Indonesia
129 N 13 Lomé, Togo
130 M 9 Lomela, Democratic Republic of Congo
129 V 15 Lomié, Cameroon
69 I 17 Lommel, Belgium
143 R 9 Lomonosov Ridge, Arctic Ocean
33 H 24 Lompoc, CA, U.S.A.
78 M 11 Łomża, Poland
57 G 15 Loncopué, Argentina
69 F 18 Londerzeel, Belgium
16 J 7 London, KY, U.S.A.
42 D 13 London, ON, Canada
63 W 10 London, U.K.
61 D 15 Londonderry, U.K.
58 H 7 Londrina, Brazil
119 T 8 Long Akah, Malaysia
63 P 11 Long Ashton, U.K.
17 R 13 Long Bay, SC, U.S.A.
14 K 13 Long Beach, NY, U.S.A.
33 J 25 Long Beach, CA, U.S.A.
14 J 14 Long Beach Island, NJ, U.S.A.
46 L 2 Long Cay, Belize
32 J 11 Long Creek, OR, U.S.A.
14 L 12 Long Island, NY, U.S.A.
37 T 10 Long Island, NU, Canada
48 M 4 Long Island, The Bahamas
135 V 6 Long Island, QLD, Australia
138 E 4 Long Island, Papua New Guinea
14 L 12 Long Island Sound, NY, U.S.A.
119 S 7 Long Lama, Malaysia
119 S 9 Long Murum, Malaysia
119 S 8 Long Pila, Malaysia
40 I 8 Long Point, MB, Canada
42 D 14 Long Point, ON, Canada
42 E 14 Long Point, ON, Canada
121 C 18 Long Point, Philippines
63 R 1 Long Preston, U.K.
41 X 10 Long Range Mountains, NL, Canada
119 T 7 Long Semado, Malaysia
63 Y 7 Long Stratton, U.K.
119 S 7 Long Teru, Malaysia
30 J 7 Long Valley Junction, UT, U.S.A.
115 L 22 Long Xuyên, Vietnam
83 D 22 Longa, Greece
132 I 5 Longa, Angola
111 K 15 Longang Shan, China
116 L 9 Longbawan, Indonesia
113 N 7 Longchang, China
113 V 11 Longchuan, China
113 O 2 Longde, China
110 J 10 Longfeng, China
61 D 17 Longford, Republic of Ireland
111 E 15 Longhua, China
113 S 9 Longhui, China
131 V 9 Longido, Tanzania
116 L 11 Longiram, Indonesia
110 I 10 Longjiang, China
113 W 12 Longjiang, China
111 G 19 Longkou, China
40 M 11 Longlac, ON, Canada
113 R 14 Longmen, China
113 N 5 Longmen Shan, China
31 R 3 Longmont, CO, U.S.A.
113 U 11 Longnan, China
116 L 10 Longnawan, Indonesia
113 P 9 Longping, China
113 X 8 Longquan, China
135 S 6 Longreach, QLD, Australia
109 P 10 Longriba, China
113 Q 7 Longshan, China
113 R 10 Longsheng, China
43 T 3 Longue-Pointe, QC, Canada
42 L 10 Longueuil, QC, Canada
65 U 3 Longuyon, France
27 T 6 Longview, TX, U.S.A.
32 G 8 Longview, WA, U.S.A.
112 L 11 Longwu, China
69 K 26 Longwy, Belgium
113 P 3 Longxian, China
113 W 10 Longyan, China
143 T 11 Longyearbyen, Svalbard
113 X 7 Longyou, China
110 K 8 Longzhen, China
113 O 13 Longzhou, China
76 F 7 Lonigo, Italy
65 U 8 Lons-le-Saunier, France
117 S 13 Lontar, Indonesia
121 H 15 Looc, Philippines
21 H 21 Loogootee, IN, U.S.A.
61 A 19 Loop Head, Republic of Ireland
115 H 18 Lop Buri, Thailand
108 L 6 Lop Nur, China
93 R 13 Lopatin, Russian Federation
93 P 4 Lopatino, Russian Federation
139 R 11 Lopévi, Vanuatu
120 H 12 Lopez, Philippines
70 I 6 Lopphavet, Norway
66 L 11 Lora del Río, Spain
21 N 16 Lorain, OH, U.S.A.
101 U 10 Loralai, Pakistan
67 R 11 Lorca, Spain
115 F 22 Lord Loughborough Island, Myanmar
31 N 14 Lordsburg, NM, U.S.A.
117 R 15 Lore, East Timor
138 E 2 Lorengau, Papua New Guinea
100 G 7 Lorestān, Iran
44 I 7 Loreto, Mexico
52 E 11 Loreto, Peru
53 K 19 Loreto, Bolivia
54 K 12 Loreto, Brazil
121 M 17 Loreto, Philippines
50 H 3 Lorica, Colombia
64 I 6 Lorient, France
29 U 2 Loring, MT, U.S.A.
17 R 12 Loris, SC, U.S.A.
73 D 25 Lörrach, Germany
65 U 4 Lorraine, France
125 Q 8 Lorzot, Tunisia
31 Q 9 Los Alamos, NM, U.S.A.
33 H 23 Los Alamos, CA, U.S.A.
58 C 11 Los Amores, Argentina
33 J 24 Los Angeles, CA, U.S.A.
57 G 14 Los Angeles, Chile
33 J 23 Los Angeles Aqueduct, CA, U.S.A.
33 H 20 Los Banos, CA, U.S.A.
56 K 5 Los Blancos, Argentina
47 P 11 Los Chiles, Costa Rica
53 K 19 Los Cusis, Bolivia
33 G 20 Los Gatos, CA, U.S.A.
57 E 16 Los Lagos, Chile
57 H 16 Los Menucos, Argentina
44 K 7 Los Mochis, Mexico
48 G 4 Los Palacios, Cuba
44 I 5 Los Pocitos, Mexico
52 B 10 Los Ríos, Ecuador
56 J 9 Los Telares, Argentina
51 Q 2 Los Testigos, Venezuela
56 F 11 Los Vilos, Chile
141 O 15 Losap, Federated States of Micronesia
78 N 12 Łosice, Poland
80 B 11 Lošinj, Croatia
33 I 22 Lost Hills, CA, U.S.A.
62 L 14 Lostwithiel, U.K.
138 G 6 Losuia, Papua New Guinea
57 E 14 Lota, Chile
127 G 22 Lotagipi Swamp, Sudan
130 M 9 Loto, Democratic Republic of Congo
114 I 12 Louang Namtha, Laos
115 H 16 Louang Phrabang Range, Thailand
114 I 13 Louangphrabang, Laos
130 F 10 Loubomo, Congo
64 J 5 Loudéac, France
113 S 9 Loudi, China
65 N 8 Loudun, France
128 D 8 Louga, Senegal
61 D 16 Lough Allen, Republic of Ireland
61 C 16 Lough Conn, Republic of Ireland
61 C 18 Lough Corrib, Republic of Ireland
61 C 19 Lough Derg, Republic of Ireland
61 B 17 Lough Mask, Republic of Ireland
61 E 15 Lough Neagh, U.K.
61 C 17 Lough Ree, Republic of Ireland
63 T 6 Loughborough, U.K.
37 N 3 Lougheed Island, NU, Canada
143 P 7 Lougheed Island, Arctic Ocean
61 C 18 Loughrea, Republic of Ireland
133 P 9 Louis Trichardt, Republic of South Africa
16 L 5 Louisa, KY, U.S.A.
17 S 8 Louisburg, NC, U.S.A.
43 Y 8 Louisbourg, NS, Canada
138 H 7 Louisiade Archipelago, Papua New Guinea
18 I 7 Louisiana, U.S.A.
16 G 5 Louisville, KY, U.S.A.
19 N 4 Louisville, MS, U.S.A.
90 H 4 Loukhi, Russian Federation
130 H 8 Loukoléla, Congo
130 G 10 Loukouo, Congo
129 S 14 Loum, Cameroon
64 M 15 Lourdes, France
54 I 8 Lourenço, Brazil
66 G 9 Loures, Portugal
63 W 4 Louth, U.K.
83 F 20 Loutraki, Greece
42 H 7 Louvicourt, QC, Canada
65 O 4 Louviers, France
71 J 14 Lövånger, Sweden
82 H 8 Lovech, Bulgaria
82 I 8 Lovech, Bulgaria
31 R 3 Loveland, CO, U.S.A.
29 U 9 Lovell, WY, U.S.A.
33 J 16 Lovelock, NV, U.S.A.
76 E 6 Lovere, Italy
31 U 13 Lovington, NM, U.S.A.
79 C 16 Lovosice, Czech Republic
90 I 3 Lovozero, Russian Federation
86 E 10 Lovrin, Romania
132 J 1 Lóvua, Angola
132 L 3 Lóvua, Angola
131 O 8 Lowa, Democratic Republic of Congo
15 N 9 Lowell, MA, U.S.A.
28 L 6 Lowell, ID, U.S.A.
127 F 22 Lowelli, Sudan
72 L 12 Löwenberg, Germany
137 K 16 Lower Hutt, New Zealand
61 D 15 Lower Lough Erne, U.K.
23 Q 3 Lower Red Lake, MN, U.S.A.
63 Z 7 Lowestoft, U.K.
101 U 8 Lowgar, Afghanistan
78 J 13 Łowicz, Poland
28 K 10 Lowman, ID, U.S.A.
14 H 7 Lowville, NY, U.S.A.
72 F 10 Loxstedt, Germany
112 K 5 Loxur, China
139 R 13 Loyalty Islands, New Caledonia
85 N 21 Loyew, Belarus
80 J 11 Loznica, Serbia and Montenegro
82 L 7 Loznitsa, Bulgaria
87 W 6 Lozova, Ukraine
103 V 2 Lozovoye, Kazakhstan
67 O 5 Lozoyuela, Spain
113 Z 12 Lü Tao, Taiwan
54 G 11 Lua Nova, Brazil
132 K 3 Luacano, Angola
113 V 5 Lu'an, China
132 F 2 Luanda, Angola
132 G 3 Luanda, Angola
132 I 4 Luando, Angola
133 O 4 Luanshya, Zambia
111 F 17 Luanxian, China
131 P 13 Luanza, Democratic Republic of Congo
133 O 3 Luapula, Zambia
66 K 1 Luarca, Spain
130 M 14 Luashi, Democratic Republic of Congo
132 K 3 Luau, Angola
129 S 15 Luba, Equatorial Guinea
79 O 17 Lubaczów, Poland
132 J 2 Lubalo, Angola
84 I 11 Lubāna, Latvia
84 I 11 Lubānas ezers, Latvia
120 F 12 Lubang, Philippines
120 E 12 Lubang Islands, Philippines
132 G 5 Lubango, Angola
131 O 11 Lubao, Democratic Republic of Congo
79 N 14 Lubartów, Poland
78 J 10 Lubawa, Poland
26 K 5 Lubbock, TX, U.S.A.
15 T 5 Lubec, ME, U.S.A.
72 I 9 Lübeck, Germany
72 I 9 Lübecker Bucht, Germany
131 N 10 Lubefu, Democratic Republic of Congo
110 H 12 Lubei, China
120 F 12 Lubgan, Philippines
121 F 16 Lubic, Philippines
79 F 14 Lubin, Poland
79 N 14 Lublin, Poland
79 I 16 Lubliniec, Poland
87 S 4 Lubny, Ukraine
120 G 7 Lubuagan, Philippines
131 O 14 Lubudi, Democratic Republic of Congo
131 P 14 Lubumbashi, Democratic Republic of Congo
133 N 5 Lubungu, Zambia
131 O 8 Lubutu, Democratic Republic of Congo
132 H 2 Lucala, Angola
132 K 2 Lucapa, Angola
23 S 14 Lucas, IA, U.S.A.
76 E 10 Lucca, Italy
19 N 7 Lucedale, MS, U.S.A.
58 I 6 Lucélia, Brazil
67 N 12 Lucena, Spain
120 H 12 Lucena, Philippines
79 J 21 Lučenec, Slovakia
77 K 14 Lucera, Italy
53 H 16 Lucerna, Peru
112 L 9 Luchang, China
72 J 12 Lüchow, Germany
113 R 13 Luchuan, China
117 R 13 Lucipara, Indonesia
132 F 5 Lucira, Angola
73 M 14 Luckau, Germany
107 Q 12 Luckeesarai, India
73 M 14 Luckenwalde, Germany
106 M 10 Lucknow, India
18 I 5 Lucky, LA, U.S.A.
64 L 8 Luçon, France
132 K 4 Lucusse, Angola
132 H 11 Lüderitz, Namibia
132 H 11 Lüderitz Bay, Namibia
131 T 14 Ludewa, Tanzania
106 I 6 Ludhiana, India
112 M 9 Ludian, China
20 I 12 Ludington, MI, U.S.A.
14 L 7 Ludlow, VT, U.S.A.
33 L 23 Ludlow, CA, U.S.A.
63 P 7 Ludlow, U.K.
19 W 5 Ludowici, GA, U.S.A.
71 G 19 Ludvika, Sweden
73 F 22 Ludwigsburg, Germany
72 M 13 Ludwigsfelde, Germany
72 J 11 Ludwigslust, Germany
84 J 12 Ludza, Latvia
130 L 11 Luebo, Democratic Republic of Congo
131 O 10 Lueki, Democratic Republic of Congo
132 J 4 Luena, Angola
113 O 4 Lüeyang, China
113 V 12 Lufeng, China
27 T 8 Lufkin, TX, U.S.A.
90 E 11 Luga, Russian Federation
121 K 20 Lugait, Philippines
74 H 11 Lugano, Switzerland
139 Q 10 Luganville, Vanuatu
127 L 19 Lughaye, Somalia
66 J 1 Lugo, Spain
86 F 10 Lugoj, Romania
103 T 10 Lugovoy, Kazakhstan
121 G 24 Lugus, Philippines
87 Z 6 Luhans'k, Ukraine
131 V 13 Luhombero, Tanzania
112 K 6 Luhuo, China
132 L 6 Luiana, Angola
145 N 4 Luitpold Coast, Antarctica
130 L 12 Luiza, Democratic Republic of Congo
56 G 11 Luján de Cuyo, Argentina
113 W 6 Lujiang, China
80 H 11 Lukavac, Bosnia and Herzegovina
92 L 2 Lukhovitsy, Russian Federation
82 I 11 Lŭki, Bulgaria
130 I 8 Lukolela, Democratic Republic of Congo
82 H 8 Lukovit, Bulgaria
78 M 13 Łuków, Poland
93 P 2 Lukoyanov, Russian Federation
130 F 11 Lukula, Democratic Republic of Congo
132 L 5 Lukulu, Zambia
131 U 13 Lukumburu, Tanzania
70 J 12 Luleå, Sweden
70 J 11 Luleälven, Sweden
94 C 7 Lüleburgaz, Turkey
113 R 2 Lüliang Shan, China
131 P 10 Lulimba, Democratic Republic of Congo
130 J 7 Lulonga, Democratic Republic of Congo
132 K 4 Lumbala Kaquengue, Angola
132 K 5 Lumbala N'guimbo, Angola
17 R 11 Lumberton, NC, U.S.A.
18 M 6 Lumberton, MS, U.S.A.
56 I 6 Lumbrera, Argentina
107 X 11 Lumding, India
138 B 3 Lumi, Papua New Guinea
115 N 19 Lumphăt, Cambodia
137 C 24 Lumsden, New Zealand
132 I 2 Lunda Norte, Angola
132 K 3 Lunda Sul, Angola
133 Q 4 Lundazi, Zambia
118 M 10 Lundu, Malaysia
62 L 12 Lundy Island, U.K.
72 H 11 Lüneburg, Germany
73 D 15 Lünen, Germany
65 V 4 Lunéville, France
74 F 8 Lungern, Switzerland
108 I 9 Lunggar, China
128 F 12 Lungi, Sierra Leone
107 X 13 Lunglei, India
33 K 19 Luning, NV, U.S.A.
93 P 3 Lunino, Russian Federation
85 I 21 Luninyets, Belarus
106 G 8 Lunkaransar, India
128 F 12 Lunsar, Sierra Leone
75 U 5 Lunz am See, Austria
110 N 9 Luobei, China
113 Q 11 Luocheng, China
113 Q 2 Luochuan, China
113 O 10 Luodian, China
113 R 12 Luoding, China
113 U 4 Luohe, China
113 R 4 Luonan, China
113 S 3 Luoning, China
112 M 11 Luoping, China
113 U 5 Luoshan, China
113 V 6 Luotian, China
113 U 9 Luoxiao Shan, China
113 S 3 Luoyang, China
113 Y 9 Luoyuan, China
130 G 11 Luozi, Democratic Republic of Congo
133 O 7 Lupane, Zimbabwe
113 N 9 Lupanshui, China
133 R 3 Lupilichi, Mozambique
112 M 3 Luqu, China
132 I 2 Luremo, Angola
61 F 16 Lurgan, U.K.
53 D 17 Lurín, Peru
131 R 9 Lusahunga, Tanzania
133 O 5 Lusaka, Zambia
133 O 5 Lusaka, Zambia
130 M 11 Lusambo, Democratic Republic of Congo
113 R 4 Lushi, China
81 J 19 Lushnjë, Albania
131 W 10 Lushoto, Tanzania
112 I 10 Lushui, China
111 H 18 Lushunkou, China
29 Z 12 Lusk, WY, U.S.A.
65 O 9 Lussac-les-Châteaux, France
74 I 6 Lustenau, Austria
73 L 14 Lutherstadt Wittenberg, Germany
131 Q 8 Lutiba, Democratic Republic of Congo
72 H 8 Lütjenburg, Germany
63 V 9 Luton, U.K.
119 R 7 Lutong, Malaysia
38 I 12 Lutselk'e, NT, Canada
86 K 3 Luts'k, Ukraine
63 T 7 Lutterworth, U.K.
87 Z 6 Lutuhyne, Ukraine
72 I 10 Lützow, Germany
145 U 2 Lützow-Holm Bay, Antarctica
132 J 14 Lutzville, Republic of South Africa
127 K 23 Luuq, Somalia
23 P 10 Luverne, MN, U.S.A.
131 O 12 Luvua, Democratic Republic of Congo
132 K 4 Luvuei, Angola
131 S 7 Luwero, Uganda
117 P 11 Luwuk, Indonesia
69 L 25 Luxembourg, Luxembourg
69 K 25 Luxembourg, Europe
69 L 26 Luxembourg, Luxembourg
69 I 23 Luxembourg, Belgium
65 V 6 Luxeuil-les-Bains, France
112 I 11 Luxi, China
112 M 11 Luxi, China
113 R 8 Luxi, China
126 F 11 Luxor, Egypt
91 O 10 Luza, Russian Federation
74 F 7 Luzern, Switzerland
113 N 8 Luzhou, China
55 J 16 Luziânia, Brazil
120 G 8 Luzon, Philippines
120 G 3 Luzon Strait, Philippines
86 I 4 L'viv, Ukraine
143 V 5 Lyakhovskiye Ostrova, Russian Federation
82 J 8 Lyaskovets, Bulgaria
71 I 14 Lycksele, Sweden
63 Y 12 Lydd, U.K.
85 K 22 Lyel'chytsy, Belarus
85 K 15 Lyepyel', Belarus
83 F 21 Lygourio, Greece
63 O 14 Lyme Bay, U.K.
63 P 13 Lyme Regis, U.K.
63 S 13 Lymington, U.K.
78 K 8 Łyna, Poland
17 R 6 Lynchburg, VA, U.S.A.
63 S 13 Lyndhurst, U.K.
25 P 4 Lyndon, KS, U.S.A.
71 A 21 Lyngdal, Norway
40 I 6 Lynn Lake, MB, Canada
87 R 3 Lynovytsya, Ukraine
63 N 11 Lynton, U.K.
85 H 15 Lyntupy, Belarus
65 T 10 Lyon, France
19 V 5 Lyons, GA, U.S.A.
24 M 5 Lyons, KS, U.S.A.
85 M 15 Lyozna, Belarus
87 T 3 Lypova Dolyna, Ukraine
69 B 19 Lys, Belgium
93 P 1 Lyskovo, Russian Federation
91 U 12 Lys'va, Russian Federation
87 Y 5 Lysychans'k, Ukraine
63 O 2 Lytham St Anne's, U.K.
137 H 20 Lyttelton, New Zealand
39 G 21 Lytton, BC, Canada
85 J 20 Lyuban', Belarus
86 M 4 Lyubar, Ukraine
87 P 1 Lyubech, Ukraine
92 L 1 Lyubertsy, Russian Federation
86 K 1 Lyubeshiv, Ukraine
90 G 12 Lyubytine, Russian Federation
92 J 2 Lyudinovo, Russian Federation

M

105 B 26 Maalhosmadulu Atoll, Maldives
133 N 6 Maamba, Zambia
96 G 12 Ma'an, Jordan
129 T 15 Ma'an, Cameroon
70 M 11 Maaninkavaara, Finland
113 X 5 Ma'anshan, China
69 J 16 Maarheeze, Netherlands
71 J 19 Maarianhamina, Finland
96 I 3 Ma'arrat an Nu'mān, Syria
68 I 12 Maarssen, Netherlands
69 H 14 Maas, Netherlands
69 K 18 Maaseik, Belgium
121 L 18 Maasin, Philippines
68 F 13 Maasland, Netherlands
69 K 18 Maasmechelen, Belgium
69 K 19 Maastricht, Netherlands
117 S 10 Maba, Indonesia
120 F 10 Mabalacat, Philippines

Country · Internal administrative region: State/Province/Territory/Dependent territory · Capital city · Mountain range/Undersea ridge · Mountain peak/Volcano/Seamount · Geographic feature · Headland/Point/Cape/Peninsula · Desert · Island/Island group · Antarctic base · Ocean · Sea · Bay/Gulf/Channel/Strait · Lake · Salt pan/Dry/Intermittent lake · River

Mabalane – Markoye

133 Q 10 Mabalane, Mozambique
131 P 7 Mabana, Democratic Republic of Congo
114 E 10 Mabein, Myanmar
121 N 22 Mabini, Philippines
63 W 4 Mablethorpe, U.K.
133 R 9 Mabote, Mozambique
43 X 8 Mabou, NS, Canada
125 U 9 Mabrūk, Libya
120 H 1 Mabudis, Philippines
145 V 5 Mac Robertson Land, Antarctica
49 A 18 Macachin, Argentina
58 O 6 Macaé, Brazil
133 S 4 Macaloge, Mozambique
118 C 5 Macang, Malaysia
54 I 9 Macapá, Brazil
52 A 11 Macará, Ecuador
47 V 15 Macaracas, Panama
52 C 10 Macas, Ecuador
113 U 13 Macau, China
55 L 15 Macaúbas, Brazil
57 L 23 Macbride Head, Falkland Islands
19 V 7 Macclenny, FL, U.S.A.
63 Q 4 Macclesfield, U.K.
134 N 6 MacDonnell Ranges, NT, Australia
66 J 4 Macedo de Cavaleiros, Portugal
82 C 11 Macedonia (F.Y.R.O.M.), Europe
54 O 13 Maceió, Brazil
76 I 11 Macerata, Italy
89 S 11 Macha, Russian Federation
52 B 8 Machachi, Ecuador
133 Q 9 Machaila, Mozambique
131 V 9 Machakos, Kenya
52 A 10 Machala, Ecuador
111 E 18 Machang, China
133 R 8 Machanga, Mozambique
46 I 3 Machaquilá, Guatemala
127 F 20 Machar Marshes, Sudan
53 L 22 Machareti, Bolivia
113 U 6 Macheng, China
105 J 16 Machhagan, India
15 S 5 Machias, ME, U.S.A.
105 G 19 Machilipatnam, India
133 R 5 Machinga, Malawi
50 K 3 Machiques, Venezuela
63 N 7 Machynlleth, U.K.
133 Q 10 Macia, Mozambique
87 N 12 Măcin, Romania
29 N 10 Mackay, ID, U.S.A.
135 U 5 Mackay, QLD, Australia
38 D 10 Mackenzie, NT, Canada
38 B 8 Mackenzie Bay, YT, Canada
145 X 6 Mackenzie Bay, Antarctica
37 N 3 Mackenzie King Island, NT, Canada
38 C 11 Mackenzie Mountains, YT, Canada
20 I 5 Mackinaw City, MI, U.S.A.
39 K 18 Macklin, SK, Canada
137 D 26 Maclennan, New Zealand
132 H 1 Macocola, Angola
21 D 18 Macomb, IL, U.S.A.
77 B 17 Macomer, Italy
133 U 4 Macomia, Mozambique
19 T 4 Macon, GA, U.S.A.
19 N 4 Macon, MS, U.S.A.
21 L 20 Macon, OH, U.S.A.
25 U 2 Macon, MO, U.S.A.
65 T 9 Mâcon, France
132 L 4 Macondo, Angola
135 T 10 Macquarie, NSW, Australia
61 B 20 Macroom, Republic of Ireland
46 J 5 Macuelizo, Honduras
50 J 10 Macuje, Colombia
96 G 10 Mādabā, Jordan
133 P 12 Madadeni, Republic of South Africa
133 W 7 Madagascar, Africa
133 W 8 Madagascar, Madgascar
129 U 5 Madama, Niger
82 I 12 Madan, Bulgaria
138 D 4 Madang, Papua New Guinea
138 D 4 Madang, Papua New Guinea
129 Q 9 Madaoua, Niger
107 U 13 Madaripur, Bangladesh
102 I 13 Madau, Turkmenistan
15 R 1 Madawaska, ME, U.S.A.
10 L 7 Madeira, Portugal
54 D 13 Madeira, Brazil
33 H 15 Madeline, CA, U.S.A.
20 E 8 Madeline Island, WI, U.S.A.
95 O 11 Maden, Turkey
103 W 6 Madeniyet, Kazakhstan
33 I 20 Madera, CA, U.S.A.
44 K 4 Madera, Mexico
107 R 11 Madhepura, India
107 Q 10 Madhubani, India
106 M 12 Madhya Pradesh, India
105 C 21 Madikeri, India
25 O 13 Madill, OK, U.S.A.
130 H 11 Madimba, Democratic Republic of Congo
96 M 3 Ma'din', Syria
96 K 3 Madinat ath Thawrah, Syria
130 E 10 Madingo-Kayes, Congo
53 I 17 Madini, Bolivia
19 U 3 Madison, GA, U.S.A.
19 U 7 Madison, FL, U.S.A.
21 F 14 Madison, WI, U.S.A.
21 J 20 Madison, IN, U.S.A.
23 O 9 Madison, SD, U.S.A.
17 R 6 Madison Heights, VA, U.S.A.
16 E 6 Madisonville, KY, U.S.A.
19 J 10 Madisonville, TN, U.S.A.
27 R 8 Madisonville, TX, U.S.A.
116 J 14 Madiun, Indonesia
130 G 7 Madjingo, Gabon
63 G 11 Madliena, Latvia
131 W 7 Mado Gashi, Kenya
42 H 12 Madoc, ON, Canada
109 O 9 Madoi, China
84 H 11 Madona, Latvia
30 H 11 Madras, OR, U.S.A.
53 H 16 Madre de Dios, Peru
53 G 17 Madre de Dios, Bolivia/Peru
67 O 6 Madrid, Spain
67 O 7 Madrid, Spain
131 U 10 Madukani, Tanzania
116 K 14 Madura, Indonesia
134 K 10 Madura, WA, Australia
105 E 23 Madurai, India
115 F 14 Mae Hong Son, Thailand
115 F 15 Mae Sariang, Thailand
115 F 16 Mae Sot, Thailand
123 J 15 Maebashi, Japan
133 X 6 Maevatanana, Madgascar
139 R 10 Maéwo, Vanuatu
40 H 8 Mafeking, MB, Canada
133 N 13 Mafeteng, Lesotho
131 W 13 Mafia Channel, Tanzania
131 X 12 Mafia Island, Tanzania
132 M 11 Mafikeng, Republic of South Africa
131 U 12 Mafinga, Tanzania
58 I 9 Mafra, Brazil
89 X 10 Magadan, Russian Federation
131 V 9 Magadi, Kenya
57 F 24 Magallanes, Chile
67 X 8 Magalluf, Spain
120 H 8 Magat, Philippines
25 T 10 Magazine Mountain, AR, U.S.A.
130 M 6 Magbakele, Democratic Republic of Congo
89 T 13 Magdagachi, Russian Federation
31 P 11 Magdalena, NM, U.S.A.
44 I 3 Magdalena, Mexico
44 I 3 Magdalena, Mexico
50 I 2 Magdalena, Colombia
50 I 4 Magdalena, Colombia
53 L 17 Magdalena, Bolivia
59 D 16 Magdalena, Argentina
73 J 14 Magdeburg, Germany
123 C 25 Mage-shima, Japan
76 C 7 Magenta, Italy
70 K 5 Magerøya, Norway
126 E 9 Maghâgha, Egypt
128 F 8 Maghama, Mauritania
124 K 6 Maghnia, Algeria
67 O 11 Magina, Spain
77 O 17 Maglie, Italy
138 F 4 Magma Point, Papua New Guinea
135 T 4 Magnetic Island, QLD, Australia
88 I 11 Magnitogorsk, Russian Federation
25 T 14 Magnolia, AR, U.S.A.
139 Y 11 Mago, Fiji
133 P 6 Màgoé, Mozambique
42 M 11 Magog, QC, Canada
128 F 7 Magta' Lahjar, Mauritania
133 Q 10 Magude, Mozambique
129 U 10 Magumeri, Nigeria
40 K 4 Maguse Lake, NU, Canada
114 C 13 Magwe, Myanmar
114 C 13 Magwe, Myanmar
114 A 13 Magyichaung, Myanmar
115 J 17 Maha Sarakham, Thailand
100 F 4 Mahābād, Iran
133 W 6 Mahabe, Madgascar
107 N 9 Mahabharat Range, Nepal
105 B 18 Mahad, India
127 M 24 Mahaddayweyne, Somalia
131 R 6 Mahagi Port, Democratic Republic of Congo
106 G 8 Mahajan, India
133 X 6 Mahajanga, Madgascar
133 X 7 Mahajanga, Madgascar
116 L 10 Mahakam, Indonesia
100 H 7 Mahallāt, Iran
100 M 10 Māhān, Iran
105 H 13 Mahanadi, India
133 Y 8 Mahanoro, Madgascar
107 P 10 Maharajganj, India
105 D 17 Maharashtra, India
96 H 10 Mahaṭṭat Dab'ah, Jordan
127 D 18 Mahbub, Sudan
105 F 19 Mahbubnagar, India
125 R 6 Mahdia, Tunisia
105 D 22 Mahe, India
131 V 13 Mahenge, Tanzania
137 F 23 Maheno, New Zealand
136 O 12 Mahia, New Zealand
136 O 12 Mahia Peninsula, New Zealand
85 M 17 Mahilyow, Belarus
85 M 18 Mahilyowskaya Voblasts', Belarus
128 G 9 Mahina, Mali
72 M 13 Mahlow, Germany
100 J 5 Mahmudabad, Iran
106 M 10 Mahmudabad, India
23 P 4 Mahnomen, MN, U.S.A.
106 K 11 Mahoba, India
136 K 11 Mahoenui, New Zealand
67 Z 7 Mahon, Spain
67 R 9 Mahora, Spain
128 K 10 Mahou, Burkina Faso
105 B 16 Mahuva, India
106 I 10 Mahwa, India
117 S 13 Mai, Indonesia
140 D 2 Maiana, Kiribati
50 K 2 Maicao, Colombia
54 H 9 Maicuru, Brazil
63 U 10 Maidenhead, U.K.
63 X 11 Maidstone, U.K.
129 U 10 Maiduguri, Nigeria
106 M 12 Maihar, India
107 V 13 Maijdi, Bangladesh
105 G 16 Maikala Range, India
116 D 12 Maileppe, Indonesia
65 S 5 Mailly-le-Camp, France
73 F 20 Main, Germany
42 C 10 Main Channel, ON, Canada
73 K 23 Mainburg, Germany
15 P 4 Maine, U.S.A.
60 H 7 Mainland, U.K.
60 J 4 Mainland, U.K.
106 K 10 Mainpuri, India
133 W 7 Maintirano, Madgascar
73 E 19 Mainz, Germany
59 D 17 Maipú, Argentina
51 O 2 Maiquetía, Venezuela
75 W 2 Maissau, Austria
56 F 10 Maitencillo, Chile
133 N 8 Maitengwe, Botswana
135 V 11 Maitland, NSW, Australia
135 P 11 Maitland, SA, Australia
145 Q 1 Maitri, Antarctica
123 G 17 Maizuru, Japan
81 J 20 Maja e Çikes, Albania
81 K 15 Maja Jezercë, Albania
45 Z 12 Majahual, Mexico
80 N 11 Majdanpek, Serbia and Montenegro
117 N 12 Majene, Indonesia
80 H 10 Majevica, Bosnia and Herzegovina
110 O 11 Majiagang, China
113 S 12 Majiang, China
113 S 8 Majitang, China
67 X 8 Majorca, Spain
141 Z 3 Majuro, Marshall Islands
141 Z 3 Majuro, Marshall Islands
129 T 14 Makak, Cameroon
117 N 12 Makale, Indonesia
131 Q 10 Makamba, Burundi
103 Y 7 Makanchi, Kazakhstan
130 J 7 Makanza, Democratic Republic of Congo
136 O 12 Makaraka, New Zealand
87 O 3 Makariv, Ukraine
89 X 14 Makarov, Russian Federation
143 R 8 Makarov Basin, Arctic Ocean
93 O 5 Makarovo, Russian Federation
81 F 14 Makarska, Croatia
90 M 13 Makar'yev, Russian Federation
117 N 11 Makassar Strait, Indonesia
102 J 6 Makat, Kazakhstan
114 E 7 Makaw, Myanmar
128 G 11 Makeni, Sierra Leone
93 R 14 Makhachkala, Russian Federation
102 I 6 Makhambet, Kazakhstan
97 S 3 Makhmūr, Iraq
137 F 22 Makikihi, New Zealand
140 D 1 Makin, Kiribati
131 V 9 Makindu, Kenya
103 R 3 Makinsk, Kazakhstan
139 N 7 Makira, Solomon Islands
41 V 7 Makkovik, NL, Canada
79 L 25 Makó, Hungary
130 F 7 Makokou, Gabon
131 S 13 Makongolosi, Tanzania
131 Q 6 Makoro, Democratic Republic of Congo
138 H 9 Makotipoko, Congo
130 H 7 Makoua, Congo
83 K 24 Makra, Greece
83 D 18 Makrakomi, Greece
101 O 13 Makran, Iran
101 N 14 Makran Coast, Iran
83 H 20 Makronisi, Greece
90 H 13 Maksatikha, Russian Federation
100 E 2 Mākū, Iran
131 T 13 Makumbako, Tanzania
130 K 11 Makumbi, Democratic Republic of Congo
131 V 14 Makunguwiro, Tanzania
105 L 16 Makunudhoo Atoll, Maldives
123 B 24 Makurazaki, Japan
129 S 12 Makurdi, Nigeria
34 J 13 Makushin Volcano, AK, U.S.A.
127 K 25 Makuungo, Somalia
107 T 10 Mal, India
53 C 17 Mala, Peru
80 C 10 Mala Kapela, Croatia
121 K 21 Malabang, Philippines
105 C 21 Malabar Coast, India
129 S 14 Malabo, Equatorial Guinea
79 G 21 Malacky, Slovakia
29 P 13 Malad City, ID, U.S.A.
85 I 16 Maladzyechna, Belarus
67 N 13 Málaga, Spain
67 O 9 Malagón, Spain
133 X 8 Malaimbandy, Madgascar
138 M 6 Malaita, Solomon Islands
139 N 6 Malaita, Solomon Islands
127 E 20 Malakal, Sudan
106 I 9 Malakhera, India
106 L 8 Malakheti, Nepal
139 P 11 Malakula, Vanuatu
138 D 4 Malalamai, Papua New Guinea
138 B 6 Malam, Papua New Guinea
117 O 12 Malamala, Indonesia
121 D 19 Malanao, Philippines
116 J 14 Malang, Indonesia
132 H 3 Malanje, Angola
132 H 2 Malanje, Angola
56 H 10 Malanzán, Argentina
71 H 20 Mälaren, Sweden
56 G 13 Malargüe, Argentina
42 G 7 Malartic, QC, Canada
85 E 22 Malaryta, Belarus
95 N 11 Malatya, Turkey
106 G 7 Malaut, India
105 E 21 Malavalli, India
119 W 4 Malawali, Malaysia
133 Q 4 Malawi, Africa
127 H 17 Malawiya, Sudan
118 D 7 Malay Peninsula, Malaysia
90 G 11 Malaya Vishera, Russian Federation
121 L 21 Malaybalay, Philippines
100 G 6 Malāyer, Iran
118 D 7 Malaysia, Asia
95 R 10 Malazgirt, Turkey
78 I 9 Malbork, Poland
72 L 10 Malchin, Germany
72 K 10 Malchow, Germany
69 D 17 Maldegem, Belgium
25 Y 8 Malden, MO, U.S.A.
69 K 14 Malden, Netherlands
141 Q 4 Malden Island, Kiribati
105 K 19 Maldives, Asia
63 X 9 Maldon, U.K.
59 F 16 Maldonado, Uruguay
59 G 16 Maldonado, Uruguay
105 L 18 Male, Maldives
105 L 17 Male Atoll, Maldives
79 G 21 Malé Karpaty, Slovakia
105 E 17 Malegaon, India
105 C 16 Malegaon, India
131 O 9 Malela, Democratic Republic of Congo
131 O 13 Malemba Nkulu, Democratic Republic of Congo
101 T 8 Mālestān, Afghanistan
127 B 17 Malha, Sudan
97 R 5 Malḥāt, Iraq
32 J 13 Malheur Lake, OR, U.S.A.
128 F 10 Mali, Africa
131 O 9 Mali, Democratic Republic of Congo
115 F 20 Mali Kyun, Myanmar
113 S 6 Maliangping, China
121 J 22 Maligay Bay, Philippines
61 E 14 Malin, Republic of Ireland
61 D 14 Malin Head, Republic of Ireland
131 X 9 Malindi, Kenya
130 F 9 Malinga, Gabon
109 Q 14 Malipo, China
81 L 20 Maliq, Albania
121 M 23 Malita, Philippines
82 L 13 Malkara, Turkey
60 F 11 Mallaig, U.K.
126 E 9 Mallawi, Egypt
40 K 3 Mallery Lake, NU, Canada
61 C 20 Mallow, Republic of Ireland
138 G 4 Malmal, Papua New Guinea
69 L 21 Malmédy, Belgium
63 R 10 Malmesbury, U.K.
132 J 15 Malmesbury, Republic of South Africa
71 E 25 Malmö, Sweden
91 Q 14 Malmyzh, Russian Federation
86 K 10 Malnaș, Romania
139 Q 10 Malo, Vanuatu
54 G 9 Maloca, Brazil
141 Z 2 Maloelap, Marshall Islands
120 G 11 Malolos, Philippines
14 J 5 Malone, NY, U.S.A.
130 M 14 Malonga, Democratic Republic of Congo
90 J 7 Maloshuyka, Russian Federation
71 A 16 Måløy, Norway
91 O 4 Malozemel'skaya Tundra, Russian Federation
104 D 12 Malpura, India
29 U 3 Malta, MT, U.S.A.
77 I 25 Malta, Europe
77 K 25 Malta, Malta
84 I 12 Malta, Latvia
77 I 24 Malta Channel, Italy
132 I 10 Maltahöhe, Namibia
63 T 3 Maltby, U.K.
63 W 4 Maltby le Marsh, U.K.
63 U 1 Malton, U.K.
117 R 13 Maluku, Indonesia
71 F 19 Malung, Sweden
121 H 23 Maluso, Philippines
138 M 6 Malu'u, Solomon Islands
105 B 19 Malvan, India
25 U 12 Malvern, AR, U.S.A.
87 O 3 Malyn, Ukraine
93 T 1 Mamadysh, Russian Federation
121 L 19 Mambajao, Philippines
131 Q 7 Mambasa, Democratic Republic of Congo
130 H 5 Mambéré-Kadéï, Central African Republic
120 F 13 Mamburao, Philippines
133 O 11 Mamelodi, Republic of South Africa
129 S 13 Mamfé, Cameroon
56 G 3 Mamiña, Chile
103 Q 1 Mamlyutka, Kazakhstan
95 W 10 Mammadbajli, Azerbaijan
30 L 13 Mammoth, AZ, U.S.A.
29 R 8 Mammoth Hot Springs, WY, U.S.A.
85 A 16 Mamonovo, Russian Federation
53 K 15 Mamoré, Bolivia
54 C 10 Mamori, Brazil
54 C 12 Mamoriá, Brazil
128 G 11 Mamou, Guinea
128 M 13 Mampong, Ghana
117 N 12 Mamuju, Indonesia
99 X 10 Ma'mūl, Oman
128 I 12 Man, Côte d'Ivoire
52 A 9 Manabí, Ecuador
54 F 11 Manacapuru, Brazil
67 Y 8 Manacor, Spain
117 Q 10 Manado, Indonesia
47 N 9 Managua, Nicaragua
133 Y 9 Manakara, Madgascar
99 P 13 Manākhah, Yemen
138 C 3 Manam, Papua New Guinea
133 X 10 Manambondro, Madgascar
121 F 16 Manamoc, Philippines
133 Z 6 Mananara Avaratra, Madgascar
133 Y 9 Mananjary, Madgascar
128 I 11 Manankoro, Mali
133 X 10 Manantenina, Madgascar
137 C 24 Manapouri, New Zealand
108 K 3 Manas Hu, China
17 T 3 Manassas, VA, U.S.A.
54 F 10 Manaus, Brazil
94 F 13 Manavgat, Turkey
127 B 18 Manawashei, Sudan
136 L 13 Manawatu-Wanganui, New Zealand
96 K 2 Manbij, Syria
20 J 11 Mancelona, MI, U.S.A.
14 L 8 Manchester, VT, U.S.A.
15 N 8 Manchester, NH, U.S.A.
16 J 6 Manchester, KY, U.S.A.
16 G 10 Manchester, TN, U.S.A.
63 R 3 Manchester, U.K.
111 H 14 Manchurian Plain, China
94 M 10 Mancilik, Turkey
101 P 14 Mand, Pakistan
133 W 8 Mandabe, Madgascar
118 A 13 Mandai, Singapore
101 P 8 Mandal, Afghanistan
114 C 12 Mandalay, Myanmar
114 D 11 Mandalay, Myanmar
109 Q 4 Mandalgovi, Mongolia
97 V 6 Mandalī, Iraq
22 J 5 Mandan, ND, U.S.A.
121 J 15 Mandaon, Philippines
77 C 18 Mandas, Italy
121 K 17 Mandaue, Philippines
131 Y 5 Mandera, Kenya
48 K 8 Mandeville, Jamaica
104 B 12 Mandha, India
127 L 20 Mandheera, Somalia
106 J 6 Mandi, India
133 Q 6 Mandié, Mozambique
133 S 5 Mandimba, Mozambique
130 E 9 Mandji, Gabon
105 G 15 Mandla, India
71 B 25 Mandø, Denmark
133 Z 6 Mandritsara, Madgascar
105 D 14 Mandsaur, India
134 G 11 Mandurah, WA, Australia
77 O 17 Manduria, Italy
105 A 14 Mandvi, India
105 E 21 Mandya, India
126 E 10 Manfalût, Egypt
77 L 14 Manfredonia, Italy
138 H 3 Manga, Papua New Guinea
130 K 10 Mangai, Democratic Republic of Congo
138 G 3 Mangai, Papua New Guinea
141 P 11 Mangaia, Cook Islands
136 L 11 Mangakino, New Zealand
107 V 10 Mangaldai, India
87 N 14 Mangalia, Romania
129 Y 10 Mangalmé, Chad
105 C 21 Mangalore, India
136 I 5 Mangamuka, New Zealand
133 N 12 Mangaung, Republic of South Africa
136 M 13 Mangaweka, New Zealand
136 K 7 Mangawhai, New Zealand
73 J 26 Mangfallgebirge, Germany
116 H 12 Manggar, Indonesia
138 M 8 Manggautu, Solomon Islands
102 J 10 Mangistau, Kazakhstan
126 G 4 Mangla Reservoir, India/Pakistan
108 L 7 Mangnai, China
129 N 11 Mango, Togo
133 R 5 Mangochi, Malawi
117 R 11 Mangole, Indonesia
136 I 5 Mangonui, New Zealand
48 K 3 Mangrove Cay, The Bahamas
66 J 6 Mangualde, Portugal
58 H 9 Mangueirinha, Brazil
110 H 5 Mangui, China
24 J 11 Mangum, OK, U.S.A.
102 G 8 Mangyshlakskiy Zaliv, Kazakhstan
25 O 3 Manhattan, KS, U.S.A.
69 K 22 Manhay, Belgium
76 H 6 Maniago, Italy
133 Q 7 Manica, Mozambique
133 P 7 Manicaland, Zimbabwe
54 E 12 Manicoré, Brazil
43 P 3 Manicouagan, QC, Canada
131 O 9 Maniema, Democratic Republic of Congo
99 S 4 Manīfah, Saudi Arabia
112 J 5 Maniganggo, China
40 J 10 Manigotagan, MB, Canada
141 O 7 Manihiki, Cook Islands
142 M 12 Maniitsoq, Greenland
107 W 13 Manikchhari, Bangladesh
106 M 12 Manikpur, India
30 M 2 Manila, UT, U.S.A.
120 G 11 Manila, Philippines
120 G 11 Manila Bay, Philippines
117 V 11 Manim, Indonesia
135 N 1 Maningrida, NT, Australia
117 R 12 Manipa, Indonesia
107 X 11 Manipur, India
107 X 12 Manipur Hills, India
94 B 10 Manisa, Turkey
55 H 14 Manissauá-Miçu, Brazil
20 H 10 Manistee, MI, U.S.A.
20 J 12 Manistee, MI, U.S.A.
20 I 8 Manistique, MI, U.S.A.
20 J 9 Manistique Lake, MI, U.S.A.
40 I 7 Manitoba, Canada
20 I 11 Manitou Islands, MI, U.S.A.
42 C 10 Manitoulin Island, ON, Canada
40 M 11 Manitouwadge, ON, Canada
42 I 9 Maniwaki, QC, Canada
117 W 12 Maniwori, Indonesia
50 H 6 Manizales, Colombia
133 W 9 Manja, Madgascar
100 F 3 Manjil, Iran
134 G 12 Manjimup, WA, Australia
23 R 9 Mankato, MN, U.S.A.
129 U 14 Mankim, Cameroon
128 J 12 Mankono, Côte d'Ivoire
105 G 24 Mankulam, Sri Lanka
105 C 16 Manmad, India
116 E 13 Manna, Indonesia
105 F 24 Mannar, Sri Lanka
105 F 24 Mannar Island, Sri Lanka
73 F 21 Mannheim, Germany
17 P 13 Manning, SC, U.S.A.
22 H 5 Manning, ND, U.S.A.
128 G 12 Mano, Sierra Leone
128 G 12 Mano River, Liberia
117 V 11 Manokwari, Indonesia
86 L 7 Manoleasa, Romania
131 P 12 Manono, Democratic Republic of Congo
65 V 13 Manosque, France
111 K 15 Manp'o, North Korea
140 K 4 Manra, Kiribati
67 W 4 Manresa, Spain
106 H 7 Mansa, India
133 O 3 Mansa, Zambia
128 E 9 Mansa Konko, Gambia
128 E 9 Mansabá, Guinea-Bissau
101 X 7 Mansehra, Pakistan
41 P 4 Mansel Island, NU, Canada
14 F 10 Mansfield, PA, U.S.A.
18 G 5 Mansfield, LA, U.S.A.
21 N 17 Mansfield, OH, U.S.A.
25 S 11 Mansfield, AR, U.S.A.
63 T 5 Mansfield, U.K.
114 D 9 Mansi, Myanmar
128 E 10 Mansôa, Guinea-Bissau
94 K 12 Mansurlu, Turkey
52 A 9 Manta, Ecuador
33 H 19 Manteca, CA, U.S.A.
50 M 5 Mantecal, Venezuela
17 W 8 Manteo, NC, U.S.A.
65 P 4 Mantes-la-Jolie, France
30 K 4 Manti, UT, U.S.A.
47 N 5 Manto, Honduras
83 G 18 Mantoudi, Greece
76 E 7 Mantova, Italy
90 M 12 Manturovo, Russian Federation
140 K 8 Manua Islands, American Samoa
141 P 10 Manuae, Cook Islands
54 H 12 Manuelzinho, Brazil
117 P 12 Manui, Indonesia
100 M 12 Manūjān, Iran
121 E 25 Manuk Manka, Philippines
136 K 8 Manukau, New Zealand
136 J 9 Manukau Harbour, New Zealand
138 D 2 Manus, Papua New Guinea
138 D 2 Manus Island, Papua New Guinea
18 H 6 Many, LA, U.S.A.
131 T 11 Manyoni, Tanzania
67 P 9 Manzanares, Spain
45 N 12 Manzanillo, Mexico
100 I 6 Manẓariyeh, Iran
110 E 7 Manzhouli, China
76 G 13 Manziana, Italy
133 P 11 Manzini, Swaziland
129 V 9 Mao, Chad
113 R 13 Maoming, China
112 J 11 Maotou Shan, China
133 Q 9 Mapai, Mozambique
45 W 13 Mapastepec, Mexico
117 Y 14 Mapi, Indonesia
117 Y 14 Mapi, Indonesia
121 D 22 Mapin, Philippines
133 R 9 Mapinhane, Mozambique
39 L 20 Maple Creek, SK, Canada
19 P 4 Maplesville, AL, U.S.A.
138 B 3 Maprik, Papua New Guinea
137 H 16 Mapua, New Zealand
54 G 9 Mapuera, Brazil
133 Q 11 Maputo, Mozambique
133 Q 10 Maputo, Mozambique
112 L 3 Maqu, China
67 N 7 Maqueda, Spain
120 K 12 Maqueda Channel, Philippines
132 G 1 Maquela do Zombo, Angola
57 H 17 Maquinchao, Argentina
23 W 12 Maquoketa, IA, U.S.A.
59 E 18 Mar del Plata, Argentina
131 T 9 Mara, Tanzania
54 D 10 Maraã, Brazil
54 J 11 Marabá, Brazil
50 J 2 Maracaibo, Venezuela
55 H 18 Maracaju, Brazil
51 N 3 Maracay, Venezuela
125 W 9 Marādah, Libya
129 R 9 Maradi, Niger
129 R 9 Maradi, Niger
100 F 4 Marāgheh, Iran
140 D 2 Marakei, Kiribati
131 V 7 Maralal, Kenya
130 J 4 Marali, Central African Republic
144 H 3 Marambio, Antarctica
118 D 8 Maran, Malaysia
30 K 14 Marana, AZ, U.S.A.
67 Q 5 Maranchón, Spain
100 F 3 Marand, Iran
54 K 12 Maranhão, Brazil
52 C 11 Marañón, Peru
86 L 10 Mărășești, Romania
77 L 17 Maratea, Italy
19 X 15 Marathon, FL, U.S.A.
26 I 10 Marathon, TX, U.S.A.
40 M 12 Marathon, ON, Canada
136 O 11 Marau Point, New Zealand
121 L 21 Marawi, Philippines
99 U 12 Mar'ayt, Yemen
95 Y 8 Mărază, Azerbaijan
66 M 14 Marbella, Spain
134 H 6 Marble Bar, WA, Australia
30 K 9 Marble Canyon, AZ, U.S.A.
133 O 10 Marble Hall, Republic of South Africa
21 N 16 Marble Head, OH, U.S.A.
25 Y 6 Marble Hill, MO, U.S.A.
29 R 12 Marbleton, WY, U.S.A.
73 F 17 Marburg, Germany
55 H 14 Marcelândia, Brazil
63 W 7 March, U.K.
75 Z 3 March, Austria
76 I 11 Marche, Italy
69 J 22 Marche-en-Famenne, Belgium
75 Z 3 Marchegg, Austria
66 L 12 Marchena, Spain
53 E 18 Marcona, Peru
59 B 14 Marcos Juárez, Argentina
101 W 7 Mardan, Pakistan
95 P 12 Mardin, Turkey
95 P 12 Mardin Dağlari, Turkey
139 R 14 Maré, New Caledonia
45 V 14 Mare Muerto, Mexico
21 D 19 Maredosia, IL, U.S.A.
135 T 3 Mareeba, QLD, Australia
56 H 10 Mareyes, Argentina
26 H 9 Marfa, TX, U.S.A.
134 F 12 Margaret River, WA, Australia
19 Y 13 Margate, FL, U.S.A.
63 Z 11 Margate, U.K.
133 P 13 Margate, Republic of South Africa
107 Y 9 Margherita, India
131 R 7 Margherita Peak, Uganda
86 G 8 Marghita, Romania
121 J 21 Margosatubig, Philippines
144 I 5 Marguerite Bay, Antarctica
97 X 9 Marhaj Kahlīl, Iraq
87 U 8 Marhanets', Ukraine
124 L 6 Marhoum, Algeria
138 A 6 Mari, Papua New Guinea
56 G 5 María Elena, Chile
135 T 15 Maria Island, TAS, Australia
75 P 8 Maria Luggau, Austria
140 A 8 Mariana Islands, Northern Mariana Islands
48 G 4 Marianao, Cuba
19 S 7 Marianna, FL, U.S.A.
71 G 23 Mariannelund, Sweden
58 D 12 Mariano Loza, Argentina
79 A 17 Mariánské Lázně, Czech Republic
75 V 5 Mariazell, Austria
99 Q 12 Ma'rib, Yemen
80 D 6 Maribor, Slovenia
30 J 13 Maricopa, AZ, U.S.A.
33 I 23 Maricopa, CA, U.S.A.
127 D 22 Maridi, Sudan
144 L 9 Marie Byrd Land, Antarctica
49 Y 9 Marie-Galante, Guadeloupe, France
48 G 4 Mariel, Cuba
69 G 23 Mariembourg, Belgium
73 M 18 Marienberg, Germany
132 J 10 Mariental, Namibia
71 F 21 Mariestad, Sweden
19 S 2 Marietta, GA, U.S.A.
21 O 19 Marietta, OH, U.S.A.
85 E 16 Marijampolė, Lithuania
58 I 6 Marília, Brazil
132 H 2 Marimba, Angola
33 G 21 Marina, CA, U.S.A.
76 D 10 Marina di Carrara, Italy
85 J 18 Mar"ina Horka, Belarus
120 H 13 Marinduque, Philippines
20 H 11 Marinette, WI, U.S.A.
57 I 7 Maringá, Brazil
66 G 7 Marinha Grande, Portugal
16 D 6 Marion, KY, U.S.A.
16 M 9 Marion, NC, U.S.A.
17 Q 12 Marion, SC, U.S.A.
17 N 7 Marion, VA, U.S.A.
21 F 22 Marion, IL, U.S.A.
21 J 18 Marion, IN, U.S.A.
21 M 18 Marion, OH, U.S.A.
23 V 12 Marion, IA, U.S.A.
51 X 7 Maripasoula, French Guiana
33 I 20 Mariposa, CA, U.S.A.
117 P 10 Marisa, Indonesia
66 K 12 Marismas del Guadalquivir, Spain
82 K 11 Maritsa, Bulgaria
87 X 8 Mariupol', Ukraine
120 F 11 Mariveles, Philippines
84 F 7 Märjamaa, Estonia
96 G 7 Marjayoun, Lebanon
25 W 3 Mark Twain Lake, MO, U.S.A.
127 L 24 Marka, Somalia
128 J 9 Markala, Mali
112 J 7 Markam, China
105 F 19 Markapur, India
100 H 7 Markazi, Iran
68 M 12 Markelo, Netherlands
68 I 10 Markermeer, Netherlands
63 Q 6 Market Drayton, U.K.
63 T 7 Market Harborough, U.K.
63 V 4 Market Rasen, U.K.
63 U 2 Market Weighton, U.K.
42 F 12 Markham, ON, Canada
108 H 6 Markit, China
87 Z 4 Markivka, Ukraine
68 K 9 Marknesse, Netherlands
130 I 3 Markounda, Central African Republic
89 Y 7 Markovo, Russian Federation
129 N 9 Markoye, Burkina Faso

Country · Internal administrative region: State/Province/Territory/Dependent territory · Capital city · Mountain range/Undersea ridge · Mountain peak/Volcano/Seamount · Geographic feature · Headland/Point/Cape/Peninsula · Desert · Island/Island group · Antarctic base · Ocean · Sea · Bay/Gulf/Channel/Strait · Lake · Salt pan/Dry/Intermittent lake · R

Marks – Mikashevichy

Q 5 Marks, Russian Federation
J 6 Marksville, LA, U.S.A.
K 19 Marktredwitz, Germany
N 8 Marla, SA, Australia
S 11 Marlborough, U.K.
V 6 Marlborough, QLD, Australia
I 17 Marlborough, New Zealand
S 10 Marlborough Downs, U.K.
Q 8 Marlin, TX, U.S.A.
P 4 Marlinton, WV, U.S.A.
U 10 Marlow, U.K.
C 19 Marmagao, India
N 12 Marmande, France
C 8 Marmara, Turkey
C 8 Marmara, Turkey
N 13 Marmaraereğlisi, Turkey
C 13 Marmaris, Turkey
G 5 Marmolada, Italy
F 9 Marne, Germany
U 7 Marneuli, Georgia
X 12 Maro, Chad
N 8 Maroa, Venezuela
Z 6 Maroantsetra, Madgascar
Z 5 Maromokotro, Madgascar
P 7 Marondera, Zimbabwe
X 8 Maroni, French Guiana
W 8 Maroochydore, QLD, Australia
O 5 Maroon Peak, CO, U.S.A.
I 6 Maropiu, New Zealand
N 13 Maros, Indonesia
V 11 Maroua, Cameroon
X 6 Marovoay, Madgascar
W 15 Marquesas Keys, FL, U.S.A.
H 8 Marquette, MI, U.S.A.
R 8 Marquez, TX, U.S.A.
A 17 Marra Plateau, Sudan
G 10 Marradi, Italy
G 8 Marrakech, Morocco
S 15 Marrawah, TAS, Australia
P 9 Marree, SA, Australia
S 7 Marromeu, Mozambique
S 4 Marrupa, Mozambique
W 8 Marsa al Burayqah, Libya
G 11 Marsa Alam, Egypt
C 7 Marsa Matrūḩ, Egypt
V 6 Marsabit, Kenya
G 22 Marsala, Italy
H 8 Marsdiep, Netherlands
U 14 Marseille, France
L 1 Marsh Harbour, The Bahamas
J 8 Marsh Island, LA, U.S.A.
P 9 Marshall, MN, U.S.A.
T 3 Marshall, MO, U.S.A.
U 9 Marshall, AR, U.S.A.
T 6 Marshall, TX, U.S.A.
W 4 Marshall Islands, Oceania
T 12 Marshalltown, IA, U.S.A.
E 11 Marshfield, WI, U.S.A.
V 4 Martanai Besar, Malaysia
L 12 Martapura, Indonesia
F 13 Martapura, Indonesia
K 24 Martelange, Belgium
F 8 Marten River, ON, Canada
O 11 Martha's Vineyard, MA, U.S.A.
C 7 Martigny, Switzerland
C 8 Martin, TN, U.S.A.
I 11 Martin, SD, U.S.A.
I 19 Martin, Slovakia
K 10 Martin Peninsula, Antarctica
N 16 Martina Franca, Italy
L 16 Martinborough, New Zealand
S 11 Martinez, Mexico
Y 11 Martinique, France, France
Y 10 Martinique Passage, Dominica
F 19 Martino, Greece
O 18 Martins Ferry, OH, U.S.A.
S 2 Martinsburg, WV, U.S.A.
Q 7 Martinsville, VA, U.S.A.
I 20 Martinsville, IN, U.S.A.
L 14 Marton, New Zealand
K 4 Martuk, Kazakhstan
U 9 Martuni, Armenia
E 19 Marugame, Japan
O 14 Maruim, Brazil
N 14 Mary, Turkmenistan
W 8 Maryborough, QLD, Australia
T 3 Maryland, U.S.A.
J 6 Marysvale, UT, U.S.A.
L 18 Marysville, OH, U.S.A.
O 2 Marysville, KS, U.S.A.
H 6 Marysville, WA, U.S.A.
G 18 Marysville, CA, U.S.A.
J 9 Maryville, TN, U.S.A.
R 1 Maryville, MO, U.S.A.
N 15 Maryyskiy Velayat, Turkmenistan
G 6 Masagua, Guatemala
R 8 Masaka, Uganda
L 13 Masalembu Besar, Indonesia
L 13 Masalembu Kecil, Indonesia
Y 10 Masalli, Azerbaijan
O 12 Masamba, Indonesia
M 21 Masan, South Korea
W 14 Masasi, Tanzania
L 21 Masavi, Bolivia
N 9 Masaya, Nicaragua
J 14 Masbate, Philippines
J 15 Masbate, Philippines
N 12 Maseru, Lesotho
S 1 Masham, U.K.
O 6 Mashhad, Iran
L 10 Mashiz, Iran
P 6 Mashonaland Central, Zimbabwe
Q 6 Mashonaland East, Zimbabwe
O 6 Mashonaland West, Zimbabwe
K 7 Masi, Norway
J 10 Masi-Manimba, Democratic Republic of Congo
J 6 Masiáca, Mexico
R 7 Masindi, Uganda
T 9 Masis, Armenia
E 14 Masisea, Peru
G 8 Masjed Soleymān, Iran
D 11 Maslenica, Croatia
S 13 Masna'ah, Yemen
W 7 Masoarivo, Madgascar
M 3 Mason, WV, U.S.A.
N 9 Mason, TX, U.S.A.
B 26 Mason Bay, New Zealand
F 18 Mason City, IL, U.S.A.
T 10 Mason City, IA, U.S.A.
E 10 Massa, Italy
F 12 Massa Marittimo, Italy
N 9 Massachusetts, U.S.A.
15 O 9 Massachusetts Bay, MA, U.S.A.
129 V 10 Massaguet, Chad
129 W 9 Massakory, Chad
133 Q 9 Massangena, Mozambique
133 R 4 Massangulo, Mozambique
127 I 16 Massawa, Eritrea
127 I 16 Massawa Channel, Eritrea
14 I 5 Massena, NY, U.S.A.
129 W 10 Massenya, Chad
39 C 19 Masset, BC, Canada
42 C 9 Massey, ON, Canada
65 R 11 Massif Central, France
49 N 8 Massif de la Hotte, Haiti
129 S 6 Massif de L'aïr, Niger
130 L 3 Massif des Bongo, Central African Republic
129 Z 8 Massif du Kapka, Chad
128 G 10 Massif du Tamgué, Guinea
130 H 4 Massif du Yadé, Central African Republic
129 Z 7 Massif Ennedi, Chad
128 J 10 Massigui, Mali
133 R 9 Massinga, Mozambique
133 Q 10 Massingir, Mozambique
145 Y 9 Masson Island, Antarctica
98 L 8 Mastābah, Saudi Arabia
95 Z 8 Mastağa, Azerbaijan
137 L 15 Masterton, New Zealand
48 K 2 Mastic Point, The Bahamas
101 W 5 Mastuj, Pakistan
101 T 11 Mastung, Pakistan
98 L 7 Mastūrah, Saudi Arabia
123 C 19 Masuda, Japan
133 P 8 Masvingo, Zimbabwe
133 P 8 Masvingo, Zimbabwe
96 H 4 Maşyāf, Syria
85 E 21 Masyevichy, Belarus
140 H 8 Matā 'Utu, Wallis and Futuna Islands
133 N 7 Matabeleland North, Zimbabwe
133 O 8 Matabeleland South, Zimbabwe
42 E 7 Matachewan, ON, Canada
130 G 11 Matadi, Democratic Republic of Congo
26 L 4 Matador, TX, U.S.A.
47 N 8 Matagalpa, Nicaragua
41 P 11 Matagami, QC, Canada
27 R 12 Matagorda Bay, TX, U.S.A.
27 R 12 Matagorda Island, TX, U.S.A.
27 R 12 Matagorda Peninsula, TX, U.S.A.
103 U 5 Matak, Kazakhstan
116 G 9 Matak, Indonesia
136 M 9 Matakana Island, New Zealand
136 O 10 Matakaoa Point, New Zealand
132 H 5 Matala, Angola
128 F 8 Matam, Senegal
136 L 10 Matamata, New Zealand
129 R 9 Matamey, Niger
45 S 7 Matamoros, Mexico
121 I 23 Matanal Point, Philippines
43 Q 5 Matane, QC, Canada
48 H 4 Matanzas, Cuba
105 G 25 Matara, Sri Lanka
83 C 19 Mataragka, Greece
116 L 15 Mataram, Indonesia
135 N 2 Mataranka, NT, Australia
67 X 4 Mataró, Spain
136 M 10 Matata, New Zealand
137 D 25 Mataura, New Zealand
137 C 24 Mataura, New Zealand
136 N 11 Matawai, New Zealand
103 W 8 Matay, Kazakhstan
53 L 17 Mategua, Bolivia
45 Q 9 Matehuala, Mexico
131 V 14 Matemanga, Tanzania
77 M 16 Matera, Italy
79 N 21 Mátészalka, Hungary
125 Q 5 Mateur, Tunisia
42 E 6 Matheson, ON, Canada
17 V 6 Mathews, VA, U.S.A.
27 P 13 Mathis, TX, U.S.A.
106 I 9 Mathura, India
121 N 22 Mati, Philippines
55 L 15 Matias Cardoso, Brazil
41 T 8 Matimekosh, QC, Canada
47 R 12 Matina, Costa Rica
84 G 9 Matiši, Latvia
101 U 14 Matli, Pakistan
63 S 5 Matlock, U.K.
121 K 14 Matnog, Philippines
55 H 14 Mato Grosso, Brazil
58 F 6 Mato Grosso do Sul, Brazil
66 H 5 Matosinhos, Portugal
75 P 8 Matrei in Osttirol, Austria
132 J 15 Matroosberg, Republic of South Africa
113 Y 10 Matsu Tao, Taiwan
123 D 18 Matsue, Japan
122 I 8 Matsumae, Japan
123 I 16 Matsumoto, Japan
123 H 18 Matsusaka, Japan
123 D 20 Matsuyama, Japan
42 F 9 Mattawa, ON, Canada
15 R 4 Mattawamkeag, ME, U.S.A.
33 M 15 Matterhorn, NV, U.S.A.
74 D 11 Matterhorn, Switzerland
75 Y 5 Mattersburg, Austria
139 S 14 Matthew Island, Vanuatu
49 N 6 Matthew Town, The Bahamas
75 Q 4 Mattighofen, Austria
21 G 19 Mattoon, IL, U.S.A.
119 O 9 Matu, Malaysia
53 D 16 Matucana, Peru
139 Y 12 Matuku, Fiji
132 I 4 Matumbo, Angola
51 R 3 Maturín, Venezuela
117 Q 8 Matutuang, Indonesia
107 O 11 Mau, India
104 F 13 Mau Rampur, India
133 S 5 Maúa, Mozambique
65 S 2 Maubeuge, France
115 D 16 Maubin, Myanmar
106 L 11 Maudaha, India
54 G 11 Maués, Brazil
140 A 5 Maug Islands, Northern Mariana Islands
107 N 12 Mauganj, India
34 D 7 Maui, HI, U.S.A.
141 P 10 Mauke, Cook Islands
56 F 13 Maule, Chile
57 F 17 Maullín, Chile
21 L 16 Maumee, OH, U.S.A.
132 L 8 Maun, Botswana
34 E 8 Mauna Kea, HI, U.S.A.
34 E 9 Mauna Loa, HI, U.S.A.
136 J 6 Maungatapere, New Zealand
115 F 19 Maungmagan Islands, Myanmar
32 H 10 Maupin, OR, U.S.A.
65 Q 11 Mauriac, France
128 F 6 Mauritania, Africa
11 Q 11 Mauritius, Indian Ocean
20 E 13 Mauston, WI, U.S.A.
75 R 7 Mauterndorf, Austria
131 O 6 Mava, Democratic Republic of Congo
133 S 4 Mavago, Mozambique
132 J 6 Mavengue, Angola
132 K 6 Mavinga, Angola
130 I 11 Mawanga, Democratic Republic of Congo
113 P 10 Mawei, China
145 X 4 Mawson, Antarctica
145 W 4 Mawson Coast, Antarctica
145 T 15 Mawson Peninsula, Antarctica
22 J 4 Max, ND, U.S.A.
56 I 8 Maxán, Argentina
45 Y 10 Maxcanú, Mexico
71 K 15 Maxmo, Finland
89 U 11 Maya, Russian Federation
112 M 4 Maya, China
116 I 11 Maya, Indonesia
46 I 4 Maya Mountains, Guatemala
49 O 4 Mayaguana Island, The Bahamas
49 T 8 Mayagüez, Puerto Rico
129 R 9 Mayahi, Niger
103 T 14 Mayakovskogo, Tajikistan
130 H 10 Mayama, Congo
100 L 5 Mayamey, Iran
127 I 18 Maych'ew, Ethiopia
127 M 9 Maydh, Somalia
64 M 5 Mayenne, France
16 C 7 Mayfield, KY, U.S.A.
137 F 21 Mayfield, New Zealand
82 M 11 Mayha Dağl, Turkey
31 R 13 Mayhill, NM, U.S.A.
103 U 4 Maykain, Kazakhstan
92 L 12 Maykop, Russian Federation
103 T 11 Mayluu-Suu, Kyrgyzstan
103 N 8 Maylybas, Kazakhstan
114 E 11 Maymyo, Myanmar
93 R 3 Mayna, Russian Federation
19 U 8 Mayo, FL, U.S.A.
38 B 12 Mayo, YT, Canada
129 T 12 Mayo-Belwa, Nigeria
129 V 11 Mayo-Kébbi, Chad
130 F 9 Mayoko, Congo
59 B 19 Mayor Buratovich, Argentina
136 M 9 Mayor Island, New Zealand
55 F 17 Mayor Pablo Lagerenza, Paraguay
133 X 4 Mayotte, France
120 G 5 Mayraira Point, Philippines
75 N 7 Mayrhofen, Austria
89 U 13 Mayskiy, Russian Federation
103 V 4 Mayskoye, Kazakhstan
16 J 4 Maysville, KY, U.S.A.
121 E 16 Maytiguid, Philippines
117 R 10 Mayu, Indonesia
130 E 10 Mayumba, Gabon
22 K 15 Maywood, NE, U.S.A.
59 A 18 Maza, Argentina
133 N 5 Mazabuka, Zambia
32 I 5 Mazama, WA, U.S.A.
65 Q 14 Mazamet, France
52 F 10 Mazán, Peru
100 J 5 Māzandarān, Iran
108 G 7 Mazar, China
101 T 5 Mazār-e Sharif, Afghanistan
77 G 22 Mazara del Vallo, Italy
67 R 12 Mazarrón, Spain
44 J 4 Mazatán, Mexico
46 F 6 Mazatenango, Guatemala
44 L 9 Mazatlán, Mexico
30 J 11 Mazatzal Peak, AZ, U.S.A.
84 D 12 Mažeikiai, Lithuania
84 D 9 Mazirbe, Latvia
44 J 4 Mazocahui, Mexico
131 W 12 Mazomora, Tanzania
133 P 9 Mazunga, Zimbabwe
85 L 21 Mazyr, Belarus
133 P 11 Mbabane, Swaziland
128 K 12 Mbahiakro, Côte d'Ivoire
130 J 5 Mbaïki, Central African Republic
129 V 15 Mbalam, Cameroon
131 T 7 Mbale, Uganda
129 T 15 Mbalmayo, Cameroon
138 M 7 Mbalo, Solomon Islands
131 T 14 Mbamba Bay, Tanzania
130 J 8 Mbandaka, Democratic Republic of Congo
129 S 14 Mbanga, Cameroon
132 G 1 M'banza Congo, Angola
130 H 11 Mbanza-Ngungu, Democratic Republic of Congo
131 R 8 Mbarara, Uganda
130 J 5 Mbata, Central African Republic
131 S 12 Mbeya, Tanzania
131 T 13 Mbeya, Tanzania
130 F 9 Mbigou, Gabon
131 U 14 Mbinga, Tanzania
133 P 8 Mbizi, Zimbabwe
131 O 4 Mboki, Central African Republic
130 G 7 Mbomo, Congo
130 M 4 Mbomou, Central African Republic
128 D 8 Mbour, Senegal
128 G 8 Mbout, Mauritania
131 S 13 Mbozi, Tanzania
130 M 11 Mbuji-Mayi, Democratic Republic of Congo
131 U 10 Mbulu, Tanzania
131 U 12 Mbuyuni, Tanzania
43 R 10 McAdam, NB, Canada
25 P 11 McAlester, OK, U.S.A.
27 P 15 McAllen, TX, U.S.A.
17 P 11 McBee, SC, U.S.A.
39 G 19 McBride, BC, Canada
28 K 8 McCall, ID, U.S.A.
26 J 8 McCamey, TX, U.S.A.
29 P 12 McCammon, ID, U.S.A.
38 I 5 McClintock Channel, NU, Canada
14 F 12 McClure, PA, U.S.A.
36 L 4 McClure Strait, NT, Canada
143 O 6 McClure Strait Gulf, Arctic Ocean
22 K 4 McClusky, ND, U.S.A.
18 L 6 McComb, MS, U.S.A.
22 K 15 McCook, NE, U.S.A.
16 M 12 McCormick, SC, U.S.A.
33 K 14 McDermitt, NV, U.S.A.
25 X 13 McGehee, AR, U.S.A.
33 N 17 McGill, NV, U.S.A.
43 S 9 McGivney, NB, Canada
35 P 8 McGrath, AK, U.S.A.
131 X 13 Mchinga, Tanzania
133 Q 4 Mchinji, Malawi
22 J 7 McIntosh, SD, U.S.A.
140 I 4 McKean, Kiribati
16 C 8 McKenzie, TN, U.S.A.
35 R 7 McKinley Park, AK, U.S.A.
27 Q 5 McKinney, TX, U.S.A.
22 J 7 McLaughlin, SD, U.S.A.
21 G 21 McLeansboro, IL, U.S.A.
39 F 18 McLeod Lake, BC, Canada
115 F 21 McLeods Island, Myanmar
20 J 9 McMillan, MI, U.S.A.
16 H 9 McMinnville, TN, U.S.A.
32 F 10 McMinnville, OR, U.S.A.
145 R 12 McMurdo, Antarctica
25 N 5 Mcpherson, KS, U.S.A.
19 U 5 McRae, GA, U.S.A.
133 O 14 Mdantsane, Republic of South Africa
24 I 7 Meade, KS, U.S.A.
35 O 3 Meade, AK, U.S.A.
39 L 17 Meadow Lake, SK, Canada
14 B 10 Meadville, PA, U.S.A.
66 H 6 Mealhada, Portugal
41 V 8 Mealy Mountains, NL, Canada
65 Q 4 Meaux, France
33 L 25 Mecca, CA, U.S.A.
98 M 8 Mecca, Saudi Arabia
69 G 18 Mechelen, Belgium
124 L 7 Mecheria, Algeria
94 K 8 Mecitözü, Turkey
72 K 10 Mecklenburg-Vorpommern, Germany
72 J 8 Mecklenburger Bucht, Germany
133 T 4 Mecula, Mozambique
116 C 9 Medan, Indonesia
59 B 19 Médanos, Argentina
124 M 5 Médéa, Algeria
50 G 5 Medellín, Colombia
68 I 9 Medemblik, Netherlands
125 R 7 Medenine, Tunisia
128 E 7 Mederdra, Mauritania
20 E 11 Medford, WI, U.S.A.
32 F 13 Medford, OR, U.S.A.
52 I 12 Media Luna, Argentina
86 I 10 Mediaș, Romania
76 G 9 Medicina, Italy
29 X 13 Medicine Bow, WY, U.S.A.
39 K 20 Medicine Hat, AB, Canada
24 L 7 Medicine Lodge, KS, U.S.A.
14 D 8 Medina, NY, U.S.A.
22 L 5 Medina, ND, U.S.A.
98 M 6 Medina, Saudi Arabia
66 M 4 Medina de Rioseco, Spain
66 M 5 Medina del Campo, Spain
128 F 9 Medina Gounas, Senegal
67 Q 5 Medinaceli, Spain
107 R 14 Medinipur, India
85 G 16 Medininkai, Lithuania
130 E 7 Médouneu, Gabon
81 M 15 Medveda, Serbia and Montenegro
90 H 8 Medvezh'yegorsk, Russian Federation
92 J 2 Medyn', Russian Federation
134 G 8 Meekatharra, WA, Australia
31 N 4 Meeker, CO, U.S.A.
69 H 16 Meer, Belgium
68 I 13 Meerkerk, Netherlands
69 J 19 Meerssen, Belgium
106 J 8 Meerut, India
29 T 10 Meeteetse, WY, U.S.A.
127 I 23 Mēga, Ethiopia
127 H 23 Mega Escarpment, Ethiopia
127 J 21 Megalo, Ethiopia
83 D 21 Megalopoli, Greece
83 B 18 Meganisi, Greece
83 G 20 Megara, Greece
107 V 11 Meghalaya, India
107 U 13 Meghna Shahbazpur, Bangladesh
95 V 10 Meghri, Azerbaijan
94 D 14 Megisti, Greece
86 G 12 Mehadica, Romania
70 L 5 Mehamn, Norway
101 U 13 Mehar, Pakistan
107 O 10 Mehndawal, India
100 L 8 Mehr Jān, Iran
100 F 7 Mehrān, Iran
113 Y 7 Meicheng, China
129 U 13 Meiganga, Cameroon
112 M 8 Meigu, China
111 K 14 Meihekou, China
114 D 12 Meiktila, Myanmar
73 H 18 Meiningen, Germany
112 M 7 Meishan, China
73 M 16 Meissen, Germany
110 M 9 Meixi, China
113 V 11 Meizhou, China
56 H 9 Mejicana, Argentina
56 F 5 Mejillones, Chile
141 Z 2 Mejit Island, Marshall Islands
130 G 7 Mékambo, Gabon
127 I 18 Mek'elē, Ethiopia
128 D 8 Mékhé, Senegal
101 U 10 Mekhtar, Pakistan
124 I 7 Meknès, Morocco
115 L 20 Mekong, Asia
118 C 10 Melaka, Malaysia
118 C 9 Melaka, Malaysia
119 U 6 Melalap, Malaysia
138 H 2 Melanesia, Oceania
19 X 10 Melbourne, FL, U.S.A.
25 W 9 Melbourne, AR, U.S.A.
135 S 13 Melbourne, VIC, Australia
46 J 2 Melchor de Mencos, Guatemala
42 B 9 Meldrum Bay, ON, Canada
93 W 3 Meleuz, Russian Federation
129 X 10 Mélfi, Chad
39 M 17 Melfort, SK, Canada
66 I 2 Melide, Spain
83 D 22 Meligalas, Greece
67 P 15 Melilla, Spain
56 F 12 Melipilla, Chile
40 H 10 Melita, MB, Canada
77 L 22 Melito di Porto Salvo, Italy
87 V 9 Melitopol', Ukraine
82 I 12 Melivoia, Greece
75 V 4 Melk, Austria
127 I 23 Melka Guba, Ethiopia
63 R 11 Melksham, U.K.
74 J 7 Mellau, Austria
69 E 18 Melle, Belgium
20 E 9 Mellen, WI, U.S.A.
71 E 21 Mellerud, Sweden
22 M 8 Mellette, SD, U.S.A.
72 E 10 Mellum, Germany
79 D 17 Mělník, Czech Republic
59 G 14 Melo, Uruguay
29 O 7 Melrose, MT, U.S.A.
29 U 5 Melstone, MT, U.S.A.
70 L 10 Meltaus, Finland
135 S 13 Melton, VIC, Australia
63 U 6 Melton Mowbray, U.K.
65 Q 5 Melun, France
127 E 19 Melut, Sudan
39 O 18 Melville, SK, Canada
37 N 4 Melville Island, NU, Canada
134 M 1 Melville Island, NT, Australia
41 O 1 Melville Peninsula, NU, Canada
116 J 11 Memala, Indonesia
133 U 5 Memba, Mozambique
117 X 11 Memberamo, Indonesia
73 H 25 Memmingen, Germany
116 I 10 Mempawah, Indonesia
16 A 10 Memphis, TN, U.S.A.
26 L 3 Memphis, TX, U.S.A.
25 S 12 Mena, AR, U.S.A.
87 R 2 Mena, Ukraine
62 M 4 Menai Bridge, U.K.
129 O 8 Ménaka, Mali
117 Q 11 Menanga, Indonesia
65 R 12 Mende, France
127 I 22 Mendebo Mountains, Ethiopia
127 I 17 Mendefera, Eritrea
143 S 6 Mendeleyev Ridge, Arctic Ocean
93 T 1 Mendeleyevsk, Russian Federation
18 M 5 Mendenhall, MS, U.S.A.
45 R 7 Méndez, Mexico
127 G 20 Mendi, Ethiopia
138 B 5 Mendi, Papua New Guinea
63 P 11 Mendip Hills, U.K.
33 E 17 Mendocino, CA, U.S.A.
21 F 16 Mendota, IL, U.S.A.
56 H 11 Mendoza, Argentina
56 H 12 Mendoza, Argentina
69 B 19 Menen, Belgium
141 U 1 Meneng Point, Nauru
77 H 22 Menfi, Italy
119 U 5 Mengalum, Malaysia
113 V 4 Mengcheng, China
116 G 13 Menggala, Indonesia
112 J 13 Menghai, China
112 K 13 Mengla, China
113 R 11 Mengshan, China
113 W 2 Mengyin, China
112 J 13 Mengzhe, China
112 M 12 Mengzi, China
135 R 10 Menindee, NSW, Australia
135 R 10 Menindee Lake, NSW, Australia
89 S 9 Menkere, Russian Federation
21 G 14 Menomonee Falls, WI, U.S.A.
132 I 5 Menongue, Angola
116 G 12 Mentok, Indonesia
109 P 7 Menyuan, China
93 U 1 Menzelinsk, Russian Federation
134 I 10 Menzies, WA, Australia
68 L 9 Meppel, Netherlands
72 D 12 Meppen, Germany
64 G 5 Mer d'Iroise, France
116 G 13 Merak, Indonesia
76 F 5 Merano, Italy
117 Y 15 Merauke, Indonesia
50 F 8 Mercaderes, Colombia
33 H 20 Merced, CA, U.S.A.
58 D 11 Mercedes, Argentina
59 D 15 Mercedes, Uruguay
14 A 11 Mercer, PA, U.S.A.
20 E 9 Mercer, WI, U.S.A.
136 L 8 Mercury Bay, New Zealand
136 L 8 Mercury Islands, New Zealand
139 R 9 Mere Lava, Vanuatu
127 N 23 Mereeg, Somalia
136 K 9 Meremere, New Zealand
115 F 20 Mergui, Myanmar
115 E 21 Mergui Archipelago, Myanmar
82 L 12 Meriç, Turkey
45 Y 10 Mérida, Mexico
50 K 4 Mérida, Venezuela
50 L 4 Mérida, Venezuela
66 K 9 Mérida, Spain
14 L 11 Meriden, CT, U.S.A.
19 N 5 Meridian, MS, U.S.A.
124 J 8 Meridja, Algeria
71 J 17 Merikarvia, Finland
73 I 24 Mering, Germany
139 I 15 Merir, Palau
119 R 9 Merit, Malaysia
103 T 10 Merke, Kazakhstan
85 F 17 Merkinė, Lithuania
127 E 15 Merowe, Sudan
134 H 11 Merredin, WA, Australia
20 F 10 Merrill, WI, U.S.A.
22 I 11 Merriman, NE, U.S.A.
39 G 21 Merritt, BC, Canada
19 X 10 Merritt Island, FL, U.S.A.
127 J 17 Mersa Fatma, Eritrea
127 I 16 Mersa Gulbub, Eritrea
69 L 25 Mersch, Luxembourg
63 Y 9 Mersea Island, U.K.
63 P 4 Mersey, U.K.
94 J 13 Mersin, Turkey
118 E 9 Mersing, Malaysia
84 E 10 Mērsrags, Latvia
104 C 12 Merta, India
63 O 10 Merthyr Tydfil, U.K.
131 W 7 Merti, Kenya
66 I 11 Mértola, Portugal
131 V 9 Meru, Tanzania
131 V 7 Meru, Kenya
119 W 7 Merutai, Malaysia
94 K 8 Merzifon, Turkey
73 B 21 Merzig, Germany
30 J 12 Mesa, AZ, U.S.A.
31 S 12 Mesa, NM, U.S.A.
45 P 9 Mesa Central, Mexico
23 S 4 Mesabi Range, MN, U.S.A.
77 O 16 Mesagne, Italy
73 E 16 Meschede, Germany
20 J 12 Mesick, MI, U.S.A.
83 F 14 Mesimeri, Greece
74 H 10 Mesocco, Switzerland
83 C 19 Mesolongi, Greece
58 D 13 Mesopotamia, Argentina
27 Q 6 Mesquite, TX, U.S.A.
33 N 21 Mesquite, NV, U.S.A.
125 N 7 Messaad, Algeria
77 L 21 Messina, Italy
133 P 9 Messina, Republic of South Africa
83 D 22 Messiniakos Kolpos, Greece
82 G 11 Mesta, Bulgaria
76 G 7 Mestre, Italy
50 J 7 Meta, Colombia
50 M 6 Meta, Colombia
41 R 3 Meta Incognita Peninsula, NU, Canada
42 M 6 Métabetchouan, QC, Canada
18 L 8 Metairie, LA, U.S.A.
56 I 6 Metán, Argentina
133 R 4 Metangula, Mozambique
46 I 6 Metapan, El Salvador
133 S 5 Metarica, Mozambique
43 S 12 Meteghan, NS, Canada
127 H 18 Metema, Ethiopia
138 G 3 Meteran, Papua New Guinea
137 G 20 Methven, New Zealand
81 G 14 Metković, Croatia
125 P 7 Metlaoui, Tunisia
133 U 4 Metoro, Mozambique
116 G 13 Metro, Indonesia
21 F 23 Metropolis, IL, U.S.A.
83 C 16 Metsovo, Greece
127 G 21 Metu, Ethiopia
65 V 4 Metz, France
69 H 21 Meuse, Belgium
62 K 15 Mevagissey, U.K.
27 R 7 Mexia, TX, U.S.A.
44 F 2 Mexicali, Mexico
30 L 7 Mexican Hat, UT, U.S.A.
14 G 7 Mexico, NY, U.S.A.
25 V 3 Mexico, MO, U.S.A.
45 N 8 Mexico, North America
45 Q 12 México, Mexico
45 R 12 Mexico City, Mexico
101 R 6 Meymaneh, Afghanistan
100 I 7 Meymeh, Iran
45 V 13 Mezcalapa, Mexico
82 G 8 Mezdra, Bulgaria
90 M 5 Mezen', Russian Federation
90 M 5 Mezen', Russian Federation
90 M 4 Mezenskaya Guba, Russian Federation
45 S 7 Mezquital, Mexico
133 Q 4 Mfuwe, Zambia
77 K 25 Mgarr, Malta
133 Q 11 Mhlume, Swaziland
123 C 19 Mi-shima, Japan
121 H 17 Miagao, Philippines
45 T 14 Miahuatlán, Mexico
66 L 9 Miajadas, Spain
19 Y 13 Miami, FL, U.S.A.
25 R 7 Miami, OK, U.S.A.
19 Y 13 Miami Beach, FL, U.S.A.
101 X 10 Mian Chanmum, Pakistan
100 F 4 Miandowāb, Iran
133 X 8 Miandrivazo, Madgascar
110 H 8 Mianduhe, China
100 G 4 Mīāneh, Iran
117 R 8 Miangas, Indonesia
121 O 24 Miangas, Philippines
112 L 8 Mianning, China
78 G 8 Mianowice, Poland
101 W 8 Mianwali, Pakistan
113 O 4 Mianxian, China
113 N 6 Mianyang, China
111 G 18 Miaodao Qundao, China
113 Z 11 Miaoli, Taiwan
133 Y 8 Miarinarivo, Madgascar
88 I 11 Miass, Russian Federation
78 G 9 Miastko, Poland
113 O 5 Micang Shan, China
79 M 20 Michalovce, Slovakia
20 J 12 Michigan, U.S.A.
21 I 16 Michigan City, IN, U.S.A.
42 A 7 Michipicoten Bay, ON, Canada
40 M 12 Michipicoten Island, ON, Canada
42 A 6 Michipicoten River, ON, Canada
45 O 12 Michoacán, Mexico
92 M 4 Michurinsk, Russian Federation
47 P 9 Mico, Nicaragua
49 Z 11 Micoud, St Lucia
107 O 8 Mid Western, Nepal
116 H 9 Midai, Indonesia
69 D 15 Middelburg, Netherlands
132 M 14 Middelburg, Republic of South Africa
68 H 8 Middenmeer, Netherlands
105 N 21 Middle Andaman, India
137 E 24 Middlemarch, New Zealand
135 U 6 Middlemount, QLD, Australia
16 K 7 Middlesboro, KY, U.S.A.
61 K 15 Middlesbrough, U.K.
46 K 2 Middlesex, Belize
16 B 10 Middleton, TN, U.S.A.
43 T 10 Middleton, NS, Canada
135 Q 6 Middleton, QLD, Australia
14 J 11 Middletown, NY, U.S.A.
14 J 13 Middletown, NJ, U.S.A.
14 L 11 Middletown, CT, U.S.A.
17 W 2 Middletown, DE, U.S.A.
63 Q 4 Middlewich, U.K.
124 I 7 Midelt, Morocco
63 U 12 Midhurst, U.K.
65 O 14 Midi-Pyrénées, France
20 K 13 Midland, MI, U.S.A.
26 J 7 Midland, TX, U.S.A.
42 E 11 Midland, ON, Canada
133 O 7 Midlands, Zimbabwe
27 O 12 Midlothian, TX, U.S.A.
133 X 10 Midongy Atsimo, Madgascar
121 L 22 Midsayap, Philippines
29 X 11 Midwest, WY, U.S.A.
25 N 10 Midwest City, OK, U.S.A.
46 K 1 Midwinters Lagoon, Belize
95 Q 12 Midyat, Turkey
82 F 7 Midzhur, Bulgaria
123 D 21 Mie, Japan
78 F 12 Międzychód, Poland
78 N 13 Międzyrzec Podlaski, Poland
78 E 12 Międzyrzecz, Poland
79 L 17 Mielec, Poland
131 V 13 Miembwe, Tanzania
66 L 1 Mieres, Spain
69 J 16 Mierlo, Netherlands
78 I 7 Mierzeja Helska, Poland
78 I 8 Mierzeja Wiślana, Poland
113 O 3 Migang Shan, China
107 Y 8 Miging, India
76 G 8 Migliarino, Italy
45 O 8 Miguel Auza, Mexico
47 V 13 Miguel de la Borda, Panama
114 C 13 Migyaunye, Myanmar
123 E 19 Mihara, Japan
68 H 12 Mijdrecht, Netherlands
85 I 21 Mikashevichy, Belarus

Country | Internal administrative region: State/Province/Territory/Dependent territory | Capital city | Mountain range/Undersea ridge | Mountain peak/Volcano/Seamount | Geographic feature | Headland/Point/Cape/Peninsula | Desert | Island/Island group | Antarctic base | Ocean | Sea | Bay/Gulf/Channel/Strait | Lake | Salt pan/Dry/Intermittent lake | River

Mikhaylov – Mount Capotoah

92 L 2 Mikhaylov, Russian Federation
93 O 7 Mikhaylovka, Russian Federation
103 U 2 Mikhaylovka, Kazakhstan
88 L 13 Mikhaylovskiy, Russian Federation
145 Y 7 Mikhaytov Island, Antarctica
71 N 17 Mikkeli, Finland
131 V 12 Mikumi, Tanzania
91 P 8 Mikun', Russian Federation
123 L 18 Mikura-jima, Japan
23 S 6 Milaca, MN, U.S.A.
105 B 25 Miladhunmadulu Atoll, Maldives
16 B 8 Milan, TN, U.S.A.
25 T 1 Milan, MO, U.S.A.
76 C 7 Milan, Italy
133 S 6 Milange, Mozambique
80 N 11 Milanovac, Serbia and Montenegro
94 B 12 Milas, Turkey
85 H 19 Milavidy, Belarus
23 O 8 Milbank, SD, U.S.A.
15 R 5 Milbridge, ME, U.S.A.
63 W 7 Mildenhall, U.K.
135 R 11 Mildura, VIC, Australia
112 M 11 Mile, China
127 J 19 Milē, Ethiopia
135 V 8 Miles, QLD, Australia
29 X 6 Miles City, MT, U.S.A.
14 I 11 Milford, PA, U.S.A.
14 L 12 Milford, CT, U.S.A.
15 N 10 Milford, MA, U.S.A.
15 N 8 Milford, NH, U.S.A.
17 W 3 Milford, DE, U.S.A.
30 I 6 Milford, UT, U.S.A.
62 K 9 Milford Haven, U.K.
25 N 3 Milford Lake, KS, U.S.A.
137 A 22 Milford Sound, New Zealand
137 B 22 Milford Sound, New Zealand
141 Z 4 Mili, Marshall Islands
79 G 14 Milicz, Poland
134 M 1 Milikapiti, NT, Australia
89 Z 11 Mil'kovo, Russian Federation
41 P 3 Mill Island, NU, Canada
145 Y 10 Mill Island, Antarctica
65 R 13 Millau, France
23 R 6 Mille Lacs, MN, U.S.A.
19 U 4 Milledgeville, GA, U.S.A.
141 S 6 Millennium, Kiribati
92 M 8 Millerovo, Russian Federation
14 F 13 Millersburg, PA, U.S.A.
21 N 17 Millersburg, OH, U.S.A.
76 B 9 Millesimo, Italy
135 Q 13 Millicent, SA, Australia
15 R 3 Millinocket, ME, U.S.A.
19 O 3 Millport, AL, U.S.A.
38 G 13 Mills Lake, NT, Canada
43 R 10 Milltown, NB, Canada
61 B 19 Milltown Malbay, Republic of Ireland
14 I 15 Millville, NJ, U.S.A.
21 M 18 Millwood, OH, U.S.A.
25 T 13 Millwood Lake, AR, U.S.A.
138 G 7 Milne Bay, Papua New Guinea
138 H 7 Milne Bay, Papua New Guinea
63 P 1 Milnthorpe, U.K.
15 Q 4 Milo, ME, U.S.A.
83 H 23 Milos, Greece
87 Z 4 Milove, Ukraine
14 F 12 Milton, PA, U.S.A.
19 P 7 Milton, FL, U.S.A.
137 E 25 Milton, New Zealand
32 K 9 Milton-Freewater, OR, U.S.A.
63 U 9 Milton Keynes, U.K.
25 N 3 Miltonvale, KS, U.S.A.
21 H 14 Milwaukee, WI, U.S.A.
64 L 13 Mimizan, France
130 F 8 Mimongo, Gabon
112 M 7 Min, China
33 K 19 Mina, NV, U.S.A.
99 W 5 Mina Jebel Ali, United Arab Emirates
99 S 3 Minā' Sa'ūd, Kuwait
100 M 13 Mīnāb, Iran
123 B 23 Minamata, Japan
48 K 5 Minas, Cuba
59 F 15 Minas, Uruguay
43 U 10 Minas Basin, NS, Canada
43 T 10 Minas Channel, NS, Canada
58 F 13 Minas de Corrales, Uruguay
48 F 4 Minas de Matahambre, Cuba
55 L 16 Minas Gerais, Brazil
45 V 13 Minatitlán, Mexico
114 C 13 Minbu, Myanmar
57 F 18 Minchinmávida, Chile
121 M 21 Mindanao, Philippines
121 K 22 Mindanao, Philippines
73 H 24 Mindelheim, Germany
18 H 4 Minden, LA, U.S.A.
42 F 11 Minden, ON, Canada
72 F 13 Minden, Germany
120 G 13 Mindoro, Philippines
121 F 14 Mindoro Strait, Philippines
123 C 20 Mine, Japan
61 D 20 Mine Head, Republic of Ireland
63 N 11 Minehead, U.K.
27 S 6 Mineola, TX, U.S.A.
27 O 6 Mineral Wells, TX, U.S.A.
93 O 13 Mineral'nyye Vody, Russian Federation
30 I 6 Minersville, UT, U.S.A.
77 M 15 Minervino Murge, Italy
131 P 14 Minga, Democratic Republic of Congo
95 W 8 Mingäçevir, Azerbaijan
95 W 7 Mingäçevir Su Anbari, Azerbaijan
130 L 4 Mingala, Central African Republic
134 G 10 Mingenew, WA, Australia
113 T 13 Minggang, China
114 D 9 Mingin Range, Myanmar
110 K 10 Mingshui, China
60 D 11 Mingulay, U.K.
113 W 9 Mingxi, China
115 D 15 Minhla, Myanmar
113 X 10 Minhou, China
105 B 24 Minicoy Island, India
29 N 12 Minidoka, ID, U.S.A.
134 F 7 Minilya Bridge Roadhouse, WA, Australia
106 H 2 Minimarg, India
94 C 8 Gönen, Turkey
128 I 11 Mininian, Côte d'Ivoire
109 P 7 Minle, China
129 Q 11 Minna, Nigeria
23 R 8 Minneapolis, MN, U.S.A.
24 J 6 Minneola, KS, U.S.A.
23 O 6 Minnesota, U.S.A.
23 R 8 Minnesota, MN, U.S.A.
67 Z 7 Minorca, Spain
22 J 3 Minot, ND, U.S.A.
85 J 17 Minsk, Belarus
78 L 13 Mińsk Mazowiecki, Poland
85 J 18 Minskaya Voblasts', Belarus
129 U 14 Minta, Cameroon
35 Q 7 Minto, AK, U.S.A.
43 S 9 Minto, NB, Canada
38 F 7 Minto Inlet, NT, Canada
39 N 20 Minton, SK, Canada
77 J 15 Minturno, Italy
107 Z 8 Minutang, India
130 F 6 Minvoul, Gabon
109 Q 9 Minxian, China
93 X 1 Minyar, Russian Federation
107 Z 9 Minzong, India
20 L 11 Mio, MI, U.S.A.
85 H 18 Mir, Belarus
66 H 6 Mira, Portugal
54 J 13 Miracema do Tocantins, Brazil
101 V 8 Miram Shah, Pakistan
59 D 18 Miramar, Argentina
43 T 7 Miramichi Bay, NB, Canada
65 N 12 Miramont-de-Guyenne, France
51 O 3 Miranda, Venezuela
55 G 17 Miranda, Brazil
67 P 2 Miranda de Ebro, Spain
66 J 4 Mirandela, Portugal
58 H 5 Mirandópolis, Brazil
81 M 20 Miras, Albania
99 X 11 Mirbāṭ, Oman
119 R 7 Miri, Malaysia
135 V 7 Miriam Vale, QLD, Australia
101 P 11 Mirjāveh, Iran
145 Y 8 Mirny, Antarctica
89 R 11 Mirnyy, Russian Federation
78 F 10 Mirosławiec, Poland
101 U 14 Mirpur Khas, Pakistan
101 U 15 Mirpur Sakro, Pakistan
127 N 22 Mirsale, Somalia
83 F 22 Mirtoö Pelagos, Greece
107 N 12 Mirzapur, India
123 D 21 Misaki, Japan
122 K 9 Misawa, Japan
43 U 6 Miscou Island, NB, Canada
101 Y 5 Misgar, Pakistan
106 H 1 Misgar, India
105 O 24 Misha, India
110 N 11 Mishan, China
107 Z 8 Mishmi Hills, India
138 C 5 Misiki, Papua New Guinea
58 F 10 Misiones, Argentina
99 O 6 Miskah, Saudi Arabia
79 L 21 Miskolc, Hungary
117 T 11 Misoöl, Indonesia
125 T 7 Mişrātah, Libya
22 J 11 Mission, SD, U.S.A.
41 N 9 Missisa Lake, ON, Canada
42 E 13 Mississauga, ON, Canada
13 S 11 Mississippi, U.S.A., U.S.A.
18 K 3 Mississippi, U.S.A.
18 M 9 Mississippi Delta, LA, U.S.A.
18 M 7 Mississippi Sound, MS, U.S.A.
29 N 5 Missoula, MT, U.S.A.
124 J 7 Missour, Morocco
12 M 5 Missouri, U.S.A., U.S.A.
25 S 5 Missouri, U.S.A.
27 S 10 Missouri City, TX, U.S.A.
23 P 12 Missouri Valley, IA, U.S.A.
41 R 11 Mistassini, QC, Canada
75 Y 2 Mistelbach, Austria
48 F 7 Misteriosa Bank, Cayman Islands
87 Y 5 Mistky, Ukraine
54 H 8 Mitaraka, Brazil
23 N 10 Mitchell, SD, U.S.A.
32 I 11 Mitchell, OR, U.S.A.
135 R 3 Mitchell, QLD, Australia
135 T 8 Mitchell, QLD, Australia
61 C 20 Mitchelstown, Republic of Ireland
101 V 15 Mithi, Pakistan
141 P 10 Mitiaro, Cook Islands
123 L 15 Mito, Japan
131 W 13 Mitole, Tanzania
122 K 6 Mitsuishi, Japan
123 A 20 Mitsushima, Japan
74 J 7 Mittelberg, Austria
74 L 8 Mittelberg, Austria
75 P 7 Mittersill, Austria
73 M 26 Mittlespitze, Germany
50 L 9 Mitú, Colombia
131 P 13 Mitwaba, Democratic Republic of Congo
130 E 7 Mitzic, Gabon
123 K 17 Miura, Japan
123 L 18 Miyake-jima, Japan
122 L 10 Miyako, Japan
123 O 26 Miyako-jima, Japan
123 N 26 Miyako-rettō, Japan
123 C 23 Miyakonojō, Japan
102 J 5 Miyaly, Kazakhstan
123 D 23 Miyazaki, Japan
123 G 17 Miyazu, Japan
123 D 19 Miyoshi, Japan
111 E 16 Miyun, China
127 G 21 Mizan Teferi, Ethiopia
125 S 8 Mizdah, Libya
61 A 21 Mizen Head, Republic of Ireland
86 I 6 Mizhhir"ya, Ukraine
113 R 1 Mizhi, China
86 L 12 Mizil, Romania
82 G 7 Miziya, Bulgaria
107 W 13 Mizoram, India
96 E 11 Mizpe Ramon, Israel
145 T 3 Mizuho, Antarctica
71 F 22 Mjölby, Sweden
131 W 11 Mkata, Tanzania
131 W 10 Mkomazi, Tanzania
133 O 4 Mkushi, Zambia
79 D 16 Mladá Boleslav, Czech Republic
80 L 11 Mladenovac, Serbia and Montenegro
78 K 11 Mława, Poland
81 G 15 Mljet, Croatia
81 F 15 Mljetski Kanal, Croatia
70 F 11 Mo i Rana, Norway
49 N 6 Moa, Cuba
117 S 14 Moa, Indonesia
135 R 1 Moa Island, QLD, Australia
30 M 5 Moab, UT, U.S.A.
139 Y 12 Moala, Fiji
133 Q 10 Moamba, Mozambique
137 G 18 Moana, New Zealand
130 F 8 Moanda, Gabon
100 I 8 Mobārakeh, Iran
130 L 5 Mobaye, Central African Republic
130 L 5 Mobayi-Mbongo, Democratic Republic of Congo
25 U 3 Moberly, MO, U.S.A.
19 O 7 Mobile, AL, U.S.A.
19 O 7 Mobile Bay, AL, U.S.A.
22 K 7 Mobridge, SD, U.S.A.
114 L 12 Môc Châu, Vietnam
49 Q 7 Moca, Dominican Republic
133 U 5 Moçambique, Mozambique
99 O 14 Mocha, Yemen
133 U 3 Mocimboa da Praia, Mozambique
132 H 4 Môco, Angola
50 G 9 Mocoa, Colombia
58 K 5 Mococa, Brazil
44 M 4 Moctezuma, Mexico
133 S 6 Mocuba, Mozambique
65 W 11 Modane, France
30 H 6 Modena, UT, U.S.A.
76 F 8 Modena, Italy
33 H 20 Modesto, CA, U.S.A.
46 J 4 Modesto Méndez, Guatemala
77 K 24 Modica, Italy
75 X 4 Mödling, Austria
109 R 3 Modot, Mongolia
80 H 10 Modriča, Bosnia and Herzegovina
135 S 13 Moe, VIC, Australia
136 K 7 Moehau, New Zealand
51 X 6 Moengo, Suriname
73 C 15 Moers, Germany
106 H 6 Moga, India
127 M 24 Mogadishu, Somalia
130 J 6 Mogalo, Democratic Republic of Congo
122 J 12 Mogami, Japan
114 E 8 Mogaung, Myanmar
58 J 5 Mogi-Guaçu, Brazil
82 C 12 Mogila, Macedonia (F.Y.R.O.M.)
78 H 12 Mogilno, Poland
133 U 5 Mogincual, Mozambique
89 S 13 Mogocha, Russian Federation
127 E 20 Mogogh, Sudan
114 E 10 Mogok, Myanmar
47 N 7 Mogotón, Nicaragua
110 H 9 Moguqi, China
79 I 26 Mohács, Hungary
124 H 7 Mohammedia, Morocco
14 J 8 Mohawk, NY, U.S.A.
110 H 4 Mohe, China
133 W 4 Mohéli, Comoros
132 K 7 Mohembo, Botswana
143 R 13 Mohns Ridge, Arctic Ocean
114 E 9 Mohnyin, Myanmar
53 H 18 Moho, Peru
131 W 13 Mohoro, Tanzania
86 M 6 Mohyliv-Podil's'kyy, Ukraine
107 X 12 Moirang, India
83 I 26 Moires, Greece
58 B 13 Moisés Ville, Argentina
43 S 3 Moisie, QC, Canada
129 X 12 Moïssala, Chad
33 J 23 Mojave, CA, U.S.A.
33 K 23 Mojave Desert, CA, U.S.A.
112 K 12 Mojiang, China
123 C 20 Mojikō, Japan
81 J 14 Mojkovac, Serbia and Montenegro
107 X 10 Mokokchung, India
137 D 25 Mokoreta, New Zealand
111 L 21 Mokp'o, South Korea
129 P 11 Mokwa, Nigeria
69 I 17 Mol, Belgium
77 N 15 Mola di Bari, Italy
45 R 11 Molango, Mexico
83 F 23 Molaoi, Greece
80 B 11 Molat, Croatia
71 B 15 Molde, Norway
87 N 9 Moldova, Europe
43 T 11 Molega Lake, NS, Canada
130 K 5 Molegbe, Democratic Republic of Congo
132 M 10 Molepolole, Botswana
85 G 14 Molėtai, Lithuania
77 M 15 Molfetta, Italy
67 R 6 Molina de Aragón, Spain
21 E 16 Moline, IL, U.S.A.
25 P 7 Moline, KS, U.S.A.
131 R 12 Moliro, Democratic Republic of Congo
77 K 14 Molise, Italy
77 L 17 Moliterno, Italy
75 Q 8 Möll, Austria
53 F 20 Mollendo, Peru
67 V 4 Mollerussa, Spain
72 I 10 Mölln, Germany
87 V 8 Molochans'k, Ukraine
87 V 9 Molochnyy Lyman, Ukraine
145 V 2 Molodezhnaya, Antarctica
103 T 4 Molodezhnyy, Kazakhstan
34 D 7 Molokai, HI, U.S.A.
83 E 18 Molos, Greece
129 V 15 Moloundou, Cameroon
133 N 13 Molteno, Republic of South Africa
117 U 14 Molu, Indonesia
117 Q 11 Molucca Sea, Indonesia
117 T 10 Moluccas, Indonesia
133 S 5 Molumbo, Mozambique
133 T 6 Moma, Mozambique
131 X 10 Mombasa, Kenya
107 X 12 Mombi New, India
82 J 12 Momchilgrad, Bulgaria
120 H 12 Mompog Passage, Philippines
130 L 8 Mompono, Democratic Republic of Congo
50 I 3 Mompós, Colombia
89 U 8 Momskiy Khrebet, Russian Federation
71 E 26 Møn, Denmark
115 E 16 Mon, Myanmar
65 X 13 Monaco, Monaco
65 W 13 Monaco, Europe
51 R 3 Monagas, Venezuela
26 I 8 Monahans, TX, U.S.A.
133 U 5 Monapo, Mozambique
77 B 19 Monastir, Italy
125 R 6 Monastir, Tunisia
122 K 6 Monbetsu, Japan
129 U 11 Monboré, Cameroon
90 H 3 Monchegorsk, Russian Federation
73 B 16 Mönchengladbach, Germany
75 Y 4 Mönchhof, Austria
17 Q 14 Moncks Corner, SC, U.S.A.
45 P 6 Monclova, Mexico
43 U 9 Moncton, NB, Canada
77 I 21 Mondello, Italy
130 L 6 Mondjamboli, Democratic Republic of Congo
129 V 9 Mondo, Chad
66 J 1 Mondoñedo, Spain
76 A 9 Mondovì, Italy
77 I 15 Mondragone, Italy
75 R 5 Mondsee, Austria
83 F 23 Monemvasia, Greece
14 B 13 Monessen, PA, U.S.A.
66 J 2 Monforte, Spain
66 I 9 Monforte, Portugal
114 N 11 Mong Cai, Vietnam
114 F 13 Mong Hang, Myanmar
114 H 12 Mong Hpayak, Myanmar
114 F 11 Mong Hsu, Myanmar
114 F 11 Mong Kung, Myanmar
114 E 10 Möng Mir, Myanmar
114 F 13 Mong Pan, Myanmar
114 G 12 Mong Ping, Myanmar
114 G 12 Mong Pu, Myanmar
114 F 11 Mong Yai, Myanmar
130 M 5 Monga, Democratic Republic of Congo
127 E 22 Mongalla, Sudan
107 V 10 Mongar, Bhutan
131 Q 6 Mongbwalu, Democratic Republic of Congo
76 A 9 Mongioie, Italy
129 X 10 Mongo, Chad
109 N 4 Mongolia, Asia
129 T 15 Mongomo, Equatorial Guinea
129 U 10 Mongonu, Nigeria
101 W 7 Mongora, Pakistan
129 Z 12 Mongororo, Chad
132 L 5 Mongu, Zambia
20 F 10 Monico, WI, U.S.A.
46 I 6 Monjas, Guatemala
134 E 8 Monkey Mia, WA, Australia
121 N 21 Monkeyo, Philippines
78 N 10 Mońki, Poland
130 L 9 Monkoto, Democratic Republic of Congo
21 E 17 Monmouth, IL, U.S.A.
63 P 9 Monmouth, U.K.
33 J 19 Mono Lake, CA, U.S.A.
15 Q 11 Monomoy Island, MA, U.S.A.
77 N 15 Monopoli, Italy
79 J 23 Monor, Hungary
129 Z 7 Monou, Chad
65 O 12 Monpazier, France
67 S 6 Monreal del Campo, Spain
14 J 11 Monroe, NY, U.S.A.
17 P 10 Monroe, NC, U.S.A.
18 J 4 Monroe, LA, U.S.A.
21 L 15 Monroe, MI, U.S.A.
21 F 15 Monroe, WI, U.S.A.
25 V 2 Monroe City, MO, U.S.A.
21 I 20 Monroe Lake, IN, U.S.A.
14 B 13 Monroeville, PA, U.S.A.
19 P 6 Monroeville, AL, U.S.A.
128 G 13 Monrovia, Liberia
69 E 21 Mons, Belgium
73 B 18 Monschau, Germany
68 F 13 Monster, Netherlands
65 W 11 Mont Blanc, France/Switzerland
129 S 14 Mont Cameroun, Cameroon
41 S 10 Mont de Babel, QC, Canada
64 M 13 Mont-de-Marsan, France
143 O 13 Mont Forel, Greenland
130 E 8 Mont Iboundji, Gabon
43 S 5 Mont Jacques Cartier, QC, Canada
43 Q 6 Mont-Joli, QC, Canada
42 J 9 Mont-Laurier, QC, Canada
43 S 5 Mont Louis, QC, Canada
65 W 12 Mont Pelat, France
51 Y 8 Mont St-Marcel, French Guiana
125 O 13 Mont Tahat, Algeria
65 W 11 Mont Thabor, France
130 M 2 Mont Toussoro, Central African Republic
65 U 13 Mont Ventoux, France
41 T 9 Mont Wright, QC, Canada
41 R 9 Mont Yapeitso, QC, Canada
35 O 10 Montague Island, AK, U.S.A.
64 L 8 Montaigu, France
67 S 6 Montalbán, Spain
76 F 13 Montalto di Castro, Italy
52 C 10 Montalvo, Ecuador
29 Q 5 Montana, U.S.A.
82 G 7 Montana, Bulgaria
82 F 7 Montana, Bulgaria
47 P 5 Montañas de Colón, Honduras
65 Q 6 Montargis, France
65 O 13 Montauban, France
14 M 12 Montauk, NY, U.S.A.
15 N 12 Montauk Point, NY, U.S.A.
65 S 6 Montbard, France
65 V 6 Montbéliard, France
67 V 5 Montblanc, Spain
65 S 8 Montceau-les-Mines, France
54 H 10 Monte Alegre, Brazil
76 J 13 Monte Amaro, Italy
55 M 16 Monte Azul, Brazil
52 E 12 Monte Bello, Peru
57 F 24 Monte Burney, Chile
65 X 13 Monte Carlo, Monaco
76 I 13 Monte Carno, Italy
58 D 12 Monte Caseros, Argentina
65 Y 14 Monte Cinto, France
49 P 6 Monte Cristi, Dominican Republic
57 H 25 Monte Darwin, Chile
57 H 24 Monte Dinero, Argentina
65 Y 15 Monte Incudine, France
57 F 19 Monte Macá, Chile
57 F 18 Monte Melimoyu, Chile
77 J 15 Monte Miletto, Italy
55 N 16 Monte Pascoal, Brazil
56 K 7 Monte Quemado, Argentina
65 Y 15 Monte Rotondo, France
77 L 14 Monte Sant'Angelo, Italy
55 N 14 Monte Santo, Brazil
76 A 8 Monte Viso, Italy
31 Q 7 Monte Vista, CO, U.S.A.
42 J 10 Montebello, QC, Canada
134 F 6 Montebello Islands, WA, Australia
58 F 9 Montecarlo, Argentina
76 F 13 Montefiascone, Italy
48 K 8 Montego Bay, Jamaica
65 T 12 Montélimar, France
20 F 13 Montello, WI, U.S.A.
66 H 9 Montemor-o-novo, Portugal
45 Q 7 Montemorelos, Mexico
58 G 12 Montenegro, Brazil
81 I 15 Montenegro, Serbia and Montenegro
133 T 4 Montepuez, Mozambique
17 Q 4 Monterey, VA, U.S.A.
33 G 21 Monterey, CA, U.S.A.
33 G 21 Monterey Bay, CA, U.S.A.
50 H 4 Montería, Colombia
53 L 20 Montero, Bolivia
45 Q 7 Monterrey, Mexico
55 L 16 Montes Claros, Brazil
23 P 8 Montevideo, MN, U.S.A.
59 E 16 Montevideo, Uruguay
24 I 6 Montezuma, KS, U.S.A.
19 R 5 Montgomery, AL, U.S.A.
63 O 7 Montgomery, U.K.
74 C 10 Monthey, Switzerland
14 I 11 Monticello, NY, U.S.A.
16 I 7 Monticello, KY, U.S.A.
18 L 6 Monticello, MS, U.S.A.
23 V 11 Monticello, IA, U.S.A.
25 V 2 Monticello, MO, U.S.A.
25 W 13 Monticello, AR, U.S.A.
30 M 6 Monticello, UT, U.S.A.
66 G 9 Montijo, Portugal
65 P 9 Montluçon, France
65 R 4 Montmirail, France
135 V 7 Monto, QLD, Australia
67 N 11 Montoro, Spain
14 L 6 Montpelier, VT, U.S.A.
29 Q 13 Montpelier, ID, U.S.A.
65 S 14 Montpellier, France
42 L 10 Montréal, QC, Canada
39 M 17 Montreal Lake, SK, Canada
39 M 17 Montreal Lake, SK, Canada
42 A 8 Montreal River, ON, Canada
74 C 9 Montreux, Switzerland
14 H 10 Montrose, PA, U.S.A.
25 W 14 Montrose, AR, U.S.A.
31 O 6 Montrose, CO, U.S.A.
60 J 11 Montrose, U.K.
129 S 7 Monts Bagzane, Niger
125 Q 7 Monts des Ksour, Tunisia
125 N 12 Monts du Mouydir, Algeria
131 Q 12 Monts Mitumba, Democratic Republic of Congo
131 O 13 Monts Mulumbe, Democratic Republic of Congo
43 P 8 Monts Notre Dame, QC, Canada
49 X 9 Montserrat, U.K.
67 N 5 Montuenga, Spain
30 M 7 Monument Valley, UT, U.S.A.
130 L 6 Monveda, Democratic Republic of Congo
114 D 11 Monywa, Myanmar
76 C 6 Monza, Italy
53 D 14 Monzón, Peru
67 U 4 Monzón, Spain
133 N 10 Mookane, Botswana
135 Q 9 Moolawatana, SA, Australia
135 Q 9 Moomba, SA, Australia
135 T 9 Moonie, QLD, Australia
134 G 10 Moora, WA, Australia
27 N 11 Moore, TX, U.S.A.
29 N 10 Moore, ID, U.S.A.
29 S 5 Moore, MT, U.S.A.
17 R 3 Moorefield, WV, U.S.A.
23 O 5 Moorhead, MN, U.S.A.
29 R 11 Moose, WY, U.S.A.
41 O 10 Moose, ON, Canada
35 R 10 Moose Pass, AK, U.S.A.
15 Q 3 Moosehead Lake, ME, U.S.A.
41 O 10 Moosonee, ON, Canada
133 S 7 Mopeia, Mozambique
128 K 9 Mopti, Mali
128 L 9 Mopti, Mali
101 T 8 Moqor, Afghanistan
53 G 20 Moquegua, Peru
53 H 19 Moquegua, Peru
79 H 23 Mór, Hungary
31 R 9 Mora, NM, U.S.A.
66 H 9 Mora, Portugal
67 O 8 Mora, Spain
71 F 18 Mora, Sweden
129 V 10 Mora, Cameroon
106 K 8 Moradabad, India
133 W 7 Morafenobe, Madgascar
78 J 9 Morąg, Poland
46 J 5 Morales, Guatemala
133 Y 8 Moramanga, Madgascar
29 R 10 Moran, WY, U.S.A.
135 U 6 Moranbah, QLD, Australia
105 F 25 Moratuwa, Sri Lanka
79 G 17 Morava, Czech Republic
79 G 19 Moravia, Czech Republic
79 E 19 Moravské Budějovice, Czech Republic
134 F 10 Morawa, WA, Australia
60 H 9 Moray Firth, U.K.
46 L 5 Morazán, Honduras
73 C 20 Morbach, Germany
105 B 14 Morbi, India
75 Y 5 Mörbisch, Austria
77 J 15 Morcone, Italy
92 M 5 Mordovo, Russian Federation
22 I 8 Moreau, SD, U.S.A.
63 P 1 Morecambe, U.K.
63 P 1 Morecambe Bay, U.K.
135 U 9 Moree, NSW, Australia
16 K 5 Morehead, KY, U.S.A.
138 A 6 Morehead, Papua New Guinea
17 U 11 Morehead City, NC, U.S.A.
45 P 11 Morelia, Mexico
67 T 6 Morella, Spain
45 R 12 Morelos, Mexico
106 J 10 Morena, India
39 C 20 Moresby Island, BC, Canada
63 S 9 Moreton- in-Marsh, U.K.
135 W 8 Moreton Island, QLD, Australia
65 V 8 Morez, France
94 H 15 Morfou, Cyprus
94 G 15 Morfou Bay, Cyprus
135 Q 11 Morgan, SA, Australia
18 K 8 Morgan City, LA, U.S.A.
33 G 20 Morgan Hill, CA, U.S.A.
17 V 8 Morgans Corner, NC, U.S.A.
17 N 9 Morganton, NC, U.S.A.
17 P 2 Morgantown, WV, U.S.A.
74 B 9 Morges, Switzerland
122 J 7 Mori, Japan
31 Q 10 Moriarty, NM, U.S.A.
118 B 9 Morib, Malaysia
128 H 11 Moribaya, Guinea
50 L 8 Morichal, Colombia
122 K 10 Morioka, Japan
64 I 4 Morlaix, France
77 M 18 Mormanno, Italy
135 P 3 Mornington Island, QLD, Australia
101 U 13 Moro, Pakistan
121 J 22 Moro Gulf, Philippines
138 E 5 Morobe, Papua New Guinea
138 E 5 Morobe, Papua New Guinea
21 H 17 Morocco, IN, U.S.A.
124 F 8 Morocco, Africa
86 K 1 Morochne, Ukraine
131 V 12 Morogoro, Tanzania
131 V 12 Morogoro, Tanzania
45 P 11 Moroleón, Mexico
117 Q 10 Moromaho, Indonesia
133 V 9 Morombe, Madgascar
48 J 5 Morón, Cuba
109 P 2 Mörön, Mongolia
52 C 10 Morona, Ecuador
52 C 10 Morona-Santiago, Ecuador
133 W 8 Morondava, Madgascar
128 J 11 Morondo, Côte d'Ivoire
133 W 4 Moroni, Comoros
117 S 9 Morotai, Indonesia
131 T 6 Moroto, Uganda
131 T 6 Moroto, Uganda
93 N 9 Morozovsk, Russian Federation
55 L 14 Morpara, Brazil
136 L 10 Morrinsville, New Zealand
23 P 7 Morris, MN, U.S.A.
40 I 11 Morris, MB, Canada
14 J 12 Morristown, NY, U.S.A.
16 K 8 Morristown, TN, U.S.A.
33 H 22 Morro Bay, CA, U.S.A.
55 M 14 Morro do Chapéu, Brazil
93 N 3 Morshanka, Russian Federation
70 G 10 Mørsvikboth, Norway
65 N 5 Mortagne-au-Perche, France
62 M 12 Morte Bay, U.K.
58 B 13 Morteros, Argentina
49 N 4 Mortimer's, The Bahamas
141 P 15 Mortlock Islands, Federated States of Micronesia
26 I 4 Morton, TX, U.S.A.
32 G 8 Morton, WA, U.S.A.
131 T 5 Morungole, Uganda
135 T 8 Morven, QLD, Australia
92 J 2 Mosal'sk, Russian Federation
29 U 5 Mosby, MT, U.S.A.
16 B 10 Moscow, TN, U.S.A.
28 J 5 Moscow, ID, U.S.A.
92 K 1 Moscow, Russian Federation
145 X 12 Moscow University Ice Shelf, Antarctica
73 C 19 Mosel, Germany
32 J 8 Moses Lake, WA, U.S.A.
131 V 10 Moshi, Tanzania
87 R 5 Moshny, Ukraine
78 G 13 Mosina, Poland
70 F 12 Mosjøen, Norway
70 F 9 Moskenesøy, Norway
92 K 1 Moskovskaya Oblast', Russian Federation
79 G 22 Moson-magyaróvár, Hungary
41 P 5 Mosquito Bay, QC, Canada
47 R 8 Mosquito Coast, Nicaragua
19 X 9 Mosquito Lagoon, FL, U.S.A.
71 D 20 Moss, Norway
137 C 24 Mossburn, New Zealand
132 L 15 Mossel Bay, Republic of South Africa
130 F 9 Mossendjo, Congo
54 O 12 Mossoró, Brazil
124 L 6 Mostaganem, Algeria
81 G 14 Mostar, Bosnia and Herzegovina
58 I 13 Mostardas, Brazil
87 Q 8 Mostove, Ukraine
92 M 13 Mostovskoy, Russian Federation
86 H 4 Mostys'ka, Ukraine
97 R 2 Mosul, Iraq
127 I 19 Mot'a, Ethiopia
67 P 8 Mota del Cuervo, Spain
139 Q 9 Mota Lava, Vanuatu
46 I 5 Motagua, Guatemala
85 G 21 Motal', Belarus
71 F 21 Motala, Sweden
106 K 11 Moth, India
107 P 10 Motihari, India
67 R 8 Motilla del Palancar, Spain
136 M 10 Motiti Island, New Zealand
67 Q 1 Motrico, Spain
86 G 12 Motru, Romania
122 I 7 Motsuta-misaki, Japan
22 H 6 Mott, ND, U.S.A.
136 N 11 Motu, New Zealand
137 H 16 Motueka, New Zealand
136 J 12 Motunui, New Zealand
138 I 5 Motupena Point, Papua New Guinea
130 I 6 Mouali Gbangba, Congo
128 G 7 Moudjéria, Mauritania
71 K 17 Mouhijärvi, Finland
130 E 9 Mouila, Gabon
127 K 18 Moulhoulé, Djibouti
65 R 8 Moulins, France
115 F 16 Moulmein, Myanmar
19 O 2 Moulton, AL, U.S.A.
19 T 6 Moultrie, GA, U.S.A.
21 F 23 Mound City, IL, U.S.A.
25 Q 1 Mound City, MO, U.S.A.
129 W 12 Moundou, Chad
17 O 2 Moundsville, WV, U.S.A.
56 G 11 Mount Aconcagua, Argentina
45 K 23 Mt Adam, Falkland Islands
32 H 8 Mt Adams, WA, U.S.A.
17 O 8 Mount Airy, NC, U.S.A.
138 E 6 Mt Albert Edward, Papua New Guinea
145 Y 10 Mt Amundsen, Antarctica
137 C 26 Mt Anglem, New Zealand
121 M 22 Mount Apo, Philippines
95 T 9 Mt Ararat, Turkey
137 F 20 Mt Arrowsmith, New Zealand
20 G 8 Mt Arvon, MI, U.S.A.
137 C 22 Mt Aspiring, New Zealand
39 J 20 Mt Assiniboine, BC, Canada
134 F 7 Mt Augustus, WA, Australia
121 G 14 Mount Baco, Philippines
32 H 5 Mt Baker, WA, U.S.A.
138 I 4 Mt Balbi, Papua New Guinea
120 H 12 Mount Banahao, Philippines
138 E 5 Mt Bangeta, Papua New Guinea
30 H 8 Mt Bangs, AZ, U.S.A.
134 H 12 Mount Barker, WA, Australia
134 K 3 Mount Barnett Roadhouse, WA, Australia
135 V 10 Mt Barrington, NSW, Australia
41 V 7 Mt Benedict, NL, Canada
144 M 11 Mt Berlin, Antarctica
130 F 9 Mt Berongou, Congo
35 T 8 Mt Blackburn, AK, U.S.A.
135 T 12 Mt Bogong, VIC, Australia
35 T 9 Mt Bona, AK, U.S.A.
138 B 5 Mt Bosavi, Papua New Guinea
134 J 4 Mt Broome, WA, Australia
121 I 17 Mount Canlaon, Philippines
121 L 14 Mount Capotoah, Philippines

Country · Internal administrative region: State/Province/Territory/Dependent territory · Capital city · Mountain range/Undersea ridge · Mountain peak/Volcano/Seamount · Geographic feature · Headland/Point/Cape/Peninsula · Desert · Island/Island group · Antarctic base · Ocean · Sea · Bay/Gulf/Channel/Strait · Lake · Salt pan/Dry/Intermittent lake · Ri

Mt Cardrona – Namysłów

C 22 **Mt Cardrona**, New Zealand
S 7 **Mount Carleton**, NB, Canada
I 21 **Mount Carmel**, IN, U.S.A.
F 8 **Mt Carmel**, Israel
U 5 **Mt Caubvick**, NL, Canada
N 9 **Mt Chapman**, Antarctica
N 2 **Mount Cleveland**, MT, U.S.A.
W 3 **Mt Codrington**, Antarctica
H 19 **Mt Columbia**, BC/AB, Canada
K 5 **Mt Coman**, Antarctica
E 20 **Mount Cook**, New Zealand
E 20 **Mt Cook**, New Zealand
W 4 **Mt Cook**, Antarctica
J 20 **Mount Dapiak**, Philippines
P 6 **Mount Darwin**, Zimbabwe
C 14 **Mt Davis**, PA, U.S.A.
R 6 **Mount Desert Island**, ME, U.S.A.
Q 5 **Mt Doonerak**, AK, U.S.A.
P 11 **Mt Douglas**, AK, U.S.A.
E 2 **Mt Dremsel**, Papua New Guinea
C 22 **Mt Earnslaw**, New Zealand
Q 4 **Mount Elbert**, CO, U.S.A.
W 3 **Mt Elkins**, Antarctica
L 6 **Mt Ellen**, UT, U.S.A.
Q 12 **Mt Erebus**, Antarctica
D 5 **Mt Eruki**, Papua New Guinea
K 22 **Mount Etna**, Italy
N 6 **Mount Evans**, MT, U.S.A.
R 9 **Mt Everest**, China/Nepal
H 8 **Mt Fairweather**, Canada/U.S.A.
D 12 **Mount Forest**, ON, Canada
L 10 **Mt Frakes**, Antarctica
J 16 **Mt Fuji**, Japan
Q 13 **Mount Gambier**, SA, Australia
C 5 **Mt Giluwe**, Papua New Guinea
M 14 **Mt Graham**, AZ, U.S.A.
L 9 **Mount Greylock**, MA, U.S.A.
I 14 **Mount Guitinguitin**, Philippines
L 9 **Mt Guyot**, TN, U.S.A.
C 4 **Mount Hagen**, Papua New Guinea
G 13 **Mount Halcon**, Philippines
S 7 **Mt Harper**, AK, U.S.A.
P 5 **Mt Harvard**, CO, U.S.A.
A 15 **Mt Hay**, BC, Canada
S 7 **Mt Hayes**, AK, U.S.A.
K 15 **Mt Hector**, New Zealand
Q 10 **Mt Hehaṇ**, Burundi
H 20 **Mt Herbert**, New Zealand
H 7 **Mt Hermon**, Syria
M 19 **Mount Hilonghilong**, Philippines
H 10 **Mt Hood**, OR, U.S.A.
F 14 **Mount Horeb**, WI, U.S.A.
Q 14 **Mt Humboldt**, New Caledonia
U 14 **Mt Hunt**, Antarctica
G 20 **Mount Hutt**, New Zealand
F 20 **Mt Hutt**, New Zealand
Q 5 **Mount Isa**, QLD, Australia
J 12 **Mount Isarog**, Philippines
K 5 **Mt Jackson**, Antarctica
H 10 **Mt Jefferson**, OR, U.S.A.
L 18 **Mt Jefferson**, NV, U.S.A.
Q 3 **Mt Katahdin**, ME, U.S.A.
P 11 **Mt Katmai**, AK, U.S.A.
V 8 **Mt Kenya**, Kenya
V 5 **Mt Kinabalu**, Malaysia
Q 10 **Mt Kirkpatrick**, Antarctica
T 13 **Mt Kosciuszko**, NSW, Australia
I 12 **Mount Labo**, Philippines
Q 12 **Mt Lister**, Antarctica
H 9 **Mt Livermore**, TX, U.S.A.
A 14 **Mt Logan**, YT, Canada
B 23 **Mt Lyall**, New Zealand
R 13 **Mt Mackintosh**, Antarctica
G 9 **Mount Magnet**, WA, Australia
J 20 **Mount Malindang**, Philippines
L 5 **Mt Mansfield**, VT, U.S.A.
B 19 **Mount Mantalingajan**, Philippines
R 9 **Mt Marcus Baker**, AK, U.S.A.
J 6 **Mt Marcy**, NY, U.S.A.
K 5 **Mt Marvine**, UT, U.S.A.
L 23 **Mount Matutum**, Philippines
M 10 **Mount Maunganui**, New Zealand
K 13 **Mount Mayon**, Philippines
R 11 **Mt McClintock**, Antarctica
M 8 **Mount McGuire**, ID, U.S.A.
Q 8 **Mt McKinley**, AK, U.S.A.
G 7 **Mt Meharry**, WA, Australia
U 5 **Mt Menzies**, Antarctica
S 3 **Mt Michelson**, AK, U.S.A.
Q 10 **Mt Miller**, Antarctica
R 14 **Mt Minto**, Antarctica
M 9 **Mt Mitchell**, NC, U.S.A.
M 8 **Mt Moore**, Antarctica
A 14 **Mount Morris**, PA, U.S.A.
E 9 **Mount Morris**, NY, U.S.A.
T 7 **Mt Mulu**, Malaysia
U 14 **Mt Murchison**, Antarctica
D 14 **Mt Murray**, YT, Canada
L 12 **Mt Ngauruhoe**, New Zealand
T 10 **Mount Olive**, NC, U.S.A.
F 6 **Mt Olympus**, WA, U.S.A.
E 15 **Mt Olympus**, Greece
F 22 **Mt Orr**, New Zealand
S 15 **Mt Ossa**, TAS, Australia
P 13 **Mt Panié**, New Caledonia
F 10 **Mount Pinatubo**, Philippines
I 23 **Mt Pinos**, CA, U.S.A.
B 13 **Mount Pleasant**, PA, U.S.A.
Q 14 **Mount Pleasant**, SC, U.S.A.
K 13 **Mount Pleasant**, MI, U.S.A.
V 13 **Mount Pleasant**, IA, U.S.A.
S 5 **Mount Pleasant**, TX, U.S.A.
K 4 **Mount Pleasant**, UT, U.S.A.
M 7 **Mt Popomanaseu**, Solomon Islands
G 8 **Mount Pulog**, Philippines
F 20 **Mt Queen Bess**, BC, Canada
L 21 **Mount Ragang**, Philippines
J 11 **Mt Ragged**, WA, Australia
H 7 **Mt Rainier**, WA, U.S.A.
C 16 **Mt Ratz**, BC, Canada
H 19 **Mt Robson**, BC, Canada
N 7 **Mt Rogers**, VA, U.S.A.
F 19 **Mt Rolleston**, New Zealand
S 6 **Mt Roraima**, Brazil/Guyana
L 16 **Mt Ross**, New Zealand
K 12 **Mt Ruapehu**, New Zealand
G 10 **Mt Rushmore**, SD, U.S.A.
X 9 **Mt Sandow**, Antarctica
E 20 **Mt Saugstad**, BC, Canada
L 11 **Mt Scott**, OK, U.S.A.
G 13 **Mt Scott**, OR, U.S.A.
N 8 **Mt Seelig**, Antarctica
G 15 **Mount Shasta**, CA, U.S.A.
33 G 15 **Mt Shasta**, CA, U.S.A.
120 G 6 **Mount Sicapoo**, Philippines
144 L 10 **Mt Sidley**, Antarctica
138 G 7 **Mt Simpson**, Papua New Guinea
138 H 4 **Mt Sinewit**, Papua New Guinea
144 K 11 **Mt Siple**, Antarctica
38 D 13 **Mt Sir James MacBrian**, NT, Canada
138 B 5 **Mt Sisa**, Papua New Guinea
137 B 24 **Mt Solitary**, New Zealand
145 S 14 **Mt Southard**, Antarctica
35 T 9 **Mt St Elias**, AK, U.S.A.
32 G 8 **Mt St Helens**, WA, U.S.A.
137 D 22 **Mt St Mary**, New Zealand
16 K 5 **Mount Sterling**, KY, U.S.A.
137 J 16 **Mt Stokes**, New Zealand
145 X 9 **Mt Strathcona**, Antarctica
138 E 5 **Mt Strong**, Papua New Guinea
127 H 16 **Mount Suara**, Eritrea
24 G 3 **Mount Sunflower**, KS, U.S.A.
39 E 16 **Mt Sylvia**, BC, Canada
138 D 5 **Mt Tabletop**, Papua New Guinea
139 P 10 **Mt Tabwemasana**, Vanuatu
138 J 5 **Mt Takuan**, Papua New Guinea
136 J 12 **Mt Taranaki (Mt Egmont)**, New Zealand
31 O 10 **Mt Taylor**, NM, U.S.A.
30 H 9 **Mt Tipton**, AZ, U.S.A.
136 L 12 **Mt Tongariro**, New Zealand
35 Q 9 **Mt Torbert**, AK, U.S.A.
124 G 8 **Mt Toubkal**, Morocco
94 G 15 **Mount Troödos**, Cyprus
30 I 8 **Mt Trumbull**, AZ, U.S.A.
144 L 7 **Mt Tyree**, Antarctica
138 G 4 **Mt Ulawun**, Papua New Guinea
137 H 18 **Mt Una**, New Zealand
14 E 13 **Mt Union**, PA, U.S.A.
57 L 23 **Mt Usborne**, Falkland Islands
35 N 12 **Mt Veniaminof**, AK, U.S.A.
19 O 6 **Mount Vernon**, AL, U.S.A.
21 F 21 **Mount Vernon**, IL, U.S.A.
21 G 22 **Mount Vernon**, IN, U.S.A.
21 M 18 **Mt Vernon**, OH, U.S.A.
25 S 7 **Mount Vernon**, MO, U.S.A.
32 H 6 **Mount Vernon**, WA, U.S.A.
145 T 3 **Mt Victor**, Antarctica
114 C 12 **Mt Victoria**, Myanmar
138 E 6 **Mt Victoria**, Papua New Guinea
139 X 11 **Mt Victoria**, Fiji
138 F 6 **Mt Victory**, Papua New Guinea
36 I 12 **Mt Waddington**, BC, Canada
15 N 6 **Mt Washington**, NH, U.S.A.
33 K 21 **Mt Whitney**, CA, U.S.A.
20 E 9 **Mt Whittlesey**, WI, U.S.A.
138 C 4 **Mt Wilhelm**, Papua New Guinea
39 D 16 **Mt Will**, BC, Canada
31 O 7 **Mt Wilson**, CO, U.S.A.
134 M 8 **Mt Woodroffe**, SA, Australia
144 M 8 **Mt Woollard**, Antarctica
35 T 8 **Mt Wrangell**, AK, U.S.A.
134 M 6 **Mt Zeil**, NT, Australia
31 P 2 **Mt Zirkel**, CO, U.S.A.
28 K 11 **Mountain Home**, ID, U.S.A.
25 V 9 **Mountain View**, AR, U.S.A.
125 T 13 **Mountains of Tummo**, Libya
62 J 15 **Mount's Bay**, U.K.
54 E 10 **Moura**, Brazil
66 I 10 **Moura**, Portugal
135 V 7 **Moura**, QLD, Australia
129 Z 10 **Mouraya**, Chad
128 I 9 **Mourdiah**, Mali
136 M 10 **Mourea**, New Zealand
69 C 19 **Mouscron**, Belgium
129 W 10 **Mousgougou**, Chad
127 K 18 **Moussa Ali**, Djibouti
129 W 9 **Moussoro**, Chad
67 V 6 **Mouth of the Ebro**, Spain
61 A 19 **Mouth of the Shannon**, Republic of Ireland
113 Z 5 **Mouth of the Yangtze**, China
54 J 9 **Mouths of the Amazon**, Brazil
107 U 15 **Mouths of the Ganges**, Bangladesh
105 H 19 **Mouths of the Godavari**, India
101 T 15 **Mouths of the Indus**, Pakistan
115 B 17 **Mouths of the Irrawaddy**, Myanmar
105 G 19 **Mouths of the Krishna**, India
115 M 23 **Mouths of the Mekong**, Vietnam
129 Q 14 **Mouths of the Niger**, Nigeria
74 D 7 **Moutier**, Switzerland
65 V 10 **Moûtiers**, France
83 D 17 **Mouzaki**, Greece
132 J 5 **Moxico**, Angola
127 I 23 **Moyale**, Ethiopia
124 H 8 **Moyen Atlas**, Morocco
129 X 11 **Moyen-Chari**, Chad
130 D 8 **Moyen-Ogooué**, Gabon
133 N 13 **Moyeni**, Lesotho
128 F 10 **Moyenne-Guinée**, Guinea
116 M 15 **Moyo**, Indonesia
131 R 5 **Moyo**, Uganda
52 C 12 **Moyobamba**, Peru
70 G 9 **Møysalen**, Norway
103 T 9 **Moyynkum**, Kazakhstan
103 T 7 **Moyynty**, Kazakhstan
133 Q 9 **Mozambique**, Africa
133 T 8 **Mozambique Channel**, Mozambique
93 P 13 **Mozdok**, Russian Federation
92 J 1 **Mozhaysk**, Russian Federation
91 R 14 **Mozhga**, Russian Federation
131 Q 12 **Mpala**, Democratic Republic of Congo
131 R 11 **Mpanda**, Tanzania
132 M 7 **Mpandamatenga**, Botswana
130 H 9 **Mpé**, Congo
107 Z 9 **Mpen**, India
131 S 7 **Mpigi**, Uganda
133 P 3 **Mpika**, Zambia
133 P 2 **Mporokoso**, Zambia
130 H 9 **Mpouya**, Congo
133 O 10 **Mpumalanga**, Republic of South Africa
131 U 11 **Mpwapwa**, Tanzania
78 L 9 **Mrągowo**, Poland
93 W 3 **Mrakovo**, Russian Federation
82 D 12 **Mrešičko**, Macedonia (F.Y.R.O.M.)
80 F 11 **Mrkonjić-Grad**, Bosnia and Herzegovina
87 Q 2 **Mryn**, Ukraine
125 N 6 **M'sila**, Algeria
85 N 17 **Mstsislaw**, Belarus
131 W 14 **Mtama**, Tanzania
92 J 3 **Mtsensk**, Russian Federation
95 T 6 **Mts'khet'a**, Georgia
131 W 14 **Mtwara**, Tanzania
131 X 14 **Mtwara**, Tanzania
130 F 11 **Muanda**, Democratic Republic of Congo
115 L 15 **Muang Khammouan**, Laos
115 M 18 **Muang Không**, Laos
115 L 17 **Muang Khôngxédôn**, Laos
114 J 12 **Muang Khoua**, Laos
114 J 12 **Muang Ngoy**, Laos
114 I 11 **Muang Ou Nua**, Laos
114 H 13 **Muang Pakbeng**, Laos
115 K 14 **Muang Pakxan**, Laos
115 L 16 **Muang Phalan**, Laos
115 M 16 **Muang Phin**, Laos
115 I 14 **Muang Phôn-Hông**, Laos
114 H 12 **Muang Sing**, Laos
114 J 13 **Muang Souy**, Laos
115 I 14 **Muang Xaignabouri**, Laos
114 I 12 **Muang Xay**, Laos
118 C 10 **Muar**, Malaysia
118 D 9 **Muar**, Malaysia
116 E 12 **Muaraaman**, Indonesia
116 F 12 **Muarabeliti**, Indonesia
116 E 11 **Muarabungo**, Indonesia
116 F 13 **Muaradua**, Indonesia
116 F 12 **Muaraenim**, Indonesia
116 C 11 **Muarasiberut**, Indonesia
103 P 13 **Mubarek**, Uzbekistan
129 U 11 **Mubi**, Nigeria
63 P 7 **Much Wenlock**, U.K.
134 G 11 **Muchea**, WA, Australia
112 M 8 **Muchuan**, China
60 F 11 **Muck**, U.K.
133 U 4 **Mucojo**, Mozambique
132 K 3 **Muconda**, Angola
132 H 6 **Mucope**, Angola
94 J 10 **Mucur**, Turkey
55 N 17 **Mucuri**, Brazil
22 H 8 **Mud Butte**, SD, U.S.A.
118 A 5 **Muda**, Malaysia
110 M 12 **Mudanjiang**, China
94 D 8 **Mudanya**, Turkey
29 V 13 **Muddy Gap**, WY, U.S.A.
105 D 19 **Mudhol**, India
115 F 17 **Mudon**, Myanmar
127 N 21 **Mudug**, Somalia
133 U 3 **Mueda**, Mozambique
113 U 7 **Mufu Shan**, China
133 O 4 **Mufulira**, Zambia
132 M 4 **Mufumbwe**, Zambia
95 Y 9 **Muğan Düzü**, Azerbaijan
133 S 6 **Mugeba**, Mozambique
107 O 12 **Mughal Sarai**, India
100 J 7 **Mūghār**, Iran
94 C 12 **Muğla**, Turkey
127 B 18 **Muhagiriya**, Sudan
126 G 13 **Muhammad Qol**, Sudan
97 O 7 **Muḩaywīr**, Iraq
145 Q 2 **Mühlig-Hofmann Mountains**, Antarctica
75 S 3 **Mühlviertel**, Austria
96 H 4 **Muḩradah**, Syria
84 E 7 **Muhu**, Estonia
131 P 8 **Muhulu**, Democratic Republic of Congo
127 G 22 **Mui**, Ethiopia
115 L 24 **Mui Ca Mau**, Vietnam
133 T 5 **Muite**, Mozambique
86 H 6 **Mukacheve**, Ukraine
119 P 9 **Mukah**, Malaysia
119 P 9 **Mukah**, Malaysia
115 L 16 **Mukdahan**, Thailand
134 G 10 **Mukinbudin**, WA, Australia
116 E 12 **Mukomuko**, Indonesia
106 G 6 **Muktsar**, India
112 K 7 **Mula**, China
47 Z 13 **Mula-tupo**, Panama
105 L 18 **Mulakatholhu Atoll**, Maldives
110 L 11 **Mulan**, China
120 I 13 **Mulanay**, Philippines
133 R 6 **Mulanje**, Malawi
133 S 5 **Mulanje**, Malawi
97 W 8 **Mūlat al Mashkhūr**, Iraq
106 I 3 **Mulbekh**, India
35 O 10 **Mulchatna**, AK, U.S.A.
57 F 14 **Mulchén**, Chile
29 Z 10 **Mule Creek**, WY, U.S.A.
131 S 9 **Muleba**, Tanzania
44 I 6 **Mulegé**, Mexico
26 I 4 **Muleshoe**, TX, U.S.A.
67 P 12 **Mulhacén**, Spain
65 W 6 **Mulhouse**, France
110 M 11 **Muling**, China
60 F 12 **Mull**, U.K.
61 G 15 **Mull of Galloway**, U.K.
61 F 14 **Mull of Kintyre**, U.K.
60 F 13 **Mull of Oa**, U.K.
134 F 9 **Mullewa**, WA, Australia
73 D 25 **Müllheim**, Germany
61 D 17 **Mullingar**, Republic of Ireland
62 J 15 **Mullion**, U.K.
132 M 6 **Mulobezi**, Zambia
105 F 15 **Multai**, India
101 W 10 **Multan**, Pakistan
130 M 5 **Muma**, Democratic Republic of Congo
101 O 14 **Mūmān**, Iran
105 B 17 **Mumbai**, India
132 L 5 **Mumbeji**, Zambia
132 G 3 **Mumbondo**, Angola
133 N 5 **Mumbwa**, Zambia
138 E 5 **Mumeng**, Papua New Guinea
93 R 11 **Mumra**, Russian Federation
45 Y 11 **Muna**, Mexico
117 P 13 **Muna**, Indonesia
104 A 12 **Munabao**, India
112 J 12 **Munai**, China
123 B 21 **Munakata**, Japan
102 H 9 **Munayshy**, Kazakhstan
39 E 15 **Muncho Lake**, BC, Canada
111 L 17 **Munch'ŏn**, North Korea
21 J 18 **Muncie**, IN, U.S.A.
14 F 11 **Muncy**, PA, U.S.A.
101 W 10 **Munda**, Pakistan
26 M 5 **Munday**, TX, U.S.A.
63 X 7 **Mundford**, U.K.
58 F 7 **Mundo Novo**, Brazil
134 K 10 **Mundrabilla**, WA, Australia
135 V 8 **Mundubbera**, QLD, Australia
67 Q 9 **Munera**, Spain
16 G 6 **Munfordville**, KY, U.S.A.
133 Q 6 **Mungári**, Mozambique
131 P 6 **Mungbere**, Democratic Republic of Congo
107 R 11 **Munger**, India
135 P 8 **Mungerannie Hotel**, SA, Australia
135 U 9 **Mungindi**, NSW, Australia
73 J 24 **Munich**, Germany
20 I 9 **Munising**, MI, U.S.A.
71 D 21 **Munkedal**, Sweden
61 B 20 **Munster**, Republic of Ireland
72 H 12 **Münster**, Germany
73 D 14 **Münster**, Germany
74 F 9 **Münster**, Switzerland
120 F 11 **Muntinglupa**, Philippines
70 N 11 **Muojärvi**, Finland
114 K 12 **Muong Het**, Laos
70 K 9 **Muonio**, Finland
111 H 19 **Muping**, China
96 K 8 **Muqāţ**, Jordan
99 Q 14 **Muqaybirah**, Yemen
95 T 10 **Muradiye**, Turkey
106 J 8 **Muradnagar**, India
118 A 13 **Murai Reservoir**, Singapore
122 J 13 **Murakami**, Japan
131 Q 9 **Muramvya**, Burundi
91 P 11 **Murashi**, Russian Federation
65 Q 11 **Murat**, France
95 R 10 **Murat**, Turkey
82 M 12 **Muratli**, Turkey
75 T 7 **Murau**, Austria
77 C 18 **Muravera**, Italy
100 I 8 **Murchek-Khort**, Iran
134 F 9 **Murchison**, WA, Australia
137 H 17 **Murchison**, New Zealand
134 F 9 **Murchison Roadhouse**, WA, Australia
67 R 11 **Murcia**, Spain
67 S 11 **Murcia**, Spain
22 J 10 **Murdo**, SD, U.S.A.
43 S 5 **Murdochville**, QC, Canada
75 W 8 **Mureck**, Austria
86 J 9 **Mureș**, Romania
65 O 14 **Muret**, France
16 F 9 **Murfreesboro**, TN, U.S.A.
17 U 8 **Murfreesboro**, NC, U.S.A.
103 U 13 **Murghob**, Tajikistan
135 V 8 **Murgon**, QLD, Australia
74 F 7 **Muri**, Switzerland
58 N 5 **Muriaé**, Brazil
132 K 3 **Muriege**, Angola
141 O 14 **Murilo Atoll**, Federated States of Micronesia
95 P 10 **Mürit Dağlari**, Turkey
72 L 10 **Müritz**, Germany
136 O 12 **Muriwai**, New Zealand
90 I 2 **Murmansk**, Russian Federation
143 U 12 **Murmansk Rise**, Arctic Ocean
90 H 2 **Murmanskaya Oblast'**, Russian Federation
90 I 2 **Murmanskiy Bereg**, Russian Federation
90 H 2 **Murmashi**, Russian Federation
93 N 1 **Murom**, Russian Federation
131 R 8 **Murongo**, Tanzania
122 J 7 **Muroran**, Japan
123 F 20 **Muroto**, Japan
123 F 21 **Muroto-zaki**, Japan
16 J 10 **Murphy**, NC, U.S.A.
28 J 11 **Murphy**, ID, U.S.A.
16 C 7 **Murray**, KY, U.S.A.
135 R 12 **Murray**, NSW, Australia
135 Q 12 **Murray Bridge**, SA, Australia
43 W 9 **Murray Harbour**, PE, Canada
21 E 19 **Murrayville**, IL, U.S.A.
101 X 7 **Murree**, Pakistan
133 T 5 **Murrupula**, Mozambique
80 E 6 **Murska Sobota**, Slovenia
39 G 19 **Murtle Lake**, BC, Canada
105 B 17 **Murud**, India
136 M 11 **Murupara**, New Zealand
105 G 14 **Murwara**, India
135 W 9 **Murwillumbah**, NSW, Australia
125 S 11 **Murzūq**, Libya
75 W 5 **Mürzzuschlag**, Austria
95 Q 11 **Muş**, Turkey
84 E 12 **Mūša**, Lithuania
101 R 9 **Musa Qala**, Afghanistan
130 M 9 **Musadi**, Democratic Republic of Congo
82 G 10 **Musala**, Bulgaria
97 X 9 **Musallam**, Iraq
111 M 14 **Musan**, North Korea
99 X 4 **Musandam Peninsula**, Oman
99 P 14 **Musaymir**, Yemen
99 Z 6 **Muscat**, Oman
23 V 13 **Muscatine**, IA, U.S.A.
41 Y 9 **Musgrave Harbour**, NL, Canada
134 L 8 **Musgrave Ranges**, SA, Australia
101 U 8 **Mūshakī**, Afghanistan
96 I 10 **Mushāsh Ḩadraj**, Jordan
130 I 9 **Mushie**, Democratic Republic of Congo
138 C 3 **Mushu**, Papua New Guinea
21 I 14 **Muskegon**, MI, U.S.A.
25 Q 10 **Muskogee**, OK, U.S.A.
39 F 15 **Muskwa**, BC, Canada
127 G 15 **Musmar**, Sudan
131 T 8 **Musoma**, Tanzania
131 T 12 **Musombe**, Tanzania
41 W 10 **Musquaro**, QC, Canada
138 F 2 **Mussau Island**, Papua New Guinea
29 U 4 **Musselshell**, MT, U.S.A.
132 H 3 **Mussende**, Angola
65 N 11 **Mussidan**, France
94 C 9 **Mustafakemalpaşa**, Turkey
127 L 22 **Mustahīl**, Ethiopia
74 K 9 **Müstair**, Switzerland
49 Z 12 **Mustique**, St Vincent and the Grenadines
84 D 7 **Mustjala**, Estonia
84 H 8 **Mustla**, Estonia
84 I 7 **Mustvee**, Estonia
135 V 11 **Muswellbrook**, NSW, Australia
94 I 13 **Mut**, Turkey
126 D 11 **Mut**, Egypt
133 Q 7 **Mutare**, Zimbabwe
50 G 5 **Mutis**, Colombia
133 W 4 **Mutsamudu**, Comoros
131 N 14 **Mutshatsha**, Democratic Republic of Congo
122 K 8 **Mutsu**, Japan
122 J 8 **Mutsu-wan**, Japan
135 S 6 **Muttaburra**, QLD, Australia
137 B 26 **Muttonbird Islands**, New Zealand
105 F 20 **Muttukuru**, India
133 S 5 **Mutuali**, Mozambique
129 T 12 **Mutum Biyu**, Nigeria
105 G 24 **Mutur**, Sri Lanka
108 K 8 **Mutztag Feng**, China
132 H 2 **Muxaluando**, Angola
132 F 3 **Muxima**, Angola
129 S 10 **Muya**, Nigeria
131 R 9 **Muyinga**, Burundi
102 L 10 **Muynak**, Uzbekistan
131 O 12 **Muyumba**, Democratic Republic of Congo
101 X 7 **Muzaffarabad**, Pakistan
101 W 10 **Muzaffargarh**, Pakistan
106 K 8 **Muzaffarnagar**, India
107 P 11 **Muzaffarpur**, India
64 J 6 **Muzillac**, France
45 P 5 **Múzquiz**, Mexico
129 T 15 **Mvangan**, Cameroon
127 D 22 **Mvolo**, Sudan
131 V 11 **Mvomero**, Tanzania
133 P 7 **Mvuma**, Zimbabwe
131 S 9 **Mwanza**, Tanzania
131 S 9 **Mwanza**, Tanzania
130 L 10 **Mweka**, Democratic Republic of Congo
133 O 3 **Mwenda**, Zambia
130 M 12 **Mwene-Ditu**, Democratic Republic of Congo
133 P 8 **Mwenezi**, Zimbabwe
131 P 9 **Mwenga**, Democratic Republic of Congo
130 M 13 **Mwimba**, Democratic Republic of Congo
132 M 3 **Mwinilunga**, Zambia
141 Q 15 **Mwokil**, Federated States of Micronesia
115 M 22 **My Tho**, Vietnam
85 I 15 **Myadzyel**, Belarus
19 V 11 **Myakka City**, FL, U.S.A.
114 C 12 **Myanmar (Burma)**, Asia
115 C 16 **Myaungmya**, Myanmar
114 D 12 **Myingyan**, Myanmar
115 F 19 **Myinmoletkat**, Myanmar
114 E 8 **Myitkyina**, Myanmar
115 F 19 **Myitta**, Myanmar
114 D 12 **Myittha**, Myanmar
87 V 8 **Mykhaylivka**, Ukraine
86 I 5 **Mykolayiv**, Ukraine
87 R 9 **Mykolayiv**, Ukraine
83 J 21 **Mykonos**, Greece
83 J 21 **Mykonos**, Greece
91 P 5 **Myla**, Russian Federation
107 U 12 **Mymensingh**, Bangladesh
103 T 8 **Mynaral**, Kazakhstan
114 B 12 **Myohaung**, Myanmar
111 M 15 **Myŏnggan**, North Korea
84 J 13 **Myory**, Belarus
70 B 12 **Myrdalsjökull**, Iceland
87 T 4 **Myrhorod**, Ukraine
83 I 15 **Myrina**, Greece
87 Q 4 **Myrne**, Ukraine
87 X 8 **Myrne**, Ukraine
17 R 13 **Myrtle Beach**, SC, U.S.A.
32 F 12 **Myrtle Creek**, OR, U.S.A.
32 E 12 **Myrtle Point**, OR, U.S.A.
89 X 10 **Mys Alevina**, Russian Federation
89 X 14 **Mys Aniva**, Russian Federation
87 T 13 **Mys Ayya**, Ukraine
89 Y 5 **Mys Blossom**, Russian Federation
87 W 12 **Mys Chauda**, Ukraine
89 R 5 **Mys Chelyuskin**, Russian Federation
89 W 10 **Mys Duga-Zapadnaya**, Russian Federation
89 W 12 **Mys Elizavety**, Russian Federation
89 Z 9 **Mys Govena**, Russian Federation
90 M 2 **Mys Kanin Nos**, Russian Federation
87 W 11 **Mys Kazantip**, Ukraine
87 S 13 **Mys Khersones**, Ukraine
89 X 14 **Mys Kril'on**, Russian Federation
89 Y 5 **Mys Litke**, Russian Federation
89 V 7 **Mys Lopatka**, Russian Federation
89 Z 12 **Mys Lopatka**, Russian Federation
89 Z 7 **Mys Navarin**, Russian Federation
90 L 4 **Mys Orlovskiy**, Russian Federation
102 H 10 **Mys Peschanyy**, Kazakhstan
102 H 10 **Mys Sengirli**, Kazakhstan
89 X 6 **Mys Shelagskiy**, Russian Federation
89 Y 5 **Mys Shmidta**, Russian Federation
102 H 11 **Mys Suz**, Kazakhstan
90 K 3 **Mys Svyatoy Nos**, Russian Federation
89 X 13 **Mys Terpeniya**, Russian Federation
89 X 10 **Mys Tolstoy**, Russian Federation
102 G 8 **Mys Tyub-Karagan**, Kazakhstan
87 S 12 **Mys Yevpatoriys'kyy**, Ukraine
89 Y 10 **Mys Yuzhnyy**, Russian Federation
89 N 5 **Mys Zhelaniya**, Russian Federation
79 K 18 **Myślenice**, Poland
78 D 11 **Myślibórz**, Poland
105 D 21 **Mysore**, India
83 L 17 **Mytilini**, Greece
92 L 1 **Mytishchi**, Russian Federation
30 M 3 **Myton**, UT, U.S.A.
133 Q 3 **Mzimba**, Malawi
133 Q 3 **Mzuzu**, Malawi

N

114 F 10 **Na-lang**, Myanmar
68 F 13 **Naaldwijk**, Netherlands
34 E 9 **Naalehu**, HI, U.S.A.
124 K 7 **Naama**, Algeria
71 K 19 **Naantali**, Finland
68 I 11 **Naarden**, Netherlands
121 H 15 **Nabas**, Philippines
131 V 10 **Naberera**, Tanzania
93 U 1 **Naberezhnyye Chelny**, Russian Federation
35 T 8 **Nabesna**, AK, U.S.A.
125 Q 5 **Nabeul**, Tunisia
106 I 7 **Nabha**, India
117 W 12 **Nabire**, Indonesia
96 G 9 **Nāblus**, Israel
128 M 11 **Nabolo**, Ghana
139 X 11 **Nabouwalu**, Fiji
133 U 5 **Nacala**, Mozambique
46 L 7 **Nacaome**, Honduras
133 U 5 **Nacaroa**, Mozambique
113 P 13 **Nachen**, China
131 W 14 **Nachingwea**, Tanzania
104 B 11 **Nachna**, India
79 F 16 **Náchod**, Czech Republic
105 N 22 **Nachuge**, India
27 T 7 **Nacogdoches**, TX, U.S.A.
44 J 3 **Nacozari de García**, Mexico
139 W 11 **Nadi**, Fiji
105 C 15 **Nadiad**, India
95 V 9 **Nadirchanly**, Azerbaijan
86 E 10 **Nădlac**, Romania
124 J 6 **Nador**, Morocco
86 J 6 **Nadvirna**, Ukraine
88 L 8 **Nadym**, Russian Federation
71 D 26 **Naestved**, Denmark
83 D 19 **Nafpaktos**, Greece
83 F 21 **Nafplio**, Greece
99 P 5 **Nafy**, Saudi Arabia
126 F 11 **Nag' Hammadi**, Egypt
120 J 12 **Naga**, Philippines
107 Y 10 **Naga Hills**, India
123 D 20 **Nagahama**, Japan
123 H 17 **Nagahama**, Japan
105 D 18 **Nagaj**, India
107 Y 10 **Nagaland**, India
123 I 15 **Nagano**, Japan
123 J 14 **Nagaoka**, Japan
107 W 10 **Nagaon**, India
105 F 22 **Nagappattinam**, India
105 F 19 **Nagarjuna Sagar**, India
123 B 22 **Nagasaki**, Japan
123 C 20 **Nagato**, Japan
104 C 12 **Nagaur**, India
105 E 24 **Nagercoil**, India
101 R 13 **Nagha Kalat**, Pakistan
106 K 8 **Nagina**, India
123 N 24 **Nago**, Japan
106 L 12 **Nagod**, India
73 F 23 **Nagold**, Germany
91 Q 11 **Nagorsk**, Russian Federation
123 H 17 **Nagoya**, Japan
105 F 16 **Nagpur**, India
108 L 10 **Nagqu**, China
88 M 3 **Nagurskoye**, Russian Federation
79 G 25 **Nagyatád**, Hungary
79 M 21 **Nagyhalász**, Hungary
79 G 25 **Nagykanizsa**, Hungary
79 J 23 **Nagykáta**, Hungary
123 N 25 **Naha**, Japan
96 F 7 **Nahariyya**, Israel
20 I 10 **Nahma Junction**, MI, U.S.A.
96 H 3 **Nahr al Āṣī**, Syria
97 U 7 **Nahr Diyālá**, Iraq
113 S 13 **Nahuo**, China
44 M 5 **Naica**, Mexico
86 F 12 **Naidăș**, Romania
63 R 10 **Nailsworth**, U.K.
111 G 14 **Naiman Qi**, China
41 U 7 **Nain**, NL, Canada
100 J 8 **Nā'īn**, Iran
105 G 15 **Nainpur**, India
60 H 10 **Nairn**, U.K.
131 V 8 **Nairobi**, Kenya
84 F 5 **Naissaar**, Estonia
131 U 8 **Naivasha**, Kenya
100 I 8 **Najafābād**, Iran
110 I 9 **Naji**, China
106 K 7 **Najibabad**, India
111 N 14 **Najin**, North Korea
99 P 11 **Najrān**, Saudi Arabia
123 A 22 **Nakadōri-shima**, Japan
123 E 21 **Nakamura**, Japan
123 I 15 **Nakano**, Japan
123 B 26 **Nakano-shima**, Japan
123 D 17 **Nakano-shima**, Japan
122 M 4 **Nakashibetsu**, Japan
131 S 7 **Nakasongola**, Uganda
123 C 21 **Nakatsu**, Japan
123 I 17 **Nakatsugawa**, Japan
127 I 16 **Nakfa**, Eritrea
126 F 8 **Nakhl**, Egypt
100 I 12 **Nakhl-e Taqī**, Iran
89 V 15 **Nakhodka**, Russian Federation
107 W 10 **Nakhola**, India
115 I 19 **Nakhon Nayok**, Thailand
115 K 15 **Nakhon Phanom**, Thailand
115 I 18 **Nakhon Ratchasima**, Thailand
115 G 17 **Nakhon Sawan**, Thailand
115 H 24 **Nakhon Si Thammarat**, Thailand
105 A 14 **Nakhtarana**, India
78 G 11 **Nakło nad Notecią**, Poland
35 O 11 **Naknek**, AK, U.S.A.
35 O 11 **Naknek Lake**, AK, U.S.A.
106 H 6 **Nakodar**, India
133 Q 2 **Nakonde**, Zambia
71 D 26 **Nakskov**, Denmark
71 F 16 **Näkten**, Sweden
131 U 8 **Nakuru**, Kenya
39 I 21 **Nakusp**, BC, Canada
101 S 12 **Nal**, Pakistan
93 O 14 **Nal'chik**, Russian Federation
105 A 14 **Naliya**, India
94 G 9 **Nallihan**, Turkey
125 R 8 **Nālūt**, Libya
108 L 10 **Nam Co**, China
114 M 13 **Nam Đinh**, Vietnam
115 J 14 **Nam Ngum Reservoir**, Laos
115 J 16 **Nam Phong**, Thailand
132 H 7 **Namacunde**, Angola
133 S 6 **Namacurra**, Mozambique
107 N 9 **Namai**, Nepal
23 S 2 **Namakan Lake**, MN, U.S.A.
105 E 22 **Namakkal**, India
131 V 9 **Namanga**, Kenya
103 S 11 **Namangan**, Uzbekistan
103 S 11 **Namangan Wiloyati**, Uzbekistan
133 U 5 **Namapa**, Mozambique
132 J 11 **Namaqualand**, Namibia
138 G 3 **Namatanai**, Papua New Guinea
135 W 10 **Nambucca Heads**, NSW, Australia
107 R 9 **Namche Bazar**, Nepal
111 K 18 **Namch'ŏn**, North Korea
132 G 8 **Namib Desert**, Namibia
132 F 6 **Namibe**, Angola
132 F 6 **Namibe**, Angola
132 H 9 **Namibia**, Africa
133 S 7 **Namidobe**, Mozambique
108 M 10 **Namjagbarwa**, China
114 E 11 **Namlan**, Myanmar
117 R 12 **Namlea**, Indonesia
135 T 10 **Namoi**, NSW, Australia
141 O 15 **Namoluk**, Federated States of Micronesia
141 N 14 **Namonuito**, Federated States of Micronesia
141 X 4 **Namorik**, Marshall Islands
28 J 10 **Nampa**, ID, U.S.A.
128 K 8 **Nampala**, Mali
111 J 18 **Namp'o**, North Korea
133 U 5 **Nampula**, Mozambique
133 T 5 **Nampula**, Mozambique
114 F 12 **Namsang**, Myanmar
71 E 14 **Namsos**, Norway
89 T 10 **Namtsy**, Russian Federation
114 E 10 **Namtu**, Myanmar
141 X 3 **Namu**, Marshall Islands
133 S 5 **Namuli**, Mozambique
133 T 4 **Namuno**, Mozambique
69 H 22 **Namur**, Belgium
69 H 21 **Namur**, Belgium
132 I 7 **Namutoni**, Namibia
133 N 6 **Namwala**, Zambia
111 L 21 **Namwŏn**, South Korea
114 E 6 **Namya Ra**, Myanmar
79 H 15 **Namysłów**, Poland

Country · Internal administrative region: State/Province/Territory/Dependent territory · Capital city · Mountain range/Undersea ridge · Mountain peak/Volcano/Seamount · Geographic feature · Headland/Point/Cape/Peninsula · Desert · Island/Island group · Antarctic base · Ocean · Sea · Bay/Gulf/Channel/Strait · Lake · Salt pan/Dry/Intermittent lake · River

Nan – Nordkapp

115 H 14 Nan, Thailand
130 J 3 Nana-Grébizi, Central African Republic
130 H 4 Nana-Mambéré, Central African Republic
39 F 22 Nanaimo, BC, Canada
111 N 15 Nanam, North Korea
113 X 11 Nan'an, China
123 H 15 Nanao, Japan
113 O 6 Nanbu, China
110 M 9 Nancha, China
113 V 8 Nanchang, China
113 W 9 Nancheng, China
113 O 6 Nanchong, China
113 P 7 Nanchuan, China
105 O 24 Nancowry, India
65 V 4 Nancy, France
106 L 7 Nanda Devi, India
113 P 11 Nandan, China
105 E 17 Nanded, India
105 C 15 Nandurbar, India
105 F 19 Nandyal, India
111 I 16 Nanfen, China
113 V 9 Nanfeng, China
108 L 11 Nang, China
129 U 14 Nanga Eboko, Cameroon
101 Y 6 Nanga Parbat, Pakistan
121 F 16 Nangalao, Philippines
101 V 7 Nangarhār, Afghanistan
116 J 11 Nangatayap, Indonesia
111 K 17 Nangnim-sanmaek, North Korea
113 U 1 Nangong, China
112 H 5 Nangqên, China
131 W 13 Nangulangwa, Tanzania
112 K 10 Nanhua, China
113 Z 6 Nanhui, China
105 E 21 Nanjangud, India
113 X 5 Nanjing, China
113 U 10 Nankang, China
123 F 20 Nankoku, Japan
132 J 6 Nankova, Angola
113 U 2 Nanle, China
113 X 6 Nanling, China
113 P 12 Nanning, China
142 M 14 Nanortalik, Greenland
113 N 11 Nanpan, China
111 G 16 Nanpiao, China
113 N 4 Nanping, China
113 Y 10 Nanri Dao, China
143 T 9 Nansen Basin, Arctic Ocean
143 S 10 Nansen Cordillera, Arctic Ocean
37 O 1 Nansen Sound, NU, Canada
131 S 9 Nansio, Tanzania
64 L 7 Nantes, France
42 E 14 Nanticoke, ON, Canada
39 J 20 Nanton, AB, Canada
113 Y 5 Nantong, China
15 P 11 Nantucket, MA, U.S.A.
15 P 11 Nantucket Island, MA, U.S.A.
15 P 11 Nantucket Sound, MA, U.S.A.
63 Q 5 Nantwich, U.K.
140 E 5 Nanumanga, Tuvalu
140 E 5 Nanumea, Tuvalu
134 E 6 Nanutarra Roadhouse, WA, Australia
113 S 7 Nanxian, China
113 U 11 Nanxiong, China
113 T 5 Nanyang, China
122 K 13 Nanyo, Japan
131 V 7 Nanyuki, Kenya
113 S 5 Nanzhang, China
113 S 4 Nanzhao, China
110 J 5 Naodahan, China
107 T 12 Naogaon, Bangladesh
106 H 4 Naoshera, India
33 G 19 Napa, CA, U.S.A.
38 H 9 Napaktulik Lake, NU, Canada
136 N 13 Napier, New Zealand
145 W 3 Napier Mountains, Antarctica
19 W 13 Naples, FL, U.S.A.
28 K 2 Naples, ID, U.S.A.
77 J 16 Naples, Italy
52 B 8 Napo, Ecuador
52 D 9 Napo, Ecuador/Peru
113 O 12 Napo, China
21 L 16 Napoleon, OH, U.S.A.
22 K 6 Napoleon, ND, U.S.A.
99 Q 13 Naqūb, Yemen
123 H 18 Nara, Japan
128 J 8 Nara, Mali
31 U 9 Nara Visa, NM, U.S.A.
85 I 15 Narach, Belarus
135 Q 13 Naracoorte, SA, Australia
105 G 17 Narainpur, India
110 C 12 Naran Bulag, China
52 B 10 Naranjal, Ecuador
52 D 11 Naranjal, Peru
45 S 10 Naranjos, Mexico
123 A 22 Narao, Japan
105 I 18 Narasannapeta, India
115 I 26 Narathiwat, Thailand
107 U 13 Narayanganj, Bangladesh
65 R 15 Narbonne, France
105 O 20 Narcondam Island, India
58 C 13 Naré, Argentina
37 Q 1 Nares Strait, NU, Canada
78 L 11 Narew, Poland
105 D 19 Nargund, India
132 J 10 Narib, Namibia
101 U 6 Narin, Afghanistan
50 F 9 Nariño, Colombia
123 L 16 Narita, Japan
106 J 6 Narkanda, India
105 D 15 Narmada, India
139 Y 12 Naro, Fiji
92 K 1 Naro-Fominsk, Russian Federation
131 U 8 Narok, Kenya
135 U 13 Narooma, NSW, Australia
135 U 10 Narrabri, NSW, Australia
135 T 12 Narrandera, NSW, Australia
134 G 11 Narrogin, WA, Australia
135 T 11 Narromine, NSW, Australia
17 O 6 Narrows, VA, U.S.A.
142 M 13 Narsarsuaq, Greenland
107 U 13 Narsingdi, Bangladesh
111 D 14 Nart, China
123 F 19 Naruto, Japan
84 J 5 Narva, Estonia
84 J 5 Narva Bay, Estonia
120 F 7 Narvacan, Philippines
70 H 9 Narvik, Norway
91 P 3 Nar'yan-Mar, Russian Federation
103 T 11 Naryn, Kyrgyzstan
103 V 11 Naryn, Kyrgyzstan
103 V 11 Narynskaya Oblast', Kyrgyzstan
92 J 4 Naryshkino, Russian Federation
139 Y 11 Nasau, Fiji
32 G 8 Naselle, WA, U.S.A.
105 C 16 Nashik, India
15 N 9 Nashua, NH, U.S.A.
29 W 3 Nashua, MT, U.S.A.
16 F 8 Nashville, TN, U.S.A.
21 F 21 Nashville, IL, U.S.A.
25 T 13 Nashville, AR, U.S.A.
80 H 8 Našice, Croatia
127 F 20 Nasir, Sudan
41 U 8 Naskaupi, NL, Canada
107 P 12 Nasmganj, India
77 K 21 Naso, Italy
131 N 14 Nasondoye, Democratic Republic of Congo
129 R 12 Nassarawa, Nigeria
48 L 2 Nassau, The Bahamas
140 M 7 Nassau, Cook Islands
71 F 23 Nässjö, Sweden
41 Q 7 Nastapoca, QC, Canada
41 P 7 Nastapoka Islands, ON, Canada
123 K 14 Nasu-dake, Japan
120 F 12 Nasugbu, Philippines
133 N 8 Nata, Botswana
50 H 7 Natagaima, Colombia
54 O 12 Natal, Brazil
116 C 10 Natal, Indonesia
100 I 7 Naṭanz, Iran
43 V 3 Natashquan, QC, Canada
18 K 6 Natchez, MS, U.S.A.
18 I 5 Natchitoches, LA, U.S.A.
138 D 7 National Capital District, Papua New Guinea
129 N 11 Natitingou, Benin
122 K 12 Natori, Japan
14 B 12 Natrona Heights, PA, U.S.A.
105 E 23 Nattam, India
115 E 14 Nattaung, Myanmar
116 H 9 Natuna Besar, Indonesia
132 I 10 Nauchas, Namibia
74 K 8 Nauders, Austria
72 L 13 Nauen, Germany
104 C 11 Naukh, India
141 U 1 Nauru, Oceania
52 E 11 Nauta, Peru
45 T 11 Nautla, Mexico
101 R 9 Nauzad, Afghanistan
67 N 8 Navahermosa, Spain
85 H 18 Navahrudak, Belarus
31 O 8 Navajo Lake, NM, U.S.A.
30 L 7 Navajo Mount, UT, U.S.A.
121 K 16 Naval, Philippines
66 L 7 Navalmoral de la Mata, Spain
85 K 14 Navapolatsk, Belarus
67 R 2 Navarra, Spain
49 N 7 Navassa Island, U.S.A., U.S.A.
85 G 18 Navavel'nya, Belarus
56 F 12 Navidad, Chile
105 A 14 Navlakhi, India
92 I 4 Navlya, Russian Federation
103 P 12 Navoi, Uzbekistan
44 J 6 Navojoa, Mexico
105 C 16 Navsari, India
139 W 12 Navua, Fiji
96 H 8 Nawá, Syria
107 S 12 Nawabganj, Bangladesh
107 U 12 Nawabganj, Bangladesh
101 U 13 Nawabshah, Pakistan
107 Q 12 Nawada, India
101 T 9 Nāwah, Afghanistan
106 H 9 Nawalgarh, India
105 H 16 Nawapara, India
114 F 10 Nawngleng, Myanmar
103 O 10 Nawoiy Wiloyati, Uzbekistan
95 V 10 Naxşşivan, Azerbaijan
113 N 8 Naxi, China
83 J 22 Naxos, Greece
83 J 22 Naxos, Greece
50 G 7 Naya, Colombia
101 T 7 Nayak, Afghanistan
45 N 10 Nayar, Mexico
44 M 10 Nayarit, Mexico
122 K 4 Nayoro, Japan
105 F 20 Nayudupeta, India
96 G 8 Nazareth, Israel
53 E 18 Nazca, Peru
123 O 22 Naze, Japan
94 C 11 Nazilli, Turkey
93 P 14 Nazran', Russian Federation
127 I 20 Nazrēt, Ethiopia
99 Y 7 Nazwá, Oman
133 O 2 Nchelenge, Zambia
132 K 9 Ncojane, Botswana
129 T 15 Ncue, Equatorial Guinea
132 G 3 N'dalatando, Angola
129 O 11 Ndali, Benin
130 K 3 Ndélé, Central African Republic
129 V 14 Ndélélé, Cameroon
130 E 9 Ndendé, Gabon
139 P 7 Ndeni, Solomon Islands
129 V 10 Ndjamena, Chad
130 E 8 Ndjolé, Gabon
130 G 8 Ndjounou, Gabon
133 O 4 Ndola, Zambia
131 Q 6 Nduye, Democratic Republic of Congo
83 F 17 Nea Anchialos, Greece
83 F 15 Nea Moudania, Greece
82 G 13 Nea Zichni, Greece
32 F 6 Neah Bay, WA, U.S.A.
83 F 23 Neapoli, Greece
83 K 26 Neapoli, Greece
34 B 11 Near Islands, AK, U.S.A.
63 N 10 Neath, U.K.
131 R 6 Nebbi, Uganda
128 M 10 Nebbou, Burkina Faso
102 I 12 Nebitdag, Turkmenistan
22 H 13 Nebraska, U.S.A.
23 P 15 Nebraska City, NE, U.S.A.
20 E 12 Necedah, WI, U.S.A.
27 T 7 Neches, TX, U.S.A.
73 F 21 Neckar, Germany
59 D 19 Necochea, Argentina
129 X 8 Nédéley, Chad
69 K 17 Nederweert, Netherlands
87 T 3 Nedryhayliv, Ukraine
29 T 10 Needle Mountain, WY, U.S.A.
33 N 24 Needles, CA, U.S.A.
40 H 10 Neepawa, MB, Canada
95 Z 9 Neftşşala, Azerbaijan
91 S 14 Neftekamsk, Russian Federation
93 P 12 Neftekumsk, Russian Federation
88 L 10 Nefteyugansk, Russian Federation
62 L 5 Nefyn, U.K.
132 G 2 Negage, Angola
116 L 15 Negara, Indonesia
127 I 21 Negēlē, Ethiopia
127 I 22 Negēlē, Ethiopia
118 C 9 Negeri Sembilan, Malaysia
96 E 12 Negev, Israel
131 W 15 Negomane, Tanzania
105 F 25 Negombo, Sri Lanka
80 O 11 Negotin, Serbia and Montenegro
86 I 12 Negreni, Romania
52 A 11 Negritos, Peru
57 H 15 Negro, South America
121 I 18 Negros, Philippines
87 N 14 Negru Vodă, Romania
101 O 9 Nehbandān, Iran
110 J 8 Nehe, China
86 K 11 Nehoiu, Romania
132 H 6 Nehone, Angola
140 J 10 Neiafu, Tonga
49 P 8 Neiba, Dominican Republic
113 N 7 Neijiang, China
105 N 22 Neill Island, India
50 H 8 Neiva, Colombia
113 S 4 Neixiang, China
45 T 14 Nejapa Tequisistlán, Mexico
127 H 20 Nek'emtē, Ethiopia
90 F 14 Nelidovo, Russian Federation
23 N 12 Neligh, NE, U.S.A.
105 G 20 Nellore, India
39 I 21 Nelson, BC, Canada
137 I 16 Nelson, New Zealand
137 I 16 Nelson, New Zealand
135 V 11 Nelson Bay, NSW, Australia
133 P 10 Nelspruit, Republic of South Africa
121 E 16 Nelyan Point, Philippines
128 J 7 Néma, Mauritania
85 D 15 Neman, Lithuania
85 C 15 Neman, Russian Federation
129 Q 14 Nembe, Nigeria
83 E 20 Nemea, Greece
85 G 15 Nemenčinė, Lithuania
122 N 4 Nemuro, Japan
122 N 4 Nemuro-hantō, Japan
122 M 3 Nemuro-kaikyō, Japan
122 N 4 Nemuro-wan, Japan
87 N 6 Nemyriv, Ukraine
35 R 7 Nenana, AK, U.S.A.
118 E 8 Nenasi, Malaysia
91 R 2 Nenetskiy Avtonomnyy Okrug, Russian Federation
110 J 8 Nenjiang, China
123 H 17 Neo, Japan
83 L 20 Neo Karlovasi, Greece
23 Q 13 Neola, IA, U.S.A.
107 O 8 Nepal, Asia
106 M 9 Nepalganj, Nepal
42 I 11 Nepean, ON, Canada
79 B 18 Nepomuk, Czech Republic
89 S 14 Nerchinsk, Russian Federation
84 G 12 Nereta, Latvia
81 G 14 Neretva, Bosnia and Herzegovina
132 K 6 Neriquinha, Angola
85 F 15 Neris, Lithuania
67 N 13 Nerja, Spain
89 T 12 Neryungri, Russian Federation
68 K 5 Nes, Netherlands
82 N 9 Nesebŭr, Bulgaria
24 J 5 Ness City, KS, U.S.A.
85 D 15 Nesterov, Russian Federation
40 J 11 Nestor Falls, ON, Canada
82 H 12 Nestos, Greece
96 F 8 Netanya, Israel
68 H 10 Netherlands, Europe
49 S 12 Netherlands Antilles, The Netherlands, The Netherlands
41 Q 2 Nettilling Lake, NU, Canada
73 J 23 Neuberg, Germany
72 M 10 Neubrandenburg, Germany
72 J 9 Neubukow, Germany
74 C 7 Neuchâtel, Switzerland
72 M 13 Neuenhagen, Germany
65 U 5 Neufchâteau, France
69 J 24 Neufchâteau, Belgium
65 O 2 Neufchâtel-en-Bray, France
75 S 3 Neufelden, Austria
75 W 4 Neulengbach, Austria
73 J 21 Neumarkt, Germany
145 O 1 Neumayer, Antarctica
72 H 9 Neumünster, Germany
65 P 6 Neung-sur-Beuvron, France
73 C 21 Neunkirchen, Germany
75 W 5 Neunkirchen, Austria
57 H 15 Neuquén, Argentina
57 G 15 Neuquén, Argentina
57 G 14 Neuquén, Argentina
72 L 12 Neuruppin, Germany
75 Y 5 Neusiedler See, Austria
73 C 16 Neuss, Germany
72 G 13 Neustadt, Germany
72 I 9 Neustadt, Germany
73 J 17 Neustadt, Germany
73 K 22 Neustadt, Germany
73 E 21 Neustadt, Germany
73 I 20 Neustadt an der Aisch, Germany
72 L 11 Neustrelitz, Germany
72 F 9 Neuwerk, Germany
73 D 18 Neuwied, Germany
25 S 6 Nevada, MO, U.S.A.
33 J 18 Nevada, U.S.A., U.S.A.
33 H 17 Nevada City, CA, U.S.A.
45 N 12 Nevada de Colima, Mexico
53 F 19 Nevado Ampato, Peru
56 G 13 Nevado Campanario, Argentina
53 F 18 Nevado Coropuna, Peru
56 H 5 Nevado de Chañi, Argentina
56 H 5 Nevado de Poquis, Chile
45 Q 12 Nevado de Tolúca, Mexico
50 H 8 Nevado del Huila, Colombia
50 I 6 Nevado del Ruiz, Colombia
53 C 14 Nevado Huascarán, Peru
53 I 19 Nevado Illampu, Bolivia
56 H 8 Nevado Ojos del Salado, Argentina
53 I 20 Nevado Sajama, Bolivia
56 H 6 Nevados de Cachi, Argentina
90 E 14 Nevel', Russian Federation
65 R 8 Nevers, France
93 N 12 Nevinnomyssk, Russian Federation
49 X 8 Nevis, St Kitts and Nevis
94 J 11 Nevşehir, Turkey
19 N 2 New Albany, MS, U.S.A.
21 J 21 New Albany, IN, U.S.A.
63 T 12 New Alresford, U.K.
51 V 5 New Amsterdam, Guyana
15 O 11 New Bedford, MA, U.S.A.
17 U 10 New Bern, NC, U.S.A.
27 T 4 New Boston, TX, U.S.A.
27 P 10 New Braunfels, TX, U.S.A.
138 F 4 New Britain, Papua New Guinea
43 S 8 New Brunswick, Canada
139 N 14 New Caledonia, New Caledonia
139 O 15 New Caledonia, France
43 T 6 New Carlisle, QC, Canada
14 A 11 New Castle, PA, U.S.A.
16 H 4 New Castle, KY, U.S.A.
14 J 12 New City, NY, U.S.A.
106 J 8 New Delhi, India
17 N 13 New Ellenton, SC, U.S.A.
15 N 9 New England, NH, U.S.A.
63 S 12 New Forest, U.K.
138 K 6 New Georgia, Solomon Islands
138 J 6 New Georgia Islands, Solomon Islands
138 K 5 New Georgia Sound, Solomon Islands
43 W 9 New Glasgow, NS, Canada
138 A 4 New Guinea, Indonesia/Papua New Guinea
15 N 7 New Hampshire, U.S.A.
138 G 2 New Hanover, Papua New Guinea
14 L 11 New Haven, CT, U.S.A.
39 D 18 New Hazelton, BC, Canada
18 J 8 New Iberia, LA, U.S.A.
138 G 3 New Ireland, Papua New Guinea
138 H 2 New Ireland, Papua New Guinea
14 I 14 New Jersey, U.S.A.
21 N 19 New Lexington, OH, U.S.A.
42 F 7 New Liskeard, ON, Canada
14 M 11 New London, CT, U.S.A.
20 G 12 New London, WI, U.S.A.
17 R 4 New Market, VA, U.S.A.
28 J 8 New Meadows, ID, U.S.A.
31 O 11 New Mexico, U.S.A.
135 S 15 New Norfolk, TAS, Australia
18 L 8 New Orleans, LA, U.S.A.
21 N 18 New Philadelphia, OH, U.S.A.
33 I 14 New Pine Creek, CA, U.S.A.
136 J 12 New Plymouth, New Zealand
48 K 2 New Providence, The Bahamas
62 L 8 New Quay, U.K.
43 S 6 New Richmond, QC, Canada
18 K 7 New Roads, LA, U.S.A.
14 K 12 New Rochelle, NY, U.S.A.
22 L 4 New Rockford, ND, U.S.A.
63 Y 12 New Romney, U.K.
43 U 11 New Ross, NS, Canada
61 E 20 New Ross, Republic of Ireland
89 T 6 New Siberia Islands, Russian Federation
19 X 9 New Smyrna Beach, FL, U.S.A.
135 T 10 New South Wales, Australia
22 H 3 New Town, ND, U.S.A.
23 R 9 New Ulm, MN, U.S.A.
14 F 9 New York, U.S.A.
14 K 12 New York, NY, U.S.A.
137 I 14 New Zealand, Oceania
131 W 14 Newala, Tanzania
14 J 12 Newark, NJ, U.S.A.
14 F 8 Newark, NY, U.S.A.
17 W 2 Newark, DE, U.S.A.
21 N 18 Newark, OH, U.S.A.
33 M 17 Newark Lake, NV, U.S.A.
63 U 5 Newark-on-Trent, U.K.
32 G 10 Newberg, OR, U.S.A.
17 N 12 Newberry, SC, U.S.A.
42 I 11 Newboro, ON, Canada
14 J 11 Newburgh, NY, U.S.A.
63 T 11 Newbury, U.K.
15 O 9 Newburyport, MA, U.S.A.
63 P 1 Newby Bridge, U.K.
29 Z 10 Newcastle, WY, U.S.A.
42 F 12 Newcastle, ON, Canada
43 S 8 Newcastle, NB, Canada
61 F 16 Newcastle, U.K.
135 V 11 Newcastle, NSW, Australia
62 L 9 Newcastle Emlyn, U.K.
63 Q 5 Newcastle-under-Lyme, U.K.
61 J 15 Newcastle upon Tyne, U.K.
14 D 8 Newfane, NY, U.S.A.
41 X 10 Newfoundland, NL, Canada
41 V 9 Newfoundland and Labrador, Canada
63 W 13 Newhaven, U.K.
21 G 19 Newman, IL, U.S.A.
134 H 7 Newman, WA, Australia
15 O 8 Newmarket, NH, U.S.A.
42 E 12 Newmarket, ON, Canada
63 W 8 Newmarket, U.K.
19 S 3 Newnan, GA, U.S.A.
14 F 13 Newport, PA, U.S.A.
14 M 5 Newport, VT, U.S.A.
14 M 8 Newport, NH, U.S.A.
15 N 11 Newport, RI, U.S.A.
16 K 9 Newport, TN, U.S.A.
25 W 10 Newport, AR, U.S.A.
32 F 10 Newport, OR, U.S.A.
32 L 6 Newport, WA, U.S.A.
62 K 8 Newport, U.K.
63 T 13 Newport, U.K.
63 Q 6 Newport, U.K.
62 K 8 Newport Bay, U.K.
17 V 7 Newport News, VA, U.S.A.
63 U 8 Newport Pagnell, U.K.
62 J 14 Newquay, U.K.
61 F 16 Newry, U.K.
15 O 10 Newton, MA, U.S.A.
23 T 13 Newton, IA, U.S.A.
25 N 5 Newton, KS, U.S.A.
63 Q 2 Newton, U.K.
63 N 14 Newton Abbot, U.K.
61 G 15 Newton Stewart, U.K.
63 O 7 Newtown, U.K.
90 M 13 Neya, Russian Federation
100 J 8 Neyestānak, Iran
101 N 6 Neyshābūr, Iran
105 E 24 Neyyattinkara, India
116 I 10 Ngabang, Indonesia
130 H 10 Ngabé, Congo
114 E 7 Ngagahtawng, Myanmar
140 J 14 Ngajangel, Palau
129 V 10 Ngala, Nigeria
129 W 11 Ngam, Chad
129 W 10 Ngama, Chad
132 L 8 Ngamiland, Botswana
127 E 23 Ngangala, Sudan
108 I 8 Nganglong Kangri, China
115 H 14 Ngao, Thailand
129 U 13 Ngaoundal, Cameroon
129 U 12 Ngaoundéré, Cameroon
131 R 9 Ngara, Tanzania
130 H 6 Ngbala, Congo
141 P 15 Ngetik Atoll, Federated States of Micronesia
138 L 6 Nggatokae, Solomon Islands
130 H 9 Ngo, Congo
115 O 18 Ngoc Linh, Vietnam
129 U 12 Ngong, Cameroon
130 I 5 Ngoto, Central African Republic
130 E 9 Ngounié, Gabon
129 W 9 Ngoura, Chad
129 U 8 Ngourti, Niger
131 N 4 Ngouyo, Central African Republic
130 H 5 Nguia Bouar, Central African Republic
129 U 9 Nguigmi, Niger
134 L 1 Nguiu, NT, Australia
135 O 2 Ngukurr, NT, Australia
140 J 14 Ngulu, Federated States of Micronesia
133 P 8 Ngundu, Zimbabwe
129 S 9 Nguru, Nigeria
114 M 11 Nguyên, Vietnam
115 O 20 Nha Trang, Vietnam
133 R 7 Nhamatanda, Mozambique
54 G 10 Nhamundá, Brazil
132 I 4 N'harea, Angola
135 R 12 Nhill, VIC, Australia
135 O 1 Nhulunbuy, NT, Australia
131 P 7 Nia-Nia, Democratic Republic of Congo
14 C 8 Niagara Falls, NY, U.S.A.
42 F 13 Niagara Falls, ON, Canada
119 R 7 Niah, Malaysia
107 P 9 Niak, Nepal
129 P 9 Niamey, Niger
131 P 5 Niangara, Democratic Republic of Congo
113 O 3 Niangniangba, China
128 K 11 Niangoloko, Burkina Faso
110 I 9 Nianzishan, China
130 F 9 Niari, Congo
116 B 10 Nias, Indonesia
133 S 4 Niassa, Mozambique
141 U 1 Nibok, Nauru
47 P 8 Nicaragua, North America
77 M 19 Nicastro, Italy
65 X 13 Nice, France
19 Q 7 Niceville, FL, U.S.A.
123 D 23 Nichinan, Japan
17 R 12 Nichols, SC, U.S.A.
105 N 24 Nicobar Islands, India
77 J 22 Nicosia, Italy
94 H 15 Nicosia, Cyprus
47 O 12 Nicoya, Costa Rica
79 K 16 Nida, Poland
85 B 14 Nida, Lithuania
82 D 13 Nidže Kožuf, Macedonia (F.Y.R.O.M.)
78 K 10 Nidzica, Poland
72 F 7 Niebüll, Germany
69 M 25 Niederanven, Luxembourg
75 U 3 Niederösterreich, Austria
72 F 12 Niedersachsen, Germany
79 M 15 Niedrzwica, Poland
130 H 4 Niem, Central African Republic
72 G 13 Nienburg, Germany
73 O 16 Niesky, Germany
68 K 11 Nieuw-Milligen, Netherlands
51 V 6 Nieuw Nickerie, Suriname
68 I 13 Nieuwegein, Netherlands
69 E 15 Nieuwerkerk, Netherlands
68 G 13 Nieuwerkerk aan den IJssel, Netherlands
68 N 6 Nieuwolda, Netherlands
69 A 17 Nieuwpoort, Belgium
94 J 12 Niğde, Turkey
129 R 8 Niger, Africa
129 Q 11 Niger, Nigeria
129 Q 12 Niger, Africa
129 R 11 Nigeria, Africa
122 K 13 Nihonmatsu, Japan
123 K 18 Nii-jima, Japan
122 J 13 Niigata, Japan
123 I 15 Niigata-yake-yama, Japan
123 E 20 Niihama, Japan
34 A 7 Niihau, HI, U.S.A.
123 E 18 Niimi, Japan
122 J 13 Niitsu, Japan
67 Q 13 Níjar, Spain
68 J 12 Nijkerk, Netherlands
69 K 14 Nijmegen, Netherlands
68 M 11 Nijverdal, Netherlands
83 E 16 Nikaia, Greece
90 H 1 Nikel', Russian Federation
70 I 9 Nikkaluokta, Sweden
129 O 11 Nikki, Benin
123 K 14 Nikkō, Japan
89 W 12 Nikolayevsk-na-Amure, Russian Federation
93 Q 3 Nikol'sk, Russian Federation
82 I 7 Nikopol, Bulgaria
87 U 8 Nikopol', Ukraine
94 M 8 Niksar, Turkey
101 O 13 Nīkshahr, Iran
81 I 15 Nikšić, Serbia and Montenegro
140 I 4 Nikumaroro, Kiribati
140 E 3 Nikunau, Kiribati
117 T 14 Nila, Indonesia
105 L 18 Nilandhoo Atoll, Maldives
126 E 10 Nile, Egypt/Sudan
127 F 16 Nile, Sudan
126 E 7 Nile Delta, Egypt
21 I 16 Niles, MI, U.S.A.
45 U 14 Niltepec, Mexico
128 I 12 Nimba Mountains, Côte d'Ivoire/Guinea
65 S 13 Nîmes, France
101 Q 10 Nīmrūz, Afghanistan
127 E 23 Nimule, Sudan
132 K 5 Ninda, Angola
105 A 23 Nine Degree Channel, India
110 M 12 Ning'an, China
113 Z 7 Ningbo, China
111 F 15 Ningcheng, China
113 Y 9 Ningde, China
113 V 9 Ningdu, China
113 X 6 Ningguo, China
113 Z 7 Ninghai, China
113 W 10 Ninghua, China
109 R 14 Ningming, China
112 L 9 Ningnan, China
113 O 5 Ningqiang, China
113 Q 4 Ningshan, China
113 O 2 Ningxia, China
113 P 3 Ningxian, China
113 S 8 Ningxiang, China
113 S 10 Ningyuan, China
114 M 13 Ninh Binh, Vietnam
115 O 20 Ninh Hoa, Vietnam
138 C 2 Ninigo Group, Papua New Guinea
122 K 9 Ninohe, Japan
22 I 11 Niobrara, NE, U.S.A.
23 N 12 Niobrara, NE, U.S.A.
107 X 9 Nioko, India
128 J 9 Niono, Mali
128 H 8 Nioro, Mali
64 M 9 Niort, France
39 M 17 Nipawin, SK, Canada
40 L 11 Nipigon, ON, Canada
33 M 23 Nipton, CA, U.S.A.
105 F 17 Nirmal, India
107 R 11 Nirmali, India
80 N 13 Niš, Serbia and Montenegro
97 U 14 Nişāb, Iraq
99 Q 13 Nişab, Yemen
123 C 25 Nishino-omote, Japan
123 F 18 Nishiwaki, Japan
123 C 22 Nisi-mera, Japan
79 M 16 Nisko, Poland
71 E 24 Nissan, Sweden
138 I 4 Nissan Island, Papua New Guinea
71 B 20 Nisser, Norway
83 M 23 Nisyros, Greece
123 E 18 Nita, Japan
58 N 7 Niterói, Brazil
79 H 21 Nitra, Slovakia
140 I 9 Niua Group, Tonga
140 I 9 Niuafo'ou, Tonga
140 I 9 Niuatoputapu, Tonga
140 K 10 Niue, Niue
140 K 10 Niue, New Zealand
110 H 5 Niu'erhe, China
140 G 7 Niulakita, Tuvalu
140 F 5 Niutao, Tuvalu
69 F 20 Nivelles, Belgium
25 T 7 Nixa, MO, U.S.A.
27 P 11 Nixon, TX, U.S.A.
105 E 17 Nizam Sagar, India
105 F 17 Nizamabad, India
90 M 13 Nizhegorodskaya Oblast', Russian Federation
93 S 1 Nizhnekamsk, Russian Federation
89 O 13 Nizhneudinsk, Russian Federation
88 L 10 Nizhnevartovsk, Russian Federation
89 T 7 Nizhneyyansk, Russian Federation
93 N 8 Nizhniy Chir, Russian Federation
93 O 3 Nizhniy Lomov, Russian Federation
93 P 1 Nizhniy Novgorod, Russian Federation
88 J 10 Nizhniy Tagil, Russian Federation
91 N 4 Nizhnyaya Pesha, Russian Federation
89 N 9 Nizhnyaya Tunguska, Russian Federation
87 R 2 Nizhyn, Ukraine
94 M 13 Nizip, Turkey
81 I 14 Njegoš, Serbia and Montenegro
133 P 12 Njesuthi, Lesotho
131 W 13 Njinjo, Tanzania
131 T 13 Njombe, Tanzania
131 R 12 Nkasi, Tanzania
133 O 7 Nkayi, Zimbabwe
133 R 3 Nkhata Bay, Malawi
133 R 4 Nkhotakota, Malawi
131 R 11 Nkondwe, Tanzania
129 S 14 Nkongsamba, Cameroon
132 J 7 Nkurenkuru, Namibia
114 F 8 Nmai Hka, Myanmar
105 J 15 Noamundi, India
123 D 22 Nobeoka, Japan
122 J 7 Noboribetsu, Japan
55 G 15 Nobres, Brazil
135 R 8 Noccundra, QLD, Australia
45 S 13 Nochixtlán, Mexico
77 N 16 Noci, Italy
123 K 15 Noda, Japan
42 E 9 Noelville, ON, Canada
30 K 15 Nogales, AZ, U.S.A.
44 I 3 Nogales, Mexico
65 O 5 Nogent-le-Rotrou, France
89 O 10 Noginsk, Russian Federation
92 L 1 Noginsk, Russian Federation
59 C 14 Nogoyá, Argentina
106 H 8 Nohar, India
73 C 20 Nohfelden, Germany
66 H 2 Noia, Spain
64 K 7 Noirmoutier-en-l'Île, France
123 L 17 Nojima-zaki, Japan
101 Q 12 Nok Kundi, Pakistan
104 C 11 Nokha, India
71 L 18 Nokia, Finland
129 V 9 Nokou, Chad
107 U 11 Nokrek Peak, India
77 J 16 Nola, Italy
130 H 5 Nola, Central African Republic
91 P 13 Nolinsk, Russian Federation
123 B 24 Noma-misaki, Japan
34 M 7 Nome, AK, U.S.A.
123 B 22 Nomo-zaki, Japan
140 I 10 Nomuka Group, Tonga
141 O 14 Nomwin, Federated States of Micronesia
115 I 16 Nong Bua Lamphu, Thailand
115 J 15 Nong Khai, Thailand
110 J 12 Nong'an, China
107 V 11 Nongstoin, India
140 E 3 Nonouti, Kiribati
115 H 19 Nonthaburi, Thailand
65 N 10 Nontron, France
68 G 8 Nooderhaaks, Netherlands
69 I 15 Noord-Brabant, Netherlands
68 H 9 Noord-Holland, Netherlands
35 N 5 Noorvik, AK, U.S.A.
135 W 8 Noosa Heads, QLD, Australia
103 R 13 Norak, Tajikistan
121 L 23 Norala, Philippines
42 F 6 Noranda, QC, Canada
129 U 12 Nord, Cameroon
70 I 6 Nord-Kvaløy, Norway
129 T 13 Nord-Ouest, Cameroon
65 Q 1 Nord-pas-de-Calais, France
143 U 11 Nordaustlandet, Svalbard
72 D 10 Norden, Germany
72 C 10 Norderney, Germany
72 F 8 Norderoogsand, Germany
71 B 17 Nordfjordeid, Norway
70 G 10 Nordfold, Norway
72 E 8 Nordfriesische Inseln, Germany
73 I 15 Nordhausen, Germany
72 C 13 Nordhorn, Germany
70 K 5 Nordkapp, Norway

Country · Internal administrative region: State/Province/Territory/Dependent territory · Capital city · Mountain range/Undersea ridge · Mountain peak/Volcano/Seamount · Geographic feature · Headland/Point/Cape/Peninsula · Desert · Island/Island group · Antarctic base · Ocean · Sea · Bay/Gulf/Channel/Strait · Lake · Salt pan/Dry/Intermittent lake · Ri

Nordkivu – Opheim

P 8 Nordkivu, Democratic Republic of Congo
F 14 Nordli, Norway
I 22 Nördlingen, Germany
I 15 Nordmaling, Sweden
B 15 Nordmøre, Norway
B 16 Nordøyane, Norway
E 15 Nordrhein-Westfalen, Germany
F 8 Nordstrand, Germany
R 7 Nordvik, Russian Federation
C 19 Noresund, Norway
V 7 Norfolk, VA, U.S.A.
N 12 Norfolk, NE, U.S.A.
V 8 Norfork Lake, AR, U.S.A.
P 14 Norias, TX, U.S.A.
O 8 Noril'sk, Russian Federation
F 11 Norland, ON, Canada
P 8 Norlina, NC, U.S.A.
G 18 Normal, IL, U.S.A.
N 10 Norman, OK, U.S.A.
R 4 Norman, QLD, Australia
D 11 Norman Wells, NT, Canada
G 7 Normanby Island, Papua New Guinea
L 4 Normandy, France
R 4 Normanton, QLD, Australia
G 17 Ñorquinco, Argentina
F 19 Norra Ny, Sweden
G 12 Norra Storfjället, Sweden
G 14 Norråker, Sweden
C 23 Nørresundby, Denmark
J 8 Norris Lake, TN, U.S.A.
G 21 Norrköping, Sweden
I 20 Norrtälje, Sweden
I 11 Norseman, WA, Australia
C 20 Norsjø, Norway
Q 10 Norsup, Vanuatu
J 4 Norte de Santander, Colombia
L 9 North Adams, MA, U.S.A.
N 20 North Andaman, India
M 13 North Augusta, SC, U.S.A.
A 21 North Balabac Strait, Philippines
L 18 North Battleford, SK, Canada
F 9 North Bay, ON, Canada
S 10 North Belcher Islands, NU, Canada
E 12 North Bend, OR, U.S.A.
T 7 North Branch, MN, U.S.A.
P 5 North Caicos, Turks and Caicos Islands
I 4 North Cape, New Zealand
P 9 North Carolina, U.S.A.
G 24 North Central, Sri Lanka
B 9 North Channel, ON, Canada
E 14 North Channel, Republic of Ireland/United Kingdom
P 14 North Charleston, SC, U.S.A.
I 4 North Dakota, U.S.A.
U 12 North Downs, U.K.
B 9 North East, PA, U.S.A.
N 8 North East, Botswana
X 6 North-Eastern, Kenya
Z 11 North Foreland, U.K.
M 15 North Fork, NV, U.S.A.
J 7 North Head, New Zealand
V 6 North Horr, Kenya
L 20 North Huvadhu Atoll, Maldives
B 23 North Island, India
H 1 North Island, Philippines
M 11 North Island, New Zealand
E 20 North Islet, Philippines
M 17 North Korea, Asia
X 9 North Lakhimpur, India
L 17 North Maalhosmadulu Atoll, Maldives
N 2 North Magnetic Pole, NU, Canada
L 16 North Miladunmadulu Atoll, Maldives
G 13 North Platte, NE, U.S.A.
I 9 North Point, MI, U.S.A.
R 7 North Pole, AK, U.S.A.
S 8 North Pole, Arctic Ocean
K 10 North Powder, OR, U.S.A.
N 21 North Reef Island, India
J 9 North Rim, AZ, U.S.A.
I 6 North Ronaldsay, U.K.
K 18 North Saskatchewan, SK, Canada
N 20 North Sentinel Island, India
J 4 North Solomons, Papua New Guinea
W 3 North Somercotes, U.K.
W 9 North Stradbroke Island, QLD, Australia
J 12 North Taranaki Bight, New Zealand
O 9 North Twin Island, QC, Canada
F 23 North Ubian, Philippines
E 10 North Uist, U.K.
D 18 North Verde, Philippines
J 20 North Vernon, IN, U.S.A.
Z 5 North Walsham, U.K.
L 11 North West, Republic of South Africa
E 6 North West Cape, WA, Australia
W 6 North West Frontier, Pakistan
G 11 North West Highlands, U.K.
F 24 North Western, Sri Lanka
M 4 North-Western, Zambia
F 13 North York, ON, Canada
S 1 Northallerton, U.K.
G 11 Northam, WA, Australia
L 9 Northampton, MA, U.S.A.
U 8 Northampton, U.K.
E 9 Northampton, WA, Australia
K 7 Northeast Cape, AK, U.S.A.
F 15 Northeim, Germany
G 23 Northern, Sri Lanka
J 11 Northern, Sudan
G 11 Northern, Sierra Leone
M 12 Northern, Ghana
O 10 Northern, Republic of South Africa
P 3 Northern, Zambia
Q 3 Northern, Malawi
F 6 Northern, Papua New Guinea
C 20 Northern Bahr el Ghazal, Sudan
K 13 Northern Cape, Republic of South Africa
L 2 Northern Cay, Belize
L 7 Northern Cook Islands, Cook Islands
B 15 Northern Darfur, Sudan
L 8 Northern Dvina, Russian Federation
E 15 Northern Ireland, U.K.
D 16 Northern Kordofan, Sudan
K 2 Northern Lagoon, Belize
Y 11 Northern Lau Group, Fiji
A 6 Northern Mariana Islands, U.S.A.
D 8 Northern Plain, Italy
N 4 Northern Territory, Australia
S 8 Northfield, MN, U.S.A.
J 6 Northland, New Zealand
43 U 8 Northumberland Strait, PE, Canada
14 J 8 Northville, NY, U.S.A.
34 K 7 Northwest Cape, AK, U.S.A.
38 H 11 Northwest Territories, Canada
63 Q 4 Northwich, U.K.
143 R 4 Northwind Plain, Arctic Ocean
24 J 2 Norton, KS, U.S.A.
34 M 7 Norton Sound, AK, U.S.A.
16 E 6 Nortonville, KY, U.S.A.
14 K 12 Norwalk, CT, U.S.A.
21 M 17 Norwalk, OH, U.S.A.
71 B 19 Norway, Europe
40 J 8 Norway House, MB, Canada
143 S 15 Norwegian Basin, Arctic Ocean
71 A 16 Norwegian Sea, Norway
14 M 11 Norwich, CT, U.S.A.
63 Z 6 Norwich, U.K.
82 N 9 Nos Emine, Bulgaria
82 O 7 Nos Kaliakra, Bulgaria
82 O 7 Nos Shabla, Bulgaria
122 N 4 Nosapu-misaki, Japan
122 I 2 Noshappu-misaki, Japan
122 J 10 Noshiro, Japan
91 Q 2 Nosovaya, Russian Federation
101 O 11 Nosratābād, Iran
60 I 8 Noss Head, U.K.
128 I 9 Nossombougou, Mali
133 Y 5 Nosy Bé, Madgascar
133 Z 7 Nosy Boraha, Madgascar
133 Y 8 Nosy-Varika, Madgascar
30 I 4 Notch Peak, UT, U.S.A.
78 E 11 Noteć, Poland
83 J 23 Notio Aigaio, Greece
83 A 16 Notio Steno Kerkyras, Greece
83 G 19 Notios Evvoïkos Kolpos, Greece
77 K 24 Noto, Italy
123 H 15 Noto-hantō, Japan
122 M 3 Notoro-ko, Japan
41 Y 9 Notre Dame Bay, NL, Canada
42 E 11 Nottawasaga Bay, ON, Canada
41 P 10 Nottaway, QC, Canada
63 T 5 Nottingham, U.K.
41 P 4 Nottingham Island, NU, Canada
124 A 14 Nouâdhibou, Western Sahara
128 D 5 Nouâdhibou, Mauritania
128 E 6 Nouakchott, Mauritania
128 E 6 Nouâmghâr, Mauritania
115 N 17 Nouei, Vietnam
139 Q 14 Nouméa, New Caledonia
103 R 12 Nov, Tajikistan
55 J 15 Nova, Brazil
58 G 5 Nova Alvorada, Brazil
132 F 2 Nova Caipemba, Angola
58 N 6 Nova Friburgo, Brazil
80 G 9 Nova Gradiška, Croatia
58 M 6 Nova Iguaçu, Brazil
133 R 8 Nova Mambone, Mozambique
133 T 6 Nova Nabúri, Mozambique
87 R 8 Nova Odesa, Ukraine
43 W 10 Nova Scotia, Canada
80 K 13 Nova Varoš, Serbia and Montenegro
82 K 9 Nova Zagora, Bulgaria
76 B 7 Novara, Italy
33 F 19 Novato, CA, U.S.A.
88 L 6 Novaya Zemlya, Russian Federation
78 H 22 Nové Zámky, Slovakia
90 G 12 Novgorodskaya Oblast', Russian Federation
87 S 1 Novhorod-Sivers'kyy, Ukraine
87 S 7 Novhorodka, Ukraine
80 K 8 Novi Bečej, Serbia and Montenegro
82 G 9 Novi-Iskŭr, Bulgaria
76 C 8 Novi Ligure, Italy
81 L 14 Novi Pazar, Serbia and Montenegro
82 M 7 Novi Pazar, Bulgaria
80 K 9 Novi Sad, Serbia and Montenegro
54 E 10 Novo Airão, Brazil
54 F 11 Novo Aripuanã, Brazil
58 H 12 Novo Hamburgo, Brazil
80 C 8 Novo Mesto, Slovenia
82 F 12 Novo Selo, Macedonia (F.Y.R.O.M.)
93 N 6 Novoanninskiy, Russian Federation
87 Q 6 Novoarkhanhel's'k, Ukraine
87 Y 8 Novoazovs'k, Ukraine
103 S 13 Novobod, Tajikistan
102 H 6 Novobogatinskoye, Kazakhstan
87 V 8 Novobohdanivka, Ukraine
93 Q 1 Novocheboksarsk, Russian Federation
92 L 9 Novocherkassk, Russian Federation
90 K 6 Novodvinsk, Russian Federation
86 M 3 Novohrad-Volyns'kyy, Ukraine
92 M 6 Novokhopersk, Russian Federation
93 S 4 Novokuybyshevsk, Russian Federation
88 M 13 Novokuznetsk, Russian Federation
145 R 1 Novolazarevskaya, Antarctica
87 V 6 Novomoskovs'k, Ukraine
92 L 3 Novomoskovsk, Russian Federation
93 N 6 Novonikolayevskiy, Russian Federation
93 P 8 Novonikol'skoye, Russian Federation
87 U 10 Novooleksiyivka, Ukraine
87 U 7 Novopokrovka, Ukraine
87 Z 4 Novopskov, Ukraine
93 K 12 Novorossiysk, Russian Federation
89 Q 7 Novorybnaya, Russian Federation
87 T 11 Novoselivs'ke, Ukraine
93 V 4 Novosergiyevka, Russian Federation
92 L 9 Novoshakhtinsk, Russian Federation
88 M 12 Novosibirsk, Russian Federation
93 R 4 Novospasskoye, Russian Federation
87 U 10 Novotroyits'ke, Ukraine
87 Q 7 Novoukrayinka, Ukraine
93 R 6 Novouzensk, Russian Federation
92 G 4 Novozybkov, Russian Federation
85 M 18 Nový Bykhaw, Belarus
79 H 18 Nový Jičín, Czech Republic
91 P 4 Novyy Bor, Russian Federation
87 S 8 Novyy Buh, Ukraine
87 R 3 Novyy Bykiv, Ukraine
92 K 6 Novyy Oskol, Russian Federation
88 M 8 Novyy Port, Russian Federation
88 M 9 Novyy Urengoy, Russian Federation
89 V 13 Novyy Urgal, Russian Federation
79 I 15 Nowa, Poland
79 M 16 Nowa Dęba, Poland
79 F 16 Nowa Ruda, Poland
78 E 10 Nowogard, Poland
135 U 12 Nowra, NSW, Australia
101 W 6 Nowshak, Pakistan
101 W 7 Nowshera, Pakistan
78 K 12 Nowy Dwór Mazowiecki, Poland
79 L 18 Nowy Sącz, Poland
79 K 18 Nowy Targ, Poland
88 M 9 Noyabr'sk, Russian Federation
65 R 3 Noyon, France
64 K 6 Nozay, France
130 I 8 Nsambi, Democratic Republic of Congo
133 R 6 Nsanje, Malawi
129 T 15 Nsoc, Equatorial Guinea
133 P 3 Nsombo, Zambia
129 Q 13 Nsukka, Nigeria
130 I 9 Ntandembele, Democratic Republic of Congo
133 R 5 Ntcheu, Malawi
130 D 7 Ntoum, Gabon
131 R 8 Ntungamo, Uganda
132 M 8 Ntwetwe Pan, Botswana
112 J 9 Nu Shan, China
127 E 18 Nuba Mountains, Sudan
127 G 14 Nubian Desert, Sudan
139 Y 10 Nubu, Fiji
45 U 13 Nudo de Zempoaltépetl, Mexico
40 J 4 Nueltin Lake, NU, Canada
46 K 5 Nueva Arcadia, Honduras
50 L 3 Nueva Bolivia, Venezuela
45 X 12 Nueva Coahuila, Mexico
51 P 2 Nueva Esparta, Venezuela
56 I 13 Nueva Galia, Argentina
48 G 5 Nueva Gerona, Cuba
47 Q 10 Nueva Guinea, Nicaragua
52 C 8 Nueva Loja, Ecuador
57 G 19 Nueva Lubecka, Argentina
46 J 6 Nueva Ocotepeque, Honduras
56 L 6 Nueva Pompeya, Argentina
45 P 5 Nueva Rosita, Mexico
46 I 7 Nueva San Salvador, El Salvador
45 R 8 Nueva Villa de Padilla, Mexico
59 C 16 Nueve de Julio, Argentina
48 L 5 Nuevitas, Cuba
45 Q 6 Nuevo Laredo, Mexico
45 R 7 Nuevo León, Mexico
127 O 20 Nugaal, Somalia
138 J 3 Nuguria Islands, Papua New Guinea
106 I 9 Nuh, India
136 O 12 Nuhaka, New Zealand
140 F 5 Nui, Tuvalu
35 Q 3 Nuiqsut, AK, U.S.A.
138 J 5 Nukiki, Solomon Islands
138 B 3 Nuku, Papua New Guinea
140 I 11 Nuku'alofa, Tonga
140 F 6 Nukufetau, Tuvalu
140 G 6 Nukulaelae, Tuvalu
138 L 4 Nukumanu Islands, Papua New Guinea
140 K 6 Nukunonu, Tokelau Islands
140 K 6 Nukunonu, Tokelau Islands
141 P 15 Nukuoro, Federated States of Micronesia
102 M 10 Nukus, Uzbekistan
134 H 6 Nullagine, WA, Australia
134 M 10 Nullarbor, SA, Australia
134 L 10 Nullarbor Plain, WA, Australia
111 F 15 Nulu'erhu Shan, China
107 R 9 Num, Nepal
117 V 11 Num, Indonesia
129 U 11 Numan, Nigeria
69 G 14 Numansdorp, Netherlands
123 J 15 Numata, Japan
123 K 17 Numazu, Japan
135 O 2 Numbulwar, NT, Australia
40 J 2 Nunavut, Canada
63 S 7 Nuneaton, U.K.
107 X 12 Nungba, India
110 F 11 Nungnain Sum, China
34 L 9 Nunivak Island, AK, U.S.A.
89 Z 6 Nunligran, Russian Federation
68 K 11 Nunspeet, Netherlands
77 C 17 Nuoro, Italy
139 P 7 Nupani, Solomon Islands
99 N 5 Nuqrah, Saudi Arabia
50 G 6 Nuquí, Colombia
103 N 6 Nura, Kazakhstan
100 I 10 Nūrābād, Iran
103 P 12 Nurata, Uzbekistan
73 I 21 Nuremberg, Germany
44 J 5 Nuri, Mexico
93 S 2 Nurlat, Russian Federation
71 N 14 Nurmes, Finland
101 W 9 Nurpur, Pakistan
106 I 5 Nurpur, India
116 M 14 Nusa Tenggara Barat, Indonesia
117 O 15 Nusa Tenggara Timur, Indonesia
95 Q 13 Nusaybin, Turkey
101 S 11 Nushki, Pakistan
143 O 11 Nuugaatsiaq, Greenland
142 M 12 Nuuk, Greenland
143 N 11 Nuussuaq, Greenland
143 O 10 Nuussuaq, Greenland
88 K 9 Nyagan', Russian Federation
131 U 7 Nyahururu, Kenya
108 K 10 Nyainqêntanglha, China
108 L 10 Nyainqêntanglha Shan, China
131 S 9 Nyakaliro, Tanzania
127 A 18 Nyala, Sudan
133 O 8 Nyamandhlovu, Zimbabwe
127 C 20 Nyamlell, Sudan
90 K 9 Nyandoma, Russian Federation
130 E 10 Nyanga, Gabon
130 F 9 Nyanga, Congo
131 T 8 Nyanza, Kenya
85 I 19 Nyasvizh, Belarus
133 O 7 Nyathi, Zimbabwe
115 E 15 Nyaunglebin, Myanmar
71 E 18 Nybergsund, Norway
71 C 25 Nyborg, Denmark
71 G 24 Nybro, Sweden
131 V 8 Nyeri, Kenya
127 E 20 Nyerol, Sudan
108 M 11 Nyingchi, China
79 N 22 Nyírbátor, Hungary
79 M 22 Nyíregyháza, Hungary
71 D 26 Nykøbing, Denmark
71 H 21 Nyköping, Sweden
71 H 21 Nynäshamn, Sweden
135 T 10 Nyngan, NSW, Australia
85 G 18 Nyoman, Belarus
74 A 9 Nyon, Switzerland
65 U 12 Nyons, France
91 S 10 Nyrob, Russian Federation
79 G 16 Nysa, Poland
122 J 10 Nyūdō-zaki, Japan
131 P 11 Nyunzu, Democratic Republic of Congo
116 M 9 Nyurang, Indonesia
89 S 10 Nyurba, Russian Federation
89 S 11 Nyuya, Russian Federation
87 U 9 Nyzhni Sirohozy, Ukraine
87 U 9 Nyzhni Torhayi, Ukraine
87 U 11 Nyzhn'ohirs'kyy, Ukraine
130 E 10 Nzambi, Congo
131 S 10 Nzega, Tanzania
128 H 12 Nzérékoré, Guinea
132 F 2 N'zeto, Angola
131 P 10 Nzingu, Democratic Republic of Congo

O

122 H 8 Ō-shima, Japan
123 K 17 Ō-shima, Japan
34 C 7 Oahu, HI, U.S.A.
15 O 11 Oak Bluffs, MA, U.S.A.
30 J 4 Oak City, UT, U.S.A.
21 H 14 Oak Creek, WI, U.S.A.
31 P 3 Oak Creek, CO, U.S.A.
32 G 6 Oak Harbor, WA, U.S.A.
21 H 16 Oak Lawn, IL, U.S.A.
16 J 8 Oak Ridge, TN, U.S.A.
18 I 7 Oakdale, LA, U.S.A.
63 U 6 Oakham, U.K.
33 I 20 Oakhurst, CA, U.S.A.
17 Q 2 Oakland, MD, U.S.A.
23 P 13 Oakland, NE, U.S.A.
32 F 12 Oakland, OR, U.S.A.
33 G 19 Oakland, CA, U.S.A.
24 I 3 Oakley, KS, U.S.A.
29 N 13 Oakley, ID, U.S.A.
134 H 5 Oakover, WA, Australia
32 G 12 Oakridge, OR, U.S.A.
136 J 12 Oakura, New Zealand
136 J 6 Oakura, New Zealand
137 F 23 Oamaru, New Zealand
123 D 19 Ōasa, Japan
33 N 15 Oasis, NV, U.S.A.
145 R 14 Oates Land, Antarctica
45 T 14 Oaxaca, Mexico
45 S 14 Oaxaca, Mexico
88 L 10 Ob', Russian Federation
42 B 5 Oba, ON, Canada
129 T 14 Obala, Cameroon
60 F 12 Oban, U.K.
137 D 23 Obelisk, New Zealand
58 F 10 Oberá, Argentina
75 Q 8 Oberdrauburg, Austria
24 I 2 Oberlin, KS, U.S.A.
75 Q 5 Oberndorf, Austria
75 Q 4 Oberösterreich, Austria
73 K 20 Oberpfälzer Wald, Germany
75 Y 6 Oberpullendorf, Austria
73 H 26 Oberstdorf, Germany
75 R 8 Obervellach, Austria
75 X 6 Oberwart, Austria
117 S 11 Obi, Indonesia
54 G 10 Óbidos, Brazil
122 L 5 Obihiro, Japan
21 G 20 Oblong, IL, U.S.A.
89 U 14 Obluch'ye, Russian Federation
92 K 1 Obninsk, Russian Federation
131 O 4 Obo, Central African Republic
131 O 8 Obokote, Democratic Republic of Congo
85 K 14 Obol', Belarus
87 S 5 Obolon', Ukraine
78 G 12 Oborniki, Poland
130 H 8 Obouya, Congo
92 J 5 Oboyan', Russian Federation
90 K 7 Obozerskiy, Russian Federation
78 E 12 Obra, Poland
80 K 11 Obrenovac, Serbia and Montenegro
33 F 14 O'Brien, OR, U.S.A.
82 N 7 Obrochishte, Bulgaria
94 H 11 Obruk, Turkey
88 L 8 Obskaya, Russian Federation
143 X 10 Obskaya Guba, Arctic Ocean
128 L 13 Obuasi, Ghana
87 P 4 Obukhiv, Ukraine
91 P 10 Ob"yachevo, Russian Federation
87 W 9 Obytichna Kosa, Ukraine
87 V 10 Obytichna Zatoka, Ukraine
19 W 9 Ocala, FL, U.S.A.
31 R 9 Ocate, NM, U.S.A.
136 K 6 Ocean Beach, New Zealand
14 J 15 Ocean City, NJ, U.S.A.
17 X 4 Ocean City, MD, U.S.A.
32 F 8 Ocean Park, WA, U.S.A.
19 N 7 Ocean Springs, MS, U.S.A.
33 K 26 Oceanside, CA, U.S.A.
87 Q 9 Ochakiv, Ukraine
95 Q 6 Och'amch'ire, Georgia
91 S 13 Ocher, Russian Federation
122 N 4 Ochiishi-misaki, Japan
48 L 8 Ocho Rios, Jamaica
19 X 13 Ochopee, FL, U.S.A.
73 H 20 Ochsenfurt, Germany
19 U 5 Ocilla, GA, U.S.A.
19 U 5 Ocmulgee, GA, U.S.A.
46 F 6 Ocos, Guatemala
45 W 13 Ocosingo, Mexico
47 N 7 Ocotal, Nicaragua
17 W 10 Ocracoke Island, NC, U.S.A.
53 J 21 Ocuri, Bolivia
123 D 18 Ōda, Japan
128 M 13 Oda, Ghana
122 J 9 Ōdate, Japan
123 K 17 Odawara, Japan
27 Q 13 Odem, TX, U.S.A.
66 G 11 Odemira, Portugal
94 C 11 Ödemiş, Turkey
71 C 25 Odense, Denmark
72 N 12 Oder, Germany/Poland
72 M 9 Oderhaff, Germany
76 H 6 Oderzo, Italy
87 Q 10 Odesa, Ukraine
26 J 7 Odessa, TX, U.S.A.
32 J 7 Odessa, WA, U.S.A.
128 I 11 Odienné, Côte d'Ivoire
115 L 21 Ŏdŏngk, Cambodia
68 N 8 Odoorn, Netherlands
86 K 10 Odorheiu Secuiesc, Romania
79 K 14 Odrzywół, Poland
80 J 9 Odžaci, Serbia and Montenegro
54 M 12 Oeiras, Brazil
22 G 11 Oelrichs, SD, U.S.A.
73 K 18 Oelsnitz, Germany
135 N 1 Oenpelli, NT, Australia
95 P 8 Of, Turkey
96 E 10 Ofaqim, Israel
129 P 12 Offa, Nigeria
73 F 19 Offenbach, Germany
73 D 23 Offenburg, Germany
83 K 23 Ofidoussa, Greece
122 L 11 Ōfunato, Japan
122 J 10 Oga, Japan
122 K 11 Ogachi, Japan
127 M 21 Ogadēn, Ethiopia
123 H 17 Ogaki, Japan
22 I 14 Ogallala, NE, U.S.A.
122 K 9 Ogawara-ko, Japan
129 P 12 Ogbomoso, Nigeria
30 J 2 Ogden, UT, U.S.A.
19 W 4 Ogeechee, GA, U.S.A.
122 I 13 Ogi, Japan
38 A 10 Ogilvie Mountains, YT, Canada
129 S 13 Ogoja, Nigeria
40 M 10 Ogoki, ON, Canada
130 G 7 Ogooué-Ivindo, Gabon
130 F 8 Ogooué-Lolo, Gabon
130 D 8 Ogooué-Maritime, Gabon
82 F 11 Ograzden, Macedonia (F.Y.R.O.M.)
84 F 11 Ogre, Latvia
80 C 9 Ogulin, Croatia
129 O 13 Ogun, Nigeria
95 W 7 Oğuz, Azerbaijan
136 L 13 Ohakune, New Zealand
125 Q 10 Ohanet, Algeria
132 I 7 Ohangwena, Namibia
137 K 15 Ohau, New Zealand
136 K 10 Ohaupo, New Zealand
56 F 12 O'Higgins, Chile
13 U 9 Ohio, U.S.A., U.S.A.
79 B 16 Ohře, Czech Republic
82 B 12 Ohrid, Macedonia (F.Y.R.O.M.)
136 K 12 Ohura, New Zealand
54 I 8 Oiapoque, Brazil
54 I 8 Oiapoque, Brazil
37 S 1 Oikiqtarjuaq, NU, Canada
69 I 15 Oirschot, Netherlands
123 C 21 Ōita, Japan
83 E 18 Oiti, Greece
20 D 10 Ojibwa, WI, U.S.A.
123 A 22 Ojika-jima, Japan
45 N 3 Ojinaga, Mexico
123 J 14 Ojiya, Japan
44 M 4 Ojo de Laguna, Mexico
138 A 4 Ok Tedi, Papua New Guinea
92 K 2 Oka, Russian Federation
117 Y 14 Okaba, Indonesia
132 I 9 Okahandja, Namibia
136 I 5 Okaihau, New Zealand
41 U 6 Okak Islands, NL, Canada
132 I 8 Okakarara, Namibia
132 I 8 Okaputa, Namibia
101 X 10 Okara, Pakistan
102 I 13 Okarem, Turkmenistan
137 E 19 Okarito Lagoon, New Zealand
132 H 8 Okaukuejo, Namibia
132 J 7 Okavango, Namibia
132 K 7 Okavango, Botswana
132 L 7 Okavango Delta, Botswana
123 I 16 Okaya, Japan
123 F 19 Okayama, Japan
123 I 17 Okazaki, Japan
19 Y 11 Okeechobee, FL, U.S.A.
62 M 13 Okehampton, U.K.
89 W 12 Okha, Russian Federation
107 Q 9 Okhaldhunga, Nepal
91 S 13 Okhansk, Russian Federation
89 W 11 Okhotsk, Russian Federation
87 V 9 Okhrimivka, Ukraine
87 U 4 Okhtyrka, Ukraine
123 D 17 Oki-shotō, Japan
123 O 24 Okinawa, Japan
123 O 25 Okinawa-shotō, Japan
123 E 22 Okino-shima, Japan
123 N 23 Okinoerabu-jima, Japan
24 L 10 Oklahoma, U.S.A.
25 N 10 Oklahoma City, OK, U.S.A.
25 Q 10 Okmulgee, OK, U.S.A.
130 G 8 Okondja, Gabon
130 H 8 Okoyo, Congo
115 D 15 Okpo, Myanmar
70 J 6 Øksfjord, Norway
91 P 3 Oksino, Russian Federation
89 Z 11 Oktyabr'skiy, Russian Federation
90 L 10 Oktyabr'skiy, Russian Federation
93 U 2 Oktyabr'skiy, Russian Federation
93 O 9 Oktyabr'skiy, Russian Federation
93 W 4 Oktyabr'skoye, Russian Federation
123 N 24 Oku, Japan
90 G 12 Okulovka, Russian Federation
122 H 7 Okushiri-tō, Japan
129 O 12 Okuta, Nigeria
25 T 11 Ola, AR, U.S.A.
47 V 14 Olá, Panama
84 F 11 Olaine, Latvia
33 L 21 Olancha, CA, U.S.A.
71 H 24 Öland, Sweden
135 Q 10 Olary, SA, Australia
25 R 4 Olathe, KS, U.S.A.
59 C 17 Olavarría, Argentina
79 G 15 Oława, Poland
77 C 16 Olbia, Italy
38 A 9 Old Crow, YT, Canada
29 R 9 Old Faithful, WY, U.S.A.
14 I 7 Old Forge, NY, U.S.A.
35 P 12 Old Harbor, AK, U.S.A.
61 C 21 Old Head of Kinsale, Republic of Ireland
15 R 4 Old Town, ME, U.S.A.
39 N 19 Old Wives Lake, SK, Canada
68 K 10 Oldebroek, Netherlands
72 E 11 Oldenburg, Germany
72 I 8 Oldenburg in Holstein, Germany
68 N 11 Oldenzaal, Netherlands
70 K 6 Olderfjord, Norway
63 R 3 Oldham, U.K.
14 D 10 Olean, NY, U.S.A.
78 M 9 Olecko, Poland
89 S 11 Olekminsk, Russian Federation
87 R 6 Oleksandrivka, Ukraine
87 W 7 Oleksandrivka, Ukraine
87 S 6 Oleksandriya, Ukraine
90 I 2 Olenegorsk, Russian Federation
89 R 8 Olenëk, Russian Federation
89 S 7 Olenekskiy Zaliv, Russian Federation
87 S 11 Olenevka, Ukraine
90 I 4 Olenitsa, Russian Federation
79 G 15 Oleśnica, Poland
79 I 16 Olesno, Poland
86 M 2 Olevs'k, Ukraine
70 G 11 Ølfjellet, Norway
108 M 2 Ölgiy, Mongolia
66 I 12 Olhão, Portugal
80 C 11 Olib, Croatia
58 I 5 Olímpia, Brazil
16 K 5 Olive Hill, KY, U.S.A.
66 J 9 Olivenza, Spain
39 L 14 Oliver Lake, SK, Canada
23 Q 8 Olivia, MN, U.S.A.
93 P 7 Ol'khovka, Russian Federation
79 J 17 Olkusz, Poland
56 H 4 Ollagüe, Chile
63 T 4 Ollerton, U.K.
130 H 8 Ollombo, Congo
67 N 5 Olmedo, Spain
52 B 12 Olmos, Peru
21 G 21 Olney, IL, U.S.A.
27 O 5 Olney, TX, U.S.A.
79 G 18 Olomouc, Czech Republic
90 G 9 Olonets, Russian Federation
120 F 11 Olongapo, Philippines
64 M 14 Oloron-Ste-Marie, France
67 X 3 Olot, Spain
79 R 14 Olovyannaya, Russian Federation
85 K 18 Ol'sa, Belarus
78 K 9 Olsztyn, Poland
78 K 10 Olsztynek, Poland
86 I 10 Olt, Romania
74 E 6 Olten, Switzerland
86 L 13 Oltenița, Romania
95 R 8 Oltu, Turkey
121 I 22 Olutanga, Philippines
32 G 7 Olympia, WA, U.S.A.
89 Z 8 Olyutorskiy, Russian Federation
89 Z 9 Olyutorskiy Zaliv, Russian Federation
127 H 17 Om Hajēr, Eritrea
122 J 8 Ōma, Japan
122 J 8 Ōma-zaki, Japan
123 J 18 Omae-zaki, Japan
122 K 11 Ōmagari, Japan
61 E 15 Omagh, U.K.
52 F 11 Omaguas, Peru
23 P 14 Omaha, NE, U.S.A.
132 J 9 Omaheke, Namibia
32 J 6 Omak, WA, U.S.A.
137 D 23 Omakau, New Zealand
137 M 14 Omakere, New Zealand
95 U 6 Omalo, Georgia
99 Y 8 Oman, Asia
137 E 22 Omarama, New Zealand
132 I 9 Omaruru, Namibia
130 I 4 Ombella-Mpoko, Central African Republic
130 D 9 Omboué, Gabon
127 F 16 Omdurman, Sudan
87 T 5 Omel'nyk, Ukraine
20 L 12 Omer, MI, U.S.A.
45 R 14 Ometepec, Mexico
100 G 9 Omīdīyeh, Iran
80 F 13 Omiš, Croatia
68 M 10 Ommen, Netherlands
109 Q 5 Ömnögovĭ, Mongolia
127 G 22 Omo Wenz, Ethiopia
89 X 8 Omolon, Russian Federation
89 X 8 Omolon, Russian Federation
88 K 11 Omsk, Russian Federation
89 X 9 Omsukchan, Russian Federation
122 K 3 Ōmū, Japan
123 B 22 Ōmura, Japan
82 L 8 Omurtag, Bulgaria
132 G 7 Omusati, Namibia
123 B 22 Ōmuta, Japan
91 Q 12 Omutninsk, Russian Federation
20 D 12 Onalaska, WI, U.S.A.
23 R 6 Onamia, MN, U.S.A.
20 K 10 Onaway, MI, U.S.A.
122 M 5 Onbetsu, Japan
132 G 6 Oncócua, Angola
132 H 7 Ondangwa, Namibia
79 M 19 Ondava, Slovakia
105 F 14 Onder, India
132 H 6 Ondjiva, Angola
129 P 13 Ondo, Nigeria
129 Q 13 Ondo, Nigeria
109 S 4 Öndörhaan, Mongolia
105 K 20 One and a Half Degree Channel, Maldives
90 J 7 Onega, Russian Federation
14 H 8 Oneida, NY, U.S.A.
14 H 8 Oneida Lake, NY, U.S.A.
22 M 12 O'Neill, NE, U.S.A.
14 I 9 Oneonta, NY, U.S.A.
19 Q 2 Oneonta, AL, U.S.A.
86 L 10 Onești, Romania
90 I 6 Onezhskaya Guba, Russian Federation
130 G 8 Onga, Gabon
136 K 12 Ongarue, New Zealand
109 O 4 Ongi, Mongolia
111 K 18 Ongjin, North Korea
105 G 19 Ongole, India
95 S 6 Oni, Georgia
129 Q 13 Onitsha, Nigeria
89 U 11 Onnes, Russian Federation
123 H 16 Ono, Japan
139 X 12 Ono, Fiji
139 Z 13 Ono-i-lau, Fiji
123 B 21 Ōnojō, Japan
123 E 19 Onomichi, Japan
110 H 8 Onor, China
140 E 3 Onotoa, Kiribati
132 J 12 Onseepkans, Republic of South Africa
134 E 6 Onslow, WA, Australia
17 T 12 Onslow Bay, NC, U.S.A.
32 L 11 Ontario, OR, U.S.A.
42 C 7 Ontario, Canada
67 T 9 Ontinyent, Spain
20 F 8 Ontonagon, MI, U.S.A.
138 L 4 Ontong Java Atoll, Solomon Islands
135 O 8 Oodnadatta, SA, Australia
127 L 20 Oodweyne, Somalia
134 M 10 Ooldea, SA, Australia
25 Q 8 Oologah Lake, OK, U.S.A.
69 D 18 Oost-Vlaanderen, Belgium
68 I 6 Oost-Vlieland, Netherlands
69 B 17 Oostende, Belgium
68 J 5 Oosterend, Netherlands
69 H 15 Oosterhout, Netherlands
69 E 15 Oosterschelde, Netherlands
69 C 15 Oosterscheldekering, Netherlands
68 L 7 Oosterwolde, Netherlands
69 C 17 Oostkamp, Belgium
69 A 18 Oostvleteren, Belgium
115 L 23 Ôp Luc, Vietnam
131 N 8 Opala, Democratic Republic of Congo
91 O 11 Oparino, Russian Federation
79 L 16 Opatów, Poland
79 H 17 Opava, Czech Republic
19 S 4 Opelika, AL, U.S.A.
18 I 7 Opelousas, LA, U.S.A.
138 G 4 Open Bay, Papua New Guinea
29 W 2 Opheim, MT, U.S.A.

Country · Internal administrative region: State/Province/Territory/Dependent territory · Capital city · Mountain range/Undersea ridge · Mountain peak/Volcano/Seamount · Geographic feature · Headland/Point/Cape/Peninsula · Desert · Island/Island group · Antarctic base · Ocean · Sea · Bay/Gulf/Channel/Strait · Lake · Salt pan/Dry/Intermittent lake · River

Opheusden – Pappadahandi

68 J 13 Opheusden, Netherlands
131 P 7 Opienge, Democratic Republic of Congo
87 U 4 Opishnya, Ukraine
90 D 13 Opochka, Russian Federation
79 K 14 Opoczno, Poland
79 H 16 Opole, Poland
102 J 8 Opornyy, Kazakhstan
136 N 10 Opotiki, New Zealand
19 Q 6 Opp, AL, U.S.A.
71 D 16 Oppdal, Norway
77 M 21 Oppido Mamertina, Italy
136 J 13 Opunake, New Zealand
132 G 7 Opuwo, Namibia
30 L 14 Oracle, AZ, U.S.A.
86 G 8 Oradea, Romania
106 K 11 Orai, India
30 L 9 Oraibi, AZ, U.S.A.
56 J 5 Orán, Argentina
124 K 6 Oran, Algeria
87 P 2 Orane, Ukraine
27 V 9 Orange, TX, U.S.A.
65 T 13 Orange, France
132 M 13 Orange, Republic of South Africa
135 U 11 Orange, NSW, Australia
46 K 1 Orange Walk, Belize
17 O 13 Orangeburg, SC, U.S.A.
138 F 7 Orangerie Bay, Papua New Guinea
42 E 12 Orangeville, ON, Canada
120 F 11 Orani, Philippines
72 L 12 Oranienburg, Germany
132 I 12 Oranjemund, Namibia
49 R 13 Oranjestad, Aruba
132 M 8 Orapa, Botswana
121 M 15 Oras, Philippines
86 H 10 Orăştie, Romania
79 J 19 Orava, Slovakia
86 F 11 Oraviţa, Romania
137 B 25 Orawia, New Zealand
76 F 13 Orbetello, Italy
135 T 13 Orbost, VIC, Australia
144 I 1 Orcadas, Antarctica
67 Q 10 Orcera, Spain
134 L 4 Ord, WA, Australia
66 H 1 Ordes, Spain
94 M 8 Ordu, Turkey
31 T 6 Ordway, CO, U.S.A.
103 N 3 Ordzhonikidze, Kazakhstan
95 X 9 Ordzonikidze, Azerbaijan
79 A 17 Ore Mountains, Czech Republic
71 G 20 Örebro, Sweden
21 F 14 Oregon, WI, U.S.A.
32 H 12 Oregon, U.S.A., U.S.A.
32 G 10 Oregon City, OR, U.S.A.
87 T 6 Orel, Ukraine
92 J 3 Orel, Russian Federation
52 D 13 Orellana, Peru
94 C 12 Ören, Turkey
93 W 5 Orenburg, Russian Federation
93 V 4 Orenburgskaya Oblast', Russian Federation
59 C 19 Orense, Argentina
82 L 12 Orestiada, Greece
137 C 25 Oreti, New Zealand
136 K 8 Orewa, New Zealand
31 Q 14 Organ Peak, NM, U.S.A.
51 Y 6 Organabo, French Guiana
101 U 8 Orgūn, Afghanistan
87 N 8 Orhei, Moldova
67 S 2 Orhi, Spain
46 M 6 Orica, Honduras
33 E 15 Orick, CA, U.S.A.
131 O 6 Orientale, Democratic Republic of Congo
59 C 17 Oriente, Argentina
67 S 11 Orihuela, Spain
87 V 8 Orikhiv, Ukraine
87 V 5 Oril', Ukraine
87 V 5 Oril'ka, Ukraine
42 F 12 Orillia, ON, Canada
29 Y 12 Orin, WY, U.S.A.
51 O 4 Orinoco, Venezuela
138 B 6 Oriomo, Papua New Guinea
105 I 16 Orissa, India
84 E 7 Orissaare, Estonia
77 B 18 Oristano, Italy
71 O 16 Orivesi, Finland
54 G 10 Oriximiná, Brazil
45 S 12 Orizaba, Mexico
71 E 24 Örkelljunga, Sweden
60 H 7 Orkney Islands, U.K.
26 H 7 Orla, TX, U.S.A.
58 K 5 Orlândia, Brazil
19 W 10 Orlando, FL, U.S.A.
15 P 10 Orleans, MA, U.S.A.
33 F 15 Orleans, CA, U.S.A.
65 P 6 Orléans, France
92 K 4 Orlovskaya Oblast', Russian Federation
93 N 10 Orlovskiy, Russian Federation
65 Q 4 Orly, France
101 R 14 Ormara, Pakistan
121 L 16 Ormoc, Philippines
19 X 9 Ormond Beach, FL, U.S.A.
63 P 3 Ormskirk, U.K.
83 G 14 Ormylia, Greece
78 K 9 Orneta, Poland
71 I 21 Ornö, Sweden
31 P 3 Orno Peak, CO, U.S.A.
71 I 15 Örnsköldsvik, Sweden
128 K 10 Orodara, Burkina Faso
28 K 5 Orofino, ID, U.S.A.
109 P 4 Orog Nuur, Mongolia
31 Q 14 Orogrande, NM, U.S.A.
141 P 15 Oroluk, Federated States of Micronesia
127 H 20 Oromia, Ethiopia
43 S 9 Oromocto, NB, Canada
96 F 11 Oron, Israel
129 S 14 Oron, Nigeria
140 J 4 Orona, Kiribati
121 K 20 Oroquieta, Philippines
83 J 26 Oros Kofinas, Greece
77 D 17 Orosei, Italy
79 L 25 Orosháza, Hungary
33 K 15 Orovada, NV, U.S.A.
33 G 17 Oroville, CA, U.S.A.
110 H 7 Orqohan, China
35 M 16 Orsha, Belarus
74 D 11 Orsières, Switzerland
88 H 11 Orsk, Russian Federation
86 G 12 Orşova, Romania
94 H 13 Orta Toroslar, Turkey
94 I 12 Ortaköy, Turkey
75 Y 3 Orth an der Donau, Austria
64 L 14 Orthez, France
53 I 16 Orthon, Bolivia
66 I 1 Ortigueira, Spain
44 J 5 Ortiz, Mexico
76 J 13 Ortona, Italy
23 O 7 Ortonville, MN, U.S.A.
100 F 3 Orūmīyeh, Iran
53 J 20 Oruro, Bolivia
53 I 21 Oruro, Bolivia
71 D 22 Orust, Sweden
76 G 12 Orvieto, Italy
144 K 6 Orville Coast, Antarctica
21 O 16 Orwell, OH, U.S.A.
82 H 6 Oryakhovo, Bulgaria
76 D 7 Orzinuovi, Italy
78 M 9 Orzysz, Poland
91 S 13 Osa, Russian Federation
23 T 10 Osage, IA, U.S.A.
123 G 18 Ōsaka, Japan
123 G 18 Ōsaka-wan, Japan
103 S 4 Osakarovka, Kazakhstan
24 L 3 Osborne, KS, U.S.A.
77 C 16 Oschiri, Italy
20 L 12 Oscoda, MI, U.S.A.
80 J 11 Osečina, Serbia and Montenegro
42 I 11 Osgoode, ON, Canada
103 T 12 Osh, Kyrgyzstan
132 H 7 Oshakati, Namibia
122 I 7 Oshamambe, Japan
132 H 7 Oshana, Namibia
42 F 12 Oshawa, ON, Canada
122 L 12 Oshika-hantō, Japan
132 H 7 Oshikango, Namibia
132 I 7 Oshikoto, Namibia
122 I 7 Oshima-hantō, Japan
20 G 12 Oshkosh, WI, U.S.A.
22 H 14 Oshkosh, NE, U.S.A.
129 P 12 Oshogbo, Nigeria
103 T 12 Oshskaya Oblast', Kyrgyzstan
130 K 10 Oshwe, Democratic Republic of Congo
80 I 8 Osijek, Croatia
23 T 13 Oskaloosa, IA, U.S.A.
71 G 23 Oskarshamn, Sweden
87 X 4 Oskol, Ukraine
71 D 20 Oslo, Norway
71 C 21 Oslofjorden, Norway
94 J 8 Osmancık, Turkey
94 E 8 Osmaneli, Turkey
94 L 13 Osmaniye, Turkey
84 E 6 Osmussaar, Estonia
72 E 13 Osnabrück, Germany
82 D 10 Osogovske Planine, Macedonia (F.Y.R.O.M.)
58 I 12 Osório, Brazil
57 E 16 Osorno, Chile
67 N 3 Osorno, Spain
35 H 22 Osoyoos, BC, Canada
70 A 19 Osøyra, Norway
69 J 14 Oss, Netherlands
20 D 11 Osseo, WI, U.S.A.
89 Y 9 Ossora, Russian Federation
90 F 13 Ostashkov, Russian Federation
87 P 3 Oster, Ukraine
72 J 12 Osterburg, Germany
71 F 16 Östersund, Sweden
72 C 10 Ostfriesische Inseln, Germany
71 I 19 Östhammar, Sweden
76 F 8 Ostiglia, Italy
79 H 18 Ostrava, Czech Republic
78 J 9 Ostróda, Poland
86 L 4 Ostroh, Ukraine
78 L 11 Ostrołęka, Poland
89 Q 5 Ostrov, Russian Federation
90 D 13 Ostrov, Russian Federation
89 N 6 Ostrov Arkticheskogo Instituta, Russian Federation
89 X 6 Ostrov Ayon, Russian Federation
89 T 6 Ostrov Bel'kovskiy, Russian Federation
88 M 6 Ostrov Belyy, Russian Federation
89 U 5 Ostrov Bennetta, Russian Federation
89 Z 10 Ostrov Beringa, Russian Federation
89 U 6 Ostrov Bol'shaya Lyakhovskiy, Russian Federation
89 R 7 Ostrov Bol'shoy Begichev, Russian Federation
95 Z 8 Ostrov Bulla, Azerbaijan
91 R 1 Ostrov Dolgiy, Russian Federation
89 N 4 Ostrov Dzheksona, Russian Federation
90 D 10 Ostrov Gogland, Russian Federation
89 O 3 Ostrov Greem-Bell, Russian Federation
89 O 5 Ostrov Isachenko, Russian Federation
89 Y 14 Ostrov Iturup, Russian Federation
89 Z 9 Ostrov Karaginskiy, Russian Federation
90 I 1 Ostrov Kil'din, Russian Federation
91 O 2 Ostrov Kolguyev, Russian Federation
89 P 4 Ostrov Komsomolets, Russian Federation
89 T 6 Ostrov Kotel'nyy, Russian Federation
102 G 8 Ostrov Kulaly, Kazakhstan
89 Y 14 Ostrov Kunashir, Russian Federation
89 U 6 Ostrov Malyy Lyakhovskiy, Russian Federation
89 R 5 Ostrov Malyy Taymyr, Russian Federation
89 Z 10 Ostrov Mednyy, Russian Federation
88 K 6 Ostrov Mezhdusharskiy, Russian Federation
90 L 4 Ostrov Morzhovets, Russian Federation
89 U 6 Ostrov Novaya Sibir', Russian Federation
102 H 12 Ostrov Ogurchinskiy, Turkmenistan
89 P 5 Ostrov Oktyabr'skoy Revolyutsii, Russian Federation
89 N 7 Ostrov Oleniy, Russian Federation
89 Z 12 Ostrov Onekotan, Russian Federation
89 Z 12 Ostrov Paramushir, Russian Federation
89 P 4 Ostrov Pioner, Russian Federation
89 N 3 Ostrov Rudol'fa, Russian Federation
89 Z 13 Ostrov Shiashkotan, Russian Federation
89 P 4 Ostrov Shmidta, Russian Federation
89 N 7 Ostrov Sibiryakova, Russian Federation
89 Z 13 Ostrov Simushir, Russian Federation
89 T 6 Ostrov Stolbovoy, Russian Federation
89 Y 14 Ostrov Urup, Russian Federation
89 O 4 Ostrov Ushakova, Russian Federation
89 O 5 Ostrov Uyedineniya, Russian Federation
91 R 1 Ostrov Vaygach, Russian Federation
89 N 6 Ostrov Vil'kitskogo, Russian Federation
89 O 4 Ostrov Vise, Russian Federation
102 L 9 Ostrov Vozrozhdeniya, Uzbekistan
89 V 5 Ostrov Zhokhova, Russian Federation
89 U 5 Ostrova De-Longa, Russian Federation
89 O 6 Ostrova Izvestiy Ts. I. K., Russian Federation
89 W 6 Ostrova Medvezh'i, Russian Federation
102 H 8 Ostrova Tyulen'i, Kazakhstan
90 L 13 Ostrovskoye, Russian Federation
78 M 11 Ostrów Mazowiecki, Poland
79 H 14 Ostrów Wielkopolski, Poland
79 L 15 Ostrowiec Świętokrzyski, Poland
79 H 14 Ostrzeszów, Poland
72 M 8 Ostseebad Göhren, Germany
75 O 8 Osttirol, Austria
77 O 16 Ostuni, Italy
82 I 8 Osŭm, Bulgaria
123 C 24 Ōsumi-hantō, Japan
123 C 24 Ōsumi-kaikyō, Japan
123 B 25 Ōsumi-shotō, Japan
129 P 13 Osun, Nigeria
66 M 12 Osuna, Spain
14 G 7 Oswego, NY, U.S.A.
63 P 6 Oswestry, U.K.
87 W 9 Osypenko, Ukraine
137 E 22 Otago, New Zealand
137 F 24 Otago Peninsula, New Zealand
136 J 6 Otaika, New Zealand
137 K 15 Otaki, New Zealand
103 U 9 Otar, Kazakhstan
122 J 5 Otaru, Japan
52 B 8 Otavalo, Ecuador
132 I 8 Otavi, Namibia
123 K 14 Ōtawara, Japan
137 E 22 Otematata, New Zealand
84 H 8 Otepää, Estonia
32 J 8 Othello, WA, U.S.A.
83 A 15 Othonoi, Greece
137 G 19 Otira, New Zealand
132 I 8 Otjiwarongo, Namibia
132 J 8 Otjozondjupa, Namibia
63 S 2 Otley, U.K.
109 R 7 Otog Qi, China
122 J 3 Otoineppu, Japan
136 K 11 Otorohanga, New Zealand
137 E 20 Otorokua Point, New Zealand
71 B 20 Otra, Norway
77 O 17 Otranto, Italy
89 Y 7 Otrozhnyy, Russian Federation
21 J 15 Otsego, MI, U.S.A.
123 G 18 Ōtsu, Japan
71 D 17 Otta, Norway
21 F 17 Ottawa, IL, U.S.A.
25 Q 4 Ottawa, KS, U.S.A.
42 I 10 Ottawa, ON, Canada
42 H 9 Ottawa, QC, Canada
37 S 9 Ottawa Islands, NU, Canada
71 G 25 Ottenby, Sweden
75 V 3 Ottenschlag, Austria
72 F 10 Otterndorf, Germany
76 D 8 Ottone, Italy
23 U 14 Ottumwa, IA, U.S.A.
129 R 13 Otukpa, Nigeria
129 R 13 Otukpo, Nigeria
56 K 8 Otumpa, Argentina
78 L 13 Otwock, Poland
74 K 8 Ötztaler Alpen, Austria
123 K 16 Ōu-sanmyaku, Japan
25 U 13 Ouachita, AR, U.S.A.
25 S 11 Ouachita Mountains, AR, U.S.A.
128 G 5 Ouadâne, Mauritania
130 L 3 Ouadda, Central African Republic
129 Y 9 Ouaddaï, Chad
128 M 10 Ouagadougou, Burkina Faso
128 L 9 Ouahigouya, Burkina Faso
130 K 4 Ouaka, Central African Republic
128 J 7 Oualâta, Mauritania
129 O 9 Ouallam, Niger
51 Z 7 Ouanary, French Guiana
131 O 4 Ouanda, Central African Republic
130 J 3 Ouandago, Central African Republic
130 M 2 Ouandja, Central African Republic
130 L 5 Ouango, Central African Republic
128 K 11 Ouangolodougou, Côte d'Ivoire
129 N 10 Ouargaye, Burkina Faso
125 O 8 Ouargla, Algeria
69 F 14 Oude-Tonge, Netherlands
69 D 19 Oudenaarde, Belgium
132 L 15 Oudtshoorn, Republic of South Africa
124 H 7 Oued Zem, Morocco
128 I 10 Ouéléssébougou, Mali
130 H 7 Ouésso, Congo
129 T 13 Ouest, Cameroon
130 I 3 Ouham, Central African Republic
130 H 3 Ouham-Pendé, Central African Republic
124 K 6 Oujda, Morocco
128 G 5 Oujeft, Mauritania
124 G 9 Oulad Teïma, Morocco
128 G 8 Ould Yenjé, Mauritania
125 N 7 Ouled Djellal, Algeria
70 L 13 Oulu, Finland
71 M 14 Oulujärvi, Finland
70 L 13 Oulujoki, Finland
129 Y 8 Oum-Chalouba, Chad
125 O 6 Oum el Bouaghi, Algeria
129 Y 9 Oum-Hadjer, Chad
124 F 8 Ounara, Morocco
70 K 10 Ounasjoki, Finland
63 U 7 Oundle, U.K.
129 X 6 Ounianga Kébir, Chad
129 Y 6 Ounianga Sérir, Chad
110 J 4 Oupu, China
71 C 18 Øure Ardel, Norway
66 I 3 Ourense, Spain
54 N 13 Ouricuri, Brazil
55 J 19 Ourinhos, Brazil
69 J 22 Ourthe, Belgium
63 T 2 Ouse, U.K.
61 D 10 Outer Hebrides, U.K.
20 E 8 Outer Island, WI, U.S.A.
20 I 10 Outer Island, MI, U.S.A.
132 I 8 Outjo, Namibia
137 E 24 Outram, New Zealand
139 Q 13 Ouvéa, New Caledonia
135 R 12 Ouyen, VIC, Australia
94 I 14 Ovacik, Turkey
139 X 11 Ovalau, Fiji
56 F 10 Ovalle, Chile
132 G 7 Ovamboland, Namibia
130 F 7 Ovan, Gabon
66 H 5 Ovar, Portugal
129 U 15 Oveng, Cameroon
69 G 19 Overijse, Belgium
68 M 11 Overijssel, Netherlands
70 K 11 Överkalix, Sweden
25 R 4 Overland Park, KS, U.S.A.
134 F 8 Overlander Roadhouse, WA, Australia
69 J 17 Overpelt, Belgium
33 N 21 Overton, NV, U.S.A.
87 N 13 Ovidiu, Romania
49 Q 8 Oviedo, Dominican Republic
66 L 1 Oviedo, Spain
84 C 9 Ovišrags, Latvia
109 P 4 Övörhangay, Mongolia
70 J 9 Övre Soppero, Sweden
87 O 2 Ovruch, Ukraine
137 E 25 Owaka, New Zealand
130 H 8 Owando, Congo
123 H 19 Owase, Japan
23 S 9 Owatonna, MN, U.S.A.
137 C 26 Owen Head, New Zealand
115 F 21 Owen Island, Myanmar
137 H 17 Owen River, New Zealand
33 D 11 Owen Sound, ON, Canada
138 E 6 Owen Stanley Range, Papua New Guinea
33 K 21 Owens Lake, CA, U.S.A.
16 E 5 Owensboro, KY, U.S.A.
129 R 14 Owerri, Nigeria
129 Q 13 Owo, Nigeria
21 L 14 Owosso, MI, U.S.A.
32 K 13 Owyhee, OR, U.S.A.
33 M 14 Owyhee, NV, U.S.A.
39 O 19 Oxbow, SK, Canada
71 H 21 Oxelösund, Sweden
14 H 9 Oxford, NY, U.S.A.
17 S 8 Oxford, NC, U.S.A.
18 M 2 Oxford, MS, U.S.A.
21 L 14 Oxford, MI, U.S.A.
63 S 10 Oxford, U.K.
137 G 20 Oxford, New Zealand
33 I 24 Oxnard, CA, U.S.A.
63 W 11 Oxted, U.K.
103 U 12 Oy Tal, Kyrgyzstan
123 H 15 Oyabe, Japan
123 K 15 Oyama, Japan
130 E 7 Oyem, Gabon
39 K 19 Oyen, AB, Canada
71 D 20 Øyeren, Norway
129 P 12 Oyo, Nigeria
129 P 12 Oyo, Nigeria
130 H 8 Oyo, Congo
53 C 15 Oyón, Peru
114 A 13 Oyster Island, Myanmar
95 T 11 Özalp, Turkey
121 K 21 Ozamiz, Philippines
25 T 10 Ozark, AR, U.S.A.
25 T 7 Ozark, MO, U.S.A.
25 S 8 Ozark Plateau, MO, U.S.A.
79 K 21 Ózd, Hungary
89 Z 12 Ozernovskiy, Russian Federation
92 H 1 Ozernyy, Russian Federation
103 Q 9 Ozero Akzhaykyn, Kazakhstan
103 X 7 Ozero Alakol', Kazakhstan
102 G 5 Ozero Aralsor, Kazakhstan
103 Q 12 Ozero Aydarkul', Uzbekistan
90 I 10 Ozero Beloye, Russian Federation
90 F 12 Ozero Il'men', Russian Federation
90 H 3 Ozero Imandra, Russian Federation
102 I 6 Ozero Inder, Kazakhstan
102 I 5 Ozero Itmurinkol', Kazakhstan
103 R 8 Ozero Karakoyyn, Kazakhstan
103 U 5 Ozero Karasor, Kazakhstan
90 H 4 Ozero Kovdozero, Russian Federation
90 J 8 Ozero Kozhozero, Russian Federation
90 K 11 Ozero Kubenskoye, Russian Federation
103 P 3 Ozero Kusmurun, Kazakhstan
90 J 9 Ozero Lacha, Russian Federation
90 G 7 Ozero Leksozero, Russian Federation
90 I 3 Ozero Lovozero, Russian Federation
93 O 10 Ozero Manych-Gudilo, Russian Federation
103 Z 5 Ozero Markakol', Kazakhstan
90 G 4 Ozero Pyaozero, Russian Federation
103 X 7 Ozero Sasykkol, Kazakhstan
90 H 7 Ozero Segozerskoye, Russian Federation
89 Y 14 Ozero Shikotan, Russian Federation
103 S 3 Ozero Siletiteniz, Kazakhstan
103 P 8 Ozero Solonchak, Kazakhstan
89 Q 6 Ozero Taymyr, Russian Federation
103 S 2 Ozero Teke, Kazakhstan
103 Q 5 Ozero Tengiz, Kazakhstan
90 G 5 Ozero Topozero, Russian Federation
103 S 2 Ozero Ul'ken Karoy, Kazakhstan
90 I 3 Ozero Umbozero, Russian Federation
90 J 8 Ozero Vodlozero, Russian Federation
90 J 10 Ozero Vozhe, Russian Federation
90 I 7 Ozero Vygozero, Russian Federation
87 N 11 Ozero Yalpuh, Ukraine
103 Y 6 Ozero Zaysan, Kazakhstan
85 C 16 Ozersk, Russian Federation
92 L 2 Ozery, Russian Federation
103 T 12 Özgön, Kyrgyzstan
77 C 16 Ozieri, Italy
79 H 16 Ozimek, Poland
93 S 5 Ozinki, Russian Federation
26 K 9 Ozona, TX, U.S.A.
78 J 13 Ozorków, Poland
123 D 21 Ōzu, Japan
45 S 10 Ozuluama, Mexico
95 R 7 Ozurget'i, Georgia

P

115 F 16 Pa-an, Myanmar
139 R 11 Paama, Vanuatu
142 M 13 Paamiut, Greenland
132 J 15 Paarl, Republic of South Africa
79 J 14 Pabianice, Poland
107 T 13 Pabna, Bangladesh
85 G 15 Pabradė, Lithuania
52 B 13 Pacasmayo, Peru
83 K 24 Pachia, Greece
77 K 24 Pachino, Italy
53 E 14 Pachitea, Peru
83 H 26 Páchnes, Greece
45 R 11 Pachuca, Mexico
8 C 9 Pacific Ocean, 0
121 K 17 Pacijan, Philippines
135 R 10 Packsaddle, NSW, Australia
32 H 8 Packwood, WA, U.S.A.
47 X 13 Pacora, Panama
116 D 11 Padang, Indonesia
116 D 10 Padangsidimpuan, Indonesia
116 I 11 Padangtikar, Indonesia
90 H 7 Padany, Russian Federation
119 U 6 Padas, Malaysia
53 K 23 Padcaya, Bolivia
73 F 15 Paderborn, Germany
53 K 21 Padilla, Bolivia
86 L 10 Padina, Romania
76 G 7 Padova, Italy
27 Q 14 Padre Island, TX, U.S.A.
77 D 16 Padru, Italy
62 K 14 Padstow, U.K.
16 C 6 Paducah, KY, U.S.A.
26 M 4 Paducah, TX, U.S.A.
106 J 4 Padum, India
111 L 14 Paektu-san, China/North Korea
111 J 19 Paengnyŏng-do, South Korea
136 L 9 Paeroa, New Zealand
94 G 15 Pafos, Cyprus
133 P 9 Pafuri, Mozambique
80 C 11 Pag, Croatia
80 C 11 Pag, Croatia
54 H 11 Paga-Conta, Brazil
121 J 21 Pagadian, Philippines
116 D 12 Pagai Selatan, Indonesia
116 D 12 Pagai Utara, Indonesia
140 B 6 Pagan, Northern Mariana Islands
83 F 17 Pagasitikos Kolpos, Greece
116 L 12 Pagatan, Indonesia
82 L 13 Pağayiğit, Turkey
30 K 8 Page, AZ, U.S.A.
85 C 14 Pagėgiai, Lithuania
17 P 11 Pageland, SC, U.S.A.
140 K 8 Pago Pago, American Samoa
31 P 7 Pagosa Springs, CO, U.S.A.
108 K 11 Pagri, China
18 D 8 Pahang, Malaysia
118 D 8 Pahang, Malaysia
137 L 15 Pahiatua, New Zealand
105 N 21 Pahlagaon, India
115 F 14 Pai, Thailand
84 G 7 Paide, Estonia
63 N 14 Paignton, U.K.
136 J 5 Paihia, New Zealand
71 M 17 Päijänne, Finland
115 J 20 Pailin, Cambodia
57 F 16 Pailiaco, Chile
64 J 4 Paimpol, France
116 D 11 Painan, Indonesia
21 O 16 Painesville, OH, U.S.A.
30 K 9 Painted Desert, AZ, U.S.A.
16 L 5 Paintsville, KY, U.S.A.
67 Q 2 País Vasco, Spain
32 I 13 Paisley, OR, U.S.A.
52 A 12 Paita, Peru
70 K 10 Pajala, Sweden
115 I 18 Pak Thong Chai, Thailand
51 Q 7 Pakaraima Mountains, Brazil/Venezuela
42 E 10 Pakesley, ON, Canada
129 R 10 Paki, Nigeria
101 U 12 Pakistan, Asia
114 C 12 Pakokku, Myanmar
79 I 25 Paks, Hungary
101 U 8 Paktiā, Afghanistan
101 U 9 Paktīkā, Afghanistan
115 L 18 Pakxé, Laos
129 V 11 Pala, Chad
27 S 12 Palacios, TX, U.S.A.
53 K 17 Palacios, Bolivia
67 Y 4 Palafrugell, Spain
94 H 15 Palaichóri, Cyprus
83 G 26 Palaiochora, Greece
83 B 18 Palairos, Greece
106 I 5 Palam Pur, India
83 D 16 Palamas, Greece
67 X 4 Palamós, Spain
89 Y 9 Palana, Russian Federation
120 I 7 Palanan, Philippines
120 I 7 Palanan Point, Philippines
84 B 13 Palanga, Lithuania
116 K 12 Palangkaraya, Indonesia
105 B 14 Palanpur, India
133 N 9 Palapye, Botswana
101 X 6 Palas, Pakistan
19 W 8 Palatka, FL, U.S.A.
89 X 10 Palatka, Russian Federation
77 C 15 Palau, Italy
140 I 15 Palau, Oceania
140 I 15 Palau Islands, Palau
120 H 5 Palaui, Philippines
115 F 19 Palauk, Myanmar
115 F 20 Palaw, Myanmar
121 D 19 Palawan, Philippines
121 B 19 Palawan Passage, Philippines
84 F 6 Paldiski, Estonia
117 O 10 Paleleh, Indonesia
116 G 12 Palembang, Indonesia
33 M 25 Palen Dry Lake, CA, U.S.A.
57 F 18 Palena, Chile
67 N 3 Palencia, Spain
77 I 21 Palermo, Italy
27 S 7 Palestine, TX, U.S.A.
96 F 10 Palestine, Israel
114 B 12 Paletwa, Myanmar
105 D 22 Palghat, India
132 G 8 Palgrave Point, Namibia
104 C 11 Pali, India
141 P 15 Palikir, Federated States of Micronesia
121 K 23 Palimbang, Philippines
69 I 24 Paliseul, Belgium
105 B 15 Palitana, India
105 F 23 Palk Strait, Sri Lanka
105 I 17 Palkonda, India
93 Q 7 Pallasovka, Russian Federation
105 G 21 Pallavaram, India
131 T 7 Pallisa, Uganda
29 Q 11 Pallisades Reservoir, ID, U.S.A.
137 K 16 Palliser Bay, New Zealand
106 G 8 Pallu, India
33 L 25 Palm Springs, CA, U.S.A.
67 Y 9 Palma, Spain
66 M 11 Palma del Río, Spain
48 M 6 Palma Soriano, Cuba
47 R 13 Palmar, Costa Rica
58 I 12 Palmares do Sul, Brazil
54 K 13 Palmas, Brazil
58 H 9 Palmas, Brazil
33 J 24 Palmdale, CA, U.S.A.
58 G 10 Palmeira das Missões, Brazil
54 L 12 Palmeiras, Brazil
58 I 8 Palmeiras, Brazil
35 Q 9 Palmer, AK, U.S.A.
144 H 4 Palmer, Antarctica
144 I 5 Palmer Land, Antarctica
134 L 1 Palmerston, NT, Australia
137 F 24 Palmerston, New Zealand
141 N 10 Palmerston, Cook Islands
137 L 15 Palmerston North, New Zealand
77 L 21 Palmi, Italy
50 H 7 Palmira, Colombia
96 K 5 Palmyra, Syria
33 F 20 Palo Alto, CA, U.S.A.
47 Z 15 Palo de las Letras, Panama
50 G 4 Palo de las Letras, Colombia
56 M 7 Palo Santo, Argentina
119 O 9 Paloh, Malaysia
127 F 19 Paloich, Sudan
70 K 9 Palojoensuu, Finland
53 H 18 Palomani, Peru
45 U 13 Palomares, Mexico
117 O 12 Palopo, Indonesia
53 E 18 Palpa, Peru
95 P 11 Palu, Turkey
117 N 11 Palu, Indonesia
117 O 15 Palu, Indonesia
120 F 13 Paluan, Philippines
116 H 14 Pamanukan, Indonesia
117 X 12 Pamdai, Indonesia
105 H 15 Pamgarh, India
75 Z 5 Pamhagen, Austria
65 P 15 Pamiers, France
103 U 14 Pamir, Tajikistan
17 V 10 Pamlico Sound, NC, U.S.A.
26 L 2 Pampa, TX, U.S.A.
56 K 7 Pampa de los Guanacos, Argentina
53 K 20 Pampa Grande, Bolivia
56 I 13 Pampas, Argentina
50 J 5 Pamplona, Colombia
67 R 2 Pamplona, Spain
106 I 3 Pampur, India
94 E 8 Pamukova, Turkey
21 F 20 Pana, IL, U.S.A.
130 F 9 Pana, Gabon
45 Z 10 Panabá, Mexico
121 H 21 Panabutan Bay, Philippines
33 N 20 Panaca, NV, U.S.A.
121 D 18 Panagtaran Point, Philippines
82 H 9 Panagyurishte, Bulgaria
116 G 14 Panaitan, Indonesia
105 C 19 Panaji, India
47 V 14 Panama, North America
47 W 13 Panama Canal, Panama
19 R 8 Panama City, FL, U.S.A.
47 X 14 Panama City, Panama
121 L 18 Panaon, Philippines
121 I 16 Panay, Philippines
121 I 18 Panay Gulf, Philippines
80 L 10 Pančevo, Serbia and Montenegro
86 F 9 Pâncota, Romania
133 R 10 Panda, Mozambique
120 K 12 Pandan, Philippines
121 I 15 Pandan, Philippines
121 B 20 Pandanan, Philippines
116 L 11 Pandang, Indonesia
116 G 14 Pandeglang, Indonesia
84 G 13 Pandėlys, Lithuania
105 D 18 Pandharpur, India
105 F 15 Pandhurna, India
53 I 16 Pando, Bolivia
47 S 12 Pandora, Costa Rica
107 V 11 Pandu, India
130 J 5 Pandu, Democratic Republic of Congo
84 F 13 Panevėžys, Lithuania
115 G 15 Pang, Thailand
131 O 6 Panga, Democratic Republic of Congo
140 I 10 Pangai, Tonga
131 W 11 Pangani, Tanzania
121 I 21 Panganuran, Philippines
131 O 9 Pangi, Democratic Republic of Congo
116 C 9 Pangkalanbrandan, Indonesia
116 J 12 Pangkalanbuun, Indonesia
116 G 12 Pangkalpinang, Indonesia
118 A 7 Pangkor, Malaysia
121 K 19 Panglao, Philippines
41 S 2 Pangnirtung, NU, Canada
130 J 5 Pangonda, Central African Republic
110 I 4 Pangu, China
57 F 16 Panguipulli, Chile
30 J 6 Panguitch, UT, U.S.A.
138 J 5 Panguna, Papua New Guinea
121 F 23 Pangutaran, Philippines
121 F 23 Pangutaran Group, Philippines
26 K 2 Panhandle, TX, U.S.A.
131 P 12 Pania-Mwanga, Democratic Republic of Congo
106 I 7 Panipat, India
103 R 14 Panj, Tajikistan
101 T 7 Panjāb, Afghanistan
103 Q 13 Panjakent, Tajikistan
101 R 13 Panjgur, Pakistan
111 H 15 Panjin, China
129 S 11 Pankshin, Nigeria
106 L 12 Panna, India
107 X 10 Golaghat, India
134 F 6 Pannawonica, WA, Australia
58 H 5 Panorama, Brazil
111 K 14 Panshi, China
118 A 7 Pantai Remis, Malaysia
55 G 17 Pantanal, Brazil
117 Q 15 Pantar, Indonesia
77 G 24 Pantelleria, Italy
117 Q 15 Pantemakassar, East Timor
114 C 9 Pantha, Myanmar
116 D 10 Panti, Indonesia
45 S 10 Pánuco, Mexico
45 R 10 Pánuco, Mexico
113 N 10 Panxian, China
112 L 9 Panzhihua, China
130 J 12 Panzi, Democratic Republic of Congo
46 I 5 Panzos, Guatemala
77 M 19 Paola, Italy
21 I 21 Paoli, IN, U.S.A.
79 G 23 Pápa, Hungary
60 I 6 Papa Westray, U.K.
55 F 14 Papagaio, Brazil
136 L 12 Papakai, New Zealand
136 J 7 Paparoa, New Zealand
72 D 11 Papenburg, Germany
23 P 14 Papillion, NE, U.S.A.
84 G 13 Papilys, Lithuania
56 F 6 Paposo, Chile
105 H 17 Pappadahandi, India

Country · Internal administrative region: State/Province/Territory/Dependent territory · Capital city · Mountain range/Undersea ridge · Mountain peak/Volcano/Seamount · Geographic feature · Headland/Point/Cape/Peninsula · Desert · Island/Island group · Antarctic base · Ocean · Sea · Bay/Gulf/Channel/Strait · Lake · Salt pan/Dry/Intermittent lake

176

Country ■ Internal administrative region: State/Province/Territory/Dependent territory   ⚓ Capital city   ▲▲ Mountain range/ Undersea ridge   ▲ Mountain peak/ Volcano/Seamount   ◇ Geographic feature   ▶ Headland/Point/ Cape/Peninsula   ▲ Desert   ⚏ Island/Island group   ⚎ Antarctic base   ⊘ Ocean   ⊃ Sea   ≈ Bay/Gulf/Channel/Strait   ⌇ Lake   ⚊ Salt pan/Dry/ Intermittent lake   ⌇ River

□ Country   ● Internal administrative region: State/Province/Territory/Dependent territory   ▲ Capital city   ▲ Mountain range/Undersea ridge   ▲ Mountain peak/Volcano/Seamount   ◆ Geographic feature   ▲ Headland/Point/Cape/Peninsula   ▦ Desert   ≢ Island/Island group   ▦ Antarctic base   ≋ Ocean   ≈ Sea   ≈ Bay/Gulf/Channel/Strait   ⌇ Lake   ⌐ Salt pan/Dry/Intermittent lake

Puerto Lempira – Raudhatain

Q 5 Puerto Lempira, Honduras
H 4 Puerto Libertad, Mexico
I 17 Puerto Lobos, Argentina
K 1 Puerto Lopez, Colombia
A 9 Puerto López, Ecuador
W 15 Puerto Madero, Mexico
I 18 Puerto Madryn, Argentina
H 16 Puerto Maldonado, Peru
A 11 Puerto Máncora, Peru
F 17 Puerto Montt, Chile
L 8 Puerto Morazáno, Nicaragua
B 14 Puerto Morin, Peru
F 24 Puerto Natáles, Chile
L 6 Puerto Nuevo, Colombia
Z 14 Puerto Obaldia, Panama
L 5 Puerto Padre, Cuba
N 5 Puerto Páez, Venezuela
D 11 Puerto Pardo, Peru
G 2 Puerto Peñasco, Mexico
J 10 Puerto Pizarro, Colombia
Q 6 Puerto Plata, Dominican Republic
F 15 Puerto Portillo, Peru
D 18 Puerto Princesa, Philippines
Q 13 Puerto Quepos, Costa Rica
T 8 Puerto Rico, U.S.A., U.S.A.
F 10 Puerto Rico, Argentina
H 22 Puerto San Julián, Argentina
M 9 Puerto Sandino, Nicaragua
H 22 Puerto Santa Cruz, Argentina
G 18 Puerto Sastre, Paraguay
K 17 Puerto Siles, Bolivia
H 10 Puerto Socorro, Peru
O 21 Puerto Suárez, Bolivia
M 11 Puerto Vallarta, Mexico
E 15 Puerto Victoria, Peru
S 12 Puerto Viejo, Costa Rica
A 19 Puerto Villamil, Ecuador
I 19 Puerto Visser, Argentina
H 25 Puerto Yartou, Chile
N 10 Puertollano, Spain
R 5 Pugachev, Russian Federation
L 9 Puge, China
G 6 Puget Sound, WA, U.S.A.
M 15 Puglia, Italy
V 9 Pugwash, NS, Canada
O 16 Puhos, Finland
W 3 Puigcerdà, Spain
P 15 Puigmal, France
X 3 Puigmal d'Err, Spain
G 12 Pujehun, Sierra Leone
M 7 Pukapuka, Cook Islands
H 7 Pukatawagan, MB, Canada
M 16 Pukch'ŏng, North Korea
K 16 Pukë, Albania
K 9 Pukekohe, New Zealand
E 19 Pukekura, New Zealand
L 16 Puksubaek-san, North Korea
C 19 Pula, Italy
A 10 Pula, Croatia
J 22 Pulacayo, Bolivia
N 10 Pulai, Indonesia
J 15 Pulanduta Point, Philippines
L 12 Pulangpisau, Indonesia
N 15 Pulap, Federated States of Micronesia
G 7 Pulaski, NY, U.S.A.
E 10 Pulaski, TN, U.S.A.
O 7 Pulaski, VA, U.S.A.
X 14 Pulau Dolak, Indonesia
Y 7 Pulau Gaya, Malaysia
N 9 Pulau Maratua, Indonesia
N 15 Pulawat, Federated States of Micronesia
M 14 Puławy, Poland
V 13 Pulborough, U.K.
M 14 Pulkkila, Finland
L 8 Pullman, WA, U.S.A.
I 15 Pulo Anna, Palau
L 12 Pultusk, Poland
I 7 Pulu, China
P 10 Pülümür, Turkey
N 15 Pulusuk, Federated States of Micronesia
H 6 Puna de Atacama, Argentina
F 18 Punakaiki, New Zealand
U 9 Punakha, Bhutan
J 20 Punata, Bolivia
W 12 Puncak Jaya, Indonesia
Y 13 Puncak Mandala, Indonesia
X 13 Puncak Trikora, Indonesia
I 7 Pundri, India
C 17 Pune, India
B 13 Punggol, Singapore
M 15 P'ungsan, North Korea
O 8 Punia, Democratic Republic of Congo
X 10 Punjab, Pakistan
H 6 Punjab, India
H 19 Puno, Peru
G 18 Puno, Peru
G 6 Punta Abreojos, Mexico
N 19 Punta Alice, Italy
Z 11 Punta Allen, Mexico
L 15 Punta Almina, Spain
B 19 Punta Alta, Argentina
J 9 Punta Arena, Mexico
G 25 Punta Arenas, Chile
E 19 Punta Atico, Peru
F 3 Punta Baja, Mexico
B 21 Punta Bermeja, Argentina
S 15 Punta Burica, Costa Rica
S 12 Punta Cahuita, Costa Rica
H 2 Punta Canoas, Colombia
B 15 Punta Caprara, Italy
N 4 Punta Caxinas, Honduras
F 17 Punta Chirambirá, Colombia
L 8 Punta Cosigüina, Nicaragua
F 12 Punta Curaumilla, Chile
H 24 Punta de Arenas, Argentina
P 13 Punta de las Entinas, Spain
M 11 Punta de Mita, Mexico
R 9 Punta de Perlas, Nicaragua
N 6 Punta de Quemado, Cuba
R 10 Punta del Mono, Nicaragua
G 15 Punta del Palmar, Uruguay
J 18 Punta Delgada, Argentina
H 22 Punta Desengaño, Argentina
F 5 Punta Eugenia, Mexico
A 8 Punta Galera, Ecuador
E 16 Punta Galera, Chile
K 1 Punta Gallinas, Colombia
Y 15 Punta Garachiné, Panama
J 4 Punta Gorda, Belize
R 10 Punta Gorda, Nicaragua
R 6 Punta Gorda, Nicaragua

56 F 2 Punta Gorda, Chile
47 O 12 Punta Guiones, Costa Rica
45 Z 11 Punta Herrero, Mexico
56 F 5 Punta Jorjino, Chile
57 E 14 Punta Lavapié, Chile
56 F 10 Punta Lengua de Vaca, Chile
57 H 23 Punta León, Argentina
47 W 15 Punta Mala, Panama
50 E 9 Punta Manglares, Colombia
47 X 12 Punta Manzanillo, Panama
47 V 15 Punta Mariato, Panama
66 L 14 Punta Marroquí, Spain
57 I 21 Punta Medanosa, Argentina
52 A 12 Punta Negro, Peru
57 J 18 Punta Ninfas, Argentina
57 J 17 Punta Norte, Argentina
57 J 17 Punta Norte, Argentina
52 A 11 Punta Pariñas, Peru
47 Q 4 Punta Patuca, Honduras
44 G 4 Punta Prieta, Mexico
59 B 21 Punta Rasa, Argentina
50 F 8 Punta Reyes, Colombia
45 U 12 Punta Roca Partida, Mexico
44 J 6 Punta Rosa, Mexico
46 L 4 Punta Sal, Honduras
53 C 16 Punta Salinasó Lachay, Peru
44 G 6 Punta San Hipólito, Mexico
46 J 8 Punta San Juan, El Salvador
47 Q 14 Punta San Pedro, Costa Rica
52 A 10 Punta Santa Elena, Ecuador
53 D 18 Punta Santa Maria, Peru
59 E 17 Punta Sur, Argentina
45 N 13 Punta Tejupan, Mexico
56 F 12 Punta Topocalma, Chile
47 O 12 Puntarenas, Costa Rica
50 L 2 Punto Fijo, Venezuela
14 C 12 Punxsutawney, PA, U.S.A.
70 M 13 Puolanka, Finland
137 H 15 Puponga, New Zealand
109 T 11 Puqi, China
53 E 18 Puquio, Peru
56 G 8 Puquios, Chile
106 L 9 Puranpur, India
138 C 6 Puratu Island, Papua New Guinea
75 Y 4 Purbach, Austria
84 G 5 Purekkari neem, Estonia
57 F 15 Purén, Chile
105 J 17 Puri, India
75 X 3 Purkersdorf, Austria
68 H 10 Purmerend, Netherlands
107 R 11 Purnia, India
57 E 17 Purranque, Chile
45 P 12 Puruarán, Mexico
116 L 11 Purukcahu, Indonesia
107 Q 13 Puruliya, India
54 D 12 Purus, Brazil
71 O 16 Puruvesi, Finland
82 J 10 Pürvomay, Bulgaria
116 H 14 Purwakarta, Indonesia
119 O 10 Pusa, Malaysia
111 N 21 Pusan, South Korea
121 O 22 Pusan Point, Philippines
93 Q 6 Pushkino, Russian Federation
90 D 14 Pustoshka, Russian Federation
109 W 13 Putai, Taiwan
114 F 6 Putao, Myanmar
136 L 10 Putaruru, New Zealand
113 X 10 Putian, China
53 H 18 Putina, Peru
136 N 12 Putorino, New Zealand
56 G 2 Putre, Chile
105 F 24 Puttalam, Sri Lanka
68 J 11 Putten, Netherlands
72 I 8 Puttgarden, Germany
105 D 21 Puttur, India
50 H 9 Putumayo, Colombia
50 J 11 Putumayo, Colombia
116 K 10 Putusibau, Indonesia
87 T 2 Putyvl', Ukraine
71 M 17 Puula, Finland
71 N 17 Puumala, Finland
41 P 5 Puvurnituq, QC, Canada
113 R 2 Puxian, China
113 U 2 Puyang, China
57 F 16 Puyehue, Chile
52 C 9 Puyo, Ecuador
137 A 25 Puysegur Point, New Zealand
91 R 8 Puzla, Russian Federation
131 W 12 Pwani, Tanzania
131 Q 13 Pweto, Democratic Republic of Congo
62 M 5 Pwllheli, U.K.
90 K 5 Pyalitsa, Russian Federation
90 I 8 Pyal'ma, Russian Federation
115 D 17 Pyapon, Myanmar
89 O 6 Pyasinskiy Zaliv, Russian Federation
93 O 13 Pyatigorsk, Russian Federation
87 T 6 P"yatykhatky, Ukraine
114 D 12 Pyawbwe, Myanmar
115 C 14 Pyè, Myanmar
85 K 21 Pyetrykaw, Belarus
71 L 14 Pyhäjoki, Finland
71 M 15 Pyhäsalmi, Finland
71 O 16 Pyhäselkä, Finland
70 M 10 Pyhätunturin, Finland
114 D 13 Pyinmana, Myanmar
83 D 22 Pylos, Greece
111 L 18 P'yŏnggang, North Korea
111 K 17 P'yŏngsong, North Korea
111 M 19 P'yŏngt'aek, South Korea
111 J 17 P'yŏngyang, North Korea
33 I 16 Pyramid Lake, NV, U.S.A.
64 K 15 Pyrenees, France/Spain
83 E 15 Pyrgetos, Greece
83 K 19 Pyrgi, Greece
83 C 21 Pyrgos, Greece
87 R 4 Pyriatyn, Ukraine
78 D 11 Pyrzyce, Poland
85 J 15 Pyshna, Belarus
87 V 7 Pys'menne, Ukraine
90 D 13 Pytalovo, Russian Federation
71 C 16 Pyttegga, Norway
115 D 14 Pyu, Myanmar

Q

98 L 7 Qaḑimah, Saudi Arabia
97 U 4 Qādir Karam, Iraq
110 F 8 Qagan, China
110 B 13 Qagan Nur, China
110 C 13 Qagan Nur, China
110 J 11 Qagan Nur, China
111 C 14 Qagan Nur, China
110 B 13 Qagan Teg, China
112 J 4 Qagca, China

101 R 6 Qaisar, Afghanistan
97 U 2 Qalā Diza, Iraq
103 S 13 Qal'aikhum, Tajikistan
99 W 14 Qalansīyah, Yemen
101 T 9 Qalāt, Afghanistan
97 W 12 Qal'at Abū Ghar, Iraq
98 J 4 Qal'at al Azlam, Saudi Arabia
96 H 4 Qal'at al Ḩiṣn, Syria
99 O 9 Qal'at Bīshah, Saudi Arabia
97 Y 10 Qal'at Şāliḩ, Iraq
97 W 9 Qal'at Sukkār, Iraq
101 Q 7 Qal'eh-ye, Afghanistan
96 F 9 Qalqilya, Israel
38 M 9 Qamanittuaq, NU, Canada
112 I 6 Qamdo, China
125 W 8 Qaminis, Libya
127 O 18 Qandala, Somalia
95 V 10 Qapiciğ Dağl, Armenia
97 U 5 Qara Tepe, Iraq
98 M 2 Qārah, Saudi Arabia
97 Q 1 Qaratshuk, Syria
127 N 20 Qardho, Somalia
103 U 13 Qarokŭl, Tajikistan
110 H 10 Qarsan, China
103 P 13 Qashqadaryo Wiloyati, Uzbekistan
111 A 16 Qasq, China
96 I 9 Qaşr al Azraq, Jordan
96 H 10 Qaşr al Kharānah, Jordan
99 S 2 Qaşr aş Şabiyah, Kuwait
126 D 10 Qasr Farafra, Egypt
99 Q 8 Qaşr Ḩimām, Saudi Arabia
125 S 11 Qaşr Larocu, Libya
96 H 7 Qatanā, Syria
99 U 5 Qatar, Asia
100 K 11 Qatrūyeh, Iran
126 C 9 Qattâra Depression, Egypt
95 W 7 Qax, Azerbaijan
101 N 8 Qāyen, Iran
97 S 3 Qayyārah, Iraq
95 U 7 Qazax, Azerbaijan
95 Y 8 Qazimämmäd, Azerbaijan
100 H 5 Qazvīn, Iran
100 H 5 Qazvin, Iran
126 F 10 Qena, Egypt
143 N 12 Qeqertarsuaq, Greenland
100 L 13 Qeshm, Iran
100 L 13 Qeshm, Iran
112 K 6 Qêyi, China
100 J 13 Qeys, Iran
96 E 11 Qeẓi'ot, Israel
113 J 12 Qian'an, China
113 P 7 Qianjiang, China
113 T 6 Qianjiang, China
112 L 6 Qianning, China
112 K 10 Qiansuo, China
112 M 7 Qianwei, China
111 F 17 Qianxi, China
113 O 9 Qianxi, China
113 P 3 Qianxian, China
113 P 3 Qianyang, China
113 Q 2 Qiaozhen, China
113 V 7 Qichun, China
113 S 9 Qidong, China
113 Z 5 Qidong, China
109 N 9 Qidukou, China
108 J 7 Qiemo, China
113 O 7 Qijiang, China
108 M 5 Qijiaojing, China
101 Q 12 Qila Ladgasht, Pakistan
101 P 11 Qila Safed, Pakistan
101 U 10 Qila Saifullah, Pakistan
109 N 7 Qilian Shan, China
113 W 7 Qimen, China
113 P 4 Qin Ling, China
113 O 3 Qin'an, China
113 L 10 Qing'an, China
111 G 20 Qingdao, China
110 K 10 Qinggang, China
109 N 8 Qinghai, China
109 O 8 Qinghai Hu, China
113 R 1 Qingjian, China
111 F 16 Qinglong, China
111 B 16 Qingshuihe, China
113 Y 8 Qingtian, China
113 S 1 Qingxu, China
113 P 2 Qingyang, China
111 J 15 Qingyuan, China
113 T 12 Qingyuan, China
113 X 8 Qingyuan, China
111 F 20 Qingzhou, China
111 G 17 Qinhuangdao, China
113 S 1 Qinxian, China
113 T 3 Qinyang, China
113 S 2 Qinyuan, China
113 Q 13 Qinzhou, China
113 R 15 Qionghai, China
112 M 6 Qionglai, China
112 L 5 Qionglai Shan, China
110 G 5 Qiqian, China
110 I 10 Qiqihar, China
100 J 11 Qīr, Iran
96 F 10 Qiryat Gat, Israel
99 U 12 Qishn, Yemen
108 L 5 Qitai, China
110 N 10 Qitaihe, China
112 M 11 Qiubei, China
111 G 19 Qixia, China
113 S 1 Qixian, China
113 U 3 Qixian, China
110 G 4 Qiyahe, China
113 S 9 Qiyang, China
110 J 7 Qizhan, China
103 V 14 Qizilrabot, Tajikistan
100 J 5 Qolleh-ye Damāvand, Iran
100 I 6 Qom, Iran
100 I 6 Qom, Iran
127 O 21 Qooriga Neegro, Somalia
102 L 10 Qoraqalpog'iston Respublikasi, Uzbekistan
96 H 5 Qornet es Saouda, Lebanon
97 T 2 Qosh Tepe, Iraq
14 M 9 Quabbin Reservoir, MA, U.S.A.
72 E 12 Quakenbrück, Germany
115 K 23 Quân Đao Nam Du, Vietnam
113 S 4 Quanbao Shan, China
115 O 17 Quang Ngai, Vietnam
115 N 16 Quang Tri, Vietnam
113 X 11 Quanzhou, China
113 S 10 Quanzhou, China
41 R 5 Quaqtaq, QC, Canada
58 E 12 Quarai, Brazil
137 D 25 Quarry Hills, New Zealand
77 C 19 Quartu Sant'Elena, Italy

33 M 20 Quartzite Mountain, NV, U.S.A.
30 G 12 Quartzsite, AZ, U.S.A.
95 X 7 Quba, Azerbaijan
101 N 5 Quchan, Iran
96 K 4 Qudaym, Syria
135 U 12 Queanbeyan, NSW, Australia
42 K 7 Québec, Canada
43 N 8 Québec, QC, Canada
73 I 15 Quedlinburg, Germany
39 C 19 Queen Charlotte, BC, Canada
57 J 23 Queen Charlotte Bay, Falkland Islands
39 B 19 Queen Charlotte Islands, BC, Canada
39 D 20 Queen Charlotte Sound, BC, Canada
36 M 3 Queen Elizabeth Islands, NU, Canada
145 W 8 Queen Mary Land, Antarctica
40 J 1 Queen Maud Gulf, NU, Canada
145 O 3 Queen Maud Land, Antarctica
145 O 9 Queen Maud Mountains, Antarctica
135 R 6 Queensland, Australia
135 S 15 Queenstown, TAS, Australia
137 C 23 Queenstown, New Zealand
32 F 7 Queets, WA, U.S.A.
132 I 2 Quela, Angola
133 S 7 Quelimane, Mozambique
57 F 18 Quellón, Chile
31 N 11 Quemado, NM, U.S.A.
57 F 17 Quemchi, Chile
59 D 19 Quequén, Argentina
45 Q 11 Querétaro, Mexico
45 Q 11 Querétaro, Mexico
73 J 16 Querfurt, Germany
67 P 11 Quesada, Spain
39 G 19 Quesnel, BC, Canada
39 G 19 Quesnel Lake, BC, Canada
101 T 10 Quetta, Pakistan
57 F 16 Queule, Chile
52 A 9 Quevedo, Ecuador
46 F 5 Quezaltenango, Guatemala
46 J 6 Quezaltepeque, Guatemala
121 C 19 Quezon, Philippines
120 G 11 Quezon City, Philippines
124 I 6 Quezzane, Morocco
113 V 2 Qufu, China
114 L 13 Qui Châu, Vietnam
115 O 19 Qui Nhon, Vietnam
132 G 2 Quibaxe, Angola
50 G 6 Quibdó, Colombia
64 J 6 Quiberon, France
72 H 10 Quickborn, Germany
69 D 21 Quiévrechain, Belgium
55 G 20 Quiindy, Paraguay
132 G 5 Quilengues, Angola
39 N 18 Quill Lakes, SK, Canada
53 F 17 Quillabamba, Peru
56 G 4 Quillagua, Chile
65 Q 15 Quillan, France
59 D 16 Quilmes, Argentina
105 D 24 Quilon, India
135 S 8 Quilpie, QLD, Australia
56 F 11 Quilpue, Chile
132 H 1 Quimbele, Angola
56 K 8 Quimili, Argentina
64 H 6 Quimper, France
64 I 6 Quimperlé, France
32 F 7 Quinault, WA, U.S.A.
53 G 17 Quince Mil, Peru
19 S 7 Quincy, FL, U.S.A.
21 D 19 Quincy, IL, U.S.A.
33 H 17 Quincy, CA, U.S.A.
56 I 11 Quines, Argentina
133 U 6 Quinga, Mozambique
34 M 10 Quinhagak, AK, U.S.A.
121 G 16 Quiniluban, Philippines
45 Z 11 Quintana Roo, Mexico
67 P 8 Quintanar, Spain
132 F 1 Quinzau, Angola
133 U 3 Quionga, Mozambique
132 G 5 Quipungo, Angola
57 F 14 Quirihue, Chile
53 K 21 Quiroga, Bolivia
59 B 16 Quiroga, Argentina
132 I 3 Quitapa, Angola
132 H 6 Quiteve, Angola
19 N 5 Quitman, MS, U.S.A.
19 T 7 Quitman, GA, U.S.A.
52 B 8 Quito, Ecuador
54 N 11 Quixadá, Brazil
112 M 10 Qujing, China
103 Q 13 Qullai Chimtarha, Tajikistan
103 S 13 Qullai Garmo, Tajikistan
103 T 14 Qullai Karl Marks, Tajikistan
112 I 5 Qu'nyido, China
135 P 10 Quorn, SA, Australia
99 Z 6 Qurayat, Oman
103 R 14 Qŭrghonteppa, Tajikistan
58 I 7 Qurinhos, Brazil
95 X 7 Qusar, Azerbaijan
99 T 13 Qusāy'ir, Yemen
126 G 10 Quseir, Egypt
113 P 6 Quxian, China
113 X 7 Quzhou, China
113 U 2 Quzhou, China
113 P 2 Quzi, China
95 V 6 Qvareli, Georgia

R

75 V 2 Raabs an der Thaya, Austria
70 L 13 Raahe, Finland
68 L 11 Raalte, Netherlands
116 L 14 Raas, Indonesia
80 C 10 Rab, Croatia
80 C 10 Rab, Croatia
79 K 18 Raba, Poland
79 G 23 Rába, Hungary
117 N 15 Raba, Indonesia
127 F 18 Rabak, Sudan
77 J 26 Rabat, Malta
124 H 7 Rabat, Morocco
138 H 3 Rabaul, Papua New Guinea
134 L 5 Rabbit Flat Roadhouse, NT, Australia
116 B 9 Rabi, Indonesia
139 Y 11 Rabi, Fiji
98 L 7 Rābigh, Saudi Arabia
46 H 5 Rabinal, Guatemala
79 K 18 Rabka, Poland
18 L 8 Raceland, LA, U.S.A.
115 L 23 Rach Gia, Vietnam
27 P 15 Rachal, TX, U.S.A.
79 H 17 Racibórz, Poland
21 H 14 Racine, WI, U.S.A.
99 P 13 Radā', Yemen
85 I 17 Radashkovichy, Belarus

16 G 5 Radcliff, KY, U.S.A.
86 J 4 Radekhiv, Ukraine
17 O 7 Radford, VA, U.S.A.
105 B 14 Radhanpur, India
93 R 4 Radishchevo, Russian Federation
41 P 9 Radisson, QC, Canada
50 E 8 Rado de Tumaco, Colombia
79 L 14 Radom, Poland
127 B 19 Radom, Sudan
82 F 9 Radomir, Bulgaria
79 J 15 Radomsko, Poland
82 L 11 Radovets, Bulgaria
82 E 11 Radoviš, Macedonia (F.Y.R.O.M.)
75 R 6 Radstadt, Austria
85 F 17 Radun', Belarus
84 E 13 Radviliškis, Lithuania
78 N 13 Radzyń Podlaski, Poland
106 M 11 Rae Bareli, India
38 H 12 Rae-Edzo, NT, Canada
38 G 11 Rae Lakes, NT, Canada
17 R 10 Raeford, NC, U.S.A.
137 D 24 Raes Junction, New Zealand
136 K 13 Raetihi, New Zealand
58 B 13 Rafaela, Argentina
99 O 2 Rafḩā', Saudi Arabia
83 H 20 Rafina, Greece
100 L 10 Rafsanjān, Iran
127 B 20 Raga, Sudan
120 I 12 Ragay Gulf, Philippines
63 P 10 Raglan, U.K.
136 K 10 Raglan, New Zealand
18 H 7 Ragley, LA, U.S.A.
77 K 23 Ragusa, Italy
117 P 13 Raha, Indonesia
85 M 19 Rahachow, Belarus
127 F 17 Rahad Canal, Sudan
129 S 13 Rahama, Nigeria
101 V 12 Rahimyar Khan, Pakistan
100 H 6 Rāhjerd, Iran
106 I 6 Rahon, India
105 E 19 Raichur, India
107 S 11 Raiganj, India
105 H 15 Raigarh, India
117 O 15 Raijua, Indonesia
39 G 15 Rainbow Lake, AB, Canada
23 R 2 Rainy Lake, MN, U.S.A.
71 J 15 Raippaluoto, Finland
105 G 16 Raipur, India
105 G 16 Raj-Nandgaon, India
105 I 15 Rajagangapur, India
105 H 18 Rajahmundry, India
119 P 10 Rajang, Malaysia
101 V 11 Rajanpur, Pakistan
105 E 23 Rajapalaiyam, India
105 C 18 Rajapur, India
106 G 8 Rajasthan, India
107 Q 12 Rajauli, India
107 R 10 Rajbiraj, Nepal
106 H 8 Rajgarh, India
105 B 15 Rajkot, India
105 D 15 Rajpur, India
107 T 12 Rajshahi, Bangladesh
107 T 12 Rajshahi, Bangladesh
141 O 6 Rakahanga, Cook Islands
131 R 8 Rakai, Uganda
137 G 21 Rakaia, New Zealand
137 F 20 Rakaia, New Zealand
86 I 7 Rakhiv, Ukraine
113 Q 6 Three Gorges Dam, China
103 P 6 Rakhmet, Kazakhstan
79 C 17 Rakovník, Czech Republic
84 H 6 Rakvere, Estonia
17 S 9 Raleigh, NC, U.S.A.
17 V 11 Raleigh Bay, NC, U.S.A.
141 W 2 Ralik Chain, Marshall Islands
26 K 4 Ralls, TX, U.S.A.
100 I 5 Rām-Sar, Iran
47 Q 9 Rama, Nicaragua
96 G 7 Rama, Israel
96 F 9 Ramallah, Israel
105 F 23 Ramanathapuram, India
105 H 14 Ramanuj Ganj, India
138 E 2 Rambutyo Island, Papua New Guinea
62 L 15 Rame Head, U.K.
107 Q 10 Ramechhap, Nepal
92 L 1 Ramenskoye, Russian Federation
90 H 13 Rameshki, Russian Federation
107 Q 13 Ramgarh, India
107 V 13 Ramgarh, Bangladesh
100 H 9 Rāmhormoz, Iran
135 O 1 Ramingining, NT, Australia
96 F 9 Ramla, Israel
99 Q 13 Ramlat as Sab'atayn, Yemen
99 P 11 Ramlat Dahm, Yemen
96 G 13 Ramm, Jordan
106 K 8 Ramnagar, India
86 L 11 Râmnicu Sărat, Romania
86 I 11 Râmnicu Vâlcea, Romania
47 P 12 Ramon, Costa Rica
33 L 26 Ramona, CA, U.S.A.
106 K 8 Rampur, India
106 K 6 Rampur, India
107 S 12 Rampur Hat, India
115 B 14 Ramree Island, Myanmar
42 C 7 Ramsey, ON, Canada
61 H 16 Ramsey, U.K.
62 J 9 Ramsey Island, U.K.
42 C 8 Ramsey Lake, ON, Canada
63 Z 11 Ramsgate, U.K.
100 G 9 Rāmshīr, Iran
71 G 17 Ramsjö, Sweden
107 W 15 Ramu, Bangladesh
138 C 4 Ramu, Papua New Guinea
104 D 13 Rana Pratap Sagar, India
56 G 12 Rancagua, Chile
69 F 23 Rance, Belgium
107 P 13 Ranchi, India
45 O 9 Rancho Grande, Mexico
77 K 22 Randazzo, Italy
71 C 24 Randers, Denmark
70 H 11 Randijaure, Sweden
128 F 8 Ranérou, Senegal
137 E 23 Ranfurly, New Zealand
115 I 26 Rangae, Thailand
107 V 14 Rangamati, Bangladesh
107 W 10 Rangapara North, India
136 J 10 Rangaunu Bay, New Zealand
15 O 5 Rangeley, ME, U.S.A.
31 N 3 Rangely, CO, U.S.A.
27 O 6 Ranger, TX, U.S.A.
42 B 8 Ranger, ON, Canada
107 V 10 Rangia, India
136 L 12 Rangipo, New Zealand

136 K 9 Rangiriri, New Zealand
136 M 12 Rangitaiki, New Zealand
137 F 21 Rangitata, New Zealand
136 L 13 Rangitikei, New Zealand
115 E 16 Rangoon, Myanmar
107 T 11 Rangpur, Bangladesh
46 K 3 Ranguana Cay, Belize
105 D 20 Ranibennur, India
107 R 13 Raniganj, India
26 K 8 Rankin, TX, U.S.A.
40 L 4 Rankin Inlet, NU, Canada
105 A 14 Rann of Kachchh, India
93 U 5 Ranneye, Russian Federation
133 W 9 Ranohira, Madgascar
115 F 23 Ranong, Thailand
138 J 6 Ranongga, Solomon Islands
115 H 25 Ranot, Thailand
117 V 11 Ransiki, Indonesia
116 L 12 Rantau, Indonesia
21 G 18 Rantoul, IL, U.S.A.
70 M 12 Ranua, Finland
97 U 2 Rānya, Iraq
110 O 9 Raohe, China
76 C 9 Rapallo, Italy
105 A 14 Rapar, India
22 G 9 Rapid City, SD, U.S.A.
20 H 9 Rapid River, MI, U.S.A.
84 I 8 Räpina, Estonia
84 G 6 Rapla, Estonia
74 H 7 Rapperswil, Switzerland
120 K 13 Rapurapu, Philippines
14 I 7 Raquette Lake, NY, U.S.A.
141 O 11 Rarotonga, Cook Islands
126 F 9 Rās, Egypt
98 K 6 Rās Abū Madd, Saudi Arabia
126 H 13 Rās Abu Shagara, Sudan
99 Z 9 Rās al Daqm, Oman
97 N 1 Ra's al 'Ayn, Syria
96 H 3 Rās al Basīţ, Syria
99 Z 7 Rās al Ḩadd, Oman
99 Z 7 Rās al Ḩadd, Oman
99 S 13 Rās al Kalb, Yemen
99 X 5 Rās al Khaimah, United Arab Emirates
99 Z 10 Rās al Madrakah, Oman
99 S 3 Rās al Mish'āb, Saudi Arabia
125 Y 7 Rās al Muraysah, Libya
126 B 7 Rās al Muraysah, Egypt
96 G 12 Rās an Naqb, Jordan
98 I 3 Rās ash Shaykh Humayd, Saudi Arabia
125 X 7 Rās at Tīn, Libya
99 S 4 Rās az Zawr, Saudi Arabia
99 O 15 Rās Bāb al Mandab, Yemen
126 G 12 Rās Banās, Egypt
98 K 6 Rās Barīdī, Saudi Arabia
127 O 22 Rās Cabaad, Somalia
127 O 18 Rās Caluula, Somalia
127 O 18 Rās Caseyr, Somalia
127 I 18 Rās Dashen, Ethiopia
127 O 20 Rās Durdura, Somalia
100 G 10 Rās-e Barkan, Iran
100 H 11 Rās-e Halileh, Iran
101 N 14 Rās-e Meydani, Iran
126 D 7 Rās el Kanāyis, Egypt
128 K 7 Rās el Mā, Mali
99 V 12 Rās Fartak, Yemen
127 O 20 Rās Gabbac, Somalia
126 H 13 Rās Hardāba, Sudan
98 L 8 Rās Ḩāţibah, Saudi Arabia
127 O 21 Rās Ilig, Somalia
99 O 13 Rās 'Īsá, Yemen
101 Q 14 Ras Jaddi, Pakistan
100 M 14 Rās Jagīn, Iran
98 K 5 Rās Karkūmā, Saudi Arabia
127 I 15 Rās Kasar, Sudan/Eritrea
127 M 19 Rās Khansiir, Somalia
127 O 20 Rās Macbar, Somalia
99 X 11 Rās Mirbāţ, Oman
99 X 14 Rās Momi, Yemen
101 T 15 Ras Muari, Pakistan
126 G 10 Rās Muhammad, Egypt
99 X 11 Rās Naws, Oman
124 A 14 Rās Nouâdhibou, Western Sahara
128 E 5 Rās Nouâdhibou, Mauritania
101 P 14 Ras Nuh, Pakistan
101 R 14 Ras Ormara, Pakistan
100 H 11 Ras osh Shaţţ, Iran
99 W 11 Rās Sājir, Oman
99 Y 10 Rās Şawqirah, Oman
131 X 9 Ras Shaka, Kenya
99 Y 10 Rās Sharbithāt, Oman
99 V 14 Rās Shu'ab, Yemen
99 Z 9 Rās Şirāb, Oman
127 N 19 Ras Surud, Somalia
99 S 3 Rās Tanāqib, Saudi Arabia
99 T 4 Rās Tannūrah, Saudi Arabia
128 E 6 Rās Timirist, Mauritania
127 O 19 Rās Xaafuun, Somalia
121 C 19 Rasa, Philippines
85 D 14 Raseiniai, Lithuania
127 E 19 Rashad, Sudan
87 T 4 Rashivka, Ukraine
100 K 6 Rashm, Iran
100 H 4 Rasht, Iran
115 K 17 Rasi Salai, Thailand
81 L 14 Raška, Serbia and Montenegro
101 Q 11 Raskoh, Pakistan
40 L 1 Rasmussen Basin, NU, Canada
38 L 7 Rasmussen Bay, NU, Canada
85 L 16 Rasna, Belarus
86 J 11 Râşnov, Romania
93 N 4 Rasskazovo, Russian Federation
73 E 22 Rastatt, Germany
70 L 6 Rásttigáisa, Norway
115 G 19 Rat Buri, Thailand
34 C 13 Rat Island, AK, U.S.A.
34 C 12 Rat Islands, AK, U.S.A.
137 I 14 Rata, New Zealand
141 X 2 Ratak Chain, Marshall Islands
106 H 9 Ratangarh, India
71 F 16 Rätansbyn, Sweden
106 L 11 Rath, India
114 A 12 Rathedaung, Myanmar
72 K 13 Rathenow, Germany
105 D 14 Ratlam, India
105 C 18 Ratnagiri, India
105 G 25 Ratnapura, Sri Lanka
86 J 1 Ratne, Ukraine
101 U 12 Rato Dero, Pakistan
31 S 8 Raton, NM, U.S.A.
75 N 6 Rattenberg, Austria
118 C 8 Raub, Malaysia
59 D 17 Rauch, Argentina
99 R 2 Raudhatain, Kuwait

Country ▪ Internal administrative region: State/Province/Territory/Dependent territory ▪ Capital city ▪ Mountain range/Undersea ridge ▪ Mountain peak/Volcano/Seamount ▪ Geographic feature ▪ Headland/Point/Cape/Peninsula ▪ Desert ▪ Island/Island group ▪ Antarctic base ▪ Ocean ▪ Sea ▪ Bay/Gulf/Channel/Strait ▪ Lake ▪ Salt pan/Dry/Intermittent lake ▪ River

Raukumara Range – Russell Springs

136 O 11 **Raukumara Range**, New Zealand
71 J 18 **Rauma**, Finland
105 I 15 **Raurkela**, India
122 M 3 **Rausu**, Japan
136 O 10 **Rautoria**, New Zealand
86 I 3 **Rava-Rus'ka**, Ukraine
28 M 4 **Ravalli**, MT, U.S.A.
100 M 9 **Rāvar**, Iran
69 H 16 **Ravels**, Belgium
33 I 16 **Ravendale**, CA, U.S.A.
76 G 9 **Ravenna**, Italy
73 G 25 **Ravensburg**, Germany
135 T 4 **Ravenshoe**, QLD, Australia
134 H 11 **Ravensthorpe**, WA, Australia
101 X 10 **Ravi**, Pakistan
103 N 14 **Ravnina**, Turkmenistan
97 Q 5 **Rāwah**, Iraq
101 W 8 **Rawalpindi**, Pakistan
97 T 1 **Rawāndiz**, Iraq
117 U 11 **Rawas**, Indonesia
106 G 8 **Rawatsar**, India
79 G 14 **Rawicz**, Poland
134 K 10 **Rawlinna**, WA, Australia
29 V 13 **Rawlins**, WY, U.S.A.
57 I 18 **Rawson**, Argentina
109 N 11 **Rawu**, China
22 H 3 **Ray**, ND, U.S.A.
96 H 6 **Rayak**, Lebanon
89 U 14 **Raychikhinsk**, Russian Federation
99 P 12 **Raydah**, Yemen
93 V 2 **Rayevskiy**, Russian Federation
63 Y 10 **Rayleigh**, U.K.
32 F 8 **Raymond**, WA, U.S.A.
27 P 15 **Raymondville**, TX, U.S.A.
115 I 20 **Rayong**, Thailand
18 J 4 **Rayville**, LA, U.S.A.
101 V 8 **Razani**, Pakistan
82 L 7 **Razgrad**, Bulgaria
82 L 7 **Razgrad**, Bulgaria
82 G 11 **Razlog**, Bulgaria
14 H 13 **Reading**, PA, U.S.A.
21 K 20 **Reading**, OH, U.S.A.
63 U 11 **Reading**, U.K.
20 E 13 **Readstown**, WI, U.S.A.
56 J 13 **Realicó**, Argentina
115 J 20 **Reăng Kesei**, Cambodia
125 Q 8 **Rebaa**, Algeria
70 I 7 **Rebbenesøy**, Norway
125 W 12 **Rebiana Sand Sea**, Libya
90 G 7 **Reboly**, Russian Federation
122 I 3 **Rebun-tō**, Japan
85 M 20 **Rechytsa**, Belarus
54 O 13 **Recife**, Brazil
57 F 14 **Recinto**, Chile
58 C 12 **Reconquista**, Argentina
56 I 9 **Recreo**, Argentina
13 P 12 **Red**, TX, U.S.A.
114 K 11 **Red**, Asia
16 H 10 **Red Bank**, TN, U.S.A.
19 O 2 **Red Bay**, AL, U.S.A.
41 X 8 **Red Bay**, NL, Canada
33 G 16 **Red Bluff**, CA, U.S.A.
22 M 15 **Red Cloud**, NE, U.S.A.
39 J 19 **Red Deer**, AB, Canada
24 J 7 **Red Hills**, KS, U.S.A.
30 H 9 **Red Lake**, AZ, U.S.A.
40 J 10 **Red Lake**, ON, Canada
29 S 8 **Red Lodge**, MT, U.S.A.
126 H 11 **Red Sea**, Africa/Asia
127 G 14 **Red Sea**, Sudan
23 T 8 **Red Wing**, MN, U.S.A.
118 D 5 **Redang**, Malaysia
61 K 15 **Redcar**, U.K.
33 G 16 **Redding**, CA, U.S.A.
63 R 8 **Redditch**, U.K.
54 J 12 **Redenção**, Brazil
54 L 13 **Redenção do Gurguéia**, Brazil
22 M 8 **Redfield**, SD, U.S.A.
90 H 14 **Redkino**, Russian Federation
33 K 24 **Redlands**, CA, U.S.A.
32 H 11 **Redmond**, OR, U.S.A.
21 L 20 **Redoak**, OH, U.S.A.
62 J 15 **Redruth**, U.K.
23 Q 8 **Redwood Falls**, MN, U.S.A.
33 F 17 **Redwood Valley**, CA, U.S.A.
20 J 13 **Reed City**, MI, U.S.A.
22 H 6 **Reeder**, ND, U.S.A.
32 E 11 **Reedsport**, OR, U.S.A.
17 V 5 **Reedville**, VA, U.S.A.
137 G 17 **Reefton**, New Zealand
73 B 15 **Rees**, Germany
95 N 9 **Refahiye**, Turkey
19 O 3 **Reform**, AL, U.S.A.
27 Q 12 **Refugio**, TX, U.S.A.
78 E 9 **Rega**, Poland
73 M 22 **Regen**, Germany
73 K 22 **Regensburg**, Germany
124 L 11 **Reggane**, Algeria
76 E 8 **Reggio**, Italy
77 L 21 **Reggio di Calabria**, Italy
86 J 9 **Reghin**, Romania
39 N 19 **Regina**, SK, Canada
101 R 10 **Registan**, Afghanistan
58 K 8 **Registro**, Brazil
107 X 8 **Regong**, India
66 I 10 **Reguengos de Monsaraz**, Portugal
132 I 10 **Rehoboth**, Namibia
17 X 3 **Rehoboth Beach**, DE, U.S.A.
17 Q 8 **Reidsville**, NC, U.S.A.
63 V 11 **Reigate**, U.K.
65 S 3 **Reims**, France
74 F 7 **Reinach**, Switzerland
39 M 16 **Reindeer**, SK, Canada
39 M 14 **Reindeer Lake**, SK, Canada
67 N 2 **Reinosa**, Spain
75 Y 2 **Reinthal**, Austria
38 J 12 **Reliance**, NT, Canada
124 L 6 **Relizane**, Algeria
125 Q 8 **Remada**, Tunisia
73 C 18 **Remagen**, Germany
116 J 14 **Rembang**, Indonesia
125 Q 8 **Remel el Abiod**, Tunisia
74 M 26 **Remich**, Luxembourg
21 H 17 **Remington**, IN, U.S.A.
65 V 6 **Remiremont**, France
93 O 10 **Remontnoye**, Russian Federation
73 C 16 **Remscheid**, Germany
114 F 6 **Renam**, Myanmar
21 F 21 **Rend Lake**, IL, U.S.A.
138 K 6 **Rendova**, Solomon Islands
72 G 8 **Rendsburg**, Germany
42 H 10 **Renfrew**, ON, Canada
116 E 11 **Rengat**, Indonesia
56 G 12 **Rengo**, Chile
113 T 10 **Renhua**, China
87 N 11 **Reni**, Ukraine
135 Q 11 **Renmark**, SA, Australia
138 L 8 **Rennell**, Solomon Islands
64 L 5 **Rennes**, France
40 J 10 **Rennie**, MB, Canada
33 I 17 **Reno**, NV, U.S.A.
14 E 11 **Renovo**, PA, U.S.A.
111 D 18 **Renqiu**, China
113 N 7 **Renshou**, China
117 O 15 **Reo**, Indonesia
103 N 13 **Repetek**, Turkmenistan
54 F 10 **Represa de Balbina**, Brazil
58 H 9 **Represa de Foz de Areia**, Brazil
58 L 5 **Represa de Furnas**, Brazil
58 F 8 **Represa de Itaipu**, Brazil/Paraguay
58 G 8 **Represa de Salto Santiago**, Brazil
58 G 7 **Represa Ilha Grande**, Brazil
58 H 4 **Represa Porto Primavera**, Brazil
58 I 3 **Represa São Simão**, Brazil
55 J 15 **Represa Serra da Mesa**, Brazil
55 L 17 **Represa Três Marias**, Brazil
54 J 11 **Represa Tucuruí**, Brazil
46 L 5 **Repressa el Cajón**, Honduras
20 G 9 **Republic**, MI, U.S.A.
32 J 6 **Republic**, WA, U.S.A.
132 M 12 **Republic of South Africa**, Africa
80 F 10 **Republica Srpska**, Bosnia and Herzegovina
41 N 2 **Repulse Bay**, NU, Canada
52 E 12 **Requena**, Peru
67 S 8 **Requena**, Spain
65 Q 13 **Réquista**, France
94 M 9 **Reşadiye**, Turkey
95 S 11 **Reşadiye**, Turkey
82 C 12 **Resen**, Macedonia (F.Y.R.O.M.)
58 H 8 **Reserva**, Brazil
31 N 12 **Reserve**, NM, U.S.A.
42 I 8 **Réservoir Baskatong**, QC, Canada
42 I 8 **Réservoir Cabonga**, QC, Canada
42 H 8 **Réservoir Dozois**, QC, Canada
42 K 6 **Réservoir Gouin**, QC, Canada
41 P 9 **Réservoir la Grande Deux**, QC, Canada
41 Q 9 **Réservoir la Grande Trois**, QC, Canada
43 P 4 **Réservoir Manic Trois**, QC, Canada
43 P 2 **Réservoir Manicouagan**, QC, Canada
41 Q 9 **Réservoir Opinaca**, QC, Canada
43 O 4 **Réservoir Outardes Quatre**, QC, Canada
43 N 4 **Réservoir Pipmuacan**, QC, Canada
87 T 5 **Reshetylivka**, Ukraine
58 C 10 **Resistencia**, Argentina
86 F 11 **Reşiţa**, Romania
78 E 9 **Resko**, Poland
37 P 4 **Resolute Bay**, NU, Canada
41 T 4 **Resolution Island**, NU, Canada
137 A 24 **Resolution Island**, New Zealand
92 L 12 **Respublika Adygeya**, Russian Federation
88 M 13 **Respublika Altay**, Russian Federation
93 W 2 **Respublika Bashkortostan**, Russian Federation
89 R 13 **Respublika Buryatiya**, Russian Federation
93 R 15 **Respublika Dagestan**, Russian Federation
93 Q 10 **Respublika Kalmykiya**, Russian Federation
90 H 6 **Respublika Kareliya**, Russian Federation
89 N 13 **Respublika Khakasiya**, Russian Federation
91 R 7 **Respublika Komi**, Russian Federation
91 O 14 **Respublika Mariy El**, Russian Federation
93 O 3 **Respublika Mordoviya**, Russian Federation
89 R 10 **Respublika Sakha**, Russian Federation
93 O 14 **Respublika Severnaya Osetiya-Alaniya**, Russian Federation
93 S 1 **Respublika Tatarstan**, Russian Federation
89 O 13 **Respublika Tyva**, Russian Federation
46 F 6 **Retalhuleu**, Guatemala
56 F 13 **Retén Llico**, Chile
63 T 4 **Retford**, U.K.
65 S 3 **Rethel**, France
83 H 26 **Rethymno**, Greece
75 W 2 **Retz**, Austria
11 Q 11 **Réunion**, France
73 G 23 **Reutlingen**, Germany
74 L 6 **Reutte**, Austria
22 H 7 **Reva**, SD, U.S.A.
65 P 14 **Revel**, France
39 H 20 **Revelstoke**, BC, Canada
52 A 12 **Reventazón**, Peru
96 E 11 **Revivim**, Israel
106 M 12 **Rewa**, India
106 I 9 **Rewari**, India
29 P 10 **Rexburg**, ID, U.S.A.
53 I 18 **Reyes**, Bolivia
70 A 11 **Reykanestá**, Iceland
143 N 14 **Reykjanes Basin**, Arctic Ocean
143 N 15 **Reykjanes Ridge**, Arctic Ocean
70 B 11 **Reykjavík**, Iceland
45 R 7 **Reynosa**, Mexico
84 I 12 **Rēzekne**, Latvia
87 N 8 **Rezina**, Moldova
80 N 12 **Rgotina**, Serbia and Montenegro
63 N 8 **Rhayader**, U.K.
72 D 13 **Rheine**, Germany
74 E 6 **Rheinfelden**, Switzerland
73 D 20 **Rheinland-Pfalz**, Germany
74 H 9 **Rheinwaldhorn**, Switzerland
65 W 5 **Rhine**, Europe
20 F 10 **Rhinelander**, WI, U.S.A.
131 R 6 **Rhino Camp**, Uganda
72 K 12 **Rhinow**, Germany
69 H 21 **Rhisnes**, Belgium
15 N 11 **Rhode Island**, U.S.A.
15 O 11 **Rhode Island Sound**, RI, U.S.A.
83 O 24 **Rhodes**, Greece
82 G 11 **Rhodope Mountains**, Bulgaria
73 G 19 **Rhön**, Germany
63 N 10 **Rhondda**, U.K.
65 T 12 **Rhône**, France/Switzerland
65 U 11 **Rhône-Alpes**, France
63 O 5 **Rhosllanerchrugog**, U.K.
62 L 10 **Rhossili**, U.K.
61 I 18 **Rhyl**, U.K.
63 O 4 **Rhyl**, U.K.
129 S 15 **Riaba**, Equatorial Guinea
54 K 12 **Riachão**, Brazil
55 L 14 **Riachão das Neves**, Brazil
55 J 15 **Rialma**, Brazil
66 G 2 **Rias Bajas**, Spain
116 E 10 **Riau**, Indonesia
67 O 5 **Riaza**, Spain
55 H 18 **Ribas do Rio Pardo**, Brazil
133 T 5 **Ribáuè**, Mozambique
63 Q 2 **Ribble**, U.K.
71 B 25 **Ribe**, Denmark
58 J 8 **Ribeira**, Brazil
66 G 2 **Ribeira**, Spain
58 K 5 **Ribeirão Preto**, Brazil
53 J 16 **Riberalta**, Bolivia
67 X 3 **Ribes de Freser**, Spain
80 C 8 **Ribnica**, Slovenia
87 O 8 **Ribniţa**, Moldova
72 K 8 **Ribnitz-Damgarten**, Germany
44 L 4 **Ricardo Flores Magón**, Mexico
76 H 10 **Riccione**, Italy
20 D 10 **Rice Lake**, WI, U.S.A.
25 S 11 **Rich Mountain**, AR, U.S.A.
19 U 2 **Richard B. Russell Lake**, GA, U.S.A.
128 E 7 **Richard Toll**, Senegal
133 Q 12 **Richards Bay**, Republic of South Africa
17 O 11 **Richburn**, SC, U.S.A.
28 M 11 **Richfield**, ID, U.S.A.
14 I 8 **Richfield Springs**, NY, U.S.A.
43 T 8 **Richibucto**, NB, Canada
27 R 7 **Richland**, TX, U.S.A.
20 E 13 **Richland Center**, WI, U.S.A.
16 M 7 **Richlands**, VA, U.S.A.
16 J 5 **Richmond**, KY, U.S.A.
17 T 6 **Richmond**, VA, U.S.A.
42 M 10 **Richmond**, QC, Canada
132 L 13 **Richmond**, Republic of South Africa
135 S 5 **Richmond**, QLD, Australia
137 I 16 **Richmond**, New Zealand
19 W 5 **Richmond Hill**, GA, U.S.A.
137 H 17 **Richmond Range**, New Zealand
63 V 10 **Richmond upon Thames**, U.K.
28 K 8 **Riddle**, ID, U.S.A.
33 K 22 **Ridgecrest**, CA, U.S.A.
17 N 15 **Ridgeland**, SC, U.S.A.
14 D 11 **Ridgway**, PA, U.S.A.
75 R 4 **Ried im Innkreis**, Austria
73 G 24 **Riedlingen**, Germany
73 M 16 **Riesa**, Germany
84 C 13 **Rietavas**, Lithuania
76 H 13 **Rieti**, Italy
31 O 4 **Rifle**, CO, U.S.A.
70 C 9 **Rifstangi**, Iceland
131 U 6 **Rift Valley**, Kenya
129 V 9 **Rig-Rig**, Chad
84 F 11 **Rīga**, Latvia
28 K 7 **Riggins**, ID, U.S.A.
84 E 6 **Riguldi**, Estonia
145 N 3 **Riiser-Larsen Ice Shelf**, Antarctica
145 U 2 **Riiser-Larsen Peninsula**, Antarctica
84 F 6 **Riisipere**, Estonia
129 Q 10 **Rijau**, Nigeria
80 B 9 **Rijeka**, Croatia
68 M 11 **Rijssen**, Netherlands
122 L 4 **Rikubetsu**, Japan
82 G 10 **Rila**, Bulgaria
25 O 3 **Riley**, KS, U.S.A.
32 J 12 **Riley**, OR, U.S.A.
69 F 16 **Rilland**, Netherlands
79 K 21 **Rimavská Sobota**, Slovakia
76 H 10 **Rimini**, Italy
43 Q 6 **Rimouski**, QC, Canada
117 N 15 **Rinca**, Indonesia
112 K 6 **Rinda**, China
83 J 21 **Rineia**, Greece
104 D 12 **Ringas**, India
18 H 4 **Ringgold**, LA, U.S.A.
27 P 4 **Ringgold**, TX, U.S.A.
129 S 10 **Ringim**, Nigeria
71 B 24 **Ringkøbing**, Denmark
24 M 12 **Ringling**, OK, U.S.A.
29 R 6 **Ringling**, MT, U.S.A.
71 D 25 **Ringsted**, Denmark
70 I 7 **Ringvassøy**, Norway
63 S 13 **Ringwood**, U.K.
54 C 13 **Rio Branco**, Brazil
58 J 8 **Rio Branco do Sul**, Brazil
55 H 18 **Rio Brilhante**, Brazil
57 F 16 **Río Bueno**, Chile
49 Z 14 **Rio Claro**, Trinidad and Tobago
58 K 6 **Rio Claro**, Brazil
59 A 19 **Río Colorado**, Argentina
56 J 11 **Río Cuarto**, Argentina
58 N 7 **Rio de Janeiro**, Brazil
58 N 6 **Rio de Janeiro**, Brazil
47 U 15 **Río de Jesús**, Panama
58 I 10 **Rio do Sul**, Brazil
57 H 23 **Río Gallegos**, Argentina
12 L 12 **Rio Grande**, U.S.A., U.S.A.
45 O 8 **Río Grande**, Mexico
57 I 25 **Río Grande**, Argentina
59 H 14 **Rio Grande**, Brazil
27 O 15 **Rio Grande City**, TX, U.S.A.
45 N 10 **Río Grande de Santiago**, Mexico
54 O 12 **Rio Grande do Norte**, Brazil
58 F 11 **Rio Grande do Sul**, Brazil
47 W 14 **Río Hato**, Panama
58 G 12 **Rio Jacuí**, Brazil
45 Z 10 **Río Lagartos**, Mexico
66 G 8 **Rio Maior**, Portugal
53 J 21 **Río Mulatos**, Bolivia
57 I 16 **Río Negro**, Argentina
58 I 9 **Rio Negro**, Brazil
59 D 14 **Río Negro**, Uruguay
58 H 12 **Rio Pardo**, Brazil
31 P 10 **Rio Rancho**, NM, U.S.A.
52 D 10 **Río Tigre**, Peru
121 B 20 **Rio Tuba**, Philippines
45 Q 10 **Río Verde**, Mexico
55 I 17 **Rio Verde**, Brazil
57 G 24 **Río Verde**, Chile
52 B 9 **Riobamba**, Ecuador
50 J 2 **Riohacha**, Colombia
52 C 12 **Rioja**, Peru
65 R 10 **Riom**, France
67 Q 10 **Riópar**, Spain
87 Q 1 **Ripky**, Ukraine
16 A 9 **Ripley**, TN, U.S.A.
17 N 4 **Ripley**, WV, U.S.A.
21 L 20 **Ripley**, OH, U.S.A.
63 S 1 **Ripley**, U.K.
63 S 5 **Ripley**, U.K.
67 X 3 **Ripoll**, Spain
63 S 1 **Ripon**, U.K.
69 K 15 **Rips**, Netherlands
86 M 7 **Rîşcani**, Moldova
47 S 13 **Risco**, Panama
122 I 3 **Rishiri-tō**, Japan
122 I 3 **Rishiri-yama**, Japan
96 F 9 **Rishon Le Ẕiyyon**, Israel
71 D 15 **Rissa**, Norway
71 N 17 **Ristiina**, Finland
70 N 13 **Ristijärvi**, Finland
84 C 6 **Ristna**, Estonia
105 N 21 **Ritchie's Archipelago**, India
32 K 7 **Ritzville**, WA, U.S.A.
76 F 6 **Riva del Garda**, Italy
56 K 6 **Rivadavia**, Argentina
56 G 9 **Rivadavia**, Chile
59 A 16 **Rivadavia**, Argentina
47 N 10 **Rivas**, Nicaragua
128 H 13 **River Cess**, Liberia
20 C 11 **River Falls**, WI, U.S.A.
59 E 16 **River Plate**, Argentina/Uruguay
58 F 13 **Rivera**, Brazil
58 F 13 **Rivera**, Uruguay
58 E 13 **Rivera**, Uruguay
59 A 18 **Rivera**, Argentina
14 L 12 **Riverhead**, NY, U.S.A.
20 H 12 **Rivers**, WI, U.S.A.
129 Q 14 **Rivers**, Nigeria
137 D 24 **Riversdale**, New Zealand
137 L 16 **Riversdale Beach**, New Zealand
27 S 8 **Riverside**, TX, U.S.A.
33 K 25 **Riverside**, CA, U.S.A.
29 U 11 **Riverton**, WY, U.S.A.
43 U 9 **Riverview**, NB, Canada
27 P 14 **Riviera**, TX, U.S.A.
43 T 5 **Rivière-au-Renard**, QC, Canada
41 Q 7 **Rivière aux Feuilles**, QC, Canada
41 R 7 **Rivière aux Mélèzes**, QC, Canada
43 V 4 **Rivière-aux-Saumons**, QC, Canada
43 P 7 **Rivière-du-Loup**, QC, Canada
43 R 4 **Rivière-Pentecôte**, QC, Canada
49 Z 11 **Rivière-Pilote**, Martinique
86 L 3 **Rivne**, Ukraine
76 A 7 **Rivoli**, Italy
132 K 6 **Rivungo**, Angola
99 R 6 **Riyadh**, Saudi Arabia
95 P 8 **Rize**, Turkey
113 X 2 **Rizhao**, China
94 J 15 **Rizokarpason**, Cyprus
49 V 7 **Road Town**, Virgin Islands, U.K.
30 M 5 **Roan Plateau**, UT, U.S.A.
65 S 9 **Roanne**, France
13 W 9 **Roanoake**, VA, U.S.A.
17 Q 6 **Roanoke**, VA, U.S.A.
19 R 4 **Roanoke**, AL, U.S.A.
17 W 9 **Roanoke Island**, NC, U.S.A.
17 T 8 **Roanoke Rapids**, NC, U.S.A.
47 N 3 **Roatán**, Honduras
63 O 10 **Roath**, U.K.
135 S 14 **Robbins Island**, TAS, Australia
25 R 10 **Robert S. Kerr Reservoir**, OK, U.S.A.
145 R 14 **Roberts Butte**, Antarctica
107 O 12 **Robertsganj**, India
144 I 3 **Robertson Island**, Antarctica
128 G 13 **Robertsport**, Liberia
42 M 6 **Roberval**, QC, Canada
135 R 12 **Robinvale**, VIC, Australia
67 Q 9 **Robledo**, Spain
40 H 9 **Roblin**, MB, Canada
53 N 21 **Robore**, Bolivia
27 P 13 **Robstown**, TX, U.S.A.
77 J 14 **Roccaraso**, Italy
59 F 15 **Rocha**, Uruguay
59 G 15 **Rocha**, Uruguay
63 R 3 **Rochdale**, U.K.
65 O 10 **Rochechouart**, France
55 H 17 **Rochedo**, Brazil
64 L 9 **Rochefort**, France
69 I 23 **Rochefort**, Belgium
90 M 8 **Rochegda**, Russian Federation
14 E 8 **Rochester**, NY, U.S.A.
15 O 8 **Rochester**, NH, U.S.A.
21 I 17 **Rochester**, IN, U.S.A.
23 T 9 **Rochester**, MN, U.S.A.
63 X 11 **Rochester**, U.K.
137 D 24 **Rock and Pillar Range**, New Zealand
21 E 16 **Rock Falls**, IL, U.S.A.
17 O 11 **Rock Hill**, SC, U.S.A.
29 T 14 **Rock Springs**, WY, U.S.A.
29 W 5 **Rock Springs**, MT, U.S.A.
27 Q 9 **Rockdale**, TX, U.S.A.
21 F 15 **Rockford**, IL, U.S.A.
135 V 7 **Rockhampton**, QLD, Australia
17 Q 11 **Rockingham**, NC, U.S.A.
22 L 2 **Rocklake**, ND, U.S.A.
15 Q 6 **Rockland**, ME, U.S.A.
21 H 22 **Rockport**, IN, U.S.A.
32 H 6 **Rockport**, WA, U.S.A.
26 M 10 **Rocksprings**, TX, U.S.A.
21 H 19 **Rockville**, IN, U.S.A.
23 R 12 **Rockwell City**, IA, U.S.A.
16 I 9 **Rockwood**, TN, U.S.A.
42 B 8 **Rocky Island Lake**, ON, Canada
17 T 8 **Rocky Mount**, NC, U.S.A.
29 O 3 **Rocky Mountain**, MT, U.S.A.
39 I 19 **Rocky Mountain House**, AB, Canada
12 J 4 **Rocky Mountains**, MT, U.S.A.
132 G 8 **Rocky Point**, Namibia
31 N 15 **Rodeo**, NM, U.S.A.
56 G 10 **Rodeo**, Argentina
65 Q 12 **Rodez**, France
73 L 21 **Roding**, Germany
86 J 8 **Rodna**, Romania
82 H 13 **Rodolivos**, Greece
83 O 23 **Rodos**, Greece
11 R 11 **Rodrigues Island**, Mauritius
134 F 6 **Roebourne**, WA, Australia
134 I 4 **Roebuck Bay**, WA, Australia
134 I 4 **Roebuck Plains Roadhouse**, WA, Australia
69 K 17 **Roermond**, Netherlands
41 N 3 **Roes Welcome Sound**, NU, Canada
69 A 18 **Roesbrugge-Haringe**, Belgium
69 B 18 **Roeselare**, Belgium
77 L 17 **Rofrano**, Italy
80 I 13 **Rogatica**, Bosnia and Herzegovina
25 S 8 **Rogers**, AR, U.S.A.
20 L 10 **Rogers City**, MI, U.S.A.
33 K 23 **Rogers Lake**, CA, U.S.A.
28 M 13 **Rogerson**, ID, U.S.A.
65 Y 14 **Rogliano**, France
77 M 19 **Rogliano**, Italy
86 J 5 **Rohatyn**, Ukraine
75 S 3 **Rohrbach**, Austria
101 U 12 **Rohri**, Pakistan
106 I 8 **Rohtak**, India
84 E 6 **Rohuküla**, Estonia
115 K 17 **Roi Et**, Thailand
107 Z 8 **Roing**, India
84 D 10 **Roja**, Latvia
59 B 15 **Rojas**, Argentina
84 G 13 **Rokiškis**, Lithuania
122 K 8 **Rokkasho**, Japan
123 H 14 **Rokkō-zaki**, Japan
86 M 2 **Rokytne**, Ukraine
71 A 19 **Røldal**, Norway
25 W 5 **Rolla**, MO, U.S.A.
74 B 9 **Rolle**, Switzerland
135 U 7 **Rolleston**, QLD, Australia
42 F 7 **Rollet**, QC, Canada
70 K 5 **Rolvsøya**, Norway
13 O 15 **Roma**, TX, U.S.A.
117 R 14 **Roma**, Indonesia
135 U 8 **Roma**, QLD, Australia
86 G 10 **Romania**, Europe
89 R 13 **Romanovka**, Russian Federation
121 I 14 **Romblon**, Philippines
121 I 14 **Romblon**, Philippines
121 H 14 **Romblon Passage**, Philippines
14 H 8 **Rome**, NY, U.S.A.
19 R 2 **Rome**, GA, U.S.A.
77 H 14 **Rome**, Italy
21 M 14 **Romeo**, MI, U.S.A.
63 W 10 **Romford**, U.K.
65 R 5 **Romilly-sur-Seine**, France
17 R 2 **Romney**, WV, U.S.A.
87 S 3 **Romny**, Ukraine
71 B 25 **Rømø**, Denmark
93 P 2 **Romodanovo**, Russian Federation
65 P 7 **Romorantin-Lanthenay**, France
118 D 9 **Rompin**, Malaysia
63 S 12 **Romsey**, U.K.
115 M 15 **Ron**, Vietnam
66 M 13 **Ronda**, Spain
50 K 5 **Rondón**, Colombia
55 E 14 **Rondônia**, Brazil
55 H 16 **Rondonópolis**, Brazil
113 Q 11 **Rong'an**, China
112 J 5 **Rongbacha**, China
111 I 19 **Rongcheng**, China
141 W 1 **Rongelap Atoll**, Marshall Islands
113 Q 10 **Rongjiang**, China
141 X 1 **Rongrik**, Marshall Islands
113 R 12 **Rongxian**, China
71 F 26 **Rønne**, Denmark
144 I 7 **Ronne Entrance**, Antarctica
144 L 7 **Ronne Ice Shelf**, Antarctica
71 G 24 **Ronneby**, Sweden
71 F 15 **Rönnöfors**, Sweden
69 D 19 **Ronse**, Belgium
106 J 7 **Roorkee**, India
69 G 15 **Roosendaal**, Netherlands
30 K 12 **Roosevelt**, AZ, U.S.A.
145 O 11 **Roosevelt Island**, Antarctica
79 M 17 **Ropczyce**, Poland
135 N 2 **Roper Bar**, NT, Australia
64 M 13 **Roquefort**, France
54 E 8 **Roraima**, Brazil
70 E 16 **Røros**, Norway
71 Q 5 **Ros'**, Ukraine
52 B 8 **Rosa Zárate**, Ecuador
48 I 9 **Rosalind Bank**, Jamaica
58 G 6 **Rosana**, Brazil
44 M 9 **Rosario**, Mexico
50 K 3 **Rosario**, Venezuela
50 C 14 **Rosario**, Argentina
120 F 9 **Rosario**, Philippines
120 G 12 **Rosario**, Philippines
48 E 8 **Rosario Bank**, Cayman Islands
56 J 7 **Rosario de la Frontera**, Argentina
58 F 12 **Rosário do Sul**, Brazil
44 E 2 **Rosarito**, Mexico
44 G 5 **Rosarito**, Mexico
44 I 6 **Rosarito**, Mexico
77 L 20 **Rosarno**, Italy
22 L 7 **Roscoe**, SD, U.S.A.
26 L 6 **Roscoe**, TX, U.S.A.
20 K 11 **Roscommon**, MI, U.S.A.
61 C 17 **Roscommon**, Republic of Ireland
61 D 19 **Roscrea**, Republic of Ireland
140 L 8 **Rose**, American Samoa
30 M 2 **Rose Peak**, AZ, U.S.A.
49 Y 10 **Roseau**, Dominica
32 F 12 **Roseburg**, OR, U.S.A.
69 H 22 **Rosée**, Belgium
127 G 19 **Roseires Reservoir**, Sudan
27 S 10 **Rosenberg**, TX, U.S.A.
73 K 25 **Rosenheim**, Germany
67 Y 3 **Roses**, Spain
76 J 12 **Roseto degli Abruzzi**, Italy
39 L 19 **Rosetown**, SK, Canada
21 D 17 **Roseville**, IL, U.S.A.
132 I 12 **Rosh Pinah**, Namibia
76 E 11 **Rosignano Marittimo**, Italy
86 J 13 **Roşiori de Vede**, Romania
92 H 2 **Roslavl'**, Russian Federation
90 M 11 **Roslvatino**, Russian Federation
135 T 15 **Ross**, TAS, Australia
137 F 19 **Ross**, New Zealand
145 O 11 **Ross Ice Shelf**, Antarctica
145 Q 12 **Ross Island**, Antarctica
63 Q 9 **Ross-on-Wye**, U.K.
38 C 13 **Ross River**, YT, Canada
145 N 12 **Ross Sea**, Antarctica
61 C 15 **Rossan Point**, Republic of Ireland
138 I 7 **Rossel Island**, Papua New Guinea
61 E 20 **Rosslare**, Republic of Ireland
128 E 7 **Rosso**, Mauritania
92 L 7 **Rossosh'**, Russian Federation
70 F 12 **Røssvatnet**, Norway
100 J 13 **Rostāq**, Iran
72 J 9 **Rostock**, Germany
90 J 14 **Rostov**, Russian Federation
92 L 10 **Rostov-na-Donu**, Russian Federation
92 M 9 **Rostovskaya Oblast'**, Russian Federation
19 S 2 **Roswell**, GA, U.S.A.
31 S 12 **Roswell**, NM, U.S.A.
140 A 9 **Rota**, Northern Mariana Islands
117 P 15 **Rote**, Indonesia
72 G 11 **Rotenburg**, Germany
73 E 17 **Rothaargebirge**, Germany
73 H 21 **Rothenburg ob der Tauber**, Germany
144 H 5 **Rothera**, Antarctica
63 S 4 **Rotherham**, U.K.
144 I 6 **Rothschild Island**, Antarctica
63 U 7 **Rothwell**, U.K.
117 P 15 **Roti**, Indonesia
137 G 19 **Rotomanu**, New Zealand
77 N 17 **Rotondella**, Italy
136 M 11 **Rotorua**, New Zealand
75 T 6 **Rottenmann**, Austria
68 G 13 **Rotterdam**, Netherlands
68 M 5 **Rottumeroog**, Netherlands
68 L 4 **Rottumerplaat**, Netherlands
73 F 24 **Rottweil**, Germany
139 W 8 **Rotuma**, Fiji
65 Q 1 **Roubaix**, France
65 O 3 **Rouen**, France
16 F 6 **Rough River Lake**, KY, U.S.A.
27 P 9 **Round Rock**, TX, U.S.A.
30 M 8 **Round Rock**, AZ, U.S.A.
29 T 6 **Roundup**, MT, U.S.A.
60 I 6 **Rousay**, U.K.
42 F 7 **Rouyn**, QC, Canada
70 L 11 **Rovaniemi**, Finland
90 L 9 **Rovdino**, Russian Federation
87 Z 7 **Roven'ky**, Ukraine
74 H 10 **Roveredo**, Switzerland
76 F 6 **Rovereto**, Italy
115 L 19 **Rôvieng Tbong**, Cambodia
76 G 8 **Rovigo**, Italy
86 H 12 **Rovinari**, Romania
80 A 9 **Rovinj**, Croatia
93 Q 6 **Rovnoye**, Russian Federation
17 R 11 **Rowland**, NC, U.S.A.
41 O 1 **Rowley Island**, NU, Canada
121 I 16 **Roxas**, Philippines
121 E 17 **Roxas**, Philippines
121 H 14 **Roxas**, Philippines
17 R 8 **Roxboro**, NC, U.S.A.
135 P 10 **Roxby Downs**, SA, Australia
29 T 14 **Roy**, MT, U.S.A.
31 S 9 **Roy**, NM, U.S.A.
63 S 8 **Royal Leamington Spa**, U.K.
63 X 12 **Royal Tunbridge Wells**, U.K.
14 M 7 **Royalton**, VT, U.S.A.
64 L 10 **Royan**, France
65 Q 3 **Roye**, France
19 U 2 **Royston**, GA, U.S.A.
63 W 9 **Royston**, U.K.
81 L 15 **Rožaje**, Serbia and Montenegro
78 L 11 **Różan**, Poland
87 T 11 **Rozdol'ne**, Ukraine
79 K 20 **Rožňava**, Slovakia
68 F 13 **Rozenburg**, Netherlands
68 K 13 **Rozendaal**, Netherlands
86 K 3 **Rozhyshche**, Ukraine
81 K 17 **Rrëshen**, Albania
93 O 5 **Rtishchevo**, Russian Federation
63 P 5 **Ruabon**, U.K.
132 G 7 **Ruacana**, Namibia
137 L 14 **Ruahine Range**, New Zealand
136 J 6 **Ruakaka**, New Zealand
137 C 26 **Ruapuke Island**, New Zealand
136 M 11 **Ruatahuna**, New Zealand
136 J 7 **Ruawai**, New Zealand
99 Q 10 **Rub' al Khālī**, Saudi Arabia
87 Y 5 **Rubizhne**, Ukraine
88 L 13 **Rubtsovsk**, Russian Federation
35 P 7 **Ruby**, AK, U.S.A.
33 M 17 **Ruby Mountains**, NV, U.S.A.
86 J 11 **Rucăr**, Romania
84 B 12 **Rucava**, Latvia
113 U 10 **Rucheng**, China
17 S 4 **Ruckersville**, VA, U.S.A.
101 Q 11 **Rudbar**, Afghanistan
92 G 1 **Rudnya**, Russian Federation
93 P 6 **Rudnya**, Russian Federation
103 O 3 **Rudnyy**, Kazakhstan
73 J 17 **Rudolstadt**, Germany
113 Z 5 **Rudong**, China
65 P 2 **Rue**, France
127 F 17 **Rufa'a**, Sudan
65 N 9 **Ruffec**, France
59 A 16 **Rufino**, Argentina
133 O 5 **Rufunsa**, Zambia
113 Y 5 **Rugao**, China
22 K 3 **Rugby**, ND, U.S.A.
61 K 20 **Rugby**, U.K.
63 T 7 **Rugby**, U.K.
63 R 6 **Rugeley**, U.K.
72 L 8 **Rügen**, Germany
131 Q 8 **Ruhengeri**, Rwanda
84 E 9 **Ruhnu**, Estonia
113 Z 8 **Rui'an**, China
113 V 7 **Ruichang**, China
31 R 13 **Ruidoso**, NM, U.S.A.
113 V 10 **Ruijin**, China
112 H 11 **Ruili**, China
131 U 12 **Ruipa**, Tanzania
44 M 10 **Ruiz**, Mexico
84 G 9 **Rūjiena**, Latvia
70 N 11 **Ruka**, Finland
131 R 12 **Rukwa**, Tanzania
60 E 11 **Rum**, U.K.
49 N 3 **Rum Cay**, The Bahamas
80 K 10 **Ruma**, Serbia and Montenegro
99 R 5 **Rumāh**, Saudi Arabia
97 Y 12 **Rumaila**, Iraq
127 D 21 **Rumbek**, Sudan
138 A 4 **Rumginae**, Papua New Guinea
122 J 4 **Rumoi**, Japan
133 R 3 **Rumphi**, Malawi
113 U 4 **Runan**, China
63 P 4 **Runcorn**, U.K.
132 J 7 **Rundu**, Namibia
131 P 6 **Rungu**, Democratic Republic of Cong
131 T 12 **Rungwa**, Tanzania
112 L 4 **Ru'nying**, China
71 O 17 **Ruokolahti**, Finland
108 K 6 **Ruoqiang**, China
70 M 6 **Ruostefjelbma**, Norway
116 E 10 **Rupat**, Indonesia
86 J 10 **Rupea**, Romania
17 O 5 **Rupert**, WV, U.S.A.
144 M 12 **Ruppert Coast**, Antarctica
53 I 18 **Rurrenabaque**, Bolivia
133 Q 7 **Rusape**, Zimbabwe
86 I 7 **Ruscova**, Romania
82 K 6 **Ruse**, Bulgaria
82 K 6 **Ruse**, Bulgaria
111 H 20 **Rushan**, China
63 U 8 **Rushden**, U.K.
21 D 18 **Rushville**, IL, U.S.A.
85 C 14 **Rusnė**, Lithuania
84 I 12 **Rušonu ezers**, Latvia
16 L 4 **Russell**, KY, U.S.A.
24 L 4 **Russell**, KS, U.S.A.
138 L 6 **Russell Islands**, Solomon Islands
16 H 7 **Russell Springs**, KY, U.S.A.

Country · Internal administrative region: State/Province/Territory/Dependent territory · Capital city · Mountain range/Undersea ridge · Mountain peak/Volcano/Seamount · Geographic feature · Headland/Point/Cape/Peninsula · Desert · Island/Island group · Antarctic base · Ocean · Sea · Bay/Gulf/Channel/Strait · Lake · Salt pan/Dry/Intermittent lake

F 7	Russellville, KY, U.S.A.
O 2	Russellville, AL, U.S.A.
U 10	Russellville, AR, U.S.A.
J 19	Russian Federation, Europe ◘
M 12	Russkaya, Antarctica
V 7	Russkoye Ust'ye, Russian Federation
U 7	Rust'avi, Georgia
N 11	Rustenburg, Republic of South Africa
I 4	Ruston, LA, U.S.A.
C 17	Ruten, Norway ▲
O 15	Ruteng, Indonesia
M 8	Ruth, NV, U.S.A.
L 7	Rutherfordton, NC, U.S.A.
L 7	Rutland, VT, U.S.A.
N 22	Rutland Island, India
H 8	Rutog, China
D 9	Rutter, ON, Canada
R 15	Rutul, Russian Federation
M 12	Ruurlo, Netherlands
U 14	Ruvuma, Tanzania
S 3	Ruvuma, Mozambique/Tanzania
V 6	Ruweis, United Arab Emirates
P 3	Ruzayevka, Russian Federation
F 19	Ruzhany, Belarus
J 19	Ružomberok, Slovakia
Q 9	Rwanda, Africa ◘
M 2	Ryazan', Russian Federation
M 2	Ryazanskaya Oblast', Russian Federation
M 3	Ryazhsk, Russian Federation
J 7	Ryberg Peninsula, Antarctica
J 13	Rybinsk, Russian Federation
J 13	Rybinsk Reservoir, Russian Federation
I 17	Rybnik, Poland
T 13	Ryde, U.K.
Y 12	Rye, U.K.
S 13	Rye, VIC, Australia
Y 13	Rye Bay, U.K. ≈
T 6	Ryegate, MT, U.S.A.
M 14	Ryki, Poland
I 5	Ryl'sk, Russian Federation
I 13	Ryōtsu, Japan
J 11	Rypin, Poland
N 24	Ryukyu Islands, Japan ≇
D 12	Rzepin, Poland
M 17	Rzeszów, Poland
G 14	Rzhev, Russian Federation

L 13	's-Heerenberg, Netherlands
I 14	's-Hertogenbosch, Netherlands
I 5	Sa de las Minas, Guatemala ▲▲
M 22	Sa Đec, Vietnam
D 18	Sa del Tandil, Argentina ▲▲
J 19	Sa Kaeo, Thailand
K 24	Saacow, Somalia
J 15	Saale, Germany
J 18	Saalfeld, Germany
Q 6	Saalfelden, Germany
C 21	Saarbrücken, Germany
B 20	Saarburg, Germany
D 9	Sääre, Estonia
D 8	Saaremaa, Estonia
L 16	Saarijärvi, Finland
C 21	Saarland, Germany
E 10	Saas Fee, Switzerland
J 6	Sab' Ābār, Syria
W 8	Saba, Netherlands Antilles ≇
J 10	Šabac, Serbia and Montenegro
W 4	Sabadell, Spain
G 16	Sabae, Japan
W 6	Sabah, Malaysia ◙
E 12	Sabalgarh, India
M 7	Sabana Grande, Venezuela
I 2	Sabanalarga, Colombia
I 2	Sabaneta, Venezuela
B 8	Sabang, Indonesia
L 9	Sabangan, Philippines
G 25	Sābāoani, Romania
H 15	Sabaudia, Italy
H 9	Sabaya, Bolivia
T 11	Sabḥā, Jordan
N 11	Sabhā, Libya
T 3	Sabinal, U.S.A.
T 3	Sabiñánigo, Spain
N 11	Sabinas Hidalgo, Mexico
H 6	Sabine, LA, U.S.A.
I 4	Sabine Lake, U.S.A. ≈
T 8	Sabkhat al Haysháh, Libya ≋
X 9	Sabkhat Ghuzayyil, Libya ≋
S 9	Sablayan, Philippines
M 13	Sabres, France
X 12	Sabrina Coast, Antarctica ◇
J 6	Sabtang, Philippines ≇
J 6	Sabugal, Portugal
L 9	Sabulu, Indonesia
O 11	Şabyā, Saudi Arabia
M 6	Sabzevār, Iran
K 10	Sacajawea Peak, OR, U.S.A. ▲
Q 6	Sacedón, Spain
M 21	Sach'ŏn, South Korea
M 16	Sachsen, Germany
J 12	Sachsen-Anhalt, Germany ◙
G 6	Sackets Harbor, NY, U.S.A.
V 2	Saco, MT, U.S.A.
I 22	Sacol, Philippines ≇
G 17	Sacramento, CA, U.S.A.
G 17	Sacramento, CA, U.S.A.
R 13	Sacramento Mountains, NM, U.S.A. ▲▲
G 16	Sacramento Valley, CA, U.S.A. ◇
I 5	Şadad, Syria
O 11	Şa'dah, Yemen
H 26	Sadao, Thailand
E 18	Sadaseopet, India
T 8	Sadd Darband-i Khān, Iraq ≋
T 8	Saddat al Hindiyah, Iraq ≋
X 11	Sadḩ, Oman
G 20	Sadi, Ethiopia
V 12	Sadiqabad, Pakistan
Y 9	Sadiya, India
I 13	Sadoga-shima, Japan ≇
U 11	Sadove, Ukraine
O 4	Sadovoye, Russian Federation
V 4	Safed Khirs, Afghanistan ▲▲
P 7	Safed Koh, Afghanistan ▲▲
E 21	Säffle, Sweden
X 3	Safford, AZ, U.S.A.
X 3	Saffron Walden, U.K.

G 8	Safi, Morocco
O 10	Safīdabeh, Iran
H 4	Şāfītā, Syria
N 11	Safonovo, Russian Federation
Z 12	Safwān, Iraq
E 4	Sag Sag, Papua New Guinea
I 10	Saga, China
B 21	Saga, Japan
B 21	Saga, Japan
K 12	Sagae, Japan
C 10	Sagaing, Myanmar
D 11	Sagaing, Myanmar
K 17	Sagami-nada, Japan ≈
K 16	Sagami-wan, Japan ≈
U 2	Saganaga Lake, MN, U.S.A. ≋
F 21	Saganthif Kyun, Myanmar
F 14	Sagar, India
S 7	Sagastyr, Russian Federation
P 10	Sagauli, India
L 8	Saghand, Iran
L 13	Saginaw, MI, U.S.A.
L 13	Saginaw Bay, MI, U.S.A. ≈
Z 2	Sagiz, Kazakhstan
G 9	Sagola, MI, U.S.A.
P 11	Sagra, Spain ▲
G 12	Sagres, Portugal
C 13	Sagu, Myanmar
M 6	Sagua de Tánamo, Cuba
M 6	Sagua la Grande, Cuba
Q 6	Saguache, CO, U.S.A.
N 6	Saguenay, QC, Canada
N 6	Saguenay, QC, Canada
T 8	Sagunto, Spain
R 3	Sagwon, AK, U.S.A.
H 9	Sahāb, Jordan
I 13	Sahara, Algeria ◇
J 7	Saharanpur, India
R 11	Saharsa, India
V 10	Sahbuz, Azerbaijan
M 9	Sahel, Burkina Faso ◇
S 12	Sahibganj, India
X 10	Sahiwal, Pakistan
W 9	Sahiwal, Pakistan
O 9	Sahlābād, Iran
T 12	Şahra' al Ḩijāra, Iraq ◇
A 4	Sahuaripa, Mexico
O 11	Sahuayo, Mexico
B 20	Sa'id Bundas, Sudan
G 6	Saïda, Lebanon
L 6	Saïda, Algeria
E 17	Saigō, Japan
X 14	Saiha, India
B 14	Saihan Tal, China
C 19	Saijō, Japan
D 21	Saiki, Japan
N 17	Saimaa, Finland ≋
P 11	Saindak, Pakistan
60 / L 3	St Abb's Head, U.K. ◇
W 5	St Aegyd am Neuwalde, Austria
J 3	St Agnes, U.K.
O 7	St-Aignan, France
M 4	St Albans, WV, U.S.A.
Y 10	St Alban's, NL, Canada
V 10	St Albans, U.K.
R 14	St Alban's Head, U.K. ◇
M 9	St-Amand-Montrond, France
U 9	St-Amour, France
O 7	St André, Austria
X 6	St Andrew Sound, GA, U.S.A. ≈
I 12	St Andrews, U.K.
R 5	Ste-Anne-des-Monts, QC, Canada
W 3	St Anthony, NL, Canada
K 7	St Anton am Arlberg, Austria
R 13	St Arnaud, VIC, Australia
H 17	St Arnaud, New Zealand
Q 1	St Asaph, U.K.
W 8	St-Augustin, QC, Canada
X 8	St Augustine, FL, U.S.A.
K 15	St Austell, U.K.
K 15	St Austell Bay, U.K. ≈
X 8	St Barthélémy, France, France ◙
N 5	St-Béat, France
J 9	St-Bride's Bay, U.K. ≈
J 5	St-Brieuc, France
F 13	St-Calais, France
F 13	St Catharines, ON, Canada
T 14	St Catherine's Point, U.K. ◇
P 12	St-Céré, France
R 5	St Charles, MO, U.S.A.
Q 13	Saint Charles, ID, U.S.A.
R 7	St Cloud, MN, U.S.A.
X 8	St Croix, Virgin Islands, U.S.A. ≇
C 10	St Croix Falls, WI, U.S.A.
O 9	St-Damien-de-Buckland, QC, Canada
J 9	St David's, U.K.
H 2	St David's Head, U.K. ◇
W 5	St-Dié, France
T 5	St Dizier, France
T 10	St-Étienne, France
X 8	St Eustatius, Netherlands Antilles ≇
J 5	St-Fabien, QC, Canada
M 6	St-Félicien, QC, Canada
M 6	St-Florentin, France
G 5	St-Flour, France
G 2	St Francis, KS, U.S.A.
E 8	St Gallen, Switzerland
N 15	St-Gaudens, France
P 14	St George, SC, U.S.A.
H 7	St George, UT, U.S.A.
S 10	St George, NB, Canada
U 9	St George, QLD, Australia
S 8	St George Island, FL, U.S.A. ≇
J 11	St George Island, AK, U.S.A. ≇
U 3	St Georges, Austria
O 9	St-Georges, QC, Canada
Y 13	St George's, Grenada ■
S 7	St Georges, French Guiana
W 11	St Georges Bay, NL, Canada ≈
N 5	St George's Bay, NS, Canada ≈
E 21	St George's Channel, Republic of Ireland/United Kingdom ≈
H 3	St George's Channel, Papua New Guinea ≈
R 5	St Gilgen, Austria
F 17	St-Gillis-Waas, Belgium
J 6	St-Girons, France
K 10	St Govan's Head, U.K. ◇
K 12	Saint Helen, MI, U.S.A.
L 11	St Helena, U.K.
J 14	Saint Helena Bay, Republic of South Africa ≈

P 15	St Helena Sound, SC, U.S.A. ≈
F 9	St Helens, U.K.
P 3	St Helens, U.K.
T 15	St Helens, TAS, Australia
J 26	St Helier, U.K.
J 23	St-Hubert, QC, Canada
L 10	St-Hyacinthe, QC, Canada
K 10	St Ignace, MI, U.S.A.
J 15	St Ives, U.K.
W 7	St Ives, U.K.
J 15	St Ives Bay, U.K. ≈
J 6	St Jacobiparochie, Netherlands
O 8	St Jakob, Austria
K 14	St-Jean-de-Luz, France
V 11	St-Jean-de-Maurienne, France
K 8	St-Jean-de-Monts, France
O 8	St-Jean-de-Port-Joli, QC, Canada
L 11	St-Jean-sur-Richelieu, QC, Canada
K 10	St-Jérôme, QC, Canada
P 6	St Johann in Tirol, Austria
L 13	Saint John, MI, U.S.A.
K 5	St John, KS, U.S.A.
S 10	Saint John, NB, Canada
V 8	St John, Virgin Islands, U.S.A. ≇
K 14	Saint Johns, MI, U.S.A.
A 11	St Johns, AZ, U.S.A.
Z 10	St John's, U.K.
Y 9	St John's, Antigua and Barbuda ■
E 10	St Joseph, TN, U.S.A.
K 5	St Joseph, LA, U.S.A.
R 2	St Joseph, MO, U.S.A.
R 8	St Joseph Bay, FL, U.S.A. ≈
Q 13	St Joseph Island, TX, U.S.A. ≇
A 9	St Joseph Island, ON, Canada ≇
J 10	St-Jovité, QC, Canada
O 10	St-Junien, France
J 15	St Keverne, U.K.
X 8	St Kitts, St Kitts and Nevis
X 9	St Kitts and Nevis, North America ■
X 6	St-Laurent-du-Maroni, French Guiana
W 11	St Lawrence, QC, Canada
K 7	St Lawrence Island, AK, U.S.A. ≇
K 25	St-Léger, Belgium
M 9	St-Léonard, QC, Canada
Q 8	St-Léonard, NB, Canada
L 4	St-Lô, France
X 4	St Louis, MO, U.S.A.
D 7	St-Louis, Senegal
Z 11	St Lucia, North America ■
Y 11	St Lucia Channel, St Lucia ≈
W 8	St Maarten, Netherlands Antilles ≇
K 4	St-Malo, France
O 7	St Marc, Haiti
P 8	St-Marcel, France
E 19	St-Maria-Lierde, Belgium
N 9	Ste-Marie, QC, Canada
T 7	St Marks, FL, U.S.A.
X 8	St Martin, France, France ◙
P 10	St Mary Peak, SA, Australia ▲
P 3	Saint Marys, U.K.
Z 11	St Mary's Bay, NL, Canada ≈
J 9	St Matthew Island, U.S.A. ≇
F 2	St Matthias Group, Papua New Guinea ≇
K 15	St Mawes, U.K.
M 9	St-Maxient-l'École, France
W 14	Ste-Maxime, France
R 7	St Michael, Austria
U 6	St Michael, Austria
K 9	St-Michel-des-Saints, QC, Canada
J 9	St Moritz, Switzerland
K 7	St-Nazaire, France
V 8	St Neots, U.K.
F 17	St Niklaas, Belgium
E 10	St Niklaus, Switzerland
S 6	St Nikolai, Austria
Q 1	St-Omer, France
O 8	St-Pacôme, QC, Canada
L 14	St-Palais, France
O 7	St-Pascal, QC, Canada
M 14	St Paul, NE, U.S.A.
S 8	St Paul, MN, U.S.A.
J 11	St Paul Island, AK, U.S.A. ≇
Y 7	St Paul Island, NS, Canada ≇
F 8	St Peter-Ording, Germany
J 25	St Peter Port, U.K.
Y 9	St Peter's, NS, Canada
W 8	St Peters, PE, Canada
V 11	St Petersburg, Russian Federation
P 7	St Petersburg, FL, U.S.A.
Z 10	St-Pierre, St Pierre and Miquelon
Y 11	St-Pierre, France
X 11	St Pierre and Miquelon, France ◙
L 9	St-Pierre-d'Oléron, France
I 4	St-Pol-en-Ter, France
W 4	St Pölten, Austria
Q 14	St-Pons-de-Thomières, France
R 9	St-Pourçain-sur-Sioule, France
Q 7	St-Quentin, NB, Canada
R 2	St-Quentin, France
W 14	St-Raphaël, France
L 4	Saint Regis, MT, U.S.A.
O 7	St Siméon, QC, Canada
Q 13	St Stephen, SC, U.S.A.
W 10	St Terese, AK, U.S.A.
L 10	Ste-Thérèse, QC, Canada
C 14	St Thomas, ON, Canada
V 8	St Thomas, Virgin Islands, U.S.A. ≇
N 8	St-Tite-des-Caps, QC, Canada
W 14	St-Tropez, France
I 19	St-Truiden, Belgium
O 2	St-Valery-en-Caux, France
T 8	St Veit an der Glan, Austria
Y 12	St Vincent, St Vincent and the Grenadines
X 12	St Vincent and the Grenadines, North America ◙
R 8	St Vincent Island, FL, U.S.A. ≇
Y 11	St Vincent Passage, St Lucia ≈
L 17	St Walburg, SK, Canada
Z 10	Sainte-Marie, Martinique
Y 9	Sainte-Rose, Guadeloupe
M 10	Saintes, France
A 8	Saipan, Northern Mariana Islands ≇
A 8	Saipan, Northern Mariana Islands ≇
B 11	Saitlai, Myanmar
C 23	Saito, Japan
H 20	Sajama, Bolivia
J 6	Sajó, Hungary
G 18	Sakai, Japan
F 16	Sakaide, Japan
E 18	Sakaiminato, Japan
M 2	Sakākah, Saudi Arabia
W 9	Sakaraha, Madagascar

K 12	Sakassou, Côte d'Ivoire
J 12	Sakata, Japan
X 13	Sakhalin, Russian Federation ≇
R 7	Şäki, Azerbaijan
O 12	Saki, Nigeria
P 5	Šakiai, Lithuania
M 26	Sakishima-shotō, Japan ≇
N 16	Sakon Nakhon, Thailand
U 14	Sakrand, Pakistan
K 13	Sakrivier, Republic of South Africa
L 15	Saku, Japan
L 16	Sakura, Japan
O 8	Saky, Ukraine
H 20	Sala, Sweden
K 11	Salaberry-de-Valleyfield, QC, Canada
F 9	Salacgrīva, Latvia
D 11	Saladas, Argentina
C 16	Saladillo, Argentina
P 5	Salado, Mexico
B 12	Salado, Argentina ⟿
D 13	Saladou, Guinea
T 2	Salahuddin, Iraq
W 8	Salal, Chad
K 13	Salālā, Sudan
W 11	Şalālah, Oman
H 5	Salamá, Guatemala
D 10	Salamanca, NY, U.S.A.
F 11	Salamanca, Chile
L 5	Salamanca, Spain
V 10	Salamat, Chad ⟿
I 4	Salamīyah, Syria
C 12	Salantai, Lithuania
H 6	Salar de Arizaro, Argentina ≋
H 6	Salar de Ascotán, Chile ≋
G 5	Salar de Atacama, Chile ≋
I 21	Salar de Coipasa, Bolivia ≋
I 22	Salar de Uyuni, Bolivia ≋
O 3	Salas de los Infantes, Spain
J 14	Salatiga, Indonesia
W 3	Salavat, Russian Federation
T 11	Salawati, Indonesia ≇
A 5	Salaya, India
O 13	Salayar, Indonesia ≇
N 15	Salcombe, U.K.
D 11	Saldanha, Republic of South Africa
D 11	Saldus, Latvia
T 5	Sale, VIC, Australia
L 8	Salekhard, Russian Federation
S 9	Salem, MA, U.S.A.
F 21	Salem, IL, U.S.A.
N 4	Salem, MO, U.S.A.
K 3	Salem, UT, U.S.A.
G 10	Salem, OR, U.S.A.
E 22	Salem, India
N 2	Salentina Peninsula, Italy ◇
O 16	Salentina Peninsula, Italy ◇
Q 3	Salford, U.K.
J 20	Salgótarján, Hungary
N 13	Salgueiro, Brazil
J 9	Sali, Algeria
R 9	Salibabu, Indonesia ≇
C 7	Salida, CO, U.S.A.
J 20	Salihorsk, Belarus
N 4	Salima, Malawi
N 4	Salina, KS, U.S.A.
J 5	Salina, KS, U.S.A.
L 3	Salina, UT, U.S.A.
U 14	Salina Cruz, Mexico
I 16	Salina Gualicho, Argentina ≋
G 21	Salinas, Mexico
P 9	Salinas, Mexico
A 10	Salinas, Ecuador
I 6	Salinas Grandes, Argentina ≋
K 9	Salinópolis, Brazil
W 4	Salisbury, MD, U.S.A.
M 5	Salisbury, NC, U.S.A.
Q 5	Salisbury, U.K.
P 3	Salisbury Island, NU, Canada ≇
R 12	Salisbury Plain, U.K. ◇
I 11	Săliște, Romania
U 8	Salkhad, Syria
W 4	Sallent, Spain
J 18	Salliqueló, Argentina
R 10	Sallisaw, OK, U.S.A.
Q 11	Sallūm, QC, Canada
N 9	Sallyana, Nepal
U 7	Salmān Pāk, Iraq
E 3	Salmās, Iran
D 8	Salme, Estonia
S 6	Salmon, ID, U.S.A.
N 8	Salmon, ID, U.S.A. ⟿
M 8	Salmon Arm, BC, Canada
M 8	Salmon River Mountains, ID, U.S.A. ▲▲
E 6	Salò, Italy
U 14	Salon-de-Provence, France
F 9	Salonta, Romania
M 11	Sal'sk, Russian Federation
K 25	Salsacate, Argentina
F 13	San Clemente, Chile
Z 12	Salsk, AZ, U.S.A. ⟿
F 7	Salt Basin, TX, U.S.A. ≋
F 7	Salt Flat, TX, U.S.A.
J 2	Salt Lake City, UT, U.S.A.
R 4	Salt Range, Pakistan ◇
I 6	Salta, Argentina
I 6	Salta, Argentina ◙
M 14	Saltash, U.K.
P 7	Saltillo, Mexico
D 13	Salto, Uruguay
E 13	Salto, Uruguay ◙
C 15	Salto, Argentina
Y 12	Salto del Guairá, Paraguay
M 25	Salton Sea, CA, U.S.A. ≋
J 19	Saltvik, Finland
N 12	Saluda, SC, U.S.A.
M 2	Salūq, Syria
S 8	San Fernando, Mexico
Y 11	San Fernando, Trinidad and Tobago
L 17	St Walburg, SK, Canada
Z 10	Salvador, Brazil
N 12	Salvador Mazza, Argentina
T 6	Salwah, Saudi Arabia
V 9	Salween, Myanmar ⟿
L 5	Salyersville, KY, U.S.A.
Q 7	Salzach, Austria ⟿
D 13	Salzburg, Austria
D 13	Salzburg, Austria ◙
H 5	Salzgitter, Germany
G 16	Salzkammergut, Austria ▲▲
J 6	Salzwedel, Germany
G 16	Sam Ngao, Thailand
M 13	Sam Rayburn Reservoir, TX, U.S.A. ≋
M 13	Sâm Son, Vietnam
K 21	Samaipata, Bolivia
P 12	Samal, Philippines ≇

H 23	Samales Group, Philippines ≇
N 19	San Giovanni in Fiore, Italy
R 7	Samaná, Dominican Republic
R 1	Samangán, Afghanistan ◙
L 15	Samar, Philippines ≇
S 3	Samara, Russian Federation ⟿
S 3	Samara, Russian Federation
G 7	Samarai, Papua New Guinea
M 11	Samarinda, Indonesia
O 3	Samarkand, Uzbekistan
T 2	Sámarrā', Iraq
S 6	Sámarrā', Iraq
Y 5	Samarskoye, Kazakhstan
Q 11	Samastipur, India
V 8	Şämaxi, Azerbaijan
O 10	Samba, Democratic Republic of Congo
N 2	Samba Cajú, Angola
I 16	Sambalpur, India
I 16	Sambas, Indonesia
Z 5	Sambava, Madagascar
N 5	Sambir, Ukraine
E 22	Sambre, Belgium ⟿
N 19	Samch'ŏk, South Korea
O 3	Samfya, Zambia
M 15	Samjiyŏn, North Korea
V 8	Şämkir, Azerbaijan
T 11	Samnū, Libya
J 7	Samoa, Oceania ◙
J 8	Samoa Islands, Samoa/American Samoa ≇
D 11	Samobor, Croatia
G 10	Samokov, Bulgaria
G 21	Šamorín, Slovakia
M 20	Samos, Greece
L 26	Samos, Greece ≇
I 14	Samothraki, Greece ≇
K 12	Sampit, Indonesia
H 4	Sampun, Papua New Guinea
O 13	Sampwe, Democratic Republic of Congo
D 25	Samsø, Denmark ≇
H 9	Samsun, Turkey
H 19	Samut Prakan, Thailand
H 19	Samut Sakhon, Thailand
H 19	Samut Songkhram, Thailand
N 19	Samut, Poland
K 9	San, Mali
K 18	San Agustín, Argentina
H 19	San Agustín de Valle Fértil, Argentina
H 19	San Andreas, U.S.A.
M 12	San Andrés, Guatemala
K 18	San Andrés, Bolivia
I 13	San Andrés, Philippines
G 9	San Andrés, Philippines
I 11	San Andres Mountains, NM, U.S.A. ▲▲
U 12	San Andrés Tuxtla, Mexico
M 8	San Angelo, TX, U.S.A.
O 11	San Antonio, TX, U.S.A.
P 12	San Antonio, TX, U.S.A. ⟿
P 12	San Antonio, NM, U.S.A.
L 23	San Antonio, Belize
J 5	San Antonio, Honduras
L 6	San Antonio, Honduras
N 8	San Antonio, Venezuela
O 3	San Antonio, Venezuela
H 11	San Antonio, Argentina
I 9	San Antonio, Chile
F 11	San Antonio, Philippines
W 9	San Antonio Abad, Spain
B 20	San Antonio Bay, Philippines ≈
G 16	San Antonio de los Cobres, Argentina
M 6	San Antonio de Oriente, Honduras
E 16	San Benedetto del Tronto, Italy
J 12	San Benedetto del Tronto, Italy
H 9	San Bernardino, Switzerland
K 24	San Bernardino, CA, U.S.A.
K 24	San Bernardino Mountains, CA, U.S.A. ▲▲
K 14	San Bernardino Strait, Philippines ≈
G 12	San Bernardo, Chile
J 18	San Borja, Bolivia
K 6	San Camilo, Argentina
H 7	San Carlos, Mexico
H 7	San Carlos, Costa Rica
P 10	San Carlos, Nicaragua
W 14	San Carlos, Panama
O 9	San Carlos, Venezuela
L 20	San Carlos, Bolivia
F 14	San Carlos, Chile
J 9	San Carlos, Uruguay
G 9	San Carlos, Philippines
G 9	San Carlos, Philippines
G 17	San Carlos de Bariloche, Argentina
O 8	San Carlos del Zulia, Venezuela
O 16	San Cataldo, Italy
K 25	San Clemente, CA, U.S.A.
F 13	San Clemente, Chile
F 13	San Clemente, Spain
H 5	San Crisóbal Verapaz, Guatemala
K 4	San Cristóbal, Venezuela
O 3	San Cristóbal, Argentina
B 12	San Cristóbal, Argentina
I 6	San Cristóbal, Argentina
I 6	San Cristóbal, Argentina
O 11	San Cristóbal, Solomon Islands ≇
W 13	San Cristóbal de las Casas, Mexico
P 13	San Cristóbal Frontera, Guatemala
K 26	San Diego, CA, U.S.A.
K 26	San Diego, CA, U.S.A. ⟿
H 7	San Donà di Piave, Italy
G 3	San Felipe, Mexico
M 2	San Felipe, Venezuela
G 11	San Felipe, Chile
Y 14	San Fernando, Trinidad and Tobago
G 12	San Fernando, Chile
D 15	San Fernando, Argentina
K 13	San Fernando, Spain
F 8	San Fernando, Philippines
F 8	San Fernando, Philippines
Q 7	San Fernando de Apure, Venezuela
N 7	San Fernando de Atabapo, Venezuela
B 13	San Francisco, Argentina
J 9	San Francisco, CA, U.S.A. ≈
J 9	San Francisco del Chañar, Argentina
D 15	San Francisco de Macorís, El Salvador
W 10	San Francisco Javier, Spain
C 8	San Gabriel, Ecuador
T 8	San Germán, Puerto Rico

E 11	San Gimignano, Italy
N 19	San Giovanni in Fiore, Italy
H 6	San Ignacio, Mexico
B 12	San Ignacio, Belize
B 12	San Ignacio, Peru
M 19	San Ignacio, Bolivia
H 9	San Ildefonso Peninsula, Philippines ◇
G 13	San Isidro, Costa Rica
K 14	San Jacinto, Philippines
K 18	San Javier, Bolivia
B 13	San Javier, Argentina
H 20	San Joaquin, CA, U.S.A. ⟿
H 20	San Joaquin Valley, CA, U.S.A. ◇
E 14	San Jorge, Argentina
R 10	San Jose, IL, U.S.A.
S 14	San Jose, NM, U.S.A.
G 20	San Jose, CA, U.S.A.
M 5	San José, Honduras
U 22	San José, Costa Rica ■
E 15	San José, Uruguay
G 9	San Jose, Philippines
G 14	San Jose, Philippines
A 8	San Jose, Northern Mariana Islands
H 17	San Jose de Buenavista, Philippines
N 20	San José de Chiquitos, Bolivia
D 12	San José de Feliciano, Argentina
J 4	San José de Gracia, Mexico
H 10	San José de Jáchal, Argentina
J 10	San José de la Dormida, Argentina
E 15	San José de Mayo, Uruguay
D 16	San José de Quero, Peru
Q 8	San José de Raíces, Mexico
J 8	San José del Cabo, Mexico
T 13	San José del Guaviare, Colombia
Q 11	San Juan, Mexico
U 7	San Juan, Puerto Rico ◙
Q 7	San Juan, Argentina
H 10	San Juan, Argentina
G 20	San Juan Bautista, Paraguay
H 5	San Juan de los Morros, Venezuela
J 25	San Juan de Salvamento, Argentina
Q 11	San Juan del Norte, Nicaragua
Q 11	San Juan del Río, Mexico
I 9	San Juan del Sur, Nicaragua
G 4	San Juan Ixcoy, Guatemala
P 7	San Juan Mountains, CO, U.S.A. ▲▲
H 6	San Juanico, Mexico
L 7	San Justo, Argentina
H 5	San Lorenzo, Honduras
L 7	San Lorenzo, Ecuador
J 18	San Lorenzo, Bolivia
H 16	San Lorenzo, Peru
E 9	San Lorenzo, Argentina
J 9	San Lucas, Mexico
K 22	San Lucas, Bolivia
I 11	San Luis, Argentina
I 12	San Luis, Argentina ◙
G 10	San Luis de la Paz, Mexico
J 6	San Luis del Palmar, Argentina
H 23	San Luis Obispo, CA, U.S.A.
P 6	San Luis Peak, CO, U.S.A. ▲
P 10	San Luis Potosí, Mexico
P 10	San Luis Potosí, Mexico ◙
G 1	San Luis Río Colorado, Mexico
H 3	San Luisito, Mexico
P 10	San Marcos, TX, U.S.A.
R 14	San Marcos, Mexico
F 5	San Marcos, Guatemala
M 7	San Marcos de Colón, Honduras
H 6	San Marino, Europe ◙
C 13	San Martín, Peru
L 18	San Martín, Bolivia
H 11	San Martín, Argentina
I 9	San Martín, Argentina
I 5	San Martín de los Andes, Argentina
N 6	San Martín de Valdeiglesias, Spain
F 20	San Mateo, CA, U.S.A.
F 4	San Mateo Ixtatán, Guatemala
O 19	San Matías, Bolivia
K 7	San Miguel, El Salvador
X 14	San Miguel, Panama
M 20	San Miguel, Bolivia
J 12	San Miguel Bay, Philippines ≈
J 7	San Miguel de Huachi, Bolivia
I 7	San Miguel de Tucumán, Argentina
H 6	San Miguel del Monte, Argentina
H 24	San Miguel Island, CA, U.S.A. ≇
C 21	San Miguel Islands, Philippines ≇
P 10	San Miguelito, Nicaragua
X 13	San Miguelito, Panama
B 15	San Nicolás de los Arroyos, Argentina
I 25	San Nicolas Island, CA, U.S.A. ≇
C 18	San Nicolò Gerrei, Italy
L 19	San Pablo, Bolivia
G 12	San Pablo, Philippines
K 18	San Pedro, Belize
I 6	San Pedro, Argentina
C 15	San Pedro, Argentina
G 14	San Pedro, Philippines
K 14	San-Pédro, Côte d'Ivoire
H 4	San Pedro Carchá, Guatemala
O 12	San Pedro de las Colonias, Mexico
R 7	San Pedro de Macorís, Dominican Republic
G 7	San Pedro del Pinatar, Spain
K 4	San Pedro Sula, Honduras
P 11	San Quintín, Mexico
P 11	San Rafael, Costa Rica
N 7	San Rafael del Norte, Nicaragua
K 20	San Ramón, Bolivia
M 20	San Ramón, Bolivia
O 4	San Remo, Italy
T 8	San Saba, TX, U.S.A.
K 7	San Salvador, El Salvador ◙
N 3	San Salvador, The Bahamas
I 6	San Salvador de Jujuy, Argentina
K 25	San Sebastián, Argentina
L 14	San Severo, Italy
K 22	San Simeon, Chile
F 2	San Vicente, Mexico
J 7	San Vicente, El Salvador
H 5	San Vicente, Philippines

☐ Country   ▣ Internal administrative region: State/Province/Territory/Dependent territory   ◼ Capital city   ⛰ Mountain range/Undersea ridge   ▲ Mountain peak/Volcano/Seamount   ◆ Geographic feature   ▶ Headland/Point/Cape/Peninsula   ⬚ Desert   ⬗ Island/Island group   ⌂ Antarctic base   〰 Ocean   ◡ Sea   ≈ Bay/Gulf/Channel/Strait   ⌇ Lake   ⬓ Salt pan/Dry/Intermittent lake

Country | Internal administrative region: State/Province/Territory/Dependent territory | Capital city | Mountain range/Undersea ridge | Mountain peak/Volcano/Seamount | Geographic feature | Headland/Point/Cape/Peninsula | Desert | Island/Island group | Antarctic base | Ocean | Sea | Bay/Gulf/Channel/Strait | Lake | Salt pan/Dry/Intermittent lake | River

Legend:
☐ Country
☐ Internal administrative region: State/Province/Territory/Dependent territory
▲ Capital city
▲▲ Mountain range/Undersea ridge
▲ Mountain peak/Volcano/Seamount
◇ Geographic feature
▷ Headland/Point/Cape/Peninsula
▬ Desert
☷ Island/Island group
Antarctic base
≋ Ocean
Sea
≈ Bay/Gulf/Channel/Strait
Lake
Salt pan/Dry/Intermittent lake